COLD CASE HOMICIDES

Practical Investigative Techniques

CRC SERIES IN
**PRACTICAL ASPECTS OF CRIMINAL
AND FORENSIC INVESTIGATIONS**

VERNON J. GEBERTH, BBA, MPS, FBINA *Series Editor*

Richard H. Walton

COLD CASE HOMICIDES

Practical Investigative Techniques

Taylor & Francis
Taylor & Francis Group
Boca Raton   London   New York

CRC is an imprint of the Taylor & Francis Group,
an informa business

Note: author Karen T. Taylor retains copyright to Chapter 28.

Published in 2006 by
CRC Press
Taylor & Francis Group
6000 Broken Sound Parkway NW, Suite 300
Boca Raton, FL 33487-2742

International Standard Book Number-10: 0-8493-2209-X (Hardcover)
International Standard Book Number-13: 978-0-8493-2209-9 (Hardcover)
Library of Congress Card Number 2005055954

Library of Congress Cataloging-in-Publication Data

Walton, Richard H.
    Cold Case homicides : practical investigative techniques / Richard H. Walton.
        p. cm. -- (Practical aspects of criminal and forensic investigation ; 43)
    Includes bibliographical references and index.
    ISBN 0-8493-2209-X (alk. paper)
    1. Criminal investigation. 2. Homicide investigation. 3. Forensic sciences. I. Title. II. CRC Series in practical aspects of criminal and forensic investigations ; 43.

HV8073.W345 2006
363.25'952--dc22   2005055954

Taylor & Francis Group
is the Academic Division of Informa plc.

Visit the Taylor & Francis Web site at
http://www.taylorandfrancis.com

and the CRC Press Web site at
http://www.crcpress.com

Series Editor's Note

This book is part of a series entitled *Practical Aspects of Criminal and Forensic Investigation*. This series was created by Vernon J. Geberth, New York City Police Department Lieutenant Commander (Retired), who is an author, educator, and consultant on homicide and forensic investigations.

This series, written by authors who are nationally recognized experts in their respective fields, has been designed to provide contemporary, comprehensive, and pragmatic information to the practitioner involved in criminal and forensic investigations.

Dedication

In Memoriam
Sergeant Rudy Ortega
Los Angeles County Sheriff's Department Unsolved Unit
1974–2005

Preface

This book provides practical and convenient information to investigators, detectives, prosecutors, and others responsible for the investigation and resolution of previously investigated but unsolved "cold case" homicides. This text is based upon my 31 years in California law enforcement as a deputy sheriff, district attorney investigator, instructor in cold case homicide investigation techniques, and extensive networking and research with some of the finest homicide investigators in the United States. In presenting this material, I also draw upon a 13-year quest in which I reactivated perhaps America's oldest active homicide investigation, a series of murders and alleged rapes set amidst official corruption in the heart of the Prohibition era in 1925.

HOMICIDE INVESTIGATION: HOT OR COLD

Homicide investigation has long been considered to be the zenith for an investigator dedicated to solving violent crime. Not all who enter police work strive to be a detective or an investigator, and not all possess the drive, the energy, or the zeal to succeed in this duty slot. Nor do all possess the ability. Chief among these abilities is the capacity to look, to see, and to think independently.

Investigation of the death of another human being is unlike any other responsibility, and homicide investigation requires a special person. A homicide investigator must be able to look at a live crime scene and read it; a cold case investigator may do so only through photographs or informational documents and revisiting the locale years or decades later. Each must have that ability to see beyond the obvious, to "feel" it. Likewise, homicide investigation calls for strategies—how to approach the investigation and how to approach and interact with people. Yet these strategies and approaches must be elastic and allow the investigator necessary freedom of thought and movement in the quest to seek the truth. This is true whether it is a hot case or a cold case. Throughout, the investigator must balance education, training and experience, flexibility, and common sense with a knowledge of applicable law and techniques.

A cold case homicide investigator also demands special attributes perhaps not found even among other successful homicide investigators. For those who aspire to either role—and succeed— this is perhaps the pinnacle of their career. It is a duty that bears heavy responsibility for professional investigators as they combine knowledge of the law, police practices, and the dynamics of human nature.

Investigators faced with a hot homicide confront human tragedy set in violence that those who are not accustomed to such cannot comprehend. Theirs is an environment that oftentimes encompasses a scenario of bloody bodies and intense human emotions. In this arena they must sort out the basic elements of investigation: who, what, why, how, when, and where. They ponder questions such as "MOM," meaning motive, opportunity, and means.

In doing so, they dedicate themselves, and sometimes their relationships with their own families, as they seek to fulfill their obligations, their mission. This mission is to conduct a professional and intelligent investigation that seeks to bring a sense of justice to the deceased and their surviving families through identification of the perpetrators and accountability through the criminal justice system. If they succeed, in the end, they identify and apprehend killers who are successfully prosecuted and adjudicated in a court of law. If they are unable to do so, someone else may pick up the pieces, often decades later. Many times there are viable reasons for the lack of success that do not necessarily reflect negatively upon the efforts of those who strove to solve yet were unable to conclude these cases. They tried hard, they did their best, but they didn't have that one piece of evidence, that one cooperative witness or bit of information. As a result, the case went "cold."

While the immediate crime scene and resultant immediate emotional roller coaster of those involved has been somewhat affected by time, the mission of cold case investigators is the same. Although the blood has been cleaned up and the body buried, they relive the crime through photographs and reports and follow-up interviews. What was the past is now once again the present. Like hot homicide investigators, they must detach themselves clinically, and concentrate objectively on a variety of topics that may or may not be answered in the reports they read. Cold case investigators spend a lot of hours reviewing and thinking, and do so both on and off duty. In this realm, they must struggle not to personalize the case, to remain objective and focus on the dynamics of the event as they reject emotional involvement in the crime. Modern cold case detectives must blend experience and "street smarts" with knowledge of computer systems, data banks, and rapidly changing forensic sciences. They must think forensically and still be able to exhibit skilled interview and interrogation skills with all segments of society from hardened convicts to senior citizens. They will work days off, nights, and weekends and will be subjected to the enduring stress of the homicide investigative paradigm.

Yet, in fulfilling this mission, they are subject to additional frustrations. These include files and reports that are lost, evidence unaccounted for, and what may now appear to have been viable and obvious leads that were not followed up or acted upon. In some instances, the attitudes and unofficial policies of the law enforcement agency or individual commanders and supervisors may appear to downplay the need to reinvestigate these crimes. Budgetary or other considerations sometimes appear to take precedence over this most heinous of interpersonal crime, murder. Cold case investigations demand resource expenditure that may surpass those encountered during a hot homicide investigation. Any manipulation or "burp" in pre-designed budgetary categories can confound and annoy those in charge of the budget and its management. At other times, sheer incompetence or bureaucracy stalls or stonewalls investigations, and, on occasion, cold cases can suffer such treatment no less. Some administrators have even suggested they see no need to go back and revisit older murder cases.

With most cold cases, the media (that fourth branch of government) is not standing in the chief's office demanding to know why these crimes are not being solved. A sad fact of reality is that public pressure is sometimes a solvability factor when law enforcement agencies dedicate resources to solving a particular high-profile crime. When I was defending the proposal for my doctoral dissertation, one of my professors asked why law enforcement agencies don't allocate more resources to solving cold case homicides. Another professor, a retired chief of police for a major American city, interjected. He advised that he once had a group of women come into his office who wanted him to allocate more resources to combat domestic violence and to increase officer awareness and training in this arena. He noted that, due to their proactive measures, he did so, and within a short time period they had a successful domestic-violence program in operation. I asked him if a group of people had ever entered his office and demanded that he allocate more resources to solving a substantial backlog of older, unsolved murders, some of which were nationally high profile. No, he said, they never had.

TEAMWORK AND ORGANIZATION

The days of the one-man, jack-of-all-trades homicide investigator are over. Hot- and cold case homicide investigations reflect modern, professional investigation methods and techniques. Both entail positive interpersonal relationships among working professionals in the law enforcement, legal, and forensic spectrums. Hot case or cold case investigators must exhibit teamwork that fosters a positive exchange of information and knowledge and disregards personal or personality differences.

Professional homicide investigators strive to remain objective and to seek the truth. In doing so, however, they may be confronted with vestiges from the past, practices and attitudes that were more commonplace in some law enforcement decades ago. Such professionals must refrain from being opinionated, tainted by racial prejudice, or prone to prejudgment. They must let the facts guide their actions and the course of the investigation. Patience and flexibility are a requisite for professional and personal success. Cold case homicide investigators must be open to new suggestions, ideas and concepts that might be out of sync with their counterparts in previous investigations.

The concept of assigning investigators dedicated to the task of identifying and resolving older homicide cases that were once investigated yet shelved for lack of evidence or information leading to the identification and arrest of a murder suspect is a relatively recent trend in law enforcement. The degree of support and devotion of resources to this arena is reflective of organizational leadership. While murder has no statute of limitations, law enforcement agencies have, through the years, routinely investigated homicides to the degree thought possible and, when no further action was available, filed and shelved these cases. As new homicides drained department resources, in many instances, these cases were forgotten. However, they were not forgotten by the victims' families or the perpetrators. And they were not forgotten by the investigators. This book presents some of these cases, how they were reactivated and how they were solved.

The book focuses on perhaps the two major elements that have combined to offer the opportunity to solve cold case homicides. These are changes in technology and changes in relationships that came about through the passage of time. The advent of DNA and other advanced forensic techniques has breathed new life into many of these old cases. However, these advances will never replace the homicide detective. "Shoe leather," knowledge of the human character, and basic criminal investigation will continue to solve cases. These traditional methods, combined with advances in forensics, may ultimately bring some justice to those who have thought they got away with murder. It is the purpose of this book to aid and assist the good guys in their pursuit of those bad guys.

Part One of this book addresses the background of the cold case homicide problem in America. Understanding the past helps us to understand where we came from and why we have the cold case problem we have today, and why we find what we do (or do not) in old case files. In addition, this section presents an overview of previous forensics, a field that has changed so much in less than two decades. It explores some of the older technology that cold case investigators may encounter when reviewing a decades-old file. In this review, the text seeks to identify what a cold case homicide *is*, and to explore some of the various means and methods that law enforcement agencies have utilized in identifying, and solving these cases. In addition, this segment explores the experiences of cold case detectives in reopening and understanding the case file and forensic and legal considerations that may be readily apparent.

Part One also explores updated database systems that may assist in further identification of other cases perhaps related to the reopened case or its perpetrator, through discussion on ViCAP, HITS, and TracKRS. The expanded role of NCIC and the National Criminal Justice Information Service is explored, as well as specialized techniques and resources involving areas not regularly encountered in a homicide investigation. These include discussion of interviewing senior citizens, review of the death certificate and coroner's inquest, use of specialized cold case squads, and the role of media in the investigation of cold case homicides.

Part Two presents changes in technology, changes that have contributed greatly to law enforcement's ability to solve cold case homicides. What we once lumped under a general label of "fingerprints" is now "friction ridge impressions," a field greatly expanded since many of the cold cases we now revisit occurred. Similarly, the role of computerized fingerprint technology and automated fingerprint identifications systems is presented. Building on this, this section presents the evolution we have seen from the groupings of serology to the specificity of DNA, and the future this science holds in the identification of criminal suspects. This portion concludes with a review of the expanding data banks that have so enabled the linking of previously unknown suspects to crimes they committed.

Part Three presents tools and techniques that may be utilized in the investigation of cold case homicides. The contributing authors for this section are outstanding practitioners in their respective fields, and this text is a grateful acknowledgement and recognition of their expertise, dedication, and professional excellence. There is no one-size-fits-all method of homicide investigation, nor is there such for cold case investigation. Each case brings with it a different set of circumstances, and, in cold case in particular, a surviving level of documentation, original people, and evidence. The tools these authors present can contribute enormously to making an unsolved cold case homicide into a solved cold case homicide. This part concludes with the presentation of an outstanding reinvestigation of a murder case that took the lives of two young police officers in 1957, a case solved over four decades later by utilizing many of the tools and techniques presented in this book. The investigators involved in this case's solution gave graciously and willingly of their time to share with others what they did so that we all can learn.

Part Four presents additional resources that may be available to law enforcement in the course of cold case investigation. While many of these might be known to those who investigate homicide, their role in cold case investigation might be more significant. These organizations are representative of the willingness of others who contribute to help their fellow citizens and to solve unsolved crimes. This part ends with my reflective concluding thoughts.

This Preface cannot conclude, however, without a tribute to Vernon Geberth, and my acknowledgment and profound gratitude to this one individual who has contributed so much to the betterment of law enforcement, and especially to professional homicide investigation. Vernon had the wisdom, the foresight, and the vision for this book. Throughout more than three decades in law enforcement, and after his retirement from the New York City Police Department as a Lieutenant Commander, Vernon Geberth has continued to raise the bar for those who seek to conduct criminal investigations, especially in sexual assault and homicide. In addition to numerous professional recognitions, accolades, and achievements, Vernon Geberth has published extensively on topics relating to practical criminal investigation and forensic techniques and applied psychology. He is a nationally and internationally renowned author, lecturer, educator, consultant, and expert witness on the subject of death investigation. I am proud to call him a friend.

Acknowledgments

I wish to express my deepest appreciation to the many persons and agencies who have contributed to *Cold Case Homicide: Practical Investigative Techniques*. I wish to acknowledge each individual for his or her professional expertise, suggestions, comments, photos, and case histories, which have encouraged and aided me in the completion of this first-of-its-kind book. The pages that follow are a testament to the quality of law enforcement, forensics, and their supporting disciplines in the United States, so exemplified by the following individuals. I have listed them alphabetically and apologize earnestly to any whom I have unintentionally omitted.

Detective Steve Ainsworth, Boulder County Sheriff's Office, Boulder, Colorado. Officer Robert Anderson (formerly of El Cajon, California, Police Department), Murrieta Police Department, Murrieta, California. Michael Arena, Criminal Intelligence Bureau, California Attorney General's Office, Division of Law Enforcement, Sacramento, California.

District Attorney Investigator Steve Baker, San Diego County District Attorney's Office, San Diego, California. Frank Bender, forensic sculptor, Philadelphia, Pennsylvania. Bennett Blum, M.D., Tucson, Arizona. Captain Tom Bevel (retired), Oklahoma City Police Department, Norman, Oklahoma. Detective Gerry Biehn, Los Angeles County Sheriff's Department Unsolved Unit, Commerce, California. Deborah Bloch, Ph.D., University of San Francisco, San Francisco, California. Fred Bornhofen, Chairman, Vidocq Society, Philadelphia, Pennsylvania. Sgt. Ana Peñaloza-Brackpool, Los Angeles County Sheriff's Department Homicide Bureau, Commerce, California. Tim Bradshaw, Deputy District Attorney, King County District Attorney's Office, Seattle, Washington. Donna Brant, "America's Most Wanted," FOX Television. David Browning, news and documentary producer, CBS News, Los Angeles, California. Brian Burritt, San Diego Police Department Crime Lab, San Diego, California.

Major George C. Cadavid, Miami Police Department, Miami, Florida. Tom Callaghan, Chief, CODIS Unit, Federal Bureau of Investigation, Quantico, Virginia. Detective Victor Caloca, San Diego County Sheriff's Department, San Diego, California. Sgt. Alfredo Castro, Unsolved Unit, Los Angeles County Sheriff's Department, Commerce, California. Danielle Carwell, CaseSoft®, Newport Beach, California. William Casper, Laboratory Director, California Department of Justice, Division of Law Enforcement, Bureau of Forensic Services, Eureka, California. Judge George Clark, San Diego County Superior Court, San Diego, California. Bonnie Collins, Analyst, California Department of Justice, Sacramento, California. Lieutenant Craig Cleary, El Segundo Police Department, El Segundo, California. Detective Bob Conrad, Chula Vista Police Department, Chula Vista, California. District Attorney Steve Cooley, Los Angeles County District Attorney's Office, Los Angeles, California. Gary Cordner, Ph.D, Eastern Kentucky University, Richmond, Kentucky. Special Agent Brad Cordts, Kansas Bureau of Investigation, Topeka, Kansas. Investigator Carl Craig, Richland County Sheriff's Department, Columbia, South Carolina. Al Crnich, Eureka, California.

Katherine Danalakis, Artists Rights Society, New York, New York. Heather Davies, Ph.D (formerly of Police Executive Research Forum, Washington, D.C), Alexandria, Virginia. Duayne J. Dillon, D.Crim., Chief Criminalist (retired), Alameda County Crime Laboratory, Martinez, California. Joseph Di Zinno, DDS, Deputy Assistant Director, FBI Laboratory, Quantico, Virginia. Detective Bob Donaldson, San Diego Police Department, Paul Dougherty, Chief Criminalist (retired), San Mateo County, California, Sheriff's Department laboratory, Ojai, California. Lieutenant (formerly Detective Sergeant) Jorge Duran, H.E.A.T. Team, San Diego Police Department, San Diego, California. Jeff Dusek, Division Chief, Deputy District Attorney, Cold Case Homicide

Unit, San Diego County District Attorney's Office, San Diego, California. John Dehaan, Chief (retired), Bureau of Forensic Services, California Department of Justice, Vallejo, California.

Detective Paul Edholm (retired), Beverly Hills Police Department, La Palma, California. Rod Englert, (Chief Deputy and Commander Operations Division, retired), Multnomah County Sheriff's Department, Portland, Oregon. Louis N, Eliopulos, Senior Homicide Analyst, Naval Criminal Investigative Service, Mayport Naval Station, Jacksonville, Florida. Julio Estrada, Senior Medical Examiner Investigator, San Diego County Medical Examiner's Office, San Diego, California.

Deputy Sheriff Dale Falicon, Los Angeles County Sheriff's Department, Los Angeles, California. Detective Sergeant James Ferguson, Cold Case Homicide Unit, El Cajon Police Department, El Cajon, California. John Firman, International Association of Chiefs of Police, Washington, D.C. Detective Vivian Flores, Cold Case Homicide Unit, Robbery-Homicide Division, Los Angeles Police Department, Los Angeles, California. Steve Fischer, Unit Chief, Multimedia Group, Criminal Justice Information Services, Federal Bureau of Investigation, Clarksburg, West Virginia. William Fleisher, Commissioner, Vidocq Society, Philadelphia, Pennsylvania. Gary Fong, *San Francisco Chronicle*, San Francisco, California. Kenneth Foote, Ph.D., Chair, Department of Geography, University of Colorado, Boulder, Colorado. Melitta Franceschini, South Tyrol Museum of Archeology.

Norman Gahn, Assistant District Attorney, Milwaukee District Attorney's Office, 1st Judicial District, Milwaukee, Wisconsin. James Gannon, Deputy Chief of Investigations, Morris County Prosecutor's Office, Morristown, New Jersey. Detective Ron Garvick, Sacramento County Sheriff's Department, Sacramento, California. Zach Gaskin, CEO United Forensics, Inc., Rockwood, Pennsylvania. Captain Duino Giordano (retired), Los Gatos Police Department, Los Gatos, California. David Godfordson, News Producer, KFMB television, San Diego, California. Scott J. Goetz, Department of Geography, University of Maryland. Officer Anna Gonzales, Miami Police Department, Miami, Florida. Detective Frank Gonzales, Unsolved Unit, Los Angeles County Sheriff's Department, Commerce, California. David Griffith, Commander (retired), Texas Department of Public Safety, Austin, Texas. Richard Grzybowski, ATF laboratory, Walnut Creek, California. Michael Grubb, Crime Lab Manager, San Diego Police Department, San Diego, California.

Sharon Pagaling Hagan, Supervising Special Agent (retired), California Department of Justice, Bureau of Investigations, Rancho Cordova, California. Rockne "Rock" Harmon, Senior Deputy District Attorney, Alameda County District Attorney's Office, Oakland, California. Captain Murl Harpham, Eureka Police Department, Eureka, California. Detective Steve Harshberger, Michigan State Police, Alpeni, Michigan. Lieutenant Joseph Hartshorne, Homicide Bureau, Los Angeles County Sheriff's Department, Commerce, California. Tori Heflin, Museum of Man, San Diego, California. Lieutenant John Hennessey, Officer-in-Charge, Homicide Detail, San Francisco Police Department, San Francisco, California. Robert Hickey, Deputy District Attorney, Gang Prosecutions Unit, San Diego County District Attorney's Office, San Diego, California. Madeleine Hinkes, Ph.D., D-ABFA, Forensic Anthropologist, San Diego, California. Detective Steve Hodel (retired), Los Angeles Police Department, Los Angeles, California. Sergeant William Holmes, Robbery Division, San Diego Police Department, San Diego, California. Professor Frank Horvath, Ph.D, School of Criminal Justice, Michigan State University, East Lansing, Michigan. Detective Neil Hubbard, Eureka Police Department, Eureka, California. Detective Technician Lisa Hudson, Wauwatosa Police Department, Wauwatosa, Wisconsin. Mary Ann Hunt, Homicide Analyst, Robbery-Homicide Division, Los Angeles Police Department, Los Angeles, California. Sgt. Mike Huff, Homicide Unit Supervisor, Tulsa Police Department, Tulsa, Oklahoma. Harold Hunt, Burnt Ranch, California. Robert Hutton, Chief of Police (retired), Coronado Police Department, Coronado, California.

Jack Irvine, M.D., Eureka, California.

Sergeant John Jackson, Cold Case Homicide Unit, Kansas City Police Department, Kansas City, Missouri. Detective Rick Jackson, Cold Case Homicide Unit, Robbery-Homicide Division,

Los Angeles Police Department, Los Angeles, California. Earl James, J.D., Ph.D., Michigan State Police (retired), Lansing, Michigan.

Robert Keppell, Ph.D., Chief Investigator (retired), Washington State Attorney General's Office, Seattle, Washington; Associate Professor, Sam Houston State University, Huntsville, Texas. Principal Criminal Attorney Eric Kindall, Sacramento County District Attorney's Office, Sacramento, California. Venetia King, Criminal Information and Transition Unit, Federal Bureau of Investigation, Clarksburg, West Virginia. Captain David Kelly, Commander, Investigative Services Bureau, New Hampshire State Police, Concord, New Hampshire. Supervising Special Agent Lisa Kincaid, ATF. Peter Komarinski, Manager (retired) Automated Fingerprint Identification Systems, New York State Division of Criminal Justice Services, Rotterdam, New York.

Detective Dave Lambkin, Cold Case Homicide Unit, Robbery-Homicide Division, Los Angeles Police Department, Los Angeles, California. Daniel G. Lamborn, Deputy District Attorney, Cold Case Homicide Unit, San Diego County District Attorney's Office, San Diego, California. Eugene J. LaChimia, Criminalist, Forensic Science Section, San Diego Police Department Crime Lab, San Diego, California. Gerry Laporte, U.S. Secret Service Laboratory, Washington, D.C. Lieutenant Tony Leal, Texas Rangers, San Antonio, Texas. Dr. Henry Lee, Chief Emeritus, Connecticut State Crime Lab, Meridan, Connecticut. Paul Levikow, Public Affairs Officer, San Diego County District Attorney's Office, San Diego, California. Detective Dave Lewis (retired), Homicide Bureau, Los Angeles County Sheriff's Department, Commerce, California. Darren Levine, Senior Deputy District Attorney, Los Angeles County District Attorney's Office, Los Angeles, California. Steve Loftin, Forensic Imaging Specialist, National Center for Missing and Exploited Children, Alexandria, Virginia. Sergeant Richard Longshore, Unsolved Unit, Los Angeles County Sheriff's Department, Commerce, California. Sheriff Leon Lott, Richland County Sheriff's Department, Columbia, South Carolina. Detective Kevin Lowe, Homicide Bureau, Los Angeles County Sheriff's Department, Commerce, California. Special Agent Ray Lundin, Kansas Bureau of Investigation, Topeka, Kansas.

Detective Tim Marcia, Cold Case Homicide Unit, Robbery-Homicide Division, Los Angeles Police Department, Los Angeles, California. Dan Martell, Ph.D., Clinical Assistant Professor of Psychiatry and Behavioral Sciences, Neuropsychiatric Institute, UCLA School of Medicine, Newport Beach, California. Ranger John Martin, Texas Rangers, San Antonio, Texas. Mitch Morrissey, District Attorney, Denver, Colorado. Special Agent Mike Matassa, ATF, Los Angeles. Jamie Sigler McDevitt, Acting Section Chief, Programs Development Section, CJIS, Federal Bureau of Investigation, Clarksburg, West Virginia. Sergeant Mitch McKay, Coronado Police Department, Coronado, California. Terry Melton, Ph.D., President and CEO, Mitotyping Technologies LLC, State College, Pennsylvania. Detective Dan McElderry, Homicide Bureau, Los Angeles County Sheriff's Department, Commerce, California. Glen Miller, Supervisor, Forensic Imaging Unit, National Center for Missing and Exploited Children, Alexandria, Virginia. Connie Milton, Criminalist, Crime Lab, San Diego County Sheriff's Department, San Diego, California. Matthew Mitchell, Ph.D., University of San Francisco, San Francisco, California. Patricia Mitchell, Ph.D., University of San Francisco, San Francisco, California.

Sergeant Paul Mondry, Unsolved Unit, Los Angeles County Sheriff's Department, Commerce, California. Sergeant Tim Morgan, Los Gatos Police Department, Los Gatos, California. Jeff Muckenthaler, Crime Analyst, Kansas Bureau of Investigation, Topeka, Kansas. Ander Murane, *Rocky Mountain News*, Denver, Colorado. Captain Tim Murray, Boston Police Department, Boston, Massachusetts.

Gerald Nance, Case Manager, Special Case Unit, National Center for Missing and Exploited Children, Alexandria, Virginia. Linda Nance, Criminal Justice Statistics Center, California Department of Justice, Sacramento, California. David O. Norris, Ph.D, Forensic Botany LLC, Boulder, Colorado. Sergeant John Neff, Cold Case Homicide Unit, Austin Police Department, Austin, Texas.

Bo Odea, i2 Investigative Analysis Software®, Springfield, Virginia. Marcutris Otani, Analyst, California Department of Justice, Sacramento, California. Patrick O'Donnell, Supervisor, DNA Unit, Crime Lab, San Diego Police Department, San Diego, California.

Edwardo Palma, Certified Latent Print Examiner, Latent Print Unit, Crime Lab, San Diego Police Department, San Diego, California. Paul Pane, Information Services Manager, California Department of Justice, Sacramento, California. Detective David Parris, Eureka Police Department, Eureka, California. William Paul, Assistant Civil Engineer, City of San Diego, San Diego, California. Captain Raymond Peavy, Homicide Bureau, Los Angeles County Sheriff's Department, Commerce, California. Kim Peterson, Sund/Carrington Foundation, Modesto, California. Silvia Pettem, Ward, Colorado. Sheriff Gary Philp, Humboldt County Sheriff's Department, Eureka, California.

Lieutenant Ray Rawlins, San Diego County Sheriff's Department, San Diego, California. Paul Redden, Polygraph Examiner, Crime Lab, San Diego Police Department, San Diego, California. Tony Ribera, Ph.D, Chief of Police (retired) San Francisco Police Department, San Francisco, California; Institute for International Justice, University of San Francisco, San Francisco, California. D. Kim Rossmo, Ph.D., Research Professor and Director Center for Geospatial Intelligence and Investigation, Department of Criminal Justice, Texas State University, San Marcos, Texas. David Reynolds, Boulder, Colorado. Detective Edward Reynolds, Phoenix Police Department, Phoenix, Arizona. Jeff Rose, Assistant Chief Deputy District Attorney, Sacramento County District Attorney's Office, Sacramento, California. Detective Richard Rouleau, Cold Case Unit, El Cajon Police Department, El Cajon, California.

Detective Arnold Sauro (retired), Los Angeles Police Department, Los Angeles, California. Special Agent Katie Schuetz, Kansas Bureau of Investigation, Topeka, Kansas. Sergeant Christopher Serritella, San Diego County Sheriff's Department, San Diego, California. Bonnie Shaffer, Management Analyst, Criminal Justice Information Service, Federal Bureau of Investigation, Clarksburg, West Virginia. Investigator Ron Shave (retired), Orange County District Attorney's Office, Santa Ana, California. Michigan. Anne-Marie Schubert, Deputy District Attorney, Sacramento County District Attorney's Office, Sacramento, California. Susan Snyder, Bancroft Library, Berkeley, California. Norman "Skip" Sperber, DDS., Forensic Odontologist, Forensic Dental Consultant, La Jolla, California. James Stam, Supervising Criminalist, Crime Laboratory, San Diego Police Department, San Diego, California. David Steitz, Public Information Officer, National Aeronautics and Space Administration. Ann Stewart, FBI Laboratory, Press Section, Washington, D.C. John Stewart, Ph.D., DNA Laboratory, Unit II, Federal Bureau of Investigation, Washington, D.C. Clay Strange, Attorney At Law, Austin, Texas.

Karen T. Taylor, Forensic Artist, Austin, Texas. District Attorney Investigator Ron Thill, San Diego Police Department H.E.A.T. Cold Case Homicide Unit/San Diego County District Attorney's Office, San Diego, California. Assistant Director Larry Thomas, Kansas Bureau of Investigation, Topeka, Kansas. Investigator Paul Tippin, Orange County District Attorney's Office, Santa Ana, California. Katie Tobin, Student Intern, San Diego County Medical Examiner's Office, San Diego, California. Detective James Trainum, Metropolitan Police Department, Washington, D.C. Major Larry C. Turner, Commander, Criminal Investigative Division, Indiana State Police, Indianapolis, Indiana.

Calvin Vine, Supervising Medical Examiner Investigator, San Diego County Medical Examiner's Office, San Diego, California.

Detective Tom Wagner, San Diego Police Department, San Diego, California. Special Agent Stanley Walker, FBI (retired), Eureka, California. William Walser, Evidence Technician (retired), Eureka Police Department, Eureka, California. Richard Walter, Prison psychologist (retired) Montrose, Pennsylvania. Director Larry Welch, Kansas Bureau of Investigation, Topeka, Kansas. Lieutenant Phil West, Boulder County Sheriff's Department, Boulder, Colorado. Jane Whitmore, Critical Incident Response Unit, FBI Academy, Quantico, Virginia. Eric Whitzig, Major Case Specialist (ViCAP), FBI Academy, Quantico, Virginia. Glen W. Wildey, Jr., Major Case Specialist (ViCAP), FBI Quantico, Virginia. Dan Williams, Mortuary Manager, Greenwood Memorial Park and Mortuary, San Diego, California. Detective Jon Woodell, El Cajon Police Department, El Cajon, California. Captain Paul Ybarrondo (Retired), San Diego Police Department, San Diego, California.

In addition, I wish to extend my deepest appreciation to the editors and staff at CRC Press for their untiring efforts in the design and production of this textbook. I wish to especially thank Erika Dery and Kari Budyk, Project Coordinators; Sylvia Wood, Project Editor; and Senior Editor Becky McEldowney-Masterson for their guidance, kindness, and support throught the writing, editing, and publishing process.

I especially wish to extend my deepest gratitude to Mr. Vernon Geberth, author of *Practical Homicide Investigation: Tactics, Procedures, and Forensic Techniques* for his unfailing confidence, wisdom, and support. I hope he is as proud of this book as I am.

Contributing Authors

Tom Bevel
Captain (retired)
Oklahoma City Police Department
Norman, Oklahoma

Paul Edholm
Detective (retired)
Beverly Hills Police Department
Beverly Hills, California

Rod Englert
Deputy Chief (retired)
Multnomah County Sheriff's Department
Portland, Oregon

Zach Gaskin
United Forensics Inc.
Rockwood, Pennsylvania

Mike Grubb
San Diego Police Department
Forensic Sciences Division
San Diego, California

Sharon Pagaling Hagan
Special Agent (retired)
Supervisor, California Department of Justice
Sacramento, California

Robert Hickey
Deputy District Attorney
Gang Prosecution Unit
San Diego County District Attorney's Office
San Diego, California

Madeleine Hinkes
Forensic Anthropologist,
San Diego County Medical Examiner's Office
   and Imperial County Coroner
San Diego, California

Steve Hodel
Detective III (retired)
Los Angeles Police Department
Studio City, California

Peter Komarinski
Komarinski & Associates, LLC
Rotterdam, New York

Terry Melton
Mitotyping Technologies, LLC
State College, Pennsylvania

Edwardo Palma
San Diego Police Department
Forensic Science Division
San Diego, California

Paul Redden
San Diego Police Department
Forensic Sciences Division
San Diego, California

Kim Rossmo
Department of Criminal Justice
Texas State University
San Marcos, Texas

Anne Marie Schubert
Deputy District Attorney
Sacramento County District Attorney's
   Office
Sacramento, California

Ron Shave
Investigator (Retired)
Orange County District Attorney's
   Office
Santa Ana, California

Norman D. " Skip" Sperber
Chief Forensic Dentist
San Diego County Medical Examiner's Office
San Diego, California

Karen T. Taylor
Facial Images
Forensic and Portrait Artist
Austin, Texas

Introduction

My introduction to cold case homicide investigation began one afternoon in the early 1980s in a rural village on the north coast of California as the result of a chance conversation on a street corner while on patrol. A woman had recently died and, before passing, recanted her accusations of rape against a young Native American six decades before. If true, it meant a man had gone to prison for crimes he did not commit and justice had not been served. Everyone *knew* Jack Ryan was railroaded, I was told. If this was true, I wondered, did he deserve to have his name cleared?

There were no records remaining, and the current homicide rate and administrative philosophy precluded any official interest in revisiting such an old crime. Certain questions immediately needed answers. Where to go? How to start?

I knew nothing of this local legend, but only blocks from that street corner lived an elderly retired newspaperman. With just a few months to live, Andy Genzoli listened to my information, retired to his study, and came back with a handful of papers. They were a start. "The law was crooked, and so was the district attorney," he told me as he handed me the bundle. The carbon-paper documents were the district attorney's written account of his solution to a series of murders and rapes that had occurred in the heart of Prohibition, crimes that had been reported nationwide in the sensational journalism of the day.

As I was to learn, these events ultimately led to the imprisonment of a young Native American whose only crime was being in the wrong place at the wrong time. For this, Jack Ryan spent over 40 years in prison and on parole for crimes later proven he did not commit. For him justice was slow. He was commuted to time served in 1969 by Governor Reagan, and granted perhaps America's first innocence pardon of its kind by Governor Pete Wilson in 1996. Posthumously. In between lay a period in which the real killers lived out their lives in freedom, yet always looking over their shoulders.

My interest was piqued. The next 13 years would be spent reading old newspaper accounts, tracking down surviving participants or their descendants, and reconstructing a case that was never meant to be reopened. I learned the original document was removed by the chief prosecutor when he himself left office under federal indictment. In all, I would conduct more than 400 interviews, over half of these with people aged 65 or more.

For the following 2 years I found myself in the newspaper morgue on my off-duty time, reading each issue of the area's two daily newspapers. These were the only surviving record that detailed what happened, the trial proceedings, and subsequent events. I copied the yellowed, dusty pages and noted names of individuals, who they were and what they did. In this manner, I unknowingly began to build what would ultimately become, perhaps, America's oldest active homicide case. As the months became years, I filled file folders and ultimately learned to operate a revolutionary new machine, the personal computer.

The series of events that transcended the decades began with the murders of a beautiful 17-year-old girl, Carmen Wagner, and her 21-year-old male companion, Henry Sweet. The couple was shot to death while deer hunting in the remote mountains in October, 1925. Jack Ryan and his half-brother, Walter David, "half breed" Indians, as they were reported in the press of the day, were arrested "on suspicion." David was later released but Ryan was held to answer for shooting the girl. The preliminary hearing took place 1 month after his arrest, and trial began 3 months later. Events moved quickly in the 1920s.

I learned from the newspaper accounts that Ryan was acquitted in less than 24 hours after a lengthy trial by a jury of white men. This was a trial marked by perjury and planted evidence. The case was my introduction to Edward Oscar Heinrich, perhaps America's first academically trained forensic scientist. He collected and examined the evidence. Decades after his death, Heinrich's records allowed an in-depth review of this aspect of these events. In these pages I saw the infancy of forensics as we know it today. —the idea of blood spatter analysis and of the ability to allegedly match a fired shell casing or bullet to a specific firearm.

After the trial, Ryan returned to being a cowboy. But the politics of Prohibition had doomed him. A new DA was elected and immediately set out to solve the crimes, all the while running the biggest bootlegging ring in the county from inside the District Attorney's Office. Walter David was murdered shortly thereafter in a torture killing, most likely committed by bad cops. Ultimately, Ryan was arrested and charged with several rapes of young girls. To stay alive, he pled guilty to the rapes. Held overnight in the county jail, Ryan was interrogated under conditions and circumstances not uncommon for the period. Shortly after daybreak on September 14, 1928, Jack Ryan confessed to the murders. Within hours he was given a preliminary hearing, and later that same afternoon—without an attorney—pled guilty to the murder of Sweet and was immediately sentenced to life in prison. By 7 p.m., he was enroute out of county to San Quentin State Prison, where he would spend the next 26 years, before being paroled in 1953.

Ultimately, my efforts would officially reopen perhaps America's oldest active homicide case. The rape victim's role in a series of Prohibition-era murders, rapes, and political corruption became apparent, as indeed, the guilty suspects escaped while an innocent man served time. As events unfolded, I found myself going to lengths not encountered when conducting a current homicide investigation, but that complement modern homicide investigation techniques.

Homicide cases can rise or fall on tiny bits of information or evidence. Without realizing it, I found myself combining current homicide investigation techniques with the fields of history, anthropology, and perhaps archeology. I was digging up the past, events that more than a few wished left undisturbed. My landscape was not only the remote mountain crime scenes, but also state and federal archives. City directories and assessor's maps, civil and probate files, and other arenas not normally encountered in a homicide investigation were exhumed to reveal the hidden skeletons left behind by parties identified in my investigation.

And, of course, I pored over years of daily newspaper review as each article was photocopied, its contents computerized for informational purposes, time line content, and value. I found myself searching for photos in old family photo albums, diaries and notes, crime scene maps, and evidence files, as well as stepping outside the box to find remnants of aged official records filed far from the scene of the crime. Original investigator notebooks were uncovered in attics. In the course of this, I began to meet people who wanted to tell me what they had known, but had never told anyone else. I found myself interviewing people with direct first-hand knowledge. These were original witnesses from a series of events that took place 60 years in the past. Slowly, the truth—and the coverup—began to emerge.

From the White House to Wall Street, and from the Governor's office in Sacramento to university archives and an old mining town in Idaho, I found myself compiling information from a myriad of sources that seem distant from those events that occur when a homicide has just been reported. As in the investigation of a current homicide, however, I was looking for evidence. I was looking for witnesses, physical evidence, and persons with first-hand knowledge. There were no patrol cars with flashing lights, no crime scene tape, and no crime scene specialists responding to recover trace evidence.

I did not have the benefit of face-to-face interviews with major original participants so that I could gauge reactions to my questions or watch the body language. I did not have the benefit of experienced investigators leading me through the steps involved in my undertaking. There was no mentoring that told me I was on the right track or off on a wild goose chase. This was my first homicide investigation. Indeed, some questioned my sanity, and certainly, the department had no interest in supporting my investigation. The more questions I asked, however, the more wrong everything seemed to be. People were evasive and some were downright untruthful, even my own captain of operations. Why? I wondered. It happened so long ago. Who cares?

It would be years, however, before I learned that my supervising captain was related to the woman who had recanted her statements before death. "You're on your own in this one," he admonished me sternly. Interestingly enough, while never revealing what he did know, he never attempted to discourage me either. In one of the many quirks that can happen over the years in these cases, I would come to learn that a sole surviving grand juror who participated in the investigation of this case in the late 1920s had only recently been murdered. He and his wife were bludgeoned to death in their farmhouse by a relative of the recently deceased "rape victim."

As I tried to combine a current homicide investigation with historical research, I had one luxury. I had no TV cameras or media looking for sound bites and film clips for the evening news. Years later, I would realize how much this helped me recreate a series of infamous events that polarized the community and that had seen numerous reinvestigations, state and federal, in the succeeding decades. The case was written up in the true crime magazines over the decades. Few believed, it seemed, that Ryan was guilty.

As I conducted scores of interviews with people in their 70s through their 90s, I learned a lot about life and the human experience as we age. I learned what worked and what did not when trying to elicit information under these circumstances. Theirs was a different perspective on life than it had been 6 decades before. I came to understand that I had to overcome perspectives of the police formed in an era of the Keystone Cops and Jimmy Cagney movies, a period of well-known corruption.

At first, naively, I thought they would open up for me. After all, the 1920s were a long time ago and the past was the past. *Wasn't it?* Surely, they did not harbor hard feelings, or fears, from so long ago. *Did they?* I came to realize that, yes, they did. Some were still terrified of a man who had died decades before. For some, including a killer who sat in the back seat of my car, it was yesterday. Over the years, I felt like I had one foot on a banana peel and the other on their graves as my interviews accelerated. I came to see, and to try to identify with, the emotions of those who are caught up in the fabric of murder so long ago. I didn't need clinical research and "data" to tell me that the pain and the hurt are just below the surface. It always has been and always will be, and it was increasingly visible for me. Slowly, they opened up and told what they knew. It was a lot.

For those with something to hide, the fear of buried events' coming to the surface brought forth a terror and a danger I did not immediately recognize. The fear was multifaceted. It was a fear not only for themselves but, perhaps more important, that their children and grandchildren would find out about their terrible secret. Grandfather executed a terrified 17-year-old girl with two shots to her head in a remote canyon. A life spent running and hiding was in danger of exposure. I learned that although blood can be thicker than water, there are those who know something, and, given the right circumstances, may come forward. Others, related to one of the victims, told me to "let it be." They did not want the case reopened. Ultimately, I would learn why.

Something else happened during this inquiry. I also began to uncover information on other murders, or secondary homicides, as former bootleggers and others who did not have long to live cautiously opened up. I had reviewed these cases as tangential issues to my case, and came to believe that they were telling some truths as they fed me bits and pieces of information about crimes they participated in, or seemingly had first-hand knowledge of. I began to wonder how many other unsolved murders were out there? How many killers were undetected, and still alive? Perhaps still plying their horrible crimes.

I realized that investigation of the crimes entailed understanding the era—the time, place, and circumstance in which the crimes occurred. I learned about Prohibition and the effects upon local, state, and national politics. One consequence was the trickle-down effect into the courtroom. I came to appreciate how far law enforcement practices have come in the last three quarters of a century. DNA has brought forth a whole new chapter in our ability to identify perpetrators of violent crimes. Fingerprint and DNA data banks are tremendous resources. It was not that long ago, however, when science could tell us only whether the blood on the suspect or victim came from a human or an animal, and not much else. Only in the mid 20th century did the science of blood splatter analysis gain a positive foothold in forensic circles.

Forensics is today a mainstay of current police investigative practice, but it was not many decades in the past that anyone with a camera and a test tube could call themselves an expert and consult on criminal cases for significant fees. Notorious criminal trials in the first half of the 20th century, and some into the second half, have focused on the reliability and competency of the forensic evidence and the forensic practitioners. Junk science truly was junk science, and we do not know how many wrongful convictions resulted, or how many guilty were never exposed.

Since 1930, the FBI has maintained extensive records on crime in America, including homicide. The annual FBI Uniform Crime Report (UCR) details murder in all its categories, including victim–offender relationship, time of day, weapon, and more. Similarly, state criminal justice agencies have kept a myriad of records and publish their own annual reports about murder and other crimes. Academics, policy makers, the news media and more can review this data in further-ance of their specific task. In doing so, we see that murder is reported both in the numbers of murders that occur each year and the percentage of those reported that are cleared.

Missing from these reports, however, is any finding or reporting of the numbers of murders that remain open and unsolved. Some murders are solved quickly, even within hours. Others may take weeks, months, or even years to compile enough evidence to identify the suspect, link him or her to the crime, and make an arrest.

Despite our best efforts, however, some murders are not solved. When all viable leads have been followed up and fresher cases compete for scarce resources, cases are suspended from active action. When this occurs, they are filed, pending new information. They become "cold cases." There are no national data banks of unsolved cases. They reside within the domain of the responsible investigating agency and these are not reported.

As the years pass, these cases grow colder. Investigators move on in their careers. They retire, but they do not forget. Time, once an enemy in homicide investigation, slowly becomes a friend. Technology and relationships change. In the past decade we have seen a resurgence of interest in cold case investigations as more and more agencies dust off old files and utilize our newfound knowledge in pursuit of justice for those who cannot speak. These cases become a passion for those homicide cops who investigate them, an obsession to see justice done for victims and their families. Sometimes, we find the wrong person went to jail. We need to work just as hard to exonerate the innocent as we do to convict the guilty.

There is no magic checklist, no one-size-fits-all method of cold case homicide investigation. No text can cover all the bases or consider every potential scenario involved. Some cases involve more effort than others. But in the end, they boil down to dedicated cops and prosecutors who seek justice and their partners in the crime lab.

This text attempts to discuss some of the means and techniques used in practical cold case homicide investigation, and to present the experiences of detectives who have solved cold cases. I hope that their experiences inspire and assist those who come after.

Richard H. Walton
La Jolla, California

July, 2005

Contents

PART IV Other Resources

Part I

Investigation

1 The Cold Case Problem

Richard H. Walton

CONTENTS

INTRODUCTION

The purpose of this chapter is to present the background of homicide in the U.S., how it has been identified and recorded, and the emergent basis for practical unsolved-homicide investigation. In addition, this chapter will review trends and patterns of 20th-century homicide in the U.S., and how these affect the investigations and operations of homicide investigators assigned to investigate unsolved "cold case" homicides in the 21st century. This chapter will review homicide and homicide data to identify the scope of unsolved murders in the U.S. at this time, and will review trends and advances in the forensic sciences and their application to cold case homicide investigation. The chapter will conclude by review of circumstances that contribute to cases growing cold and to recent trends to reinvestigate such cold cases.

Hot versus Cold Case Homicide

The very use of the term "cold case" is controversial among homicide investigators and others associated with the investigation of unsolved murders. Such terminology may suggest to some that unsolved cases are unworkable, impossible, and offer no hope for future solution. This term may convey a false impression to family and friends of unsolved murder victims that their cases do not count anymore, that their case will never be resolved, and that, as a result, their case is old and "cold" and has been forgotten. Counter to this philosophy is the use of the term "unsolved" when it comes to reference to such murder cases. As will be discussed in future chapters, the wounds of murder are sub-surface in the hearts and minds of those who have suffered the violent loss of a loved one or a close friend, and "closure" is a misnomer. Like the proverbial pebble cast upon still waters, the ripple effect continues. There is *no* closure.

A common perception of cold case homicides is that they are unsolved murders previously reported to law enforcement and investigated, but that failed to result in the identification and arrest of a suspect and filing of criminal charges. Due to the passage of time and lack of investigative leads, they are no longer actively pursued by investigators. To the best of my knowledge, the popular application of the phrase and of the concept of "cold case" homicide has been attributed to the news media in the Metro-Dade region of Florida.

A high-profile rape-murder of an 9-year-old girl during a surge in homicides in the 1980s prompted the homicide section to assign a four-man team of highly experienced detectives to focus solely on solving this case. They did so, and the concept of a special team of highly experienced detectives to work cases that others do not have time to work grew up. The effort was the first of a number of successes for the "Pending Case Squad." The media, however, coined a new term, calling them "The Cold Case Squad." The name stuck. Similarly, "cold" has been used in countless Western and police movies when describing a trail or a search for someone as going "cold." The Los Angeles County Sheriff's Department, however, has maintained its Unsolved Unit in the Homicide Bureau since the 1970s. In the past two decades, numerous law enforcement agencies have formed their own cold case squads, detectives and investigators tasked to reinvestigate previously investigated yet unsolved murders. For purposes of this book, we will use the term "cold case" to identify previously reported and investigated, yet unsolved, homicides.

Media focus and attention on this topic in the past decade has brought about public awareness of this aspect of homicide investigation. In a positive manner, this attention has:

- Stimulated public interest in rejuvenating older unsolved cases.
- Provided public understanding and support when law enforcement designates resources to investigate cold cases.
- Encouraged those with knowledge of unsolved homicides to come forward.
- Stimulated law enforcement organizations to become more proactive in reviewing cold cases.
- Reminded those who have so far gotten away with murder that law enforcement does not give up and their case has not been forgotten.

Conversely, "hot" homicides are those murders that have been reported to law enforcement and are in the initial active investigation phase. Most commonly in this scenario:

- A murder or finding of a body is reported to law enforcement.
- Officers and investigators respond to the scene.
- Witnesses are located and interviewed.

- Forensic services are enlisted.
- The victim is identified.
- The cause and manner of death are established.
- Investigators seek to identify what happened and who did it.
- In doing so, they write reports and document their actions, building the case day by day.
- These actions result in the identification and arrest of a suspect and filing of criminal charges. If not, the case may become an unsolved homicide.

Once the media coins a term, we are often stuck with it whether we like it and agree with it or not. In the recent decade, "cold case homicide" has come to be collectively understood by the public and the media as an older, unsolved murder. What is cold to one investigator or to one law enforcement agency, however, may not be shared by other investigators or agencies.

Murder, for purposes of this book, is the intentional non-negligent killing of one human being by another without legal justification or excuse. While it is the least frequent violent crime, it is also the ultimate crime against a person. In our culture, we value life and do not want anyone to get away with murdering another person. For the protection of society and the rule of law, it is incumbent upon the police to identify those who kill and for the criminal justice system to adjudicate their actions in accordance with law.

Murder is one of the two most common forms of willful homicide. The other is war. Murder has existed as long as man has walked on earth, when prehistoric men and women committed homicide and even cannibalism. Murder has captivated the public interest and attention and been the focus of writing since Cain killed his brother Abel in the Biblical recording perhaps identifying the first victim and perpetrator. Such crimes continue to plague our society, and, despite the passing of the years, people still kill people. It is important to realize that while the means and methods may change, the motives and reasons for killing have not. A thousand years ago, people killed other people with arrows, rocks, and knives. In ancient Greece, Socrates died from poison. These instruments, or their variations, are still in use today. They have been supplemented, however, by guns, automobiles, and more advanced and exotic chemical compounds.

In both hot and cold homicide scenarios, investigators routinely seek to answer the questions

- *What* happened?
- *Why* was the victim killed?
- *Who* had the opportunity to do it?
- *How* did it happen?
- *Why* did it happen?
- *Where* did it happen?
- *When* did it happen?

As in a hot homicide investigation, cold case investigators seek to learn why the victim was killed and who had the means, opportunity, and motive to do so (MOM). Over the centuries, these motives have not changed. People still commit murder for love, for money, or power, and in anger, rage, or for retribution of a real or imagined wrong. Cold case investigators may also consider:

- Murder-suicide
- Thrill killing
- Self defense
- Random killing
- Sex and sadism
- Love triangles
- Jealousy
- Drug connection
- Gang involvement

In recent years, interest has been shown in reexamining solved and unsolved murders dating back decades—to the 19th century or before. As in a hot homicide, however, there is no one best way or one-size fits-all method of investigation. Each cold case is investigated on its own merits and the circumstances surrounding the crime, building upon those records available to modern investigators. Modern cold case investigation teams professional law enforcement practices with forensic knowledge and technology. This combination has been applied to revisiting unsolved murders dating back 10, 20, and 30 years, or more.

"ICEMAN"

The circumstances and cause of death surrounding "Iceman" illustrate a number of lessons for those who would examine cold cases. Iceman, or Iceman Ötzi, was a preserved human being whose mummified remains were discovered in 1991 frozen in a glacier in the Ötztal Alps bordering Italy and Austria (see Figure 1.1). The reporting parties were two German hikers. It has been estimated that he died approximately 5300 years ago. The discovery of this well preserved early man 11,000 feet above sea level created a sensation among scientists and the public.

Initial reports, based in part upon the location of his remains in a glacier, suggested that he had perhaps been killed in a fall, or had perished from hypothermia or drowning. Others theorized that he had been a human sacrifice. Examination of the remains indicated that he was 46 years old and was armed with an unfinished bow, arrows, and a dagger while ascending the glacier from the

FIGURE 1.1 Iceman Ötzi. (© South Tyrol Museum of Archaeology, www.iceman.it)

valley floor. Forensic examination revealed an arrow point in his left shoulder. Years later, however, one of the two people who discovered the body subsequently stated that, when first observed, the Iceman was clutching a knife in his right hand. Such information, as in more recent cold case homicide investigations, brought a fresh examination and interpretation of the deceased and of the events surrounding his death.

A knife *had* been found at the scene but was apparently dislodged when the mummified remains were removed. A cold case investigator seeking to examine this case would inquire if there were any photographs taken *before* the body was moved? When later placed in Iceman's clenched hand, the knife did fit. Fresh forensic examination revealed what appeared to be a defensive wound on his right hand. Other injuries included a gash on his left hand, a slash on his right forearm and bruising on his torso. Thus, it appears that the victim may have been involved in a fight. DNA examination of his effects revealed different sequences of ancient human DNA, suggesting that he died from violent wounds inflicted by others. DNA taken from his cloak, a broken arrow point, the arrow shaft, and from his knife blade did not match Iceman's DNA. Ultimately, forensic examiners concluded that he was shot with an arrow from behind while fighting with at least one other assailant, and may have bled to death from the arrow wound. Ensuing examinations have included various disciplines, including plant morphology and metallurgy, that are employed in some modern homicide investigations. In many ways, this was the coldest of cold cases.

MURDER IN THE 20TH CENTURY

The number of unsolved murders in the U.S. is unknown. No comprehensive databases for reporting or recording murder existed in the U.S. throughout the 20th century, and none that track unsolved cases on a national basis exist today. The Vital Statistics Division of the National Center for Health Statistics (NCHS) currently records mortality information resulting from death certificate information as received from coroners or medical examiners.

In the early years of the 20th century, some states reported death certificate information while others did not. It was not until the 1930s that vital statistics reporting became fully national. Prior to this time, the reliability and presence of this information depended on which cities and states participated. While some eastern cities, such as Boston and Washington, D.C., furnished such information in the late 19th century, Georgia reportedly did not begin to provide this information until 1922, and Texas followed suit in 1933. Beginning in the mid 1930s, law enforcement- and mortality-based data are increasingly more reliable than the sporadic data of the first third of the century.

Interestingly enough, in the early part of the century, coroners in some locales in the U.S. practiced a "fee for service" program for enumeration. By this method, they were paid in part depending upon the manner of death they decreed for each death. A fee schedule was linked to the death reported, irrelevant of the difficulty or length of time of the case. In the case of murder, the fee was often to be collected from the convicted perpetrator. One can only imagine that when a body is found with multiple gunshot wounds in the back and no known suspect in sight, death may have been recorded as other than murder. I have reviewed some murder cases going back to the 1930s in which I wondered about the true mode of death.

MODERN CRIME REPORTING

According to the U.S. Department of Justice, Bureau of Statistics (BJS), homicide is of interest due not only to its severity but because it is a fairly reliable barometer of all violent crime, and is a crime most likely to be reported and investigated. No other crime is measured as precisely and accurately as homicide. In addition, homicide is one means by which the public gauges police operation and efficiency. In 1929, the International Association of Chiefs of Police established a system to begin to uniformly collect law enforcement statistics and record national crime information. This was done in such a way as to standardize variations in which crimes were defined in various regions of the country.

The following year, the Bureau of Investigation (later renamed the Federal Bureau of Investigation or FBI) initiated the Uniform Crime Reporting (UCR) program. Subsequently, law enforcement data at the national level began to be compiled in 1933. The UCR program collects and publishes criminal offense, arrest, and law enforcement personnel statistics. The program's principal objective is to generate a reliable set of criminal justice statistics for use in the administration and management of law enforcement. Information on the number of persons arrested includes numerous other additional crime types including drug abuse violations and driving under the influence.

Sources of early murder data are sometimes questionable or incomplete. Not every jurisdiction and police agency participated in this program in the early 1930s. Its initial objective was to provide an accounting of the nature and extent of criminal activity, and it was intended to serve as an administrative tool for better criminal justice management within law enforcement agencies. In the succeeding decades, the UCR has become a source to gauge the country's social order, and it is referenced by urban planners and scholars.

The FBI publishes an annual report, "Crime in the United States, Uniform Crime Report." The data for this report is gathered from monthly reports submitted by law enforcement as a result of information that has come to the attention of law enforcement agencies from victim reports or observation. This information is reported directly to the FBI or through respective centralized state agencies. This report summarizes the amount of violent crime and property crime reported the previous year. According to the FBI UCR, seven main offense classifications, known as Part I crimes, were chosen to gauge the state of crime in the nation. These included:

- Homicide and non-negligent manslaughter
- Forcible rape
- Robbery
- Aggravated assault

and the property crimes of Burglary, Larceny-theft, and Motor vehicle theft. Arson was added in 1979. Together, these crimes reflect and gauge fluctuations in the overall volume and rate of crime.

The annual report analyzes crime by region in the U.S. as well as analyzing many factors involved in murder and other reported offenses. These analyses, such as known victim–offender relationships, have evolved over the decades and the UCR is a continually evolving document. Awareness of victim–offender relationship is an important component of many homicide investigations, and this relationship may become more viable in cold case investigations. Much of the statistical data is derived from the Supplemental Homicide Reports (SHR) program. This supplemental information is derived from monthly submissions with detail on the victim, location, and offender characteristics (if known). In addition, these reports detail the month and year of the offense, the reporting agency and residential population, county and metropolitan information, geographic division and population group based on the age, race, and sex of victims and offenders, and on the victim–offender relationship, weapon use, and other crime circumstances.

BACKGROUND OF CURRENT COLD CASE PROBLEM

According to the BJS "Homicide Trends in the U.S.", contributing agencies provided supplemental information for 466,195 of the estimated 512,550 murders estimated to have been committed between 1976 and 2000. Additionally, supplemental information was also provided for 516,005 of the estimated 564,547 offenders. While the UCR is based on information reported by law enforcement agencies, not all agencies report data to the UCR. As a result, the data reflected in the UCR is not an absolute figure but is an *estimate*. According to the BJS, the most significant problem in using SHR data to analyze offender characteristics "is the sizeable and growing number of unsolved homicides contained in the data file."

As it was once explained to me: "There are lies, damn lies ... and the UCR."

Acting as a national clearing house for homicide data, the UCR describes the conditions by which a homicide case is considered solved or cleared (closed). These are:

- When at least one person is arrested, charged with the commission of an offense, and turned over to a court for prosecution.
- By exceptional means. This occurs when circumstances beyond the law enforcement agency's control preclude the agency from placing formal charges against an identified offender. To clear a crime in this manner, an agency must have: (1) identified the offender; (2) enough evidence to support an arrest; (3) identified the offender's location; and (4) a reason outside the agency's control that does not allow the agency to arrest, charge, and prosecute an offender. These circumstances may occur when the offender dies by suicide or is justifiably killed by police or citizenry. Official closure of the case may also result when the victim refuses to cooperate with the prosecution after the identification of the offender or denial of extradition because the offender committed a crime in another jurisdiction and is being prosecuted there.

Each of these is a potential option in closing a cold case investigation.

RATES AND TRENDS 1900–1950

HOMICIDE

Population and demographic changes and post turn-of-the-century immigration changed the nation. During this period, the nation underwent transformation from agrarian and rural to one more urban in nature, and the big cities saw concentrated pockets of those with similar ethnic and cultural origins. The crime patterns and trends that originated during this period have in part become the basis for police, legal, and forensic practices today. During this period, the murder rate has varied significantly. This is reflected in Figure 1.2.

The compilation of homicide data from death certificates for the whole of the 20th century makes it possible to view rises and falls in the homicide rate (the number of homicide victims per

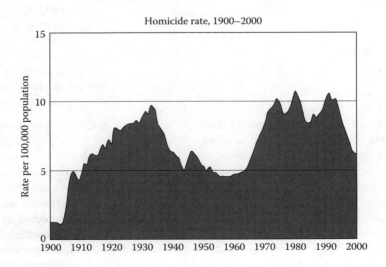

FIGURE 1.2 Homicide rate 1900–2000. (Courtesy of National Center for Health Statistics)

100,000 population). This can be viewed against a backdrop of national events. Certain major events appear to have contributed to changes in the crime rate during this period. According to the National Vital Health Statistics System, the murder rate rose from one homicide per 100,000 population to a peak of 9.8 in 1933.

Post-WWI events saw increased reporting on crime by the national press and reaction from state and federal governments. National Prohibition, that period between 1920 and 1933 when America went dry, brought organized crime to the forefront of national attention and encouraged the efforts of federal law enforcement to assume a stronger role in criminal investigation. In part due to the use of machine guns by gangsters and others during this period, America witnessed the origins of national gun control through the beginning of the National Firearms Act in 1934 that regulated private possession of fully automatic firearms. The Lindberg kidnapping brought forth federal kidnapping statutes, paving the way for future federal legislation encompassing a wide variety of topics in the later part of the century.

The subsequent period witnessed the recovery from the Great Depression and the onset of WWII. These events affected the homicide rate, as evidenced by a sharp decline during the war years and a short time rise thereafter. The rates fell during the 1950s, but the postwar baby boom generation began to mature in the early 1960s. At this time, the homicide rate began to rise sharply. Subsequently, this upward swing occurred against a backdrop of the Viet Nam War and the sharp increase in drugs and gangs.

ADVANCES IN FORENSIC SCIENCE

Trace evidence, the idea that there occurred a transfer of telltale evidence between an offender to a victim or crime scene was formally advanced in the early 20th century by Edmond Locard (1877–1866). A Frenchman, Locard was the founder of the anthropometric service within the Lyon Police Service shortly before WWI. He later served as an educator in forensics, and strongly advocated analysis and examination of microscopic "trace" evidence. He noted that inculpatory evidence of a perpetrator was to be found in the examination of soil and dust, and that examination of clothing, shoes, underclothing, body parts including skin, hair, and nails as well as weapons and vehicles, would reveal a telltale linkage between the offender and the scene or the victim. If the offender did not bring something to the scene, he certainly took something away, and proper forensic microscopic examination would reveal it. Thus, the foundation of trace, or microscopic, evidence is to be found in the contact between people, places, and objects. With the advent of DNA technology late in the century, Locard's theories became consistent with our use of this advanced technology.

BLOOD AND SEROLOGY

Scientific investigation in the 19th century recognized the forensic potential for detection of blood at crime scenes and upon the clothing of suspected perpetrators. At the beginning of the 20th century, science lacked a reliable method of distinguishing bloodstains of an animal from those of a human. Bloodstains did not mean much in most of those early investigations, as a claim could be made that bloodstains came from a nosebleed or an animal. Science could not reliably differentiate.

This changed in 1901, however, when Paul Uhlenhuth discovered a method to distinguish human blood from that of animals. This was the beginning of the branch of science called serology. The precipitin test, as it came to be known, soon became a benchmark in scientific criminology. About this same time, Karl Landsteiner discovered the existence of different blood types and the compatibility or incompatibility among certain groups of people. He identified three blood groups, A, B, and C. Shortly thereafter, C became AB and O was recognized. Thus, the four groups we know today were identified in the first years of the 20th century. The use of this knowledge was primarily applied to paternity issues, however. For criminal cases in America, the science did not go far beyond differentiating animal blood from human during the first half of the century.

Firearms Identification

The concept of matching a fired projectile to a specific firearm dates at least to the 18th century. More formal, albeit less scientific, application of this concept began to surface in the later part of the 1800s and early 20th century. A series of high-profile crimes during the first quarter of the century focused America's attention on the application of science to the criminal justice process and the courtroom. On April 15, 1920, an armored-car robbery in Braintree, Massachusetts, resulted in the shooting deaths of a guard and paymaster. Police arrested shoe factory worker Nicola Sacco and itinerant fish peddler Bartolomeo Vanzetti, and they were charged with the murders. This was the era of the Red Scare and both men were active anarchists. Racial and political overtones transcended the legal aspects of the case and the case attracted international attention.

Forensic examination presented by the prosecution affirmed that their weapon fired the fatal shots and both were sentenced to death. Others disagreed. In the courtroom process, those who testified for the prosecution that fired projectiles and shell casings came from a specific weapon were countered by experts for the defense that the suspect weapon did not fire the items. After lengthy legal appeals and controversy surrounding witness identification and forensic presentations in the courtroom, both men were executed in 1927. In this and other cases, juries were left to believe or disregard the testimony of experts. During this period, anyone with a microscope and a camera could hold themselves up to be a "criminologist" and the field was marked by charlatans and frauds. The "expert" witness had come to stay.

In June, 1925, the *Saturday Evening Post* reported upon the advances in forensics as they pertained to firearms examinations and "fingerprinting" of bullets. The public was informed of the advances in matching fired projectiles to specific firearms and of a new device, the comparison microscope. This piece of equipment was developed by Charles Waite, a former New York Attorney General's investigator; John Fisher, a student of physics; chemist Howard Gravelle; and reserve army officer Calvin Goddard, M.D. It utilized two lens systems which, when combined with prisms, allowed an examiner to bring two images side by side for comparison. Thus, an examiner could compare a suspect projectile and a known exemplar together under conditions more conducive to accurate comparison and analysis than previous methods. Goddard and others advanced the use of forensic sciences and the establishment of formal schools for training investigators in the application of science to the courtroom and in the criminal investigation process. Goddard and others were the harbingers of professional standards in the area of identifying characteristics of spent bullets and shell casings, and examination of firearms for forensic purposes.

On the west coast in this same time period, Edward O. Heinrich (see Figure 1.3) offered to law enforcement and the courtroom process the results of years of formal academic training and experience in the physical sciences. He has been called perhaps America's first academically trained forensic scientist. Upon graduation from the University of California at Berkeley with a degree in chemistry in 1908, Heinrich began to apply the field to areas in criminal investigation. As a generalist, his practice included a variety of forensic skills, including questioned document and firearms examination. During the ensuing decades, he was employed to examine evidence in a multitude of high-profile murders and other cases. Upon his death in 1953, his life works, including case files, notebooks, photo archives, and other records were bequeathed to his alma mater.

Cold case homicide investigators can benefit from Heinrich's example. When reviewing cold cases in which any or all of the law enforcement or forensic participants have died, it is suggested that investigators identify those who may still possess their files and records and review any that exist. My investigation into the 1925 murders and subsequent alleged rapes discovered the existence and location of Heinrich's case files, which included extensive notes, reports, and photographs. Among these records was the forensic case file for the Wagner-Sweet homicide case. Figure 1.4 illustrates Heinrich's file photograph of Ryan's jacket. An examination of the bloodstains by a research physician identified human and non-human stains, a fact supporting Ryan's account and discounting the prosecution's. Accompanying notes and newspaper accounts reported that the pins

FIGURE 1.3 For the first half of the 20th century, criminalist Edward Oscar Heinrich advanced the forensic sciences by his application of science and technology in many high-profile criminal and civil cases. (Courtesy of Duayne J. Dillon, D.Crim.)

FIGURE 1.4 Jack Ryan's Jacket. In 1925, technology allowed only differentiation between human or animal blood. In his report concerning analysis of blood found on a suspect's jacket, Dr. Ernest Victors determined that both human and animal blood was present. This ran counter to the prosecution's theory that only human blood was present, and helped exonerate the defendant, who had a logical explanation for the presence of both types. (Courtesy of University Archives, Bancroft Library, University of California, Berkeley)

FIGURE 1.5 1949 *FBI Law Enforcement Bulletin*. By the late 1940s, the FBI laboratory was conducting forensic examinations in a variety of fields ranging from firearms examination to fingerprints to paint analysis. Since the 1930s the FBI Laboratory has set high standards for forensic examination of evidence.

were used to denote the direction of blood spatter. This file and its contents provided detailed information about case events and case forensics. As do many such investigations, methods and techniques used involved thinking "outside the box." Successful cold case investigations are often concluded by investigators who are resourceful and use imagination not normally associated with hot homicide investigation.

Local and state government agencies slowly began to build crime labs that could analyze physical evidence. In 1932, using a microscope borrowed from Bausch and Lomb, the origins of the FBI laboratory were born. By the middle of the century, the facility was conducting examinations for federal agencies and local and state law enforcement agencies. At this laboratory and others, forensic examinations included those related to firearms, serology, toolmark, paint, questioned documents, tire treads, shoeprints, and forensic geology. In publications such as the *FBI Law Enforcement Bulletin,* the federal agency announced these and other capabilities of the FBI Laboratory (see Figure 1.5). The field had come a long way in a short time.

RATES AND TRENDS 1950–2000

MURDER RATES AND TRENDS IN HOMICIDE

By 1944, the homicide rate had decreased to 5.0 murders per 100,000 population. It rose slightly in 1945 and 1946, and then declined to 4.5 per 100,000 in 1955. This period appears to be a turning point in the second half of the century. According to the BJS, murder rates subsequently increased each year from 1960 through the mid 1970s, and peaked at 10.2 per 100,000 in 1980. They dipped

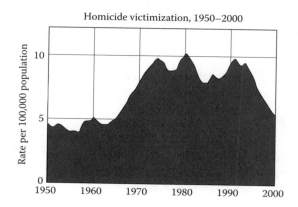

FIGURE 1.6 Homicide Victimization 1950–2000. (Courtesy of FBI Uniform Crime Reports and Bureau of Justice Statistics)

slightly in the mid 1980s, and then rose to 9.8 per 100,000 in 1991. For cold case homicide investigators, this is the birthing grounds for most of the cases they will encounter. By 1997, the nation's murder rate had fallen to the lowest level in 3 decades, with most of this occurring in cities with more than 1 million inhabitants. Nationally, murder rates had declined to 5.5 per 100,000 by 2000 and this decline has allowed law enforcement agencies the opportunity to dedicate resources to reexamination of unsolved homicides (see Figure 1.6).

FORENSIC SCIENCES AND TECHNOLOGY

In the 1950s, scientific breakthroughs laid the groundwork for significant advances in forensic and criminal investigation processes at the end of the century. In 1953, American scientist James Watson and Britain's Francis Crick demonstrated the double helix of the deoxyribonucleic acid (DNA) molecule. This was the beginning of the ability to identify individuals not by grouping, as in ABO serology, but now down to the individual. This is further discussed in Chapter 15. In 1986, British scientist Alec Jeffries first applied DNA identification to the criminal investigative process. His efforts resulted in the capture of a perpetrator for the rape-murders of two young girls in England by linking biological evidence left at the crime scene to a local baker. The forensic value of DNA quickly became apparent, but not just for conviction of criminal defendants. In 1989, the first U.S. DNA database was created, and in that year, David Vazquez reportedly became the first person in the U.S. exonerated through post-conviction DNA testing. Convicted of rape, Vazquez was freed after another individual was identified through DNA testing as responsible for the crime for which Vazquez had been sentenced. The forensic value of DNA became a highlight of forensic advances in the later half of the century.

In 1992, the FBI introduced the Combined DNA Index System (CODIS), which was designed to be a national database for linking crimes to criminals through DNA. In 1995, O.J. Simpson was acquitted of murder despite what many people saw as strong DNA evidence against him. Evidence collection and custody issues were microscopically analyzed in court and in the media, and as a result, methods of handling and testing of evidence underwent significant analysis and change. By 2003, a Justice Department survey found that two thirds of the chief prosecutors in U.S. courts were using DNA in criminal investigations and trials.

Other disciplines came into their own during the latter half of this century. In 1954, Marilyn Sheppard was murdered in Cleveland, Ohio. The investigation and subsequent trial became a media circus. Her husband, Dr. Sam Sheppard, was tried for her murder and convicted. Sheppard insisted throughout his life that a "bushy-haired intruder" committed the crime, knocking him unconscious and murdering his wife. University of California forensic scientist Paul Kirk analyzed bloodstains

Sheppard Evidence Turns Up in Bay Area

Blood from 1954 slaying in 2 vials

Associated Press

Cleveland

Missing blood evidence from the Dr. Sam Sheppard murder case has resurfaced in the Bay Area, potentially offering new clues as to whether he committed the slaying that inspired TV's "The Fugitive."

A court order says the material in Walnut Creek — forgotten for decades — includes two vials containing bloodstains taken from a wardrobe door in Marilyn Sheppard's bedroom after her 1954 slaying.

Sam Sheppard

Sheppard spent 10 years in prison for the beating death of his pregnant wife. He was acquitted at a second trial in 1966 and died four years later.

The doctor insisted throughout his life that a "bushy-haired intruder" knocked him unconscious and killed his wife.

Sheppard's estate, on behalf of the couple's only son, Sam Reese Sheppard, who lives in Oakland, is now suing the state of Ohio in civil court, claiming wrongful imprisonment.

The wardrobe bloodstains are "of huge significance," Terry Gilbert, an attorney for the younger Sheppard, said yesterday. "It is a potential source of blood from a third-party suspect in the murder room itself, something that we have not had yet in this case."

County prosecutors maintain that too much time has passed and too much evidence has been lost to make a definitive conclusion about the killer.

Cuyahoga County Common Pleas Judge Ronald Suster ordered last week that the bloodstains be sent back to Cleveland from Walnut Creek, where they are in the hands of forensic scientist John Murdoch.

Murdoch was a student at the University of California at Berkeley of Paul Kirk, a forensic scientist hired by the Sheppard family.

In 1955, Kirk collected samples and analyzed bloodstains at the crime scene. He concluded that Sheppard's blood was not present in the room.

From the shape of the bloodstain on the wardrobe, he also deduced that it came from the killer touching it, rather than from blood spattered from Marilyn Sheppard.

Kirk died in 1970, and when his office was later cleaned out, Murdoch received a box of material related to the case, including the vials with the bloodstains, Gilbert said. Murdoch, who now works for the federal Bureau of Alcohol Tobacco and Firearms, learned through another scientist about the current case and contacted the Sheppard team last month.

Murdoch was at a meeting in Maryland yesterday and could not be reached.

FIGURE 1.7 News story regarding Sam Sheppard. It is suggested that cold case investigators seek to identify the disposition of the forensic collections of deceased forensic scientists involved in now-cold case investigations. (*San Francisco Chronicle*)

and patterns at the crime scene. He concluded that Sheppard's blood was not present at the scene. He further deduced that a bloodstain on a piece of furniture was left there when the killer touched it, and not from blood spattered from the victim. Kirk's role in this notorious crime enhanced forensic and public awareness of blood spatter analysis. After serving 10 years in prison, Dr. Sheppard was acquitted at a second trial and died in 1970. This case further illustrates the value of determining the disposition of the case files, notes, and records of case personnel. Kirk died in 1970, and in the late 1990s, an unsuccessful legal action was brought to clear Dr. Sheppard's name. Two vials of blood from the crime scene were discovered in the possession of one of Kirk's students, who had acquired some of the famed scientist's property after his demise. It became a focal point in the resultant civil action (see Figure 1.7).

ROLE AND INFLUENCE OF THE MEDIA

Coupled with advances in the legal and criminal investigation processes and forensic technology, the role of the media entered into the ability of law enforcement to investigate crime. This affected investigative efforts in the field and events in the nation's courtrooms. The results have directly impacted the public perception of forensic science and how cold case investigators assemble their cases.

COPS AND THE MEDIA

In the early 1950s, television began to supplement and replace newsprint as the source of America's news. Television shows about the police, including "M-Squad" and "Dragnet" popularized and glamorized the police role, especially homicide detectives. This popularization, however, sometimes tainted and misinformed the public about the homicide investigation process and police work in general. Television shows such as "The Andy Griffith Show" and "Car 54 Where Are You?" portrayed law enforcement in a comical, non-realistic setting. While vast differences did, and do, exist between large metropolitan agencies and their rural counterparts, these images have remained to this day in the minds of the baby-boomer and subsequent generations through reruns of these episodes. These events may impact cold case investigators. Perception is reality, and perception of the police as "Andy of Mayberry" or "Joe Friday" may affect the willingness of some to speak to the police about events long ago and to cooperate with cold case investigators. This perception may also carry over into the jury pool in a courtroom.

Television shows about police work saturated the airwaves during the last quarter of the century. Programs from the 1960s and 1970s such as "Adam-12" and "Police Story" gave insight into police practices and professionalized the law enforcement image. In the last decade of the century, television programs such as "NYPD Blue" and "Law and Order" impacted the way America viewed law enforcement and the court process. True-life television coverage of events such as the Los Angeles-based SLA shootout and the Rodney King and O.J. Simpson episodes also contributed to America's perception of police and police practices.

The 1990s and beginnings of the 21st century marked a turning point in television's script-based portrayal of law enforcement. Programs such as "COPS" and "America's Most Wanted" portrayed the reality of law enforcement, and reminded viewers that the world of police work is sometimes brutal and violent, and that the police investigation process cannot be accomplished between commercials. In this evolution, however, a new trend emerged that has impacted homicide investigations, the courtroom process, and cold case investigations. This was the marriage of television with the courtroom and forensics.

Television shows based around advances in forensic sciences such as "CSI," "Cold Case," and "Cold Case Files" have emerged as among the most popular and watched in television. (However, I have never seen a crime scene investigator or technician come to a scene or the laboratory in leather pants and high heels.) Together with television coverage of live courtroom proceedings, these elements have combined to raise the public's expectation of homicide investigation to a new level. This expectation is brought to the courtroom by the potential jury pool. As a result, advances in forensics as well as law enforcement investigative methods are perhaps more closely scrutinized now than in decades past. This is significant for cold case investigators, as they must build upon the work performed during a different period and perhaps a different level of expectation, and subsequently develop it to meet today's standards. Past evidence identification and collection practices may directly affect their ability to conduct and resolve cold case investigations.

LAW ENFORCEMENT CULTURE, ORGANIZATION, AND PRACTICES

The changing landscape of American law enforcement has challenged and affected the ability of cold case investigators to solve cold case homicides. In the late 1960s, most of the nation's 40,000 police forces had 10 or fewer members. In many instances, organizational structure and practices had not changed perceptively for decades. Nationally, approximately 40 county, municipal, and state agencies had more than 1000 personnel. Coordination among agencies was sometimes sporadic

FIGURE 1.8 1950s police officer/dispatcher. (Courtesy of El Segundo Police Department)

and informal, and rivalries and jealousies between some police departments and sheriff's departments have carried over to this day. The result is a lack of communication and coordination. This
fragmentation plays into the ability of perpetrators to commit their crimes, cross jurisdictional
boundaries, and get away.

In the first few decades following WWII, many states increased selection and training standards
for police-empowered personnel. In the mid-1970s, some agencies were implementing variations
of community policing and redesigning their organizational structure. Some agencies experimented
with the abandonment of the police uniform in favor of less militaristic attire. Many, however,
remained entrenched in the traditional hierarchy of patrol, traffic, detectives, and administration
(see Figure 1.8). Standards for selection of detectives varied, and it was not uncommon that such
personnel, especially in smaller agencies, were promoted for reasons other than demonstrated
investigative ability. Knowledge of organizational structure, culture, and records and evidence
practices is of importance to cold case investigators, and this will be discussed in future chapters.

In 2000, approximately 17,000 city, county, and state law enforcement agencies representing
about 94% of the total population in America voluntarily reported data on crimes that were known
to them through reports to their agency to the UCR. America has long resisted any attempts to
create a national uniform police agency such as is found in Europe and other countries. This
patchwork condition, termed by crime writer Joseph Wambaugh as the "Balkanization" of the U.S.,
is a contributing factor in the amount and nature of the cold case homicide problem in the U.S.

The landscape of American law enforcement comprises city police departments operating within
an incorporated jurisdiction, while county sheriffs are responsible for investigation of crimes that
occur within the unincorporated regions of the state in which the county is located. In addition,
states operate their own agencies with statewide jurisdiction to investigate crimes, including murder,

and these may be known as state police, state troopers, or other names. Further, murders committed on federal reservations may not be reflected in local statistics; instead, these case files are in the custody and control of agencies such as the Federal Bureau of Investigation or Naval Criminal Investigative Service.

As a result, multiple jurisdictions, each with its own traditions, hierarchy, policies, ranks, rules, and procedures, practice their own brand of communication—or in some cases, lack of communication. Similarly, each agency maintains its own system of information retention and retrieval, as well as property and evidence rules, procedures and methods of evidence storage. Failure in intra-agency and inter-agency communications has been a contributory factor to the unsolved, or cold case, problem.

The advent of microfiche and microfilm impacted department record keeping and retrieval. In the early 1980s the computer began to revolutionize the way the world worked. Law enforcement recognized the advantages of computerizing records and communications, and a new means of recording and retrieving information evolved. These changes occurred in police agencies of all sizes, creating new sources of potential data retrieval for those investigating homicides and other serious crimes. Unfortunately, in some cases, as these records were converted to other formats, it was not uncommon for agencies to destroy the original records. These developments merged to lay the foundation for a new type of homicide investigation and murder investigator, the cold case detective.

HIGHLIGHTS OF HOMICIDE PATTERNS AND TRENDS 1976–2000

Traditional legal doctrine in the U.S. was to treat juveniles as potentially subject to rehabilitation. Even for egregious acts, the punishments for juveniles were not in proportion to adult offenders who committed the same crimes. This began to change at the federal and state levels in the 1980s as it became apparent that juveniles were committing violent crimes and hiding behind the façade of their supposedly youthful innocence. Due to changes in the laws as a result, juveniles as young as 15 years of age have now been sentenced to life in prison. The increase in street gangs and the influence of prison gangs further contributed to the murder problem during this period.

According to the BJS, murder victim and offending rates for teens and young adults rose sharply, during the later part of the 1980s and the early 1990s, then subsequently declined in the later 1990s. The rates for those older than 25, however, has declined steadily during the last 2 decades of the century. During this era, males were found to be more than nine times more likely than females to commit murder, and both male and female offenders were more likely to target males than female victims.

In 1970, an estimated 15,810 murders represented a 76% increase over the 9000 estimated murders in 1960. In 1970, 86% of these reported murders were cleared or solved.

In 1980, 23,044 murders were reported, and the homicide rate peaked at an all-time high of 10.2 per 100,000 population. In these cases according to FBI and BJS reports:

- 17,559 offenders were arrested, resulting in a 72% overall clearance rate.
- Over three quarters of all victims were male.
- 45% of those arrested for murder were under age 25.
- Those 18–24 years of age accounted for approximately 35% of those arrested in that year.

As reported by the FBI UCR and the BJS, 23,438 murders were reported in 1990, and 67% of these were cleared. In addition, it is estimated that:

- 78% of victims were male.
- 90% of victims were 18 years old or more.
- 49% of victims were ages 20–34.

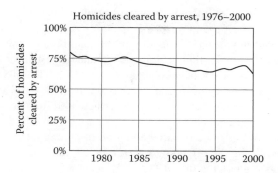

FIGURE 1.9 Homicides cleared by arrest 1976–2000. (Bureau of Justice Statistics)

- Over half of the victims were related to or acquainted with their assailant.
- 14% were murdered by strangers.
- There was an unknown relationship factor in 35% of the murders.
- 35% of female victims were slain by husbands or boyfriends. (Source: UCR 1970–2000 and Bureau of Justice Statistics)

CLEARANCE RATES

Clearance rates are the number of homicides that are cleared or solved. Law enforcement agencies like to reflect high clearance rates for homicide and other violent crimes. During these last decades, however, another trend became evident. This trend is a foundation for cold case investigators: the number of homicides cleared by arrest has been declining (see Figure 1.9). According to the BJS, 79% of all homicides were reported cleared in 1976. In 1997, the figure had dropped to 66% of all homicides' being reported as cleared, while, by 2000, the clearance rate was 63%. This was the lowest clearance rate yet. In addition:

- Males made up 76.2% of murder victims.
- 45.1% of male victims were between ages 20–34.
- Males were most often murdered by males.
- 90.8% of females were murdered by males.
- Approximately 44.3% of all victims knew their offenders.
- 13% of victims were slain by strangers. (Source: UCR and Bureau of Justice Statistics)

This is significant for understanding of the cold case problem in the U.S. It has been estimated that perhaps 40% of the murders nationwide have remained unsolved. It is important to note that arrests made subsequent to the initial offense reporting would impact the total number of unsolved cases, but, as this information is not tracked outside of the investigating agency, this information is not known. However, these numbers indicate the potential scope of the problem.

Other significant factors have emerged that, combined, further impact the cold case homicide problem that has resulted from events between 1976 and 2000. According to the UCR and BJS,:

- Approximately one third of murder victims and almost half of the offenders were under age 25.
- Killings within the family made up about one quarter of all homicides, and over one half involved spouse killing spouse.
- More than four out of ten homicides were due to argument outside the family unit.

- In husband–wife homicides, the wife was the victim in 54% of the murders; the husband was the victim in 46% of the murders.
- Males outnumbered females as victims by more than three to one.
- Five males were arrested for murder for every female arrested for murder.
- Six of every ten victims were between ages 20 and 45; 30% fell within ages 20–29.
- 10% of all persons arrested for murder were under age 18; 43% were under age 25.
- Offending rates for teenagers and young adults increased dramatically in the late 1980s while rates for older groups declined.
- 18–24-year-olds have historically had the highest offending rates and their rates doubled from 1985–1993. While the offending rate for 18–24 year olds has declined, it remains higher than levels prior to the mid–1980s.
- The homicide offending rates of 14-17 year-olds exploded after 1985.
- Homicide rates for large cities (over 100,000 population) varied by size.
- Over half the homicides occurred in cities with population of 100,000 or more.
- Approximately one quarter of the homicides occurred in cities of 1,000,000 or more.
- Stranger murders accounted for approximately 14% of all murders.
- Victim–Offender relationship was undetermined in about one third of all homicides
- Over one quarter of the victims of gang-related killings were under the age of 18.
- Juveniles were also usually involved as victims of family members, sex-related homicides, and homicide by arson or poison.
- Juveniles are especially implicated as offenders in homicides involving multiple perpetrators, or gang related.
- A large percentage of older victims suffer felony murder, workplace murder, and arson homicide.
- Large cities were much more commonly the site of drug-related and gang-related killings and relatively less likely to be the location of family-related and work-related murders.

Further statistics on intimate homicide (spouses, ex-spouses, boyfriends, and girlfriends):

- Intimate murders, while dropping in larger and small cities and suburban areas, made up a larger proportion of murders in rural areas than in suburban or urban environments.
- The number of men murdered by intimates dropped by 68% since 1976.
- The number of women killed by intimates, while stable for 2 decades, declined somewhat between 1993–1995 (coincidentally the era of the O.J. Simpson media blitz) and remained relatively stable through 2000.
- About 11% of murder victims were determined to have been killed by an intimate.
- Spouses and family members made up about 15% of all victims.
- Female murder victims were substantially more likely than male murder victims to have been killed by an intimate.
- Among all homicide victims, women were particularly at risk for intimate killings, sex-related homicides, and murder by arson or poison.

THE UNSOLVED HOMICIDE PROBLEM TODAY

The highest homicide rates of the 20th century occurred during the last 2 decades of the 20th century. FBI special Agent Charles L. Regini summarized the background and nature of the cold case problem today in his report in the *FBI Law Enforcement Bulletin* in August, 1997. During this period, traditional patterns and trends were impacted by the rise in gangs and drugs, stranger killings or drive-by shootings. The growth in drug-related homicides, crimes much more time consuming and difficult to solve, provided new challenges to law enforcement. During this era, murder became more vicious, senseless, and random. The link between victim and killer became more blurred and motives were uncommonly thin. In addition, killers were themselves not infrequently killed before they could be identified or located. Further, insufficient investigation allowed uncharged killers to be released back on the street to continue to kill.

During this period, traditional investigative approaches such as focusing on motive, were less effective in solving these cases. Practical difficulties of identifying and locating witnesses, overcoming their hostility and obtaining their confidence posed additional problems beyond the normal realm. Fear of retribution affected efforts to secure witness cooperation and obtain needed testimony in court. Additionally, the lifestyles of many of these witnesses impacted credibility and compounded the difficulties in investigation and prosecution.

The ability of law enforcement to adequately investigate the sharp rise in homicides decreased under the onslaught as a steady stream of fresh murders taxed overworked investigative, forensic, and medical examiner resources. This was especially true in some of the nation's largest cities, but also in smaller jurisdictions and more rural areas. Available resources were not sufficient to keep up with the surge and spike in homicides. As a result, many agencies found themselves unable to supply the necessary fiscal, technological, educational, or manpower resources necessary to efficiently and adequately address each new homicide. In some cases, less-experienced personnel lacking the skill and practice were assigned to investigate homicides. The growth in stranger-to-stranger homicides further exacerbated the problem, as traditional homicide investigation focused on identifying a known victim–offender relationship.

WHAT ARE COLD CASES?

Cold case is a concept, and as such, there is no one standard definition of a cold case homicide. These are those homicides that others, perhaps more experienced, tried to solve and could not. These are homicides previously reported to law enforcement and investigated; yet lack resolution. These are cases in which a suspect may have been known to the investigators, yet there was insufficient evidence for arrest and charging. These also include those cases in which no perpetrator has been identified, and the case is a "whodunit" (see Figure 1.10).

Cold case homicides are among the most difficult and frustrating cases facing investigators. In addition to having been previously reported and investigated, such cases may include homicides in which:

- The primary investigator has transferred to another area or been otherwise detached from the case and the case is not currently assigned to an investigator.
- No current investigative activity is taking place due to lack of leads or information.
- The case is at least a year old but has had no activity on it for at least 1 year.

In my experience, the "cold case" definition varies and the specific designation of what constitutes a cold case rests with guidelines used by the individual law enforcement agency responsible for the investigation of the crime. Theirs is the definition they design to designate the parameters to allow those cases to be classified and investigated as cold case homicides within the agency. Some specify that a lengthy period of time must have elapsed between the commission of the crime and present. Others require that 1 year must have passed or a change of personnel involved in the investigation process must have occurred. Among the various definitions of a cold case homicide or cases to be investigated as cold case murders are those with parameters that include:

- Unsolved cases prior to specific time period (ie., 1990).
- Unsolved cases during specific intervals (ie., 1960–1995).
- Long-term missing person's cases that have a high probability of being homicides.
- Cases wherein enough time has passed that the perpetrators begin to feel confidant enough to speak freely about their involvement, suggestively 5 years or more.

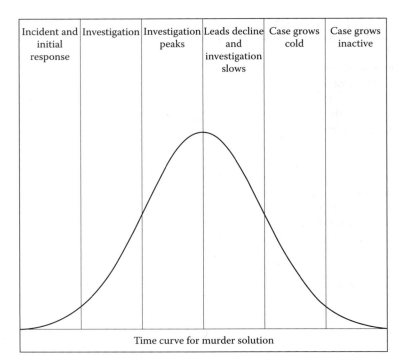

Incident and initial response	Investigation	Investigation peaks	Leads decline and investigation slows	Case grows cold	Case grows inactive

Time curve for murder solution

FIGURE 1.10 The investigation of homicides resembles the traditional bell curve. When the case is reported and investigation begins, it follows through until leads taper off and the investigation slows. As other cases consume agency resources, the case grows cold and inactive. At any time, the bell curve may again incline when new information comes in. It is not unusual that some cold case homicides, solved and unsolved, have shown a series of bell curves.

- Homicide cases older than 3 years from date of the offense in which no arrests have been made.
- Homicide cases older than 3 years from the date of the offense that are "closed-active" or cases that were closed by arrest of a suspect but the charges were dismissed without the suspect's going to trial.
- Homicide cases less than 3 years old from date of offense (including closed but active) in which all leads have been reasonably exhausted and investigation or assignment as a cold case homicide has been authorized by a responsible authority.
- Homicide cases in which the date that the death was ruled a homicide by the Medical Examiner's Office is greater than 1 year after the original event that led to the decedent's death. This would include those cases wherein the victim dies more than 1 year after the fatal injuries were received.
- Undetermined deaths of a suspicious nature older than 1 year following the death.
- Any case linked to a case under active investigation by a cold case investigation unit.
- A case at least a year old that has had no activity on it for at least 1 year.

WHY CASES GO COLD

Conventional wisdom in a homicide investigation has traditionally held that time is of the essence. For decades, this perception has guided investigators in their approach to homicide investigation.

It held that if a murder was not solved within the first 24–72 hours, the chances of solving the case rapidly diminish. Why? At the outset:

- Witnesses were still centrally located and easier to locate.
- Their recollection of events was fresh and most accurate.
- Those who may have been involved had not had a chance to get their stories and alibis straight among themselves.
- The chances of identifying and retrieving evidence are strongest at the outset, whereas as time passes, so does the evidence. In the ensuing interval, it may be damaged, lost, or destroyed.

Two primary factors may affect a homicide case's becoming a cold case. Awareness of these by cold case investigators may contribute to their understanding of the strengths and weaknesses of the initial investigation in their cold case investigation. These are: (1) case factors over which police have no control, and (2) organizational factors within the law enforcement agency over which the police have control.

1. Case factors over which the police have no control include:

- Lack of physical evidence
- Lack of witnesses
- Inability to identify victim
- Weapon used
- Gang or drug related
- Crime scene location (public vs. private)
- Previous technology inadequate to fully analyze evidence

2. Organizational factors within the law enforcement agency may include:

- Number of detectives originally assigned to case
- Detectives' case load
- Initial response and documentation
- Initial investigation and gathering of evidence
- Leads not followed up
- Retirement of investigators or other concerned personnel
- Promotion and transfer
- Leadership and organization commitment
- Budgetary and financial considerations
- Personnel management
- Politics and personal agendas

CASES MOST LIKELY TO GO COLD

Those cases most likely to go cold include cases involving:

- Missing persons
- Gang- or drug-related killings
- Immigrants, transients, and homeless victims
- Unidentified victims
- Suicides
- Accidental deaths

FIGURE 1.11 Unsolved murders of police are among some of the hardest to solve. Officer Mike Edwards was murdered in 1974 and the case remains unsolved. Use of media is one means to elicit information from the public in some of the more difficult cases. (Courtesy of Detective Rick Jackson, Los Angeles Police Department)

- Unclassified deaths
- Murders of police officers (see Figure 1.11)

How Old Is Cold?

Some departments have arbitrarily decreed that, absent compelling information and circumstances, they will not proactively review cases prior to a specific date or year. This is in part due to the rationalization that the chances of the perpetrator's remaining alive, witness availability and similar case factors are minimal or nonexistent. It is also in part due to optimizing use of available resources. Also factored into this set of guidelines is the easily recognizable availability of biological evidence suitable for DNA analysis or latent fingerprint evidence. Those who have expressed this parameter to me most often cite varying time periods in the 1960s to 1970 as the arbitrary cut-off date. This issue will be addressed in future chapters.

CASE STUDY

On the night of November 1, 1946, Miami police officer John Milledge, a male aged 48 years (see Figure 1.12), was on duty and patrolling near a city park in which a football game was being played. Milledge was among the first black officers appointed to the department during a time period when racial segregation was a predominant fact of life in the South. The presence of black police officers was a new concept in the city, and these officers were primarily assigned to the same racial areas. While on patrol, Milledge caught some local juveniles trying to sneak into the game. He reportedly struck some with his nightstick and they ran away. A short time later, an unknown assailant fired one shot from a .22 caliber weapon and struck Milledge in the neck. He died shortly thereafter at a local hospital. According to reports, witnesses reported seeing "some young negroes" nearby who might have been responsible, and another witness reported that one was carrying a rifle.

During the initial investigation, officers contacted two witnesses who advised them that on the night of the shooting, an individual known locally as "Fats" came to their residence and asked for a ride out of town. He was given a ride and never seen again. "Fats" became a prime suspect in the shooting, and officers learned his true name was Leroy Strachan. Officers learned he might have gone to New York City, but he was never located or contacted during the initial investigation. Other potential suspects were investigated, and the case went unsolved until 1989.

FIGURE 1.12 Officer John Milledge, one of the first African-American police officers in Miami, Florida, was shot from ambush in 1946. His murder was not solved until 1990, following revelations by a witness who had lived in fear of revealing what she knew. With the death of someone she feared, the witness now came forward. Change in relationships and no longer being in fear of another are significant solvability factors in solving cold case homicides. (Courtesy of Miami Police Department)

On July 27, 1989, 43 years after the murder, an anonymous caller to the local Crime Stoppers program indicated knowledge about the murder of a black police officer. The call was forwarded to the homicide unit of the Miami Police Department. The caller identified herself and gave a sworn statement. The caller was an elderly witness, a female who lived near the park. She reportedly was plagued by her conscience and wanted to tell what she knew but had withheld all these years.

On the night of the shooting, the witness was sitting on her porch with a male friend. A black teenager ran to her porch, almost out of breath. He was carrying a rifle. The witness described the teenager as having a bad eye. Upon seeing the rifle, her male friend went inside the house, and shortly afterwards, they learned a policeman had been shot. The witness initially misidentified the name of the teenager with the gun, but noted that he had a brother who was a close friend of her companion. She stated her companion subsequently told her the teen had left town. The witness further stated that she learned the teen had gone to New York, but she was afraid of her male companion and remained silent all these years. He had recently died.

The case was reopened and assigned to Detective George Cadavid of the Cold Case Squad of the City of Miami Homicide Unit. A 13-year veteran, Cadavid had been assigned to homicide for the past 10 years, and to this unit to reinvestigate unsolved cases for approximately 2 years. Cadavid located the original case on file with the police department. He reviewed the names of those contacted during the initial investigation, and reinterviewed some of these witnesses from 1946. Among those reinterviewed was the same male witness who gave "Fats" a ride out of town shortly after the shooting. With the passage of time, the witness now provided further detail of the events of that night, information not furnished to the police four decades before.

He stated that on the night of the shooting, which he remembered well, his brother and sister came home upset over the shooting of the officer. Later that night, "Fats" came to their house, nervous and scared, and wanted a ride out of town. During this conversation, "Fats" told the witness he had shot the officer. The witness stated he now knew "Fats" as Leroy Strachan, and that Leroy had a problem with one of his eyes. Except for the name, this information was consistent with information from the new witness.

Cadavid located Strachan, now age 62, in New York City. He learned that Strachan did have a problem with his left eye. A meeting was arranged and Strachan gave a taped statement. Strachan stated that on the night of the shooting, he and others tried to sneak into the game. Milledge caught them and hit a number of them with his nightstick. Strachan ran to a friend's house and retrieved a .22 caliber rifle. He and the friend returned to an alley across from the park, and his friend handed him the weapon.

He yelled for other boys in the alley to move and he fired one shot at the officer. He then ran home and left Miami the next day for New York. Strachan was indicted by a grand jury for the murder of Officer Milledge and arrested in New York City on February 15, 1990.

The police and assistant state attorney recommended waiver of the death penalty. Mitigating factors considered that Strachan had no significant criminal history prior to the murder, he was 18 years old at the time of the murder, and had not had any criminal activity for the subsequent 43 years in which he had been a law-abiding citizen with a wife and family. It is reported that some family members of the victim further believed that Strachan deserved a "break." Strachan subsequently pled guilty to manslaughter and was given credit for 19 months in custody time served and 400 hours community service each year for 5 years and 7 years' probation.

IDENTIFIED COLD CASE ISSUES

- Unsolved murder of police officer
- Media crime reporting program
- Tip from citizen due to conscience
- Department maintained case file
- Procedural assignment to experienced cold case detective
- Change in relationships due to passage of time
- Original investigation identified perpetrator yet never followed up
- Youthful age of offender
- Reinterview of original case witnesses
- New information by other witnesses
- Perpetrator now a religious person who admitted guilt
- Time, place, and social setting
- Legal, charging, and "justice" considerations

ACKNOWLEDGMENT

I wish to express my deep appreciation to Kim Rossmo, Ph.D., for his review and perspectives addressing criminal justice reporting methods and homicide trends in this chapter. Dr. Rossmo is a research professor in the Department of Criminal Justice at Texas State University, and a management consultant with the Bureau of Alcohol, Tobacco, Firearms and Explosives. Formerly, he was the Director of Research for the Police Foundation, and the Detective Inspector in Charge of the Vancouver Police Department's Geographic Profiling Section. His law enforcement experience spans more than 21 years in various assignments. Dr. Rossmo obtained his Ph.D in criminology from Simon Fraser University and has researched and published in the areas of policing, offender profiling, and environmental criminology. He is a member of the International Chiefs of Police Advisory Committee for Police Investigative Operations, and other advisory boards. He sits on the editorial board of the international journal *Homicide Studies*, and has further contributed to this book by authorship of Chapter 30, "Geographic Profiling."

SUGGESTED READING

Abrahamson, S. (2002). Using DNA to solve cold cases. Commission Report NCJ 194197. National Institute of Justice. Washington, D.C.

Anonymous (2002). Cold Case Homicide. C.P.T. Network. Sacramento, California Commission on Peace Officer Standards and Training.

AP (1997). "Sheppard evidence turns up in Bay Area." *San Francisco Chronicle,* July 17, 1997. San Francisco: A2.

Block, E.B. (1958). *The Wizard of Berkeley.* New York, Coward-McCann, Inc.

Block, E.B. (1979). *Science vs. Crime: The Evolution of the Police Lab.* San Francisco, Cragmont Publications.

Cadavid, G. (1991). Homicide Investigation F90-6184. Miami Police Report, Miami Police Department.

Carroll, R. (2002). "Wounds suggest iceman was stabbed in the back, fought attacker. (March 26, 2002). *The Guardian Unlimited*. Retrieved from http://www.nationalgeographic.com/news on August 23, 2004.

Department of Justice. Statistics (1983). Report to the Nation on Crime and Justice. Washington, D.C.

Eliopulos, L. (2003). *Death Investigators Handbook: Expanded and Updated Edition*. Boulder, CO, Palladin Press.

Ellis, K. (2004). "Kansas City cold case squad solves string of murders." *Police Executive Research Forum* 18: 1,7.

FBI (1970). Crime in the United States 1970: Uniform crime reports. Federal Bureau of Investigation. Washington, D.C.

FBI (2001). Crime in the United States 2000:Uniform crime reports. Federal Bureau of Investigation. Washington, D.C.

FBI (2002). Crime in the United States 2001: Uniform crime reports. Federal Bureau of Investigation. Washington, D.C.

Fowler, B. (2000). "The Iceman's last meal," NOVA online. http://www.pbs.org/wgbh/nova/icemummies/iceman.html. Retrieved December 9, 2003.

Fox, J.A. and M. Zawitz (1999). Homicide trends in the United States, Bureau of Justice Statistics. 2002.

Geberth, V. (1996). *Practical Homicide Investigation: Tactics, Procedures, and Forensic Techniques*. Boca Raton, FL, CRC Press.

Goddard, C. (1936). "A history of firearms identification." *Chicago Police Journal*.

Houck, M.M., Ed. (2001). *Mute Witness: Trace Evidence Analysis*. New York, Academic Press.

Lane, R. (1997). *Murder in America: A History*. Columbus, Ohio State University Press.

Lorenzi, R. (2003). "Details emerge of Iceman Otzi's death," http://dsc.discovery.com/news/briefs 20030811/iceman.html. Retrieved December 9, 2003.

McCall, P.L. and M. A. Zahn, (1999). "Trends and Patterns of Homicide in the 20th-Century United States." In M.D. Smith and M.A. Zahn, Eds. *Homicide: A Sourcebook of Social Research*. Thousand Oaks, CA, SAGE Publications.

Norrgard, D.L. (1969). *Regional Law Enforcement: A Study of Intergovernmental Cooperation and Coordination*. Danville, IL, Interstate Printers and Publishers, Inc.

Nyberg, R. (1999). "Investigations: Cold case squads re-activate old investigations." *Law and Order* 47(10): 127–130.

Regini, C.L. (1997). "The cold case concept." Federal Bureau of Investigation. Washington, D.C. *FBI Law Enforcement Bulletin* 66(8): 1–6.

Stout, W.W. (1925). "Fingerprinting bullets: The expert witness." *Saturday Evening Post*: 6–7, 193, 194, 197.

Stout, W.W. (1925). "Fingerprinting bullets: The expert witness." *Saturday Evening Post*: 18-19, 163, 165, 166, 169-170.

Thompson, G. and E. Williams (7/28/2003). "The thin blue line's new front line." *San Diego Union-Tribune*. San Diego: G1,5,6. Online at policeone.com.

Thorwald, J. 1967. *Crime and Science: The New Frontier in Criminology*. Trans. by Richard and Clava Winston New York: Harcourt, Brace and Winston.

Turner, R. and R. Kosa (2003). "Cold case squads: Leaving no stone unturned." *Bureau of Justice Assistance Bulletin*. U.S. Department of Justice. Washington, D.C.: 2–7.

Van Natta, D. (1991). "NY Man to plead guilty in 1946 Miami cop killing.' *Miami Herald*. Miami: 1, 14A.

Wambaugh, J. (2002). *Fire Lover*. New York, Avon Books.

Wellford, C. and J. Cronin (2000). "Clearing up homicide clearance rates." *National Institute of Justice Journal*(April, 2000): 3–7.

REFERENCES

Crank, J.P. (1998) *Understanding Police Culture*. Cincinnati: Ohio. Anderson Publishing Group.

Davies, H.J. (2003). Understanding variations in murder clearance rates: The influence of the political environment. Unpublished Ph.D dissertation. American University. Washington, D.C.

Fox, J.A. and Zawitz, M.W. (2003). Homicide trends in the United States. Bureau of Justice Statistics. Retrieved June 23, 2003 from http://www.ojp.usdoj.gov/bjs/homicide/html.

BJS. (2002). Homicide trends in the United States: Additional information about the data. (November 21, 2002). Bureau of Justice Statistics. Retrieved January 5, 2004 from http://www.ojp.usdoj.gov/bjs/homicide/addinfo.htm.

Fox, J.A. and Zawitz, M.W. (2003). Homicide trends in the United States: 2000 update. (January, 2003). (January, 2003) Bureau of Justice Statistics Data Brief. NCJ 197471. Washington, D.C.: Bureau of Justice Statistics.

IACP. (1994, November). Murder in America: Recommendations from the IACP murder summit. Paper presented at the IACP Murder Summit, Virginia.

Innes, M. (2002). Organizational communication and the symbolic construction of police murder investigations. *British Journal of Sociology*. 53(1), 67–87.

Langberg, R. (1967). Homicide in the United States, 1950–1964. (October, 1967). U.S. Department of Health, Education, and Welfare. U.S. Government Printing Office: Washington, D.C.

Manning, P.K. (1997). *Police work: The Social Organization of Policing* (2nd ed). Prospect Heights, Ill: Waveland Press.

Nyberg, P. (2004) Justice served cold. (October, 2004) policemag.com. 28,10. p 44, 46–48, 50–52.

Schein, E.H. (1992). *Organizational Culture and Leadership* (2nd ed.). San Francisco: Jossey-Bass.

Smith, M.D. and Zahn, M.A. (Eds.). (1999). *Homicide: A Sourcebook of Social Research*. Thousand Oaks, CA: Sage Publications.

Walton, R.H. (2005). Identification of solvability factors in twenty-first century cold case homicide investigation. Unpublished Ed.D dissertation. University of San Francisco. San Francisco, California.

Wolfgang, M.E. (1958). *Patterns in Criminal Homicide*. Philadelphia: University of Pennsylvania Press.

2 Case File Review

Richard H. Walton

CONTENTS

INTRODUCTION

Cold case investigation begins with review of the case file. The investigation of a cold case homicide is different from the investigation of a "hot" homicide in many ways. Cold case investigation is *proactive*, versus the *reactive* nature of a hot case. The cold case investigation initially builds upon the documented work of others, utilizing case files that may vary in the degree of completeness and record retention over a period of years. In addition, cold case investigation exploits the elements of time and technology in conjunction with advanced investigative techniques. While every case and each victim's family deserves the ultimate opportunity to see that justice in some form or another is rendered on their behalf, available resources require that investigation of cold cases must be selective, focused, and targeted in its method.

This chapter begins with a review of the qualities of investigator most suitable for cold case homicide investigation, and discussion of the influence and impact of time and technology as they pertain to cold case homicide investigation. It addresses the influence of past law enforcement methods in cold case investigation and how to approach a file and assess file contents. In addition, this chapter highlights administrative considerations for cold case investigation, and further discusses how to organize and prioritize multiple cases for subsequent investigation.

CAUSES FOR REVIEW AND REACTIVATION OF COLD CASES

A single cold case may be selected for reexamination based on any of the following factors:

- Inquiry, single or repeated, by a family member or friend of the victim. As time passes, the parents, siblings, or others may periodically contact the police to inquire whether anything new has arisen on their case. Family inquiries may cause a fresh review of the case.
- New information brought forth by family or friends of victim. With the passage of time, friends and family of the victim may hear or otherwise obtain information that furnishes a new lead to investigators.
- New information furnished by a member of the public.
- Institutional knowledge of detectives. With the passage of time, detectives go on to other cases, but for the most part, do not forget those they could not solve. As the years become decades, other investigators may transfer in and out of homicide and the case may have been rendered inactive due to a lack of leads. But those who initiated the investigation, or later followed it up, remember the unsolved. Through intentional or casual communication with homicide supervisors, homicide detectives, or others within the department, something is said that causes the case to be pulled and subjected to a fresh review.
- Individual investigator curiosity.
- Secondary information from other investigations, often drug- or organized-crime-related.
- Those in trouble with the law providing information to mitigate their legal burden.
- Media report.
- Political pressure.
- Purely by accident.

PRELIMINARY CONSIDERATIONS IN COLD CASE INVESTIGATION

COLD CASE INVESTIGATOR ATTRIBUTES

It is estimated that almost every law enforcement agency in the U.S. has unsolved homicide cases in its files. These are cases other investigators worked, but that went unsolved for various reasons. If they had been easy, they would have been solved. As time goes by, however, and the evidence is reviewed by a fresh set of eyes and technological advances come into play, these cases may offer fresh leads. Case review is more than just opening a file folder or carton. The review begins with *mental attitude* or *mindset* by the investigator. In addition, it includes awareness of the changes wrought by time in technology and personal relationships. The investigator's attributes include:

- The ability to think and act objectively
- The ability to ask the right questions
- A positive "can-do" spirit
- Knowledge of modern investigative methods
- Knowledge of advances in science and technology

Case file review also entails *teamwork*. The days of the one-man homicide ace-detective following gut instinct are over. Cold case homicide investigation is a team effort among law enforcement, the prosecutor's office, the medical examiner/coroner's office, and the laboratory. Each of these is an important component in the re-opening and investigation of a cold case file. In addition, cooperation and communication within the law enforcement community are required, not the territorialism or proprietary mindset of "It's my case."

To proceed expediently, investigators assigned a cold, unsolved homicide will be faced with a variety of start-up decisions and options. Depending upon the age of the case, many factors may immediately present themselves. Some of these may appear daunting, or even insurmountable. The older the case, the greater the potential for missing reports and missing or degraded evidence, deceased investigators and witnesses, and other obstacles. The law enforcement agency may have changed physical locations one or more times. Each time files, evidence, or property are moved increases the possibility that these items will be lost, misplaced, or even destroyed. Administrative and budgetary issues may also impact the presence or absence of these items. Cases that have been inactive for a few years for lack of leads present a different arena from those revived after 20 or 30 years, or more. The more recent ones are likely to be written on forms currently in use; formats to which current investigators are accustomed and that will tell them quickly where to look for desired information.

Remember: a cold case investigation builds upon the previous work of others.

Who will investigate cold case homicides is an immediate concern to law enforcement supervisors and administrators, as well as to the investigators themselves. Whenever possible, those assigned to cold case homicide investigation should be experienced homicide detectives. These investigations are often prolonged, and it is important to note that all of the problems and frustrations experienced in a hot homicide may be multiplied many times over in cold case investigation and resultant court proceedings.

Desirable personal attributes for a cold case investigator would include:

- Knowledge of the mechanics of homicide investigation
- Knowledge of the variations in homicide law
- Knowledge of the use of forensic sciences and up-to-date advances

FIGURE 2.1 Cold case investigation requires "Bulldog" tenacity. (Courtesy of Sgt. Richard Longshore, Los Angeles County Sheriff's Department)

- Skill in interview techniques
- Excellent oral and written communication skills
- Knowledge and experience in use of informants
- An open mind
- Strong deductive and reasoning skills
- Good listening skills
- A creative and innovative approach
- Knowledge of crime scene reconstruction
- Experience in use of computers and report writing
- Knowledge of courtroom procedures and testimony
- Ability and willingness to work in a team atmosphere
- Knowledge of department resources, procedures and protocols
- Good health and stamina
- Motivation and enthusiasm
- Patience, an analytical mind, and bulldog tenacity (see Figure 2.1)

In my experience, it appears to be a consensus among those involved in the investigation of cold case homicides that not all homicide investigators are suited to cold case investigation. Cold case investigations are tedious and require an investigator who can sit for hours reviewing old papers, analyzing people, events, relationships and time sequences. This is cerebral analysis. In some older cases it may be helpful to assign the task to a more senior investigator who may have knowledge and experience in the time frame of the crime, as well as trends in department systems over the years. Younger, less experienced investigators may seek faster-paced activity.

The use of senior, experienced homicide investigators for cold case homicide investigation draws upon aspects of investigative ability that can come only from practice. These more experienced investigators:

- Know what the case needs to move forward.
- Know what the prosecutor needs to prosecute the case.
- Have established contacts and rapport with the prosecutor's office.

- Have established contacts and rapport with the coroner/medical examiner's office.
- Through experience, have statewide and nationwide contacts.
- Through membership and participation in homicide investigator associations and training programs, have expanded fields of contact.
- May recognize information overlooked or blatantly obvious in the case file.

Each of these is important in all stages of file review and case investigation. *What* you know is sometimes not as important as *who* you know.

Homicide investigation is part scientific, but also part subjective. With experience comes the ability to "*feel*" or "*read*" a case beyond the words on paper. It is an ability to feel the "*pulse*" of the case. Selection of the wrong individual to pursue the investigation can further compound the difficulty in case solution. In the end, it will be the investigator who combines time, technology, and old-fashioned shoe leather to solve a cold case homicide.

AGE + EXPERIENCE = WISDOM

Investigators assigned to investigate cold cases must know that they may have no control over the cases they work, depending upon the political climate of their agency or community. Similarly, they may have little say in how their agency prioritizes which cases are more important and which are not as important. Conversely, however, investigators may have a say in which cases they reinvestigate due to their experience and ability to separate those cases with a higher potential for solution from those with less possibility of being solved with given resources.

TIME

Modern cold case investigation turns the previous liability of time into an asset. While law enforcement traditionally labored under a conventional wisdom that murders unsolved after 48–72 hours were increasingly difficult to close, the pendulum of time in cold cases has now reversed this adage. Time, once so unforgiving in homicide investigation, may now be an ally to law enforcement efforts to solve cold cases. This change is due primarily to two factors: (1) Change in relationships and (2) advances in technology.

In a hot-homicide scenario, witnesses or those with knowledge about the crime often remain silent due to a relationship with or fear of the perpetrator, their own lifestyles and standards, or fear of, hostility toward, or non-involvement with the police.

With the passage of time, relationships change. Not uncommonly in these cases, people *want* to tell what they know, yet cannot bring themselves to pick up the telephone and call the police. In some cases, all it takes is for an investigator to take the initiative and knock on their door. In a cold case scenario:

- The friendship that once existed between perpetrator and those with knowledge of the crime may have ended. It may now even be adversarial.
- Marriages and former lover-partnership relations may have ended, perhaps on a sour note.
- Business relationships dissolve.
- Formerly hostile witnesses are no longer hostile.
- Religion may have entered the life of one with information or knowledge of the crime.
- Conscience may have become a factor in the lives of those with information or knowledge of the crime.
- People mature. Witnesses may have moved away from the influence of the perpetrator and lifestyle that existed at the time of the murder. They may have married, raised a family, and become a better person.

- Witness no longer fears the perpetrator. This may be due to time having made the witness a stronger person or the perpetrator a weaker person. Or, the perpetrator may be dead.
- The perpetrator may become complacent and talk to others about crimes committed in the past.

TECHNOLOGY

Advances in technology have enabled:

- More precise examinations of evidence than was available in the past.
- DNA profiles to be extracted from amounts of biological material previously insufficient in quantity for analysis.
- DNA profiling to offer a strong potential as an investigative aid (see Chapter 17).
- DNA databanks such as CODIS to allow for comparison of known and unknown genetic profiles between crime scenes and identified or unidentified perpetrators.
- Expanded fingerprint identification capabilities. Advanced fingerprint methods can now lift prints from surfaces once considered unprintable. Among these are cyanoacrylate fuming ("superglue") and laser systems for lifting and reading fingerprints. Fingerprint databanks such as AFIS/IAFS allow for inputting and comparing fingerprints on a national level.
- Other databanks such as NIBIN and Drugfire for comparing spent shell casings and projectiles or projectile fragments.
- Expanded computer-based communications and information exchange.
- Geographical profiling.

TIME + TECHNOLOGY

Time and technology have combined in a manner no one anticipated just a few decades ago. This includes the perpetrator *and* the police, however. Suspects who considered themselves knowledgeable, or lucky, in seemingly leaving no trace behind did not anticipate DNA or computer databanks. Similarly, neither did the police. In too many instances, evidence in homicide cases was discarded after a decade or two, and records were destroyed. The mindset of many who have committed murder is such that they become confident after the passage of the years, and many have moved to other regions of the country away from where they committed their crimes. Some have gone on to raise families and become accepted or respectable members of their community. In many cases, the original investigators moved on in their careers, retired, or died. There is no free pass for those who kill, however. While those who murdered may try to forget and put their past behind them, others have not. The family and friends of the murder victim never forget, and in most cases, neither does law enforcement. Awareness of these factors is important before an investigator opens the file.

Time may not be an ally in some cases, however. If a case is 40–50 years old, is it plausible to expect that witnesses or a suspect may still be alive? Even with a thoroughly documented case and evidence in a file, does the case warrant an initial effort? In a situation such as this, a review may be justified. The investigation will involve locating friends, relatives, and other associates of the decedent. In addition, any subsequent investigation would seek to locate medical or law enforcement personnel involved in the initial investigation. These are concerns to be considered in the initial review. Regrettably, however, I have had senior administrative and command officers advise me that they would not review cases of this vintage.

What if the perpetrator in a 40-year-old homicide was 17–19 years old at the time of the crime? That person would now be 57–59 years old. Given longevity and other factors in modern life, this person may still be a suitable prospect for investigation and prosecution. Several notable investigations and convictions in these circumstances have occurred in the past few years. These include the case of Miami Police Officer John Milledge illustrated in Chapter 1, and those of defendants Freiburger, Mason, and Wilkerson, discussed elsewhere in this text.

A cold case should be evaluated on the reasonable merits of the case and not necessarily rejected solely due to its age.

ADMINISTRATIVE AND SUPERVISORY CONCERNS

Hot case homicides generate media publicity. The media is often in contact with family and friends of the victim and this is relayed in sound bites on TV or in newspaper stories. This in turn may generate a response from the law enforcement agency. In higher-profile cases such as the Beltway Sniper case in Virginia and Maryland in 2002, the sheriff or chief of police often faces the media to assure the public and answer questions.

In cold case investigations, however, the family and friends usually do not know when a case is reactivated until contacted by law enforcement. In turn, the media usually does not become aware of cold case investigations until an arrest is made. The public likes to hear that somebody did not get away with murder. The resultant publicity reflects positively on the agency and not uncommonly, law enforcement uses this time to reassure the public they are doing all they can to track down killers in unsolved cases and to protect the public. Such news may also stimulate others to come forward with information on the case, or on another case. These come with a cost, however.

Cold case investigations may incur expenses and resources exceeding those normally found in hot homicide investigation. Further, results may be longer in coming. In addition to the normal frustrations encountered when working homicide cases, additional annoyance for investigators results when an agency assigns investigators to work these cases but does not supply the necessary resources. The leadership and organizational commitment by an agency to investigate cold cases requires awareness and acceptance that such investigations often include:

- Added travel expenses. By this time, suspects, witnesses and others with important information may have scattered about the country. This may apply to former and retired officers and investigators as well. All witnesses and investigators will have to be located and reinterviewed, often face to face. These interviews and other investigation costs will require added travel, lodging, transportation, and related expenses.
- Overtime and associated expenses for investigators due to travel, telephone, and investigation.
- Use of other personnel and resources.
- Potential for increased laboratory costs or other evidentiary related expenses. All physical evidence will need to be reprocessed.
- Conflicts within the agency. There may be those who would contest revisiting cold cases when resources are drained from investigation of current cases or other individual agendas or priorities occur within the department.
- Impact on the workload or caseload of others.

In addition, one cold case investigation may be the precursor to others. These investigations are often cross-jurisdictional. Investigation in these cases may lead investigators to spend time and travel to nearby or more-distant law enforcement agencies. In other instances, the information spawned in one cold case may lead to reopening other cases within the department or in other agencies. It has not been unusual that information developed in the investigation of one cold case has also identified a serial killer.

Cold case homicide investigation is especially time consuming and labor intensive. The very nature and intensity of these investigations necessitates focus upon the written case and subsequent investigation. A cold case investigation begins with a review of the written record, often complex in size. In this regard, a cold case investigation builds upon the degree of thoroughness and completeness of previous investigators. It is also built upon the missed opportunities. This focus is necessary for an investigator to begin to digest and understand a multitude of names, dates, relationships, and who-said-what's, as well as evidence and property considerations, and to begin to formulate an investigative plan. It is a disservice to the investigator, the victims, and to the agency to distract the investigator's focus from the cold case investigation.

Because these investigations originate with review of a written record and not through on-the-spot investigation such as occurs with a hot homicide, investigators must have conducive working conditions and agency support to accomplish their task. While some agencies may assign multiple cold cases to an investigator or teams of investigators, other agencies may assign one cold case to one investigator or one team. In either circumstance, one case at a time per investigator is an ideal caseload. In either situation, cases are worked to solution or until they can be worked no further. It is highly desirable that investigators assigned to cold case investigation not be distracted or assigned other duties during the course of these investigations.

When investigators assigned by the administration to investigate cold cases, they must be free to do so with a minimum of resistance from other administrative personnel (who sometimes have no investigative experience and understanding of what homicide investigation entails). On some occasions, investigators have been directed to pursue a cold case by the head of the agency or other supervisory personnel, only to be stonewalled and rebuffed by those in charge of the budget and other agency resources. This creates added tension and is detrimental to the goal of the investigation, not to mention the negative impact it has on morale and interpersonal relations.

OPENING THE FILE

WHERE IS THE CASE FILE?

Locating the original case file and evidence is sometimes not as easy as it could be in cold case investigation. Personnel changes, individual filing habits (quirks) or procedures, facility changes, and passage of time may complicate the simple effort of retrieving a case file or evidence. Investigator experience and knowledge of past practices and patterns of the agency may be beneficial to a cold case investigator in this sequence. Beginning in-house, investigators may look in numerous places, including:

- Agency records storage area where records are normally filed
- Homicide bureau or specially designated storage facility for homicide files, solved and unsolved
- Agency property room (as well as for evidence logs and physical evidence)
- Off-site warehouses or storage facilities

Don't hesitate to ask those who have been around for a long time whether they know of any records or other places where records may have been stored over the years. Long-time secretaries and clerks are many times the best sources of information on many different subjects. If you don't ask the question, you will not get the answer.

FILE CONDITION

Subjectively, initial appearance of the case file and organization may offer an insight into the ease and potential time and resources necessary for case review and subsequent investigation. Is it together in three-ring binders (see Figure 2.2) or labeled envelopes and folders? Or is it a collection thrown haphazardly into a box? Or, *is* there a file?

Cases may be encountered in any one of three categories, or a combination of completeness:

1. *Organized.* An organized file suggests that the case will be complete and laid out in an orderly manner. Review of an organized file may begin with little or no reorganization

FIGURE 2.2 An organized case file makes cold case investigation more efficient and effective. (Courtesy of El Cajon Police Department)

by the assigned investigator. This facilitates investigator review and absorption of the case. This case may have summaries of events, evidence, and of witnesses and suspects involved in the case. These will assist the investigator in coming up to speed in a shorter period of time than otherwise. No matter which category the file appears to fall into, a cold case investigator will strive to ensure that all relevant records are identified and recovered.

Caution is warranted, however, that if or when reports or similar material seemingly not connected to the case under review are found, they should not necessarily be discarded as having no connection to the case at hand. Someone along the line may have thought this was related to the case. Whether these reasons are documented or not, the investigator should not disregard this earlier thought at this time.

As an example, detectives Jon Wooddell and Robert Anderson of the El Cajon, California, police department were reinvestigating a cold case homicide that occurred in their city in 1965. Mingled with the homicide investigation case were reports and records from other seemingly unconnected sexual assaults during this same time period. Upon review, however, these reports suggested that their predecessors, decades before, had believed there might be a connection between these crimes. These detectives ultimately succeeded in identifying and convicting serial killer-rapist Clyde Wilkerson in 2003 for the murders of two people 37 years earlier. This case is discussed further in Chapter 4.

2. *Disorganized.* These are not infrequently encountered in older unsolved cases, and may be found in departments of all sizes. These are characterized as reports and other material dumped loosely into a box or file folders (see Figure 2.3). These cases may have gone through a series of investigators over the decades and documents may be such as to suggest an uncertainty as to completeness. There may be notations or other writings on reports and documents that do not appear to be those of the original author of the document. This compounds the efforts of later investigators to determine who wrote these remarks and the significance on that particular document.

3. *Missing.* These are circumstances in which no case file may be retained in the department records. It has happened. In one study by Robert Keppell, Ph.D., data was collected on all unsolved and solved murders in the State of Washington between January, 1981, and December, 1986. Of the 1309 murder victims, 38 homicide case files were "missing" and could not be located by records personnel of the responsible agencies. This obviously poses a potential problem for investigators, and this situation has been reported to me by investigators for other agencies.

FIGURE 2.3 Disorganized files are not uncommon. Over the years, contents are scattered and dumped loosely into a box or folder. Inside these files may be found original biological or physical evidence, photos, or even bullets. (Author's collection)

Cold case investigators will often invoke methods not normally associated with homicide investigations, and may successfully reconstruct events and a case file. Reconstruction of these case files may begin with review of the death certificate, media reports, and interviews with family and friends of the victim. Other methods to reconstruct these cases will unfold throughout this text.

Additional reasons for files to be missing include:

- Files may be lost due to changes in physical storage location. This may occur when an old police station or courthouse is torn down and files are lost when records are moved. In these cases, it might be prudent to attempt to identify who may have had access to the homicide files and inquire whether the files were taken for someone's personal reading.
- Material is destroyed due to fire, flood or other natural disaster at the storage location.
- Evidence is inadvertently misfiled.
- Evidence has been stolen or intentionally removed or destroyed.
- There *never was* a case file. Yes, it has happened. Those assigned to investigate a death never wrote reports. As a result, there is no file to be found.

ORGANIZING THE DISORGANIZED FILE

The first step in this instance is to organize the remaining record. It is not uncommon to find that these cases, as well as some organized cases, have items of evidentiary value comingled with the reports. This would include film negatives, x-rays, physical items, and other case material. In one case, a detective found a spent bullet and a shell casing. There was no documentation, however, and it was unknown whether they were related to the case. Other cold case files have contained women's panties, hairs and fibers, and other items of potential physical or biological evidentiary value. If items of evidentiary value are present, contact the appropriate evidence specialist and follow evidence-handling procedures.

The initial physical opening of the file or box in any cold case may be done in a laboratory or similarly secure setting, using appropriate coverings such as gloves in case items with potential trace evidence might be present in the file or box. Teamwork begins with the file review, so the investigator should work with laboratory associates to ensure that no items are handled in such a way as to potentially destroy or contaminate evidence. These items should be secured and handled in conjunction with evidence-handling practices and department procedures.

Investigators should consider lab and legal partners in a cold case investigation to be part of the team. They must be given ownership and be kept informed.

Next, organize the paperwork into chronological order. Consider the sequence of how a current homicide investigation begins, a series of steps evolving from initial report of the crime through evidence and witness development. Begin with those records reflecting the initial report of the crime and work forward. This gives the basis of when and how the crime came to be reported and insight into how it progressed. This is the beginning of the "who, what, when, where, why, and how" of the case. This may present a problem in some instances as investigative actions might have occurred on one date while the report was not written until days later and other interviews and actions occurred in between. The date of the interview or action in relation to when the report was written should be noted. In addition, it is not uncommon to find multiple witness interviews on one document or sequence of a single report. The object of this process is to reconstruct the sequence of reported events and steps in the investigation. This will facilitate investigator review and provide a logical basis for understanding what happened and moving forward with the review or investigation. At the same time, it would be useful to also note that which is missing and to begin to construct an investigative plan as the file is reconstructed.

This sequence reflects events as earlier investigators came to know them, and latter-day detectives should not be judgmental or critical with the advantages of hindsight. Current investigators will have to spend additional time sorting documents, often having to review, assemble, and reconnect disconnected reports. Special attention, requiring additional time, must be paid to making sure that papers are reassembled correctly, and often there may be multiple copies of each report—or there may appear to be what seem to be multiple copies, but which are in fact slightly different.

Case Study

Figure 2.3 illustrates a disorganized file. This case consisted of a cardboard box upon which was written the victim's name and the 1958 case number. The victim was a white female in her 40s, a part-time prostitute and waitress in a blue-collar town in the Pacific Northwest. Most of the reports were separate from the file folders also found in the box, and many of these were unstapled and loose. There was no order to the documents and contents were scattered loosely in the box. In addition, someone at a later time had re-numbered in red letters all the report pages. The significance of this was unknown due to lack of documentation. The file folders themselves contained many notes and notations written by numerous, unidentified persons. Who were they? When were they written? What did they mean?

Photographs of the victim and other unidentified persons were scattered in the box, as well as original x-rays and personal property of the victim. Numerous envelopes of negatives of the crime scene, the victim's vehicle, and other subjects were also scattered, although it appeared none had been printed. There was an absence of documentation of the significance of what the photos may have intended to show. In addition, letters from unidentified individuals concerning a variety of topics were found in the file, including letters suggesting first-hand knowledge of events in the crime. There was no documentation to denote the status of any investigation regarding these claims.

The documents, when reassembled, revealed a pattern of investigation that began with a missing-person's report in an incorporated city and the finding of her body 6 months later in a remote rural jurisdiction. This is not an uncommon sequence of events, even today. After the initial investigation span of approximately 1 year, the case went cold. Review by local investigators was sporadic after the first year with no sign of proactive review in the succeeding decades.

Of noteworthy importance, no evidence or property logs were contained in the box. A handwritten note dated in 1979 from the property clerk to the district attorney, however, explained why: "... *because the case is now 20 years old and will never be solved, request permission to destroy all the evidence in this case.*" Permission was granted by the prosecutor.

In 2002, all the original investigators and a number of witnesses were still alive. Despite lack of physical evidence, cases such as this might be solved due to changes in relationships with passage of time. Such scenarios and their variations have been relayed to me by cold case investigators seeking to locate old case files and evidence. However, the ease with which investigators may quickly come up to speed in understanding the sequence of known events and subsequent investigation is dependent upon how the file was initially organized and maintained. This degree of organization may also indicate a carryover into the care and preservation of evidence.

OTHER CONSIDERATIONS

PAST PATTERNS AND PRACTICES

During initial review of older cases, an investigator should not be alarmed if the case file appears physically rather thin. That does not necessarily mean that it is incomplete. Once subjected to follow-up investigation incorporating modern techniques and protocols, such files quickly become much more massive in physical size and content. Other cases from the same time period may occupy many carton boxes or file cabinet drawers. It is not the size, but the *quality* that counts.

This is one area, however, that in many instances exemplifies the difference between past and present law enforcement investigative practices. Understanding these may be of importance to cold case investigators. Each law enforcement agency has traditionally set its own practices and standards for investigating homicides and documenting these investigations. In the 1950s and forward, many states began mandating changes and implementing standardization in the selection and training of law enforcement officers. This ultimately carried over into adoption of uniform means and methods of documentation and recording in police reports. This has been, and still is in some areas, an evolving process.

In many instances, especially prior to the early 1980s, law enforcement agencies did not have policies regarding required documentation in homicide investigations. As a result, what was, or was not recorded depended on the individual investigator and the degree of supervision. Some investigators wrote detailed investigative reports, while others wrote a minimum, if anything at all.

Who the victim was may, in some instances, have factored into the scope and quality of the initial investigation. Prostitutes, minorities, and known offenders or "troublemakers" may not have had the diligence applied to their investigations as was found in other homicide investigations. In a recently reactivated federal civil rights case, a forensic exhumation was undertaken due to a reported lack of an autopsy at the time of the murder of a black teenager in the 1950s South (see Figure 2.4).

In addition, it may not be uncommon to find that investigation reports were more synopsis-oriented than detail-specific in their construction. Some agencies required no documentation in a homicide investigation unless a suspect was developed. As a result, written reports for homicide investigations may be nonexistent. The entire case record might have been kept in the notes and notebooks of individual detectives, and when they retired, the notebooks went with them if the department did not require such to be turned in (see Figure 2.5). I have spoken to "old time" detectives who would tap their shirt pockets or their heads and stress that they carried their investigation "right here."

Another area in which these practices occurred was documentation of a neighborhood canvass. In decades past, if a witness reported nothing of importance, there was no requirement for any documentation. Thus, the witness who reported nothing was not identified. It was not unusual for investigators to detail uniformed officers to conduct the canvass, and any documentation of a neighborhood canvass may be a hit-or-miss affair. Further discussion of this topic is covered in Chapter 4.

When opening a cold case file, never discard any papers, worn-out file folders, or other items in the file or box that may appear unrelated or of no use in the case investigation. This should be noted in the report of the initial review. A defense attorney may ask if this occurred at some point and perhaps try to stress that the real killer's name was discarded.

NATION

Body of lynched teen Emmett Till will be exhumed for autopsy

1955 killing reopened after filmmaker claimed to have new evidence in case

By Darryl Fears
THE WASHINGTON POST

The body of Emmett Till will be exhumed within the next few weeks so an autopsy can be performed, authorities said yesterday, 50 years after the black teenager was savagely murdered in the Mississippi Delta in a case that electrified the civil rights movement.

An autopsy of Till's remains, buried in the Chicago suburb of Alsip, Ill., was ordered by District Attorney Joyce Chiles in Greenville, Miss., who is investigating the 1955 slaying with the help of the Justice Department and the FBI.

"The exhumation will take place in the next few weeks," said Deborah Madden, a spokeswoman for the FBI's office in Jackson, Miss. "Previous investigations did not perform an autopsy, even in 1955. Consequently, no cause of death was ever established."

Authorities in Mississippi and Washington announced last year that the case would be reopened after a documentary by New York filmmaker Keith Beauchamp claimed to have uncovered new evidence about the case.

Till's lynching Aug. 8, 1955, in segregated Money, Miss., touched off intense mourning throughout black America and helped give rise to the modern civil rights movement.

At the funeral, Mamie Till Mobley insisted on an open casket, to expose the brutality her son suffered. She died two years ago and is buried next to her son.

Till was a brash 14-year-old from Chicago who knew nothing of the Jim Crow South. While visiting family members, he whistled at a white woman in a local store. Frightened relatives rushed him home, but he was later abducted, and a fisherman discovered his badly beaten body in the Tallahatchie River.

Roy Bryant, the husband of the woman Till whistled at, and his half brother J.W. Milam were charged with the killing but acquitted. The all-white jury returned a verdict less than two hours after a defense attorney pleaded with them to honor their forefathers by refusing to convict white men for killing a black person.

Bryant and Milam later admitted in a *Look* magazine article to torturing Till. The two said they pistol-whipped him, shot him, tied his mutilated body to a large metal fan and tossed it into a river. Both men are now dead.

The Department of Justice failed to pursue the case before a five-year statute of limitations on federal charges expired. There is no statute of limitations on state murder charges.

Beauchamp's documentary, "The Untold Story of Emmett Louis Till," includes a claim of evidence that there was a third accomplice.

The case is one of several murders in the South from the civil rights era that have been reopened in recent years. In 2003, Earnest Avants was convicted in the 1966 killing of a 67-year-old black handyman in an attempt to try to lure Martin Luther King Jr. to the area.

In January, Edgar Ray Killen, now 80, was arrested for the murders of three civil rights workers in the case dramatized in the movie "Mississippi Burning" and faces trial this summer.

FIGURE 2.4 In some instances, homicide victims were buried without an autopsy. Forensic exhumation is one technique to be considered when reactivating a case in which no autopsy was made. (© 2005, *The Washington Post*. With permission.)

OLDER TECHNOLOGY

When reviewing older files, investigators may encounter several types of formats not normally seen today. Reports may be handwritten or typed on typewriters. Older homicide files may include both

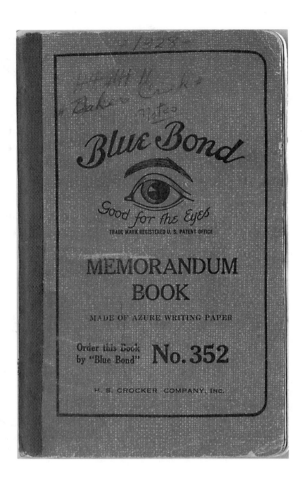

FIGURE 2.5 During review of old homicide cases, it is prudent to identify case investigators or their descendants, and enquire whether they retain any notebooks or other case memorabilia. (Author's Collection)

types. Forms may be primitive by today's standards or lacking altogether. Word processors began to attain widespread use within law enforcement in the early to mid 1980s.

- *Onionskin paper.* This is a very thin, almost transparent type of paper that was used for making multiple copies of the same document (See Figure 2.6). It is characterized by being very fragile and tears easily. Most often encountered in a typewritten format, reports on this paper were made using carbon paper. Carbon paper is a black paper that when struck on the top side leaves the impression in dark ink on a piece of paper adjacent to the bottom side. Manual (non-electric) typewriters could often make three to five legible copies using these papers. The copy most immediate to the original sheet is usually most legible and the quality of print declines with the additional copies. This format is not uncommon in reports written prior to the mid 1980s.
- *Thermal Paper.* This style of copy paper uses a heat source to impregnate the words and images into the paper (See Figure 2.7). It was invented approximately 50 years ago, and variations of it are still used today in facsimile machines. A characteristic of this paper is that it begins to fade after a few years or so, depending upon its composition and the conditions to which it has been exposed, such as light and heat. Documents reproduced on thermal paper may be identified by an overall brownish hue, and a reddish-brown

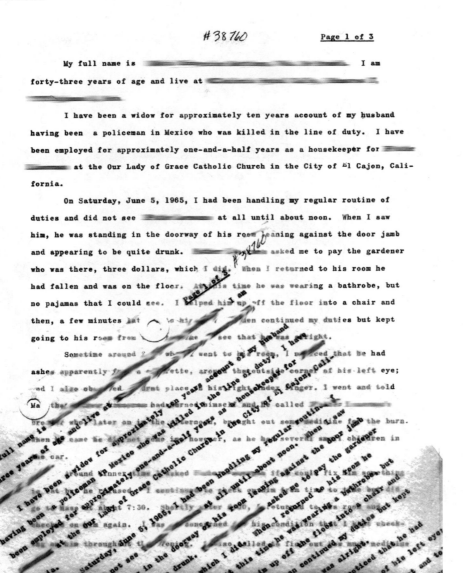

FIGURE 2.6 Older case files will contain copies made with carbon paper, and these are often encountered on onion skin paper, a semi-transparent, fragile paper. (Courtesy of El Cajon Police Department)

tinge to the letters. In addition, the paper may have a semi-glossy sheen. I have encountered these in reviewing reports from the 1950s and 1970s, and this was one of the earlier forms used in office style duplicating machines to reproduce reports or other documents now found in some older cold case files.

When thermal paper copies are found in a file, it is suggested that these be photographed or their images otherwise preserved due to the continuing degradation that may occur. In addition, a cold case investigator may ask, "Where is the original?" This may suggest possible sources for follow up or to retrieve further case documents or materials, or to identify other contacts. Why were copies made and who were the recipients?

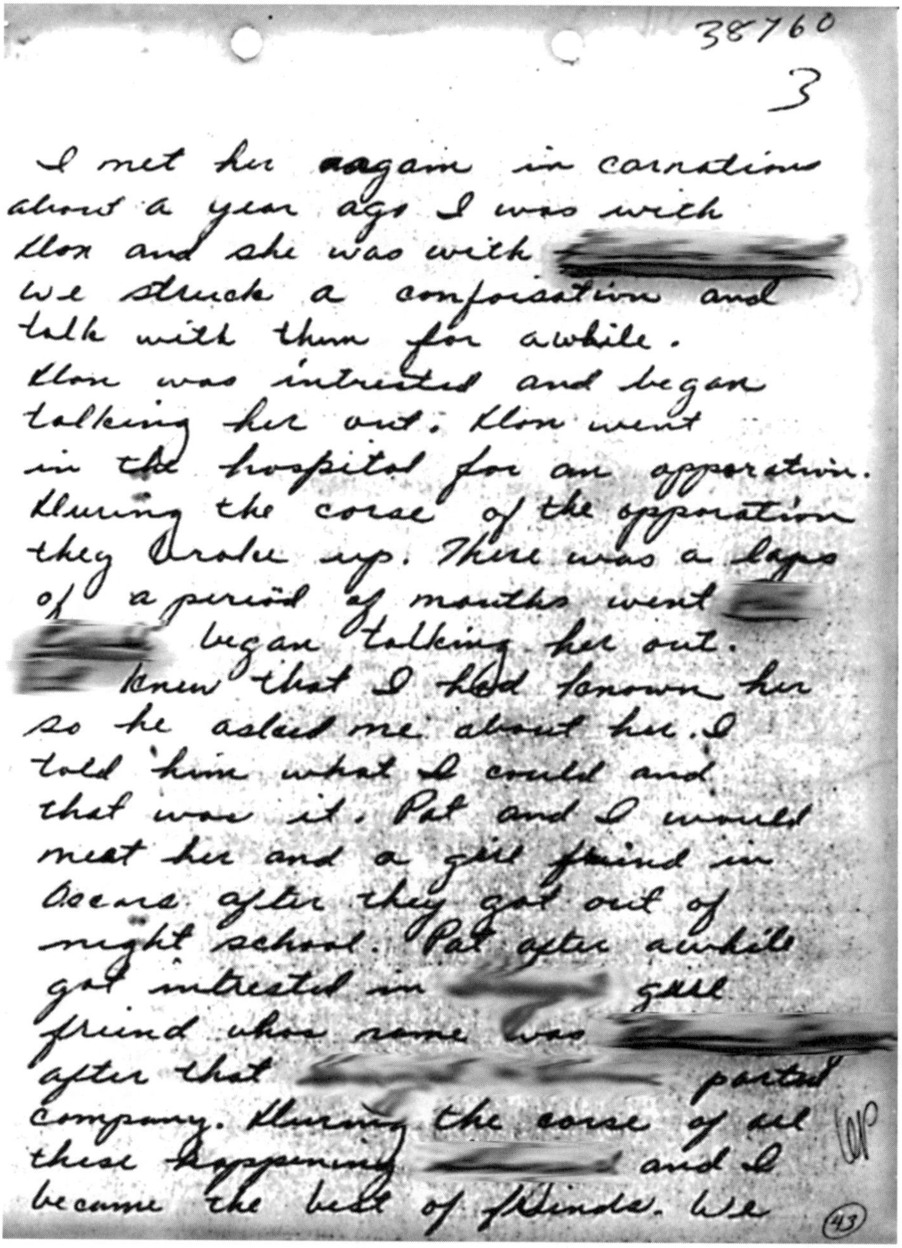

FIGURE 2.7 (See color insert following p. 216.) Note the faded quality of this paper. With time the writing will fade almost completely. (Courtesy of El Cajon Police Department)

- *Photostat.* The term is a trademark name for a style of photocopier, and copies of documents made by this process may still be found in cold case files. The device is a large camera that takes a photograph of the object. A paper negative is processed in developer, washed, and dried in a drier. The result is white letters on a black background, whereas the original of the document was black letters, such as from a typewriter, on a white background (See Figure 2.8).

FIGURE 2.8 This was essentially a paper negative produced by a particular camera. (Courtesy of Mr. Paul Edholm)

- *Shorthand*. Shorthand is a method of taking notes and reporting dialogue using a handwritten series of figures and spaces. It is a process that is formally learned through specialized training and experience and was a commonplace form for taking dictation in business and in the legal profession for many decades. The use of shorthand in the legal system dates to at least the late 1800s. In the days before courtroom reporting became mechanized, trained clerks recorded question-and-answer sessions and court proceedings using paper and pencil or pen. I have reviewed a number of cold cases in which the stenographers' notes are retained in the file. These are often the result of interrogation and interviews between investigators and witnesses or suspects.

  These notes may be encountered in loose sheet form, or in spiral or similar bound tablets. In addition, there have been different styles of shorthand. Should these be encountered in reviewing cold case files, the local court reporter's office may be able to assist in deciphering and/or transcribing these notes. In addition, they may know the whereabouts or disposition of the original stenographer as well. A cold case investigator may seek to identify the stenographer who took the notes to inquire as to what they are and ask:
  - Is this a complete statement or a partial statement?
  - Was a transcribed report made? (Is it in the file or does the stenographer have a copy?).
  - Does the stenographer retain any other records pertaining to this case?

During the course of opening and reviewing a cold case file, investigators may discover different-colored copies of report forms. When these are found, investigators may seek to determine the number of copies in the original form and their dissemination routes. This may lead investigators to other sources of case information. An example is shown in Figure 2.9. Investigators should ask: Who were the recipients? Why did they need, or get, a copy? Do they have additional documentation relevant to this case?

PRELIMINARY FILE REVIEW

The goal of a preliminary file review is to:

- Put each file into such a condition that an investigator can (1) take that file anytime following the review, (2) see a concise summary of the facts and physical evidence, and (3) begin working that case without having to track down missing information or reports.

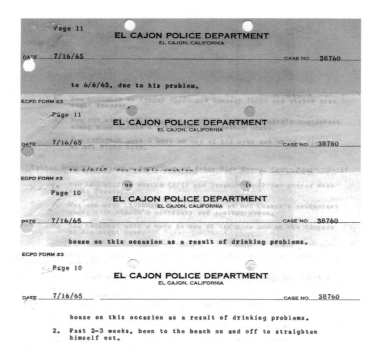

FIGURE 2.9 (See color insert following p. 216.) When colored forms are found in a file, cold case investigators should determine who might have received the copies. These recipients may retain case documents or other material. (Courtesy of El Cajon Police Department)

- Create a concise summary of the facts and physical evidence as well as results of forensic examinations previously performed upon the evidence. This summary can be downloaded into appropriate computer systems, thus allowing for an immediate review of the case without having to physically locate the file.
- Update all identifying information pertaining to witnesses, suspects, and other persons of interest, allowing for the possibility of linking these persons to other cases or alerting other investigators who might have contact with these persons of their involvement in this case.
- Download case information into the Violent Criminal Apprehension Program (ViCAP) or other local, regional, or state information-sharing system.
- Allow for rapid identification of cases for future forensic potential when new technology becomes available.
- Identify investigative leads.
- Prioritize cases based upon leads and evidence.

Review of cold case homicide files and selection of those cases for investigation may further occur through organizational circumstances. Agency leadership, size, and number of unsolved homicide cases may factor into this analysis. Not infrequently, the decision to undertake a preliminary file review might address legal considerations as well as personal relationships and evolving technological changes.

This review may also be the result of selection of (1) one or a few cases or (2) systematic review of all unsolved homicide cases.

Preliminary guidelines in a case file review may include these evidentiary considerations:

- There is a known suspect and physical evidence appears to have been preserved.
- There is no known suspect but physical evidence has been preserved.
- There is no known suspect and physical evidence is lacking or not preserved in a manner that facilitates reexamination through advanced technology.

INITIAL LEGAL CONSIDERATIONS

When conducting an initial case file review, whether it is a single case or during the course of a systematic review of all unsolved cases, cold case investigators should consider potential legal issues. While there is no statute of limitations on first-degree murder, there may be limitations to prosecution on lesser degrees of murder. Review and potential reactivation of cold case homicides may involve other legal issues as well. In conjunction with representatives of the prosecutor's office, considerations during the review process may include:

- Degree of homicide
- Jurisdiction or venue
- Changes in the law since time of offense
- Previous invocation of Miranda Rights
- Statute of limitations of premeditated vs. manslaughter
- Speedy trial
- Evidence code then and now
- Chain of custody of evidence
- Suspect status (deceased or incarcerated)
- Sexual assault statute of limitations (if this component is present)
- Allegation of prior offenses
- Ex post facto considerations
- Enhancements
- Possible change of punishment

Arrest and successful prosecution of those responsible for the murder is the ultimate goal of police and prosecutors. These are circumstantial cases at present, and cold case investigators should bear in mind that investigation and prosecution will fully illustrate the difference between "probable cause" and "beyond a reasonable doubt." Good communication between law enforcement and local prosecutors is critical when examining legal questions, and serves to build rapport for the future. Prosecutors and judges may need to be *educated* in cold case investigation.

Cold case investigators may, in some instances, need to overcome prosecutorial belief that every possible hypothesis of innocence must be overcome. This is not normally done in the course of current homicide cases, and is not necessarily so in cold case investigation and prosecution. Identifying prosecutors to assist in these cases early in the process facilitates the exchange of information, and may speed search and arrest warrants in the future. Good communication at this time will not put the investigator in a position of calling a prosecutor at 3a.m. and hearing, "…you're calling me *now* on how old a case?"

Remember, the case is not done until you get a conviction.

SYSTEMATIC REVIEW OF ALL CASES

In this method of file review, all unsolved homicide cases are identified, reviewed for potential solvability, and prioritized for further investigation. The methods and procedures utilized in this process are applicable to a single-case file review as well. During this process, reviewers may include:

- Current homicide detectives.
- Retired homicide detectives hired back by the organization to review these cases. This is an option that an agency might utilize in lieu of assigning detectives with current full

case loads. When this method is used, however, it should be noted that one of the advantages in a file review is to have someone *unfamiliar* with the case do the review. A fresh pair of eyes means a fresh perspective, something that may not be possible should original detectives be hired back and assigned their own unsolved cases.

- Civilian volunteers with homicide investigation experience. In 2002, the Charlotte, North Carolina, Police Department inaugurated a program to review unsolved homicide cases dating back to 1979. After concerns addressing confidentiality and potential judicial obstacles were resolved, these volunteers were assigned a case based on solvability factors such as DNA and fingerprints as well as examination for potential relationship changes. The volunteers reviewed their assigned cases and developed an organized case file. They prepared lead sheets addressing forensic evidence and suggested persons to interview. As a result of their work, a case summary was prepared for homicide detectives and the case was given back to a detective for continued follow-up. The agency has reported favorably upon this method.

QUALIFICATIONS TO REVIEW UNSOLVED CASES

Those persons selected to review unsolved homicide cases should be knowledgeable in homicide investigation, law, and technology. In addition, they should be:

- Knowledgeable in current computer software relating to case review including ViCAP and agency case management systems
- Knowledgeable of current sources for research of witnesses, suspects, and principals involved in unsolved cases
- Knowledgeable in locating current sources for all evidence and coroner or medical examiner documentation
- Knowledgeable in operating applicable agency computer software to document their activity

SOLVABILITY FACTORS

Cold case review focuses on people (as victims, witnesses, or suspects), and evidence (physical or biological). These are the components that may solve it. Solvability factors are those facts and circumstances of a case that influence its potential to be solved. These reviews commonly seek to maximize the potential to be gained from (1) changes in relationships that may now result in persons providing necessary information to law enforcement or (2) utilization of advanced technology in the examination and analysis of physical or biological material. Ultimately, these solvability factors can be incorporated into the parameters that are defined when a systematic case review program is instituted.

Technology as a solvability factor includes:

- DNA/CODIS (COmbined DNA Index System)
  - Potential suspect DNA recovered
  - Potential probative victim DNA recovered
  - No DNA evidence recovered
- AFIS (Automated Fingerprint Identification System)/IAFIS (Integrated Automated Fingerprint Identification System)
  - Identified fingerprints recovered
  - Unidentified fingerprints recovered
  - No fingerprints recovered

- NIBIN (National Integrated Ballistics Information Network)/DRUGFIRE (an automated, computerized forensic firearms identification system)
  - Shell casings recovered
  - Bullets recovered
  - Linked to another crime
  - No firearm evidence recovered
- ViCAP—Potential link to another crime

People as potential solvability factors may be:

- Suspect
  - Arrested but released
  - Named, no arrest
  - Incarcerated/other charge
  - Under investigation/other charge
  - Seen but unidentified
  - Deceased
  - No suspects
- Witness
  - Witness under investigation/trial
  - Witness incarcerated
  - Multiple eye-witnesses
  - Previously uncooperative
  - Previously did not tell all
  - Other

These solvability factors have been summarized by the Washington, D.C. Metro Police Department, and are shown in Figure 2.10

Those homicides that have a sexual assault or biological evidence or fingerprint component often present the highest potential for solvability.

DEFINING PARAMETERS FOR A SYSTEMATIC REVIEW

Parameters may be based on elements of time, technology, and encompassing time periods. Some agencies conduct a systematic review by:

- Reexamining all unsolved cases beginning with the most recent (cases prior to a date 1 to 3 years in the immediate past or similar criteria). The Kansas City, Missouri, Police Department has utilized this method.
- Selecting a specific encompassing time period. For example, those cases unsolved from 1960 to 1995. The Los Angeles, California, Police Department has utilized this method.

In addition, these selection criteria may be combined with:

- Selection of those cases in which there exists a potential to exploit changes in personal relationships due to passage of time.
- Selection of those cases in which evidence exists that can be exploited by advanced technology.

A systematic review is often conducted by an agency that has a large backlog of unsolved homicides. In conducting this style of review, an agency may seek to learn:

HOMICIDE CASE REVIEW SOLVABILITY CHART

SUSPECT		COMMENTS
Arrested but released	☐	_____
Named, no arrest	☐	_____
Incarcerated/other charge	☐	_____
Under Investigation/other charge	☐	_____
Deceased	☐	_____
Seen but unidentified	☐	_____
No suspects	☐	_____
WITNESS		
Witness Under Investigation/Trial	☐	_____
Witness Incarcerated	☐	_____
Multiple eye-witnesses	☐	_____
Other	☐	_____
FIREARM EVIDENCE		
Shell Casings Recovered	☐	_____
Slugs Recovered	☐	_____
Linked to Another Crime	☐	_____
No Firearm Evidence Recovered	☐	_____
FINGERPRINT EVIDENCE		
Unidentified Prints Recovered	☐	_____
No Fingerprint Evidence Recovered	☐	_____
DNA EVIDENCE		
Potential Suspect DNA Recovered	☐	_____
Potential Probative Victim DNA	☐	_____
No DNA Evidence Recovered	☐	_____
OTHER CRIMES		
Potential Link to Another Crime	☐	_____
MISC. SOLVABILITY FACTORS		
_____	☐	_____
_____	☐	_____

FIGURE 2.10 Washington, D.C. Metropolitan Police Department Solvability chart. (Courtesy of Detective Jim Trainum)

- How many qualifying cases are there in the agency?
- Where are these cases located?
- Do case summaries currently exist?

Interestingly enough, this method of review has also resulted in:

- Identification of cases reflected in the records as "unsolved" that are actually solved, but records were not current. Thus, the agency had fewer cold cases than initially thought and records are updated.
- Identification of cases considered "unsolved" that had progressed through the identification of a suspect and issuance of an arrest warrant but that the warrant had not been entered into state or national computer systems.
- Identification of cases wherein an arrest warrant had been issued but erroneously recalled and needed to be reissued.
- Recognition of previously unrecognized patterns in homicides or sexual assaults.
- Updated database that identifies the offense and other designated criteria. This may include:
  - Victim
  - Date of offense or report

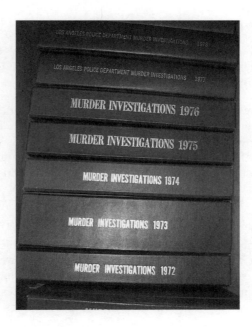

FIGURE 2.11 The larger the agency, the greater the possibility of higher numbers of unsolved homicides. (Courtesy of Detective Rick Jackson, LAPD)

- Suspect name, description, and vehicle
- Presence of physical or biological evidence
- Physical location and availability of case or evidence

This method is appropriate for any jurisdictional size, and agencies of many different sizes have utilized it to review their unsolved homicide cases. No agency, however, has unlimited means and these efforts will be affected by time, number of personnel, and other available resources. While a larger department may assign more personnel to review of cold cases, it most likely will have a proportionally larger number of cold cases to investigate (see Figure 2.11). Similarly, smaller departments may assign one, two, or more detectives, to review a smaller number of cases. They may be assigned on a full- or part-time basis to review unsolved cases. In either method, a systematic review represents a commitment by the agency to address all unsolved homicides.

CASE PRIORITIZATION BY HOMICIDE CATEGORY

During a systemic review, homicides may be prioritized by type or category of homicide. These could include:

- Sex-related. Due to DNA/CODIS potential, sexual assault-related murders may present the highest rate of solvability, depending upon existence and preservation of biological evidence.
- Stabbings. Possibility of biological evidence/DNA transfer left by suspect.
- Beating and strangulation. Possibility of DNA transfer from suspect.
- Shootings. Largest category but small potential for DNA or physical evidence.
- Closed cases. Cases closed by arrest, but should be considered whether charges were later dropped or whether more than one suspect may have been involved

Objectives Clearly Stated

In conducting a systematic review, the goal of the review should be clearly stated and understood by those who are assigned to conduct the review: (1) is the goal of the review to obtain convictions? or (2) is the goal of the review to solve and close unsolved cases regardless of whether a conviction can be obtained?

If the purpose of the review program is to obtain convictions and the statute of limitations has expired, an agency may desire to save the resources for those cases more likely to result in a conviction. If the goal of the review is to solve and close unsolved cases regardless of whether a conviction can be obtained, an agency may opt to review all cases that qualify under its guidelines. This may be an important consideration during investigations of serial killers, whose criminal depredations may span years or decades.

Identifying Unsolved Cases

Using a systematic approach, investigators give each unsolved homicide a preliminary review and subsequently prioritize or rank it for the possibility of successful investigation potential. When conducting a systematic review of all unsolved homicide cases, it is important to thoroughly and methodically identify all unsolved homicides within the agency. Sources of information to identify potential unsolved cases or to assist in corroboration of unsolved cases would include:

- Local agency logbooks
- Computer databases
- Rejected cases
- Dismissed cases
- Autopsy logbooks and coroner or medical examiner records
- Crime laboratory logbooks
- Retired homicide investigators
- Prosecutor records
- State Bureau of Vital Statistics
- Local Recorder's Office

Suggested Preliminary Case Review Procedure

The following is a synopsis of several cold case review protocols utilized by various law enforcement agencies. The cold case reviewer would consider (1) reports and documents, (2) evidence, and (3) review and updated condition of case file. In-depth discussion of these topics will occur in future chapters.

1. Reports and Documents

- Locate all case files and reports.
- Read all reports and documents to determine whether workable information exists.
- Listen to all audio tapes and determine whether transcripts should be made or existing ones are accurate. Consider making back-up copies for case work and minimizing usage of original tapes.
- Review all video recordings. Similarly, consider preserving originals and making duplicates.
- Where possible, contact original detectives to obtain their perspectives and an overview to determine whether information exists that is not reflected in the case file. During this contact, the reviewer should seek to determine whether the former detective has any notebooks, case files, photos, or other memorabilia from this case, and to recover these.

- During this contact, the previous detectives' work must not be criticized or belittled. Other events or activities that may have been concurrent with their investigation at the time are not known. In some rare circumstances, detectives have declined to cooperate based upon personal and professional circumstances at the time of their departure.
- The reviewer should determine whether contact should be made with the victim's family. This may be necessary to establish whether new information exists that was not known to original investigators. This could be especially true in gang-related homicides.
- The reviewer would prepare recommendations for a follow-up assigned investigator to obtain possible information from any specialized law enforcement units, such as gang units, narcotic investigative units, or other groups.

During the case file review, reviewers and investigators may begin to formulate their investigative plan by considering factors that may include:

- Totality of information known about the crime. Included would be:
  - Date, time, location
  - Name of victim
  - Brief profile of victim
  - Finding of body
- Identified or developed suspects:
  - Known relationship to victim
  - Known prior contacts with victim
  - Current location
- Agency jurisdiction for investigation of the offense
- Previous investigation(s)
- Autopsy and medical examiner records
- Motive
- Witness information
- Known physical evidence that may link a potential suspect to the crime
- New forensic technologies that may assist in developing known physical evidence
- Impact the passage of time might have on the case
- Whether this case has a *pulse*

2. Evidence Review

- The reviewer would determine whether evidence exists. Locations to find physical or biological evidence may include:
  - Agency evidence or property room.
  - Coroner or medical examiner office for original slides, swabs, victim clothing, or other evidence. Even when agency biological evidence has been discarded, lost, or otherwise cannot be located, check with the coroner or medical examiner for duplicate slides/swabs that may have been retained in their files.
  - Public or private crime laboratories (previously submitted or tested evidence and lab reports).
  - Hospital or medical facilities (rape kits, medical reports, slides).
  - Courthouse property rooms.
  - Prosecutor's offices (previous trial or investigations).
  - Retired investigators' files, including case notes and details not found in files.
  - Other investigating agencies.

It is incumbent during a preliminary cold case file review, or during a subsequent in-depth case examination, to identify the location of the evidence and to *personally* inspect and examine it. During this inspection and review, the cold case investigator seeks to:

- Identify the physical existence of the evidence.
- Identify the physical location of the evidence.
- Confirm the identity and description of the evidence.
- Confirm that all evidence is properly packaged and stored.
- Physically examine it to check for degradation, damage, or other conditions.
- Confirm quantity (drug evidence).
- Compare physical evidence and property to be concurrent with written case records.
- Examine chain of custody issues to ensure integrity of the evidence.
- Assure that all evidence is present and accounted for.
- Document this activity.
- Determine and recommend what analysis may be available for existing evidence, such as DNA, AFIS, etc.

"JOHN DOE" WARRANTS

During the initial file review, DNA-related legal issues may be identified. Due to advances in this technology, "John Doe" warrants might be a viable option. This is the method of issuing an arrest warrant for a DNA profile obtained from analysis of unsolved crime scene evidence. The warrant is issued for the DNA identifier, absent the name of the profile holder. This innovative approach was pioneered by Deputy District Attorney Norm Gahn in Milwaukee, Wisconsin. The method has allowed charges to be filed and permit old cases, primarily sexual assaults, to be prosecuted when the person matching the "John Doe" DNA profile is subsequently identified by name. "John Doe" DNA warrants are one way to permit cases to remain active, thus allowing them the chance to be solved through future DNA technology and databases.

3. Review and Update Case File

- Ensure that the "Murder Book" is complete and updated with all necessary reports.
- Locate and inspect all photos and negatives and ensure that they are in satisfactory condition for court purposes.
- Identify and ensure that all coroner's or medical examiner's reports and photographs and other documents are in the file and in satisfactory condition for court purposes.
- Ensure that all available investigator's notebooks and case notes are in the file and not with the original investigator (see Figure 2.12).
- Ensure that all evidence is documented and accounted for, and that requests for needed examination or reexamination are completed and filed. In addition, the reviewer would ensure that a complete copy of the evidence list, including location, is present in the case file.
- Locate and inspect all maps and diagrams to ensure that they are present and suitable for court purposes.

4. Case Synopsis and Assessment Report

Upon completion of the file review, the reviewer would prepare a complete and accurate summary of the case for entry in specified agency computer systems. This synopsis provides a review of events, the persons involved, and summary of the evidence and the case.

- *Solved Cases.* If the case has been solved or resolved, the reviewer would prepare a closing supplemental report and dispose of evidence (with the approval and supervision of the homicide-unit supervisor or commander).

FIGURE 2.12 Detective's notebook. (Courtesy of Sgt. Richard Longshore, Los Angeles County Sheriff's Department)

- *Unsolved Cases*. If the case is unsolved, the reviewer would ensure that the case is ready to be handed off to an assigned investigator for active follow-up investigation. This might include:
  - Written recommendations and offer of a comprehensive investigative plan that would suggest a high probability for the arrest and prosecution of responsible suspect(s) for criminal homicide.
  - Indication of the reviewer's preparation to give an oral overview of the case and presentation of proposed investigative plan.
- *Solved Cases with Arrest Warrants Outstanding*. The reviewer would evaluate the case and locate and confirm evidence. Also:
  - Ascertain and determine what information exists in the file to positively identify the defendant named in the outstanding arrest warrant.
  - Ensure that certified copies of identification that positively identifies the named defendant in the outstanding warrant exists in the case file. This may include:
    - Certified copy of driver's license photo with fingerprint verification.
    - Latent-fingerprint card.
    - Other (passport, etc).
  - Recommend or ensure ViCAP update when new information is received.
  - Prepare a written comprehensive recommendation so the case can be assigned to a specialized unit for active investigation. In these cases, it is important to realize the necessity for *due diligence* and to document these efforts for future legal activity.
  - Be prepared to present an oral briefing or overview of case as necessary.
  - Update case management system.
  - Ensure that warrant is valid and entered into state or national computer systems.

CASE STATUS AND REVIEW

File #: _____   Date Received: _____

                                        Date Returned: _____

Victim Name(s): _____

Location of case file: _____

                              (Library # or who has it)

Investigator responsible for   1. _____

the case or investigation: 2. _____

(Not the Reviewer)   3. _____

INFORMATION FOR CASE NARRATIVE UPDATE:

Don't rewrite case summary or narrative unless necessary. Just write additions or update narrative already in case management system.

_____

_____

_____

_____

_____

_____

_____

_____

_____

_____

FURTHER INVESTIGATION	**(Check these only if done by**
ACTIVE WITH NO WORKABLE INFORMATION	CASE ASSESSMENT REPORT (6 Pages)
SOLVED	POOR-BOY INVENTORY SHEET
(Mark Only If Requesting Lab Work)	MURDER BOOK
EVIDENCE - FIREARMS	SUPPLEMENTARY REPORT SUBMIT
EVIDENCE - DNA	CLOSE/OUT SUPP. REPORT
EVIDENCE - PHYSICAL	

REVIEWED BY: _____   DATE: _____

FIGURE 2.13 Case Status and Review Summary. (Courtesy of Lt. Joseph Hartshorne, Los Angeles County Sheriff's Department)

Figure 2.13 and Figure 2.14 are examples of forms used in the review process by the Unsolved Unit of the Los Angeles County Sheriff's Department. Additional report forms are used for case assessment and evidence evaluation and examination of evidence. This process is described further in this chapter.

CASE ASSESSMENT REPORT

FILE # _____ CRIME: _____

Murder Book: Yes No Library # _____ Crime Status: _____

Date of Occurrence: _____ Time of Occurrence: _____ Day of Occurrence: _____

LOCATION: _____ TYPE OF LOC: _____

VICTIM: _____ CC# _____
DESCRIPTION: _____

ADD'L VICTIMS: _____
_____

SUSPECT( ): _____ IN CUSTODY: YES NO
DESCRIPTION: _____

ADD'L SUSPECTS: _____
_____

****

CASE SUMMARY: _____

_____

_____

_____

_____

FIGURE 2.14 Case Assessment Report. (Courtesy of Lt. Joseph Hartshorne Los Angeles County Sheriff's Department)

PRIORITIZATION SCHEDULES

Once the preliminary case and evidence reviews have been completed, a priority of likelihood for solution building upon the designated criteria may be considered. This prioritization schedule will assist in filtering those cases that offer the highest potential for solvability with given resources from those with a lesser chance of solution. The following examples reflect three different types of prioritization schedules.

1. FIVE-PART SCHEDULE

Priority 1. These are those cases in which an offender has been identified and an arrest warrant has been issued. These cases have "fallen through the cracks." Further, this review will assure that the arrest warrant is still valid and properly entered into the National Crime Information Center (NCIC) or an Unlawful Flight to Avoid Prosecution (UFAP) warrant has been obtained. Follow-up investigation to locate the suspect will be necessary and this investigation may ultimately draw upon forensic artistry, media alerts, or national television broadcast in attempts to locate the suspect. Investigation may necessitate review of all evidence to ascertain its existence, location, and condition as well as witness location and potential reinterviews.

Priority 2. There is a known suspect and physical evidence has been preserved. Modern technology, including DNA, AFIS and other fingerprint-related technology may be enlisted to develop significant information that perhaps was previously not technically feasible. In some cases, evidence was not processed. Review and follow-through might result in successful prosecution.

Priority 3. There is no known suspect but physical evidence has been preserved. Modern technology could potentially identify the suspect(s). An example would be identifying a DNA profile in conjunction with the CODIS system.

Priority 4. There is no known suspect and insufficient physical evidence, but there are witnesses who were not previously available who may now provide material information that can assist in suspect identification. These cases may involve situations in which witnesses could not be initially located and interviewed or who now need to be reinterviewed. Investigation may be extensive.

Priority 5. There are no known witnesses and no known physical evidence that can assist in identifying the suspect(s). These are what cold case consultant Louis N. Eliopulos terms a "snowball's chance in hell."

By the very nature of these cases, the reality of cold case review and prioritization may be affected by who the victim is, degree of heinousness, media influence, and election politics.

2. 4-PART SCHEDULE

This style is exemplified by the protcol of the San Diego Police Department Cold Case Team.

Priority 1. Suspect(s) have been previously identified. A warrant of arrest has previously been issued. A suspect has been identified by forensic methods. These cases are given the highest priority for reinvestigation.

Priority 2. There are witnesses who can assist in identifying the suspect(s). Information or evidence has been developed that identifies possible suspect(s). Initial investigation identifies witnesses who could not be located or need to be reinterviewed. These cases will be reinvestigated.

Priority 3. Evidence has been preserved and modern technology, AFIS, DNA, and other methods can be utilized to process and analyze evidence. These cases will be reclassified depending on the results of the additional laboratory analysis.

Priority 4. There are no known witnesses who can assist in identifying suspect(s). There is no physical evidence that can assist in identifying suspect(s). These cases will not be reinvestigated.

3. THREE-PART SCHEDULE

This is a three-tiered level of investigative prioritization that is evidence- and case-specific-based. It may also be known as a *high-medium-low* system. The following is an example as used by the Texas Rangers:

High. There exist viable investigative option(s) that can be expected to generate leads or suspects.

Moderate. There exists reasonable investigative option(s) that might generate leads and/or suspects.

Low. Remote investigative option(s) exist and these are not expected to generate viable leads or suspects.

In this method, a case may also be *declined* due to (1) the absence of any viable investigative option(s) or (2) case facts strongly suggest that something other than a violent crime (i.e., suicide) has occurred.

Those agencies adopting a system utilizing a high-medium-low method of prioritization may also adopt a policy of investigating all high-range cases before investigating cases offering a moderate potential for solution. This can be rationalized based upon number of cases and available resources. In turn, all moderate-range cases may be investigated before dedicating resources to those cases exhibiting a low potential for solvability.

In reality, investigative efforts, due to case numbers and resources, may never arrive at the moderate level or the low level of priority. Similarly, those agencies utilizing a number tiered system may also choose to investigate those that offer the most potential before moving to those offering a lesser potential, based upon investigative resources.

The end result, however, may be that some cases are not reinvestigated.

AGENCY SAMPLES

MORRIS COUNTY PROSECUTOR'S OFFICE METHOD

Figure 2.15 identifies 10 solvability factors used by the Morris County, New Jersey, Prosecutor's Office to determine the priority of investigation of cold case homicides. This method utilizes a point system to rank and subsequently prioritize a cold case homicide in comparison with other unsolved homicides. Final determination of investigative priority, however, rests with the County Prosecutor, Chief of Investigations, or their designee. This method is in keeping with identifying all unsolved homicides, management of agency resources, and optimization of investigative resources.

KANSAS CITY, MISSOURI, POLICE DEPARTMENT METHOD

During 2002, the Kansas City, Missouri, Police Department was scrutinized as a result of the disappearance of evidence in a pending homicide trial. The Chief of Police formed a cold case squad and assigned the detectives two purposes: (1) detectives were to examine unsolved homicides to look for new leads, and (2) detectives were to audit each item of evidence and property from their assigned cold cases. In this regard, they were to determine its physical location and proper maintenance. Cases were reviewed from 2001 and working backward. The philosophy driving this directional sequence considered maximization of resources. Older cases present more difficulty due to lack of witness availability, evidence considerations, and other factors.

The department wanted the unit to be operational within a short period of time, and established a method to determine which cases would be reinvestigated. Their procedure included:

1. Each unsolved homicide would be reviewed by a detective not originally assigned to the investigation. They thought that fresh eyes offered a fresh perspective to the case.
2. A case document would be prepared upon completion of the review. This overview document would cover:
   - Crime scene information overview
   - Physical evidence description, condition, and location

Factor #	Factor	If yes, add	If no, add
1	Has the death been ruled a homicide?	+1	−9
2	Can the crime scene be located today and is it in Morris County?	+1	−9
3	Has the victim been identified?	+5	−3
4	Is there significant physical evidence that can identify a suspect?	+5	0
5	Is the evidence still preserved and available?	+1	−5
6	Can any evidence be reprocessed to yield further clues?	+5	0
7	Are the critical witnesses still available?	+7	0
8	Are their leads documented in the last 6 months?	+2	0
9	Are there named suspects in the file?	+5	0
10	Is there behavior in this crime that is unusual or significant enough to warrant a behavioral assessment that may identify the offender(s)?	+1−5	0

FIGURE 2.15 This agency has identified 10 factors to be considered in the re-opening of an unsolved case and the resulting prioritization. (Courtesy of Deputy Chief of Investigations James Gannon)

- Victim/victimology information
- Overview of witness statements
- Citizen/Informant Information
- Suspect Information
- Availability of new forensic technology
- Impact of passage of time (positive or negative)

Upon this review, a conclusion highlighting new information or details about the evidence would be prepared. It was the responsibility of the assigned detectives to physically locate property and evidence and to document their findings, including date and time. In addition, the conclusion specified the disposition of the case, including whether it was (1) submitted for prosecution, (2) maintained by the Cold Case Squad for investigation, (3) exceptionally cleared, or (4) archived due to lack of follow-up leads or evidence.

If the preliminary review suggested the likelihood of a successful investigation and solution to the crime, a more formal review and investigation would be conducted by an assigned investigator. The KCPD adopted a point system to identify cases to be worked. This system assigns a weighted value to 23 individual categories (see Figure 2.16). While 50 points are possible, cases examined with as little as two points and as many as 24 points have been successfully cleared. This format has proven to be a valuable tool for their detectives, although the overall value as a solvability indicator is unknown. The unit reported solving 22 cold case homicides within the first year of the method's implementation.

LOS ANGELES COUNTY SHERIFF METHOD

Beginning in July, 2000, the Los Angeles County, California, Sheriff's Department undertook a systematic review of all identified unsolved homicides that occurred from January 1, 1980 through December 31, 1999. Approximately 3000 unsolved homicide cases were initially believed to exist within these parameters. The concept of this program was to determine whether the passage of time since the murder had occurred might lead to the identification of a suspect in selected cases. The parameters for this concept involved (1) utilization of advances in forensic technology, including DNA, fingerprint visualization techniques, NIBIN or DRUGFIRE firearm databases; (2) previously unknown witnesses who might now come forward; (3) previously reluctant witnesses who

Offense number					
Victim					
Date of crime					

Evidence		Yes	PT.	No	UNK	N/A
1	Fingerprints recovered?		2			
2	Prints checked through afis?		-			
3	Any prints AFIS quality?		3			
4	Prints available on possible suspect?		2			
5	Trace evidence recovered for DNA analysis?		4			
6	DNA analysis requested?		-			
7	DNA profile obtained from analysis?		3			
8	DNA sample obtained from suspects?		2			
9	Murder weapon recovered?		4			
10	Projectiles/casings recovered?		2			
11	Checked through nibin system?		-			
12	Nibin identification made?		2			
13	Victim's property taken in crime?		2			
14	Stolen property entered in NCIC?		4			

Witness(s)		Yes	PT.	No	UNK	N/A
15	Eyewitness (s) to the crime?		3			
16	Cooperative witness(s)?		2			
17	Hostile witness(s)?		1			
18	Good witness(s) developed in Canvass?		2			

Suspect(s)		Yes	PT.	No	UNK	N/A
19	Suspect(s) named by witness(s)?		4			
20	Does eyewitness(s) know suspect(s)?		2			
21	Suspect(s) developed in investigation?		2			
22	Can witness(s) identify suspect(s)?		2			
23	Is suspect(s) still in Kansas city?		2			

Total solvability points (50 possible)	
Det.	Date

FIGURE 2.16 The KCPD utilizes a 23-factor table that utilizes a point system for categories of evidence, witness, and suspect in the determination of a priority ranking system for reinvestigation. (Courtesy of Sgt. John Jackson, Kansas City, Missouri, Police Department)

might now be more likely to cooperate; and (4) a multiyear review that might reveal previously unknown homicide patterns.

The Sheriff's Department re-employed six retired Sheriff's homicide detectives, "hirebacks," and devised a protocol by which they were to identify and score those cases that held potential for solution. In addition to their previous experience within the Homicide Bureau, requirements for selection included knowledge of current scientific capabilities and proficiency with law enforcement databases and other computer technology. These rehired detectives underwent a 24-hour training program and began to review these unsolved homicides.

This training instruction entailed (1) locating and cataloging homicide file contents from within Sheriff's Department sources; (2) instruction in computer software for the FBI's National Center for Analysis of Violent Crime (ViCAP) and department case management systems; (3) instruction in research sources for locating witnesses, suspects, and principals in unsolved cases; (4) locating all evidence and Coroner's Office documentation, and (5) writing and filing a "Case Assessment Report;" as shown in Figures 2.13 and 2.14, summarizing their case review activity.

A case review was then completed for each unsolved homicide case. The procedures used in this review included (1) location and receipt of case file; (2) listening to all audio tapes and determining whether transcripts should be made or whether existing ones are accurate; (3) contacting original investigators, if possible, for case overview and to determine whether additional information exists that is not in the case file. In addition, to recover any notes or notebooks still retained by the original investigator, (4) determine whether or not contact needs to be made with family of victim to establish whether new information exists that was not known to original investigators, and (5) prepare recommendation to sheriff's homicide investigator as whether to obtain information from other specialized law enforcement units.

These examiners would also systematically review and update the condition of the case file. This would include ensuring that:

- Case file folder had the appropriate information required by the Homicide Bureau and that it was up to date and complete.
- All photos and negatives were located and in satisfactory condition for investigative and court purposes.
- All Coroner's reports, photos, and other documents were present in the file, complete and in satisfactory condition for court presentation.
- All original investigators notes and notebooks were in the file and not still retained by the investigator.
- All evidence is accounted for and its location is determined, as well as need for reevaluation and reexamination.
- All progress reports were up to date and in the file.
- All maps and diagrams were inspected and in satisfactory condition for court presentation.

The reviewing detective would then prepare a case assessment report. This would provide updated information and recommend any necessary fieldwork and investigation. As a result, the file would be as complete as possible and in a condition to turn over to a homicide investigator with an oral briefing.

The agency identified in excess of 2000 homicide cases that were unsolved, and, as a result of the filtering process based on parameters of time and changes in relationships and technology, identified approximately 600 cases for further investigation. A number of the cases have subsequently been solved.

CONCLUSION

Cold case homicides are solved by a combination of time, technology, and a change in relationships. Cold case investigators begin by finding and reviewing the original case file, a feat sometimes more difficult than it may first appear to be. These files are found in a variety of conditions. For those agencies with large numbers of unsolved cases, a systematic review may be a practical method of filtering those cases with a potential for solvability with available resources from those with a lesser possibility. After the cases are reviewed, they may be prioritized, thus providing a means for the agency to proactively move forward with cold case investigations. The following chapters discuss further techniques in file reviews and investigative methods that may assist in the solution of cold case homicides.

ACKNOWLEDGMENTS

I would especially like to thank Detective Jim Trainum of the Washington D.C. Metro Police Department; Lt. Tony Leal and Ranger John Martin of the Texas Rangers; Sergeant John Jackson of the Kansas City, Missouri, Police Department; Sgt. John Neff of the Austin, Texas, Police Department; Deputy Chief of Investigations James Gannon of the Morris County, New Jersey, Prosecutor's Office; Detective Rick Jackson of the Los Angeles Police Department and Lt. Joe Hartshorne, Sergeant Paul Mondry and Sergeant Richard Longshore of the Los Angeles County Sheriff's Department, and Deputy District Attorney Jeff Dusek of the San Diego County District Attorney's Office, for their invaluable assistance in the preparation of this chapter. In addition, the KCPD method was drawn from a discussion of the Kansas City cold case squad by Sergeant Kate Ellis of that agency in the July, 2004, issue of *Subject to Debate*, published by the Police Executive Research Forum, and interviews with department personnel. Discussion of the methods used by the Charlotte, North Carolina, Police Department was drawn from an article by Mike Adams in the July, 2003, issue of *Subject to Debate*.

SUGGESTED READING

Adams, M. (2003). Cold case squad: Partnering with volunteers to solve old homicide cases. (July 2002) *Subject to Debate*. Police Executive Research Forum. Washington, DC. P. 1, 7.

Anonymous (2002). "Cold Case Homicide". C.P.T. Network. Sacramento, CA, California Commission on Peace Officer Standards and Training.

Anonymous (2003). Los Angeles sheriff's cold case unit uses old fingerprints in new ways. *Crime Control Digest*, 37(6), 1.

Barmazel, S. (1996). "Murder on coyote flat." *California Lawyer* 16(5): 42–45, 86–87.

Bowker, M. (1994). "The case of the fateful fingerprints." *Readers Digest*: 91–96.

Davies, H.J. (2003). Understanding variations in murder clearance rates: The influence of the political environment. Unpublished Ph.D dissertation. American University. Washington, D.C.

Eliopulos, L.N. (2003). *Death Investigators Handbook: Expanded and Updated Edition*. Boulder, CO, Paladin Press.

Ellis, K. (2004). "Kansas City cold case squad solves string of murders." Washington, D.C., Police Executive Research Forum. 18: 1,7.

Geberth, V. (1996). *Practical Homicide Investigation: Tactics, Procedures, and Forensic Techniques*. Boca Raton, CRC Press.

Keppell, R.D. and J.G. Weis (1994). "Time and distance as solvability factors in murder cases." *Journal of Forensic Sciences* 39(2): 386–401.

National Institute of Justice (2002) "Using DNA to solve cold cases." (Commission report No. NIJ 194197). Washington, D.C.

Nyberg, R. (1999). "Investigations: Cold case squads reactivate old investigations." *Law and Order* 47(10): 127.

Roletti, A. (1992). "Team's task is to look at long-unsolved murders." *San Diego Union-Tribune*. November 29. San Diego: B-1, B-4.

Regini, C.L. (1997). The cold case concept. *FBI Law Enforcement Bulletin*. (August, 1997). Federal Bureau of Investigation, Washington, D.C.

Spraggs, D. (2003). "How to open a cold case." *Policemag.com*: 29–31.

Turner, R. and Kosa, R. (2003). Cold case squads: Leaving no stone unturned. Bureau of Justice Assistance Bulletin (NCJ Report 199781). (July, 2003). 1–7.

Walton, R.H. (2005). Identification of solvability factors in twenty-first century cold case homicide investigations. Unpublished Ed.D. dissertation. University of San Francisco. San Francisco, California.

3 Read the Book: Learn the Case

Richard H. Walton

CONTENTS

INTRODUCTION

"Read the book. Before you do anything, read the *whole* book." With these words, the late Sergeant Rudy Ortega of the Unsolved Unit, Los Angeles County Sheriff's Department, summed it up. Before you begin to investigate a cold case, read the case file to see what you have, and what's already been done. As you do so, you will begin to *reconstruct the case* and formulate an *investigative plan* in your mind. You will read what is known about the victim and about the circumstances of the crime. You will read how it was initially handled, who responded, and what was learned in the initial investigation. You may readily identify a weakness in the investigation — perhaps witnesses who appear to be less than truthful or may have been holding back, or identification of evidence that may now offer more potential due to advanced technology. As you do so, your experience will begin to identify any potential gaps, areas that you may seek to fill.

Through understanding the case file, you are *informally* reconstructing the crime, the crime scene, and post-crime behavior. This is in contrast to a formal reconstruction as might be undertaken at a later stage of investigation. This is the beginning of the new investigation as you seek answers to the same questions you would normally ask in a homicide investigation, but are now asking years or even decades since. These questions include:

- What happened?
- How did it happen?
- When and where?
- Who found the body?
- Who had a motive?
- Did anyone gain financially from the victim's death?
- Do the witnesses' statements, or those of others, make sense?
- Where are the witnesses now?
- Has the passage of time affected the willingness of others to cooperate?
- What evidence did they have?
- Does the evidence "fit" the crime?
- What would a timeline of events reveal?
- Have there been any relationship changes that may now be exploited?
- If a suspect was developed, where is that suspect now?
- Is the suspect in custody?
- What other crimes did the suspect commit before, or after, this crime?
- Who might he or she have talked to about this crime?
- What relationship changes may have occurred in the suspect's life?

In doing this, you will see what was done by the investigators. You may also see what they did not do. You may initially sense no weakness in the case, that the original investigators did everything humanly possible at the time but were not able to make the case. It is now your turn, and you will try to exploit the advantages of time and technology to solve it. Maybe now a reexamination of the physical or biological evidence will reveal critical information not known before, or perhaps an informant can be generated or a witness enticed to tell *all* they know.

As you do, keep an open mind and do not necessarily be drawn into the theories and avenues of focus of the original investigators. I have experienced those cases, personally and through discussion with other cold case investigators, in which the focus of our predecessors was wrong. They may have had incorrect information or circumstances at the time may have suggested they were on the right track. There have been those cases, hopefully few, in which the initial investigators focused on individuals with little regard for truth or fact, and perhaps were guided by personal feelings or other motives. This is rare, but it has happened.

This chapter considers these and other issues that might be addressed by cold case investigators as they proceed with the investigation. If the case has been assigned to the investigator as a result of a systematic review, it may be in order and contains a synopsis or summary from which the investigator can readily obtain an overview of the case elements. A suggested investigative plan might already be outlined, but this is a suggestion only. Cold case investigation is cerebral and what may have sounded good at the time to a reviewer may now not seem as necessary or beneficial as it once did. All investigators have their own approaches. If a cold case investigator assumes the investigation without the benefit of a prior review, this chapter offers further assistance in understanding the file and moving forward with the investigation. If the reinvestigation is the result of specific information that has come to the attention of law enforcement, this chapter and the next address potential avenues through which to approach the case and its investigation.

INITIAL CONSIDERATIONS

No one person is an expert in every field, and those in law enforcement are no different. When studying the case file, keep in mind the various disciplines and experts that are used in homicide investigation today, and their possible role in a cold case investigation. Among these are:

- Behavioral analysis
- Legal and prosecution considerations
- Crime scene reconstruction
- Forensic laboratory
- DNA (human/plant/animal)
- Technology data banks such as CODIS/AFIS/NIBIN
- Blood-spatter experts
- Polygraph
- Specialty crime investigatory methods such as forensic document and handwriting analysis
- Medical examiners and forensic pathologists
- Firearm examiners
- Advanced fingerprint technology
- Forensic odontologists
- Forensic anthropologists
- Forensic botanists
- Forensic artists
- Child-abuse experts and resource organizations
- Non-government resources
- Media
- Technical and specialty support resources within the agency or at the state level

THE CASE FILE

The case file contains the entire written record of the investigation, including all interview reports, photographs, evidence collection and analysis reports, and other documentation. The previous chapter discussed methods and sources through which to determine that all known records have been assembled. It is imperative that all records be identified and collected for the reinvestigation. Some of the sources of these are:

- In-house agency file systems where records are normally kept
- Archives in on-site or off-site storage areas
- District attorney/prosecutor's office
- Property/evidence storage
- Coroner/medical examiner office
  - Reports
  - Biological or physical evidence
  - Coroner's Inquest
- Local laboratory
- State or FBI laboratory
- Retired investigators
- Other agencies involved in joint investigation of the homicide
  - Local
  - State
  - Federal

When reading the file, does it appear complete and is it in order? As you study the file you are beginning your investigation. Ask the following questions:

- What do you know about your victim?
- Victim's lifestyle?
  - Friends and associates?
  - Relationships?
- By what circumstances did the victim come to be a victim?
- What do you need to learn about your victim?
- What do you know about any developed suspect?

Where to Start

My experiences and those of most cold case investigators with whom I have spoken suggest that a cold case file review should begin at the start of the case. In other words, at the beginning. Whether it begins with the initial missing-person's report, the finding of a body, or a report of shots fired, start at the earliest time and date of related events. The reasoning behind this is that the cold case investigator can see the investigation as it unfolded, as the events occurred, and how the pieces began to fall into place. In doing so, you may see open windows that need to be closed.

I have spoken to a very few investigators, however, who prefer to start investigating a cold case by working *backward*. That is, once the file is in chronological order, they prefer to work backward from the most recent investigative activity to the initial report of the crime and related events. This chapter addresses the investigation in a *forward* manner from the beginning of the crime to the latest activity and to the rejuvenated investigation.

As you begin, do you have questions? Write notes down now. When you read it a second time, the same thought may not be repeated exactly as it was and may become a different thought pattern altogether. Quite often, our first thoughts are the best. Although many of your questions will be answered as you read further, these initial questions and thoughts are the beginning of your investigation. If they are not answered when you have finished reading the book, they become the basis of your investigative plan. This plan is one that identifies and organizes your investigative action. It is based upon what has been done and what you determine needs to be done.

Start to think about your own organization, also.

At the outset, place a fresh page with a photograph of your victim at the start of the file. This is the person you now represent, the victim for whom you may be the last chance for what passes for justice in our society.

Biography Sheet

With many cold cases, there are a lot of people to come to know, and their roles in the crime and the investigation. Many, if not all, will need to be located, contacted, and reinterviewed. Consider a biography sheet for each individual (see Figure 3.1). This document contains summary information about an individual and provides a quick resource for the cold case investigator in lieu of reading through numerous documents. In addition, it may be used to document those who are now deceased, and other pertinent information.

As the cold case investigation progresses, investigators may learn of relationships between persons that were previously unknown, or have developed in the interim, and this may be significant. This is a good place to note it for future investigative knowledge. As an example, while I was investigating a case, I contacted a man believed to have knowledge about past events at his residence. After some time had passed, I identified a woman who might have important information about the same event and drove to contact her. As I approached her residence, I observed that I was not very far from the man's location, which I had been to in the past. Upon interviewing my new witness, I casually noted that I had been to another nearby location in the past and inquired whether she knew the man. Whereupon my current witness said, "Oh yes, that was my uncle." This one comment tied together a number of people and opened a whole new understanding of previously unknown familial relationships that were critical to the case. Knowledge of relationships may

INDIVIDUAL BIOGRAPHY SHEET

Case No. _____   Case Name _____

[ ] New Witness
[ ] Original Participant
[ ] Relative of Participant
[ ] Other
[ ] Role

NAME:

DOB: _____   POB: _____

DOD: _____   POD: _____

Current Address:

Current Telephone:

Previous Addresses/Time of Offense:

PHOTO/DRIVERS LICENSE

Father: Address/Phone:

Mother: Address/Phone:

Notes:

Figure No. _____

FIGURE 3.1 A biography sheet provides quick access to individual information and is one way to summarize the role of people, past and present investigation. (Courtesy of El Cajon Police Department)

become important in cold case investigations, especially some gang-related homicides, and this is one means of quickly documenting who is related to whom.

This document can be used for:

- Victim
- Victim's family members, friends, and associates
- Witnesses and other parties
- Suspect
- Suspect's family members, friends, and associates
- Law enforcement officers
- Forensic/laboratory personnel
- Others for a quick reference as necessary

Information to be included:

- Case number (old and new as necessary)
- Case name
- Individual role
  - New witness
  - Original participant
  - Relative of participant
  - Other
  - Role
- Name
- Date of birth (DOB)
- Place of birth (POB)
- Date of death (DOD)
- Place of death (POD)
- Current address
- Current telephone
- Previous address/Time of offense
- Subject's picture or copy of driver's license
- Father
- Address/Telephone
- Mother
- Address/Telephone
- Ex-wives or husbands or other partners

If you establish and use a computer database for your investigation, this information can be included within your case file on the computer system.

Calendars

Consider preparing a calendar of the month and year of the crime, as well as one of the month preceding and the month(s) following. Such calendars are readily available on many desktop computer programs (see Figure 3.2). Confirming accuracy can be accomplished by comparison to a period newspaper from the time of the crime or original investigation. This serves a number of purposes, including:

- Allow investigator to picture sequences of events as they unfolded by day of the week.
- Allow investigators to correlate witness statements to dates, days, and times.
- Illustrate potential incongruencies.
- Graphically enhance investigator comprehension of the crime events and subsequent investigation.
- Aids witness recall. During witness reinterviews in the cold case investigation, it may assist the witness in recalling events and time sequences. This might be especially true when interviewing senior citizens. For instance, they may not recall the *date* of an activity, but that the activity occurred on the "*Wednesday* before her body was found." The calendar assists the witness in establishing a correct orientation of events.
- At the conclusion of the investigation, such a calendar may contribute to preparing computerized slide shows or presentations to present the case to superior officers or the prosecutor.

| | July | | | | | |
Sun	Mon	Tue	Wed	Thu	Fri	Sat
	1	2	3	4	5	6
7	8	9	10	11	12	13
14	15	16	17	18	19	20
21	22	23	24	25	26	27
28	29	30	31			

1957

FIGURE 3.2 A helpful technique, for investigators and witnesses, is to prepare a calendar of the period of the cold case. This helps related days to dates, and put events in context. They can be created on many desktop word processing programs.

In-House Changes

A complete case file is essential to moving forward. Knowledge of past filing systems and practices within the agency is important in locating and gathering all relevant written and evidentiary material. This includes records filing, maintenance and storage, as well as evidence filing and storage practices. This knowledge can be learned from more senior members of the agency as well as past employees. When reviewing property lists and property records, know how the evidence section filed and catalogued evidence and paperwork during the case and subsequent time period. When possible, investigators should become familiar with:

- Information intake systems and dispatch procedures in place at time of reporting of crime.
- 911 or similar recordings that might still be available.
- Information recording systems (handwritten logs or computer generated).
- Agency daily activity logs. Availability and accessibility of these day-to-day records of reported crimes and other activities may be of importance in reconstructing the crime or similar relevant time-frame events.
- Any "purges" or destruction of agency records since the offense.

The Case Number

Depending upon the age of the case, note whether this number style corresponds to the form still in use by the agency. If not, identify when the department or agency changed numbering systems since the homicide, and consider its relevance to the case under investigation. Identify all case file numbers associated with this case, past and present, and assure that files and evidence are located under all identified numbers. During the review and inspection of each report and document, ensure that the file or case number is accounted for. If there were additional victims, check whether separate case numbers were issued and ensure that all relevant case files pertaining to the cold case have been identified and collected.

Similarly, if the laboratory or evidence facilities have changed numbering systems, check under all their numbers also. When gathering and reviewing coroner or medical examiner files, similarly ascertain whether there have been any changes in numbering systems. In these locations, changes in numbering systems may preclude a complete search and recovery of all pertinent records and evidence.

In the case of physical evidence such as rape kits or bullets and expended cartridge casings, inquire whether, at any time, personnel filed large groups of property under a single case number. This has happened, usually when suspects are unknown.

File Contents

While the layout of a "murder book" and file conditions vary between agencies, the contents detail what was done during the initial and follow-up investigations. These records serve to reconstruct the crime scene as well as the investigation. Consider that the older case files may contain all or portions of the following, which are areas to be studied and addressed in your investigation:

- **Case chronological record.** Often, over the period of years or decades, case chronological records and summaries will be compiled by a sequence of investigators. These are informative, but should be viewed with caution. As in any instance when someone reports the work of others, misinterpretation and misreporting may result, albeit unintentionally. Always try to know and use *original* source documentation wherever possible. Upon completion of the cold case investigation, compilation of a detailed timeline and chronological record will assist those who review the completed case, as well as the prosecutor, in understanding what may often be a decades-long series of events, relationships, and technology advancements.
- **Crime scene.** Nature and extent of crime scene documentation. This would include photos and reports.
  - Initial responding officer actions and observations.
    - Was blood dry or wet upon arrival?
    - Did the responding officer see or smell anything unusual upon arrival?
    - Weather conditions at the time.
    - Who were the technicians who responded?
    - How was evidence identified — or not?
    - What evidence collection and preservation methods were used?
    - Who turned any lights on or off?
    - Were windows and doors checked?
    - Was there evidence of what we today call "staging?"
- **Crime scene log.** Nice in theory, not always done, especially in older cases. When, and if, this document is in the case file, identify and interview.
  - Who preserved the scene and their subsequent documentation.
  - Subsequent officers and other agency personnel present.
  - Others recorded in the log.
  - Other recorded events or unusual circumstances.

As with all other law enforcement or other persons involved in the response or investigation, reinterview and ask whether they retain any notes, photographs, or other records, and also any *undocumented* observations or thoughts on the crime. When reinterviewing original-scene officers and investigators:

- Ask what they first saw.
- Discuss what they did and what evidence they recovered or did not recover.
- Review original reports with each.
  - Were there discrepancies?
  - Was the original report complete?
  - Can they add any further thoughts?
  - Were there observations or perceptions that they did not report?
- **Crime report(s).** Including initial responding officer and investigator reports. Although previously described, keep in mind that older case file reports may be much different by today's standards. Changes may include:
  - Personal identification information lacking specific detail. This compounds cold case investigator's efforts to identify "John Smith" and to relocate for follow-up interview.
  - Synopsis versus detail style of reporting
  - Lack of reports

- Look for information on how the crime came to be reported, including:
  - Who discovered the body?
  - Who made the call or notified police?
- **Property and evidence reports.** Review all property reports and compare these with what was seized and has since been maintained. How complete, and how detailed, are these reports? Consider the source of seizure and its relationship in the crime. In addition, consider what advances in technology may be used in an attempt to obtain further information from the property or evidence. During your physical inspection of each item, note whether its weight (narcotics) or other description is sufficiently detailed.
- **Forensic logs and reports.** Review the evidence gathered at the time and cross-check to other evidence and property logs. Does the case file reflect all copies of logs and reports? Compare any original requests for forensic examination to what was done, or not done, and to copies maintained by the forensic facility. Inquire whether they retain:
  - Examination notebooks.
  - Work journals.
  - Photographs and diagrams.
  - Reports.
  - Slides.

Consider what might be accomplished by reexamination using more advanced technology. When reviewing this with laboratory personnel, explore advances such as DNA testing now as opposed to the serology grouping in previous decades or earlier DNA methods. Consider the present ability to identify fingerprints or trace evidence that was technically not possible even within the past decade. If a knife recovered from a suspect was tested for the victim's DNA yet none was found, would advanced technology now be able to recover victim DNA from *within* the hilt of the knife due to advances in STR DNA (see Figure 3.3)?

- **Vehicle reports.** Identify all vehicles involved in the case and their disposition. Were they released to family members or sold at auction? In addition to family or friends information, consider running the Vehicle Identification Number or license plate through motor vehicle registrations to relocate vehicle if title has changed hands. This may be useful in reconstructing the crime scene or other events. If the case is old and the vehicle cannot be located, consider on-line Web searches for similar vehicles through car-collector clubs, local car clubs, auto enthusiasts, etc.
- **Related crime reports.** When reviewing names and reports, note whether other crime reports may be associated with this offense. Were there co-victims whose case might have been assigned a separate case number? Were there other victims at the same period as the homicide, or other cases suspected by original investigators to be related?
- **Follow-up and progress reports.** During the review of these reports, original investigator focus and theories may become evident. Are there numerous reports of interviews with one or a few subjects? Does the same name reappear? Are there investigator synopses detailing case progress, including their thoughts and theories?
- **Crime scene canvass.** Was a canvass completed? How complete and thorough was it? Are the records present?
- **Victim information.** Victim information found in the file may provide insight into motive or a possible contributing role to the homicide. Keep in mind that there is an approximately 50%–70% chance that victim and attacker knew one another. An original profile of the victim may be portrayed in the reports through interviews with family, friends, co-workers, classmates, teacher, and others. Consider the width and depth of what is known about the victim in the case file and consider followup investigation addressing the victim. Considerations include:

FIGURE 3.3 With advances in DNA technology, it may now be possible to retrieve a usable DNA profile from within recesses, such as this knife handle, that previously could not be accomplished. (Courtesy of Detective Bob Donaldson, San Diego Police Department)

- Was a psychological autopsy addressed?
- More complete victim profile.
- Current personal relationship at time of offense.
- Previous or other relationships.
- Perhaps more so than men, females have a *"best"* or close friend to whom they may confide and share private thoughts, including secrets, fears, or other intimate information. This person is not necessarily a family member. While reviewing witness statements, consider identifying and interviewing (or reinterviewing) the victim's best or closest friend. What *more* might he or she say now?
- When viewing photos of victim, note other persons in the photo. Identify these people and ascertain whether they are known to the investigation.
- Background and biographical information.
- Criminal history including probation and parole reports.
- Other civil or criminal reports previously reported by victim or family.
- Any reported stalking of victim.
- Rap sheet.
- What *don't* you know about your victim and the circumstances?
- Victim activity within 24 hours before death.
- **Suspect information.**
  - Statements.
  - Alibis and witness statements.
  - Photos or forensic artist/composite drawings.
  - Criminal history including probation and parole reports.
  - Rap sheet.
  - Current custody status.
  - Custody history to identify past incarcerations and identify possible cellmates, institution intelligence reports, etc.
  - Other identified relationships that may now be changed due to passage of time, including friends, intimate partners, spouses, business associates.
  - Suspect activity within 24 hours prior to victim's murder.
- **Photo lineups.** Were photo lineups conducted in the previous investigation? Are they in the file? Who were they shown to? What identifications were made? What reports were generated as a result of these lineups? What processes were utilized during the procedure? Were any admonitions similar to current practice given to witnesses?

- **Witness statements and lists.** Are the reports of these statements sufficiently detailed? During the review of witness statements, cold case investigators should note closely what questions were asked and what answers were given (and how these were subsequently documented).
  - What was *not* asked may be more important than what was asked.
  - Note the number of interviews with repeat witnesses or suspect. Consider statement analysis of repeat interviews as discussed later in this chapter.
  - Is there sufficient information to identify and relocate the witness?
- **Crime scene notes and surveys.** Are these preserved in the file? Review and cross-check to the crime-scene log, if possible. Identify officers or crime-scene personnel who may have made or maintained any notes, surveys, or other documents not in the file.
- **Crime-scene sketches.** Are these present in the file? If so, are they detailed and to scale? In older cases, these may be general overview and not measurement-specific (see Figure 3.4). Consider that in some agencies, other city or county resources may have been called upon for assistance in this regard (See Figure 3.5). These might include:
  - City/county engineers (see Figure 3.6)
  - Public works
  - Private architects/draftsmen
  - State architects, engineers, or draftsmen

In *"Practical Homicide Homicide: Tactics, Procedures, and Forensic Techniques,"* homicide investigation expert Vernon Geberth stressed the role of crime scene sketches in homicide investigation, and these hold true for cold case homicide investigations. The crime scene sketch can be used in cold case investigations to:

1. Refresh the memory of the investigator.
2. Refresh the memory of the witness(es).
3. Refresh the memory of the cooperative suspect to assist in detailing his or her actions at the scene.
4. Develop a clearer understanding of what happened and determine the relative likelihood of various possibilities. As shown by Geberth, persons may be requested to trace their particular movements on copies of the original sketch.
5. Explain to a jury or witness the specifics of a case that may otherwise be too complex or confusing. The value of the crime scene sketch is that its clarity and simplicity motivate understanding.

- **Crime-scene photos.** Does the case file reflect a number of photographs that sufficiently detail the crime scene in macro and micro detail? Are they adequately documented to reflect:
  - What they represent (see Figure 3.7).
  - The significance of this photo (see Figure 3.8).
  - When it was taken.
  - By whom it was taken.
  - What you now see as evidence shown in the photos that was never collected.
- **Ambulance run records.** Were ambulance and similar emergency personnel identified and interviewed? Were their run records obtained?
- **Medical records.**
  - Emergency room records.
  - Doctor reports.
- **Coroner's records.**
  - Autopsy reports.
  - Toxicology reports.

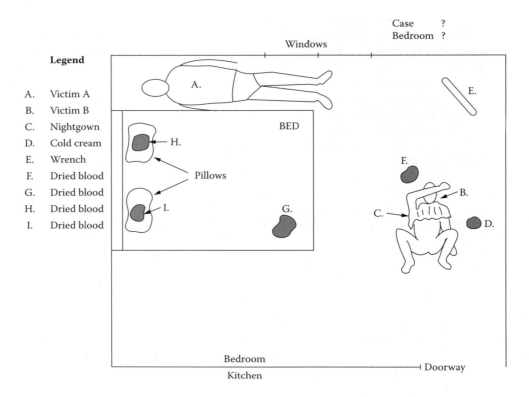

FIGURE 3.4 Older crime scene sketches lack the measurement and detail present in later investigations. However, even rough sketches, coupled with photographs, can provide an informational picture of the crime scene. (Courtesy of El Cajon Police Department)

FIGURE 3.5 Maps of crime scene drawn by city engineers.

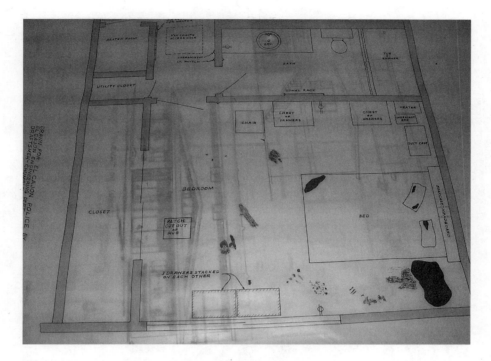

FIGURE 3.6 When reviewing cold cases, consider that outside resources may have been utilized for crime scene mapping. These detailed crime scene maps were prepared by the city engineer's office in the Wilkerson case shown in Chapter Four. (Courtesy of El Cajon Police Department)

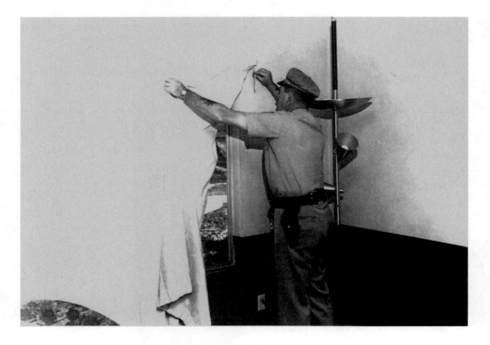

FIGURE 3.7 It is not uncommon in older crime scene photos to observe police practices no longer utilized. Here an officer handles a drapery cord from which a ligature was cut by a suspect, and stands within the crime scene. (Courtesy of El Cajon Police Department)

FIGURE 3.8 Although there appear to be footprints in the picture, a lack of documentation makes this photo almost worthless. We do not know where it was, when it was taken, by whom, or its significance. No measurement instrument is included in the photo. (Courtesy of El Cajon Police Department)

- Photos.
- Retained clothing.
- Retained biological samples.
- **Death certificate and obituary.** These documents may not always be found in the cold case file, but may provide valuable information for the course of investigation. They are further described in Chapter 9.
- **Communications.**
  - Initial crime report intake information.
  - Teletypes.
  - Press releases.
  - Newspaper clippings.
  - Police bulletins.
  - Other computer runs.
- **Affidavit for search warrants and search warrants.** Affidavits contain detailed information about known case events and investigator knowledge at a specific time during the investigation when the affidavit is drafted and submitted. Is there evidence in the case file that affidavits for search warrants were ever prepared?
  - Are these documents still retained in the file?
  - Were they served?
  - Do court clerk or court copies remain?
  - Are there search warrant returns listing any property recovered.

- **Investigation notes.** Are any, part, or all in the file? During the follow-up interviews, cold case investigators should seek to gather all remaining notes from initial responding officers, investigators and other persons connected with the case or its investigation.

ADDITIONAL CONSIDERATIONS

CASE ORGANIZATION

While investigators have their own method of doing so, many prefer to initially organize cold cases chronologically. After doing this, it may be helpful to segregate persons, or topics, into groups and to proceed in this manner. In this way, cold case investigators can identify all persons whose names are reflected in the reports, and subsequently identify a plan of action that needs to take place with each. This will illuminate the process of the original investigation as well as identify those who need to be reinterviewed. These persons can be categorized as:

- Law enforcement.
- Medical and ambulance.
- Crime scene and evidence.
- Coroner or medical examiner.
- Laboratory and forensic.
- Witnesses.
- Victim family, friends, and associates.
- Suspects.
- Legal.
- Other persons or topics developed during the course of previous and current investigation.

Some investigators find it helpful to organize the file utilizing a simple system of file folders that address each individual or topic (e.g., evidence) by category. All reports, news clippings, and any document mentioning the individual name, can be included in this file. As the records are reviewed and filed, this simple system may bring together relationships or identify contradictory statements, as well as illuminate the full role of the individual in the investigation. This is a simple system, but it could ultimately consume boxes of files. Each investigator has a system that works, however. What works is what is best.

Homicide investigators and cold case homicide investigators are guided by experience, training, and decades of insight into human nature. From this experience comes intuition and "gut feeling." When reviewing the case reports, ask yourself:

- Were the right questions asked of the right people?
- Which interviews are less than incomplete now in context with the investigation to date?
- Who might have more to say now than what the original report noted?

Listen to original taped interviews (it is suggested that copies be made first to preserve the original tapes). Do you perhaps hear something on the tape the original investigators did not? If there is a transcript, is it complete? Is it accurate? A simple phrase may be something that slipped out but was not caught by the investigator. Look for anonymous letters and phone calls or messages that were not returned.

Reexamination of Evidence

The importance of reexamining all physical and biological evidence is discussed throughout this book. This is necessary to update and confirm examination results due to technological or other changes. The results of these examinations may influence the investigative plan and direction of the investigation. Because of the age of many unsolved homicides, successful prosecution may depend greatly upon the use of scientific evidence. Despite old lab reports attesting that no trace evidence (such as semen) was found, or that the results are inconclusive or negative, you should *retest.* Reexamination using the latest technology and forensic know-how not only provides updated results, it also provides the prosecution with an expert to subpoena when it comes time for trial.

The investigator should keep in mind that the presence of the potential evidence in the case under review and findings of original examination are subject to (1) mistaken filing, tagging, or other association of the evidence with the case under review; (2) original error on the part of the examiner, including misidentification or inaccurate conclusions based upon, among other factors, the state-of-the-art techniques and procedures in effect at the time of the examination; and (3) other factors that have arisen due to passage of time. In cases such as Freiburger, discussed later in this chapter, reexamination of firearms evidence provided a positive match between the weapon linked to the suspect and bullet fragments recovered from the victim, as opposed to previously inconclusive examination results.

As a result of a fresh analysis, potentially new exculpatory or inculpatory evidence may be discovered. A previous negative finding for presence of semen that, upon reexamination, provides a DNA profile resulting in a CODIS hit can significantly alter the direction of the investigation. Reexamination of evidence can save investigators valuable time and other resources when review of the evidence discounts that which was previously thought possible. This includes circumstances in which suspect items were associated with a homicide when in fact they were not. Conversely, reanalysis could yield new information through discovery of new evidence that might assist police in identifying the suspect(s) and solution of the case.

CASE STUDY

While searching the evidence room in another case, officers in a small California police department discovered an old Colts revolver in a box with items from another case (see Figure 3.9). The number on the evidence tag indicated that the weapon was associated with a case number that was not

FIGURE 3.9 Discovery of an old revolver in the evidence room prompted re-investigation of a cold case homicide.

known to the agency. Documentation was sparse, but found in the same box were the original investigator's notebooks for an unsolved homicide that had occurred in the early 1980s.

A transcript of an interview marked with the case number of the other agency was also located in the box. These items suggested that this case encompassed investigation by at least one or more jurisdictions. Contact with the other agency discovered that their case file remained, although the original recording from which the transcript was made was no longer in their custody. Their reports, plus the original investigator's notebook, were the beginnings of a cold case homicide investigation in the late 1990s. When contacted, the original investigator, now retired, recalled little of the case. Officers began by reviewing all the names in the investigator's notebook, reports from the other agency, and the remaining physical evidence in the evidence room.

Also recovered from the box was the victim's clothing. The victim had been recovered from a large body of water when released to the medical examiner. The clothing was subsequently bagged in plastic and returned to the agency. It was stored in this condition for almost 20 years. It had not been properly dried for storage and was now in a moldy condition.

Cold case homicide investigation builds on the life and career experience of cold case investigators. An x-ray showing a number of bullets in the victim's torso was also found in the box (see Figure 3.10). When I reviewed the x-ray and was given a description of the revolver, it immediately became doubtful that the bullets had been fired from this weapon. Observation of the bullets in the x-ray indicated that they were round-nose projectiles. The Colt was now an antique, and was

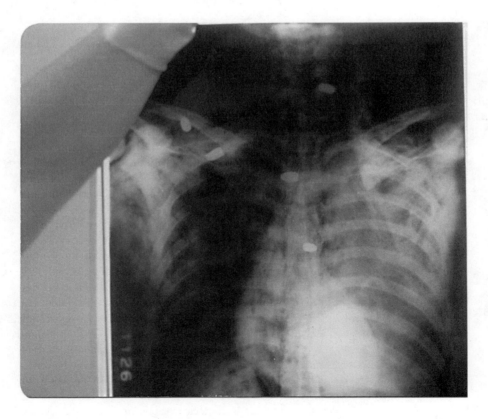

FIGURE 3.10 While scant documentation existed, an x-ray of the victim was also present. Officers initially thought the gun belonged with the case and had fired the fatal rounds. Subsequent firearms examination dispelled this supposition, however, and the gun proved to have no role in the homicide.

chambered for the 32WCF round. This frontier-era cartridge saw double duty as a rifle cartridge in tubular-feed, lever-action-style rifles that necessitated the use of flat-nose bullets. When it was suggested that the weapon be reexamined to determine whether it could have fired the bullets, modern forensic examination corroborated my review and the weapon was discovered to have no relationship to the crime.

The case remains open.

Photos and Photo Analysis

While the value of crime scene photos in homicide investigation has long been recognized, nowhere is this more important than in reconstruction of a cold case homicide. The presence of sharp, quality photos that thoroughly document the crime scene in micro and macro detail provide investigators with the best representation of what the scene looked like years or decades before. While investigator or witness memory can serve to augment words on paper, nothing takes the place of original crime-scene photos.

As with other trends in law enforcement, this aspect may be observed in some cold cases by a general lack of crime-scene photographs, or especially of *detailed* crime scene photos. In addition, the written record to support and authenticate these photographs may be lacking in detail, if present at all. When this occurs, investigators have photographs that may not necessarily be fully relied upon for future courtroom value due to lack of authenticating documentation. They are, however, valuable for investigative purposes, as quite often the subject or topic that the photograph seeks to represent may be apparent. In other cases, however, it may not be (see Figure 3.11).

FIGURE 3.11 This person is unidentified and there is no documentation to suggest the relevance of this photo. It may be surmised that the man is pointing to the shoeprints in the ground shown in Figure 3.8, but without documentation, the investigative and evidentiary value is significantly lessened. (Courtesy of El Cajon Police Department)

When reviewing the photo file, it is prudent to identify agency photographic protocol at the time of the original homicide investigation. Who took crime scene photos? Was it:

- Full time photographic and crime scene/evidence personnel?
- Responding officers responsible for own crime scene processing?
- Contract or on-call photographers from local camera shop?
- Local news media photographers?
- Others?

Depending upon agency size, organization, and other factors, there may or may not have been a formal protocol. What was done may have varied from scene to scene, depending on the circumstances and availability of a photographer. In reviewing the photographic record Vernon Geberth lists desired photographic information. This includes:

- Identity of Photographer.
- Date and time of photograph.
- Exact location.
- Written record of detail being photographed.
- Compass orientation.
- Camera and film description.
- Specialized equipment used.
- Weather and light conditions.
- Processing sequences including chain of custody.
- Development record including number of prints.
- Print distribution.
- What were the processing standards? Was the film automatically developed or was it developed and printed only at the discretion of the investigators, or the photographer?
- Where were the negatives stored?
- Where are the copies now?

If the photographer is known and available:

- Meet with the person to review each photo.
- Attempt to learn what additional information the photographer may have to offer that is not already known.
- Does the photographer have any additional photos not found in the case file?
- Does the photographer maintain any notes or other records of the crime or photography session?

Review of available case file photographs will reveal whether they are ground-based photos or aerial photos (see Figure 3.12 and Figure 3.13), and whether they are in black-and-white or color.

Aerial Photos

While the concept and earliest experiments at aerial photography date to the mid 19th century, aerial photos have been practically utilized in some regions of the U.S. since the 1920s for government and private purposes. They became more commonplace in the 1940s and 1950s with reflights to update the photo files often taking place every so many years. Aerial photos can be very useful in reconstructing a crime scene decades later, especially in those areas where urban growth has redefined the landscape. Local tax assessor's offices are sometimes the best sources of aerial photos. While they were most likely obtained from private contractors, there could be photos going back many

FIGURE 3.12 Aerial photos may be a valuable resource in reconstructing a period crime scene. This practice dates back many decades, and these may be readily available. (Author's collection)

decades in these offices. If they do not have what you are looking for, they may be able to suggest sources of older local regional aerial photos. Other sources of these photos include:

- Local governments, including city and county planning departments
- Local universities and colleges
- State highway departments
- Utility companies
- Local large industries and developers
- Railroads
- Bureau of Mines
- Bureau of Reclamation
- U.S. Army Corp of Engineers
- National Park Service
- U.S. Geological Survey
- U.S. Forest Service
- Bureau of Land Management
- U.S. Department of Agriculture including National Agriculture Imagery Program
- National Environmental Satellite, Data, and Information Service
- NASA
- SpaceImaging Corporation

FIGURE 3.13 Consider using a computer to magnify areas of interest, or consult with other resources such as the National Law Enforcement and Corrections Technology Center. (Author's collection)

Photo Degradation

When reviewing the crime scene photographs in older cases, consider doing so with someone knowledgeable in applicable forensic or image-enhancement techniques. Due to age, crime scene photographs may be faded. This is especially true in older instant-development photographs, such as those commonly referred to as Polaroids®. This problem is also encountered in 35mm color photos. When faded or less legible photos are found in the file, consider consulting with in-agency photographic or forensic resources, the state or FBI crime laboratory, or the National Law Enforcement and Corrections Technology Center (NLECTC).

Other Considerations in Photo Analysis

- Carefully study the photo to see what it *really* shows you in relation to what you know from reading the case reports.
- Study the photo from the center out.
- Enlarge or blowup photos. This often reveals significant detail not otherwise noticed.
- Consider reprinting from negatives without cropping the picture. Cropping may have removed vital detail.
- Is there evidence of posing the scene?
- Evidence that victim killed, dragged, or carried to location.
- Number of perpetrators.
- Weapon used.

- Opportunity or planned.
- Ingress and egress for victim and suspect.
- Drag marks, including direction.
- What evidence do you see in the photo that you do not have today?
- Suggestion of motive.
- Possibility of witnesses.
- Primary crime scene is the body.
  - State of decomposition.
  - Bug activity.
  - Wounds or mutilation.
  - Secondary scene around the body.
  - Tertiary or third level including blood spatter in surrounding area.

Take all photos and put them in sequence of the events during the crime. What do they tell you? Do you see anything not reflected in reports?

If persons are present in the photo, identify and reinterview to ascertain scene value and meaning of the photograph. In past decades, it was not unusual or uncommon for officers and investigators to stand in the crime scene or related locations as pictures were being taken (see Figure 3.14). Other persons that might be found in crime scene photographs might be family members, coroner or medical examiner personnel, fire and ambulance personnel, or news photographers. Or they might be suspects.

Review the photos with a crime scene reconstruction expert. What does he or she see that perhaps you do not?

For example, I had occasion to review a series of photographs from a late 1970s homicide. These were 35mm color photographs, and many were now fading. The female victim had been left in a remote area that had previously been used for body dumps. A suspect had been identified in the case, but evidence to place him at the scene was lacking. Photographs of the suspect, a biker, taken prior to the homicide, had been recovered during the initial investigation. When the victim's body was recovered, a man's belt was wrapped around her legs and had been left behind, as if the

FIGURE 3.14 When reviewing old crime scene pictures, consider identifying persons present. In this photo, a man holding a camera may be a newsperson. Who is he? What other crime scene pictures might he still have? (Courtesy of El Segundo Police Department and LASD)

suspect might have been interrupted or scared off while disposing of the body. The unusual buckle was multisided and irregular in shape, and had the name and logo of a popular motorcycle brand embossed on it in a wavy manner. In addition, the leather belt also was stamped with an ornate pattern. Although other circumstantial evidence was present, the prosecutor wanted more evidence to link the suspect to the victim, and to the scene.

Review of the photographs recovered from the suspect showed one of him wearing a belt and belt buckle seemingly identical to the belt and buckle recovered with the victim's body. This was forwarded to the laboratory for further analysis that confirmed that the buckle and belt pattern recovered with the victim were apparently identical to that worn by the biker suspect in the photograph.

Photos Can Turn up in the Strangest of Places

During review and investigation of cold case homicides, originals or copies of photographs not in the case file have turned up in places normally beyond the practical range of sources explored by cold case investigators. Sometimes this is the result of publicity or word-of-mouth information resulting from investigator actions. They have been found in:

- Old newspapers no longer in publication.
- Off-campus university publications. (see Figure 3.15).

FIGURE 3.15 This 1954 off-campus university magazine contained the only then-known picture of "Boulder Jane Doe" when the cold case was re-activated. This case is further discussed in Chapter 22. (Name withheld by request)

FIGURE 3.15A When recontacting persons involved or living near old crime scenes, inquire whether they have any relevant photos in family albums. The photos shown are original pictures recovered in a family album and published in the newspapers in the 1925 Wagner-Sweet case. (Author's collection)

- Pawn shops.
- *True Detective* and similar crime magazines (see Figure 12.7)
- Private collections of local photographers.
- Historical societies.
- Family photograph albums of those who participated in the crime or its investigation (see Figure 3.15A). When interviewing family members, witnesses, and others, ask whether they have any photographs regarding the case and its investigation.

PRACTICAL STATEMENT ANALYSIS

When a case file contains more than one statement by the same individual, or follow-up investigation results in additional statements, I have found it useful to combine these in an individual file and to subject them to line-by-line scrutiny that may reveal discrepancies and inconsistencies. As an example, use of the phrase "I did ..." during the course of the initial interview that subsequently changes to "I did *not* ..." when reinterviewed in regard to the original statement, or in the course of a cold case investigation, years or decades later. While this avenue of approach is not uncommon in normal day-to-day interviews, in cold case investigation, identification of such inconsistencies may be even more valuable. While this sounds simple, consider that some cold cases consume cartons of files concerning the crime, evidence, and witness statements. Also consider that while cold case investigators are the best in the field, they are not machines. When the statements are spread out over a sequence of files, the full impact and value of what they say may not necessarily be realized. If individuals have been interviewed, then reinterviewed, over a period of time, their statements may reveal these variations, variations that may be a segue to breaking down their discrepancies and learning the truth.

Sources of statements are not necessarily confined to just interview statements given to police during the course of the specific investigation. There are other sources of potential statement information that may offer opportunities to identify these discrepancies and variations. Among these are:

- Initial police interview
- Follow-up police interview
- News media interviews or statements
- Statements made to other parties, including their own families or the family of the victim
- Written memorabilia including diaries, notes, or book and short-story drafts
- Interviews to investigators from other agencies
- Probation and parole statements
- Wiretap conversations
- Civil actions including deposition statements
- Criminal trial actions including testimony
- Coroner's inquest testimony
- Post-arrest interviews

CASE STUDY

On the afternoon of February 28, 1961, U.S. Army Private Edward Freiburger purchased a new .32 caliber H&R Model 722 revolver and a box of S&W Lubaloy ammunition at a Columbia, South Carolina, pawn shop. That same night, John Orner, a Fort Jackson, South Carolina-area taxicab driver (see Figure 3.16) did not arrive home at midnight, as was his custom. His family reported him missing the next morning to the Columbia Police Department.

In the meantime, Orner's taxicab had been found abandoned on a Columbia street, and a large-scale search was under way for its driver. There was evidence of blood on the back of the driver's seat, and an empty wallet was found on the back seat. The wallet's contents were scattered about, but all the money was missing. The Columbia Police Department processed the vehicle, and in doing so, observed a muddy substance on the undercarriage. A sample of this was sent to the South Carolina State Law Enforcement Division (SLED) laboratory. Chief chemist James Wilson concluded that the substance was mica. He suggested that this substance might be found in the lower

FIGURE 3.16 A military veteran, the taxi driver was murdered for about $45, $7 less than what his killer paid for the gun that killed him. (Courtesy of Investigator Carl Craig, Richland County, South Carolina, Sheriff's Department)

FIGURE 3.17 Black-and-white photo of original crime scene showing victim's body as well as the slope and drainage. (Courtesy of Investigator Carl Craig, Richland County, South Carolina, Sheriff's Department)

FIGURE 3.18 The surviving crime scene photo offered pictorial evidence that robbery was a motive in this crime, and preserved a record for cold case investigators decades later. (Courtesy of Investigator Carl Craig, Richland County, South Carolina, Sheriff's Department)

part of Richland County near the Wateree River area. Thus, the case now became multi-jurisdictional in scope. Sheriff Strother S. Sligh and numerous members of local law enforcement, along with every available cab driver in the area, formed a search group and directed their efforts to the area described by Wilson. On March 3, 1961, Orner's body was found partially hidden on a steep embankment about 30 miles south of Columbia in southern Richland County (see Figure 3.17). His body was face down, and his pants pockets were turned inside out, indicating that he had apparently been robbed (see Figure 3.18).

The autopsy revealed that the victim had been shot once in the back of the head. The single bullet fragmented into three pieces and lodged in the brain. These fragments were removed by the attending pathologist and turned over to investigators. No one at the time considered the additional value of these fragments, a value that would further contribute to solving this murder with the advent of DNA.

The bullet fragments were submitted for examination to the laboratory of the South Carolina Division of Law Enforcement. Officers were subsequently advised that the fatal weapon was an H&R 732 revolver and the type of ammunition was S&W Lubaloy.

Sheriff Sligh and two deputies began a canvass of local gun dealers and pawn shops. Within 10 days of the homicide, they found that Freiburger had purchased such a weapon, giving an Indiana address. The clerk who sold the gun remembered that Freiburger was wearing a U.S. Army uniform and that his nametag matched the name he signed on the purchase record. The sheriff requested assistance from the U.S. Army CID, and with this began a series of events that would take almost 40 years to bring Freiburger to justice. A U.S. Army CID Agent at Fort Jackson, Carl Craig, became familiar with a case that he and others would finally conclude in 2002 (see Figure 3.19). Freiburger was already under suspicion by military authorities for housebreaking and grand larceny and was AWOL. On March 29th, 1961, Freiburger was apprehended in Newport, Tennessee, by Trooper

FIGURE 3.19 This photo of Investigator Carl Craig, taken from the same general direction as the 1961 crime scene photo, illustrates the relative lack of change in the 40 years between the crime and when Freiburger was convicted. (Courtesy of Investigator Carl Craig, Richland County, South Carolina, Sheriff's Department)

FIGURE 3.20 H&R .32 revolver used in the crime, seized by Trooper Meredith, and the center of investigation almost four decades later. The ability of the authorities to place Freiburger with the murder weapon, to show his purchase of the gun, and to prove it had fired the fatal projectile was critical evidence that evolved over the decades. (Courtesy of Investigator Carl Craig, Richland County, South Carolina, Sheriff's Department)

Don Meredith for hitchhiking. Freiburger was dressed in civilian clothing, and as the trooper patted him down, he discovered the H&R revolver concealed in his pocket (see Figure 3.20). During the course of this arrest, Trooper Meredith seized the weapon and wrote Freiburger a receipt for it. Almost four decades later, long after Meredith's retirement, follow-up investigators would locate the trooper and he would provide a critical original document linking Freiburger to this specific weapon. He still possessed his copy of the receipt.

Freiburger was arrested and pled guilty to carrying the concealed weapon and was sentenced to 30 days. He confided to a cellmate that he was AWOL and this was relayed to authorities, who notified the military police in Knoxville, Tennessee. The military police apprehension team picked Freiburger up, but instead of returning him to his post at Fort Jackson, transferred him to Atlanta. This complicated the sheriff's efforts to question him about the murder. After a month and a half, the sheriff was finally allowed to interview Freiburger, but with no success. In the meantime, Freiburger was convicted of being AWOL and sentenced to one year in the Fort Leavenworth, Kansas, stockade.

Freiburger's H&R revolver was examined by an SLED examiner who ultimately concluded that the weapon revealed "… a extremely close match as being the murder weapon." However, he did not tender a conclusive written report that Freiburger's gun was the murder weapon. Sheriff Sligh reinterviewed Freiburger at Fort Leavenworth in August, 1961, resulting in an 82-page typed transcript, but the officer did not have the firearms examiner's report when he conducted this interview. During this session, Freiburger made only one admission, that he had bought the gun on March 22, 1961, 3 weeks *after* the murder of victim Orner.

The records obtained by the investigators, however, revealed otherwise (see Figure 3.21). Freiburger had signed a purchase card and the transaction was recorded in the Alcohol-Tobacco-Firearms (ATF) Register for the gun and ammunition on the afternoon of February 28, 1961, using his U.S. Army ID card and Army serial number for identification. The weapon was described by make, model, and serial number, and was the same as recovered by Trooper Meredith. In the absence of a more conclusive laboratory finding or admission of guilt, however, and lack of further information, the case was not resolved.

A New Investigation

By 1997, Carl Craig had retired from a career in the U.S. Army CID. He had also retired again as a criminal investigator for the South Carolina State Police. During Leon Lott's campaign for Sheriff

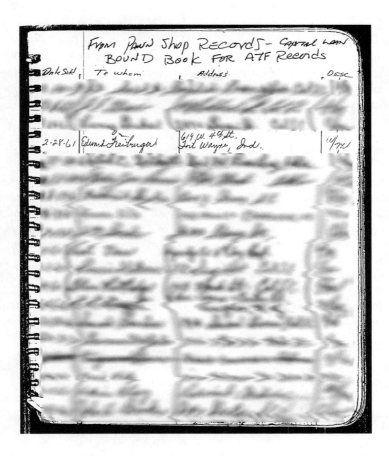

FIGURE 3.21 Cold case investigation builds on the work of earlier investigators, and this is a prime example of the good investigation shown by now-deceased law enforcement officers. Their recovery, and the preservation, of these documents, helped link Freiburger conclusively to this crime. (Courtesy of Investigator Carl Craig, Richland County, South Carolina, Sheriff's Department)

of Richland County, Craig and candidate Lott had discussed the possibility of forming a cold case homicide unit if Lott was elected sheriff. Lott won the election and on March 1st, 1997, Craig began working pro bono to review unsolved homicides. In September, 1999, sheriff's captain Bill Brown asked Craig whether he recalled the 1960s murder of a taxi driver. Craig advised the captain of the victim and suspect's name immediately. A relative of Orner attended church with the captain, and had inquired whether they could take another look at the case.

Brown retrieved the original case file and gave it to Craig. The file contained several individual folders in an accordion file folder, but the ravages of time, older technology, and storage conditions had taken their toll. Approximately two thirds of the reports were on Thermofax paper, and had deteriorated significantly. The file had been stored for decades in an unshaded trailer storage facility with no heat or air conditioning. The photographs and newspaper clippings were still good, but reports and pages were about to fall apart. Office personnel were able to carefully reconstruct a working copy of the now-fragile documents. Included within the original file were black and white photos of the crime scene, Thermofax copies of numerous pawn shop documents and registers, photos of the suspect murder weapon, and a photo of Freiburger.

Craig studied the file in depth for 2 weeks to familiarize himself with it and to formulate an investigative plan. He discovered that all nine of the original law enforcement investigators, medical, and forensic persons involved in the original investigation were now deceased. The original file had noted Freiburger's ties to Indiana, and a check with the State Police confirmed that Freiburger now resided near Fort Wayne. A relative of his still lived at the same address Freiburger had used in 1961. Craig also learned that a close friend who had joined the army with Freiburger also lived in the same vicinity. Craig further discovered the whereabouts of one other witness, as well as that of Trooper Meredith. Craig located three living relatives of the victim and began to conduct a victim profile.

Craig could not find the gun and bullet fragments and contacted the state crime laboratory. A search of microfiche records revealed that, after 38 years, the lab still retained the weapon, the bullet fragments, and the test bullets. All were in pristine condition. Craig and his partner, investigator Brian Metz, reviewed the evidence, and subsequently requested that a reexamination of the gun and fragments be conducted using advanced technology now available.

It is not unusual in cold cases to find that suspects have moved to another state, and this was no exception. Craig and Metz contacted investigator Rocky Stotts of the Indiana State Police in Fort Wayne, and asked for assistance. Stotts conducted a background check on Freiburger and the investigators confirmed that the Freiburger from the 1961 homicide case was the *same* Freiburger now living in Fort Wayne. The two South Carolina detectives traveled to Indiana to meet with Investigator Stotts and to interview Freiburger.

On October 20, 2000, Investigator Stotts contacted Freiburger at home and requested that he come to the Whitley County Sheriff's Office to meet with investigators from Columbia, South Carolina. Freiburger drove there in his personal vehicle and met with Craig and Metz. The officers told him that they wanted to speak to him about a murder that occurred near Columbia on February 28, 1961, while he was there as an army trainee. He was further advised that there were neither warrants nor restraints for him and he was free to leave at any time. Investigators noted, and documented, Freiburger's *immediate* reaction. He first turned pale, then red, and beads of sweat appeared on his forehead. He was visibly shaking and momentarily had trouble talking. When asked about his service in the army, he responded "I was in the Army?" When asked about ever being in Columbia, South Carolina, he replied "I was in Columbia, South Carolina?"

It appeared he was faking memory loss and Craig showed him a black-and-white picture of himself in uniform (see Figure 3.22). He then bowed his head and admitted he had been in the Army. When asked about his sentence in Fort Leavenworth, he again asked whether he had been there. The investigators had been prepared, and showed him a copy of his FBI rap sheet. He then acknowledged he had been in the stockade.

Investigator Craig then showed him a photo of the revolver and purchase record bearing his name and Indiana address. He denied buying the gun, but his facial expressions indicated otherwise to the experienced detectives. He was shown the purchase signature and asked if it appeared to be his own, and after first declining to answer, indicated it might or might not be his signature.

Investigators switched tracks and began talking about other events in his life since childhood and he answered without hesitation. He discussed his life after discharge from the Army in 1962, as well as his family and work history. He was specifically asked whether he was seeing a medical doctor or psychiatrist and he replied that he was not. Freiburger appeared to become edgy, and then the investigators showed him a picture of the victim. Freiburger actually gasped and said, "I think I need to talk to a lawyer."

This cold case occurred before Escobedo and Miranda, but the theory and issues surrounding these U.S. Supreme Court decisions addressing the rights of criminal suspects have, in my opinion, improved the quality of law enforcement in this country as well as contributing to improved safeguards for all citizens. These rules, however, do apply in pre-Miranda era investigations, and the investigators were aware of this as they terminated further interviews. Freiburger drove home. Investigators had observed apparent "selective" memory loss and that his body language, expressions, and reactions to certain questions and answers suggested perpetration, involvement, or knowledge of the murder of John Orner.

The day after their return to Columbia, however, a private attorney representing Freiburger called the investigators, intimating that he and his client were open to a plea bargain on a lesser

FIGURE 3.22 When interviewed, the gun store clerk recalled that Freiburger purchased the weapon while in uniform and used his military identification for the transaction. The original investigators documented this fact. During interview with investigators in 2000, however, he did not at first seem to recall having served in the Army, nor having been sentenced to Fort Leavenworth prison. Preservation of this photograph in the file proved an important piece of evidence. (Courtesy of Investigator Carl Craig, Richland County, South Carolina, Sheriff's Department)

charge than murder one. This did not materialize, but further reinforced the investigators' belief that they were on the right track.

Upon their return, Investigators Craig and Metz learned the results of the reexamination of Freiburger's H&R revolver. The laboratory had excluded a second suspect revolver, but again concluded Freiburger's gun was "a very close match, and may or may not be the murder weapon."

As the laboratory had not *excluded* the weapon, Freiburger's gun and the other weapon were submitted to a qualified private-sector firearms examiner in an attempt to obtain a definitive answer. This is a different situation, however, from what might be concluded when dealing with "experts." Experienced investigators have encountered situations in which some persons involved in the criminal justice process, both prosecution and defense, have "shopped around" until they find an "expert" who will tell them what they want to hear. This has led to hard feelings on both sides of the aisle, but has also contributed to some gross miscarriages of justice. No conclusion had been formally rendered by a firearms expert, and the issue was still open. Experts rely upon experience to form their opinions, but they rely on technology as well.

A third examiner examined both guns as well as the fragments removed from the victim. On April 2, 2001, the examiner notified investigators that he had excluded the second revolver, but had made a positive match on the Freiburger revolver. A consideration in cold cases, as in others, is chain-of-custody issues. In these cases, there may be additional opportunity for misfiling, mislabeling, loss, or contamination of evidence depending upon circumstances over the years and decades. A potential defense that the fragments belonged to someone else, however, was eliminated when DNA recovered from the bullet fragments was matched to that of the victim, Orner. An arrest warrant was obtained for Freiburger.

Freiburger had in the meantime secured the services of an attorney who in turn secured the services of a local attorney. Arrangements were made for the suspect's surrender to Richland County authorities on April 10, 2001. He was subsequently arraigned and released on $50,000 bond.

The case was assigned to Richland County Deputy Solicitors Knox McMahon and Ms. Luck Campbell. The investigators made contact with now-retired Tennessee Trooper Meredith and obtained the documents he still retained from his encounter with Freiburger. Trial began on July 29, 2002 in Richland County General Sessions Court and lasted 3 days. Mr. McMahon and Ms. Luck were able to lay the necessary legal foundations and enter evidence almost 40 years old, and to reconstruct for the jury a decade-long series of events. After only 2 hours' deliberation, the jury reached a unanimous verdict of guilty and Freiburger was shortly sentenced to spend the rest of his natural life in the South Carolina Department of Corrections. Under current South Carolina sentencing guidelines, however, he will be eligible for parole in 10 years. According to Investigator Craig, this may be the nation's oldest adjudicated cold case wherein a jury has convicted a defendant.

Cold cases may be fraught with irony. In this case, Investigator Craig was in on the beginning, and the end, of this investigation. Craig, now an experienced cold case investigator, *just happened* to be in his office the day a superior officer commented casually and asked if he knew anything about a murder of a taxi driver in the 1960s. The nexus for this resulted from an encounter in church between a member of the victim's family and the captain. By chance, Investigator Craig was familiar with it already. Such knowledge is important at the start, simply identifying who and when, and building upon this knowledge. Such a chain of events was the sole factor in the reactivation of this murder, one that in most likelihood would not have been otherwise reopened due to the age of the case and other factors.

In additional irony, this investigation and conviction made headline news. This news was noticed by another cold case killer, Gerald Mason, also living in the region. What officers and neighbors did not know was that this now-retired local businessman had murdered two police officers in El Segundo, California, 4 years prior to Freiburger's murder of Orner. Just 6 months after Freiburger's conviction, California investigators would visit Richland County in January, 2003, to arrest Gerald Mason for these cold case homicides. Mason would later tell officers that Freiburger's fate weighed heavily on his mind. This investigation is presented in detail in Chapter 31 of this text.

In one other irony, victim Orner was robbed of about $45, $7 less than Freiburger had paid for the revolver. In the end, only three remaining survivors of the victim were able to see what passes for "closure" in these cases.

The Richland County Sheriff's Office ultimately has created a specialized Cold Crimes Unit with the services of a full-time lieutenant, two full-time investigators, and three part-time (retired) investigators. From the start, Investigator Carl Craig has donated his services pro bono to this law enforcement agency and its quest to solve unsolved homicides.

SIGNIFICANT COLD CASE ISSUES

The case history given above offers a significant number of issues encountered by these and other cold case homicide investigators.

- Organizational leadership and commitment to proactive cold case homicide investigation.
- Case reactivation as a result of effort initiated by the victim's family through casual conversation with a law enforcement official.
- Quality and thoroughness of initial investigation and retention of case file, including physical evidence, photographs, and firearm purchase records.

- Ability to save therma-fax documents and make a working case copy.
- Initial role of forensic geology.
- Thorough search for and location of physical evidence.
- Review and retesting of all evidence utilizing advanced technology. This resulted in a match of the weapon to the fragments, and the fragments, through DNA, to the victim.
- Witness re-contact and interview, and the discovery of Trooper Meredith's retention of documents that further linked Freiburger to the weapon.
- Although the nine principal investigators and other personnel were deceased, cold case investigators were able to reinvestigate this case and, through the efforts of the prosecutor, to establish foundation for admission into evidence of almost 40-year-old documents and events. To my knowledge, this is the oldest cold case homicide adjudicated through the jury process that resulted in a finding of guilt.
- A check of the defendant's 1961 address revealed relatives still residing at same location.
- Suspect returned to his home state.
- Interstate law enforcement cooperation so necessary in these cases.
- Reinterview with suspect and recording of immediate reaction and responses to questions, including statements and body language.
- Interview preparation by investigators including photographs and records to show suspect.
- Denials and apparent selective memory loss feigned by suspect.
- Investigator knowledge of suspect background and interview methodology.
- Dedication and perseverance of cold case investigators.
- Fate and luck.

I wish to extend my gratitude to Investigator Carl Craig and his partner, Brian Metz, for their work in this case, and for providing the material used in compiling the case history. This investigation is a credit to cold case homicide investigation and to law enforcement. I further wish to acknowledge the leadership role demonstrated by Sheriff Leon Lott, Richland County Sheriff's Office, Columbia, South Carolina, in cold case homicide investigation, and to express my gratitude for his assistance in providing this case material.

ACKNOWLEDGMENTS

I wish to express my gratitude and appreciation to the late Sergeant Rudy Ortega of the Unsolved Unit, Los Angeles County Sheriff's Department, as well as his partner Deputy Frank Gonzales and sergeants Paul Mondry and Alfredo Castro of the same unit. In addition, I wish to acknowledge and continue this appreciation to Detective Rick Jackson of the Los Angeles Police Department, Cold Case Squad; District Attorney Investigator Ron Thill of the San Diego County, California, district attorney's office; Lieutenant Jorge Duran of the San Diego, California, Police Department; Detective Richard Rouleau of the El Cajon, California, Police Department; Investigator Carl Craig of the Richland County, South Carolina, Sheriff's Department; and Anne-Marie Schubert of the Sacramento County, California, district attorney's office for sharing their thoughts, experiences, and perspectives on the investigation of cold case homicides.

SUGGESTED READING

Anonymous. (2003). Los Angeles sheriffs cold case unit uses old fingerprints in new ways. *Crime Control Digest*, 37(6), 1.

Anonymous (2002). Cold case homicide. C.P.T. Network, Sacramento, California. Commission on Peace Officer Standards and Training.

Dieckmann, E.A. (1961). *Practical Homicide Investigation*. Springfield: Charles C. Thomas.

Eliopulos, L.N. (2003). *Death Investigators Handbook: Expanded and Updated edition*. Boulder, CO: Paladin Press.

Geberth, V.J. (1996). *Practical Homicide Investigation: Tactics, Procedures, and Forensic Techniques*. (3rd ed.). Boca Raton, FL: CRC Press.

Keppell, R.D. and Weis, J.G. (1994). Time and distance as solvability factors in murder cases. *Journal of Forensic Sciences*, 39(2), 386–401.

Lee, H., Palmbach, T.M., and Miller, M. (2003). *Henry Lee's Crime Scene Handbook*. New York: Academic Press.

Leonard, V.A. (1970). *The Police Detective Function*. Springfield: Charles C. Thomas.

Lochyer, B. (1999). Cold case investigations. Sacramento, California: California Attorney General.

NIJ. (2002). Using DNA to solve cold cases. (Commission report No. NCJ 194197). Washington, D.C.: National Institute of Justice.

Nyberg, R. (1999). Investigations: Cold case squads re-activate old investigations. *Law and Order*, 47(10), 127–130.

Spraggs, D. (2003). How to open a cold case. *Policemag.com*: 29–31.

Walton, R.H. (2005). Identification of solvability factors in twenty-first century cold case homicide investigation. Unpublished Ed.D. dissertation. University of San Francisco. San Francisco, California.

4 Investigation

Richard H. Walton

CONTENTS

INTRODUCTION

The investigation sequence and methods in a cold case homicide investigation will vary, depending upon a number of factors. These factors include those forces that caused this specific case to be reexamined (i.e., specific information has come forward regarding this specific case) and individual methods of investigation based on each investigator's training and experience, as well as perceived investigative plan based upon file review. As no two hot homicides are investigated in exactly the same manner, neither are cold case homicides. Each takes place within an overall similar framework, however. This framework includes people, places, and evidence.

This chapter explores various considerations that may be involved in the reinvestigation of a cold case homicide. Not all cases will use all of the methods or sources of potential information presented here. Perhaps they will use others. In addition, investigators may "color outside the box" as they utilize combinations of other means and methods.

RECONSTRUCTING THE CRIME AND INVESTIGATION

After reading and studying the case file, the cold case investigator is familiar with the *documented* record that has been preserved. This includes what officers and investigators did, what witnesses and others said, what evidence was collected, analyzed, and preserved, and what was photographed. In this way, the investigator has *informally* and *informationally* reconstructed the crime scene. During the course of this investigation, it may be appropriate to further consult with qualified reconstruction experts to *formally* reconstruct the crime. Reconstruction will depend upon the nature of the crime, the types of events that occurred, and the questions that need to be answered. This may involve physical or psychological reconstruction (victim and suspect). Such reconstruction may involve:

- Gunshot trajectory
- Muzzle-to-target distance
- Ejection pattern and other firearm-related analyses
- Blood-spatter patterns
- Sharp object injuries, including depths, angles, clothing damage, defense wounds, and ante- or postmortem injuries
- Arson and fire burn
- Furniture and objects
- Vehicle impact
- Vehicle tire and skid mark patterns
- Clothing or article patterns
- Bitemark

VISIT THE CRIME SCENE

Reports and photographs provide the cold case investigator with a two-dimensional, informational view of the crime scene and the crime. In my experience, nothing serves to orient the investigator, and the investigation, more forcefully than a visit to the crime scene. Decades later, the scene may be little changed from where only a rural cabin stood (see Figure 4.1 and Figure 4.2), or condos may now stand in place of an old office building. Regardless, returning to "the scene of the crime" provides an insight that words and photographs cannot quite equal. While reading the case may allow the cold case investigator to feel the "pulse" of the crime, visiting the scene allows one to sense the scene of the crime (see Figure 4.3).

Reconstructing the Scene

If the location has changed, consider reconstructing the scene through interviews with those who knew the scene and through the use of photographs. Such photos may be found:

- With family members of victims (if crime occurred in or near residence)
- With neighbors of scene
- In city planning or building departments, including aerial photos
- In newspapers or local magazines of the time

FIGURE 4.1 In some cold cases, the area that contained the crime scene is preserved only in photographs found outside the case file. These can provide investigators an insight into what the scene looked like at the time, and aid in informational reconstruction of the crime. Pictured here is the scene of a 1925 homicide case reactivated in the 1980s. (Courtesy: Irvine collection)

- In other media
- In historical societies
- In libraries
- In private collections

FIGURE 4.2 Although the ravages of time may alter the original scene of the crime, photographs and returning to the scene with original participants or witnesses may further investigator understanding and provide information not found in the case file. In this photo, a member of the 1925 posse returns to the scene of a murder with the author to walk through the events from over 60 years before. (Author's collection)

FIGURE 4.3 Vegetation changes and remodeling are not uncommon in decades following a homicide. In many cases, such as this 1960s case resurrected decades later, current homeowners have allowed law enforcement to reenter the residence to familiarize themselves with the "ins and outs" of the scene. Contact of scene owners or those who control access might be a delicate situation, as they may have had no knowledge of the prior homicide. (Courtesy of El Cajon Police Department)

When Visiting the Scene of the Crime

Revisit all scenes that are known to be associated with the crime. These may include:

- Homicide location.
- Body recovery location(s).
- Victim's residence or last known location.
- Suspect's residence or last known location.
- All locations where evidence was located.
- Consider geographic profiling.
- Consider behavioral assessment of both victim and suspect.

Time and Distance

- Note the ingress and egress for victim and suspect.
- Visit at the time of day or night the crime occurred.
  - Lighting?
  - Who else may have been present?
  - Where?
  - Businesses hours or routine activities by others that might have allowed for unknown witnesses to be present.
- Also, for a different perspective, visit in the daytime if crime was at night and vice versa.
- Take the crime scene pictures with you and orient yourself and the pictures to the scene.
- Observe surrounding terrain or buildings.
- Look up, down, and around
- Slope and lay of the land.
- Compare witness statements to the scene. Do they appear realistic as to what they said, did and saw?
- Is evidence still present? For instance, in a rural location with tall grass and brief scene investigation, perhaps evidence was missed and never recovered.
- Have witnesses or reporting party walk through the scene with you.

THE NEIGHBORHOOD CANVASS

According to homicide expert Vernon Geberth, a neighborhood canvass is the door-to-door questioning of those in the general area after a crime has been committed in an attempt to gain information about the specific incident. During this brief contact and interview with residents and others, officers or investigators attempt to locate witnesses or individuals who might provide information about the specific incident. Although this knowledge may not appear important to them, when coupled with other information known to investigators, could play a significant role in an investigation. The canvass, according to Geberth, may provide:

- An actual eyewitness to the crime.
- Information about the circumstances of the crime.
- An approximate time of occurrence and/or estimate time of death.
- Information about the deceased, including identity, habits, friends, etc.
- A motive for the crime.

This important investigative technique has been utilized in both rural and urban areas for many decades, perhaps if not centuries. Normally a canvass is conducted shortly after the crime or incident. A canvass, then or now, could provide additional information, including information about unusual observations or individual behavior at the time or information about a suspect, if not the identity of a suspect. Remember, due to the passage of time, those with information to contribute to the investigation may now be more willing to divulge what they know.

A canvass may have been done by the investigators, but also may have been done by other officers who would then forward the names and addresses of potential witnesses to the investigators along with a brief summary of what each witness may have to offer. The investigators would then conduct a more thorough, detailed, interview.

A neighborhood canvass could be a hit-or-miss affair, depending upon the diligence of those assigned this duty, or other priorities. If a neighborhood resident had nothing to offer, the canvassing officer may not have written anything down. If a resident was not home, perhaps no one went back. Some agencies may have used a standard form, a canvass questionnaire, in the course of this activity, and case file review should attempt to identify this practice. Not uncommonly, however, the canvassing officers used their notebooks or perhaps index cards to make note of any information. Transmission to the investigators of the identity of persons to be contacted could be verbal, and subsequently forgotten and never followed up.

In one instance, a man hit his wife and she died. A neighbor who knew the couple well approached uniformed officers at the scene and stated that she had information the investigators should be aware of. She was told that investigators would contact her. Some weeks later, she telephoned the police agency to state that she had never been contacted and possessed information regarding the couple that police should be aware of. She was never contacted.

Approximately a year later, the case was going to trial. The suspect stated he had never hit his wife before. District attorney investigators were conducting pretrial investigation in the neighborhood of the crime when they were approached by the same neighbor, who then told of past domestic violence toward the victim and how, just days before the homicide, she had observed the suspect hit her so hard he knocked the victim across the room. At this time, he had said that next time he would kill her. The suspect pled guilty.

Reconstructing the Canvass

Going back to a neighborhood years, even decades, after the crime may yield valuable information. If the results of a neighborhood canvass have been found in the file, use this as a starting point to begin. What addresses were checked? Which were not? Go to the neighborhood and look around. Look for neatly maintained older homes. Attempt to identify the older residents of the neighborhood and elicit their help. Choose a time of day that most optimizes the chance of finding people at home. When reconstructing a canvass, ascertain whether the addresses or numbering sequences may have changed since the time of the crime.

Start going door to door as you would a primary canvass today. Attempt to identify those who might have been living in the neighborhood at the time of the crime. In some instances, they may have moved but the current resident may be their tenant, or know how to contact them. In some circumstances, a son or daughter might now live there, if not the same resident from the time period. In the 45-year-old El Segundo case, summarized in Chapter 31 of this book, one witness still resided in the same residence as he had in 1957. In other cases, including the Wilkerson case study, witnesses from the 1960s still resided in the same residence as when they first reported information to police.

Call the telephone number in the report. Check the address.

Remember, while some may possess knowledge of the crime or persons involved, they can't bring themselves to pick up the telephone to call but may be just waiting for the investigator to knock on their doors to tell all they know.

When conducting the canvass, start at the point where the crime occurred. Look around, from what locations might someone see something? Don't forget to look up, also. Consider the time of day, or night, of the crime.

To reconstruct the neighborhood for a canvass, consider:

- City or county directories for the time period
- Public works for street maps
- Planning department
- Public utilities
- Local historical societies
- Fire department
- Post Office
- Local resident input

Suggested Questions

- Did you reside here at the time of the crime?
- Knowledge of crime?
- Know anyone involved?
- First-hand knowledge of events or the crime?
- Heard of anything about the crime or individuals over the years?
- Did anybody move away suddenly after the crime?
- Any suspicious persons at that time, or other suspicious events?
- Any similar crimes before or after?
- Do you suspect anyone of this crime?

After the canvass, check criminal histories on any names that may have developed.

City or County Directories

City or county directories are publications produced by commercial companies that provide information about people living within the boundaries as designated by the directory (see Figure 4.4).

FIGURE 4.4 These published directories offer cold case investigators a variety of information about people and the local community during previous decades. Such directories date to the 19th century in many areas and are useful in researching people and places and may also be useful in construction of timelines. (Author's collection)

These directories have been around since the late 1800s and were offered nationwide in many locales, both urban and more rural. It is not unusual to find that directories for more urban-designated regions may include suburban areas as well. These publications are especially useful in reconstructing information about physical locations, including neighboring addresses and intersections as well as personal data about individuals. The cold case investigator should keep in mind that, like other print sources, the information to be found in these sources is only as good as the original source of information.

These directories were compiled and published on an annual basis. They were sold commercially, often by subscription, and may have been produced in association with local chambers of commerce. They offered commercial and demographic information about a community, as well as personal information about its occupants. Among these directories, one can find:

- Alphabetical directory of business names
- Alphabetical directory of private citizens
- Directory of householders
- Occupants of office buildings and other business places
- Street name and number guide
- Numerical telephone directory
- Classified advertising
- Other miscellaneous information

For example, if an investigator knows that subject of interest operated a barber shop in San Diego, California, in 1959, a review of the city directory for that year includes a list of barber shops in alphabetical order, as compiled by this data source. Although city or state licensing and business-operation records may normally be destroyed or discarded after such a length of time, city directories offer a means to locate reported information about people and places in a specific time period.

As a source of personal information, city directories offer a cold case investigator a thumbnail picture of people. Persons are listed in alphabetical order by last name, followed by first name, middle initial, name of spouse (common-law, "significant other" or other nonmarried cohabitants will probably not be included in these older listings), address, place of employment, or occupation. The listing of a spouse or employment information may offer cold case investigators additional names or sources of information heretofore unknown, especially in older cases.

These directories detailed the numerical sequencing of streets and intersections. In addition, they listed individual house numbers, name of occupant, and telephone number (see Figure 4.5). City or county directory listings may also include not only the address of apartment structures, but also the names of individual occupants and their telephone numbers. The passage of time between the period when the information was obtained and when it was published, however, may impact the accuracy of this information. This may be especially true in more transient populations. These listings may be useful when attempting to reconstruct addresses and occupants surrounding a subject location or crime scene. Development of this information may provide cold case investigators with names and addresses of persons not reflected in original police reports or statements. This information might be useful in preparing diagrams showing scene locations or when used in conjunction with aerial photographs. The directories might also offer confirmation or non-confirmation of information and aid in constructing time lines and occupational profiles.

Sources of old city directories may include:

- In-agency archives and library
- Local libraries
- Local chamber of commerce
- Local historical societies

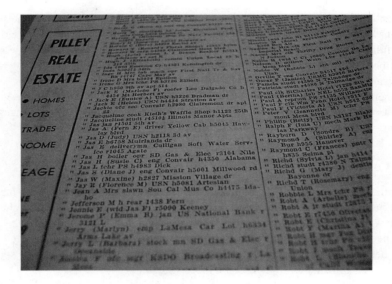

FIGURE 4.5 In addition to listing people by name and phone number, city directories also provide sequential street address information. This may aid in identifying neighbors to a particular address or in reconstructing an area cold case canvass. (Author's Collection)

- Local law enforcement agency archives
- Local offices of the FBI and other federal agencies

Telephone Directories

The style and format of telephone directories has changed in the decades since the 1940s. Older telephone directories may list persons by last name, full first name, middle initial, physical location address for the specified telephone number, and the telephone number. In more recent decades, there has been a transition from such inclusive personal information to a listing that includes last name, first initial, and telephone number only. As a consequence, old telephone directories may offer more assistance to cold case investigators in some cases than more recent editions.

Telephone directories may provide cold case investigators with information useful when:

- Establishing residency confirmation or disconfirmation, or locations of suspects, witnesses, or other persons
- Cross-checking or indexing telephone numbers
- Yellow Pages business information

VICTIM AND FAMILY CONSIDERATIONS

Contacting the Victim's Family

Cold case investigators hold differences of opinion as to investigator-initiated contact with a victim's family. To contact or *not* to contact depends upon the circumstances of the case and the investigative plan of action as it is conceived and carried out. While perhaps no such contact is planned at the start of the cold case investigation, circumstances may change and contact then becomes necessary.

When contacting the family of a victim in these investigations, keep in mind that the pain and anxiety, the feelings from that first day of the crime, are just below their emotional surface. The family never forgets. To the family of homicide victims, the hurt is still present, even after 60 years or more. In the initial period after the crime, they sought answers from the police, from friends, and from each other. How they *perceived* their treatment by law enforcement can affect how they react to a renewed investigation. Their feelings may run the scale from desiring no contact with authority to full cooperation. On some occasions, they may not wish the case to be reopened, and to just "let it be." There may be reasons for this, and these might include family secrets or matters they do not want exposed, or culpability or involvement by a family member.

If and when contact is made with family, consider utilizing the services of the Victim/Witness Unit. When a cold case is solved, involve this unit with the family in the post-arrest and media-interest phase.

Reasons to Contact Victim's Family

- Over the years, the victim's family may have learned direct information or have second-hand information that could be of interest to the investigation. They might also have previously contacted law enforcement investigators who did not give them the perception that their input was considered valuable at the time. This information may or may not have been documented in the file. In later years, with other information subsequently known, that information may now be more valuable.
- To obtain diaries, notes, photographs, or other material that now may be of importance to the investigation. These might identify previous relationships, relationship status, other friends and acquaintances, or identify specific concerns or fears held by the victim (see Figure 4.6).
- To learn more about the victim and circumstances at the time of the homicide.
- To identify or learn more about other persons of interest who may have surfaced during the initial or subsequent investigation.
- To verify or eliminate other information from consideration.

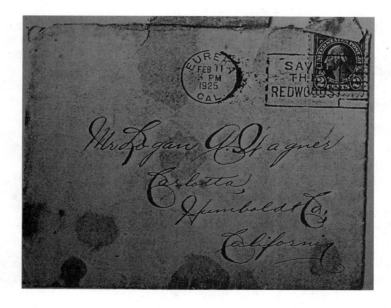

FIGURE 4.6 During a cold case investigation, investigators seek to learn as much as they can about a victim's movements prior to the crime, as well as previous relationships. Contact with the family may provide notes, letters, and diaries with information previously unknown to investigators. In this 1925 case, a letter from the victim to her brother provided personal information and detailed a relationship that was important in the case reconstruction 8 decades later. (Author's collection)

- To inform the family that their case has not been forgotten.
- To obtain a photo of the victim for use when later confronting suspect.
- To stimulate communications in the family or immediate circle of friends.

Arguments against Contacting Victim's Family

- Raises false hopes and expectations.
- Family members begin to call every day to learn whether anything is new.
- Family begins to discuss it and word may get to the suspect(s) and they further cover their tracks.
- If the cold case goes nowhere and remains unsolved, they do not ride another emotional roller coaster.
- A family member may be involved in the case, or may even be the suspect.

Learning More about the Victim (and the Suspect)

When studying the unsolved case, investigators try to learn as much about their victim as they can. This *may* begin to identify the suspect. Consider the *victimology* in the course of investigation, and try to come to know who the victims were before the murder and identify and assess what role they may have played in this chain of events. Apply your experience as you would in a fresh case.

- **Physical.** This includes evidence transfer from the crime and recovered at the scene, at autopsy, or other circumstances. This may include:
  - Seminal or other body fluids
  - Bruises
  - Bitemarks
  - Bullet wounds and tracks
  - Contact distance
  - Defense wounds
  - Blood spatter or patterns
  - Foreign objects
  - Hair and fibers

Interview the autopsy pathologist for case review and discussion.

- **Lifestyle.** This is learned through observations, interviews, and document analysis and may assist in learning more about the victim as well as contributing to the identification of a suspect. As a suspect is identified, these considerations could also apply to building the case.
  - Physical residential environment.
  - Environment where the crime occurred.
  - Notes, diaries, letters.
  - Church associates.
  - Employment.
  - Circle of friends, acquaintances and co-workers.
    - Any outliers.
    - Anybody who moved away suddenly.
    - Anybody who underwent a noticeable lifestyle change.
  - Anyone who had access to victim.
  - Then-current relationships and prior relationships (including former spouses).
  - Victim's fears and phobias.
  - Mental and physical history.

- Behavior changes.
- Hobbies and sports.
- Habits and routines.
- Neighbors.
- Social clubs and organizations.
- Physical abilities and capabilities.
- Hairdressers.
- Financial profile and credit check.
- Review of credit card records including spending and last uses or usage profile.
- School or work problems.
- Telephone records or cell phone records reviewed.
- Sexual fetishes or interests.
- Sexual orientation.
- Drug or alcohol abuse.
- Cellmates and co-defendants.
- Probation and parole reports.
- Institution intelligence reports.
- Violence or illegal activity in background.
- Enemies and adversaries.
- Former business partners and associates.
- Social services.
- Civil files.
- Known trial testimony.
- Activity within 24 hours prior to the murder.

Other Family Dynamics

- Did any family ever hire private investigators (PIs)?
  - Were witnesses contacted by PIs?
  - Were PIs used in any aspect of the case (civil or criminal)?

- Who benefited financially from the victim's death?
  - Life insurance?
  - Mortgage insurance?
  - Review last will and testament and probate file or trusts.
  - Business insurance policies.
  - Property transfers or money movements.
- Identify family tree.
  - Refer to obituary.
  - Siblings.
  - Step-parents and relations.
  - Other relations including "black sheep" who may tell what others will not.

INTERVIEWS AND REINTERVIEWS

Reinterviewing witnesses is an important component of the reinvestigation of cold case homicides. By this process, investigators seek to:

- Affirm previous witness statement and update contact and identifier information,
- Obtain information *held back* by previously identified witnesses who may now tell more due to changes in their own life style, maturity, distancing from the previous crowd they ran around with, or no longer fear suspect.

- Identify previously unidentified witnesses or associates of suspect,
- Obtain cooperation of previously uncooperative witnesses,

Interview Sequence

- Cold case investigators may consider the order of the witness interview process.
- Begin with law enforcement and other officials as necessary.
- Consider those witnesses on the outside periphery of those initially contacted and work toward the center, those most immediate to the victim. These on the outside may know more than they told, or have picked up new information over the years. Of course, remember, the more people you contact, the more likely that word may get back to the suspect.
- Material witnesses. Prior to contacting material witnesses, compile as much background information on them as possible. Ascertain any pending legal difficulties, including custody, probation, or parole status.
- *Before you begin the interviews*, run background checks on *all* subjects, including witnesses, family members, or others involved in the case as you would if the case were a fresh homicide. Use the advantage of time to obtain further insight into various individuals.

During the background and interview process, look for:

- Lifestyle changes. These include downhill slides as well as improved lifestyle and relationships or religious embracement.
- Movements out of city, county, or state. It has been my interesting observation that many of those who commit their crimes in the vicinity of where they were raised may often move out of state, and those who commit their crimes far from where they were raised may return to their comfort zone of family and friends.
- Arrests.
- Violence.
- Changes in personal relationship or inability to maintain relationships. Keep in mind that former friends, lovers, and secretaries can be the most valuable sources of information. Identify these when possible and as necessary.
- Other evidence of self-destructive behavior.
- Be careful not to give out more than you receive.

MODUS OPERANDI (M.O.) IN THE 21ST
CENTURY — "THOUGHTPRINTS"

In his international bestseller, *Black Dahlia Avenger: A Genius for Murder,* retired Los Angeles Police Department homicide detective Steve Hodel introduces us to the term, *"thoughtprints."* Beginning in 1999, Hodel began to research the possibility that his father, the late Dr. George Hodel, was responsible for one of the most infamous unsolved homicides in Los Angeles history, the 1947 "Black Dahlia" murder. In doing so, he uncovered compelling evidence that suggested his father was responsible for this and other unsolved murders. During his investigation, he conceived the idea of "thoughtprints" and provides this definition:

Our thought patterns determine what we do each day, each hour, each minute. While our actions may appear simple, routine, and automatic, they really are not. Behind and within each of our thoughts is an aim, an intent, a motive.

The motive within each thought is unique. In all of our actions, each of us leaves behind traces of our self. Like our fingerprints, these traces are identifiable. I call them thoughtprints. They are the ridges, loops, and whorls of our mind. Like the individual "points" that a criminalist examines in a fingerprint, they mean little by themselves and remain meaningless, unconnected shapes in a jigsaw puzzle until they are pieced together to reveal a clear picture.

If we are careful and clever in committing our crime, we may remember to wear gloves and not leave any fingerprints behind. But rarely are we clever enough to mask our motives, and we will almost certainly leave behind our thoughtprints. A collective of our motives, a paradigm constructed from our individual thoughts, these illusive prints construct the signature that will connect or link us to a specific time, place, crime, or victim."

In his book, Hodel cites numerous examples of Dr. George Hill Hodel's thoughtprints. I asked Hodel if he might provide us with a few examples of thoughtprints, and if he would explain how they might be useful to cold case investigators. Here is his response:

First let me clarify a misconception. Thoughtprints have absolutely nothing to do with anything psychic or metaphysical. They can apply to any crime. However, in the specialized field of homicide investigation, they should be thought of as a tool to complement M.O. and signatures.

As with the "Zodiac" unsolved murders in the San Francisco area in the 1960s and early 1970s, the slayer in the Black Dahlia case taunted police with notes and documents mailed to the news media. Figure 4.7 shows notes mailed to a local newspaper after the homicide. I believe the sender reveals training as a journalist and crime reporter through the pasted headline "copy" he sent to the press and the police as the "Black Dahlia Avenger." During the investigation, I learned that my father had training as a journalist and crime reporter for newspapers.

In another instance, as illustrated in Figure 4.8, the careful posing of the victim's arms and body mimicked the surrealist photograph, The Minotaur, created by Dr. Hodel's personal friend Man Ray. This artist's photograph illustrated a nude woman bisected at the waist (see Figure 4.9). The nude victim was found bisected at the waist and similarly posed.

Within months of the murder, George Hodel's 11-year-old daughter asked him to help her name her play doll. Interviewed decades later, the woman recalled that Hodel told her to name the doll, "Elizabeth Ann." As revealed during my investigation, The Black Dahlia's dossier from the FBI revealed the victim's name as Elizabeth Ann Short.

In another instance, I discovered a witness statement that described attendance at a "Hollywood" party at George Hodel's Hollywood house. The witness told officers that the doctor used lipstick to write words on the bare breasts of a partygoer. After concluding that the evidence strongly suggested Dr. Hodel stomped a woman to death months later, my research indicated that Dr. Hodel wrote a taunting message to the police on her nude body—using lipstick.

The concept of thoughtprints can best be utilized by cold-case investigators, by providing them a fresh start, and emphasizing the need to "think outside the box." I suggest that investigators should look for connections in a suspect's background, profession, or personal life. These could link him or her, to the crime, the victim, or the location. One of the best sources for finding potential thoughtprints comes through the reinterview of close friends. In very cold cases, careful research and review of all newspaper articles from the period can be invaluable. In the Dahlia-related serial killings from the 1940s, I extracted the documented statements of over seventy-five witnesses, and after placing them in chronological order, discovered they yielded critical information on both the victim and the suspect. Another huge potential source for latent thoughtprints is the original crime-scene photographs. Investigators can re-scan them at high-resolution, then magnify and zoom in, and conduct a present day "walk-through," right from a laptop. Reexamine the scene, inch by inch, quadrant by quadrant.

Good luck and good hunting.

Steve Hodel
Los Angeles, California
January, 2005

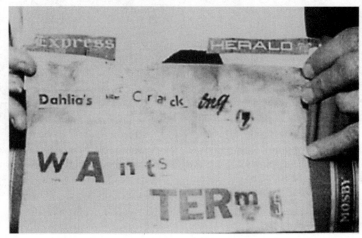

FIGURE 4.7 Detective Hodel's investigation revealed that the prime suspect, his father, Dr. George Hodel, had training as a journalist and crime reporter as well as that of a surgeon. (Courtesy of Steve Hodel)

FIGURE 4.8 During photo review and the case investigation, cold case investigators may consider "posing" in cold cases as well as in those more recent. (Courtesy of Steve Hodel)

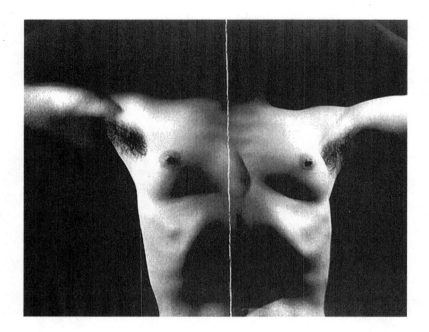

FIGURE 4.9 Cold case investigators often "think outside the box" when studying the case file, and, during the conduct of the subsequent investigation. Detective Steve Hodel reasoned that the surrealist painting "The Minotaur" by an artist and close friend of Dr. George Hodel was the model for the manner in which the victim was bisected and posed. (© 2005 Man Ray Trust/Artists Rights Society (ARS) New York/ADAGP, Paris)

ADDITIONAL BACKGROUND RESOURCES FOR VICTIM AND SUSPECT INFORMATION AND DEVELOPMENT

- Marriage and divorce records
- Real estate records including grantee/grantor
- Birth certificate
- Civil liens and judgments
- Local Fire/police/ambulance reportings of victim/witness/suspect
- Assessor
- Treasurer/tax collector
- City/County clerk
- Professional licensing and certification
- Trade Unions
- Post Office
- Schools
- Local voter registration

ADDITIONAL INVESTIGATIVE MEANS AND METHODS FOR SUSPECT DEVELOPMENT

Time and changes in relationships as well as technology are the primary solvability factors identified in the successful resolution of cold case homicides. Many of these topics discussed in victim and witness development in this chapter are applicable to further suspect development. As the suspect is identified, many of these investigative avenues may prove useful to the investigation.

In addition to reexamination of evidence and use of databases such as CODIS and AFIS/IAFIS, other means and methods may assist the cold case investigator. These include:

- Wiretaps
- Off-line NCIC checks
- Law enforcement criminal intelligence services at local, state, and federal level
- Law enforcement computer data bases
- Corrections Institution/incarceration records
- Corrections Institution staff interviews
- Psychological Profiling and Behavioral Assessment
- Cellmate informants and street informants
- Accomplices and co-defendants in prior criminal activity
- Internet searches
- Physical surveillance
- Use of Grand Jury
- Federal Organized Crime Statutes
- Undercover operations
- Search Warrants
  - Home and work computers
  - Telephone records
  - Cell phone records

When investigating crime, remember crime is like water. Crooks, for the most part, are inherently lazy. Like water, they will take the path of least resistance. Don't make more out of a particular crime than it is. The easiest answer that makes sense, is usually the answer.

—Lieutenant Tony Leal, Texas Rangers

INTERVIEW CONSIDERATIONS

Once the suspect has been identified and located, a number of considerations occur as investigators attempt to conduct an interview or to effect arrest.

Chief among these is whether to arrest *then* interview, or interview and *then* follow with arrest to follow. At this stage of the investigation the interview process should involve both law enforcement and prosecutorial perspectives. Each has its own perspective and concerns, although ultimately the same end result.

Law Enforcement Perspective

- Is the interview *within* the investigating agency jurisdiction or outside, including out of state?
  - If out of state or jurisdiction, arrangements must be made with appropriate authorities.
  - Contact strategy.
    - Direct approach.
    - Indirect approach (i.e., the Freiburger case study).
  - Availability of surreptitious video or recording devices.
- Type of setting for interview (formal or informal).
- Recording or video options or availability.
- Custodial Interview. Arrest and then interview with possibility of suspect invoking Miranda Rights.
- Non-custodial interview.
  - Further inculpatory statements that may conflict with previous statements.
  - Observations and appraisal of demeanor and the person.
  - Negative statements.
  - Admissions or confession.
- Use of *forensic* psychologist to frame interview questions, techniques, and tactics.
- Strategize how to approach suspect.

- Strategize *who* will interview suspect.
  - Selection of investigator most likely to elicit suspect's cooperation and not alienate suspect from the start. As an example, perhaps it would not be wise to utilize an African-American investigator to interview a white supremacist.
  - Interviewer must be thoroughly familiar with *all* aspects of the case.

Strategize Interview and Interrogation

- Determine suspect's interview style. Identify and interview previous authorities who have interviewed suspect to see how he reacts — what "pushes his buttons" and what does not.
  - Police officers and investigators.
  - Probation and parole officers.
  - Former prosecutor insight.
  - Pull all prior reports and read interviews.
  - Former psych reports.
  - Listen to previous interview tapes.
  - Determine what works and what does not.
    - Confrontation.
    - Accusation.
    - Bluff.
    - Use of props such as photo of:
      - Victim.
      - Crime Scene.
      - Grave.
- Suspect's interview and interrogation history.
  - How many arrests?
  - Circumstances.
  - Locations.
  - Custodial or non-custodial.
  - When/how long ago was suspect's last interview or law enforcement contact?
- Time span since crime.
  - Suspect's life style then/now.
  - Stability as expressed through family, relationships, religion, children, career.
  - Known or identified medical/mental conditions.
  - Known criminal history since the cold case homicide.
- Methods that have appeared to be successful.

The element of surprise is a prime consideration for a successful interview.

Prosecution Perspective

- Ideally would like admissions or confession with corroborating evidence.
- Must consider additional evidence admissibility problems due to passage of time.
- Must consider how suspect's post-crime behavior may affect jury. If suspect went on to become a respectable member of the community, church, and family figure, prosecutor must keep jury focused on the *deed* and *accountability*.
- May strongly conflict with police perspective.

It is recommended to form a partnership with your Fugitive Unit, which performs extraditions. A cold case detective can travel to the state of the extradition and complete a cold case interview along with the Fugitive Unit detective. This is one way to multi-task and save money.

—James Gannon, Deputy Chief of Investigations,
Morris County Prosecutor's Office, New Jersey

ARREST CONSIDERATIONS

Most law enforcement agencies have guidelines, policies, and procedures for arrest and apprehension of suspects in violent crimes. If the arrest is to occur within your jurisdiction, you would most likely invoke normal arrest procedures. This is an area where history of the case and investigation, and post-crime behavior coupled with investigator experience and perceptions influences how, when, and where the arrest is to be made. These options may range from negotiated surrender to high-risk entry tactics. In this arrest situation, you would consider potential:

- Hazard Assessment.
  - Time of day or night.
  - Type of location.
  - Firearms.
  - Possibility of pursuit.
  - Neighbors.
  - Pedestrian or other vehicular traffic.
  - Hostage potential.
- Tactical Plan.
  - Totality of knowledge of the suspect; previous arrest history, propensity for fight or flight.
  - Assistance from specialized units, allied investigation agency or neighboring agency.
  - Surveillance and reconnaissance of suspect and location.
  - Approach. Best method to minimize hazards and execute surprise.
  - Communications systems.
  - Availability of ambulance and medical personnel.
  - Briefing and personnel assignment.
  - Coordination.
  - Execution of plan.
- Cold case considerations.
  - Advanced age and potential medical condition of suspect and spouse.
  - Search warrant (sealed until service to minimize leaks).
  - Documents and memorabilia pertaining to the crime.
  - Documents to establish identity as same person in original investigation.
  - Documents that show dominion and control of residence.
  - Diaries, records, letters, notes correspondence that may indicate suspect knowledge of victim or relationship, or commission of the crime.
  - Travel and movement documents.
  - Documents that exhibit suspect's original handwriting.
  - Documents or photos that show interest in any particular aspects of the crime, i.e., bondage, torture, etc.
  - Photos of subject then and now.
  - Firearms and ammunition or other weapons.
  - DNA.
  - Other items particularly related to the offense.

CASE STUDY — WILKERSON

El Cajon is a "bedroom" community along the interstate highway that runs east out of San Diego, California. The city has long maintained its own police department, as have many similar communities in the region, including neighboring La Mesa. The larger San Diego Police Department and county sheriff's office border these small Southern California departments in a patchwork of jurisdictional boundaries. On June 6, 1965, a 19-year-old mother was murdered in her bottom-floor apartment in El Cajon. She had been out with friends until approximately midnight, and one of

FIGURE 4.10 The murder weapon was brought to the scene of the crime, and afterward released back to its owner. This was a not uncommon practice, perhaps depriving cold case investigators in some instances of the chance to apply advanced technology. (Courtesy of El Cajon Police Department)

these friends stayed with her until approximately 3a.m. Before dawn, an intruder entered through a sliding glass door and beat her with a cocktail-mix bottle. He then used a drapery cord (see Figure 3.7) cut from a living room window to strangle the victim, then raped her. The victim was left in a "staged" position, with candles left to burn in a "last-rite" orientation and a candle was inserted into her vagina. The apartment was ransacked, although there was no sign of a struggle. The contents of the victim's purse were dumped on the living room floor, although cash and jewelry were not taken. The only items taken were a camera and a crucifix.

The homicide was discovered when neighbors saw the victim's young son wandering outside her apartment the next morning. She was found partially sprawled across the corner of her bed, and her legs kept her propped up off the floor. Evidence recovered at the scene indicated that she had been sexually assaulted, and, decades later, that evidence provided a DNA profile. While processing the crime scene, investigators recovered the ligature and it was booked into evidence. There it remained for over 3 decades.

Two weeks after the murder, a husband, age 63, and his 57-year-old wife were preparing for bed in their apartment when an intruder entered the residence. Armed with a long-handled socket wrench (see Figure 4.10) he had stolen in a vehicle burglary a short time before, he beat the husband to death, raped the wife, and beat her viciously with the wrench before leaving her for dead. An open jar of hand cream was next to her, and cream smeared about her vagina. Her legs were doubled underneath her with the heels of her feet resting on her buttocks and her legs spread apart. She was found about 20 hours later when neighbors heard her moans and cries. Numerous individuals were investigated and cleared, but despite the best efforts of a number of detectives and other personnel, no suspects were identified. Serology and fingerprints (see Figure 4.11) were the two primary means of identification utilized at this time, and no leads were developed. The socket wrench was released to its owner, and the other evidence was boxed up and put into storage.

The next month, a man in the nearby community of La Mesa reported to police that his son had seen a suspicious man emerging from some bushes. When asked what he was doing, the man replied that he was looking for his lighter. The boy did not believe him and told his father. They copied the license number from the man's red Triumph and called police. Not long after, a similar-looking man was seen near a red Triumph in La Mesa outside the apartment of a 23-year-old nurse.

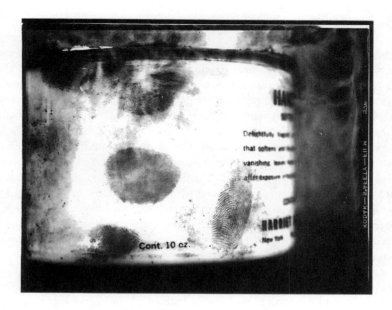

FIGURE 4.11 Although latent prints were observed on the jar, it was broken when crushed in a vise being used to hold it. (Courtesy of El Cajon Police Department)

Before dawn, the nurse heard noises within her apartment, and dialed the telephone operator. The suspect had broken into her apartment and attempted to rape and murder her. As she fought him off, the operator heard the fight and called police, but the suspect was gone on their arrival. Based on the boy's observation and witness information regarding the red Triumph, Clyde Wilkerson, a recently released parolee, was brought in for questioning.

Wilkerson was arrested and charged for this crime after the victim positively identified him as her assailant. Although questioned in the two homicides and rapes, there was no evidence to link him to these crimes. He was convicted on the La Mesa offense in November, 1965, and sentenced to 5 years to life in prison (see Figure 4.12). He subsequently paroled to Oklahoma in 1973.

In the meantime, the homicide cases remained unsolved.

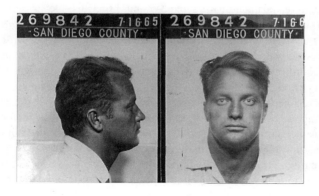

FIGURE 4.12 Serial killer Clyde Wilkerson after his 1965 arrest for rape. Authorities could not link him to the homicides and rapes at this time. Only the advent of DNA and the tenacity of determined investigators enabled this case to be solved. (Courtesy of El Cajon Police Department)

In 1997, El Cajon Police Department (ECPD) Lieutenant Pat Sprecco began to assign some of the older, unsolved crimes to investigators. He believed that advanced forensic technology might assist in resolving some of these crimes. The officers' reviews of the cases, however, had to be accomplished while carrying their normal caseloads and other assigned duties. In January, 1999, Detective Jon Wooddell received the homicide case of the young mother. Sometime after, Detective Robert Anderson observed a box of news clippings about the case of the older couple and began reading them. Neither case file contained a death certificate for the victims. While each officer began working his respective case separately, they soon had reason to believe they might be connected. During their review of the evidence, they found that items were commingled between the two cases, suggesting that earlier detectives had considered them linked. Wilkerson was the apparent linchpin.

During this review, they encountered a situation not uncommon in cold case investigation. Although items were individually tagged and bagged, some from one case were mixed with the other case. In addition, the cold cream jar with fingerprints had been broken when crushed in a vise. Loose reports, photographs, correspondence, and other material were dumped into boxes and there was no apparent chain of custody. Some pages of some reports were lost and never found. During this process, Anderson contacted other agencies mentioned in the reports to ascertain whether they possessed related documents. The district attorney's office still retained reports, as did the Probation Department. In addition, the California Department of Justice retained important documents and reports.

The detectives began by putting everything on a table and sorting the two cases. In this process, they began to reassemble the record *chronologically*. As they reviewed the reports, they observed a lack of uniformity in reporting. Some reports were handwritten and some were typed (misspellings not infrequent), and there was a noticeable lack of identifying information to be used in their efforts to relocate persons of interest. Thermofax paper documents were fading badly, and onionskin carbon paper documents were fragile to handle. In addition, certain report entries were not "politically correct" by today's standards, with detective's opinions freely inserted into the reports. In those days, suspects were not "alleged." Like the photos, the case was black and white to some earlier investigators, but the focus ultimately shifted with the later investigation.

The photo review similarly showed investigative actions far different from today's. Officers handled crime scene evidence without gloves or stood in the middle of the crime scene smoking a cigarette while the picture was being taken. The photos were generally more overall than specific in nature. Similarly, crime scene sketches and diagrams were lacking by today's standards. The sketches showed no measurements or other detail (see Figure 4.13), but for the present, did provide an overview of the scene as encountered by responding investigators.

During the course of their review and investigation to locate persons and documents, Anderson discovered that city engineers had subsequently diagramed the scene and their drawings had been entered into evidence. These were illustrated in Figures 3.5 and 3.6. Thus, the investigators recovered more detailed drawings to supplement the photo record that could be utilized to more accurately reconstruct the scene. Although they were unable to locate the engineer who actually drew the diagrams, they did locate his supervisor, who was able to authenticate the period work as a course of business document.

An additional record of the crime and investigation was discovered when Wooddell contacted media from the time period. They discovered that a local television station still retained film footage from broadcasts of the period. As this was previously aired material, the station converted the footage to a video tape and furnished it to the investigators. A similar review of the newspapers was conducted by Anderson. Microfilm copies were located, and many hours were spent in the library reviewing old newspaper reports in an effort to identify overlooked witnesses and information, as well as to learn what was in the public domain. Some of the newspaper reports provided better witness identification than did the police reports, as reporters had interviewed neighbors and reported in detail. These reports were copied and placed in the file.

The investigators continued to search for original persons who had figured in the initial investigations. They located and brought on board the original detectives, who were elated at the reinvestigation of their unsolved cases. Among those contacted was one detective who had interviewed

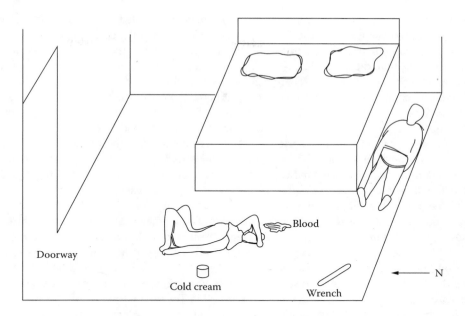

FIGURE 4.13 Like other crime-scene sketches of the period, no measurements were included on this sketch. However, when combined with a minimal number of photographs, it does depict the crime scene. (Courtesy of El Cajon Police Department)

Clyde Wilkerson in 1965. In addition, they located the boy who had observed Wilkerson emerge from the bushes, a grown man now living in his father's house, the same house as in 1965.

Like other smaller agencies, the El Cajon department utilized the San Diego County Sheriff's Department crime laboratory to conduct forensic examinations. Very early in the investigation, the detectives consulted with a DNA specialist, Criminalist Connie Milton, in the Sheriff's Crime Lab. Anderson was interested in DNA recovered from his crime scene. He had read the reports that earlier detectives suspected Clyde Wilkerson, and wanted to locate him to obtain a sample of his DNA. At this stage of the investigation, the two detectives were in constant contact, yet handled aspects of their own investigations independently as time allowed.

Review of the remaining case file indicated that period investigators had suspected family members of the murdered couple, and reports indicated that polygraph examinations had been utilized to clear them (the actual polygraph reports were not found in the file). The polygraph examinations had been administered by police officers and not by State Department of Justice personnel, as was often the case during this time period for smaller agencies. Similarly, the polygraph was mentioned as being used in the young mother's case, but further documentation was again lacking.

In Wooddell's investigation, events were a bit more complicated. During the course of their file review and investigation, cold case investigators seek to develop as much information on the victim as they can, and to learn more about the victimology. They attempt to identify anything victims might have done to contribute to their victimization, and that might subsequently contribute to the identification of the perpetrator. While the older couple's case was an apparent "whodunit," the victim's family was fully cooperative in the investigation. In Wooddell's case, the cooperation was less. The little boy found wandering outside the crime scene was now an ex-con, and when located, did not want anything to do with police or the investigation. "Let it be," he told investigators.

In addition, Wooddell's investigation revealed that some earlier detectives had a different prime suspect, a Catholic priest. Apparently the young mother was being tutored in catechism. The priest, an alcoholic, had made comments to various persons in the bars he frequented that he was responsible for her death. When word of this reached period detectives, they began to focus on him as a suspect. "Responsible" equated in some minds to "I killed her." The earlier detectives tried relentlessly to pursue the priest, without success. He repeatedly denied that he killed her, and ultimately, the church transferred him to another locale outside the easy reach of local law enforcement. The man died in 1972, and the question remained for cold case investigators decades later — was he the guilty person? There was one way to find out: DNA.

A forensic exhumation is a means to disinter a body, a process that is presented in Chapter 22. Early in the investigation, the investigators had involved a deputy district attorney, Dan Lamborn, in their efforts. Detective Wooddell sought a court order to exhume the body, and this was accomplished. DNA excluded, once and for all, the priest as a source of the DNA in the victim. In addition, it was also necessary to disinter the other victims as well, and permission was granted by family members in lieu of court action. As in similar cases, there were other suspects, and these were tracked down and tested, with negative results. Slowly, everyone was eliminated except for Clyde Wilkerson.

Wilkerson was a career criminal, one we now recognize as a serial killer. He had a lengthy rap sheet and the only time he was not committing crimes was when he was in custody for previous offenses. A long-distance truck driver, Wilkerson's livelihood took him all around the nation, and to this day, there is no way of knowing how many other murders he is responsible for. He was arrested in Oklahoma in 1973 on suspicion of robbery, although charges were later dropped, and in April, 1976, he was convicted and sentenced for rape in Arkansas. After serving 7 years in prison, he was paroled in 1983. In June, 1985, he was arrested in Texas on suspicion of aggravated assault, and in March, 1987, convicted of selling a controlled substance in Florida and sentenced to 3 years in prison, including time for violating parole.

As he began to focus on Wilkerson, Anderson formulated a timeline to assist in the investigation (see Figure 4.14).

Timelines and Visual Investigative Analysis (VIA) Charts

A useful and valuable tool in many situations, a timeline is an asset in homicide cases, perhaps even more so in cold case homicide investigations. These cases often involve developing, and understanding, an abundance of dates, times, events, places, and more. In a hot homicide scenario, investigators develop the information first hand and absorb it as it happens. In a cold case investigation, the information is contained not only in the often voluminous reports and other files, but in the develop-ment of the investigation. Timelines and VIA charts can show the linkages, time flows, and relation-ships among people, places, and events, and can aid in the visual, informational reconstruction. They can take an apparent unconnected series of events and graphically illustrate a clear visual picture of the entire case, relating apparently unrelated events and activities. They can illuminate an individual's presence or motive. This method can depict missing details and information and show investigators where to focus their efforts to fill these gaps. They can help reduce duplication of effort and increase investigative efficiency. In addition, they are highly effective for prosecutor and court presentations. Today, these have been upgraded through use of programs such as Microsoft PowerPoint®.

According to the California Department of Justice, the concept of VIA reportedly originated in the mid 1960s by the Los Angeles Police Department, the source of many advanced law enforcement concepts and techniques. This notion evolved from previous approaches, the Critical Path Method (CPM) and the Program Evaluation and Review Techniques (PERT). The VIA idea was picked up the California Department of Justice and the Federal Law Enforcement Training Center at Glynco, Georgia, and has now become a standard investigative tool. VIA methods involving the concept of networking were reportedly first incorporated in a major criminal inves-tigation as a result of the Robert Kennedy assassination in 1968, and in the still-unsolved Zodiac killings of the late 1960s and early 1970s.

Timelines may be especially useful in understanding victim movements, as well as suspect movements and how they converge

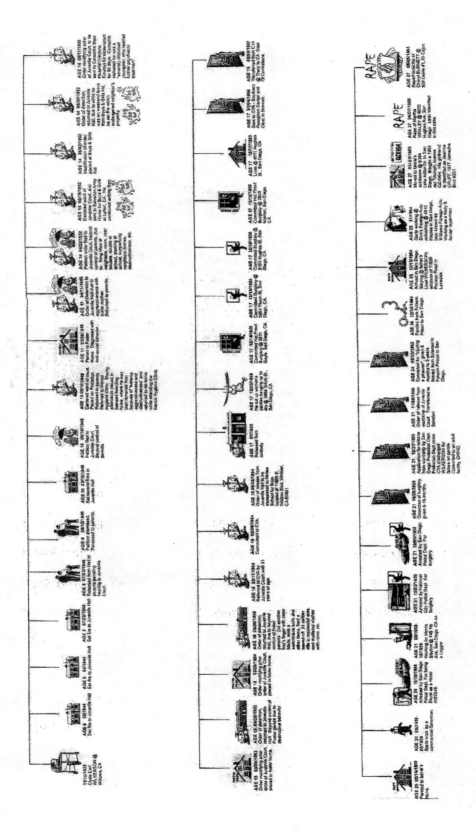

FIGURE 4.14A Clyde Wilkerson timeline. Timelines are an invaluable tool for investigators, prosecutors, and juries. They can illustrate and illuminate a great deal. (Courtesy of FBI)

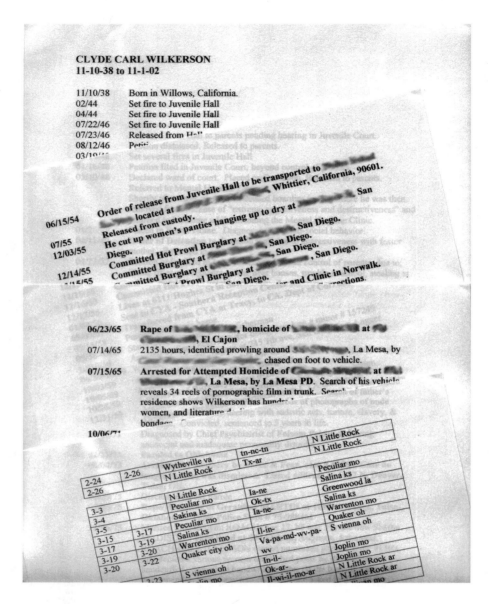

FIGURE 4.14B

The ability to construct useful timelines has been enhanced greatly by computers. What was once done on legal pads or rolls of butcher paper is now accomplished on desktop computer software, such as i2®, Casesoft®, or Microsoft Visio®. Other software may assist in documenting and organizing clue information (see Figure 4.15). The sources of detailed time and date information for timelines include:

- Law enforcement reports
- Booking sheets
- Witness statements
- Probation and parole documents
- Rap sheets

FIGURE 4.15 Clue Management Program. The Los Angeles County Sheriff's Department provides free software to law enforcement agencies to assist in clue management. This program is well suited to cold case homicide investigation. (Courtesy of Detective Gerry Biehn, Los Angeles County Sheriff Unsolved Unit)

- Telephone and cell phone records
- Residence locations
- Employment records
- Trip logs
- In-custody records
- Public utility records
- Traffic/parking tickets
- Drivers license
- Department of motor vehicle registrations and related documents
- Receipts (motel, gas, grocery etc)
- Suspect statements
- Diaries, notes and journals
- Accomplice and informant information

As the detectives discovered, Wilkerson began his life of crime at an early age, displaying behavior that later criminal profilers would come to identify as not uncommon among violent predators. This included setting fires and mutilating animals. Much of his teen years was spent in juvenile reformatories and foster homes. Every event and every known movement was now being compiled into a timeline that chronicled the life and movements of Clyde Wilkerson. Overviews provided investigators with a profile of his life, and specific timelines such as monthly trucking route, broken down by date, time, and location were compiled (see Figure 4.16).

As Wilkerson's profile developed, Anderson sought interstate assistance from San Diego FBI Agent Matt Brown. The FBI and U.S Marshall's service are excellent cold case homicide investigative resources.

Locating suspects can sometimes be difficult, at other times relatively easy. Based upon case file information for suspected places he might reside, Anderson conducted a driver's license search of various states where Wilkerson might be licensed — if he was still alive. He was, and when they located him, he was 62 years old and living in Arkansas.

TEXAS

Date	Time	Location-City	State	Date	Time	Location-City	State
09/03/99	21:36:00	Waxzahachie	TX	12/05/99	5:38:00	Horizon Cy	TX
09/03/99	22:32:00	Waxahachie	TX	12/05/99	10:11:00	Saragosa	TX
09/03/99	22:40:00	Red Oak	TX	12/05/99	15:02:00	Ingram	TX
09/14/99	5:10:00	Horizon Cy	TX	12/06/99	5:21:00	Kirby	TX
09/14/99	10:36:00	Van Horn	TX	12/06/99	7:33:00	San Antonio	TX
09/14/99	15:44:00	Sweetwater	TX	12/06/99	10:48:00	Kirby	TX
09/15/99	0:11:00	Weatherford	TX	12/06/99	15:35:00	San Antonio	TX
09/15/99	1:19:00	Blue Mound	TX	12/06/99	15:56:00	Kirby	TX
09/15/99	7:53:00	Ft Worth	TX	12/06/99	19:18:00	San Antonio	TX
09/15/99	9:03:00	Ft Worth	TX	12/06/99	19:46:00	Kirby	TX
09/15/99	11:35:00	Rockwall	TX	12/07/99	5:58:00	Sealy	TX
09/20/99	15:30:00	Cumby	TX	12/07/99	9:44:00	Hilshire V	TX
09/20/99	19:33:00	Rockwall	TX	12/07/99	10:46:00	Houston	TX
09/21/99	7:14:00	Irving	TX	12/08/99	5:21:00	Marshall	TX
09/21/99	13:18:00	Irving	TX	12/10/99	5:16:00	Amarillo	TX
09/21/99	13:33:00	Mesquite	TX	12/17/99	5:50:00	Carthage	TX
09/21/99	15:06:00	Rockwall	TX	12/17/99	7:34:00	Burke	TX
09/21/99	15:27:00	CadoMills	TX	12/17/99	9:47:00	Hillshire V	TX
10/08/99	10:28:00	Alanreed	TX	12/17/99	16:45:00	Houston	TX
10/16/99	7:23:00	Post	TX	12/17/99	16:47:00	Hilshire V	TX
10/16/99	9:11:00	Hermleigh	TX	12/17/99	17:49:00	Jacinto Cy	TX
10/16/99	15:13:00	Elgin	TX	01/16/00	5:41:00	Amarillo	TX
10/17/99	10:16:00	Houston	TX	03/09/00	10:01:00	Tyler	TX
10/18/99	10:00:00	Heights	TX	03/09/00	11:27:00	Tyler	TX
10/18/99	11:24:00	Houston	TX	03/09/00	15:56:00	Strawn	TX
10/18/99	13:49:00	Cheek	TX	03/10/00	5:52:00	Pecos	TX
11/07/99	0:00:00	Amarillo	TX	03/10/00	8:47:00	Van Horn	TX
				03/10/00	10:56:00	Horizon Cy	TX

FIGURE 4.16 Timelines are constructed from multiple sources of information, and may portray a period of one day to weeks to months or years and decades. Shown is a timeline compiled from trucking logs to show locations. (Courtesy of El Cajon Police Department)

Investigation revealed that Wilkerson had long been employed as an Arkansas-based truck driver. Anderson obtained a court order for employment records, and through FBI Agent Brown and the Little Rock, Arkansas, FBI Agent, obtained Wilkerson's employment application and route invoices. Then the Arkansas agent inquired whether the company still retained any envelopes in which Wilkerson had mailed their invoices. They did.

Anderson conducted a further background check on Wilkerson, one that sought to determine any *relationships* that might now yield information about the crimes. Anderson located and interviewed the officers who had interviewed Wilkerson's Oklahoma rape victim, but when he attempted to talk to a relative of Wilkerson, the door was slammed in his face.

Chain-of-custody documentation is now different from that in the 1960s, and while reviewing the evidence, Detective Anderson discovered a thermos bottle that he suspected contained original cotton swabs. For fear of contaminating any potential evidence, the thermos was sent unopened to the FBI lab. Nationwide, the events of 9/11 impacted many facets of police work, and changed the priorities for FBI operations. This investigation was no different, and ultimately, the thermos was returned unopened. Wooddell recontacted criminalist Connie Milton.

When reviewing the original forensic reports, Milton had not suspected that any usable evidence had remained. The method used in rape examinations during the time period of the crimes was no longer even a part of a modern sexual assault examination. She considered that, for lack of another container, an examining physician had emptied his thermos and stored evidence in it. It was not the usual evidence container, even then.

Inside the thermos were glass vials containing cotton swabs and a dried residue (see Figure 4.17). Examination revealed the presence of sperm, but the source of the sperm was unknown. After more than 30 years, Criminalist Milton extracted and typed the DNA. Although Wilkerson had been questioned after both rapes and murders, there was not enough evidence to link him to the crime scenes at the time.

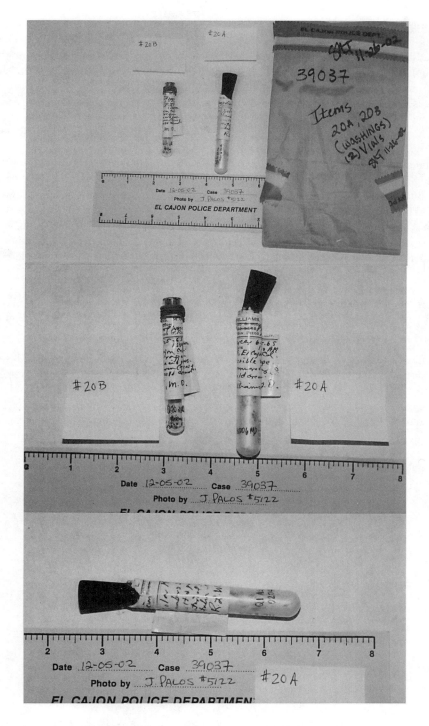

FIGURE 4.17 These vials containing cotton swabs were recovered in a coffee thermos that had been used to contain them for over 30 years. Criminalist Connie Milton was able to extract and type DNA, closing the forensic net on serial killer Clyde Wilkerson. (Courtesy of El Cajon Police Department)

Milton had previously processed the semen evidence found on the bed sheet collected at the scene from where the young mother was raped and murdered. On a Saturday afternoon, she made the match. She now had the DNA from the trucking company envelopes as well as from the murder of the couple and the young mother. Clyde Wilkerson was the common denominator among the samples from the victims as well as the trucking company envelopes.

The case had taken over 37 years to reach this point. *Technology* had now enabled law enforcement to make an identification from sources almost a nation, and decades, apart. It had taken 3 years to complete the reinvestigation, one complicated by a process of eliminating numerous other potential suspects as the focus narrowed on Wilkerson.

Not unheard of in cold cases, Anderson and Wooddell were toddlers at the time of the crime, and those who had collected the evidence decades before were now quite elderly or deceased. Connie Milton had not even been born when the murders occurred. Her skills, however, now identified Wilkerson's DNA print as having been at both crime scenes. The frequency of occurrence of this DNA profile for Caucasian males was now estimated at one in 57 quadrillion.

An arrest warrant was obtained, and the detectives, Deputy District Attorney Lamborn, District Attorney Investigator Steve Baker, and San Diego-based FBI agent Matt Brown traveled to Benton, Arkansas.

With the cooperation of local authorities, Wilkerson was arrested without incident on his rural property on October 29, 2002 (see Figure 4.18). Time had not improved his social behavior, and arresting officers discovered a small methamphetamine lab when he was taken into custody (see Figure 4.19).

Post-Arrest Interview

In cold cases, investigators have the advantage of being able to compile background history on an identified suspect and to study all aspects of the crime. As have other cold case killers, Wilkerson claimed no memory of the events, admitting that *if* he had committed these vicious crimes, he would surely have remembered. "If you get arrested, you remember it. If you don't get arrested, you don't," he said. As far as any other crimes, he told them, they would have to prove that on their own and stopped talking.

FIGURE 4.18 Clyde Wilkerson at his arrest. Thanks to the efforts of detectives, prosecutors, and criminalists, a serial killer's decades-long rampage came to an end. Wilkerson was arrested and subsequently pled guilty to one 1965 California murder as well as a 1975 Oklahoma murder. The investigation into his activities has continued. (Courtesy of El Cajon Police Department)

FIGURE 4.19 Officers recovered this low-budget methamphetamine lab setup at the time of Wilkerson's arrest. (Courtesy of El Cajon Police Department)

During the arrest period, identification and interview of those who know the suspect is a suggested tactic. At the time of Wilkerson's arrest, District Attorney investigator Steve Baker interviewed a tenant who resided on Wilkerson's property. On his own, the tenant then contacted Wilkerson in jail. He asked Wilkerson whether he had committed the crimes. "Yeah, but it took 'em 37 years to catch me," the tenant later reported his landlord had said.

Wilkerson was returned to San Diego. On March 17, 2003, almost 40 years after his crime spree, Clyde Carl Wilkerson pled guilty in a plea agreement to the murder of the husband and rape against his wife. Under the law *at the time of the murder* in 1965, Wilkerson could only be sentenced to 7 years to life in prison. The other charges were not pursued, as he would receive no additional prison time, and would most likely die in prison for this offense.

Continuing Investigation — The Internet

The investigation into Wilkerson's decades-long crime spree did not end with his arrest and return to San Diego. Detective Robert Anderson believed that Wilkerson was responsible for more murders when he was not in custody, and set out to identify other unsolved cases that fit Wilkerson's M.O. He was already suspected in another unsolved San Diego homicide from July, 1965, as well as a 1954 Los Angeles-area murder and attempted murder.

On his own time, from his home computer, Detective Anderson began to search the Internet and the Web pages of law enforcement agencies and unsolved homicides. He discovered that the Tulsa, Oklahoma, Police Department had an unsolved rape-homicide of a junior college student from February, 1975. The victim had been abducted from the parking lot of her downtown campus, and her body was found 3 weeks later in a vacant apartment. She had been raped and strangled. The victim suffered numerous facial injuries due to blunt-force trauma, as well as sexual mutilation. The official cause of death was ligature strangulation. The victim's clothes, jewelry, purse, checkbook, and other identification were gone. A day after the victim was reported missing, a white male cashed one of her checks and attempted to use one of her credit cards in the Tulsa area. Evidence seized from the crime scene provided a DNA profile of the offender.

Anderson contacted the Oklahoma agency, and as a result of his diligence and tenacity, the authorities there reopened their unsolved case. DNA linked Wilkerson to this crime, and on April 28, 2004, Clyde Carl Wilkerson pled guilty to the Oklahoma crime and was sentenced to life in prison. His prison time was to run concurrently with his California sentence. Under the California law, Wilkerson will be eligible for parole after 6 years, and after 20 years in Oklahoma. In 2005, he is still being investigated for other unsolved homicides.

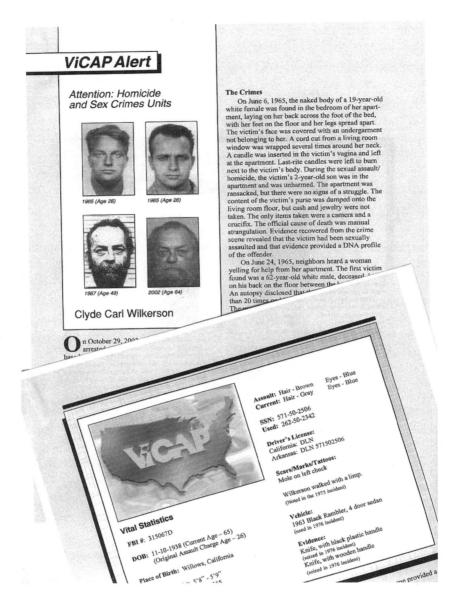

ViCAP Alert

Attention: Homicide and Sex Crimes Units

1965 (Age 26)   1965 (Age 26)

1987 (Age 49)   2002 (Age 64)

Clyde Carl Wilkerson

On October 29, 2002 arrested based...

The Crimes

On June 6, 1965, the naked body of a 19-year-old white female was found in the bedroom of her apartment, laying on her back across the foot of the bed, with her feet on the floor and her legs spread apart. The victim's face was covered with an undergarment not belonging to her. A cord cut from a living room window was wrapped several times around her neck. A candle was inserted in the victim's vagina and left at the apartment. Last-rite candles were left to burn next to the victim's body. During the sexual assault/homicide, the victim's 2-year-old son was in the apartment and was unharmed. The apartment was ransacked, but there were no signs of a struggle. The content of the victim's purse was dumped onto the living room floor, but cash and jewelry were not taken. The only items taken were a camera and a crucifix. The official cause of death was manual strangulation. Evidence recovered from the crime scene revealed that the victim had been sexually assaulted and that evidence provided a DNA profile of the offender.

On June 24, 1965, neighbors heard a woman yelling for help from her apartment. The first victim found was a 62-year-old white male, deceased on his back on the floor between the... An autopsy disclosed that... than 20 times...

Eyes - Blue
Eyes - Blue

Assault: Hair - Brown
Current: Hair - Gray

SSN: 571-50-2506
Used: 262-50-2342

Driver's License:
California: DLN
Arkansas: DLN 571502506

Scars/Marks/Tattoos:
Mole on left cheek.

Wilkerson walked with a limp.
(Noted in the 1975 incident)

Vehicle:
1963 Black Rambler, 4 door sedan
(used in 1976 incident)

Evidence:
Knife, with black plastic handle
(seized in 1976 incident)
Knife, with wooden handle
(seized in 1976 incident)

Vital Statistics
FBI #: 315067D
DOB: 11-10-1938 (Current Age – 65)
(Original Assault Charge Age – 26)
Place of Birth: Willows, California
5'8" - 5'9"

...e provided a

FIGURE 4.20 Wilkerson is a "poster child" for the need for this agency and similar state programs. The more law enforcement learns about people like this, and communicates this knowledge, the better the chances that killers such as Wilkerson will be identified and removed from society. (ViCAP Alert in *FBI Law Enforcement Bulletin*)

Due to the serious crimes and his interstate movements, Wilkerson was the subject of the FBI's Violent Criminal Apprehension Program (ViCAP) Alert in the *FBI Law Enforcement Bulletin* in August, 2003 (see Figure 4.20). This notice to the nation's law enforcement community detailed events of his numerous crimes, including method of operation, personal identifying information, known vehicles, and evidence. It was disseminated to alert law enforcement to Wilkerson's existence so that local agencies could review any unsolved homicides or other crimes in light of what was now known about him.

The ViCAP Alert provided additional detail regarding Wilkerson's M.O., and further information may be obtained from ViCAP. Wilkerson's DNA profile has also been entered into CODIS.

CONCLUSION

The means and methods of cold case homicide investigation are based upon the crime, evidence, original investigation, and subsequent events. Each cold case must be weighed and evaluated on its own merits. *How to* proceed is based upon the experience, training, and best investigative plan as conceived by the investigator or investigative team. Different cases call for different tactics and there can be no one "best way." The investigation of these cases exploits the advantage of time as it is primarily revealed through changes in relationships and changes in technology. Various tools are at the disposal of the cold case investigator, and the combination of these factors has allowed some cold cases to be solved. Not all will be solved, however, and many will be reshelved as unsolved cold case homicides.

ACKNOWLEDGMENTS

I wish to express my gratitude and appreciation to Mr. Steve Hodel for his authorship and contribution of "Thoughtprints," his thoughts and perspective in the application of homicide expertise and how to "think outside the box" when it comes to the investigation of cold case homicides. Prior to his retirement in 1986, Steve Hodel investigated over 300 homicides as a detective and supervisor with the Los Angeles Police Department. It is through the learning experiences of others that we may come to solve yet unsolved homicides. Hodel presents insights into the more uncommon methods we may encounter and utilize during these investigations. Further cold case investigative techniques can be found in his book *Black Dahlia Avenger: A Genius for Murder.*

I further wish to express my appreciation to Sergeant Richard Longshore and Lieutenant Joseph Hartshorne of the Los Angeles County Sheriff's Department, and Mr. Rod Englert for their input and review of this section. In addition, I wish to also recognize and extend my thanks to Lieutenant Tony Leal of the Texas Rangers for sharing his thoughts and perspectives on cold case homicide investigation.

The investigation of Clyde Wilkerson by Detectives Anderson and Wooddell exemplifies the highest abilities of cold case investigators. Their teamwork with criminalist Connie Milton, Deputy District Attorney Dan Lamborn, FBI Agent Matt Brown, and others showed the results of team effort applied to cold case investigation. In addition, I wish to acknowledge the leadership of the El Cajon Police Department for its proactive efforts in identifying and reinvestigating unsolved cold case homicides.

The case history was compiled from extensive inverviews with Detectives Anderson and Wooddell and Criminalist Milton, and review of records. In addition, I wish to acknowledge Mr. Paul Levikov of the San Diego County District Attorney's Office and his report "How a Thermos Helped Catch a Killer" in the Winter-Spring 2003–2004 edition of *Law Enforcement Quarterly.*

SUGGESTED READING

Anonymous (2002). Cold Case Homicide. C.P.T. Network. Sacramento, California Commission on Peace Officer Standards and Training.

Anonymous. (2003). ViCAP Alert. FBI Law Enforcement Bulletin (August, 2003). V72.n.8.

Eliopulos, L. N. (2003). *Death Investigator's Handbook: Expanded and Updated Edition.* Boulder, CO. Paladin Press.

Geberth, V. (1996). *Practical Homicide Investigation: Tactics, Procedures, and Forensic Techniques. (Third Edition).* Boca Raton, CRC Press.

Jackson, I.M. (2002). 1965 Crime Spree May Be Solved. (October 30, 2002). *San Diego Union.* A1,9.

Jackson, I.M. (2003). Plea is Guilty in '65 Rape, Murder. (March 18, 2003). *San Diego Union.* B3.

Johnson, R.S. (1995). *How to Locate Anyone Who Is or Has Been in the Military.* San Antonio, Texas. MIE Publishing.

Keppell, R.D. and Weis, J.G. (1994). Time and distance as solvability factors in murder cases. *Journal of Forensic Sciences* 32 (2): 386–401.

Lee, H.C., Palmbach, T. and Miller, M. (2001). *Henry Lee's Crime Scene Handbook*. New York. Academic Press.

Levikow, P. Special Report: How a Thermos Helped Catch a Killer. *Law Enforcement Quarterly*. (Winter 2003–2004). San Diego District Attorney. San Diego, California.

Newcombe, B. (1990). Paper Trails: A Guide to Public Records in California. Oakland, CA. Center for Investigative Reporting, California Newspaper Publisher's Association.

Nyberg, R. (2004). Justice Served Cold. Police. *The Law Enforcement Magazine*. (October, 2004). V28, N10. p44.

Poole, H. and Jurovics, S. (1993). MUST: A Team for Unsolved Homicides. *FBI Law Enforcement Bulletin*. (March, 1993). V62 N3. Federal Bureau of Investigation. Washington, D.C.

Ray, D. (1995). *California Investigator's Handbook: A Public Records Primer*. (6th ed.). Burbank, CA. ENG Press.

Spraggs, D. (2003). How To Open A Cold Case. Policemag.com (May, 2003).

Turner, R. and Kosa, R. (2003). Cold Case Squads: Leaving No Stone Unturned. (July, 2003). *Bulletin NCJ* 199781. Washington, D.C. Bureau of Justice Assistance.

Walton, R.H. (2005). Identification of solvability factors in twenty-first century cold case homicide investigations. Unpublished Ed.D dissertation. University of San Francisco. San Francisco, CA.

Westvear, A. (unknown). Death Investigation. Federal Bureau of Investigation. Washington, D.C.

5 The Prosecution of Cold Case Murders

Anne Marie Schubert

CONTENTS

INTRODUCTION

On May 7, 1977, 15-year-old Penny Parker went out to collect money for her paper route with the *Sacramento Bee* newspaper (see Figure 5.1). She never returned home. Two days later, Penny's body was found in a rural field in Sacramento County. She had been sexually assaulted and stabbed to death. For 25 years, her murder remained unsolved the despite diligent and persistent efforts of law enforcement to find her killer. For 20 years, Penny's family waited for justice. Finally, in 2002, as a result of Sacramento County's Cold Case Prosecution Program, Penny's murderer was identified and charged with her murder.

Cold case murders present unique and interesting challenges for both investigators and prosecutors. Unlike active homicide cases, there are many legal and evidentiary issues that would never arise in a fresh homicide that must be addressed both in the investigation and the prosecution to effectively present an old murder case to a jury.

The most significant factor in the investigation and prosecution of cold cases is — not surprisingly — the passage of time, which can both help and hinder a cold case. While time clearly has an adverse impact on the memories of witnesses, it also may become an ally if once-reluctant witnesses become forthright and cooperative. While some investigative leads can be lost with time, perhaps because physical evidence was lost or destroyed or because witnesses have died or become

FIGURE 5.1 Photograph of Penny Parker.

disabled, other avenues may open up. The most important advancement of recent years has been provided by DNA technology, which has revolutionized the ability of investigators to evaluate physical evidence. DNA has, in essence, become the silent witness to the truth.

While the investigation of a cold case presents distinctive challenges, so too does the prosecution. In addition to learning and briefing legal issues that must be mastered in many ordinary murder trials, the prosecutor in a cold murder trial may also have to deal with legal issues arising from sometimes extensive pretrial delay, which will be governed by the statute of limitations and constitutional standards of due process.

Additionally, the prosecutor must master the facts, and in doing so, take into account the expectations of the jury. With the introduction of cold cases in television media, jurors expect scientific evidence on par with what television writers and producers have presented to them. Satisfying these expectations in any murder case, let alone an old one, can be very difficult.

EARLY INVOLVEMENT OF A PROSECUTOR

Due to the legal, evidentiary, and modern-day challenges presented by cold cases, it is critical for law enforcement and the prosecution to work together at the earliest phase of the investigation. This should be done as soon as the cold case is reopened. Through this team approach, the investigator and prosecutor can effectively anticipate and prepare for any legal or evidentiary challenges that may arise in court once an individual is charged. Coordination and cooperation may involve discussing the necessity and sufficiency of search warrants, photographic or live lineups and the chain of custody for forensic evidence. It might also involve discussing what scientific tests should be used, as well as what defenses may be raised. Through this coordination and cooperation during the investigative stage, the likelihood of a successful prosecution will increase dramatically.

Additionally, many of these cold cases will involve hundreds, if not thousands of pages of police reports. This will be for several reasons: (1) the case was initially investigated by law enforcement at the time of the murder; (2) the investigation may have continued over several years by many different investigators; and (3) the case was ultimately solved. Further, once perpetrators are identified, police reports will be generated not only connecting the suspects to the crimes but also detailing their criminal background. If defendants are charged with capital murder, a thorough review of their backgrounds will be required for the penalty phase. Obtaining and organizing these materials in a manner sufficient to justify arrest, conviction, and perhaps even the imposition of the death penalty, requires prosecutorial involvement — and the sooner the better.

Because of the complexity of cold cases, the involvement of a local prosecutor during the investigation will assist in the organization of the case and the presentation of evidence to a jury.

PROSECUTING THE COLD CASE MURDER

Charging Cold Case Murders

Several considerations must be taken into account when charging a cold case murder:

1. **Statute of Limitations:** In many murder cases, additional crimes have been committed along with the homicide. In both the homicide charge and the other offenses, the prosecutor must determine the appropriate statute of limitations for all charges.

   In general, there is no statute of limitations for murder. There can be exceptions to the general rule, however, depending on the jurisdiction and the date of the offense. For instance, in October of 2000, Michael Skakel was charged by the State of Connecticut with the 1975 murder of 15-year-old Martha Moxley. At the time of his arrest, Skakel was 39 years old — he was barely 15 at the time of the crime. Numerous legal motions were filed by the defense seeking a dismissal based upon statute of limitations. In particular, the defense claimed the prosecution of the murder was time barred by a 5-year statute of limitation in effect in Connecticut in 1975. While the trial court denied the motion to dismiss, the claim was the defendant's primary contention on appeal.

   In addition to the statute of limitations for murder, the prosecution must also become familiar with the statute of limitations for any lesser and included offenses to murder (such as manslaughter), and for any other crimes that were connected to the murder. These statutes will vary according to the jurisdiction. As a result, in many jurisdictions, the charging document may be limited to the murder charge alone.

   However, even if the statute of limitations precludes the charging of related offenses, in many jurisdictions the prosecution can still allege special circumstances that might qualify the defendant for capital punishment. For instance, a murder case from 1981 may involve the kidnap, rape, and murder of a young female. While the statute of limitations may bar the filing of kidnap and rape as separate counts, it may not bar the filing of kidnap and rape as *special circumstances* attached to the count of murder.

2. **Law of Murder:** One of the most important issues that must be confronted when charging a cold case murder is determining what the law of murder was at the time of the crime. This includes the degree of murder and any lesser included offense to the crime of murder, such as manslaughter. The simplest means of determining this is to consult the Penal Code for the year of the crime. Additionally, the prosecutor must determine what jury instructions will be provided to the jury at trial. This may require finding jury instructions that were in use at the time of the crime and determining whether some more modern variant of those jury instructions must be used.

3. **Law of Special Circumstances:** In jurisdictions that have capital punishment, it is imperative to know what special circumstances existed at the time of the crime. In many jurisdictions, the list of special circumstances has been expanded over the years. For instance, if a murder that occurred in 1982 involved a kidnapping and carjacking, it is necessary to know whether the kidnapping and carjacking were on the list of special circumstances law in 1982. If they were not, but some related charge was (such as robbery), the prosecutor might be able to allege robbery as an alternative special circumstance in the charging document.

Additionally, even if the death penalty was authorized under the Penal Code at the time of the murder, there are jurisdictions where court rulings nullified those statutes, finding that the law was unconstitutional. In such jurisdictions, the death penalty cannot be sought for offenses committed before the court ruling. For instance, in California, the California Supreme Court found the death penalty statute of that state unconstitutional in August 1977. As a result, no defendant in California who committed murder before August 1977 can be put to death and, in fact, face a maximum term of 7 years to life in prison. Thus, in Penny Parker's murder, the prosecution was precluded from seeking the death penalty because the crime occurred in May 1977.

Clearly, the potential charges and sentence will have a significant impact on both the investigation and prosecution of a cold case. Understanding the laws that existed at the time of the murder is critical.

4. **Proper Court for Filing Charges:** In some murder cases, the defendant may have been a juvenile at the time of the murder. In those instances, the prosecutor must determine whether his or her jurisdiction requires that charges first be filed in juvenile court or adult court. The determination of whether a juvenile defendant may be tried in adult court presents many complex issues that must be fully explored by the prosecutor.

NECESSARY ELEMENTS OF THE INVESTIGATION

The successful prosecution of a cold murder case is dependant upon the investigation conducted by law enforcement. From a prosecutor's perspective, there are several key elements to a successful cold case investigation. These include the following:

Thorough Review of Case File

- A thorough review of the case file is necessary to effectively investigate and prosecute a cold case. From an investigator's point view, this is necessary to complete the investigation. From a prosecutor's perspective, this review is necessary not only for an effective prosecution but to ensure compliance with the rules of discovery, which, in most jurisdictions, impose upon the prosecutor an ethical obligation to provide all reports associated with the case file to the defense. In this case review, the following steps should be taken:
  - Obtain all reports, including:
    - Police reports: this includes reports in the original case file as well as those maintained in the police records division. It is not uncommon for reports in the original case file not to have been submitted to the records division. It is highly recommended that the prosecutor personally review the original police file to verify that all records have been obtained.
    - Autopsy reports.
    - Laboratory reports: this includes all final reports as well as laboratory notes generated or relied upon by the laboratory analyst.
    - Medical records.
    - Psychological records.

- Records in possession of prosecution: In some instances, the prosecutor's office may have a copy of the case file. This may be for several reasons. The case might have been filed and later dismissed, or might have been submitted for filing but rejected by a prosecutor. In many instances, the prior prosecutor may have obtained records that were never seen by the original investigator.
- Locate all Photographs, Videotapes, Audiotapes, and Composites: These include from the following agencies:
  - Law enforcement: This can include original reports, photographs, tapes, composites or Polaroid photographs of suspects or vehicles. These items should be in the records division. As noted above, however, items sometimes do not make it from the original case file to the records division.
  - Medical Examiner/Coroner's Office: The original autopsy photographs should also be obtained. While the law enforcement agency might also have taken photographs at the autopsy, the photographs taken by the medical examiner may be more comprehensive. In particular, the medical examiner could have taken photographs depicting the collection of evidence and the internal examination of the victim. Many times, these photographs will become critical for the prosecution in demonstrating the proper chain of custody in the collection of evidence or for identifying particular wound patterns for the victim.
  - Hospital Photographs: In some instances, a hospital might have taken photographs of injuries of the victim prior to or after death.
  - Other Sources of Photographs: The investigator and prosecutor should also determine whether other individuals have photographs relevant to the investigation. These include media sources (TV or newspapers) or those in possession of civilian witnesses. For instance, it may be necessary to obtain photographs from the victim or suspect's family demonstrating events around the time of the homicide.

Thorough Review and Analysis of Physical Evidence

One of the most critical steps in the investigation and prosecution of a cold case involves review of the physical evidence. In many cases, the identity of the suspect is determined through forensic evidence. In particular, the introduction of forensic DNA testing and the use of convicted offender DNA databanks have allowed investigators to identify suspects in cases that might otherwise remain unsolved. Therefore, it is important that both the investigator and prosecutor understand how to handle and evaluate physical evidence. In many cases, the reliability of the evidence testing and the chain of custody will be aggressively attacked by the defense. For this reason, it is imperative that this review be thorough and that all necessary and relevant items of evidence be analyzed.

In reviewing the state of the physical evidence, the following steps should be taken:

- Consider all possible locations where the evidence could be located. This might include the following locations:
  - Law enforcement property room.
  - Coroner's office: In many jurisdictions, the Coroner's office provides the autopsy kit to either the crime laboratory or police agency at the time of the autopsy. However, in some jurisdictions, the Coroner's office keeps additional biological samples (such as smears of biological fluids placed on slides) in its own possession. Additionally, the Coroner's office may have tissue samples from the victim. These autopsy and tissue samples may become vital to the investigation of the case. This is particularly true where the law enforcement autopsy kit has been either lost or destroyed. For instance, in Penny Parker's murder, the law enforcement agency was unable to locate the autopsy kit taken in 1977. However, the Sacramento County Coroner's Office

retained autopsy samples in its possession. These samples became the vital piece of evidence for identifying Penny's killer.

- Crime Laboratory or specific laboratory analyst's possession: this should include all laboratories that have conducted analysis in the case. In many cases, several laboratories may have conducted analysis over many years. It is vital to determine whether any of these laboratories have retained any evidence in the case.
- Prosecutor's office.
- Previous investigator's possession.
- Court file.

Additionally, in reviewing the physical evidence, both the investigator and prosecutor should consider the following:

- Do not assume evidence has been lost or destroyed. It is not uncommon for investigators to be told that the evidence is lost or destroyed when in fact it is not. The evidence may have been misplaced or the property clerk may not know where to find it. The investigator should personally seek the evidence by going to all the possible locations in which it might be stored. A diligent and meticulous search can oftentimes result in locating the critical items of evidence.
- Seek the assistance of an expert when conducting an inventory and review of the evidence. To fully explain the significance of physical evidence in a cold case, an expert will need to be consulted. The analysts employed in law enforcement crime labs will likely be able to either provide this expertise personally or know someone who can. The expert can also evaluate whether potential defenses are scientifically viable. For instance, in many cold case murders, the defendant may claim that he had consensual sex with the victim prior to her death but did not kill her. This defense, however, may be undermined by an understanding of the significance of the physical evidence that only an expert can provide. If a large amount of semen belonging to the defendant is found in the victim's body, the expert may understand that this indicates recent sexual relations between the defendant and the victim. This finding may thereby defeat a consent defense wherein the defendant claims his sexual contact with the victim occurred several hours or days prior to the victim's death.
- Reevaluate old lab reports. Forensic science has changed dramatically over the last 20 to 30 years. Tests, particularly of biological substances, are much more definitive and reliable than they once were. For instance, some of the following factors should be considered in reviewing forensic testing performed in the original case:
  - If a lab report indicates "no semen or sperm" was *found*, do not automatically assume that no semen or sperm was present. It may be that the laboratory performed only a "presumptive" test (such as acid phosphatase) at the time. In many cases, the lack of a positive response on this presumptive test does not mean there is no semen or sperm present. The investigator or prosecutor should confirm this through a microscopic analysis by the laboratory.

    In the Penny Parker case, for example, the victim's underwear was analyzed in 1977, and at that time, the laboratory reported that no seminal fluid was detected on the underwear (see Figure 5.2). A review of the analysis revealed that this conclusion was based solely on a presumptive test. In 2002, the laboratory performed a microscopic analysis of the underwear, revealing a large amount of sperm. DNA testing of the sperm conclusively identified the individual later charged with Penny's murder.
  - Do not rely exclusively on the autopsy or medical sexual assault examination to determine whether sperm is present. In many old cases, the method of evidence collection by the medical examiner may have precluded the observation of sperm. While the autopsy report may indicate "no sperm" *found*, this does not necessarily

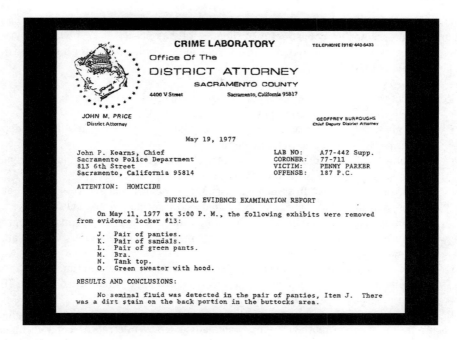

FIGURE 5.2 1977 laboratory report.

mean that there is no sperm *present* or there was no sexual assault. Thus, the autopsy kit may well have to be retested using current forensic technology.

- View and photograph the condition of the existing evidence. By viewing the evidence in person, both the investigator and prosecutor can better understand the significance of items that either were not photographed before or that cannot be adequately portrayed in photographs. This may provide a better understanding of the circumstances surrounding the crime.

   Additionally, viewing and photographing the evidence can assist in determining the chain of custody. In many cold cases, the chain of custody is difficult to establish. In some instances, property sheets may have been lost or destroyed—if they were ever prepared at all. By viewing the evidence in person, the investigator and prosecutor can see what documentation relating to chain of custody was maintained with the evidence itself. Photographing these items as well as documentation relating to the chain of custody will often help the prosecution in court proceedings.

- Determine whether additional forensic testing is available and advisable. Both law enforcement and the prosecution should consult about whether additional testing is possible and is needed in a particular cold case. For instance, further analysis may reveal additional sexual acts committed against the victim. As a result, it may be possible to allege additional special circumstances against the defendant. Furthermore, additional testing may provide greater insight into the circumstances surrounding the crime and the defendant's connection to it. This could provide useful information when the case is presented to a jury.

Reconstruct the Crime and the Defendant's Connection to the Crime

One of the most challenging aspects in both the investigation and prosecution of a cold case murder is reconstructing the crime and the defendant's connection to it. Presenting a cold case homicide to a jury offers unique challenges because many jurors expect that even an investigation conducted years ago will meet the latest scientific standards. Defense attorneys are sure to contrast modern standards with those that were actually used at the time. One way to address this issue is for the investigator and prosecutor to reconstruct the crime as fully as possible.

There are several ways that a cold case homicide can be reconstructed for a successful prosecution. These include the following:

- Reconstruct the Crime Scene: This can be accomplished in several ways:
  - Original crime scene photographs.
  - Aerial photographs taken at or near the time (often by a government planning department or private aerial photography company).
  - Maps drawn at or near the time of the crime. This can be from the original investigation or by obtaining plot maps from private or public agencies.
  - Revisit the crime scene. In some instances, the scene has changed very little, if at all. As such, current photographs may provide useful information that may not have been photographed in the original investigation. In some instances, the original photographs taken have been lost or destroyed. As a result, current photographs will be all the investigator or prosecutor can get.
  - Video Footage: In many instances, video footage was taken at the time by either law enforcement or the news media. If possible, this footage should be obtained. If the footage is unavailable, new video photography may be useful.
- Reconstruct the circumstances surrounding the crime. Understanding *why* the homicide occurred is a question that every jury wants answered. While a prosecutor technically does not have to establish that a motive exists, because motive is not an element of the crime of murder, the *absence* of motive may present a viable defense to the crime. In reconstructing the circumstances of the homicide, a prosecutor may therefore want the following investigation conducted:
  - A thorough analysis of the victim's background ("victimology").
  - Interviews of the original investigators and medical examiners.
  - Current background investigation and interviews with witnesses interviewed at the time of the crime (if possible).
  - Re-analysis of all forensic evidence.
  - A complete background investigation of the defendant.
- Background investigation of the defendant. In cold cases, as in all murder cases, the defendant must be connected to both the victim and the crime scene. This is particularly true in "cold hit" cases, where the primary evidence will typically be a DNA match between biological samples obtained from the victim's body and a reference sample taken from the suspect. While it might be tempting for resource-strapped investigators and prosecutors to conclude that that is all the jury *needs,* that may not be all the evidence they *want.* In presenting a cold case to a jury, a complete background investigation of the defendant will provide the jury with a thorough understanding of the defendant's connection to the murder. Sources of information that should be considered in obtaining a complete background of the defendant include the following:
- Interviews with the defendant's family, friends, co-workers and previous sexual partners both before and after the homicide.
- Police reports of all crimes committed by or involving the defendant.
- Field identification ("FI") cards on the defendant. This may assist in determining the whereabouts of the defendant around the time of the murder.
- Registration cards, such as sexual offender-, drug- or arson-registration cards.
- Records relating to the defendant, including medical, mental health and employment records.
- A complete copy of the defendant's prison file. This should include:
- Visitation logs.
- Information regarding addresses used for parole or family members.

- Family history.
- Old prison photos (particularly those near the time of the murder).
- Psychological reports.

Special Considerations in DNA Cold Hit Cases

In cold cases that are solved by way of a DNA "cold hit," the defendant is identified through the use of an offender database, where the DNA from crime scene evidence is linked to the defendant's DNA. In these cases, several factors should be considered. They include the following:

- Once the "hit" is made, the most critical concern is a determination of whether the suspect is in or out of custody. Clearly, if out of custody, the law enforcement agency will need to expedite the investigation. If, however, the suspect is in custody, law enforcement will have more time, and can more effectively and thoroughly prepare the case for prosecution.
- Once a "hit" is made, law enforcement should obtain and test an additional DNA sample from the defendant. This will confirm the analysis conducted in the case. In addition, it will allow the local DNA laboratory that conducted testing on the crime scene evidence to provide the all the necessary testimony in court.
- Prior to filing criminal charges, law enforcement and the prosecution should also determine whether additional DNA testing should be conducted. If additional items of evidence will be consumed through DNA testing, the prosecutor must also determine whether this testing should be done before or after criminal charges are filed. If additional items of evidence will be consumed through DNA testing, the prosecutor must also determine whether this testing should be done before or after criminal charges are filed. For example, if only one vaginal swab collected at the victim's autopsy remains in police evidence, the DNA testing may exhaust this evidence. As a result, the defense would be unable to conduct their own independent testing of this sample. If the testing is done after the filing of criminal charges, and the evidence will be consumed through this testing, the prosecutor should be aware that the defense may have a right to be present during the testing analysis. If the testing is done after the filing of the criminal charges, and the evidence will be consumed through this testing, the prosecutor should be aware that the defense may have a right to be present during the testing analysis.

PREPARATION FOR PENALTY PHASE

In many cold cases, the defendant may be facing capital punishment. Because many of the solved cold case murders involve sexual assault, the prosecution may seek the death penalty against the defendant. Like many other death cases, preparation for the penalty phase is critical. One benefit for the prosecution in cold cases is that, where the defendant is already in custody for other offenses, much of this preparation can be done before the murder charges are even filed. This may be very beneficial since some witnesses—particularly the defendant's family and friends—may be more cooperative before the charges are filed.

In preparation for the penalty phase, the following avenues of investigation should be considered:

- **Interview family and friends of the defendant:** While the family and friends of the defendant will often resist providing law enforcement with any helpful information, this is not always the case. Some may cooperate because they dislike the defendant or dislike what he has done. Others may try to limit disclosures to innocuous information but, because they don't know all the facts (particularly before charges are filed), may in fact provide information of great value. These individuals may be able to provide relevant information for the guilt phase of the trial, information that might connect the defendant to the murder. They could also provide useful information regarding the defendant's background, childhood, and any mental health issues. Once the defendant is charged, the defense will conduct an extensive background of the defendant's life in an effort to avoid the death penalty. In cold cases, having these individuals interviewed *prior* to the filing of charges may provide useful information that can be later used at trial.

- **Interview Other Victims.** In all death penalty cases, it is imperative to locate and interview every person victimized by the defendant who survived encounters with him. These other crimes may be relevant in the guilt phase as evidence of such facts as common modus operandi (M.O.) or intent, and will certainly be relevant during the penalty phase as the jury weighs the appropriate verdict. In cold cases, it is suggested that these witnesses be identified and contacted in person at the earliest possible time. It should be anticipated that this contact may be emotionally traumatic for them.

- **Obtain all Necessary Records.** In preparation for the penalty phase, the prosecution should obtain all records pertaining to the defendant. In cold cases, this can be very challenging given the age of the case and the fact that many businesses or agencies have destroyed records over the years. The following types of records should be obtained, if possible:
  - Prison and jail records
  - School records
  - Employment records
  - Military records
  - Medical records
  - Mental health records
  - Police records

LEGAL ISSUES IN COLD CASES

Several legal issues may be present in cold cases that are rarely seen in other homicide cases, including the following:

1. **John Doe Warrants.** John Doe warrants, which identify the defendants by their physical characteristics rather than by name, are rare, but have been used for over a century. In the California case of *People v. Montoya*, 255 Cal.App.2d 137 (1967), for example, the Court of Appeals said that it was legal to issue a warrant describing the defendant as "John Doe, white male, dark hair, medium build, 30–35."

   With the introduction of DNA tests in criminal cases, John Doe warrants have been revived, with a twist. Instead of providing a physical description of the defendant in a traditional sense, these warrants have spelled out the defendant's "type" at specific genetic locations. This has proved to be a useful tool in preventing the statute of limitations from expiring. The first John Doe DNA warrant was filed in 1999 by Norm Gahn, a prosecutor in the Milwaukee County District Attorney's Office. Since that time, numerous jurisdictions have filed these warrants. Several courts have upheld the use of John Doe DNA warrants reasoning that, while individuals can readily change their identities, names, addresses or even their physical appearances, they cannot change their DNA. Therefore, there is no better way to describe a defendant than by his genetic code.

2. **DNA Admissibility Hearings.** In cold cases that are based primarily on the use of DNA evidence, the defense may challenge the admissibility on the ground that the technology is new or novel. In some jurisdictions, the court must find that such scientific technique

is "generally accepted" in the relevant scientific community.[1] In other jurisdictions, the court must first find that the DNA testing was reliable.[2] Even if these hurdles are overcome, the defense may argue that there are problems with the testing so grave that no jury should hear it. When a cold case is filed, the prosecutor must be aware of the possibility of a pretrial challenge to the DNA evidence. In particular, the defense may challenge the strength of the evidence where a cold hit is made. The prosecution must be prepared for the testimony of expert witnesses retained by the defense.

3. **Evidentiary Issues in Cold Cases.** Cold cases present several potential evidentiary issues for the prosecution. Because these issues may have significant impact on the outcome of the case, the prosecution and investigation team should work closely throughout the investigation and prosecution of the case. The following are potential evidentiary issues that may arise in a cold case:

- **Chain of Custody:** One of the most common concerns in cold case homicides is the chain of custody. In many instances, items of evidence were packaged or stored inappropriately. Additionally, there is often an incomplete log detailing the chain of custody. In some cases, items of evidence were removed from law enforcement's possession without any record of their removal. In other cases, witnesses integral to the chain of custody are unavailable or deceased. While an improper chain of custody should not result in exclusion of evidence, it may present defense claims that the integrity of the evidence has been compromised. Therefore, the prosecution must be prepared to address this with a jury.

- **Loss or Destruction of Evidence:** In many cold cases, evidence may be lost or destroyed. While this presents obvious challenges for the investigator, it also presents challenges for the prosecution. If items of evidence have been destroyed, the defense may seek sanctions against the prosecution, alleging a Due Process violation. In some instances, the defense may seek dismissal of the charges. For the defense to win this motion, however, it must demonstrate that the evidence both possessed an exculpatory value that was apparent before the evidence was destroyed, and be of such a nature that the defendant would be unable to obtain comparable evidence by other reasonably available means.[3] While it is rare that a defendant can succeed in a dismissal of charges on these grounds, both the investigator and prosecutor should be prepared to litigate the motion when it is made.

- **Use of Hypnosis:** In many cold cases, the investigators relied upon hypnosis to develop information from witnesses. While this practice may have aided the investigation, it will create problems for the prosecution in many states. If a prosecutor has hypnosis evidence in his or her case, it is imperative to consult the rules of evidence regarding that evidence. For instance, in California, the testimony of a witness who has been previously hypnotized is limited to events that the witness "recalled and related prior to the hypnotic session."[4] Clearly, the limitations on admissibility of such evidence can have a significant and adverse impact on the prosecution's case.

- **Insufficient Memories of Witnesses:** One of the most common concerns in cold cases is the inability of witnesses to recall the events surrounding the homicide. In most cases, witnesses can refresh their memories by reviewing the statements they gave previously to law enforcement. However, in cold cases, there may be little or no memory left to refresh, and reviewing the police report will do little or no good.

In cases where a witness gave a prior statement to law enforcement but no longer recalls that statement, the contents of the written statement itself may nevertheless be

---

[1] *Frye v. United States,* 293 Fed. 1013 (D.C.Cir. 1923).
[2] *Daubert v. Merrell,* 509 U.S. 579 (1993).
[3] *California v. Trombetta,* 467 U.S. 479 (1984).
[4] *People v. Hayes,* 49 Cal.3d 1260, 1263, 1270–73 (1989).

admissible through an exception to the hearsay rule called "past recollection recorded."[5] Through this exception, the investigator may be allowed to read the witness's statement into evidence if certain factors have been proved. Most notably, if the prosecution can show that the statement of the witness was made at or near the time of the events and the events were still fresh in the witness's mind at the time of the statement, then the statement should be admissible.

The older the case, the more likely that witness memories will fail, and the more likely that the prosecutor will have to rely on the "past recollection recorded" hearsay exception at trial. Investigators must therefore anticipate this issue and determine whether the facts necessary to prove this exception can be met as they meet and reinterview witnesses so that the prosecutor can later prove to the court that all the requirements of this exception have been met.

- **Admissibility of Prior/Post Crimes Evidence.** In many cold cases, the defendant has a criminal history that includes similar crimes that occurred either before or even after the homicide. This type of evidence, particularly in sexually motivated homicide cases, can play a decisive role in the prosecution's case if it demonstrates the defendant's M.O. In some jurisdictions, the prosecution may use evidence of other sexual assaults to demonstrate that the defendant has a propensity to commit such crimes.[6]

  In a cold case prosecution, a complete background investigation of the defendant's criminal behavior, whether reported to law enforcement or not, is vital. This background investigation should not only include reports made to law enforcement but interviews with family and friends of the defendant. In many instances, the defendant may have committed crimes against family or friends but it was never reported to law enforcement.

  The use of prior/post criminal behavior may not only be used during the guilt phase of the prosecution's case but may also play a significant role in the penalty phase of a capital murder case.

4. **Defense Motion to Dismiss for Pre-Complaint Delay.** In many cold cases, years pass before the defendant is ever arrested or charged with the murder. In that time, evidence may have been lost or destroyed, memories have faded and some witnesses may have died.

   A pre-arrest or pre-filing delay in prosecution may constitute a denial of the defendant's right to a fair trial and to due process under the state and federal Constitutions.[7] If the defense moves to dismiss charges for such delay, the court will likely undertake a three-step analysis to determine whether the delay violated the defendant's due process rights to a fair trial: (1) The defendant must show that he has been prejudiced by the delay; (2) if prejudice is established, then the burden shifts to the prosecution to justify the delay; and (3) finally, the court balances the prejudice to the defendant caused by the delay against the justification for that delay.[8] In addition, for the defendant to make a claim of a due process violation under the federal constitution, he must show that the delay was undertaken to gain a tactical advantage over the defendant.[9]

   In cold cases, the prosecution must be prepared for a motion to dismiss for delay in prosecution. The prosecutor should be prepared to present evidence at a pretrial hearing to justify any delay in prosecution. In many cold cases, the prosecutor will need to establish that the charges could not have been filed without the use of new scientific tests. Further, the prosecution may also need to determine whether potential defense witnesses are really unavailable or "material" to the defense. In doing so, the prosecution can demonstrate to the court that the defendant has not been prejudiced by the delay.

---

[5] Federal Rules of Evidence section 803.
[6] California Evidence Code section 1108.
[7] *People v. Caitlin,* 26 Cal.4th 81, 108 (2001); *see also United States v. Marion,* 401 U.S. 307 (2001).
[8] *United States v. Lovasco,* 431 U.S. 783, 789–790 (1977).
[9] *United States v. Lovasco,* 431 U.S. at p. 795 (1977).

DISCOVERY ISSUES IN COLD CASES

The prosecution has a legal and ethical duty to disclose evidence favorable to a defendant.[10] With this ethical obligation, it is imperative that all discovery be provided or made available to the defense once a defendant is charged in a cold case murder. In many cold cases, because of the passage of time, it may be very difficult to find all the documents related to the investigation. In some instances, reports, photographs, or tapes have been lost or destroyed. In some cases, reports were never written at all; rather, notes from the original investigator may be found in the original investigation file.

To comply with the prosecution's obligation under *Brady*, the following suggestions are made:

- **Obtain and copy original "murder" book:** In most cold cases, the police agency maintains an original "murder" book that was the working copy of the homicide detective. While the records maintained in this file should have been given to the police agency's records division, in some instances they were not. It is highly recommended that the prosecutor obtain, review, and copy the original file. This file will oftentimes contain such items as investigator notes, phone logs, suspect lead information, Polaroid photographs, and composites.
- **Record keeping for the Prosecutor:** Cold cases can often involve hundreds, if not thousands of pages of documents. As a result, it is important for the prosecutor to organize these documents for trial in a logical format. In addition to an organized file, it may be helpful for the prosecutor to keep a "master discovery" file that documents exactly what items have been discovered or made available to the defense. This practice will ensure that all discovery obligations have been satisfied.

SENTENCING IN COLD CASES

In cold cases, the defendant will be sentenced according to the law at the time of the crime. Therefore, while a first-degree murder conviction may currently result in a 25 to life sentence, it may be significantly different for a first-degree murder that occurred 25 years ago. Thus, in Penny Parker's murder, if the defendant were convicted of first-degree murder, his resulting sentence would have been 7 years to life.

CONCLUSION

Cold cases are exciting and challenging cases to investigate and prosecute. Law enforcement and prosecutors have an obligation to the families of murder victims to thoroughly investigate and prosecute those responsible for these crimes. With an effective investigation and prosecution, justice, while delayed, will be served.

The advent of DNA testing in particular has revolutionized murder investigations. Not only are more "fresh" murder cases being solved, but cases that have long languished for lack of leads are being resurrected. The window of opportunity to reopen these cold cases, however, is closing; time continues to exact its toll on surviving evidence, witnesses, and memories. At some point, courts will find that further delay in investigating and prosecuting these cases is inexcusable.

Penny Parker's family had to wait a quarter of a century for answers, but in the end, they got them. Through a persistent and thorough investigation, the individual who killed her was identified. After charges were filed and an arrest warrant was issued for him, Penny's murderer committed suicide. With his suicide, a painful chapter in their lives could be closed. Penny mattered to the

---

[10] *Brady v. Maryland,* 373 U.S. 83 (1963).

officers charged with solving her murder and they did not allow her to be forgotten. Today there are thousands of families just like Penny's all over the country. They, too, deserve answers.

ACKNOWLEDGMENTS

I wish to acknowledge and express my gratitude to Deputy District Attorney Anne Marie Schubert of the Sacramento County, California, District Attorney's Office for authoring this chapter. Ms. Schubert is a veteran cold case homicide prosecutor with this office, and was a founding member of the Cold Case Homicide Training Program at the California Department of Justice Advanced Training Center. This program teams experienced homicide investigative, prosecution, laboratory, and behavioral personnel to review unsolved homicide cases presented by the case investigator in a classroom atmosphere. She has presented on the topic of cold case investigation and prosecution to numerous venues, including national prosecutors conferences. In addition, Ms. Schubert wishes to acknowledge and extend her gratitude and recognition to Assistant Chief Deputy Jeff Rose and Principal Criminal Attorney Eric Kindall for their contributions and review of this chapter.

6 Databases: ViCAP, HITS, and TracKRS

Richard H. Walton

CONTENTS

Due in large part to the political and local diversification of American law enforcement agencies, communication and information sharing have historically been cumbersome and inefficient. Nowhere has this been more illustrated on occasion than in the field of homicide investigation, as agencies sometimes labored to solve homicides, unaware that perhaps their information held the key to solving a murder in another jurisdiction. Or vice versa.

This chapter presents means and methods utilized to assist in the identification of related homicides through different levels of databases and increased information technology dedicated to identifying and comparing homicides, sexual assaults, and methods of operation. This chapter presents three examples of databases that have proven useful in the investigation of homicide and cold case homicides. These are the national Violent Criminal Apprehension Program (ViCAP), the Washington State Homicide Investigation and Tracking System (HITS), and the Orange County, California, Taskforce Aimed at Catching Killers, Rapists, and Sexual Offenders (TracKRS) programs.

ViCAP

THE BEGINNINGS

ViCAP originated from an idea by local law enforcement and the late Pierce R. Brooks. As a detective for the Los Angeles, California, Police Department in 1956, Detective Brooks investigated the murders of two Los Angeles women who had replied to an advertisement for photographic models. Their bodies, tied with rope in such a way as to suggest that their killer practiced bondage, were later found in the desert. Detective Brooks believed that these victims were not the killer's first murders. For 18 months he used his off-duty time to visit the Los Angeles central library and read out-of-town newspapers to look for information on murders that exhibited characteristics similar to those he was investigating. He found such an article in a newspaper, and using pieces from that case coupled with his own cases, arrested an individual who was subsequently tried, convicted, and executed for the murders.

Detective Brooks refined this idea and concluded that a computer could capture relevant information about murders. If information on both open and closed cases were stored in a computer, investigators could query the database for similar cases when confronted with new homicide investigations. In this manner, they could use clues from other cases that exhibited similar characteristics, and in turn, solve more cases. In addition, when investigators identified offenders, a search of the computer using their modus operandi (M.O.) would reveal other open cases for which they might be responsible.

In 1983, the Office of Juvenile Justice and Delinquency Prevention and the National Institute of Justice awarded a planning grant, the "National Missing/Abducted Children and Serial Murder Tracking and Prevention Program" to Sam Houston State University in Texas. From a series of workshops, the last in November, 1983, emerged the National Center for the Analysis of Violent Crime (NCAVC). Initial funding was provided by the U.S. Department of Justice, and the program was established under the direction and control of the FBI training center at Quantico, Virginia.

The NCAVC was specifically authorized to maintain a computer-assisted national clearinghouse for the analysis of violent crimes with specific interest in murder, rape, child sexual abuse, arson, and bombings. ViCAP is authorized by 28 USC 534 to collect, classify, analyze and preserve records on violent crimes and their offenders. ViCAP is a *confidential* system that is exempt under the provisions of the Privacy Act.

The NCAVC is a law enforcement-oriented behavioral science and data analysis center designed to consolidate research, training, and investigative/operational support functions for the purpose of providing expertise to law enforcement agencies confronted with unusual, bizarre and/or repetitive violent crime. This assistance is provided without charge to Federal, state, local and foreign law enforcement agencies. The NCAVC reviews crimes from both a behavioral and investigative perspective.

ViCAP was implemented at the FBI Academy on June 1, 1985, with the goal of identifying cases exhibiting similar characteristics, and providing that information to law enforcement to facilitate cooperation and communication, enhance investigative coordination, and close cases (see Figure 6.1). This goal has remained unchanged and the unit today seeks to provide support to law enforcement efforts to investigate, identify, track, apprehend, and prosecute violent serial offenders.

FIGURE 6.1 *FBI Law Enforcement Bulletin* cover December 1986. (Author's collection)

Pierce Brooks became the unit's first program manager. In its early stages, ViCAP became a part of the NCAVC, with its goal to collect and analyze information, whether or not the offender was identified or arrested, regarding:

- Solved or unsolved homicides or attempts, especially those that:
- Involved an abduction.
- Were apparently random, motiveless, or sexually oriented.
- Were known or suspected to be part of a series.
- Missing person, where the circumstances indicated a strong possibility of foul play and the victim was still missing.
- Unidentified dead bodies, where the manner of death was known or suspected to be homicide.

In cases where the offender had been arrested or identified, ViCAP requested that these cases be submitted so that unsolved cases in the ViCAP system could be linked to known offenders. Unfortunately, this was not always done. Cold case investigators, during the course of file or case review, should attempt to identify whether the case has previously been submitted to ViCAP. This report may assist the investigator in understanding what was known at the time and provide an overview of the case. If the case was never submitted to ViCAP, it is recommended that the case be submitted now.

Cases where the offender has been arrested or identified should be submitted so unsolved cases in the ViCAP system can be compared with known offenders.

The early ViCAP reporting forms (see Figure 6.2) utilized 189 questions in areas including:

- Case administration
- Victim information
- Offender information
- Identified offender information
- Vehicle description
- Offense M.O.
- Condition of victim when found
- Cause of death and/or trauma
- Forensic evidence
- Request for profile
- Other related cases
- Narrative summary

In 1994, the FBI created the Critical Incident Response Group (CIRG) to facilitate a rapid response to, and management of, crisis incidents. The CIRG is composed of three major areas:

- Operations Support Branch
- Tactical Support Branch
- NCAVC

The NCAVC is organized into components. These are:

- ViCAP
- Behavioral Analysis Unit (BAU)
  - BAU-1 (Terrorism/Threat Assessment)
  - BAU-2 (Crimes against Adults)
  - BAU-3: (Crimes against Children)

FD-676 (Rev. 3-22-91)
OMB No. 1110-0011

U.S. Department of Justice
Federal Bureau of Investigation

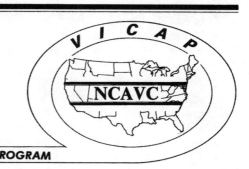

VIOLENT   CRIMINAL   APPREHENSION   PROGRAM

VICAP

Crime Analysis Report

NATIONAL   CENTER   FOR   THE   ANALYSIS   OF   VIOLENT   CRIME

FIGURE 6.2 Early ViCAP cover. (Courtesy of FBI)

THE NEW ViCAP

In the mid 1990s, a business review revealed that:

- On average, only 3% to 7% of the total numbers of annual homicides were being reported to ViCAP.
- Urban law enforcement agencies were not contributing their homicide data to the ViCAP database.
- Users were reporting that the 189-question ViCAP form was cumbersome and difficult.
- Users perceived that ViCAP case submissions entered a bureaucratic "black hole" never to emerge or be seen again.
- Chronic understaffing caused a failure to address incoming casework on a timely basis.

From this business review and legislative direction from Congress, changes were made in ViCAP to enhance user friendliness and agency utilization of this resource. Computers and software were provided to local and state law enforcement agencies under a memorandum of understanding (MOU). In this process, the system moved from a mainframe environment to an affordable client-server environment. In addition, the 189-question form was redesigned to 95 questions. To increase response time to incoming work and requests, the numbers of analyst personnel were increased. A number of these personnel have prior law enforcement experience. As a result of the system rework, ViCAP gave its new software and program a new name: the New ViCAP.

How It Works

The FBI provides the software, free of charge, to state and local law enforcement agencies to set up the ViCAP database. Some agencies run the New ViCAP system in their own departments, while others prefer to run it on a stand-alone desktop. Several put the software on their internal network. Agency networks support as few as three users, through the entire investigative staff, and up to five different boroughs and the precincts therein. New ViCAP software operating in participating agencies allows direct access to all the information they enter and offers the ability to perform their own crime analysis.

The architecture of the system varies according to the needs of its users. For instance, some states utilize a "hub-and-spoke" design. By this system, MOUs are created between a centralized, often state agency, and cities and counties within the state. Cases can be entered at the local level and uploaded to the state. Other states have implemented a regional system, whereas a larger sheriff's or police department serves as the collection point and analysis hub for cases within their county. This serves to provide a web of case-sharing information for participating law enforcement entities.

Cold case squads or investigators can store their cases without resorting to large volumes of file cabinets. With minimal information, a nickname, an address, or the name of a bar or other business, investigators can retrieve decades-old cases for further investigation. Conversely, cold case investigators looking for cases exhibiting an M.O. used by a suspect, or a series of cases matching a particular M,O., can make those searches as well.

Whatever their age, cold cases should be submitted to ViCAP today.

Standard reports include:

- Cases by day of the week, month, or district
- Case status (open or closed)
- Causative factors
- Offender age or ethnicity
- Victim age or ethnicity
- Victim-offender relationship
- All weapons used or firearms used by caliber and type

FD-676 (Rev. 4-1-98)
OMB No. 1110-0011

U.S. Department of Justice
Federal Bureau of Investigation

Crime Analysis Report

National Center for the Analysis of Violent Crime

800-634-4097

FIGURE 6.3 Later ViCap Cover. (Courtesy of FBI)

    This format utilizes a one-page New ViCAP summary report (see Figure 6.3). This document collects the main facts from a violent crime and prints them to the screen, or typically, two sheets of paper. The summary report proves an excellent briefing tool for administrators, managers, or elected officials. To overcome concerns regarding electronic storage and attendant security, the New ViCAP also provides a hard copy. This multipage report prints on screen or on paper and includes all of the information entered into the database. The printed document can be placed in the case folder or jacket and preserved indefinitely.

Unique cases require distinctive database queries. To provide for discrete, particular questions of the database, the program has a powerful ad hoc query tool, whereby any combination of New ViCAP variables and attributes can be strung together to produce a set of possibly related cases. Refinement of the ad hoc query produces more, or fewer, cases delivered to the crime analyst through the possibilities set. When the listing of cases is returned, the crime analyst can contrast and compare them in a matrix of variables specified by the analyst. Particularly valuable case matrixes can be titled and printed for more formal presentations, such as multi-agency case meetings. The ad hoc query and resulting matrix analysis prove a very powerful combination of tools for any analyst examining violent crime.

ViCAP Crime Analysis Report

The purpose of the ViCAP Crime Analysis Report is to collect data for analyses that will lead to the identification of patterns of violent crime throughout the county. Completion of the report and submission of cases is voluntary. Like any other database, however, it can only be as efficient as the data that is input into the system. A single report received and analyzed by the ViCAP staff could initiate a coordinated effort among numerous law enforcement agencies, perhaps hundreds or thousands of miles apart, to expedite identification and solution of one or more violent crimes.

Cases meeting ViCAP submission criteria with an arrested or *identified* offender can be entered into the ViCAP system by law enforcement investigators for comparison within the database to unsolved cases. Cases with an *unidentified* offender may also be submitted for database comparison.

Once a case is entered into the ViCAP database, it is continuously compared against all other entries based upon certain aspects of the crime. The purpose of this process is to detect signature aspects or traits of homicide and similar patterns of M.O., which in turn may allow ViCAP personnel to pinpoint those crimes that have been committed by the same offender. When such patterns are identified, involved law enforcement agencies will be notified to pursue the information for potential lead value.

When a pattern of criminal activity is discovered, ViCAP can assist law enforcement agencies by coordinating a multi-agency investigative conference for case review. This may become especially important when suspect(s) travel throughout the country. The discovery of such a pattern enhances:

- Information sharing
- Coordination of activities such as interview topics that might link cases
- Successful interview and interrogation techniques
- Specific evidence to be identified in search warrants
- Unique or specialty laboratory tests to be conducted

In addition, ViCAP also offers other investigative support services, including:

- Timelines
- NCIC offline searches
- NLETS searches
- Investigative matrix
- Case consultation, coordination, facilitation, and training in crime analysis

ViCAP Submission Criteria

- Solved or unsolved homicides or attempted homicides. Especially those that involve (1) an abduction; (2) are apparently random, motiveless, or sexually oriented; or (3) are known or suspected to be part of a series.

- Missing persons or kidnappings where the circumstances indicate a strong possibility of foul play and the victim is still missing.
- Unidentified dead bodies where the manner of death is known or suspected to be homicide.

The New ViCAP report forms encompass information that may or may not be present in cold case files. In this regard, this report may serve as a model or format for information to be sought by cold case investigators (see Figure 6.4).

ViCAP REPORT COMPONENTS

The New ViCAP report utilizes a series of 93 questions with multiple-selection information to provide a detailed overview of the known elements of the crime and the persons involved. In addition, the report addresses two additional narrative-summary questions and hold-back material, or information not to be released to the public. These headings are grouped as follows:

- Administrative
  - Case administration details including case numbers, personnel, etc.
- Victim Information
  - Case type (murder, attempted murder, etc.)
  - Probable crime type (financial gain, revenge, robbery, etc.)
  - Personal identifying information (aliases, addresses, sex, race, DOB, physical description, etc.)
  - Legal or illegal occupation(s)
  - Lifestyle
- Missing and Unidentified Victims
  - Physical descriptions
  - Scars, marks, tattoos
  - Clothing, jewelry, glasses, etc.
- Offender or Suspect Information
  - Known or unknown
  - Life status
  - Aliases or nicknames, addresses
  - Social Security Number (SSN), other SSNs used, FBI number
  - Race and gender
  - Date of birth (DOB) or other DOBs used
  - Physical
  - Hair description
  - Scars, marks, tattoos, or other features
  - Use of disguise or mask
- Identified Offender Information
  - Detailed dates or time of address, employment, locations of offender
  - General lifestyle
  - Relationship to victim
- Offender's M.O. (see Figure 6.5)
  - Offender's Approach to Victim
    - Unknown
    - Deception or con
    - Surprise
    - Blitz
    - Other
    - Victim's activity if relevant

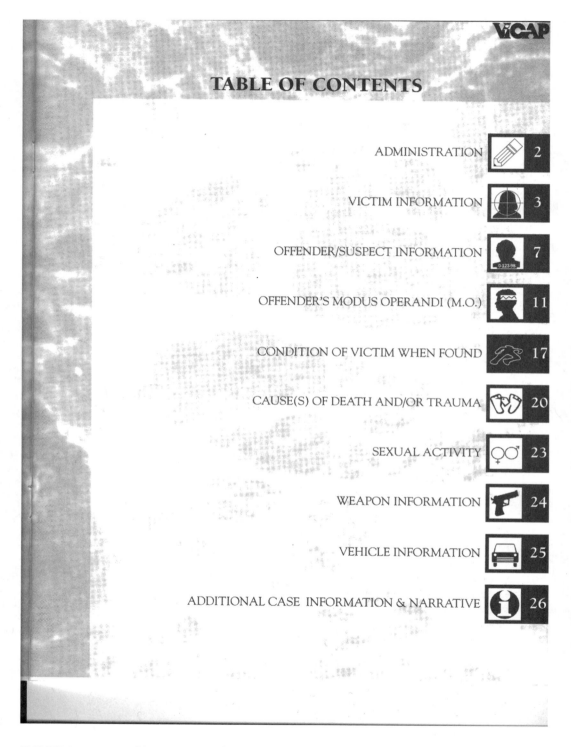

FIGURE 6.4 ViCAP table of Contents with Report components. (Courtesy of FBI)

OFFENDER'S MODUS OPERANDI (M.O.)
OFFENDER'S APPROACH TO VICTIM

54. The offender's initial approach to the victim was (check all that apply):

☐ **Unknown Approach**
☐ By **Deception or Con:**

    ☐ Posed as Authority Figure/Police Officer
    ☐ Posed as Business Person/Customer
    ☐ Asked Victim to Model/Pose for Photos
    ☐ Offered Job, Money, Treats or Toys
    ☐ Implied Family Emergency or Illness
    ☐ Wanted to Show Something
    ☐ Asked For/Offered Assistance
    ☐ Caused/Staged Traffic Accident
    ☐ Solicited for Sex
    ☐ Offered Ride/Transportation
    ☐ Placed or Responded to Advertising
    ☐ Third Person Used to Lure Victim
    ☐ Other Deception/Con (describe) _____

☐ By **Surprise:**

    ☐ Lay in Wait - Out of Doors
    ☐ Lay in Wait - In Building
    ☐ Lay in Wait - In Vehicle
    ☐ Victim Sleeping
    ☐ Other Surprise (describe) _____

☐ By **Blitz** - Direct and immediate physical assault:

    ☐ Physically Overpowered Victim (picked up, carried away, etc.)
    ☐ Hit Victim with Hand, Fist or Clubbing Weapon
    ☐ Choked Victim
    ☐ Stabbed Victim
    ☐ Shot Victim
    ☐ Other Blitz/Assault (describe) _____

☐ **Other** Approach (describe) _____

55. **If relevant to the crime** describe victim's activity at the time of the initial contact between the offender and the victim, or when the victim was last seen alive prior to incident (check all that apply):

☐ Going to/from residence
☐ Going to/from school
☐ Going to/from work
☐ Jogging/Bicycling/Walking
☐ Hitchhiking
☐ On a date
☐ Prostituting
☐ Hunting/Camping/Fishing
☐ Other (describe) _____
☐ Unknown

12

FIGURE 6.5 ViCAP report Offender Approach to Victim. (Courtesy of FBI)

- Dates and Exact Geographic Locations
  - Victim last seen alive
  - Initial contact
  - Murder/assault
  - Victim/Body recovered
- Specific Locations for Event Sites
  - Unknown
  - Living Quarters
  - Business
  - Transportation
  - Entertainment
  - Public/Other Buildings
  - Outdoor Locations
  - Water Locations
- Events at Crime Scene(s)
  - Alterations of crime scenes
  - Alterations or drawings on victim's body
  - Indications of symbolic or unusual acts or things
- Condition of Victim When Found
  - Body Disposition
    - Conditions, events, and circumstances
  - Restraints Used on Victim (see Figure 6.6)
    - Types of restraints
    - Body parts bound
    - Bindings selection
    - Bindings recovery
  - Clothing and Property of Victim
    - Stages of dress or undress
    - Indicators of re-dress
    - Indicators of victim clothing intentionally ripped, torn, or cut
    - Indicators of items of victim taken by offender
- Cause(s) of Death or Trauma
  - Cause of death/trauma
  - Official cause of death
  - Additional trauma
  - Number of wounds
  - Major trauma locations
  - Range of gunfire
  - Extent of blunt force trauma
  - Elements of unusual or additional assault, trauma or torture to victim
  - Body parts removed by offender
- Sexual Activity
  - Evidence of sexual activity or attempted sexual activity with the victim
  - Type of sexual activity or attempt
  - Body Location
  - Foreign Objects
  - Not in or on body when found
- Weapon Information
  - Use or threat of weapon
  - Weapon type
  - Weapon selection

RESTRAINTS USED ON VICTIM

72a. At any time was the victim bound?

❑ Yes   ❑ No   ❑ Unknown

72b. If yes, indicate the articles used, parts of body bound, whether binding(s) were brought to scene or found at scene by offender, and whether bindings were left at scene or taken from scene by offender.

ARTICLE USED TO BIND	PARTS OF THE BODY BOUND						BINDINGS SELECTION			BINDINGS RECOVERY		
	Hands, Wrists, or Arms	Feet, Ankles, or Legs	Hands Bound to Feet	Arms Bound to Torso	Other (describe in Item 94)	Unknown	Brought to Scene by Offender	Found at Scene by Offender	Unknown if Brought or Found	Left on Victim's Body	Left at Scene (NOT on Victim)	Taken From Scene
Chain	☐	☐	☐	☐	☐	☐	☐	☐	☐	☐	☐	☐
Clothing (describe)	☐	☐	☐	☐	☐	☐	☐	☐	☐	☐	☐	☐
Flexcuffs/ Plastic Ties	☐	☐	☐	☐	☐	☐	☐	☐	☐	☐	☐	☐
Handcuffs	☐	☐	☐	☐	☐	☐	☐	☐	☐	☐	☐	☐
Rope/Cordage (describe)	☐	☐	☐	☐	☐	☐	☐	☐	☐	☐	☐	☐
Tape (describe)	☐	☐	☐	☐	☐	☐	☐	☐	☐	☐	☐	☐
Linens (describe)	☐	☐	☐	☐	☐	☐	☐	☐	☐	☐	☐	☐
Telephone/ Electrical Cord	☐	☐	☐	☐	☐	☐	☐	☐	☐	☐	☐	☐
Wire (Non-electrical)	☐	☐	☐	☐	☐	☐	☐	☐	☐	☐	☐	☐
Other (describe)	☐	☐	☐	☐	☐	☐	☐	☐	☐	☐	☐	☐
Unknown	☐	☐	☐	☐	☐	☐	☐	☐	☐	☐	☐	☐

73. At any time was the victim tied to another object?

❑ Yes (describe) _____
❑ No
❑ Unknown

74. At any time was a gag placed in or on the victim's mouth or throat?

❑ Yes (describe) _____
❑ No
❑ Unknown

75. At any time was a blindfold placed on or over the victim's eyes?

❑ Yes (describe) _____
❑ No
❑ Unknown

18

FIGURE 6.6 ViCAP page showing information regarding restraints. (Courtesy of FBI)

- Weapon recovery
- Firearm
  - Type
  - Make
  - Caliber or gauge
  - Rifling twist or pellet size
- Vehicle Information
  - Known or unknown
  - Victim control
  - Stolen or recovered
  - License and ID
  - Make, model, year
  - Body style
  - Color
  - Distinctive features
- Additional Case Information
  - DNA/CODIS
  - Latent prints
  - Projectiles or casings
  - Knowledge or awareness of additional cases involving offender
- Narrative Summary
- Hold-Back Information

FUTURE DEVELOPMENTS AND TECHNOLOGY

SEXUAL ASSAULT DATA COLLECTION AND OTHER DEVELOPMENTS

ViCAP is currently working on a crime analysis tool for sexual assaults and designing data collection that mirrors the existing homicide-oriented form. In addition, the New ViCAP has an ability to store images and to associate them with a specific case. The images can be photographs scanned into the system or maps or other graphics imported into the system. This tool has important implications for training new investigators, refreshing case-specific recollections of experienced investigators, or exchanging precise information to identify unknown victims.

An envisioned tool, currently in the mapping stage, is a mapping capability that could be used for traditional pin maps. Alternately, investigators could use GIS (a computer technology that uses a geographic information system as an analytic framework for managing and integrating data; solving a problem; or understanding a past, present, or future situation) data to store and search offender timelines like those prepared for suspected or known serial killers. Once offender timelines are stored, GIS data for each newly entered case could be automatically compared with the timelines. For example, an automated hit system could report to the analyst that plus or minus 3 days (any arbitrary time period could be programmed), a killer was in the town where the murder occurred.

CASE HISTORY — BAG OF BONES

The following is reproduced from the June, 2003, issue of the *FBI Law Enforcement Bulletin*.

In 2001, a ViCAP crime analyst reviewed a state police publication that mentioned a bag of human bones found by hunters in a seaboard forest of an eastern state. The victim was a white male, about 40 to 60 years old, and between 5'7" and 5'9" in height. His cause of death was blunt-force trauma to the head. Recovered with the remains was a 14-carat-gold ring with engraved letters. Authorities had no leads for identification of the remains.

A ViCAP crime analyst searched the database using the physical description of the victim and then made an additional search, thinking that the letters engraved in the ring might be the initials of a name. A possible match was made with a July 1998 case where three people were reported missing from a Midwestern state. The report was made by a fourth member of the family, a son, who waited a week before reporting his mother, father, and sibling as missing persons. Personnel had exhausted all investigative leads.

Authorities in the eastern and Midwestern states contacted each other. In January, 2001, ViCAP learned that forensic odontology had identified the bones in the bag as those of the father missing from the Midwestern state. The letters in the recovered ring represented the maiden name of the missing mother and the name of the missing father.

ViCAP learned later that a suspect had been identified and charged with the murder — the oldest son who had made the report in the Midwest. The remains of his mother and his sibling have not been located.

ViCAP ALERT

The monthly *FBI Law Enforcement Bulletin* publishes this feature to alert law enforcement agencies of solved and unsolved homicides and other cases inclusive within the ViCAP system (see Figure 6.7). This alert is prepared at the request of the law enforcement agency, and provides the agency name, location, and telephone number of a contact person. Information is further disseminated through the Law Enforcement ON-Line Newsletter (www.fbi.gov/hq/isd/cirg/ncavc.htm) and other media. These notices typically address (1) offender descriptive data; (2) crime(s); (3) background; (4) M.O.; and (5) maps showing travel. In addition, photographs or composites of the offender and vehicles are broadcast when possible.

This discussion of the New ViCAP was reproduced in detail from "The New ViCAP," an article by Eric W. Witzig, M.S. that appeared in the June, 2003, issue of the *FBI Law Enforcement Bulletin*, pp. 1–7. Witzig is a former detective in the Homicide Branch of the Washington, D.C. Metropolitan Police Department and agent of the chief medical examiner for Washington, D.C. He is a major case specialist with the FBI's ViCAP. Other material was drawn from documents provided by the FBI. I wish to acknowledge and express my gratitude and appreciation to Crime Analyst Jane Whitmore for her gracious assistance in review and commentary for this segment.

For Further Information:
Critical Incident Response Group
FBI Academy
Quantico, Virginia, 22135
703-632-44 00

THE HOMICIDE INVESTIGATION AND TRACKING SYSTEM (HITS)

Washington State's HITS system relies on law enforcement agencies to voluntarily submit information to HITS investigators on murders, attempted murders, missing-persons cases in which foul play is suspected, unidentified persons believed to be murder victims, and predatory sex offenses. Detectives conducting investigations need methods and tools that will help them do their jobs as effectively and efficiently as possible. Ready access to information about the crimes being investigated is one of their needs. This information is crucial to developing good leads and in turn to solving the case.

HITS was developed by Robert D. Keppel, Ph.D., who started the program in Washington State. HITS is helping investigators work better by allowing them access via computer to a wide range of information about serious crimes and to resources that can help solve them.

Basically, HITS is a murder- and sexual-assault-investigation system that collects, collates, and analyzes the salient characteristics of all murders and predatory sexual offenses in the states of

ViCAP Alert

Attention: Homicide and Robbery Units

Unsolved Homicides/Robberies

The St. Charles, Missouri, Police Department requests assistance in an investigation of a series of unsolved commercial homicide/robberies that occurred in the spring of 1992. A lone white male entered strip mall stores near Interstate 70 in several states, shot the employees, and robbed the stores. All of the victims were females, except for one male with long hair whose appearance might have suggested the presence of a female. Firearms evidence was recovered at each location. These murders became known as the Interstate 70 Series because of their close proximity to that route.

Crime Scenes

The suspect appeared comfortable traveling long distances along Interstate 70 and selected victims in strip mall stores, several of which were only a few miles from other interstates as well. The homicides occurred in Indianapolis and Terre Haute, Indiana; St. Charles City and Raytown, Missouri; and Wichita, Kansas. The offender entered stores that had the appearance of possibly being operated by women (e.g., shoe, ceramic, and bridal shops). From April 8, 1992 to May 7, 1992, he killed six individuals on five separate occasions by shooting each of the victims in the head.

Firearms evidence from the six victims and five scenes was compared. Examination of this evidence revealed that the same firearm was used at all five scenes. Bullets recovered from the scenes were .22 caliber and exhibited marks consistent with having been fired from a barrel rifled with eight lands and grooves, right-hand twist. Casings from a .22 caliber also were recovered.

Possible Suspect Information

Witnesses described the suspect as a white male, about 5' 7" in height. At the time of the attacks, he was between 32 and 37 years of age, with blonde, red, or brown hair.

Alert to Law Enforcement

Law enforcement agencies should bring this information to the attention of all crime analysis personnel and officers investigating homicides or crimes against persons and robberies. Any agency with solved or unsolved cases similar to these should contact Detective Rich A. Plummer of the St. Charles, Missouri, Police Department at 636-949-3320, Special Agent Ann C. Pancoast of the FBI's St. Louis Division at 314-589-2540, or Major Case Specialist Eric W. Witzig of the Violent Criminal Apprehension Program (ViCAP) Unit at 703-632-4194. ✦

Agencies that have a case exhibiting similar modus operandi, even if the case is not a homicide, should contact the St. Charles, Missouri, Police Department at 636-949-3320.

FIGURE 6.7 ViCAP Alert. (Courtesy of FBI)

Washington and Oregon. The National Institute of Justice (NIJ), the research arm of the Department of Justice, played a key role in the development of this project. This same organization encouraged Pierce Brooks in the 1970s to pursue ViCAP, which was originally designed to provide local law enforcement access. HITS complements Federal research and programs against violent crime because the system generates a ViCAP report that is sent to the National Center for the Analysis of Violent Crime. ViCAP staff can then determine whether the similar pattern characteristics exist among the individual cases in the ViCAP system.

HITS provides three major services to law enforcement agencies. First, it supplies information related to a murder or predatory sexual assault case, including the following:

- Incidents with similar characteristics involving murder, attempted murder, suspected murder, or predatory sexual assault and persons missing as a result of suspected foul play.
- Evidence, victimology, offender characteristics, offender's method of operation, associates, geographical location of the case, weapons and vehicles.
- Identification of known murderers and sex offenders living in a particular community.

Second, HITS permits analysis of murder cases to identify:

- Factors that may help solve a particular murder case.
- Possible links between a single victim, offender, or case and other incidents of violence.
- Verification of statements provided by informants, offenders, or both, in which the information relating to an alleged murder is incomplete or questionable.

Third, HITS provides investigators with the following resources:

- Names of experts who can assist with a murder or sexual assault investigation.
- Advice and technical assistance on the various steps to be followed in a murder or sexual-assault investigation.

Prior to HITS use in Washington, the only way to obtain this type of crime information was through time-consuming, labor-intensive personal visits, interviews, telephone calls, teletypes, and mail. By filling out a simple form that takes less than 30 minutes, investigators save countless hours on the phone or on their feet searching for information that the HITS system locates for them. More importantly, HITS provides investigators with that important two-way communication.

HITS was founded on the premise that information plays a critical role in solving homicides. The key to solving crimes and making arrests is to understand how much and what kind of information is available and how to organize it to make it more accessible and useful. Because of the need to collect and collate violent crime information, HITS investigators and analysts work very closely with police detectives to provide assistance in their cases.

In the opinion of expert homicide investigator Vernon Geberth, the most viable alternative to ViCAP is a series of statewide or regional systems that compile all serious crimes such as rape, murder, and gang-related crime into integrated databases that provide ready access to local law enforcement. In addition, any missing-persons cases where the circumstances indicate that they are missing under suspicious circumstances, as well as unidentified bodies where the manner of death is known or suspected to be homicidal in nature should be entered into the system.

This discussion on the HITS program is reprinted with permission from Vernon Geberth and is taken from his benchmark homicide investigation textbook, *Practical Homicide Investigation: Tactics, Procedures, and Forensic Techniques, Third Edition* (published by CRC Press). Mr. Geberth is a retired Lieutenant Commander of Homicide for the NYPD and is renowned worldwide for his experience and expertise in this field. The first edition of this textbook was proclaimed "The Bible" by experts in the field of homicide investigations. Mr. Geberth is an accomplished writer and lecturer on the myriad of subjects encompassed under the umbrella of homicide investigation. In addition, this book is the outgrowth of a vision by

Vernon, a man who has enriched the law enforcement profession with his standards as well as accomplishments.

TASKFORCE REVIEW AIMED AT CATCHING KILLERS, RAPISTS AND SEXUAL OFFENDERS (TracKRS)

Investigator Ronald Shave (Retired)
Orange County, California, District Attorney's Office

In 1996 the Orange County, California, District Attorney's Office recognized that there were approximately 1,000 unsolved murders in the county and that efforts to link cases were fragmented due to rotations, retirements, promotions, and a lack of central information. The office believed that legislation, DNA science, and technology existed that could be better utilized if local law enforcement united to organize those resources. The District Attorney accepted that leadership role and responsibility.

In March 1997 the District Attorney proposed the TracKRS's Project to the Orange County Chiefs of Police and Sheriff's Office, and it was adopted unanimously. The TracKRS Unit would provide investigators access to a central M.O. database of homicide and sexual assault cases and offer a problem-solving team to assist local investigators.

Purpose of TracKRS

The Orange County District Attorney is committed to helping protect the community by providing the best available resources for investigators to obtain the highest yield from their efforts. Our premise is that "if you give good investigators good resources, you will get good results."

The Scope of TracKRS

The heart of TracKRS is an information system available to investigators from their desktop computers via a secure Internet site maintained by the District Attorney (see Figure 6.8). The TracKRS Unit has focused on providing resources to help in the investigation of our community's worst crimes, homicides, and sexual assaults. The unit identifies what investigators need, establishes a plan, and seeks to provide the solutions. It is flexible and responsive.

The TracKRS Review Committee is the team that helps the TracKRS Unit identify the problems and set priorities. The committee consists of police investigators, crime analysts, criminalists, forensic technicians, fingerprint experts, Deputy District Attorneys, District Attorney's Investigators, and other experts willing to help TracKRS identify the roadblocks that interfere with homicide and sexual assault investigations. Solutions, in light of available resources, are recommended. The TracKRS Unit implements the solution.

The team meets quarterly and any law enforcement person is welcome to attend.

Why Homicides and Sexual Assaults?

There are several reasons TracKRS has targeted homicide and sexual assault cases. The obvious is that these crimes exact a huge toll on the victims and their families, and the implications to the community are enormous. But there are also very sound statistics, technologies, and legislation that have prompted our focus.

Statistically, sexual offenders repeat their crimes. The FBI reports that if you have identified a felony sexual assault offender, he is likely to have committed 5.2 other sexual assaults he will never be linked to. If you have identified a sexual killer, the offender has a 94% chance of having had a prior felony sexual assault conviction.

For instance, if you have an unsolved sexual murder, you are likely to have a conviction of the suspect in a case with similarities. This knowledge has helped law enforcement personnel to better

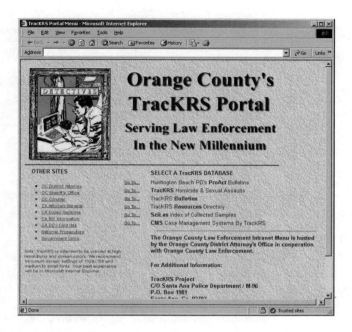

FIGURE 6.8 Orange County TracKRS Portal. (Courtesy of Investigator Ron Shave, Orange County District Attorney's Office, retired)

focus their work on cases that will improve results. However, the necessary computer technology and data must be available to the investigator to achieve better results. Fortunately, TracKRS has the technology and has made it available to local investigators, enabling them to link evidence, characteristics of a crime, and offender's M.O. and signature.

DNA technology has improved dramatically since the inception of the TracKRS Unit. DNA examinations that once took weeks can now be performed in days, if not hours. Examinations that once required a substantial amount of sample can now be performed on microscopic cells. Also, the federal, state, and Sheriff's crime labs are now using compatible DNA standards for comparison. Additionally, new legislation permits law enforcement to collect samples from previous offenders.

Each new component alone does not solve cases. They are additional tools available to Orange County investigators, and cooperation and coordination can dramatically improve their results.

The Los Angeles Times reported on April 16, 2001: "A string of arrests in old murder cases has catapulted Orange County from worst to first when it comes to solving homicides in Southern California ... Wheelock's case also underscores a dramatic improvement by investigators in Orange County, which a decade ago posted the region's worst record in clearing homicides."

This "dramatic turnaround" since TracKRS was implemented in 1997 is a direct result of an overwhelming team effort supported by Orange County administrators. The Sheriff's Crime Lab has committed extensive resources, as well as its cold case unit, C.L.U.E. Many cities have supported the reviews of cold cases and the California cities of Santa Ana, Garden Grove, Anaheim, Costa Mesa, and Newport Beach, among others, have committed investigators solely to cold case investigations.

TracKRS Development

The effort to develop the TracKRS Unit was to provide local investigators with a database of homicides and sexual assault cases that they could research themselves. In March of 1997, every Orange County chief and the Orange County Sheriff agreed to support the project by providing

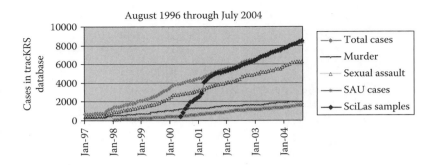

FIGURE 6.9 (See color insert following p. 216.) Graph: Cases in TracKRS Database August 1996-2004. (Courtesy of Investigator Ron Shave, Orange County District Attorney's Office, retired)

their cases for input into the TracKRS M.O. database. The District Attorney's Office began entering the descriptions of previously prosecuted offenders to support our premise that those offenders are likely often responsible for unsolved cases. The database was designed with the investigator in mind. Queries are simple and the response is immediate.

Today, the TracKRS information system contains nearly 8,800 murders and sexual assault cases going back to 1960. TracKRS has been aggressively collecting the case information investigators need to link cases (see Figure 6.9).

TracKRS has also provided a more efficient means of sharing information. The bulletin's database gives investigators the ability to immediately post online any information they believe will be able to help other investigators. This bulletin remains available and will not be deleted. Think of it as a permanent teletype (see Figure 6.10).

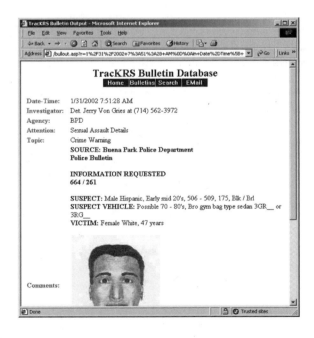

FIGURE 6.10 TracKRS Bulletin Database. (Courtesy of Investigator Ron Shave, Orange County District Attorney's Office, retired)

FIGURE 6.11 TracKRS Project Resource Menu. (Courtesy of Investigator Ron Shave, Orange County District Attorney's Office, retired)

The Resource Directory is similar to an online phone book of investigators and other experts in the law enforcement community (see Figure 6.11).

TracKRS has over 350 authorized investigators who have access to data 24 hours a day, 7 days a week, from their desktop computers over a secure Internet connection.

PROJECTS INVOLVING TracKRS

COLD CASE REVIEWS

Cold case reviews and collecting the case information for the database have been TracKRS' most difficult challenges. Investigators often have too much responsibility on current caseloads to take time out to review cold cases. In response, TracKRS has employed retired investigators to help review cold cases and get the information online. During those reviews, observations are made as to what evidence may benefit from new technology. Since inception, more than 30 murder cases have been identified with what is likely suspect DNA and more than 20 cases have had Cal-ID (an automated fingerprint identification system) fingerprint hits on prints previously entered into Cal-ID. Additionally, TracKRS does the data entry and the local investigator gets an online case summary that is available to all new investigators and supervisors that may rotate through the office.

To help with the collection of current case information, most agencies have provided TracKRS with a liaison officer. That person ensures that TracKRS is provided with copies of the appropriate cases. Without a complete set of cases, offenders may slip through the cracks.

COLD CASE INVESTIGATIONS

The Los Angeles Times' reference to the murder of Larry Wheelock in 1975 is an example of a TracKRS cold case investigation. TracKRS investigators actually investigated the case with the consent of the responsible agency. In this example, TracKRS had submitted fingerprint evidence for re-submission to Cal-ID as part of the case review process even though it had been previously entered into Cal-ID. As a result, a suspect, Larry Paige, was identified and later convicted. Although TracKRS investigated the case, TracKRS will not "take over" a case without consent. TracKRS will work only within the boundaries agreed upon by the agency "owning" the investigation.

SciLas, the Samples Collected Index — Location, Activity, and Status Database

The TracKRS Review Committee recognized that although state law authorized the collection of blood samples from certain mandated offenders and even provided reimbursement for the effort, local law enforcement was not collecting the samples from out-of-custody offenders. Translated, this meant that we might miss connecting suspects to DNA collected from crime scenes. In response, the TracKRS Review Committee determined that Orange County investigators needed assistance in getting the samples collected.

TracKRS created a database, now known as SciLas, to help track the collection effort and established an efficient system for the collection of the samples. Today, SciLas has documented nearly 20,000 offender samples and suspects whose blood is required (see Figure 6.12 and Figure 6.13).

The SciLas program at TracKRS provides investigators access to the SciLas database, a blood collection site at a local police department, and training to assure the offenders in every jurisdiction have provided samples.

The Sexual Assault Backlog Reduction Effort (SABRE)

SABRE is hosted by the Sheriff's Office. It is a project that aims to identify and collect rape kits requiring DNA examination going back to January 1995 (see Figure 6.14). TracKRS assists the Sheriff's Office in that effort. The cases are entered into the TracKRS database and enable the DA's office to guarantee that the cases with DNA can be prosecuted at any later date. Because of the SABRE project, Orange County led the state in the initiation of DNA case analysis as of June 8, 2001.

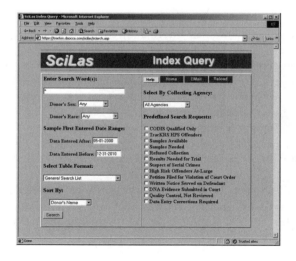

FIGURE 6.12 SciLas Indez Query. (Courtesy of Investigator Ron Shave, Orange County District Attorney's Office, retired)

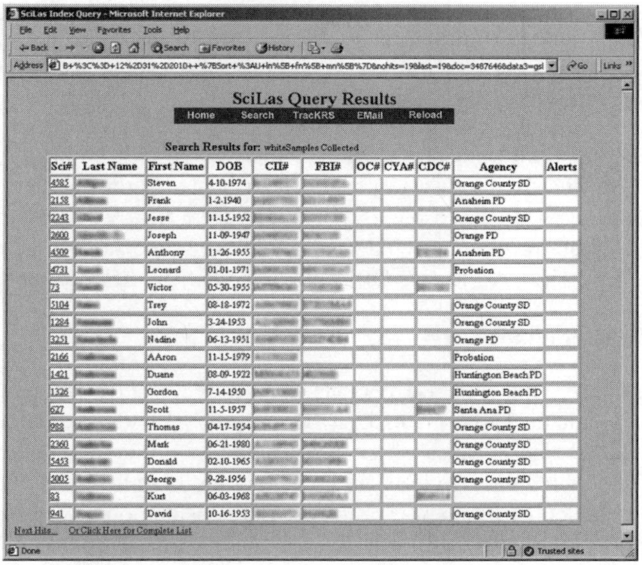

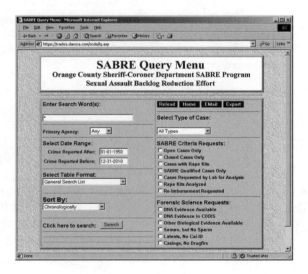

FIGURE 6.13 SiLas Query Results. (Courtesy of Investigator Ron Shave, Orange County District Attorney's Office, retired)

Prefiling Case Reviews of DNA Cases

In January of 2001 the California statute of limitations for certain sex crimes was extended from 6 years to 10 years, and, if suspect DNA was identified there was no statute of limitations on the crime. It could be prosecuted at any later date, with few restrictions.

The District Attorney's Office has established a procedure to protect those cases from the consequences of time. Since the TracKRS database is able to track the cases that have DNA, the unit will request certain qualifying cases to be submitted to the deputy DA assigned to review cases

FIGURE 6.14 SABRE Query Menu. (Courtesy of Investigator Ron Shave, Orange County District Attorney's Office, retired)

for critical evidence that can be gathered only at or about the time of the crime. The review will assure each agency that the case will not be forfeited at some later date on a technicality.

Inmates Refusing to Give Blood Samples

TracKRS discovered that California law did not authorize the collection of blood from inmates with reasonable force when they refuse to provide a mandated sample. Therefore, the California Department of Corrections had ceased blood collections from nearly 16,000 mandated inmates, a group certainly more likely to be connected to DNA crime scene samples than any other group. TracKRS prompted the District Attorney's Office involvement and helped propose new legislation.

Evidence Retention Guidelines

In meetings with property and evidence persons in Orange County, TracKRS was advised that every agency has difficult decisions to make when it comes to the retention of evidence. The problem has been exacerbated because of the new statute of limitations on sex crimes and post-conviction DNA testing of evidence legislation. Even the moral implications of destroying evidence that now may be able to identify dangerous predators is a consideration. As a response to this issue, TracKRS worked closely with the California Department of Justice and others in the preparation of the Postconviction DNA Testing Task Force Report on evidence retention guidelines issued by the California Office of the Attorney General, Bill Lockyer.

Streamlining Failure to Register Violation Filings

Investigators complained to TracKRS that the filing process for registration violations by sex offenders was difficult and inconvenient. In response, the District Attorney's Office has established guidelines for filing violations and has assigned attorneys to assist investigators with filing the cases. The same guidelines can be used for offenders who refuse to give blood samples when required to do so pursuant to law.

ViCAP

The FBI hosts a national database of significant homicide cases called ViCAP. Orange County has entered into an agreement with the FBI to provide homicide case information to the national database. TracKRS is required to collect all Orange County homicide information and put that information into the ViCAP computer. TracKRS has the ViCAP forms available and can assist in the preparation of the case information upon request.

The California State DOJ Sexual Predator Apprehension Team (SPAT)

The SPAT team is available to assist local law enforcement in locating Orange County's worst offenders. TracKRS maintains a liaison with those investigators.

Referrals

Occasionally, TracKRS investigators will make observations or obtain information that might be able to assist local investigations. As a courtesy, TracKRS will forward that information to a supervisor for evaluation. What the agency does with that referral is their decision, however, and TracKRS appreciates feedback, especially in an effort to update case information.

Murder Case Due Diligence

The District Attorney's Office has entered into agreements with local agencies to better share murder case due diligence information. The program aims to eliminate duplicated efforts by distributing

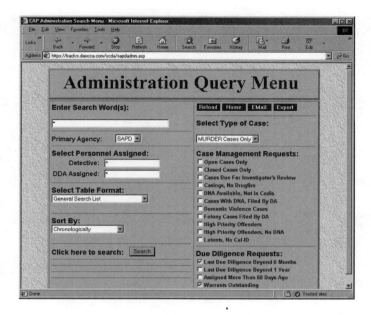

FIGURE 6.15 Administration Query Menu. The DA's Office and the primary investigating agency will be able to log on to TracKRS and determine what cases need attention. The queries are simple. Just make the menu selections for the conditions of interest. (Courtesy of Investigator Ron Shave, Orange County District Attorney's Office, retired)

the work between the originating agency that has obtained a murder warrant and the prosecuting agency. The details of the distribution are described in a memorandum of agreement signed by each of the chiefs of police and the district attorney.

The due diligence work performed is summarized on the TracKRS database. This will assure that cases are not neglected due to transfers, promotions, retirements, workload, or misunderstandings between agencies.

The DA acknowledges that the originating agency owns the case and has the right to continue the investigation when the defendant is arrested. However, case law requires the prosecutor to provide the court with justification to proceed with the prosecution. The prosecutor needs sufficient written documentation and witnesses to prove that an adequate ongoing effort was made to arrest the defendant since the warrant was issued (see Figure 6.15).

CONCLUSION

The focus of TracKRS to date has been the provision of an M.O. database of homicide and sexual assaults, a means to manage the collection of DNA samples and a system to address the backlog of casework examinations. Together, the project addresses the three components required to get the best results from DNA. The three components are:

1. An MO database to identify cases linked by leads other than DNA (see Figure 6.16).
2. A DNA collection process that helps ensure required offenders are in the CODIS database.
3. An examination process to get as much casework evidence examined as possible to connect to other cases and offender DNA.

The TracKRS Review Committee constantly evaluates the investigators' needs and works to remove obstacles and provide the coordinated efforts our community deserves. The Orange County

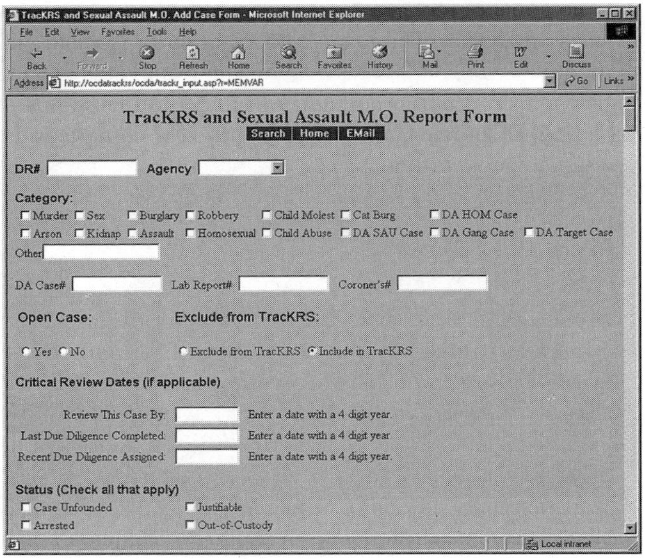

FIGURE 6.16 TracKRS and Sexual Assault M.O. Report Form. TracKRS will update case summaries and the dates relevant to due diligence. (Courtesy of Investigator Ron Shave, Orange County District Attorney's Office, retired)

District Attorney's Office believes that by taking regional responsibility for integrating law, science, and technology we are continually providing good investigators with better resources.

Contact Information:
Supervising Investigator
TracKRS Project
C/O Santa Ana Police Department/M-96
P.O. Box 1981
Santa Ana, CA 92702
714-245-8301

ACKNOWLEDGMENTS

I wish to acknowledge and extend my gratitude to Investigator Ronald Shave (retired) of the Orange County District Attorney's Office for the authorship of the foregoing segment. Investigator Shave began his law enforcement career at the Garden Grove Police Department in California in 1971. He was promoted to Detective in 1975 and worked child abuse and molestation cases for several years before being assigned to Homicide in 1981. In 1985, after several capital cases and a series of Asian murder cases presented huge volumes of documents, it became apparent that the personal computer had become powerful enough to help manage those cases. Over the next several years, while off-duty, Investigator Shave developed programs to help the homicide investigator.

In 1993, Investigator Shave transferred to the Orange County, California, District Attorney's Office. In 1994, the county was thrust suddenly into the throes of bankruptcy, resulting in a massive investigation. Investigator Shave's software was used to manage the millions of pages of evidence seized during the investigation. At the same time, a Deputy District Attorney began using the software in the District Attorney's Homicide Unit. As a result of his efforts in 1995 and 1996, the District Attorney offered to provide those programs in an Internet environment to Orange County homicide investigators. The TracKRS Project was officially implemented and housed at the Santa Ana, California, Police Department in July 1997.

Investigator Shave retired in December of 2001 and is presently contracted to assist the DA's Office in issues relating to the TracKRS Project.

In addition, I wish to recognize and extend my appreciation to the members of the HITS program and of the FBI Center for Analysis of Violent Crime at the FBI Academy for their efforts in seeking to identify suspects in unsolved crimes and contributing to our knowledge and ability to solve these cases.

SUGGESTED READING

FBI. (1994). Handbook of Forensic Science. U.S. Department of Justice, Federal Bureau of Investigation. Government Printing Office, Supt. of Documents.

Geberth, V. (1996). *Practical Homicide Investigation: Tactics, Procedures and Forensic Techniques.* (3rd ed.) Boca Raton, FL: CRC Press.

Howlett, J.B., Hanfland, K.A., Ressler, R.K. (1986). The Violent Criminal Apprehension Program — ViCAP: A Keppel Progress Report. *Law Enforcement Bulletin* (December, 1986).

Keppel, R.D. and Weis, J.G. (1994). Time and distance as solvability factors in murder cases. *Journal of Forensic Sciences,* 39(2), 386-401.

Witzig, E.W. (1993). The New ViCAP: More User Friendly and Used by More Agencies. *FBI Law Enforcement Bulletin,* June, 2003, 72/6. 1–7.

7 FBI: NCJIS and NCIC

Richard H. Walton

CONTENTS

INTRODUCTION

Operated by the Federal Bureau of Investigation, the Criminal Justice Information System (CJIS) is tasked to:

> Reduce terrorist and criminal activities by maximizing the ability to provide timely and relevant criminal justice information to the FBI and to qualified law enforcement, criminal justice, civilian, academic, employment, and licensing agencies concerning individuals, stolen property, criminal organizations and activities, and other law enforcement related data.

This division is now a consolidation of previously separate programs. This chapter presents an overview of services within this division that may be of benefit to cold case homicide investigators.

BACKGROUND AND HISTORY

The CJIS Division was established in February, 1992, to serve as a central repository for criminal justice information services in the FBI. Now the largest Division within the FBI, CJIS consolidated the National Crime Information Center (NCIC), Uniform Crime Reporting (UCR), and Fingerprint Identification into a single facility at Clarksburg, West Virginia. This consolidation became effective in June, 1992. Several ongoing technical programs were also transferred to the CJIS Division. Among these were:

- Integrated Automated Fingerprint Identification System (IAFIS).
- NCIC
- National Incident-Based Reporting System (NIBRS).

NATIONAL CRIME INFORMATION CENTER

The NCIC became operational in January, 1967, as a computerized, nationwide information system serving and supporting criminal justice agencies at the local, state, and federal level. The initial goal was to assist law enforcement in apprehending fugitives and locating stolen property. The goal has been expanded over the past 30 years to include locating missing persons and further protecting law enforcement personnel and the public.

The structure and basic procedures of the NCIC were approved by resolution of the full membership of the International Association of Chiefs of Police (IACP) in Philadelphia, Pennsylvania, in October, 1966. The previous year, a small number of local and state agencies were implementing electronic law enforcement information systems. To enable the sharing of criminal justice information across these jurisdictions, a national system was needed. The FBI conducted a feasibility and developmental study concerning the establishment of a national crime information system. The purpose of the study was to develop a system that made available to all local, state, and federal law enforcement agencies needed information on crime and criminals with data to transcend statewide and metropolitan area boundaries.

The NCIC has operated under a shared management concept between the FBI and state users since telecommunication lines to the CJIS Systems Agency (CSA) in each of the 50 states, the District of Columbia, Guam, Puerto Rico, the U.S. Virgin Islands, and Canada. Those jurisdictions, in turn, operate their own computer systems, providing NCIC access to local criminal justice agencies. The CSAs are responsible for monitoring system use, enforcing system discipline, and assuring that the NCIC operating procedures are followed by all users within their jurisdiction. Through this cooperative network, more than 94,000 law enforcement and other criminal justice agencies have direct online access to more than 30 million records. General policies concerning the philosophy, concept, and operational principles of the NCIC are based upon the recommendation of the CJIS Advisory Policy Board (APB). The APB is composed of top administrators from local, state, and federal criminal justice agencies throughout the country.

NCIC contains records entered by participating criminal justice agencies, and the individual agency is responsible for their accuracy, timeliness, and completeness. Access and input information is provided through terminals authorized by NCIC. Those authorized terminals were given an individual identifier and are known as the Originating Agency Identifier (ORI). Historically, NCIC contained information on wanted persons, missing persons, and stolen property. In recent years, the files have been expanded to include individuals who may pose a danger to others. The NCIC computer stores vast amounts of criminal justice information that can be instantly retrieved and furnished to any authorized terminal. Access to the NCIC system is through a regional or state computer system. NCIC standards require responses to be returned within seconds.

NCIC also provides inquiry-only capability to more than 30 foreign countries for access to records maintained in the Vehicle, License Plate, and Boat Files. In 1999, the system had a complete upgrade known as NCIC 2000. This is a major upgrade to those services previously offered by NCIC, and extends services to patrol cars and mobile officers. The NCIC computer receives an average of 4.2 million inquiries each day, the majority of which contain subject or vehicle information.

Although there appears to be no specific documentation addressing this issue, it is reasonable to assume that some small amount of data was lost over the years, as with any computer system operated in the 1960s and 1970s. Currently, the NCIC has a real-time backup system located at a disaster recovery site. Previously, all data in the NCIC was routinely copied to electronic media and stored off site. Additionally, a system log is maintained. If the system crashes, the NCIC would be restored using the backup data and the system log.

NCIC FILES

The NCIC computer stores records in the following files:

- **Article File.** Contains items of property with unique serial numbers. This file contains records for stolen articles for which a theft report has been made. These include:
  - Bicycles
  - Cameras
  - Tools
  - Household Appliances
  - Musical Instruments
  - Personal Accessories
  - Radios and Televisions
  - Sound Equipment Devices
  - Sports Equipment
  - Viewing Equipment
  - Data Processing Equipment
  - Furniture
  - Livestock
  - Toxic Chemicals
  - Gaming Equipment
  - Collectibles
  - Items of Identification
- **Boat File.** Records for stolen boats. Entry requires (1) an unrecovered stolen boat that has a registration number, document number, permanently attached Boat Hull Serial Number (BHN) or Owner-Applied Number (OAN) with a filed theft report or (2) a lent, rented, or leased boat with a theft report or a filed complaint that results in the issuance of a warrant charging embezzlement, theft, etc.
- **Immigration Violators File.** Added in 1996 as the Deported Felons File, included records for criminal aliens who have been deported for drugs or firearms trafficking or serious violent crimes. Reentry of these criminal aliens into the U.S. violates Title 8, USC Section 1326.
- **Foreign Fugitive File.** Records for persons wanted by another country for a crime that would be a felony if it were committed in the U.S. Wanting country must be a signatory to an extradition treaty or convention with the U.S. Generally, U.S. law enforcement officers cannot execute foreign-issued arrest warrants. However, Title 18, U.S. Code, Section 3184, states that a U.S. extradition warrant (federal arrest warrant) may be issued for the apprehension of a foreign fugitive who is found in the U.S. This holds true only if a treaty or convention for extradition exists between the U.S. and the wanting foreign country.
- **Gun File.** Records for serial-numbered stolen, lost, felony and recovered firearms. A record for a lost or missing firearm if the agency has supporting documentation.

- **Image.** Images may be of a person, property, or reference. Images may be entered for Convicted Person on Supervised Release, U.S. Secret Service Protective, Missing Person, Deported Felon, Violent Gang and Terrorist Organization, Unidentified Person, Wanted Person, Convicted Sexual Offender Registry, Article, Vehicle, Boat, or Vehicle/Boat Part Files. The types of images that may be stored for a person are:
  - Fingerprint
  - Mugshot
  - Signature
  - Identifying Images Such As Scars or Tattoos

Other images that can be entered include:

- Specific articles
- Parts
- Boats
- Vehicles

- **License Plate File.** Records for uniquely numbered stolen license plates. This includes standard passenger automobile plates and special plates that have a theft report on file.
- **Missing Persons File.** Contains records for persons meeting any of the following criteria:
  - *Juvenile.* A person who is missing and under the age of 21 years.
  - *Endangered.* A person of any age who is missing under circumstances indicating that his or her physical safety may be in danger.
  - *Disabled.* A person of any age who is missing and under proven physical or mental disability or is senile, thereby subjecting himself or herself or others to personal and immediate danger.
  - *Involuntary.* A person of any age who is missing under circumstances indicating that the disappearance may not have been voluntary (abduction or kidnapping).
  - *Catastrophe Victim.* A person of any age who is missing after a presumed or known catastrophe.
  - *Other.* A person over the age of 20 not meeting the criteria for entry into any other category who is missing and for whom there is a reasonable concern for his or her safety.

Approximately 80% of NCIC Missing Person File entries pertain to juveniles. The National Child Search Assistance Act of 1990 (the "Child Act") requires law enforcement agencies to make entries for all missing juveniles without observing any waiting period. Agencies may formulate an inquiry using non-unique identifiers, including approximate age, sex, race, height, weight, and eye and hair color. While such an inquiry may generate more than one missing person record, investigators may review to ascertain if any such has occurred. This file complements the Unidentified Person File. Records entered into the NCIC Missing Persons File are automatically searched against records in the Unidentified Person File to seek possible matches (see Figure 7.1).

- **Unidentified Person File.** This file complements the Missing Persons File. Records entered into the NCIC Missing Persons File are automatically searched against records in this file to seek possible matches. It assists law enforcement in the identification of unidentified persons and body parts. There are three different categories for entry of records into this file. These are:
  - *Unidentified Deceased Persons*, including victims of catastrophe.
  - *Unidentified Living Persons* who are unaware of their identities (i.e., amnesia victims, small children, persons with Alzheimer's Disease, etc.

Comparison of Missing Person and Unidentified Person Identifiers

The Unidentified Person File operates in conjunction with the Missing Person File. The NCIC computer daily compares the identifiers contained in new and modified Unidentified Person File with the identifiers in all Missing Person File records. Similarly, the identifiers in new and modified Missing Person File records are compared daily with all records in the Unidentified Person File. Once the computer has compared new or modified records of both files, it transmits the best possible 100 matches to the entering agency for possible leads. If more than 100 records are matched, the remaining records may be obtained by contacting NCIC directly. The identifiers used in the comparison are listed below.

Date of Birth	Estimated Year of Birth
Sex	Sex
Race	Race
Height	Estimated Height
Weight	Estimated Weight
Eye Color	Eye Color
Hair Color	Hair Color
Date of Last Contact	Estimated Date of Death
Date of Last Contact	Date Body Found
Scars, Marks, Tattoos	Scars, Marks, Tattoos
Finger print Classification	Finger print Classification
Jewelry Type	Jewelry Type
Originating Agency State Code	Originating Agency State Code
Blood Type	Blood Type
Dental Characteristics	Dental Characteristics

FIGURE 7.1 Comparison of Missing Persons and Unidentified Person Identifiers. (Courtesy of the FBI)

- *Body Parts.* In some cases, bodies have been dismembered and parts scattered in different geographic or jurisdictional regions. These records may provide an investigative link between agencies that have recovered body parts. An agency that recovers an unidentified, partial body can make inquiry by identifying the specific body part(s) that has been recovered. The system will search for other records of incomplete bodies and transmit any matches that have that part(s) missing. As with the Missing Person File, non-unique identifiers can be used when inquiring for unidentified-person records, including approximate height, weight, age, sex, race, and eye and hair color.
- **Originating Agency Identifier (ORI) File.** An ORI is a nine-character identifier assigned by NCIC to an agency to identify the agency in transactions on the NCIC system. This file addresses those records for agency information that have been assigned an NCIC ORI for purposes of accessing the NCIC System. Through this file, authorized users may identify other agencies revealed through an ORI number. The ORI File maintains pertinent information on virtually every criminal justice agency in the United States, Commonwealth of Puerto Rico, the U.S. Virgin Islands, and Canada, as well as certain foreign criminal justice agencies. In some cold case homicide investigations, this might be useful

in identifying agency source documents that contain an ORI number but no other identifying information. In addition, this file may assist to identify law enforcement agency's that may no longer exist as separate entities due to merging with another agency or termination with police services contracted to another agency.

- **Protection Order File (POF).** The Violent Crime Control and Law Enforcement Act of 1994 contained provisions that necessitated development of the NCIC POF. The CJIS Advisory Policy Board approved the design of the program in December, 1995, and the POF was implemented on May 4, 1997. Protection orders are issued to prevent acts of domestic violence against a person or to prevent a person from stalking, intimidating, or harassing another person. The types of protection orders issued and the information contained within varies from state to state. For these to be entered into this File, they *must* meet the following criteria under 18 U.S.C. §2266(5):

  PROTECTION ORDER. – The term "protection order" includes any injunction or other order issued for the purpose of preventing violent or threatening acts or harassment against, or contact or communication with or physical proximity to, another person, including any temporary or final order issued by a civil and criminal court (other than a support- or child-custody order issued pursuant to State divorce and child custody laws, except to the extent that such an order is entitled to full faith and credit under other Federal law) whether obtained by filing an independent action or as a pendent elite order in another proceeding so long as any civil order was issued in response to a complaint, petition or motion filed by or on behalf of a person seeking protection.

And under 18 U.S.C. § 2266 (6):

  Reasonable notice and opportunity to be heard must be given to the person against whom the order is sought sufficient to protect that person's right to due process. In the case of ex parte orders, notice and opportunity to be heard must be provided within the time required by State or tribal laws, and in any event within reasonable time after the order is issued, sufficient to protect the respondent's due process rights.

Inquiry of the Wanted Person or Vehicle Files will result in an automatic cross search of the POF. Active records will be returned in a positive response and inactive records will not.

- **Securities File.** This file contains serially numbered identifiable securities that have been stolen, embezzled, our counterfeited for which a report has been made. In addition, records for currency that has been stolen, used as bait money, or paid as ransom can be entered. The following do *not* meet the definition for entry in the NCIC Securities File:
  - Personal Notes
  - Bank Drafts
  - Bank Officer's Checks
  - Cashier's Checks
  - Certified Checks
  - Company Checks
  - Lost or Stolen Credit Cards
  - Gift Certificates
  - Personal Checks
  - Savings and Checking Account Passbooks
  - U.S. Treasury Checks
  - Gold or Silver Coins
  - Other Types of Government Checks
- SENTRY. Records for persons incarcerated by the Bureau of Prisons. No data has been included in this file as of early 2005.

- **Convicted Sexual Offender Registry File.** Added in 1999 with implementation of NCIC 2000. This file contains information records for a person who has been convicted of a criminal offense against a minor. This is defined as any criminal offense in a range of offenses specified by state law that is comparable to or exceeds the following range of offenses:
  - Kidnapping of a minor except by a parent
  - False imprisonment of a minor except by a parent
  - Criminal sexual conduct toward a minor
  - Solicitation of a minor to engage in sexual conduct
  - Use of a minor in a sexual performance
  - Solicitation of a minor to practice prostitution
  - Any conduct that by its nature is a sexual offense against a minor
- **Convicted Person on Supervised Release File.** Added in 1999 with implementation of NCIC 2000. Local, state, and federal supervision officers may enter records in NCIC for subjects under specific restrictions during their probation, parole, or supervised release sentence following imprisonment.
- **U.S. Secret Service Protective File.** Records for individuals who may pose a threat to the President of the United States or others afforded protection as authorized by law.
- **Vehicle File.** Records for stolen vehicles, including aircraft and trailers, as well as vehicles involved in the commission of a felony crime. The file contains information about:
  - Recovery of stolen vehicles or lent, rented, or leased vehicles that have not been returned (providing an official police theft report has been made or a filed complaint results in the issuance of a warrant charging theft or embezzlement)
  - Location of vehicles used in the commission of a felony
  - Recovery of vehicles subject to seizure based on a federally issued court order
- **Vehicle or Boat Part File.** Records for serially numbered stolen vehicle or boat parts.
- **Violent Gang and Terrorist Organization File (VGTOF).** Records for violent gangs and their members. Records for terrorist organizations and their members.
- **Wanted Persons File.** Contains records on:
  - Individuals for whom a felony, serious misdemeanor, or federal warrant is outstanding.
  - Parole and probation violators.
  - Juveniles who will be tried as adults or have been adjudged delinquent and have absconded while on probation or parole or have escaped from an institution or agency vested with legal custody or supervision, or where the Rendition Amendment to the Interstate Compact on Juveniles has been executed.
- **Interstate Identification Index (III).** This is an automated system, accessed through NCIC, that facilitates the interstate exchange of online criminal history record information among criminal justice agencies. It consists of an index containing identifying data, including:
  - Individual's name
  - Aliases
  - Physical descriptors
  - Identifying numbers
  - Fingerprint classifications
  - Names of the agency maintaining the criminal history information

NCIC RECORDS RETENTION

Upon its startup in 1967, NCIC provided a means to check items possessing serial numbers or license plates for wanted, stolen, or other status. Records entered into NCIC are retained for a specific period of time, and some of these periods have changed over the years. The length of record retention depends upon the NCIC file into which the record was entered, as well as the type of record that was entered. Cold case investigators are cautioned that information entered decades ago may not now be in the active NCIC computer databanks. Investigators who handle cases that continue for extended periods of time should be aware that their NCIC entries can automatically be retrieved. Records may be reentered if the circumstances surrounding the case warrant such an action. NCIC can retrieve old records through a process known as an "offline search."

The following list indicates current NCIC record retention policy (2005):

- **Interstate Identification Index** — This is not a part of NCIC, but records remain in file until the individual reaches the age of 99 years. Records can be removed due to expungement or 7 years after death. See IAFIS section.
- **ORI File** — Records remain indefinitely. If an agency no longer qualifies for NCIC access, the ORI record is retired but kept in an inactive status.
- **Wanted Person File**. Records of adults and juveniles remain in file indefinitely or until the originating agency clears or cancels them. Temporary felony want records will be automatically removed from the file after 48 hours.
- **Missing Person File** — Records remain in file indefinitely or until the originating agency removes the record.
- **Unidentified Person File** — Records remain in file indefinitely or until the originating agency removes the record.
- **Foreign Fugitive File** — Records remain in file indefinitely or until the originating agency removes the record.
- **U.S. Secret Service Protective File** — Records remain in file indefinitely or until the U.S. Secret Service removes their record.
- **Vehicle File** — Records containing a VIN or OAN remain in file for the year of entry plus 4 years. Felony vehicle records and records not containing a VIN or OAN will remain in file for 90 days after entry. License plate-numbered data remain in a stolen vehicle record for the year of entry plus 4 years. Non-expiring license plate data remain in a stolen vehicle record until the entire record is purged.
- **License Plate File** — Records remain in file for 1 year after the end of the plate's expiration year. Records for non-expiring license plates remain in file for the year of entry plus 4 years.
- **Boat File** — Records remain in file for the balance of the year plus 4 years. Records without a BHN or OAN remain in file for 90 days after entry.
- **Securities File** — Records remain in file for the balance of the year entered plus 4 years, except records for traveler's checks and money orders, which are retained for the balance of the year entered plus 2 years. Records entered by the U.S. Secret Service and ransom securities remain in file indefinitely or until removed by the USSS.
- **Article File** — Records remain in file for the balance of the year entered plus 1 year.
- **Gun File** — Stolen, felony, and lost records remain in file indefinitely or until the originating agency removes the record. Records for recovered weapons will remain for the balance of the year entered plus 2 years.
- **Violent Gang and Terrorist Organization File**:
  - Group Member Capability — Records for violent gang members are retained 5 years unless removed by originating agency. Only records entered by corrections agencies remain past 5 years. Terrorist member records remain in file indefinitely, or until agency cleared or cancelled.
  - Group Reference Capability — Single interest records remain indefinitely or until removed by originating agency. Multiple interest records remain indefinitely or until all agencies remove their records.

- **Immigration Violator's File** — Records remain in file indefinitely or until Immigration and Custom Enforcement (ICE) removes them.
- **Protection Order File:**
  - Active records will be retained until cancelled by the entering agency or expiration date of the order is reached.
  - Inactive records will be retained on line for the remainder of the year in which cleared/expired plus 5 years.
- **Images** — Images associated with records are subjected to the same retention periods as those records. Generic images will remain on file indefinitely unless removed by the FBI CJIS Division staff.
- **Convicted Sexual Offender Registry File** — Records will remain active until they are cleared or canceled by the entering agency or until the Ending Registration Date (ERD) is reached. Sexual offender records with the ERD Field containing NONEXP are retained as active records until they are cleared or canceled by the entering agency. Records for registered sexual predators must have an ERD value of NONEXP.
- **Convicted Person on Supervised Release** — Records have the same unlimited retention period as wanted person records. The agency is responsible for clearing a record when the terms of the probation or the parole have expired.
- **Vehicle/Boat Part File** — If a stolen vehicle/boat part record remains on file for 90 days and it does not contain an SER and OAN, the record is retired. Stolen Vehicle/Boat Part File records that contain an SER or OAN will remain on file for the balance of the year entered plus 4 years.

During the review of cold case homicide files, investigators may look for copies of older forms indicating that related crime items, such as firearms, were entered into the original NCIC data bank, or local or state systems. The presence or absence of such indicators should not mean the property was entered or was not entered, nor that it still remains accessible in these systems. An archive of entries is kept in an offline system. Recordkeeping practices or lost or misfiled forms may create an erroneous impression. When evidence that an item capable of being entered into NCIC is found in file, cold case investigators are urged to check the item for previous entry and inquiries from other law enforcement agencies. It is recommended that input items be updated when appropriate.

CASE HISTORY

Shortly after WWII, a white female in her early 50s was found in her bungalow in a small blue-collar town in the Northwest. The victim had been struck in the forehead with an axe kept in the garage for splitting kindling. She was subsequently dragged from the interior of the residence down a flight of stairs to the basement. The axe was recovered and processed for latent prints at the time with negative results. Approximately a dozen black-and-white photos of the victim and the blood spatter near the wall telephone and in the hallway leading to the garage were taken at the time (see Figure 7.2). There were no photos of the exterior of the house or of other rooms in the residence present in the case file when I reviewed it in 2001. The original case file is approximately 1 inch thick and most reports were more synopsis-oriented than detail-specific. Such a style of reporting was not uncommon in homicide investigation reports from this and subsequent decades.

Remaining physical evidence consisted of a portion of the skull cap and the axe (see Figure 7.3). The axe head was loosely wrapped in paper and had obviously been handled without thought to potentially preserving it for future evidence. Indeed, the captain of the detective bureau took it out of the remaining paper wrapper, handled it and attempted to give it to me.

FIGURE 7.2 This unsolved homicide occurred 2 decades before NCIC became operational in 1967. During case file review, any information from crimes predating this databank may, and should be entered. Note the measuring instrument. (Author's collection)

Investigation at the time of the murder indicated that the victim operated a successful small business and was married. There was a significant age difference between the younger husband and his wife. They slept in separate bedrooms, however, and her husband had an alibi for the time of the homicide. Investigators surmised that an intruder had entered through a side garage door and may have interrupted the victim while she was talking on the telephone. Original investigators discovered that the victim's bedroom was ransacked. The husband's bedroom was reportedly undisturbed. A substantial sum of cash kept by the victim was missing. Also missing were two handguns. The make, model, caliber, and serial numbers of the guns were recorded in the file (see Figure 7.4). The description of the weapons had been mailed by letter to several other law enforcement agencies, but there was no indication they had ever been submitted to any modern databanks.

The primary investigation appeared to last about 6 months. Periodic inquiry into the husband's activities and whereabouts was randomly made. The last report in the file was dated 1963, and reported the husband's location in another distant county. The town is still relatively small and the

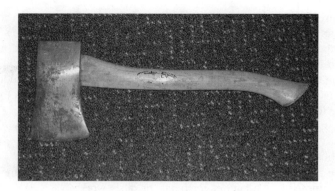

FIGURE 7.3 The murder weapon, found at the scene, with blood spatter is still in evidence. It has been handled an unknown number of times. (Author's collection)

case was well known among the surviving generation from this period. Local rumor among survivors of the period suggested that, *"the husband did it."*

In 1997, an experienced homicide detective reviewed the case evidence to ascertain that it still existed and to check its condition. As is frequently encountered in older cases, review of the reports showed that personal identifying information of those interviewed was lacking. Although there were lists of persons interviewed, there was little or no identifier information such as date of birth; many were recorded by nicknames or similar incomplete information. This is not uncommon in older cases. Present in the case, however, was a case synopsis and a list of those persons who had been interviewed.

During my later discussion, the detective advised he had no way to identify these persons, and no investigative action was taken. Subsequently, the news media broadcast a short story on the unsolved case. A local official angrily called the police department to denounce the publicity and to

FIGURE 7.4 Review of the case file indicated that, at the time of the murder, the victim's bedroom was ransacked and a large amount of cash was stolen. In addition, two pistols were also taken, including a Colt .25 similar to this pistol. The make, model, and serial numbers of both were known, and recorded in the report. In such instances, these serial numbers should be entered into NCIC, even if the crime predates NCIC's operation.

demand that no further such be made as a relative had been the person who found the body and this was distressing.

I inquired of the captain of the detective bureau regarding the guns, and he assured me they were "entered into NCIC at the time." He further advised me that they would expend no further effort to investigate this case as there were no leads and no evidence. At my request, he did reenter the weapons into NCIC after running the serial numbers through this system to ascertain whether they had been previously entered.

There are investigative actions that offer potential for this case, despite its age. Among these are:

- Run an offline NCIC check for any record of the gun.
- Contact the manufacturers with the serial numbers and ascertain whether either gun has ever been returned to the factory for repair or other work.
- Utilize resources of Bureau of Alcohol, Tobacco and Firearms (ATF) regarding any history for the weapons.
- Review remaining physical evidence with criminalist.
- Obtain a death certificate and review it for relative information.
- Obtain the newspaper obituary and review for known names and relationships.
- Contact the initial reporting party and reinterview.
- Review the names of subjects found in the case file with the initial reporting party and attempt to identify them further, who they might be related to, known associates or friends, and others who might have knowledge at this later date.
- Review newspaper accounts of the time for details and names.
- Contact retired officers, investigators, and other personnel to ascertain whether they have any records, photos, knowledge of the case, etc.
- Consider use of the news media as a source of eliciting further information.
- Attempt to identify relatives of the victim for interview.
- Attempt to learn the status of the husband, police record, and whether he is still alive.

CRITERIA EVOLUTION

Since their inception, entry qualification standards for some NCIC Files have changed. The following is a list of some, including startup dates, criteria, and evolutionary changes:

NCIC Vehicle File

Established 1967.

Criteria for Entry (1967)

1. Unrecovered stolen vehicles after 24 hours with the exception of Minnesota, Iowa, Missouri, Arkansas, Louisiana, and all other states to the East thereof where stolen unrecovered after 12 hours will be entered.
2. Vehicles wanted in conjunction with felonies for which the states will extradite will be entered into file immediately.
3. Unrecovered stolen engines and transmissions identified by all or a part of the VIN number will be entered in file on the same basis as stolen vehicles.

The Evolution

1. No documentation exists indicating why there was a delay for entry of vehicle records, but appears that sometime prior to 1975 this "waiting period" was dropped.
2. In 1996, the entry criterion was expanded to include vehicles subject to seizure based on a federally issued court order.

3. In 1999, the Vehicle/Boat Part File was implemented. Previously, part records were included in the NCIC Vehicle File.

NCIC Article File

Established in 1967.

Criteria for Entry (1967)
1. Individual serially numbered property items valued at $1000.00 or more.
2. Multiple serially numbered property items totaling $5000 or more in one theft.
3. Other serially numbered property items may be entered at the discretion of the reporting agency if (1) the circumstances of the theft indicate that there is a probability of interstate movement, or (2) where the seriousness of the crime indicates that such an entry should be made for investigative purposes.

The Evolution
1. Value reduced from $1000 to $500 sometime pre-1975.
2. Ability to enter records for office equipment, television sets, and bicycles regardless of value occurred sometime pre-1975.
3. Stolen property abroad June, 1996.

NCIC Securities File

Established in 1968.

Criteria for Entry (1968)
1. Serially numbered identifiable securities that have been stolen, embezzled, or counterfeited may be entered into the file if a theft report has been made.

The Evolution
1. The entry criteria were expanded to include securities used for ransom. This change occurred pre-1975.

NCIC Unidentified Person File

Established in 1983.

Criteria for Entry (1983)
1. Any unidentified deceased person.
2. A person of any age who is unable to ascertain his/her identity, e.g., amnesia victim, infant, etc.
3. Any unidentified disaster victim.
4. Body parts when a body has been dismembered (entered as an unidentified deceased person).

The Evolution
The entry criterion has not changed.

NCIC Violent Felon File

Established in 1992, discontinued in 1998.

Criteria for Entry (Current)

ATF Headquarters will be the only agency authorized to enter records in this file. The violent felon record subject must meet all four of the following criteria:

1. Have a minimum of three prior violent felony or serious drug offense convictions as defined in the statute.
2. Have a felony conviction for a violent crime where a firearm or other weapon was used.
3. Have a conviction for a crime where the subject has injured or killed the victim.
4. Be either on probation or parole or have been released from supervision (prison, probation, or parole) within the last 5 years.

The Evolution

There were no changes to the entry criteria for the duration of the NCIC Violent Felon File.

NCIC Violent Gang and Terrorist Organization File

Established in 1995.

Criteria for Entry (1995)

Group Reference Capability (GRC) — Two different kinds of organizations, street gangs or terrorist organizations, both of a violently criminal nature, can be entered in the GRC. Despite the definitional difference reflected by the entry criteria and by message keys, an ORI may find that certain groups may meet both definitions. In such case, the entering ORI should use the criteria and message key that best typify the activity of the subject group. In all cases, entry of a group or subgroup will be based on an approved spelling necessitating reference to the NCIC Code Manual prior to entry. Classification as a gang or terrorist organization will be determined prior to inclusion in the Code Manual. In both cases, strict adherence to the entry criteria and documentation of the information establishing the existence of the entry criteria is necessary.

A. Gang Definition

For purposes of entry in the GRC, a gang must meet the following criteria:

1. Must be an ongoing organization, association, or group of three or more persons, and
2. The group must have a common interest and/or activity characterized by the commission of or involvement in a pattern of criminal or delinquent conduct.

"Criminal or Delinquent Conduct" includes narcotics distribution, firearms or explosives violations, murder, extortion, obstruction of justice (including witness intimidation and/or tampering), and any other violent offenses such as assault, threats, burglary, or carjacking. "Delinquent Conduct," as with the Wanted Person File, is conduct of a juvenile which would be a crime if committed by an adult. "Criminal Conduct" includes acts committed during incarceration often labeled "disruptive" which could be punished as crimes.

B. Terrorist Organization Definition

For purposes of entry in the GRC, a terrorist organization must meet the following definition:

1. Group must be an ongoing organization, association, or group of three or more people, and
2. The group must be engaged in conduct or a pattern of conduct which involves the use of force or violence, and
3. The purpose of the group in using violence must be to intimidate or coerce a government, civilian population, or segment thereof, in furtherance of political or social objectives.

Effectively, those criminal activities that predicate entry as a "gang". Such as murder, extortion, firearms, or explosive offenses, assault, burglary, and similar offenses, also predicate entry of a "terrorist organization."

Terrorist Organization — Restriction on Entry

Entry of a terrorist organization or subgroup is restricted to the smallest identifiable segment, cell, or division that has been documented to be engaged or preparing to engage in qualifying terrorist activity. This restriction is intended to prevent entry of persons who may maintain political views similar to a terrorist organization's, but who do not actively support the violent part of that organization.

Group Member Capability (GMC)

The following criteria must exist for any individual to be entered in the GMC, whether a gang or terrorist organization member:

1. Must be a member of a gang or terrorist organization and subgroup thereof which meets the criteria for and is entered in the GRC (see subsection 2.2); and
2a. Has admitted membership in that gang or terrorist organization (and subgroup) at the time of his or her arrest or incarceration; or
 b. Meets any two of the following:
    i. Has been identified by an individual of proven reliability as a group member.
    ii. Has been identified by an individual of unknown reliability as a group member and that information has been corroborated in significant respects;
    iii. Has been observed by members of the entering agency to frequent a known group's area, associate with known group members, and/or affect that group's style of dress, tattoos, hand signals, or symbols;
    iv. Has been arrested on more than one occasion with known group members for offenses consistent with group activity; and/or
    v. Has admitted membership in the identified group at any time other than arrest or incarceration.

GMC — Criterion For Entry — Relationship To GRC

The first and overriding criterion for entry of a GMC record is that the GNG (Group) and SGP (Subgroup) must match a gang or terrorist organization already entered in the GRC.

The Evolution

In 2004, two additional categories for terrorist members were implemented.

1. Terrorist acting alone.
2. Subject is suspected or believed to be associated with terrorism or a terrorist organization.

Other wording has varied slightly and it is suggested that investigators review current statutes.

NCIC Protection Order File

Established in 1997.

Criteria for Entry (1997)

Each record in the POF must be supported by a protection order. Protection orders must meet the following criteria before an entry can be made into the file:

The protection order must have been issued for the purpose of preventing violent or threatening acts or harassment against, or contact or communication with or physical proximity to another person, including temporary and final orders issued by civil or criminal courts (other than support or child custody orders) whether obtained by filing an independent action or as a pendent elite order in another proceeding so long as any civil order was issued in response to a complaint, petition, or motion filed by or on behalf of a person seeking protection.

Reasonable notice and opportunity to be heard must be given to the person against whom the order is sought. In the case of ex parte orders, notice and opportunity to be heard must be provided within the time required by state laws, and in any event within reasonable time after the order is issued, sufficient to protect the respondent's due process rights.

The Evolution

The entry criterion is taken from the statutory definition of a protection order. This definition was modified by the Violence Against Women Act of 2000, which took effect on October 28, 2000.

NCIC Wanted Person File

Established 1967.

Criteria for Entry (1967)

1. Individuals for whom Federal warrants are outstanding.
2. Individuals who have committed or have been identified with an offense that is classified as a felony under existing penal statutes of the jurisdiction originating the entry and felony warrant has been issued for the individual with respect to the offense that was the basis for the entry. Agency must be ready to extradite the individual and return to jurisdiction for prosecution upon notification of the arrest and availability.
3. A "Temporary Felony Want" may be entered when a law enforcement agency has need to take prompt action to establish a "want" entry for the apprehension of a person who has committed, or the officer has reasonable ground to believe has committed a felony, who may seek refuge by escape across jurisdictional boundaries and circumstances preclude the immediate procurement of a felony warrant. A "Temporary Felony Want" shall be subsequently identified as such and subject to verification and support by a proper warrant within 48 hours following the initial entry of a temporary want. The agency originating the "Temporary Felony Want" shall be responsible for subsequent verification, or re-entry of a permanent want. A "Temporary Felony Want" will be automatically removed from the file after 48 hours.

The Evolution

1. Inclusion of warrants for serious misdemeanor sometime pre-1975.
2. In 1984, the Wanted Person File was expanded to include records on juvenile offenders.
3. In 1998, the policy was changed to permit the entry of wanted person records wherein extradition was not anticipated.

NCIC 2000

Recognizing the need to update and improve operations, the FBI completed a new project called NCIC 2000. This system went into effect July 11, 1999. NCIC 2000 provided a major upgrade to those services provided by the older version of NCIC, termed legacy NCIC, and extends these services to those serving in patrol cars as well as mobile officers. This system enhances the base capabilities of the legacy NCIC System and added new files. The additional capabilities of NCIC 2000 include:

- **Enhanced Name Search.** Uses the New York State Identification and Intelligence System (NYSIIS). Returns phonetically similar names (e.g., Marko, Marco, or Knowles, Nowles, or derivatives of names such as William, Willie, Bill).
- **Fingerprint Searches.** Stores and searches the right index fingerprint. Search inquiries compare the print to all fingerprint data on file (wanted persons and missing persons).
- **Probation/Parole.** Convicted Persons or Supervised Release File contains records of subjects under supervised release.
- **Information Linking.** Connects two or more records so that an inquiry on one retrieves the other record(s).
- **Mugshots.** One mugshot per person record may be entered into NCIC 2000. One fingerprint, one signature, and up to 10 other identifying images (scars, marks, and tattoos) may also be entered.
- **Other Images.** One identifying image for each entry in the following files: Article, Vehicle, Boat, Vehicle or Boat Part. A file of generic images (ie., picture of a 1989 Ford Mustang) is maintained in the system.
- **Convicted Sex Offender Registry.** Contains records of individuals who are convicted sexual offenders or violent sexual predators.
- **SENTRY File.** An index of persons incarcerated in the federal prison system. Response provides descriptive information and location of prison.
- **Delayed Inquiry.** Every record entered or modified is checked against the inquiry log. Provides the entering and inquiring agency with a response if any other agency inquired on the subject in the last 5 days.
- **Online Ad Hoc Inquiry.** A flexible technique that allows users to search the active databases and access the system's historical data.

SPECIAL CAPABILITIES OF NCIC

Offline Search: Online inquiries conducted by law enforcement can quickly retrieve accurate information. Frequently, however, an investigator will not have all the information necessary to perform an online inquiry of NCIC, and lacks required parameters such as date of birth, license plate number or VIN. In these and other investigative situations, online inquiries alone may not be adequate. This may be especially true in cold case investigations in which a number of years have passed. In such cases, investigators and their agencies may need to request offline searches of the NCIC database. In addition, state agencies also have offline search capabilities. Agencies can contact their state organization for further details.

An *offline search* is a special technique that can be used in a variety of situations to obtain information not available through online channels. The results may provide an investigator with information to:

- Determine if any other agency(s) has made an inquiry on a particular individual or item of property.
- Place an individual at the scene of a crime or miles away from the scene.
- Substantiate or discredit an alibi.
- Determine if a record for a person or item of property was previously entered into NCIC and subsequently removed.
- Track the route of witnesses, suspects, or other persons of interest.

Information obtained through the offline search process can be retrieved from three different sources:

1. The NCIC *active record database* that is maintained in an online mode for 24 hours a day, 7 days a week.

2. The NCIC *historical database* that includes records that have been removed from the active database as a result of cancellation, clearance, or retention expiration. From an offline search of purged records, it can be determined if a property item was entered and subsequently removed due to its retention expiration, even though an online inquiry produces a "NO RECORD" response.

3. The *transaction log* that contains historic NCIC transactions. An offline search of the NCIC transaction log will reveal whether inquiries were made on a particular individual or property item (ie., during a traffic stop) for a specified timeframe. This type of information can assist in determining if a subject was near the scene of a crime or miles away. These log searches are normally limited to a 6-month timeframe, for example, a certain month(s), day(s), or hour(s). NCIC transaction log tapes are maintained for 10 years.

Offline searches may be tailored to the unique needs of the individual case. An offline search can be made with a minimum of one search parameter, but, as with other aspects of investigation, the more information that is available to assist, the more effective results that may be produced. For example:

- Persons. To identify a wanted, missing, or deceased person, searches may be made on non-unique personal descriptors such as sex, hair color, approximate height, approximate weight, and estimated age.
- Vehicle Identification may be made on:
  - Partial license plate number
  - Partial vehicle identification number (VIN)

Even in cases in which all VINs and serial numbers have been obliterated beyond restoration, the offline search has been of value. In some cases, offline searches have provided identifying data on suspect(s). In addition, gun make, article type, securities descriptors, date of theft, and date of warrant can also be used as offline parameters.

Name-Only Offline Inquiry

NCIC has a specialized program that enables inquiries of the Wanted Person and Missing Person Files by *name only* when a date of birth or other numeric identifier is unavailable for an online inquiry. The Name Only inquiry can be requested by contacting the staff of Investigative and Operational Assistance Unit (IOAU); or by forwarding an administrative message via the National Law Enforcement Telecommunications System (NLETS). The results of the search will be furnished on a computer printout or, if circumstances require, a magnetic tape. A survey is included with the results of each survey and participants are urged to complete and return the form as soon as practical to assist the FBI in evaluating the usefulness of the NCIC offline search program.

Delayed Inquiry Program

User inquiries are stored in NCIC for 5 days. Subsequent entry or modify transactions received by NCIC are checked against the file of inquiries. If any match occurs, both the user entering or modifying a record and the user who made the initial inquiry are respectively advised by way of a delayed-inquiry notification and a delayed-inquiry hit response. Agencies should contact each other to obtain additional information.

One-Crime Inquiry

This transaction enables the user to submit an inquiry for all information related to a crime based on ORI and date of entry or case number. The inquiry can be directed to one, more than one, or all file types. If not specified, the inquiry will search all files. The inquiry will return up to 20 hits online. If the hit response contains more than 20 responses, a notification will be included to indicate that a file is being created with the additional hits.

Date and Time of Entry

This is used to inquire upon the date and time of entry of a record and is available to all users. If a record was entered prior to NCIC 2000 implementation (July 11, 1999), then the inquiry result will feature a date of entry only. If a record was entered subsequently, the response returned will include the date and time the record was entered.

Double Query Match

In October, 2002, the Beltway Sniper terrorized the Washington, D.C. area. FBI staff conducted numerous offline searches of NCIC transaction logs based upon various reporting by persons who suspected neighbors, co-workers, and even family members. These searches attempted to place the person near one of the crime scenes. They generated volumes of printouts but little useful information. On October 18, FBI staff discussed a new search strategy that would be called the *Double Query Match* technique. This was a data-mining application that would search the NCIC transaction log twice. The first search would be to extract license-plate number inquiries made by law enforcement agencies in the immediate area of each shooting limited to 5 hours before through 5 hours after each incident. The second search would list only those inquiries that contained a license plate number that had been queried by more than one agency.

By the morning of October 21, NCIC had generated a printout containing 92 sets of inquiries on different license plates. Included within the printout was the license plate registered to a blue 1990 Chevrolet belonging to John A. Muhammad. Later that night, FBI latent fingerprint examiners working on the case received four latent prints taken from a weapon's magazine found at the scene of a previous murder in Alabama. The recovered prints were searched against the Integrated Automated Fingerprint Identification System (IAFIS). The four prints were identified as belonging to John Lee Malvo. His criminal history revealed that he was a Jamaican citizen who had been arrested by the U.S. Immigration and Naturalization Service (INS) in December, 2001. The INS, now called Immigration and Custom Enforcement (ICE), was in the process of removing him from the country. Further investigation turned up his connection to Muhammad. Before the Sniper Task Force had an opportunity to review the NCIC information, however, the latent print examiner had identified Malvo as a suspect. The reign of terror was coming to an end, and one can speculate that perhaps within a few days of further investigation to eliminate the others, the Double Query Match lead could have pointed to these suspects who were later convicted for the crimes.

Since the Sniper case, the Double Query Match technique has been used in three additional cases involving serial criminals. In each case, the Double Query Match returned a relatively small number of names or license plate numbers as lead information. In one case spanning a 10-year search for a serial sex offender, a single name was returned. The subject had not previously been identified or linked to the crimes, although the man had a significant criminal history of similar crimes.

The NCIC Double Query Match has the potential to be a powerful investigative tool. Matching identical inquiries made by different law enforcement agencies on vehicles or subjects within the circumscribed areas and approximate times of crime occurrences can generate more specific investigative leads. The CJIS Division encourages investigators to contact the IOAU for assistance in using this new technique for cases in which a minimum of 4–6 incidents are involved and no suspects have been developed.

Global Transaction Inquiry

This is the same as an offline search. This is a request for records that cannot be retrieved by way of a standard inquiry transaction. The use of the Global Transaction Inquiry is restricted to authorized terminals. Searches can be made of active or retired (purged) NCIC records.

Integrated Automated Fingerprint Identification System (IAFIS)

The Integrated Automated Fingerprint Identification system, commonly known as IAFIS, is a national fingerprint and criminal history system maintained by the FBI's CJIS. The IAFIS provides automated fingerprint search capabilities, latent searching capabilities, storage of electronic latent images, and electronic exchange of fingerprints and responses. This system operates 24 hours a day, year round. This rapid response of fingerprint identification and turn-around time through IAFIS has made it possible to now identify fugitives and wanted persons while they are still in police custody rather than days or weeks later, as once was the norm.

IAFIS became operational in July, 1999. As of winter, 2002–2003, however, only 30 states were online to submit crime scene prints to the FBI, and nationwide, only about 75 agencies were electronically submitting latent prints to IAFIS. Since its inception, the system has produced some spectacular hits. Among these were D.C. Sniper Lee Malvo, and Gerald Mason, the killer of two El Segundo, California police officers in 1957 (see Chapter 31). As of the winter of 2002–2003, the IAFIS database contained over 44 million fingerprints going back 70 years. The FBI Laboratory began searching latent prints through IAFIS in July, 1999, and has since made over 1,675 identifications. Many of these hits reopened cold case homicides that had lain dormant for years.

IAFIS consists of three integrated components. These are:

1. **Identification Tasking and Networking (ITN).** This segment manages the electronic processing of fingerprint images by CJIS service providers and interacts with both the III and the Automated Fingerprint Identification System (AFIS) and links networks to the FBI.
2. **Interstate Identification Index (III).** This segment performs automated name and biographic searches in response to ITN and NCIC requests. Upgrades to this system have allowed expanded criminal history record exchange.
3. **Automated Fingerprint Identification System (AFIS).** This segment performs automated Tenprint and latent fingerprint searches. It produces ranked candidate lists in response to ITN and remote search requests.

IAFIS offers five key services. These are:

1. **Tenprint Based Fingerprint Identification Services.** (Both criminal and civil). The IAFIS system maintains the largest biometric database in the world. IAFIS utilizes two primary databases:
   a. *The Criminal Master File.* The Criminal Master File contains fingerprints acquired as a result of an arrest at a local, state, or federal level. Fingerprint and corresponding criminal history information are voluntarily submitted by local, state, and federal law enforcement agencies. This file contains fingerprint information and corresponding criminal history data for more than 47 million persons. The fingerprints are processed at the local level and then forwarded electronically to a state or other federal agency system for processing, and then transmitted electronically through the CJIS Wide Area Network (WAN) to the FBI's IAFIS for processing. Mailed Tenprint fingerprint cards are converted to an electronic format for processing in the IAFIS environment.
   b. *The Civil Tenprint Submission File.* Fingerprints are acquired as a result of submission from background checks for employment, licensing, and other non-criminal justice purposes where authorized by state and federal law and in compliance with appropriate regulations. Similar to the criminal fingerprints, civil fingerprints are processed by local, state, or federal agencies prior to being submitted to the IAFIS for processing. Civil Tenprint cards are submitted electronically, by mail, or on tape as machine readable data (MRD). An identification or a non-identification response may be generated. For submissions that require payment, a billing record is created. This file contains approximately 40 million subjects.
2. **Latent Fingerprint Services.** The IAFIS supports both electronic and hard-copy submissions of latent fingerprints. The IAFIS provides the FBI's Laboratory with enhanced search capabilities using databases that are specially designed for matching latent fingerprints. Latent fingerprint specialists return decisions to the requester and add any unidentified latent fingerprints and their features to the unsolved latent fingerprint file.

3. **Subject Search and Criminal History Services.** IAFIS maintains the III files and supports the National Fingerprint File (NFF) program. The III segment of the IAFIS is the national system designed to provide automated Criminal History Record Information (CHRI). The III stores the CHRI of federal offenders and those offenders established by participating and nonparticipating III states. Each III record is created through the submission of fingerprint images to IAFIS. The III-participating states establish and update records within III through the submission of first and subsequent fingerprint images of arrested suspects. Once these records are established, the III-participating states provide requested criminal history records when an electronic inquiry for a state-maintained record is processed by the III system. States participating in the final stage of III as NFF participants submit only the first arrest fingerprint images on a subject to establish a pointer record within the III segment. Any subsequent activity related to this NFF pointer record will be the sole responsibility of the NFF-participating state. If a direct terminal inquiry of an IAFIS fingerprint inquiry identifies a person with a criminal history in one or more NFF-participating states, a Criminal History Request is forwarded to the participating NFF state's criminal history system for the appropriate response. The NFF eliminates unnecessary processing by the FBI and allows participating states to advise the FBI of subsequent arrests of an individual rather than submitting redundant fingerprint information and detailed criminal history updates.

4. **Document and Imaging Services.**
   - *Document Services.* The IAFIS processes documents associated with criminal history records received by electronic input, hard copy, or Machine Readable Data format. These documents include arrest dispositions, expungements, and other miscellaneous updates.
   - *Fingerprint Image Services.* The IAFIS supplies electronic images of fingerprints to authorized agencies upon request.
   - *Photo Services.* The IAFIS has the capability to accept, store and distribute on demand mug shots of criminals.

5. Remote Tenprint and Latent Fingerprint Search Services. The IAFIS supports direct remote Tenprint and latent fingerprint searches by law enforcement agencies. This service is available 24 hours a day, 7 days a week. The results of remote Tenprint and latent searches are returned electronically and include a list of potential matching candidates and their corresponding fingerprints for comparison and identification by the requesting agency. The FBI will provide law enforcement agencies with free remote fingerprinting editing software packages upon request. The Remote Fingerprint Editing Software (RFES) is a complete software package that will perform remote searches of the IAFIS. RFES supports remote IAFIS transactions to include images and feature-based searches for both latent and Tenprint fingerprints. In addition, the Universal Latent Workstation (ULW) latent software package will also perform remote latent searches of the IAFIS. For further information regarding connectivity to IAFIS or latent capabilities, contact the CJIS Division.

ACKNOWLEDGMENTS

I wish to acknowledge the gracious assistance and contributions of Unit Chief Stephen Fischer, Federal Bureau of Investigation, Criminal Justice Information Services who, as well as providing the extensive research and necessary documentation, gave freely of his time in the review of this chapter. In addition, I wish to acknowledge and thank Venetia King and Bonnie Shaffer, Federal Bureau of Investigation, Criminal Justice Information Services, Criminal Information and Transition Unit for their extensive assistance in compiling the material used as a basis for this chapter.

Further, I wish to extend my appreciation to Jamie Sigler McDevitt, Acting Section Chief, Programs Development Section, of the Federal Bureau of Investigation, CJIS, for her extensive research and assistance in compiling the material contained in this section. Material that addressed the Double Query Match was taken extensively from "Double Query Match can help Catch Serial Offenders" printed in the Winter 2002–2003 issue of *The CJIS Link*.

SUGGESTED READING

Federal Bureau of Investigation. "NCIC's Double Query Match can help catch serial offenders." *The CJIS Link*, Vol. 6 No 4/Winter 2002-2003.

Federal Bureau of Investigation. The Investigative Tool. NCIC: National Crime Information Center. Booklet. Revised April 2001.

Federal Bureau of Investigation. "The Offline Search." National Crime Information Center. Revised October 2000.

Federal Bureau of Investigation. National Crime Information Center (NCIC): NCIC File Reference Card. Revised July 2000.

8 Interviewing Senior Citizens

Richard H. Walton

CONTENTS

INTRODUCTION

Interviewing senior citizens and eliciting useful information in the conduct of a criminal investigation is a form of police procedure not taught in the usual training channels. Yet it is one that police officers and investigators encounter not infrequently. Senior citizens — those above 65 years of age — are often encountered as victims of burglary, violent crimes, and especially fraud and white-collar crimes. They are also encountered as victims of sexual assault, homicide, and attempted homicide. In the course of cold case homicide investigations, investigators revisiting older cases may encounter now-older witnesses during the course the of reinterview process, or in the course of developing heretofore unknown witnesses. Successful interviews and processing of information furnished by senior citizens can often lead to arrest and successful prosecution in cold case homicides.

For a variety of reasons, senior citizens present unusual challenges to investigators. Social, health, and family considerations may govern the nature and extent to which they cooperate, or appear to cooperate, with law enforcement. In general, the passage of time is often friendly to cold case investigators in the course of these investigations. Family considerations, however, may significantly contribute to a lack of cooperation by some in this age group.

- Family Secrets. Rejuvenation of a cold case homicide may resurrect actions or activities on their part that they do not wish their family to learn. This applies to other than direct suspects or perpetrators, including family members of the homicide victim in some instances. Events thought long past and buried resurface when investigators begin asking questions. And, as investigators ask questions, family members may begin asking questions also.
- Enhanced Relationships. It is important to keep in mind during this phase of investigation and interview that, with time, relationships may change. These changes may have, in some cases, enhanced relationships that investigators are not aware of. We normally tend to believe that relationships between the offender and those with knowledge will deteriorate with the passage of time, and that those with information of the crime and events may now be more forthcoming to investigators. However, in our efforts to learn that which investigators could not acquire in decades past, relationships may have developed over the succeeding years, and these may be hidden from all but those closest to these parties.

Unfortunately, investigators may sometimes be disinclined to press beyond initial statements when faced with an apparent or perceived reluctance on the part of these persons to cooperate. This may include statements disclaiming any knowledge of the persons or events. The result is that a less than optimum exchange of information occurs. It is the purpose of this section to assist investigators in overcoming these shortcomings and to further their abilities in the course of the interview process during cold case homicide investigations. This information derives from literature on the aging and memory process, and my experiences and those of other investigators in working with senior citizens in fraud, elder abuse cases, and cold case homicide investigation.

DON'T ASSUME ANYTHING

MEMORY

The Merriam-Webster Medical Dictionary defines memory as:

> The power or process of reproducing or recalling what has been learned and retained especially through associative mechanisms ... the store of things learned and retained from an organism's activity or experience as evidenced by modification of structure or behavior or by recall and recognition.

In less formal terms, it is the retention and retrieval in the human mind of past experiences. Learning cannot occur without the function of memory. Memory, however, is not the result of a single system, but encompasses a number of functions and components within the human body. Exactly how memory works, however, is still poorly understood, and it is one of the puzzles of neurology.

Human memory utilizes systems that store and retrieve information gleaned from our senses. These include sight, sound, smell, or other tactile impressions. Noted eyewitness researcher and author Dr. Elizabeth Loftus writes that memory is less like a videotape recorder that captures an event for repeated playback than it is an interpretive process of putting together information when it is called for. According to Loftus, "When we experience an important event, we do not simply record that event in memory as a videotape recorder would. The situation is much more complex." Memory is a physiological process. There are three stages theoretically attributed to memory by researchers and those who specialize in the memory process. Understanding these may be note-worthy for the cold case investigator:

1. **The Acquisition Stage** — To recognize and absorb an event. Information is encoded and entered into a person's memory system. It is here the witness decides which aspect of the visual environment should be attended to and encoded or stored in memory. Not everything perceived is absorbed and stored evenly, however.
2. **The Retention Stage** — This is the period of time that passes between the event and the eventual recollection of some particular item of information. The information is physiologically committed to the brain. During this period, some information may remain here unchanged and some may not. The witness may subsequently be subjected to post-event conversations, media stories, or other secondary sources of input.
3. **The Retrieval Stage** — This is the period during which a person recalls stored infor-mation. This is when the acquisition and retention stages are crucial. Any answer that a person may pose to one asking a question is based upon the first two stages. A failure in the acquisition stage can be a cause for failure in the retrieval stage. If it was accurately perceived in the acquisition stage, it may have been interfered with or contaminated during the retention stage.

According to Loftus, this three-stage analysis is central to the concept of human memory and is "…virtually universally accepted among psychologists." With the passage of time, these stages may be of significant importance to cold case investigators. Loftus attributes two groups of variables during the acquisition stage that might affect the ability of a witness to perceive events accurately.

1. Event Factors
   - *Exposure Time.* This is the amount of time a witness has to observe that which is going to be later remembered.
   - *Frequency.* This is the number of opportunities an individual has to observe and perceive particular details to be remembered.
   - *Detail Salience.* Many events consist of a number of sub-events, and not all the details within that event are equally salient, or memorable to the witness. According to Loftus, a salient detail is "one that has a high probability of being spontaneously mentioned by individuals who witness a particular event."
   - *Type of Fact.* This may include length of time for the crime to occur or the height and weight of suspect, and these are facts not equally easy to perceive or recall.
   - *Violence of the Event.* The brutality and violence of the act. While the immediate affects of bearing witness to unaccustomed violence may outwardly appear to diminish with the passing of years, the cold case investigator is cautioned not to automatically assume that they have vanished and that the witness can now speak accurately and devoid of the effects of emotional impact of the event. As with friends and family of the victims of homicide, the pain may be just below the surface.

Of importance to cold case investigators are *situational factors*, which may include factors asso-ciated with:

- Physical Location and Obstacles. In this category, the cold case investigator would seek to determine whether the witness's line of sight was inhibited by any physical barriers or obstacles such as trees and vegetation or other hindrances.
- Environmental Obstacles.
- Lighting Conditions.
- Distance from the subject.

1. Witness Factors

- *Stress.* The amount and nature of stress an individual endures at the time of perception. According to the Yerkes-Dodson law, strong motivational states such as stress or other forms of emotional arousal facilitate performance and learning *"up to a point."* After this point, there is a decline in the ability to perform.
- *Expectations.* Perceptions may be influenced by expectations; what one expects to see, feel, etc.
- *Cultural Expectations.* A belief held by a large number of people within a certain culture. These are sometimes referred to as stereotyping and may be widely held and accepted within certain populations. According to Loftus, cultural expectations can affect perception, and are highly inaccurate. It is not uncommon in the course of police investigations to encounter persons who personify such stereotyping, and they may be encountered in cold case homicide investigation as well.
- *Expectations From Past Experience.* This is the role that prior experience might play in the ability of a witness to perceive an event. That perception then becomes embedded and subject to retrieval at a later date.
- *Personal Prejudices.* These are individual stereotypic beliefs that affect perception.
- *Temporary Bias.* Momentary bias that may affect perception.
- *Perceptual Activity.* The activity the witness was engaged in at the time of being a witness. This activity may be important in attempting to determine how well aspects of the event may be remembered.

Additionally, the cold case investigator may seek to determine the nature of involvement in the event to which their subjects were witnesses. These include whether they were an:

- *Active Witness.* These are witnesses who may be included as victims of the crime or those who were close enough to the crime to feel threatened.
- *Passive Witness.* These are witnesses who may be more impartial and who may have had occasion to view the event from a safe distance with no feeling of personal threat.
- *Inactive Witness.* These are those witnesses who may not have realized something they saw was significant or may not have realized a crime was taking place.

INFORMATION RETENTION

Cold case investigators should be cognizant that researchers have theorized that post-event information may factor into the ability of a witness to provide information after a long interval between acquisition and recalling the events for an investigator. Time in itself does not cause a loss or slippage of memory. Such a loss however, may occur due to other events in the intervening period.

What witnesses see or hear after the event may contaminate their original perception and subsequent retention. This post-event information can not only augment an existing memory, but also change the memory. In some instances, it may even cause nonexistent information to become incorporated into the previously acquired memory. It is suggested that the cold case investigator design the interview questions in an attempt to distinguish between the actual first-hand perception of the event and post-event contamination.

Forms of post-event information may include:

- *Enhanced Memory.* Memory enhanced by suggestion of another.
- *Compromised Memory.* This may occur when a witness to an event later learns information that potentially conflicts with that which was previously seen and may compromise the original perception with the later information. This is a compromise between what they saw

and what they were later told. During review of the case reports, investigators may seek to determine when or if witnesses were separated prior to giving statements to investigators. In addition, investigators may seek to determine if the witnesses wrote individual statements before contact with investigators or others. The cold case investigator may seek to compare these with later statements to investigators or, in some situations, defense investigators.

- *Timing of Post-Event Information.* When potential post-event information is introduced to the witness, the cold case investigator may seek to determine:
  - How long after the event the information was introduced?
  - By whom was the information introduced?
  - Under what circumstances was the information introduced?
  - Does the information introduced subsequent to the event have a different impact depending upon whether it was introduced immediately after the event or just prior to recall of the event?
- *Nonverbal Influences.* In addition to spoken influences in the post-event setting, the cold case investigator may seek to determine whether the witness's memory of events may have been subjected to nonverbal influences. These may include:
  - Tone of voice by original officers, investigators, or others whom the witness encountered.
  - Movement of body parts such as head and eyes to convey ideas to others. This could occur in the immediate post-event circumstances or indeed even during interview by cold case investigators. As a result, it is important for cold case investigators to maintain a sense or tone of neutrality during their contact with the witness.

As a result of post-event information, the cold case investigator may seek to determine whether:

- Facts and events have been added to the circumstances perceived at the time of the event or subtracted or altered in the memory of the witness.
- Has the passage of time significantly affected the accuracy of recall? Included within this category may be perceptions of the noise associated with the event or violence of the event.

Loftus has further suggested other factors that may affect retention of information in the memory. These include:

- *Intervening Thoughts of a Witness.* During the intervening time period, the witness's thoughts may tend to bend toward self-serving purposes.
- *Labeling.* How a witness labels a given situation may affect the way in which the situation is remembered. The cold case investigator may seek to determine whether the witness views the situation as serious, and thus is potentially more liable to recall the circumstances with less potential for bias. If the witness labels the event as less serious, the witness may downplay those circumstances relayed to the investigator and potentially be less forthcoming and descriptive.

In addition, the cold case investigator may attempt to learn whether the potential witness is *guessing* when recalling certain aspects of the event.

AGE AND MEMORY

There are many misconceptions regarding age and memory. Among these are:

- Old age automatically triggers memory loss.
- Forgetfulness is a symptom of old age.

- Most old people will develop Alzheimer's disease.
- A person can kill or hurt another person and never remember it.
- Each of us is born with the same memory abilities; some use it and others lose it.

Research has shown that aging does not automatically cause memory loss, and the investigator faced with the task of interviewing older people should not fall prey to common societal misconceptions concerning the aging process and memory. Memory can be likened to muscle. If it is not exercised and used, you lose it. It improves with exercise and the investigator interviewing elderly persons should take this into account during the interview.

Reactions slow with age and so does memory. With increasing age, thinking slows and paying attention becomes more difficult. Distractions may become harder to ignore and interruptions may cause older people to forget more easily. However, many memory difficulties are problems of *attention* and not necessarily retention. The investigator interviewing elderly persons must be aware of this and recognize that the period between the time the question is asked and answered is not necessarily indicative of the subject's inability to understand or that of formulating alternative responses to the truth. Nor is it necessarily an indication of difficulty in his or her ability to retrieve the desired information.

Attempts to understand memory have suggested that life may be categorized as a time for:

- Childhood
- Adolescence
- Adulthood
- Old Age

The age of witnesses involved in a cold case homicide investigation may derive from any of these groupings, and so may memory and the ability to recall. Memory is directly related to interest level. Those events that one cared about and paid attention to are more rapidly recalled than events in which there was little or no interest. As age progresses, interests change and with these changes comes the ability to retrieve. *"Concentration"* is a key factor in the quality of storage, and subsequently, memory and recall. Researchers have found that people tend to remember what at the time seemed most important or influential. Some believe fear and anxiety are linked to the ability to forget or repress, a consideration of note to the investigator. These factors are influential elements in a witness's perception of events. Although such emotions may dim with age, they do not disappear.

One of the more erroneous assumptions that an investigator can make is that interviewing elderly or senior citizens will result in a *lesser* quality product than interviews of much younger persons. Memory is one of the most important considerations to be competently recognized and understood while interviewing senior citizens and evaluating the quality and worth of their statements. A variety of influences affects the memory of people at all ages and these influences are also applicable to the memories of senior citizens. Among these are:

- Fear. This fear may stem from the event or its aftermath.
- Anxiety. This may result from the event, its aftermath, or the renewed interest on the part of law enforcement and subsequent contact with the witness.
- Physiological conditions.

MEMORY TYPES

Speculation and theories about how memory works have been evolving for at least 2000 years. Greek philosopher Aristotle reportedly believed that, while thinking took place in the head, memory was stored in the heart. Scientific investigation into this process, however, began approximately 100 years ago. Prior to the 1950s, many believed that memory was a unitary system. This thought gave way to the belief that memory was composed of a short-term memory for immediate functioning and a long-term memory for life skills, including language, mathematics, and similar abilities. Further research evolved during the 1960s and 1970s, suggesting that memory was a storage system, and later a part of a larger, more elaborate information processing system. The latter included the ability to reason, perceive, and comprehend. In the 1980s, renewed interest focused on nonverbal aspects of memory, including the fact that more than one system was involved in this process. Experts in this area of research and study do not necessarily agree on all aspects of this function, although a basic concept of memory is that it is based on practice.

Memory can be generally categorized as *short-term* or *long-term*. Some researchers have attributed a third category to this function, *sensory memory*. Awareness of these categories may be of importance to the interviewers in cold case homicide investigation.

Short-Term Memory

Short-term memory is a system to retrieve information of a recent duration, or that which is "in use." The definition is considered by some to be referring to events that occurred less than one month or so before, and is the memory most commonly in use in more current day-to-day activities. Unlike long-term memory, the ability to store information in this form is of a limited capacity, and short-term memory decays rapidly. An example would be remembering a telephone number. Unless it is rehearsed, it is usually forgotten within seconds. The very act of reading involves holding in memory the beginning of the sentence while reading to the end.

If it is rehearsed, the information is maintained and transferred to the next stage, *long-term* memory. While this form of memory often takes longer to function with increasing age, it does not necessarily deteriorate with age, although it may become increasingly susceptible to *interference*. For this reason, we may seek to complete a task stored in short-term memory as quickly as possible. The cold case investigator should be aware that short-term memory is directly affected by a number of factors. Among these are:

- Neuron breakdown
- Medical condition
- Dietetic considerations

Long-Term Memory

Long-term memory is the form of memory usually addressed during cold case homicide investigations. It is that memory associated with events long past (commonly considered to be in excess of a month or more). It is a form of memory that reportedly appears limitless, although not all the stored information may ultimately be subject to retrieval. This form of memory remains strong during the aging process, and is one in which there is little decay. This is the form of memory formulated and activated during the younger, usually more chemically and nutritionally balanced years. It is memory formed when the body and brain are growing in physical and mental condition. Many consider it to be a *learned process* that develops as a result of social stimulus.

There are two types of long-term memory. These are:

1. Episodic memory. This type of memory represents our memory of experiences and events in serial form. From this memory we are able to reconstruct the actual event(s) that occurred at a specific time in our life. It may be thought of as the how-when-where file for an event occurrence.
2. Semantic memory. This form of memory is more structured and encompasses the facts, skills, and concepts that have been acquired in life. This form of memory involves our organized knowledge about words, meanings, relations, concepts, symbols, and rules, etc. This information is derived from episodic memory, and enables us to learn new facts or concepts from our life's experiences.

There are reportedly three primary activities related to long-term memory. These are:

1. Storage. Repeated information from a stimulus is stored in the short-term memory and transferred to storage in the long-term memory.
2. Retrieval. Some researchers have debated whether we actually ever forget, or whether it just becomes increasingly more difficult to retrieve certain information from memory. Of importance to cold case homicide investigators, forgetting something may be a matter of retrieval. Information may not be immediately recalled, but may be recognized or may be recalled by prompting. Two primary types of information have been suggested. These are:
    *   Recall. By this process, information is reproduced from memory. Recall may be assisted with retrieval cues, which assist in the ability of the witness to more quickly access the information.
    *   Recognition. This is a less complex process as information is provided in response to a cue. In this process, the presence of the information stimulates knowledge that this information has previously been seen.
3. Deletion. This may be caused by decay or interference.

Long-term memory is *organized* memory. It is memory that often is retrieved by *association* with other events, times, and places. Association is the ability to associate the event or material to information learned and stored through correlation to another. Long-term memory is affected by *attention* and *association*. These factors influence the ability to recall — to retrieve — information stored in the long-term memory. If the information was learned and stored, the ability to retrieve is directly linked not only to the attention given at the time in order to learn and store the information but also to the attention required in order to retrieve this information at a later date.

Strategies such as association and *visualization* help people remember. Such time sequences, however, may be very relative and long-term memory can remain strong with increasing years. The significance of this to the cold case investigator cannot be underestimated. Often, while senior citizens are being interviewed, especially regarding events stored in long-term memory, the subject may appear to be talking incoherently or in a disorganized fashion. What they may be doing, however, is *associating* the event under discussion with other events, times, or people in order to facilitate their response to the question at hand.

This process may also work in tandem with the process of *reminiscing*. The investigator is cautioned to not misinterpret this as a sign of mental incompetence or the inability to understand and to communicate. Reminiscing involves the recall of persons and sequences of events associated with particular areas of attention. According to the Merriam Webster Dictionary, reminiscing is the "recall to mind of a long-forgotten experience or fact … the process or practice of thinking or telling about past experiences … a remembered experience … an account of a memorable experience … something so like another as to be regarded as an unconscious repetition, imitation, or survival." This process helps people to remember names, events, and places, and enhances self-confidence and esteem.

While the investigator may question a subject with the desired purpose of eliciting information about a specific person or event, such stimulation may trigger what might seem to be unrelated bits and pieces of information about other people and events. Reminiscing allows the subject to activate the recall process, associating other information with the information desired by the investigator. Depending upon the type and amount of information sought by the investigator, and the ability of those interviewed to furnish it, the amount of reminiscing undertaken may vary considerably. The interview may thus become an extended session and the interviewer is cautioned not to rush the interview. It is a good idea for the cold case investigator intent on interviewing senior citizens to allow extra time.

Reminiscing further allows the subject to cover a variety of subjects, thus activating the mind to the time period under discussion and opening avenues of thought perhaps long retired. The investigator must take extra care to remain focused upon the information desired and the efforts to elicit such, while also listening carefully for indicators of other relevant information offered unintentionally or in passing. Such may be only a word or two, a thought, or short utterance. Care and attention must thus be directed not only to what the investigator is searching for while remaining focused on the responses desired, but also to what else the subject may intentionally — or unintentionally — offer. Such offerings may be lead material for future or follow-up investigation.

To the unknowing, reminiscing can be likened to *wandering*. This is a different mechanism. While reminiscing is usually associated with events brought about by the thought processes involved in recalling certain event(s), wandering is a less organized situation wherein there is little or no cohesion to the thought process. This is more often associated with difficulty in the ability to *retrieve*, and is influenced or affected by areas noted below in the discussion of short-term memory. An investigator should not assume that the information is not there, but the ability to recall may present formidable obstacles to the investigator. Such a condition should be recorded in the course of the investigation so that follow-up investigators and prosecutors are aware of the situation. While the investigator would like to keep subjects being interviewed on track of the subject under discussion, allowances and tolerances must be given to aging people.

SENSORY MEMORY

These memories are acknowledged to act as a buffer for stimuli that are received through the senses. These are further categorized as *iconic memory* (visual stimuli), *echoic memory* (aural stimuli) and *haptic memory* (touch). Information from these memories are transmitted to the short-term memory through attention, and thus act as a filter for what is of interest at the moment.

During the aging process, a variety of factors can cause memory failure or loss. These can act together or independently of each other. Throughout the course of cold case interviews, it is suggested that investigators look for indications of these characteristics, and document them for future investigators and prosecutors. These include:

- Reaction time
- Attention
- Diet
- Medications
- Emotions and other emotional factors
- Inactivity
- Isolation
- Lost confidence
- Vision and hearing problems
- Alcohol abuse

IMPAIRED MEMORY

Forgetting. Those experienced with interviewing the elderly often encounter the *"I forget"* factor. Every investigator is aware that suspects and some witnesses may overuse the "I forget" phrase. Some are truthful, while others are not. When interviewing senior citizens, the reality of this element is one more often than not innocent in scope and not one of intent to mislead or deceive. Forgetting is a process whereby information in memory becomes inaccessible. Such memory lapses can happen at any time, especially if a person is distracted, overloaded, or busy.

Simplicity in asking the question and allowing the subject time to answer is suggested during these interviews. Rushing another question while the person is attempting to answer the preceding one may cause overload and confusion in some instances. The ability to retrieve is affected by factors that preclude instant or quick recall. Careful questioning can elicit information that may tend to substantiate or otherwise indicate that subjects being interviewed truthfully do not know, or may think they do not know because they cannot retrieve the information.

Forgetting can be influenced by a number of factors. Among these may be interference from other material learned before or after the time sequence. The amount of material forgotten increases with the amount of other distractions or other material that interferes with the smooth retrieval of the information. Occasional moments of forgetfulness or memory loss are not uncommon in many age groups. In older age groups, however, these may be indicative of senility, stroke, or diseases such as Alzheimer's, although this is not necessarily so.

Symptomatic of this is *panic* on the part of the senior citizen. In addition to verbal statements, this may be demonstrated by outward signs of alarm that include shaking or a visible look of fear or panic. This panic is a manifestation of a self-perceived deteriorating condition, which, in fact, may not be the case. Forgetfulness can afflict persons of any age, including those in their 30s and 40s. The interviewer is advised to downplay this during the course of the interview, attempting to put the subject at ease to diminish self-induced notions of declining mental ability and self worth. When this occurs, investigators may respond to their feelings, explaining that it is "okay," and downplay the significance and importance of their visit, reassuring the potential witnesses. Do not remind them they are forgetting, use slang, or argue.

Amnesia. Amnesia is a form of impaired memory. This form of impaired memory is reported as one of the most common symptoms following brain damage. This damage may arise from physical trauma, disease, a stroke, or may be attributed to the aging process. Amnesia does not affect other workings of the brain, but interferes with, and blocks, elements of the memory process. There are a number of forms of amnesia, and among these are:

- Pure amnesia. This is a quite rare form. It affects those memories acquired within the past few months or few years prior to the onset of amnesia. Access to older, more deeply embedded memories is normal.
- Post-traumatic amnesia. A stage of amnesia resulting from a head injury in which the victim emerges from a relatively confused period and encounters difficulty keeping track of ongoing activities and exhibits other degrees of confusion.
- Retrograde amnesia. This amnesia reflects difficulty in recalling events and information from the distant past. After a head injury, the victim may have trouble recalling events that occurred before the injury. The degree of this form of amnesia may be correlated to the extent of the head injury and its impact upon short-term and long-term memory.
- Anterograde amnesia. This form of amnesia refers to problems in new learning and in ongoing memory.

Dementia. According to the National Institute on Aging, dementia is a term for a group of symptoms that are usually caused by changes in the normal activity of very sensitive brain cells. The name means "without mentation." The brain suffers a breakdown in the ability to pass electrical messages. As a result, the ability to learn, remember, or retrieve is affected. This seriously interferes with a person's ability to carry out daily activities. Dementia is a progressive deterioration of the brain and is irreversible. Dementia cannot be cured. It is a syndrome in which a person suffers from impaired memory, and also at least one of the following conditions:

- Problems with executive functions such as planning, thinking abstractly, appropriately starting or stopping behavior, switching focus, or considering consequences
- Inability to recognize people or objects
- Inability to use language in an appropriate manner for time and place
- Inability to perform over-learned tasks, such as brushing one's teeth

It should be noted that dementia is not in itself a disease. Rather, it is a group of symptoms that may accompany certain diseases or physical conditions.

Alzheimer's disease is the most common cause of dementia. This progressive disease frequently starts with short-term memory impairment, but may also include impairment in the ability to recall faces, sequences of events, distances, and shapes, etc. Although Alzheimer 's disease is not curable, diagnosis and early treatment may slow the progression of cognitive losses.

Vascular disease is the second most common cause of dementia. This is a condition in which blood flow in the brain is impaired because the blood vessels become blocked or damaged, as in a stroke. This is not the same as Alzheimer's disease, although similarly, the afflicted person becomes progressively worse and eventually incapable of caring for him or herself. Alzheimer's and vascular disease account for approximately 85% of all dementias. However, dementias may also be caused by treatable conditions such as depression, certain nutritional deficiencies, and some endocrine disorders. In these cases, the cognitive problems may resolve when the underlying medical issue is addressed.

The onset of dementia may be noted by:

- A decline in reasoning and judgment
- Changes in memory, including ability to perform word problems or getting lost
- Changes in ability to handle life's functions
- Potential personality and mood changes
- Behavioral changes

There are many conditions with symptoms that resemble dementia, but which are not. Among these are loneliness, anxiety, sadness, and boredom.

ALZHEIMER'S DISEASE

This is a type of memory deficit in the form of progressive dementia. It is one of a group of diseases that make up "dementia." This disease appears to damage, and ultimately kill, many of the nerve cells in the brain. In this process, it also weakens and damages the connections between them. As a result, the patient shows increasingly pronounced symptoms affecting language, perceptual, and emotional problems, which ultimately results in a terminal stage.

The beginnings of Alzheimer's disease may be almost imperceptible, but memory loss becomes more severe with increasing time. Old memories may tend to be substituted for new ones, thus the victim of this disease repeats events from the past. As the disease progresses, old memories suffer and ultimately the damage to nerve cells and connections results in knowledge being erased. As old knowledge and information disappears, the ability to learn anything new also suffers. In addition, damage occurs in other parts of the brain, resulting in further alteration of behavior and ability to function normally. Alzheimer's disease is uncommon before age 65, but the percentage of people afflicted rises rapidly between this period and ages 80–85.

Physicians typically use some of the following criteria to diagnose Alzheimer's disease:

- Age of onset is between 40 and 90
- Problems in two or more areas of mental function, such as speech, memory, or ability to draw
- Progressive worsening of these mental problems
- Lack of evidence of other disease to explain these conditions

STROKE

A *stroke* is a sudden disruption in the flow of blood to an area of the brain. Thus deprived, the affected brain cells are damaged or die. Cell damage can be repaired, but the death of brain cells is permanent and results in disability.

Stroke victims, depending upon the severity and number of strokes, may not tape record as clearly as the interview may have seemed in person, and the resultant recordings might not transcribe clearly. Depending upon the medical condition and medication, this does not necessarily mean, however, that they cannot understand what the investigator has to say nor that they are unable to communicate in response. These people require additional time for the investigator to attempt to understand the degree of impairment, and the ability to clearly receive and understand what the interviewee may be communicating. While each affected individual must be measured and weighed upon individual merits, he or she should not necessarily be discarded as a potential source of information.

CASE HISTORY

During the reinvestigation of the series of murders and alleged rapes that occurred in a rural mountain region during the mid 1920s, as discussed in the Introduction, I had occasion to interview an elderly man in the mid 1980s.

I initially contacted Russ in a face-to-face interview at his home and told him that I wished to speak to him about events that had occurred in the period 1925–1930. At the time of the interviews, he was in his late 80s. I had been told by others that Russ possibly had critical information pertaining to the case. However, I was advised by his family that he had recently suffered two small strokes. Russ spoke with difficulty and his words were garbled. To ascertain whether he understood my questions, I asked him the same question on three different occasions, slightly rephrasing it each time so that it did not appear to be the same question yet solicited the same answer. Each time, however, he responded with the same answer.

During the interview, after asking a question and receiving an answer, I would frequently pause before asking another question. This served to downplay any stress from the interview brought up by revisiting the events that had occurred 60 years before. Despite the passage of time and the death of one of the killers in the mid 1960s, Russ was still afraid of this man and would not mention his name. At one point during the interview, Russ paused, and then asked me whether I knew that another principal figure in the case, the corrupt district attorney who convicted the innocent man, had visited him at his ranch during the period surrounding the conviction? I did not.

Russ then told me that the prosecutor had come to the ranch to go deer hunting. While there, he had told Russ and a group of other men present how he had forced a confession to murder, under fear of death, from the Indian cowboy. This information was significant as it corroborated documentary evidence with a living, eyewitness account. I subsequently reviewed Russ's family photo album. I observed two photographs of interest. One photograph depicted Russ and a group of men (see Figure 8.1) and the other photo depicted the corrupt prosecutor at the ranch (see Figure 8.2).

I showed the photos to Russ. He identified the prosecutor and stated that the man had visited the ranch on only *one* occasion, in 1929. He then identified each of the other men in the group photo. All the others were dead now. However, his memory of the event was very clear and he was able to communicate this to me, although the tape recording was very difficult to understand if one was not familiar with listening to, and understanding him.

Russ's information was very significant, and I returned 2 weeks later, accompanied by the chief investigator for the district attorney's office. The purpose of this follow-up interview was to seek a second opinion about Russ's credibility and clarity. I again asked him the series of questions from my first visit, and he answered just as he had 2 weeks before. His memory of those long ago events was clear and concise. Russ ultimately became a cornerstone witness in subsequent legal proceedings that identified two killers from the period and contributed toward a posthumous innocence pardon for a man who was wrongfully convicted for the murders almost 60 years before.

The interview process during cold case homicide investigations builds upon the experience and training of the homicide investigator and is not separate and detached. The ability to distinguish between real and artificial memory loss is a skill that enhances the proficiencies of the cold case investigator during interviews with the elderly. With age, distractions are often harder to ignore and

FIGURE 8.1 In the 1980s, Russ, back row second from left, was the only surviving member of this group photo taken in 1929. At this time, the corrupt district attorney brought illegal alcohol to the gathering. It was later shown that he was also running the biggest bootlegging ring in the county from the DA's office. He told these men how he forced a confession from a subject by fear of death. Despite his age and several strokes, Russ provided me and follow-up reviewers with a credible first-hand account of an event he had witnessed some 60 years before. (Courtesy of the Harold Hunt family)

FIGURE 8.2 This photo was taken when the corrupt district attorney visited the ranch. (Courtesy of the Harold Hunt family)

interruptions can cause older people to forget more easily. This can be a positive assurance to the investigator trained to recognize such symptoms. During the course of an interview in the cold case process, I have found that it is a useful technique to ask the same question several times, altering the wording while designing the question to elicit the same response. If the subject recognizes this tactic, it is indicative of short-term memory retention (and with such, potential clarity of memory). If they do not recognize this tactic, yet furnish the same answer, it suggests that they are truthful.

Interviewing some senior citizens may be time consuming and delicate in nature. Occasionally in the course of the interview the investigator may point out what seem to be areas of conflict in the statement. Care must be given to do this in a non-accusatory tone without suggesting that the investigator is belittling the witness. A natural tendency may be to give deference to senior citizens, even perhaps extending sympathy, compassion, and courtesy during the interview. Do not let sympathy and a false sense of respect for the elderly overcome your investigative skills and abilities.

CAPACITY

According to Dr. Bennett Blum, a psychiatrist considered by many to be the nation's top expert on geriatric forensic work, there is much more to assessing the competency of a potential elderly witness than "memory." While a battery of examinations, interviews, and observations may be needed for a complete forensic psychiatric assessment, this is not necessarily so during the witness interview process in a cold case investigation. Observation, one of the components used to assess competency, may be utilized by cold case investigators.

Investigator observation of the subject's behavior during the course of an interview may assist in assessing the capacity of a potential elderly witness. In addition to memory, observations may include:

- Daily living activities, including bathing, grooming, dressing, and eating
- Concentration and orientation
- Subjects ability to plan and strategize (including ability to understand the probable outcome of decisions)
- Speech and language
- Thought processes
- Emotional control
- Insight and judgment
- Anticipation, anxiety, irritability
- Impaired recall of recent or more remote information

INTERVIEW TECHNIQUES AND CONSIDERATIONS

Contact and interview with a senior citizen — or other witnesses for that matter — may occur in the course of a cold case homicide investigation in any of the following occasions:

- Reinterview of the witness due to reactivation of the case after an extended period of time
- Change in investigators
- Clarification and followup of information in a previous statement(s)
- Identification of the new witness

While preparing for an interview and during the interview process, I have found the following considerations to be helpful:

- Formative Years.
  - During what era or decade(s) did witnesses begin to experience life and to form opinions?

- What effect did this period have on their mindsets?
- How much effect and impact do those experiences carry over to today?
- What is their geographical, demographic, or cultural history? This may be important to the interview process. Those who have immigrated from other countries and Third World nations may have an impression of law enforcement based upon their early history and law enforcement standards and tactics far removed from those in the United States. This may impact their willingness to cooperate with law enforcement.
- Do they have criminal records during these years?

Past Law Enforcement Practices

In the United States, wide-ranging law enforcement practices and procedures marked the period from the 1930s to the 1970s. Different regions within the country witnessed a mixture of police styles and practices that were not necessarily in agreement with the standards and styles uniformly practiced in other regions of the country. Since this period, law enforcement standards and ethics of conduct have progressed significantly. However, bribery and corruption were not uncommon during the middle half of the 20th century, especially in some jurisdictions. Those raised in an inner-city environment may have different exposure and concepts of law enforcement from those in a more rural environment. Either may be more positive than the other and each must be appraised on an individual basis. The cold case investigator is advised not to generalize that a witness's upbringing or environment automatically inclines him or her to be untruthful.

A senior citizen's perception of law enforcement is important to a cold case investigator. The style of cop portrayed in old Jimmy Cagney gangster movies was not far removed from fact in decades past, and media portrayal may be a factor in a witness's willingness to speak. The "third-degree" stuff was very real, and, on rare occasions, has carried over to the present. This perception may be conscious or unconscious on the part of the interviewee.

Conversely, however, prior experiences with law enforcement may have been positive and engendered a respect for the "system." The senior citizen of today may have been raised in an atmosphere where you did not question government officials, or "buck the system." In preceding eras, there was more of a blind respect for authority of the courts and law. In decades past, few might question the actions of a judge, and did not argue with his authority or that of detectives. Investigative reporters were not as prevalent as today, and society was not as open. Policy was what one person said it was.

The Approach, Introduction, and Interviews

The significance of the initial meeting and rapport-building period of the interview cannot be underestimated. It sets the tone for the subsequent interview and post-interview relationships between law enforcement and the witness. When conducting an interview with senior citizens, it has been my experience to be especially observant and intuitive during the approach to the interview. Although it is dependent upon the style of the investigator and circumstances of the case, I have found that interviews of senior citizens as witnesses is most effective when accomplished in a face-to-face environment. This format works best because it:

- Establishes, builds, and enhances a relationship between witness and the investigator.
- Allows the investigator to observe and evaluate a number of factors that may affect the reliability and quality of the interview and the information sought and received.
- Diminishes the potential for miscommunication and misunderstanding.
- Facilitates identification of additional information.

This phase includes both verbal and non-verbal communication, as well as observation of the individual and surroundings. As they may be distrustful of your purposes or motives it is suggested that you:

- Make them feel relaxed and comfortable.
- Don't rush.
- Do a short explanation of your presence at this time.
- Be casual yet professional.
- Attempt to establish common interests.
- Spend time "warming up" with witness. Talk about a variety of matters. Some senior citizens are lonely and welcome the visit and desire conversation.
- Use initial conversation to feel out their backgrounds, attitudes and potential for cooperation.
- Be honest. Senior citizens have a good capacity to "see through" or evaluate.
- Note their concerns for future publicity or family awareness.

Spouse/relationships. Learn as much as possible about your witness as such knowledge may lead to other sources of information that might be unknown to the investigator or who may substantiate the credibility and accuracy of the witness. Some questions to ask might include:

- Any (or how many) prior spouses or relationships?
- Period of relationship(s).
- Statements to witness by former spouse or others.
- Time of separation.
  - Why? (Potential for additional witness or source of information).
  - Number of Children (Identify as potential source of information).
  - When?
  - Where?
  - How?
  - Violence in background?
- Background of their relationship with spouse's family?
- Other leads, contacts, or referrals?

Friends. The cold case investigator may seek to identify friends of the witness as these persons may become additional witnesses or corroborate the witness or provide further follow up information.

- Do they refer to other friends during the interview?
- Long-term or short-term (Identify)?
- Nearby or distant?
- Number/relationship?

Physical Condition. During the approach and subsequent interview, the cold case investigator should note the physical condition of witnesses as it may suggest their ability to see, hear, and understand the events of the interview. These may also impact the ability of witnesses for future court appearances. Among these observations might be:

- Physical appearance
- Presence of eyeglasses
- Presence of hearing aid
- Medical bracelets or necklaces
- Use of prescription drugs or other medications

Mental Condition. During the interview, the cold case investigator should take note of the apparent mental condition of witnesses. This may tend to enhance or diminish their reliability and veracity.

- Do they appear "together?"
- Observe physical appearance.
- Self concern about appearance?
- Stated medical background. What medical conditions may affect the ability of the witness to hear, understand, and communicate with the investigator? In addition, the cold case investigator seeks to identify any medical conditions that may affect the reliability and consistency of the witness such as:
  - Medication.
  - Strokes.
    - May/may not affect reliability of memory.
    - May influence response time from question to answer.
    - May affect ability to verbally communicate with interviewer.

Outlook on Life

- Desire to live?
- Desire to die?
- Live in the past?
- Live in the present?
- Live for the future?

Observation at residence or location of witness. These may provide subjective insight into the ability of the witness to present a credible presence and consistency. Note:

- Standard of living
- Self-sufficiency
- Economic status
- Style/maintenance and care of residence
- Neighborhood

Physical Surroundings. What do the physical settings of witnesses suggest about their potential credibility and reliability?

- Clean and neat
- Cluttered and dirty
- Living in past vs. present
- Furniture
- Age of furnishings and condition
- Style ("Chesterfield" instead of "couch" or "sofa")
- Age and condition of appliances
- Pictures and decorations
- Type and age
- Reflect interest of witness
- Family
- Locations
- Artwork

Pets. What does pet ownership suggest regarding the ability of the witness to present a credible and reliable presence and ability to communicate or of their ability to focus? Their pets are:

- Dogs
  - Noisy or yappy
  - Big or small
  - Purebred or mongrel
  - Attention paid to by witness during interview
- Cats
  - Number
  - Type (domestic or alley)

Family. Does the witness have other family who may provide further information, provide support to the witness, or potentially be a cause of concern or embarrassment to the witness?

- Children and grandchildren
- Are pictures abundant, sparse, or lacking?
- Attentive to or reference by witness
- Surviving
- Near or far. Identify
- Amount of contact

TAPE RECORDER

The use of a tape recorder may be desirable while conducting an interview with a senior citizen. However, the display and use may warrant additional considerations other than those perhaps found with younger individuals contacted during the course of investigations:

- Do *not* walk in and immediately pull out a tape recorder.
- Do not let them see it immediately.
- Use a warm up period of conversation and ask if they would mind if you use it. Say, "It's easier for me," or similar phrases to downplay its presence and use.
- Tape recording may be an object of distrust or uncertainty by the senior citizen. It may be too formal a technique for them.
- The tape recorder may elevate any anxiety level felt by the senior witness.
- If used, try to do so unobtrusively and don't continually look at the recorder or allow the subject to focus on the object instead of you.
- Keep in mind that the voice characteristics of senior citizens in some interviews may pose additional problems for those who later listen to the tape or attempt to transcribe it. It is suggested that specific points of interest be clarified by the investigator by repeating the conversation and eliciting a "yes" or "no" answer.

DOCUMENTS, PICTURES AND PROPS

Documents. The elderly usually need greater visual contrast and larger print to read documents than younger adults. Printing should be at least 14-point type. Documents should be in black ink, printed on white paper. Dr. Blum reported having once seen a series of bank brochures that had red writing on a black background. The creators thought this would emphasize key points for their elderly customers. Instead, most customers could not see those sections at all.

Photos. If the purpose of the interview entails showing crime-scene or other photographs to the witness, the investigator may consider using enlarged photographs, perhaps 8×10 inches in lieu of smaller photographs. In reactivating older cold case files, the investigator may encounter black-and-white photos approximately 4×4 inches. Whether the case file photos are in this format or later 4×6-inch or other format, the investigator may consider using enlarged photographs for witness review and identification.

Witnesses may be too embarrassed to admit that they cannot see as clearly as they once did. If this is the case, the investigator may run the chance of a well-meaning witness making an erroneous or mistaken identification based upon embarrassment about lack of visual acuity. Enlarged photos may enable the witness to identify or reveal information not previously known to the investigator but recognized in the photograph by the witness. Viewing photos might stimulate recall of other information by the witness. Note during the interview and observations whether the witness normally wears glasses or if glasses are worn at the time of the witness review.

Photo Lineup. If the purpose of the interview entails the investigator showing a photo lineup, it is suggested that the investigator consider:

- Use of enlarged photographs in an 8×10-inch format. This is for the same reasons noted above.
- Using a sequential lineup instead of the traditional six-pack. While this style of photo lineup has been thought to reflect a more fair and balanced format, there may be an additional advantage when used with senior citizens. This format may appear less intimidating, thus reducing stress and anxiety felt by the elderly witness.

In all cases, these photos should be marked and retained per department procedure for their evidentiary value in future court proceedings.

Calendars. When conducting an interview with a senior citizen regarding past events, a calendar of the month as well as those preceding and following that in which the crime occurred may serve as an investigative aid. The investigator may also want to include a calendar of the present year. It has been my experience that witnesses in cold cases, as well as current, may identify or associate other events with the date or time under discussion. In doing so, they may recall the day of the week, but not the date. Or, they may recall the date and not the day. It is important that these be in sync. Showing a witness a calendar may elicit further information not known to the investigator by stimulating recall of case or other period events.

For example, a senior citizen may inform the investigator that he or she found the victim dead on the afternoon of October 11th. This may be contrary to the statements of others who last saw the victim alive in the morning on October 12th. During the course of the interview, the investigator may elicit from the witness that he was coming home from church when he last saw the victim. A check of a period calendar may reveal that October 12th was a Sunday, and that the witness was in error on the date but not the day, due to association with church activity that same day. Thus, the calendar serves as an investigative aid for the investigator and the witness. The object of investigation is to obtain the facts, and with the passage of time, the use of props such as calendars enhances the investigator's ability to seek the truth.

THE INTERVIEW

The traditional police interview has often utilized a "just the facts ma'am, just the facts," question-and-answer approach. In this manner, the investigator asks questions that seek to answer the questions who, what, when, where, why and how. Depending upon the circumstances and available location, the investigator seeking to interview senior citizens may seek to do so in a physical setting most accommodating to the interviewees. Most often this may be their homes or other zones in which they feel most comfortable. The goal of the investigator in this regard should be to make the witness physically and emotionally comfortable, and to enhance witness cooperation.

When interviewing, all other distractions should be removed or turned off, especially radios and televisions. If someone has even a mild cognitive impairment, any distraction could significantly reduce the quality of information provided to investigators. Dr. Blum reports of one interview with a man who could not answer any questions while the door to his hospital room was open. The hallway noise distracted him so much that he became literally incoherent. When the door was closed, however, he was able to hold a reasonable conversation and provided information that turned out to be essential.

On occasion, seniors may wish to have a relative present during the interview. The cold case investigator must make the decision to allow such visitors depending upon the perceived importance of the witnesses, the information they may have to offer, and the anticipated or perceived assistance or interference the visitors may pose.

Make sure the person heard the question and that it was understood. Allow adequate time to respond, and if necessary, ask if they understood the question. Repeat and clarify the question if they indicate they do not, or if you are not sure. During the interview, the investigator should seek to avoid a confrontational atmosphere. If witnesses exhibit initial anxiety, consider changing the subject to a more neutral topic, such as "Did you paint that picture yourself?" When appropriate, slowly come back around to the investigation. If they appear to become upset over little things, respond positively and do not hesitate to accept blame and move forward. Let witnesses wander off the topic on occasion, guiding them back on track as necessary. During the interview, a cold case investigator may consider:

- Formulate and ask a few good questions. Look for areas they may be avoiding.
- Don't use an accusatory tone.
- Let them know that it is okay now to tell what they know.
- Ask leading questions to stimulate other thoughts, questions, and answers.
- Use any previous questions and answers and statements as guide to ascertain whether their statements now are in agreement. Know their statements in advance so you do not have to keep referring to earlier reports.
- Avoid physical barriers such as desk, table, etc., between investigator and witnesses.
- Avoid distractions such as radio, television, etc.
- Avoid sarcasm, "police humor," or comments they may interpret in different context.
- Observe how they react to questions. Note their body language at time of question and time of answer.
- Note unsolicited statements.

Once you have completed the interview, review the high points or critical areas in a "yes or no" answer format. If necessary, ask the same question a second time a few minutes later.

A WORD OF CAUTION

The experienced investigator should *not* fall prey to thinking that senior citizens are like small children; that they are simple and will always be truthful. They have a whole life experience to draw upon, a life configured by circumstances unknown to the investigator. It has not been uncommon for cold case investigators to interview witnesses and suspects in cold case homicides that occurred before the investigator was born. Like all people, some elderly persons possess an ability to lie and deceive that could fool even veteran experienced investigators. Treat them courteously and as professionally as any other victim or witness. Keep in mind that while you are interviewing them, they may be interviewing you. They may be attempting to learn how much you know (about them). In the arena of cold case homicide investigation, those with something to hide may turn deadly at any moment.

Always think and practice officer safety.

CONCLUSION

Senior citizens may offer cold case investigators valuable information. As with the interview process for others, each must be accomplished using the experience and best judgment of the investigator. Understanding what researchers believe about the memory process and how it functions may assist in the interview and evaluation by the investigator when interacting with senior citizens. Memory lapses can be completely normal, especially during the aging process. Forgetting, blurring, or invention of events is a part of the normal memory process. Knowledge and understanding of their physical, emotional, and mental states, as well as familial relationships and pressures, may contribute to the ability of the investigator to elicit important information. Keep in mind the life experiences these people possess, and be patient.

ACKNOWLEDGMENTS

I wish to gratefully acknowledge the significant material and effort contributed to this chapter by Bennett Blum, M.D. Dr. Blum is an internationally recognized expert on forensic and geriatric psychiatry, with emphasis on mental capacity and undue influence assessment. His research on forensic issues in geriatric psychiatry is widely acclaimed, and his works have been utilized by attorneys, law enforcement, and social service personnel. Dr. Blum's website, http://bennett-blummd.com offers further information for those interested in this topic. His offices are located in Tucson, Arizona, and Newport Beach, California. Dr. Blum consults throughout the U.S. and Europe on cases involving elder abuse, mental capacity assessment, and undue influence situations.

In addition, I wish to extend my gratitude and appreciation for input and review of this chapter by Dan Martell, Ph.D., A.B.P.P. and Richard Walter, M.A. Dr. Martell is a Board-certified Fellow of the American Academy of Forensic Psychology, and a Fellow of the American Academy of Forensic Sciences. In addition, he is a Clinical Assistant Professor of Psychiatry and Biobehavioral Science, Neuropsychiatric Institute, U.C.L.A. School of Medicine. He maintains a private practice in Newport Beach, California, and consults nationally on criminal and civil cases involving brain damage and related psychological issues. Richard Walter is a retired prison psychologist and consulting expert in crime assessment, as well as co-founder of The Vidocq Society.

In addition, I wish to express my deep appreciation to veteran detectives Kevin Lowe and Dan McElderry of the Los Angeles County Sheriff's Homicide Bureau for sharing their insight, experiences, and perceptions on interviewing senior citizens during homicide and cold case homicide investigations.

SUGGESTED READING

Anonymous. (1991). "Confusion and Memory Loss in Old Age: It's Not What You Think." National Institute on Aging. Gaithersburg, MD.

Anonymous. (2003). "Information from Your Family Doctor: Memory Loss." *American Family Physician.* V67, I5. March 1, 2003.

Baddeley, A. (1998). *Human Memory: Theory and Practice* (Revised edition). Allyn and Bacon. London.

Blum, B. (2005). "Geriatric psychiatry: Forensic issues." *Kaplan and Sadock's Comprehensive Textbook of Psychiatry* (8th ed.). Lippincott, Williams, and Wilkins.

Gordon, B. (1995). *Memory: Remembering and Forgetting in Everyday Life*. Mastermedia Limited. New York.

Haberlandt, K. (1999). *Human Memory: Exploration and Application*. Allyn and Bacon. Boston.

Loftus, E.F. (1996). Eyewitness Testimony. Harvard University Press. Cambridge.

Lovden, M., Ronnlund, M., Washlin, A., Backman, L., et al. *The Journals of Gerontology: Series B: Psychological Science and Social Sciences*. Washington, D.C. V59B, I3. May, 2004.

Memon, A., Barblett, J., Rose, R., Gray, C. *The Journals of Gerontology: Series B: Psychological Sciences and Social Sciences*. Washington, D.C. V. 58B, I6. Nov. 2003.

Parkin, A.J. (1993). *Memory: Phenomena, Experiment and Theory*. Blackwell Publishers. Oxford.

Taylor, K.T. (2001). *Forensic Art and Illustration*. CRC Press. Boca Raton.

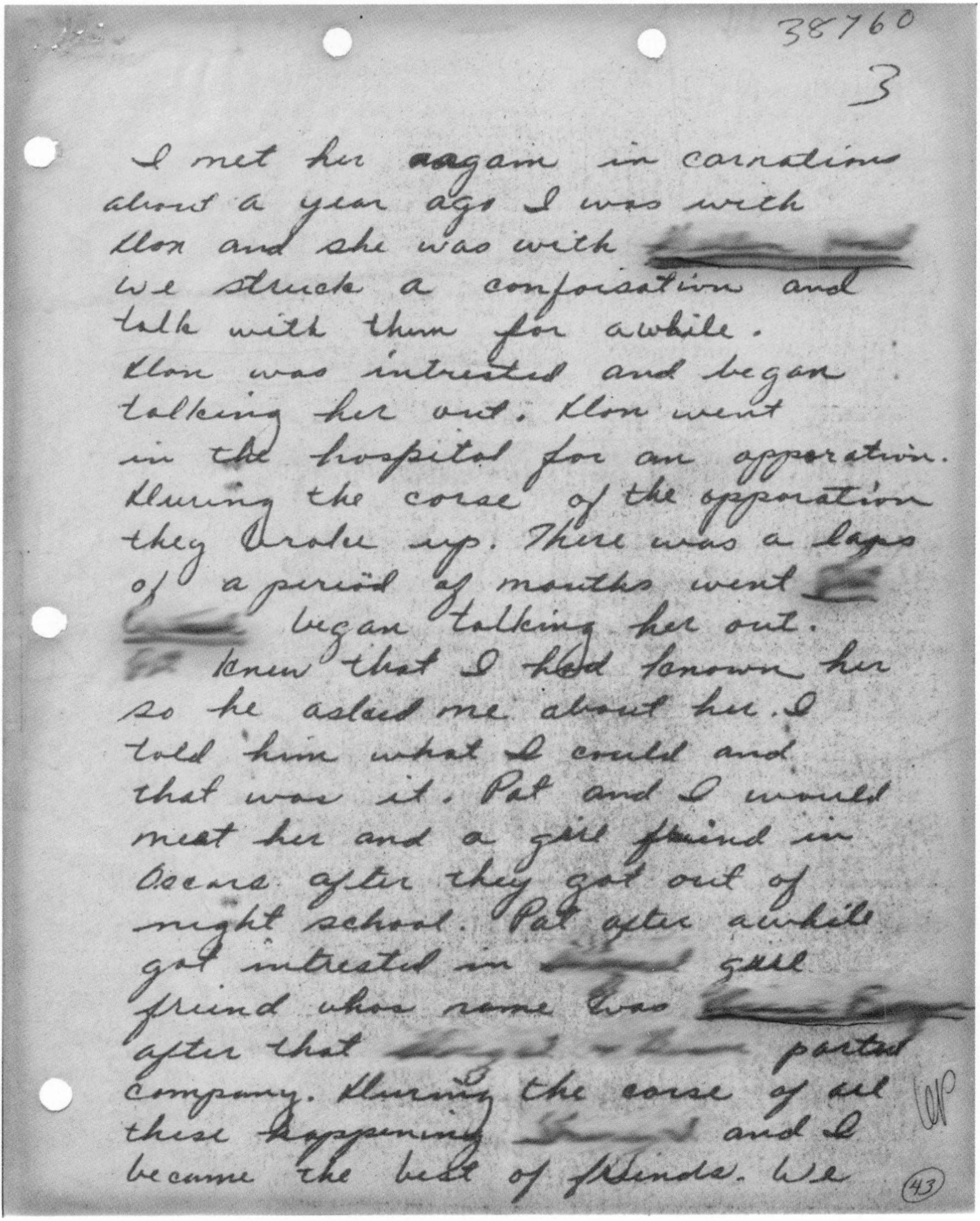

3

I met her ~~aagain~~ again in carnations
about a year ago I was with
Ron and she was with ████████
we struck a conforsation and
talk with them for awhile.
Ron was intrested and began
talking her out. Ron went
in the hospital for an opporation.
during the corse of the opporation
they broke up. There was a laps
of a period of mouths went ████
████ began talking her out.
████ knew that I had known her
so he asked me about her. I
told him what I could and
that was it. Pat and I would
meat her and a girl friend in
Oscars after they got out of
night school. Pat after awhile
got intrested in ████████ girl
friend whose name was ████████
after that ████████████ parted
company. during the corse of all
these ~~happening~~ ████████ and I
became the best of friends. We

(43)

COLOR FIGURE 2.7

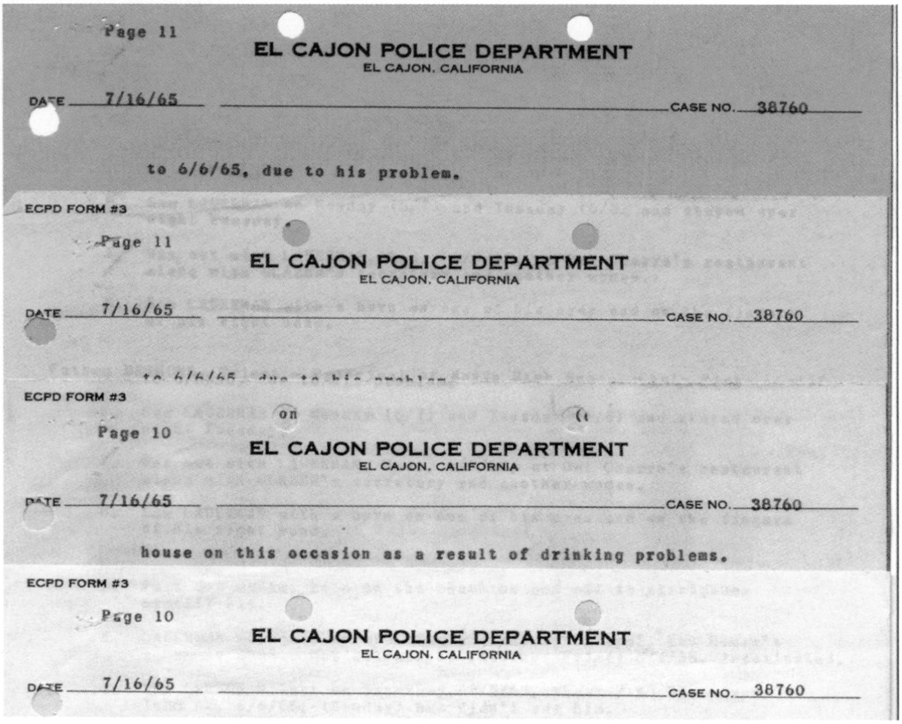

Page 11

EL CAJON POLICE DEPARTMENT
EL CAJON, CALIFORNIA

DATE   7/16/65 _____ CASE NO.   38760

to 6/6/65, due to his problem.

ECPD FORM #3

Page 11

EL CAJON POLICE DEPARTMENT
EL CAJON, CALIFORNIA

DATE   7/16/65 _____ CASE NO.   38760

to 6/6/65, due to his problem.

ECPD FORM #3

Page 10

EL CAJON POLICE DEPARTMENT
EL CAJON, CALIFORNIA

DATE   7/16/65 _____ CASE NO.   38760

house on this occasion as a result of drinking problems.

ECPD FORM #3

Page 10

EL CAJON POLICE DEPARTMENT
EL CAJON, CALIFORNIA

DATE   7/16/65 _____ CASE NO.   38760

COLOR FIGURE 2.9

Cases in TracKRS Database
August 1996 Through July 2004

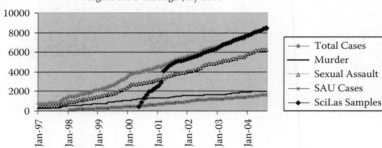

- ◆ Total Cases
- ━ Murder
- △ Sexual Assault
- ✳ SAU Cases
- ◆ SciLas Samples

COLOR FIGURE 6.9

PRESS RELEASE - Dated: July 26, 2004
LOS ANGELES POLICE DEPARTMENT
William J. Bratton, *Chief of Police*

On April 12, 1991, Soo Hoo Quon, 93 years of age,
was found brutally murdered in her residence
at 2433 N. Eastern Avenue, Los Angeles.

Victim:
Soo Hoo Quon
Case: No. DR 91-04 00591

Suspect:
Albert Rodriguez Salinas
Now 42 years old
On Parole

On July 22, 2004, Mr. Salinas was
taken into custody by the Cold Case
Homicide detectives with the
assistance of State Parole
charging him with
Ms. Quon's murder.

 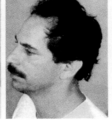

Cold Case Homicide Unit
Robbery Homicide Division
(213) 847-0970

COLOR FIGURE 12.11

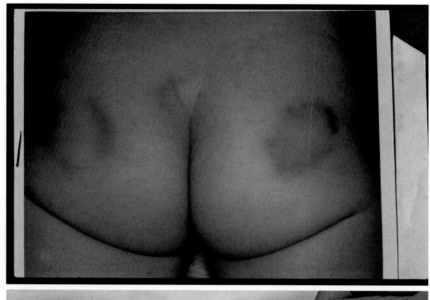

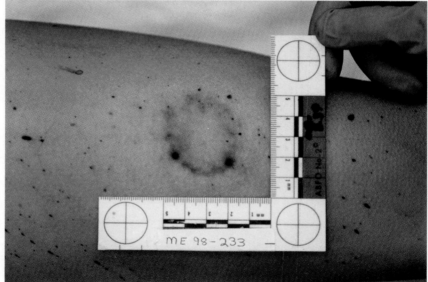

COLOR FIGURE 21.8

COLOR FIGURE 26.4

COLOR FIGURE 28.4

SAN DIEGO COUNTY SHERIFF'S DEPARTMENT
HOMICIDE DETAIL
"VALLEY CENTER JANE DOE"

Gold Cross on chain

"LAFFEL USA" Brand shirt

Two Gold Rings:
Heart with a center stone
Crucifix with a stone

Newly applied acrylic fingernails painted red

LA GEAR Hi-TOPS

"CYCLONE" Brand Jeans

k.t.taylor
2-16-02

COLOR FIGURE 28.7

COLOR FIGURE 30.1

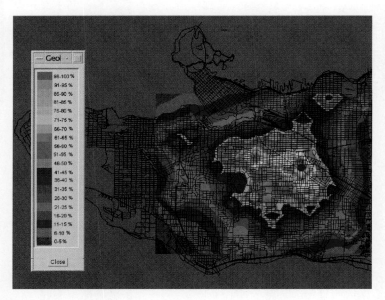

COLOR FIGURE 30.2

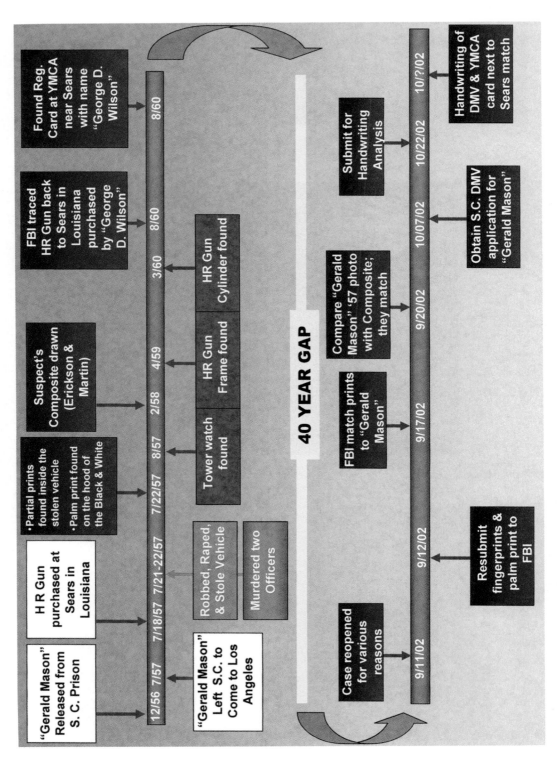

COLOR FIGURE 31.29

9 Death Certificate and Obituary

Richard H. Walton

CONTENTS

A number of documents not normally encountered in the unsolved homicide investigation case file may provide investigative direction to cold case homicide investigators. These documents may be especially valuable when, in the perception of the investigator(s), the case file is incomplete or lacking in some material areas, or as a guide for investigation and determination of relationships. Among these documents are:

- Certificate of Death
- Application and Permit for Disposition of Human Remains
- Physician or Coroner's Amendment
- Obituary

This section examines these documents and their relevance during the course of a cold case homicide investigation.

DEATH CERTIFICATE

Interestingly enough, in my experience, it is not uncommon or unusual to find the Certificate of Death, also called the *death certificate*, absent when reviewing a case file that has been inactive. During the course of the initial homicide investigation, obtaining this document for the file may not have been a high priority due to the course of the investigation and other duties encountered by the original investigators. As the case was not forwarded to the district attorney for prosecution, obtaining this document for the murder book did not get done.

With the reactivation of a cold case, obtaining and reviewing this document is an important course of action. The information in the Certificate of Death is compiled and constructed by officials involved in the course of establishing death and disposition of the remains. Unlike the obituary, this document is not directly compiled by family members, although some information on the death certificate may originate with a family member or close friends. According to the American Medical Association, a death certificate must be filed for every individual who dies, including stillborn fetuses, in most states.

There is no national system of death investigation in the U.S., nor is there a uniform system for recording the information on a Certificate of Death. There is, however, some information that is consistent across the nation. This includes basic information identifying the individual and information surrounding the cause, mode, and manner of death. All states provide for a permanent and compulsory vital statistics registration system. This system, however, depends upon the willingness and cooperation of those involved with the decedent, including physicians, hospitals, coroners or medical examiners, and funeral directors, to prepare and certify necessary information.

In some states, vital statistic information relating to births, deaths, or fetal deaths may be mandated for direct reporting to the state vital statistics unit by the primary source. This may include hospitals, coroners or medical examiners, and funeral directors. Some, but not all, states are divided into registration districts in furtherance of collecting vital statistic information and they utilize a local registrar system. These districts may be a county, city, or other geographical or political subdivision, or a combination of these. In these states, this office collects the necessary information for transmittal to the state bureau or office of vital statistics. The local registrar is required to ensure that a complete certificate for each of these events is filed. In some states, this official also issues burial and transportation permits for deceased persons (see Figure 9.1).

Not uncommonly, the Certificate of Death is initiated by the mortuary, which obtains vital information from the family (as the legal representative) as well as the attending physician. It prepares the document and forwards it to the physician for signature. After this signing, the document is returned to the mortuary and then forwarded to the registrar for assignment of a file number and permit for disposition. A sign of the times — in some locales, mortuaries are now prohibited from keeping copies of death certificates in their case files due to identity-theft concerns.

It is suggested that review of the death certificate be completed in the earliest stages of the reinvestigation of a cold case homicide. In those cases in which the identity of the victim is known yet the case must be reconstructed from "scratch," that is, with little or no information on file, this document provides a jump-off point for numerous avenues of investigation. These include:

- Identification of dates for newspaper review and subsequent identification of persons and reported events
- Dates and time frames for review of agency archives and document search
- Names of relatives
- Mortuary records or other disposition information that may contain more detailed information

At the outset of the cold case investigation, the Certificate of Death identifies:

- The name and personal information of the decedent
- The decedent's usual residence
- The place of death
- Approximate interval between onset and death
- The cause of death
- Approximate time of death
- Name and address of informant
- Physician's certifications
- Injury information
- Other Coroner's or Medical Examiner's information
- Disposition of remains
- Pertinent dates and names of those persons involved with the care and processing of decedent's remains

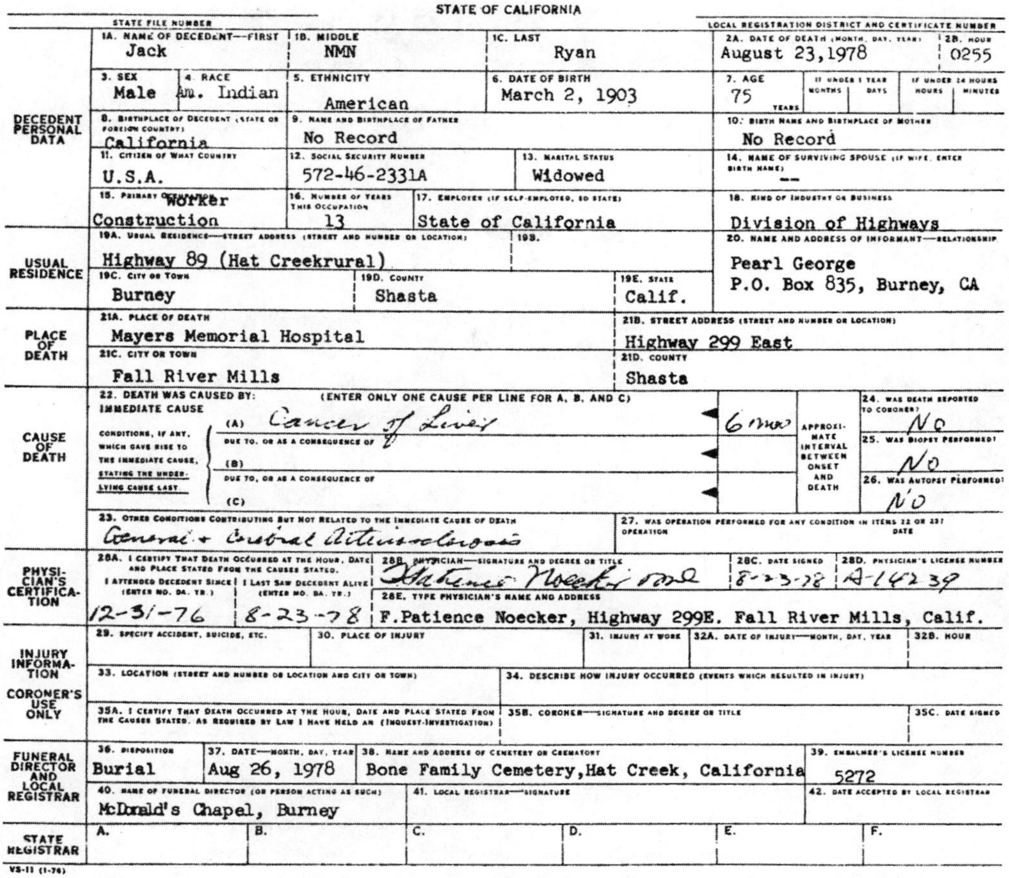

STATE OF CALIFORNIA

STATE FILE NUMBER | LOCAL REGISTRATION DISTRICT AND CERTIFICATE NUMBER

DECEDENT PERSONAL DATA

1A. NAME OF DECEDENT—FIRST: Jack | 1B. MIDDLE: NMN | 1C. LAST: Ryan | 2A. DATE OF DEATH (MONTH, DAY, YEAR): August 23,1978 | 2B. HOUR: 0255

3. SEX: Male | 4. RACE: Am. Indian | 5. ETHNICITY: American | 6. DATE OF BIRTH: March 2, 1903 | 7. AGE: 75 YEARS | IF UNDER 1 YEAR: MONTHS, DAYS | IF UNDER 24 HOURS: HOURS, MINUTES

8. BIRTHPLACE OF DECEDENT (STATE OR FOREIGN COUNTRY): California | 9. NAME AND BIRTHPLACE OF FATHER: No Record | 10. BIRTH NAME AND BIRTHPLACE OF MOTHER: No Record

11. CITIZEN OF WHAT COUNTRY: U.S.A. | 12. SOCIAL SECURITY NUMBER: 572-46-2331A | 13. MARITAL STATUS: Widowed | 14. NAME OF SURVIVING SPOUSE (IF WIFE, ENTER BIRTH NAME): —

15. PRIMARY OCCUPATION: Worker Construction | 16. NUMBER OF YEARS THIS OCCUPATION: 13 | 17. EMPLOYER (IF SELF-EMPLOYED, SO STATE): State of California | 18. KIND OF INDUSTRY OR BUSINESS: Division of Highways

USUAL RESIDENCE

19A. USUAL RESIDENCE—STREET ADDRESS (STREET AND NUMBER OR LOCATION): Highway 89 (Hat Creekrural) | 19B.

19C. CITY OR TOWN: Burney | 19D. COUNTY: Shasta | 19E. STATE: Calif.

20. NAME AND ADDRESS OF INFORMANT—RELATIONSHIP: Pearl George P.O. Box 835, Burney, CA

PLACE OF DEATH

21A. PLACE OF DEATH: Mayers Memorial Hospital | 21B. STREET ADDRESS (STREET AND NUMBER OR LOCATION): Highway 299 East

21C. CITY OR TOWN: Fall River Mills | 21D. COUNTY: Shasta

CAUSE OF DEATH

22. DEATH WAS CAUSED BY: (ENTER ONLY ONE CAUSE PER LINE FOR A, B, AND C)

IMMEDIATE CAUSE (A) Cancer of Liver — 6 mos — APPROXIMATE INTERVAL BETWEEN ONSET AND DEATH

CONDITIONS, IF ANY, WHICH GAVE RISE TO THE IMMEDIATE CAUSE, STATING THE UNDERLYING CAUSE LAST

DUE TO, OR AS A CONSEQUENCE OF (B)

DUE TO, OR AS A CONSEQUENCE OF (C)

24. WAS DEATH REPORTED TO CORONER? No | 25. WAS BIOPSY PERFORMED? No | 26. WAS AUTOPSY PERFORMED? No

23. OTHER CONDITIONS CONTRIBUTING BUT NOT RELATED TO THE IMMEDIATE CAUSE OF DEATH: General + Cerebral Arteriosclerosis

27. WAS OPERATION PERFORMED FOR ANY CONDITION IN ITEMS 22 OR 23? OPERATION | DATE

PHYSICIAN'S CERTIFICATION

28A. I CERTIFY THAT DEATH OCCURRED AT THE HOUR, DATE AND PLACE STATED FROM THE CAUSES STATED. I ATTENDED DECEDENT SINCE (ENTER MO. DA. YR.): 12-31-76 | I LAST SAW DECEDENT ALIVE (ENTER MO. DA. YR.): 8-23-78

28B. PHYSICIAN—SIGNATURE AND DEGREE OR TITLE: [signature] MD | 28C. DATE SIGNED: 8-23-78 | 28D. PHYSICIAN'S LICENSE NUMBER: A-14239

28E. TYPE PHYSICIAN'S NAME AND ADDRESS: F.Patience Noecker, Highway 299E. Fall River Mills, Calif.

INJURY INFORMATION / CORONER'S USE ONLY

29. SPECIFY ACCIDENT, SUICIDE, ETC. | 30. PLACE OF INJURY | 31. INJURY AT WORK | 32A. DATE OF INJURY—MONTH, DAY, YEAR | 32B. HOUR

33. LOCATION (STREET AND NUMBER OR LOCATION AND CITY OR TOWN) | 34. DESCRIBE HOW INJURY OCCURRED (EVENTS WHICH RESULTED IN INJURY)

35A. I CERTIFY THAT DEATH OCCURRED AT THE HOUR, DATE AND PLACE STATED FROM THE CAUSES STATED. AS REQUIRED BY LAW I HAVE HELD AN (INQUEST-INVESTIGATION) | 35B. CORONER—SIGNATURE AND DEGREE OR TITLE | 35C. DATE SIGNED

FUNERAL DIRECTOR AND LOCAL REGISTRAR

36. DISPOSITION: Burial | 37. DATE—MONTH, DAY, YEAR: Aug 26, 1978 | 38. NAME AND ADDRESS OF CEMETERY OR CREMATORY: Bone Family Cemetery,Hat Creek, California | 39. EMBALMER'S LICENSE NUMBER: 5272

40. NAME OF FUNERAL DIRECTOR (OR PERSON ACTING AS SUCH): McDonald's Chapel, Burney | 41. LOCAL REGISTRAR—SIGNATURE | 42. DATE ACCEPTED BY LOCAL REGISTRAR

STATE REGISTRAR: A. | B. | C. | D. | E. | F.

VS-11 (1-76)

FIGURE 9.1 This older Death Certificate (Ryan 1978), shows that the format of death certificates has changed over the years, but the core information has not. (Author's file)

As a result, this document provides names, dates, and known circumstances as officially recorded. This information, or portions of it, may be lacking in the present case file, and this document offers investigators potential sources for investigative information as well as, in some circumstances, potential sources to recover missing or uncollected evidence. That the death was ruled a homicide is important for investigation and prosecution, although cold case investigations can, and have, gone forward when the death certificate has initially ruled the case as accidental, suicide, or undetermined (see Figure 9.2).

At the forefront of the investigation, the death certificate informs the cold case investigators as to the medical opinion rendered at the time of the autopsy (if there was one). While required in homicide cases, they may not have been performed, depending upon the medical, legal, or — sadly — political climate at the time.

Death certificates are issued for the known death of any human being. They are normally issued only in the county and state in which the death occurred, excluding a death at sea. A *regular* state death certificate is issued for any person who has breathed on their own. A *fetal* death certificate may be issued for the death of a fetus. If a fetus took one breath of air on his or her own, a birth certificate would be issued, and then a death certificate.

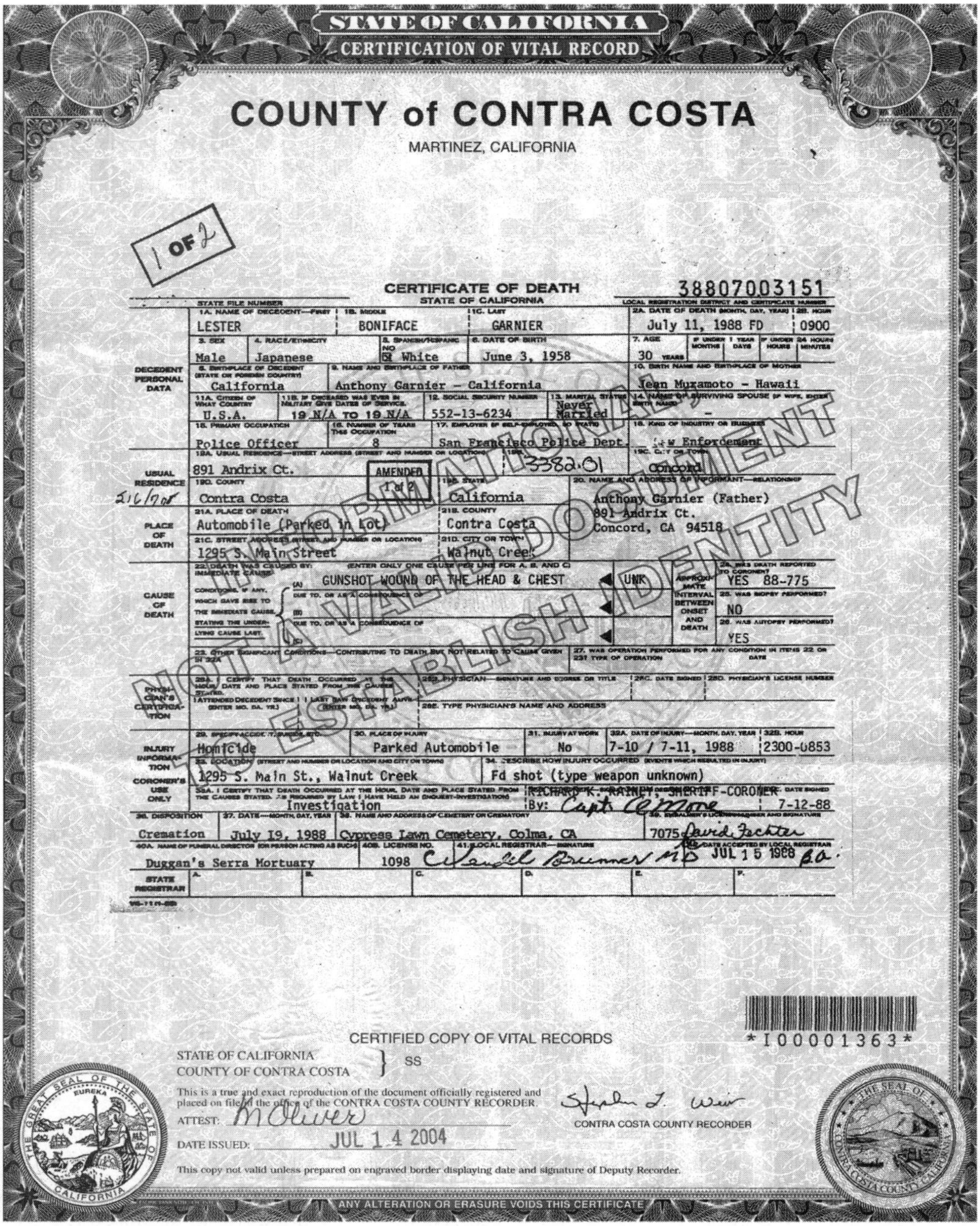
STATE OF CALIFORNIA
CERTIFICATION OF VITAL RECORD

COUNTY of CONTRA COSTA
MARTINEZ, CALIFORNIA

1 OF 2

CERTIFICATE OF DEATH 38807003151
STATE OF CALIFORNIA

1A. NAME OF DECEDENT—FIRST: LESTER | 1B. MIDDLE: BONIFACE | 1C. LAST: GARNIER | 2A. DATE OF DEATH: July 11, 1988 FD | 2B. HOUR: 0900
3. SEX: Male | 4. RACE/ETHNICITY: Japanese | 5. SPANISH/HISPANIC: NO White | 6. DATE OF BIRTH: June 3, 1958 | 7. AGE: 30 YEARS
8. BIRTHPLACE OF DECEDENT: California | 9. NAME AND BIRTHPLACE OF FATHER: Anthony Garnier - California | 10. BIRTH NAME AND BIRTHPLACE OF MOTHER: Jean Muramoto - Hawaii
11A. CITIZEN OF WHAT COUNTRY: U.S.A. | 11B. IF DECEASED WAS EVER IN MILITARY GIVE DATES OF SERVICE: 19 N/A TO 19 N/A | 12. SOCIAL SECURITY NUMBER: 552-13-6234 | 13. MARITAL STATUS: Never Married | 14. NAME OF SURVIVING SPOUSE: -
15. PRIMARY OCCUPATION: Police Officer | 16. NUMBER OF YEARS THIS OCCUPATION: 8 | 17. EMPLOYER: San Francisco Police Dept. | 18. KIND OF INDUSTRY OR BUSINESS: Law Enforcement
USUAL RESIDENCE: 19A. USUAL RESIDENCE: 891 Andrix Ct. | 3382.01 | 19C. CITY OR TOWN: Concord
19D. COUNTY: Contra Costa | 19E. STATE: California | 20. NAME AND ADDRESS OF INFORMANT—RELATIONSHIP: Anthony Garnier (Father) 891 Andrix Ct. Concord, CA 94518
AMENDED 1 of 2
PLACE OF DEATH: 21A. PLACE OF DEATH: Automobile (Parked in Lot) | 21B. COUNTY: Contra Costa
21C. STREET ADDRESS: 1295 S. Main Street | 21D. CITY OR TOWN: Walnut Creek
CAUSE OF DEATH: 22. DEATH WAS CAUSED BY: IMMEDIATE CAUSE (A) GUNSHOT WOUND OF THE HEAD & CHEST | UNK | 24. WAS DEATH REPORTED TO CORONER? YES 88-775 | 25. WAS BIOPSY PERFORMED? NO | 26. WAS AUTOPSY PERFORMED? YES
23. OTHER SIGNIFICANT CONDITIONS | 27. WAS OPERATION PERFORMED
28A. PHYSICIAN'S CERTIFICATION | 28B. PHYSICIAN—SIGNATURE AND DEGREE OR TITLE | 28C. DATE SIGNED | 28D. PHYSICIAN'S LICENSE NUMBER | 28E. TYPE PHYSICIAN'S NAME AND ADDRESS
INJURY INFORMATION: 29. SPECIFY ACCIDENT, SUICIDE, ETC.: Homicide | 30. PLACE OF INJURY: Parked Automobile | 31. INJURY AT WORK: No | 32A. DATE OF INJURY: 7-10 / 7-11, 1988 | 32B. HOUR: 2300-0853
33. LOCATION: 1295 S. Main St., Walnut Creek | 34. DESCRIBE HOW INJURY OCCURRED: Fd shot (type weapon unknown)
CORONER'S USE ONLY: 35A. Investigation | RICHARD K. RAINEY, SHERIFF-CORONER By: Capt. [signature] | 7-12-88
36. DISPOSITION: Cremation | 37. DATE: July 19, 1988 | 38. NAME AND ADDRESS OF CEMETERY OR CREMATORY: Cypress Lawn Cemetery, Colma, CA | 7075 [signature]
40A. NAME OF FUNERAL DIRECTOR: Duggan's Serra Mortuary | 40B. LICENSE NO.: 1098 | 41. LOCAL REGISTRAR—SIGNATURE: [signature] MD | 42. DATE ACCEPTED BY LOCAL REGISTRAR: JUL 15 1988

NOT A VALID DOCUMENT TO ESTABLISH IDENTITY
INFORMATIONAL

I00001363

CERTIFIED COPY OF VITAL RECORDS
STATE OF CALIFORNIA } SS
COUNTY OF CONTRA COSTA
This is a true and exact reproduction of the document officially registered and placed on file in the office of the CONTRA COSTA COUNTY RECORDER.
ATTEST: M Oliver
DATE ISSUED: JUL 14 2004
CONTRA COSTA COUNTY RECORDER
This copy not valid unless prepared on engraved border displaying date and signature of Deputy Recorder.
ANY ALTERATION OR ERASURE VOIDS THIS CERTIFICATE

FIGURE 9.2 Due to increasing concerns about identity theft and terrorism, access to copies of death certificates is increasingly more restricted. For non-family members or other non-official purposes, copies of more recent death certificates may be labeled "informational" to identify them as having been issued to third parties. (Author's file)

A legal document, the Certificate of Death is a certification of vital record and is issued in the name of the state. It might indicate the manner of death as natural, accidental, suicide, homicide, or undetermined.

Death certificates may be *amended* when erroneous information has been found to have been included on the original death certificate (see Figure 9.3). Normally, this change is at the behest of the physician or coroner. In this case, an Affidavit to Amend a Record or similar procedure may be filed to correct the error, and the Certificate of Death will subsequently reflect these changes as well as noting that this change process occurred. Only a physician can amend those portions of the certificate of death pertaining to medical aspects of the document. If a typo or other change needs to be made, the mortuary may process the amendment. When obtaining a Certificate of Death for a cold case homicide, investigators should seek to determine whether any subsequent corrections and amendments had occurred.

INFORMATION FOUND ON THE DEATH CERTIFICATE

Inspection of the death certificate may reflect detailed information that includes:

- Decedent's personal data
  - First, middle, last name
  - Date of death (month, day, year)
  - Estimated hour of death
  - Sex of decedent
  - Race or ethnicity
  - Date of birth
  - Age at time of death
  - Birthplace
  - Name and birthplace of father
  - Birth name and birthplace of mother
  - Country of citizenship
  - Dates of military service
  - Social Security Number
  - Marital status
  - Name of surviving spouse
  - Occupation
  - Number of years in occupation
  - Employer
  - Nature of business or industry
- Residence Information
  - Usual residence (street and address or location)
  - Town or city
  - County
  - State
- Place of death
  - Physical location of death (inside automobile in a parking lot, etc.)
  - Nearest street address
  - City
  - County

- Name and address of informant (and relationship)
  - Normally the legal next of kin (which goes in order from wife, adult children, parents, etc.) who provides needed information for the certificate. An exception could be a person with a medical durable power of attorney or the Public Administrator.

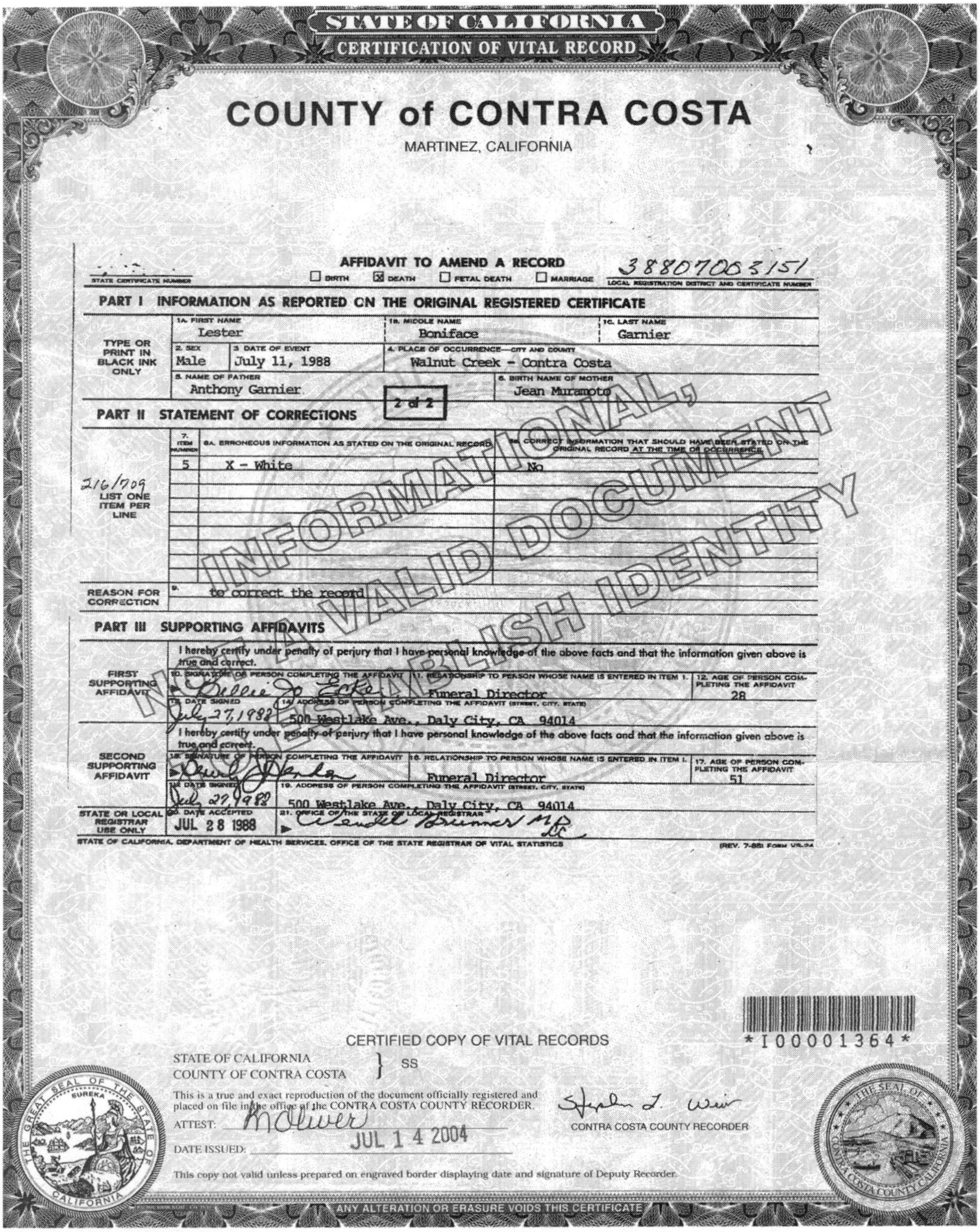

FIGURE 9.3 Amendment to Death Certificate. (Author's file)

- Cause of death
  - What caused immediate death
  - Conditions, if any, that gave rise to the immediate cause of death
  - Underlying cause of death
  - Other significant conditions contributing to death but not related to cause given
- Approximate interval between onset and death
  - Was death reported to the Coroner or Medical Examiner? (and case number)
  - Was biopsy performed?
  - Was autopsy performed?
- Physician's certification
  - Certification by physician that death occurred as described
  - Certification of attending physician, if applicable, for time period prior to death
  - Physician signature and title
  - Date signed
  - Physicians name and address (typed)
  - Physicians license number
- Injury information
  - Specific injury type (accident, suicide, etc)
  - Place of injury (parked automobile, etc)
  - Location of injury (street or other address)
  - Description of how injury occurred or events resulting in injury ("Found shot (type weapon unknown")
  - Whether work related
  - Date of injury (month/day/year)
  - Hour of death
- Disposition of remains
  - Type of disposition
  - Date (month/day/year)
  - Name and address of cemetery
  - Embalmer's name and license number
  - Name of funeral director or person acting as such
  - License number
- Other information
  - Coroner's investigation
  - Coroner's inquest
  - Signature of Coroner or Medical Examiner certifying the document and events
  - Date of signature

CERTIFICATE OF FETAL DEATH

When the deceased is a fetus, a Certificate of Fetal Death may be substituted for a regular State Certificate of Death. While the specific definition for this purpose may vary — for example, in California a fetus for this purpose would be defined as one 21 weeks of (gestational) age or older that has not breathed air on its own. In this state, if the fetus is less than 21 weeks of age, no death certificate is required. In some circumstances, if the fetus is less than 21 weeks, only a letter from an attending physician attesting to gestation may be necessary and the fetus may be buried or otherwise disposed of with no formal certificate or permit. Due to the nature of the victim in these cases, and apparent statistical reporting purposes, additional information is required on the certificate (see Figure 9.4).

CERTIFICATE OF FETAL DEATH
STATE OF CALIFORNIA
USE BLACK INK ONLY MAKE NO ERASURES, WHITEOUTS, OR OTHER ALTERATIONS

STATE FILE NUMBER   LOCAL REGISTRATION DISTRICT AND CERTIFICATE NUMBER

THIS FETUS
1A. NAME—FIRST (GIVEN) | 1B. MIDDLE | 1C. LAST (FAMILY)
2. SEX | 3A. THIS FETUS, SINGLE, TWIN, ETC. | 3B. IF MULTIPLE THIS FETUS 1ST, 2ND, ETC. | 4A. DATE OF EVENT—MONTH, DAY, YEAR | 4B. HOUR—24 HOUR CLOCK TIME

PLACE OF DELIVERY
5A. PLACE OF EVENT—NAME OF HOSPITAL OR FACILITY | 5B. STREET ADDRESS—STREET, NUMBER, OR LOCATION
5C. CITY | 5D. COUNTY | 5E. PLANNED PLACE OF DELIVERY

FATHER
6A. NAME OF FATHER—FIRST (GIVEN) | 6B. MIDDLE | 6C. LAST (FAMILY) | 7. STATE OF BIRTH | 8. DATE OF BIRTH—MONTH, DAY, YEAR

MOTHER
9A. NAME OF MOTHER—FIRST (GIVEN) | 9B. MIDDLE | 9C. LAST (MAIDEN) | 10. STATE OF BIRTH | 11. DATE OF BIRTH—MONTH, DAY, YEAR

CERTIFICATION
I CERTIFY THAT THIS FETUS WAS BORN DEAD AT THE HOUR, DATE AND PLACE STATED FROM THE CAUSES STATED. | 12A. SIGNATURE OF PHYSICIAN, CORONER, OR DEPUTY CORONER | 12B. DEGREE OR TITLE AND TYPED NAME | 12C. DATE SIGNED | 12D. LICENSE NUMBER

FUNERAL DIRECTOR AND LOCAL REGISTRAR
13A. DISPOSITION(S) | 13B. PLACE OF DISPOSITION—NAME AND ADDRESS | 13C. DATE MO, DAY, YEAR | 14A. SIGNATURE OF EMBALMER | 14B. LICENSE NUMBER
15A. NAME OF FUNERAL DIRECTOR (OR PERSON ACTING AS SUCH) | 15B. LICENSE NUMBER | 16. SIGNATURE OF LOCAL REGISTRAR | 17. REGISTRATION DATE

CONFIDENTIAL HEALTH AND MEDICAL INFORMATION

CAUSE OF DEATH
18. FETAL DEATH WAS CAUSED BY:
IMMEDIATE CAUSE (A)
DUE TO (B)
DUE TO (C)
21. OTHER SIGNIFICANT CONDITIONS OF FETUS OR MOTHER—CONTRIBUTING TO FETAL DEATH BUT NOT RELATED TO CAUSE GIVEN IN 18.
19. WAS DEATH REPORTED TO CORONER? REFERRAL NUMBER YES NO
20A. WAS AUTOPSY PERFORMED? YES NO
20B. WAS IT USED IN DETERMINING CAUSE OF DEATH? YES NO

FATHER
22. RACE | 23. HISPANIC SPECIFY YES NO | 24A. USUAL OCCUPATION | 24B. USUAL KIND OF BUSINESS OR INDUSTRY | 24C. EDUCATION—YRS. COMPLETED

MOTHER
25. RACE | 26. HISPANIC SPECIFY YES NO | 27A. USUAL OCCUPATION | 27B. USUAL KIND OF BUSINESS OR INDUSTRY | 27C. EDUCATION—YRS. COMPLETED
28A. RESIDENCE—STREET, NUMBER, OR LOCATION | 28B. CITY | 28C. STATE | 28D. ZIP | 28E. COUNTY

MEDICAL DATA
(ENTER THE APPROPRIATE CODE(S) FOR ITEMS 29D AND 32A–35 FROM THE VS 12A SUPPLEMENTAL WORKSHEET.)
29A. DATE LAST NORMAL MENSES BEGAN MONTH DAY YEAR | 29B. MONTH PRENATAL CARE BEGAN (1ST, 2ND, ...8TH, 9TH) | 29C. NUMBER OF PRENATAL VISITS | 31. PREGNANCY HISTORY (COMPLETE EACH SECTION)
LIVE BIRTHS | OTHER TERMINATIONS (EXCLUDE INDUCED ABORTIONS)
29D. PRINCIPAL SOURCE OF PAYMENT FOR PRENATAL CARE CODE: | 30. FETAL WEIGHT GRAMS | 32A. METHOD OF DELIVERY CODE(S): | NOW LIVING (NUMBER) A | NOW DEAD (NUMBER) B | BEFORE 20 WKS (NUMBER) D | AFTER 20 WKS (NUMBER) E
32B. EXPECTED PRINCIPAL SOURCE OF PAYMENT FOR DELIVERY CODE: | 33. COMPLICATIONS AND PROCEDURES OF PREGNANCY AND CONCURRENT ILLNESSES CODE(S): | DATE OF LAST LIVE BIRTH MONTH DAY YEAR C | DATE OF LAST OTHER TERM. MONTH YEAR F
34. COMPLICATIONS AND PROCEDURES OF LABOR AND DELIVERY CODE(S): | 35. ABNORMAL CONDITIONS AND CLINICAL PROCEDURES RELATING TO THE FETUS CODE(S):

STATE REGISTRAR
A. | B. | C. | D. | E. | F. | CENSUS TRACT

VS 12 (REV 7/91)   PENALTY FOR UNAUTHORIZED RELEASE, $500 FINE OR SIX MONTHS IMPRISONMENT.   OSP 00 36252

FIGURE 9.4 The Fetal Death Certificate. This form of death certificate reveals more information about mother, father, and other births. (Courtesy of Daniel Williams)

This certificate may indicate information relative to

- This fetus
  - First (given), middle, and last (family) name
  - Sex
  - Single, twin, etc.
  - If multiple birth, whether this fetus is 1st, 2nd, etc.
  - Date of event (month/day/year)
  - Hour
- Place of Delivery
  - Place of event
  - Address
  - City
  - County
  - Planned place of delivery
- Father
  - Full name
  - State of birth
  - Date of birth

- Mother
  - First, middle, last (maiden) name
  - State of birth
  - Date of birth
- Certification by physician, coroner, or deputy coroner
  - Degree or title and typed name
  - Date signed
  - License number
- Funeral director and local registrar
  - Disposition
  - Place of disposition
  - Date
  - Signature of embalmer
  - License number
  - Name of funeral director or person acting as such
  - License number
  - Signature of local registrar
  - Registration date
- Cause of Death
  - Immediate cause
  - Due to
  - Was death reported to coroner and referral number
  - Was autopsy performed
  - Was it used in determining cause of death
  - Other significant conditions of fetus or mother contributing to fetal death but not previously given
- Father
  - Race
  - Ethnicity
  - Usual occupation
  - Usual kind of business
  - Education
- Mother
  - Race
  - Ethnicity
  - Usual occupation
  - Usual kind of business
  - Education
  - Residence address
  - City, state, and zip code
  - Country
- Medical Data
  - Date last normal menses began
  - Month prenatal care began
  - Number of prenatal visits
  - Principal source of payment for prenatal care
  - Expected principal source of payment for delivery
  - Complications and procedures of pregnancy and concurrent illnesses
  - Complications and procedures of labor and delivery
  - Abnormal conditions and clinical procedures relating to the fetus
  - Fetal weight

- Method of delivery
- Pregnancy history
  - Live births
    - Now living (number)
    - Now dead (number)
    - Date of last live birth
- Other terminations
  - Before 20 weeks
  - After 20 weeks
  - Date of last other term

APPLICATION AND PERMIT FOR DISPOSITION OF HUMAN REMAINS

Normally, a permit from local health authorities is required to transport human remains. This permit may offer additional information to cold case investigators regarding the decedent, death, and disposition of the remains. This permit may be required at all stages of the handling of human remains, including the forensic exhumation. This application and permit might be issued by the city or county registrar or other designated official, including health department. Among the information to be found on this document is included:

- Decedent's full name
- Date of birth
- Date of death
- Sex
- City of death
- County of death
- Name, relationship and address of informant
- Name and address of funeral director or those acting on their behalf
- Signature and date of applicant for permit

Types of Disposition of Human Remains

There are a number of options available for the disposition of human remains, including:

- Burial (including entombment)
- Temporary envaultment
- Cremation
- Disposition of cremated remains other than in a cemetery
- Scientific use
- Transit
- Scattering or burial at sea or disposition other than in a cemetery

While a review of this application and permit denotes the disposition of the remains, it may also indicate:

- Name and address of the cemetery of burial, including
  - Date buried
  - Signature of person in charge of burial
- Cremation
  - Name and address of crematory
  - Date cremated
  - Signature of person in charge of cremation

- Scientific use
  - Name and address of facility receiving remains
  - Date received
  - Signature of person in charge of facility
- Transit
- Name and address in receiving state or country where remains or cremated remains are to be shipped.
- Date shipped
- Address and signature of person in charge of placing with the carrier
- Scattering, including burial at sea or disposition other than in a cemetery
  - Address, nearest point on shoreline, or other description sufficient to identify final place. If burial at sea, latitude and longitude.
  - If a full body burial at sea by a military service, the name of the branch of service is given.

OTHER MORTUARY AND FUNERAL HOME RESOURCES

Cold case investigators may consider visiting the funeral home or mortuary to seek further information. Among those records that may be of interest is the *case file*. This contains most of the records pertinent to the individual deceased's case. It may include:

- Cemetery records
- Copies of any checks written for funeral and interment expenses
- Worksheets
- Logs of family conversations, or any problems experienced during the handling and interment or disposition of the remains
- Embalming report. (The embalming process tends to bring out bruises that may have not been previously noticed, especially with children).
- Removal sheet. This is the document(s) that cemetery personnel fill out when picking up a body for transport. It will note the date, times, vital information of the decedent such as Social Security numbers, when the deceased was last seen by a physician, time of death, next of kin, and list of personal effects on the body.
- Hospital sheet. Similar to the Removal Sheet, vital information, Social Security numbers, DOB, etc.
- Clothing sheet. Clothing brought in by the family for dressing the decedent.

Mortuary or funeral home personnel who might possess information of interest to the investigation may include:

- Case arranger. This is generally the person responsible for overseeing the funeral/interment process.
- Funeral director. Handles the funeral as set up by the arranger. On the mortuary side, handles the arrangement, and on the cemetery side, handles markers, interment, etc.
- Super director. In some locales, this person handles both mortuary and cemetery sides, but this practice varies from place to place.

Visitor's Log

A visitor's log is often present at the time of viewing of the deceased through the interment. These names may be of interest to cold case investigators in some situations. These are normally returned to the family at the conclusion of the service. The case file may reflect to whom the log was given after the service.

OBITUARY

The obituary is a voluntary, unofficial public announcement by the family or friends of the deceased announcing their death. It is published in the local newspaper, typically in a dedicated Notices section of the paper, pursuant to that media's rules and policies. In most cases, it is published within a week and runs for a number of days, depending upon the arrangement between the family or author and newspaper.

The obituary often attests to the deceased's birth, youth, career, hobbies, military or other service, and other interests. It commonly closes by listing the names of relatives — to the grand-children level — and friends, as well as to where contributions in their memory may be sent. In cold case investigations, these obituaries might offer information of interest such as:

- Date of death
- Age at death
- Residence community
- Names of parents, siblings, and other relatives
- Names of close friends and associates
- Relationships
- Deceased children or siblings
- Residence locations and history
- Employment and military history
- Other biographical information and hobbies or interests
- Mortuary or funeral home
- Dates and location of services
- Location of interment
- Casketbearers

ACKNOWLEDGMENTS

I wish to acknowledge the support and assistance of Mr. Daniel Williams, Director of Operations for Greenwood Mortuary and Memorial Park in San Diego, California, as well as Senior Medical Examiner Julio Estrada of the San Diego County, California, Medical Examiner's Office. Daniel Williams graduated from Cypress College of Mortuary Science in Cypress, California, with a degree Mortuary Science and has practiced in this field for the past 18 years. In addition, he is licensed by the State of California as an embalmer and funeral director. Mr. Williams has contributed his knowledge and experience to this and other chapters.

Mr. Estrada's experience and professional credentials are reviewed in further detail in Chapter 10.

SUGGESTED READING

American Medical Association and Robertson, J. (2002). "Autopsy: Life's final chapter." Retrieved January 5, 2005 from http://www.medem.com/MedLB/article.

Geberth, V. (1996). *Practical Homicide Investigation: Tactics, Procedures, and Forensic Techniques*. Boca Raton, FL. CRC Press.

10 The Coroner's Inquest

Richard H. Walton

CONTENTS

CORONER AND MEDICAL EXAMINER OPERATIONS

The American medicolegal system of death investigation, founded in the English coroner's system, was brought to this country by the early colonists. In this founding period, the position of sheriff and coroner were usually combined in one office and person, and the earliest reported Coroner's Inquest was held in the colony of New Plymouth, New England, in 1635. In the late 1800s, pathology began to take an important role in death investigation, and in 1915, New York City eliminated the Coroner's Office and instituted a Medical Examiner's system. The first statewide medical examiner system was instituted in Maryland in 1939. This system has grown and expanded in the ensuing decades.

Three primary systems are in use today. They may vary from county to county within a state, and understanding the type and background of their system may be of value to cold case investigators. These are the County Coroner, the Sheriff-Coroner, and the Medical Examiner.

The role and duties of these offices can often be found in the government code or other codified sources of agency authority. Cold case investigators, when seeking to identify what material might be, or might have been present in coroner's inquest files may attempt to find the appropriate codes from the time of the homicide under investigation in an attempt to learn what might have been done. A Coroner's Inquest record could be a very informative resource during a cold case homicide investigation.

COUNTY CORONER

The county coroner is usually an elected official, and does *not* need to be a physician. Not infrequently, the minimum qualifications are to be 18 years of age or over and a resident of the county or district. There is no minimum qualification for education and training in the forensic sciences. These persons usually have primary jurisdiction within their county or district. An additional qualification is, and has always been, a need to win a popular vote. In some jurisdictions, the coroner might have additional duties such as acting as the public administrator. This office may be part-time, full-time, or on an as-needed basis. In the past, coroner's fee schedules may have been based upon the findings they officially rendered.

In my experience, especially in smaller, more rural counties, recordkeeping systems varied and record retention for periods dating to the 1980s and before may be hit or miss. The writing of reports and file organization and maintenance were at the discretion of the office holder. A search for coroner's records by investigators in older cold cases may entail identifying previous coroners and their assistants, and attempting to locate these individuals and make inquiry into possible retention of records from their tenure. Similarly, identifying their secretaries or other clerical personnel might yield helpful information. Smaller agencies are not alone in this however, and larger coroner's offices have been known to lose files, bones, and evidence.

During the course of their duties, the coroner or staff might have consulted with local medical personnel or employed qualified pathologists to conduct autopsies. In decades past, in some instances, autopsies were not always conducted by the most qualified medical personnel. Their education in forensic matters might have been minimal, and ultimately, however, the coroner made the conclusion regarding cause and manner of death as reflected upon the death certificate. I recall one report decades ago in which the coroner, a hotel owner, held a .25 caliber rifle bullet to an entrance wound and proclaimed it the fatal projectile as opposed to a .32 pistol bullet, as it most closely matched the entrance wound.

Coroners may be required by law to keep a Coroner's Register. This record contains:

- Name or alias of the deceased
- Description necessary for identification
- Property taken from person or premises
- Disposition of money or property
- Cause of death
- Information as to disposition of remains
- Persons notified of the death as well as notations of any unsuccessful attempts at notification

Sheriff-Coroner

A variation of the coroner system is the Sheriff-Coroner. This practice is less common, but still in use today in some areas. In addition to other prescribed law enforcement duties, the sheriff of such counties is also mandated to perform the duties of the coroner. Similarly, deputy sheriffs may also be empowered as deputy coroners. In these jurisdictions, a search for records may begin within the county sheriff's office.

Medical Examiner

The medical examiner may have county, district, or statewide jurisdiction. These persons must be licensed physicians and are generally forensic-trained pathologists. They are usually appointed and serve at the discretion of the appointing authority, and traditionally have been encountered in more metropolitan areas.

For purposes in this segment, the term "coroner" is used synonymously as reference to the medicolegal authority responsible for conducting the death investigation.

Despite the variations in systems, the coroner's responsibility was, and is, to take charge of the body when notified of the death, make identification, and inquire into circumstances, manner, and means of death. Classification of deaths requiring inquiry was mandated by the state in which the jurisdiction rested. Not uncommonly, the duty of the coroner, past and present, would include inquiry and determination into the circumstances and manner of:

- All violent, sudden, or unusual deaths, unattended deaths, or deceased not attended by physician within past 20 days before death, and deaths related to or suspected to be self-induced or resulting from criminal abortion
- Deaths known or suspected to be homicide, suicide, or accidental poisoning
- Deaths due to accident, injury, drowning, fire, hanging, gunshot, stabbing, cutting, exposure, starvation, acute alcoholism, drug addiction, strangulation, aspiration
- Death in whole or in part occasioned by criminal means, deaths associated with a known or alleged rape or crime against nature, deaths in prison or while under sentence
- Deaths under such circumstances as to afford reasonable grounds to suspect that the death was caused by the criminal act of another

These duties were separate from those performed by other law enforcement agencies. Review of older unsolved cases has shown a joint coroner-law enforcement participation in those cases that ultimately became cold cases. Other qualifying deaths may include those situations in which there is a possible threat to public health. In all events, the medicolegal investigation sought to learn:

- Who died?
- How and why?
- Who did it (when applicable)?

CORONER'S INQUEST

To answer these questions, coroner officials in past decades, as well as medical examiners, have utilized a process called the coroner's inquest. This centuries-old system was once more prevalent than it is today, although it is still in occasional use. Documentation that this inquest occurred may or may not be found in the cold case file.

A primary purpose of a coroner's inquest was to provide a means for the prompt securing of information for the use of those charged with the detection and prosecution of crime. In this manner, people were subpoenaed to the inquest, questioned under oath, and a transcript was made of the proceedings. Knowledge of this process and the records systems it produced may provide investigators with information in those cold cases in which this process was utilized.

These could be valuable investigative sources. While variations might occur in different states, this synopsis provides an overview of the manners and methods of coroner's inquests as may be encountered in practical cold case investigation. Issues identified with the coroner's inquest include:

- Discretion of the coroner or medical examiner to hold an inquest
- Jurisdiction and venue of the inquest
- Juror qualifications to serve on a coroner's inquest
- Oath and duties of the juror
- Inquest process
- Verdict or decision and findings

Unlike a grand jury process, there was and is no confidentiality or secrecy barrier.

For cold case investigators decades after a coroner's inquest, there is no legal barrier to identifying and attempting to contact former members of the coroner's inquest, or coroner's jury, when and where possible. As in any other cold case interview, ask about any notes or other documents or photos. Until you ask the question, you never know what might turn up.

DISCRETION

The decision to hold a coroner's inquest rested with the coroner or medical examiner and was *discretionary* at their pleasure and if circumstances warranted it. An inquest could be held using a coroner's jury, or with the coroner acting as the sole inquisitor and official, at the discretion of the coroner. The coroner needed only a reasonable ground to suspect possibility of death at the hands of another or through the instrumentality of some other person. The coroner did not need the consent or permission of the family to hold an inquest. These inquests were open to the public and, especially in more sensational investigations, attended and reported by the local media.

Such an inquest may have been mandatory, however, when requested by the sheriff or chief of police, district attorney, or attorney general. In those circumstances in which the coroner conducted the inquiry, the coroner or a deputy would personally sign the certificate of death. If the death appeared to have occurred under natural circumstances, and the inquiry determined that the physician of record possessed sufficient knowledge determine that, a coroner could authorize that physician to sign the certificate of death.

JURISDICTION AND VENUE

The inquest was limited to conducting inquiry into death in the county where the death occurred (rather than the county where the deceased may have resided). The coroner or his authorized deputy or a hearing officer would conduct the inquest. In addition, to discharge their duties as prescribed by law, coroners had the right to exhume the body of a deceased person when necessary. Depending upon authority and location, the coroner or his deputy might have exercised peace officer power. Although coroners usually did not have power to subpoena witnesses from outside their county, they have had authority to travel outside the jurisdiction to obtain information.

Juror Qualifications

No one was exempt for jury service except at the discretion of the coroner. Inquest jurors were not subject to challenge by any party. Exemptions were noted, however, and included those persons related to the decedent, charged or suspected with the killing of the decedent, and prejudiced for or against the deceased.

Oath and Duties

Upon selection, the jurors participating in a coroner's inquest took an oath in which they were sworn to inquire into who the person was; when, where, and by what means the person came to his or her death; and circumstances attending his or her death. They could also render a verdict according to the evidence offered or arising from inspection of the body.

Inquest Process

Upon notification that a death had occurred and when the coroner had determined that an inquest was to be conducted, the coroner then decided whether to conduct the inquest himself or to use a coroner's inquest jury. The coroner was authorized by law to summon a number of jurors to serve as coroner's inquest jurors, and the number varied among different jurisdictions. For instance, in California, the coroner:

… shall summon, or cause to be summoned by any sheriff, constable, or policeman, not less than nine nor more than 15 persons qualified by law to serve as jurors, to appear before him forthwith, either at the place where the body of the deceased is or at some other convenient place within the county designated by him, or at the request of the district attorney, to inquire into the cause of the death.

In the Boulder Jane Doe case cited elsewhere in this text, the recovered records indicated that the coroner's inquest jury numbered six persons. The inquest did not have to be held at the coroner's office or in a government facility. Such inquests could, and have, been held at the site where the deceased died or other locations.

Jurors could be summoned orally or in writing. A summons was a command to a person to appear at a given time and place to meet. Coroner's inquest jurors were residents of the county in which the inquest was to be held. They were compensated according to a schedule set by the county.

During the proceedings, coroner's inquest jurors were often required to view the body as a necessary part of the identification process.

Witnesses were subpoenaed to attend a coroner's inquest in a manner similar to being summoned to appear in a regular court. Upon being called, the witness would be administered an oath. Questions would be directed toward the witness by the coroner, or in some instances, by members of the coroner's jury. In some situations, witnesses also viewed the body. Those summoned to a coroner's inquest would include

- Person who discovered the body
- Law enforcement personnel
- Medical personnel
- Expert witnesses (who may provide opinion as to cause of death)
- Family members of the victim
- Friends, associates, and co-workers of the victim
- Spouse, boyfriend or girlfriend of the victim
- Others thought to have knowledge pertinent to the investigation

TRANSCRIPTS AND RECORDS

A court reporter or stenographer made a transcript of coroner's inquests. Beginning in about the late 1940s, a mechanical device could be used to make a recording of the inquest process in lieu of a written record in some locales. Upon completion of the proceedings, the transcript or tape recording was filed with the coroner or county clerk, usually within a specified time period. I have seen coroner inquest files that include original stenographic notepads.

Verdict or Finding

Upon completion of their duty, coroner's inquest jurors were to render a verdict or finding based upon what they heard and saw. This verdict, *inadmissible* in evidence in civil or criminal proceedings, was to set forth, without regard to civil or criminal responsibility:

- Name of the deceased
- Time and place of death
- Medical cause of death and whether by:
  - Natural causes
  - Suicide
  - Accident
  - Hands of another other than by accident
  - Undetermined

When the findings of the coroner's jury suggested that death came at the hands of another, the coroner would also transmit his written findings to the district attorney or police agency for the jurisdiction in which the body was recovered.

In addition, I have viewed a number of coroner's inquest verdicts in which the jurors provided additional detail, including:

- State or country of origin (birth)
- Age
- Occupation
- Marital status
- The name of the person who inflicted the fatal injuries upon the victim

ACKNOWLEDGMENTS

I wish to acknowledge the enthusiastic assistance of Senior Medical Examiner Investigator Julio Estrada of the San Diego County, California, Medical Examiner's Office. Mr. Estrada has given freely of his time and experience in several segments of this book, including the previous chapter. Mr. Estrada graduated from medical school at Autonomus University of Guadalajara, Mexico, in 1983. After graduation, he completed his internship at Mexicali General Hospital in Mexicali, Mexico, and thereafter donated a year of community service in the village of Benito Juarez, Baja California. After this, he worked for the Public Health Department for the Mexican government for 7 years before moving to the United States. In 1996, Investigator Estrada began working for the San Diego County Medical Examiner and is now a supervising medical examiner investigator with full peace officer powers.

SUGGESTED READING

Westvear, A.E. (Unk). Death Investigation. U.S. Department of Justice, Federal Bureau of Investigation. Quantico, VA.

11 Cold Case Squads

Richard H. Walton

CONTENTS

INTRODUCTION

Rising crime rates, declining clearance rates, staff shortages, and budget restrictions in the last decades of the 20th century taxed American law enforcement. This was felt across a wide spectrum of the public safety arena, including within homicide investigation and the medical examiner or coroner area. More crime and fewer resources were coupled with organizational issues within these departments, including retirements, transfers, and other personnel changes. Younger, less experienced detectives were thrust into positions for which their predecessors had heretofore been groomed and prepared for — investigation of criminal homicide. With the decline in murder rates, agencies began to explore various options to revisit unsolved homicides. One of these methods was the cold case squad.

Cold case squads are specialized units of investigators within a law enforcement agency tasked to review and investigate unsolved homicides. Such units may also be formed for proactive review and investigation of unsolved sexual assaults. This chapter presents a background on the origin and development of these units and how they may be formed, and presents guidelines and protocols that have been proven to work. This chapter draws heavily on interviews with cold case homicide investigators and supervisors from around the nation as well as review of numerous agency protocols and literature in the field. It concludes with a representative list of U.S. and Canadian cold case investigation units and contact information.

WHY FORM A COLD CASE SQUAD?

According to the National Institute of Justice (NIJ), cold case squads have been found to be a practical means for jurisdictions faced with a significant number of unsolved murders. Police agencies of all sizes can organize cold case squads. Smaller agencies usually have a smaller number of unsolved homicides, however, and a detective or two dedicated to these investigations might be a practical solution while larger departments may assign proportionately more personnel to their higher number of cases.

This concept provides a practical opportunity to identify and solve some of these cases. Some cold case squads have been formed because the volume of fresh cases or other responsibilities prevents detectives from going back and revisiting unsolved cases. In other instances, cold case squads have been formed due to a decline in the number of new murder cases, and the resultant availability of personnel and other resources. In either circumstance, these provide a mechanism to identify and investigate unsolved murders. These systems offer the agency, and individual investigators, a potential win-win arrangement for maximum utilization of departmental and human resources in the investigation of unsolved murders.

For the agency, cold case squads offer a mechanism to continue the investigation of unsolved or suspected homicides long after the lead detectives have departed from the case. In doing this, they provide a means to reduce the backlog of unsolved cases. Experience has also shown that, success in one case may also solve others. These investigative units can bring some sense of justice to the families of victims with the successful solution or resolution of a case. Further, through developed resources, cold case squads can be very useful in locating and working with witnesses in past or potential cases as well as reviewing evidence.

WHAT'S IN A NAME?

Some investigators and law enforcement agencies dislike the term "cold case squad" because it sends a negative message to the family and friends of victims — as well as the public — that their cases are old, cold, and forgotten. Unsolved homicides cases are those that were investigated as thoroughly as possible, and then shelved, suspended, or otherwise categorized in non-investigative or inactive status in department records, pending further leads and investigation. While in some instances cases have been lost, misfiled, misplaced, or have otherwise been consistently relegated behind more active investigations, they are still "open." In this regard, cases are solved or unsolved. They are open or closed. There is no legal category or definition of a "cold" case.

The name "cold case squad" is one that has apparently originated as a media term. It has become prevalent in media and literature as well as police agency protocols and jargon (see Figure 11.1). In addition to this term, however, agencies have utilized other names to define their investigative bodies dedicated to investigation of older, unsolved murder cases. Among these are:

- Unsolved Unit
- Unsolved Homicide Unit
- Old Mysteries Homicide Unit

FIGURE 11.1 Unofficial LAPD Cold Case Squad Logo. (Courtesy of Mary Ann Hunt)

- Historical Homicide Section
- Archive Unit
- Cold Case Team
- Cold Case Unit
- H.E.A.T. Team (Homicide Evidence Assessment Team)
- The Gray Squad. (Interestingly enough, this term has been used by a volunteer cold case review group in the Tulsa, Oklahoma, Police Department. It refers to cases in a gray area, not active, not solved. It does not reflect upon the hair color of the detectives.)

In addition, while some agencies may not have a formally recognized cold case unit, yet have unsolved cases, they might consider having a detective or investigator assigned to monitor or coordinate these older cases and their investigation. Such a designation provides a single contact point when agencies or citizens call in with information. This individual is familiar with all unsolved cases and serves as a specific point of contact for receiving information and coordinating inquiries from other agencies. The designation of a specific individual contributes to lessening the chance that when a tip or information comes in, it might get lost, misplaced, or misfiled, and not reviewed in context with the case and no action is taken.

FORMING THE COLD CASE SQUAD

Cold case investigation units can be a resounding success for an agency, or a costly failure (in terms of money, morale, and press exposure). Chief among contributing factors that make these units a success are: (1) organizational leadership and administration and (2) selection of personnel (see Figure 11.2).

ADMINISTRATION

Administrative commitment and support are critical to the design and implementation of a cold case squad. The concept of cold case, and that of a cold case squad, is relatively recent in origin. Members of these units must perceive that they have the support and backing of the department administration, both in fiscal and other necessary resources, and also in the flexibility required to do their job. This flexibility may involve the authority and ability to exercise independent judgment when and as required, based upon experience and case needs, and to not be hamstrung in their efforts by needless or unnecessary barriers.

In many cases, everyone identified in the initial investigation may need to be reinterviewed. Investigators will often need to travel, sometimes long distances, to conduct these interviews. Previously unknown persons may similarly have to be located and interviewed. The greater the number of cases investigated, the greater the cost. They will need to have evidence examined, or reexamined. They will incur overtime. They will possibly require the assistance of outside experts. Cold case investigators can work most effectively and efficiently when provided the resources and administrative support necessary to do their jobs.

If cold cases were easy to solve, they would have been solved before. As one cold case team leader once told me, "I'd be thrilled if my people could solve 5% of our unsolved cases." Cold case investigation requires concentration and *focus*. Those assigned to cold case investigation must be allowed to work exclusively on old, unsolved cases. When cold case investigators are assigned to rotating shifts, assigned hot calls as back-fill to regular homicide investigators, assigned to dignitary protection or other non-cold case activities, their effectiveness is greatly reduced. This translates to fewer cases solved. Administration support in providing all necessary resources and flexibility to investigate cold cases is very important to the success of the program.

A number of cold case units have suggested that one case at a time is a highly desirable case load for cold case investigators.

FIGURE 11.2 Units that specialize in the investigation use a variety of names, but Cold Case Squad or Team is a commonly used term. "Team" implies just that, that the unit works together as a team to solve unsolved homicides. (Author's file)

SELECTION OF PERSONNEL

Selection of the most qualified personnel is critical for the success of a cold case squad. This is not the place for repayment of political favors or cronyism. Nor is it a place to put someone who is looking to "coast" before retirement. Cold cases require detailed review and analysis of the previously investigated case, coupled with the "instinct" of an experienced homicide detective to identify perhaps a single avenue that may lead to a successful conclusion.

Those selected for these positions in cold case squads should be experienced homicide investigators with traits that include:

- Strong communication and interpersonal skills (interview and interrogation)
- Strong research skills
- Patience
- Creativity
- High motivation and enthusiasm
- Experienced with informants and undercover operations
- Tenacity

These desired qualities for cold case investigators have been explored in previous chapters in more detail. While many agencies employ the *team* concept for investigation of homicide, cold case investigators may approach a case with a preference for working a more *individualistic* approach. Some investigators prefer to work alone. By this time in their careers, they have demonstrated an ability for productivity in this capacity, and this is a flexibility that works well in many cases. In either method, investigators selected for cold case squad investigation may draw upon knowledge and experience in areas including:

- Firearms examination
- Medical examination
- Behavioral analysis
- Blood spatter
- Crime scene and identification
- Forensic anthropology and odontology
- Forensic botany and entomology
- Current investigative methods including wiretaps

It has been demonstrated, however, that a cold case squad can successfully utilize otherwise qualified and experienced personnel who may have incurred some forms of injury or light-duty status. This offers the investigator the ability to continue to ply his or her talent and expertise, and the department continues to benefit from his or her experience and capabilities. Neither suffers an unwanted separation. Depending upon circumstances, investigators so assigned may:

- Review cases and write case summaries.
- Review evidence and facilitate evidence processing and reprocessing.
- Compile and construct witness lists.
- Utilize computer resources for case-related tasks, including constructing time lines.
- Perform witness and suspect background checks and gather information.

This offers a win-win for both, and reaffirms commitment by the agency to its personnel as well as contributing to higher morale by personnel who see, feel, and appreciate this commitment.

SUPERVISORS AND INVESTIGATORS

A proper blend of supervisory and investigative talent optimizes the work of a cold case squad. In agencies with dedicated homicide investigation units, personnel for cold case investigation are normally drawn from this investigative pool. Smaller agencies, however, have drawn on personnel who investigate a wide variety of crimes in addition to homicide. Regardless, how these units are staffed is dependent upon the organization and makeup of the cold case squad.

Unfortunately in some instances, personnel have been assigned to supervisory duties in areas in which they have minimal or no experience and expertise. Homicide supervision has not been exempt in this area. Supervision of a cold case squad is optimized by selecting as supervisors those who have experience in homicide *and* cold case homicide experience as well as supervisory experience.

Where conditions allow, supervisors may carry a minimal investigatory load as well as their supervisory duties. As an example, the Los Angeles County, California, Sheriff's Department utilizes a single homicide bureau facility. This bureau of the department is physically separate from other components within the department. Cold case calls or inquiries from citizens or law enforcement to the Homicide Bureau are routed to the supervisor in the Unsolved Unit of the Homicide Bureau. The supervisor, an experienced homicide investigator and cold case investigator, evaluates the information and assigns the followup to an investigator. The supervisor also carries a minimum load of cold case investigations. In this manner, supervisory and investigative roles allow the supervisor to maintain professional expertise in the field as well as supervisory duties of other investigators.

Not uncommonly, cold case squads usually include the following, or a variation thereof:

- Supervisor or administrator. Usually a lieutenant or other ranking member from the homicide division who oversees police management and serves as liaison between administration, participating law enforcement agencies, the community and the media.
- Immediate Supervisor. Usually a sergeant who coordinates and oversees daily operations of the team. The sergeant is there to make day-to-day decisions and to supervise assignment of cases and to monitor investigation progress.
- Investigators. Those assigned as *investigators* within cold case squads may have previous supervisory experience from other assignments in the agency. This has fostered their abilities and experiences in a manner not shared by those who do not have this wider background. As such, they possess a different perspective and thus do not always take "no" for an answer. They have the experience to know where to go, what to do, and how to go about doing it in homicide investigation. Through their experiences and seniority, they will probably have the ability to communicate directly with upper echelons of the department, who, earlier in their careers, may have worked under or have been mentored by the cold case investigator. These investigators have contacts, know who to call, are versed in the latest in forensic technology and are up to date on the law. These should be the best of the best. Above all, they are *tenacious.*

ADDITIONAL STAFFING

Similar to other investigative units, cold case squads may benefit from the skills and abilities of other support personnel who may be assigned full- or part-time to the cold case squad, depending upon organizational circumstances. These include:

- Clerical and secretarial. The backbone of many organizational units.
- Analysts and specialized computer skills such as database research or visual illustrative analysis.
- Information technology (computer persons).
- Forensic specialists.
- Behavioral science resources.

Assignment to a Cold Case Squad

Assignment to a cold case squad can offer a variety of benefits. These might include: (1) ability to work regular Monday-Friday daytime shifts (in theory, anyway), (2) increase in rank, (3) pay incentive, (4) lack of night time callouts, (5) lack of shift rotation, and (6) use of separate office and equipment, including assigned automobile. Given agency resources, it is highly desirable that those assigned to cold case squads work out of facilities separate from the main homicide or detective division or central agency facility. This separation not only facilitates their focus on cold cases, it may serve to keep them from being drawn as resources into other "temporary" assignments or high-profile cases. In addition, this "distancing" serves to remove them from day-to-day, mainstream petty politics and unconstructive activities.

This assignment, however, should not be perceived as a "gravy" assignment. It *will* entail night work, weekends, and holidays. Nor should assignment to a cold case squad be perceived as a "retirement" position. When informants call or someone wants to talk, the opportunity must not be wasted. It is not unusual that a break on one cold case may offer up leads in other cold cases — the "snowball" or "domino" effect. The stress of working a regular homicide beat may transfer to the cold unit as well. This stress, conversely, may diminish in many cases, however.

There might be a perception by other detectives, in some instances, that cold case detectives are receiving a "plum" assignment. They may resent the working conditions and assignments enjoyed by the cold case detectives. Keep in mind, however, that cold case detectives are usually the most senior personnel. They have paid their "dues" and while they may, in some cases, not be far from retirement, they represent the most experience and ability available within the department. In addition, by handling the cold cases, they relieve their brethren from having these cases added to their caseloads.

Case Identification and Selection

Rule number 1 is to pick the easiest cases first. When a cold case squad is formed, there may be media attention. The agency administration has committed personnel and resources. The reality is that the public likes to see results. In this case, they wish to see arrests and convictions in cold cases. As cases are solved, the media reports favorably on this innovative concept and others may come forward with information on other cases. As a result, the agency may strengthen its commitment and provide more financial and personnel resources.

Cold case homicides are not investigated in the same manner as hot cases. This presents a difficulty to those assigned to initial cold case squad investigations, one that is not really portrayed in the media: (1) the nature of these cases is that they are the most difficult to solve, (2) they entail additional resources and expenditures, and (3) they are *time consuming*. The dilemma facing the establishment of these units is that they must quickly show results or face the threat of disbanding of their squad. Perception is reality, and, unfortunately, this has actually happened.

Common agency guidelines utilized to select cases for cold case squad investigation seek to identify those in which time has now become an ally to solving the case. The most common considerations in selecting these cases have been discussed in other chapters. They are (1) changes in relationships and (2) advances in technology.

Those cases in which advances in technology can utilize remaining evidence may offer cases with a stronger possibility for a speedier solution. Among these would be cases that can take advantage of:

- CODIS. This DNA-based tool would take in cases in which remaining evidence would include blood, saliva, and other biological material.
- AFIS. This fingerprint technology may maximize identification of unidentified fingerprints.
- National Integrated Ballistics Information Network (NIBIN).

A possible prioritization of a cold case squad review in these circumstances might be:

1. CODIS.
2. AFIS.
3. IBIS/NIBIN or Drugfire, where applicable.
4. Identify changes in relationships.

These databanks, which are expanding daily, present a growing opportunity for solving cold cases.

If cases have been previously identified and systematically reviewed and prioritized, case investigation may begin with selection from this list. Case review and prioritization schedules were addressed in more depth in Chapter 2. Additionally, investigator expertise and experience may refine this list and identify cases that, in their view, offer more hope for resolution than others. This is subjective, but further maximizes the cold case effort. The ability for experienced investigators to "handpick" their cases may contribute to an increased potential to solve cold cases.

Additional steps to be utilized in the identification and selection of cases may include:

- Review all open and closed files in agency archives and records.
- Assimilate case information from surrounding law enforcement agencies.
- Get input from senior detectives assigned to homicide or those previously assigned or retired.

COLD CASE SQUAD DESIGN

Experience has shown that there is no one-size-fits-all method of constructing a cold case squad. How these squads are formed depends upon a number of variables, including (1) financial resources, (2) availability of personnel, and (3) size and scope of the unsolved problem. Cold case units can be constructed within local agencies, a state agency, a federal law enforcement agency, or a combination of these.

Regardless, experience has shown that agencies aspiring to construct a cold case squad most commonly contact *other* law enforcement agencies that have successfully implemented such a unit. There is nothing like experience. In so doing, agencies may identify other jurisdictions that appear similar to theirs and contact or visit them. Following such contact, the agency seeking to set up a cold case squad may attempt to identify from their target agency:

- How did they go about setting up their unit?
- Who did *they* contact for assistance and information?
- What have they found to work best?
- What did not?
- What advice and recommendations would they make?

Differences in population bases, demographics, economics, resources, the nature and extent of the unsolved homicide problem, and other factors all contribute to each agency's need to tailor a design to fit its own needs. As reported by the NIJ, certain styles and forms of cold case squads have been successfully implemented, however. These are:

- **Single full-time investigator**. This form of a cold case squad utilizes one person assigned and dedicated full time to investigation of cold case homicides.
- **Two or more full-time investigators**. This form of a cold case squad utilizes two or more full-time qualified investigators dedicated to cold case investigations. Supervision may be among the membership or the responsibility of the supervisor or commander of a larger unit within which they operate.

- **Other investigative duties that include cold case investigation**. This form of a cold case squad recognizes the cold case problem and assigns personnel with responsibility for investigation of these cases. This responsibility, however, occurs in addition to other investigative assignments not related to cold case homicide.
- **Hired-Back squad**. This form of a cold case squad utilizes the experience of former or retired homicide detectives hired back by the agency to review or investigate cold cases. These detectives may participate on a part-time, full-time, or volunteer basis, or combination thereof.
- **One-Time squad**. This form of a cold case squad is utilized for a single case, often high-profile. The number of personnel in the complement may vary.
- **Occasional squads**. This form of squad operates on an as-needed basis or when time allows from other duties.
- **Volunteer squad**. This form uses civilian volunteers with or without law enforcement experience to review unsolved cases, identify potential leads and investigative avenues, and prepare written summaries for follow-up investigation by an assigned detective or investigator. Volunteers have included college interns or students, internal or external agency forensic specialists (firearms, fingerprints, etc.), and others retired from the criminal justice system.
- **Interagency cold case squad**. This form of cold case squad incorporates multi-jurisdictional agencies. Unlike a *task force* composed of representatives of various agencies to solve a particular crime or series of crimes, this form of unit may be made up of local, county, state or federal agencies participating in an effort to identify, review, and solve cold cases. As an example, the San Diego, California, Police Department Homicide Evidence Assessment Team (H.E.A.T.) utilizes full-time personnel assigned from the District Attorney's office and the U.S. Marshall's Office. Similarly, the Washington, D.C. Metro Police Department (MPD) has utilized a cold case team concept incorporating representatives from the Federal Bureau of Investigation (FBI) and the MPD, as well as an assistant U.S. Attorney (AUSA) assigned full time to the unit.
- **District Attorney cold case squad**. A more recent innovation in the concept of cold case investigation has been the design and implementation of a cold case squad operated by the district attorney or county prosecutor's office. These have been exemplified by the San Diego County, California, District Attorney's Office and that of the Morris County, New Jersey, Prosecutor's Office (see Figure 11.3).
- **DNA cold case squad (aka CODIS team or CODIS squad)**. This is a very recent, evolving concept designed to implement focused review and investigation into those unsolved cases in which suspects have been identified by the increasing number of "cold hits" from the CODIS system. These combine cold case homicide investigation with an initial focus on the DNA or biological-material component of the unsolved case.

Defining Responsibilities of the Cold Case Unit

Once a cold case squad has been designed, it must have parameters that define its mission, means, and goals. These include:

- Identification of the organizational unit in which the cold case squad will operate
- Date of implementation
- Authority of the unit
- Staffing of the unit
- Facilities
- Investigative priorities or direction of the unit
- Case review and investigation parameters
- Organization and administration

FIGURE 11.3 Diego County District Attorney Investigator Ron Thill is assigned on a full-time basis as part of the District Attorney's office's commitment to solving and prosecuting unsolved homicides. A veteran officer, he brings homicide experience and expertise to the team effort utilized by the San Diego Police Department Cold Case Team. (Author's file)

EXAMPLE OF A COLD CASE SQUAD SETUP

The following example is extracted from the fact sheet establishing the Cold Case Squad of the Los Angeles, California, Police Department in 2001 (see Figure 11.4). It serves as a model to illustrate the foregoing:

> To: All Operation Support Division Commanders
> From: Commanding Officer, Detective Services Group
> Subject: Robbery-Homicide Division, Cold Case Homicide Unit

At the direction of the Chief of Police, a cold case homicide unit is being formed within the Robbery-Homicide Division. This unit will be operational as of November 15, 2001. This Unit has the authority to reopen any homicide case in the City. However, due to available grant funding and advances in DNA technology, this Unit will initially focus on unsolved sexually motivated homicides.

The Cold Case Homicide Unit will systematically review all unsolved homicides and reopen cases based on solvability factors. These include: (1) Cases with suspect DNA that can be submitted to the Combined Offender DNA Information Systems (CODIS); (2) Cases with latent print evidence that can be submitted to Cal-ID, Western States, or the FBI's automated fingerprint systems; (3) Cases with ballistic evidence that can be submitted to DRUGFIRE and/or National Integrated Ballistics Information Network (NIBIN); (4) Cases with modus operandi and/or signature aspects that are sufficiently unique for matching to other cases captured through the FBI's Violent Crime Apprehension Program (ViCAP); (5) Cases that could not be filed because identified suspects and/or witnesses could not be located or were uncooperative at the time of the original crime; and, (6) Cases that originally lacked evidence for a criminal filing, but could now be proven through the application of new evidence processing techniques.

FIGURE 11.4 Cold Case Detective Rick Jackson of the Los Angeles, California, Police Department with some of the unsolved homicide cases he currently carries in his caseload. The LAPD instituted a cold case homicide investigation unit in November, 2001, to address over 8,000 homicides that were unsolved between the 1960s and 1996. (Author's file)

The memorandum fact sheet further specifies:

- The Cold Case Homicide Unit will concentrate its efforts on unsolved homicides that occurred between 1960 and 1995. If a case is reopened and the original investigating officer is still on the department, a request will be made for that officer to work with the Cold Case Homicide Unit to the degree necessary for the successful resolution of the case.
- Staffing.
  - This Unit will be under the auspices of …
  - Detective XXX will have functional responsibility for the Unit as the OIC.
  - Detective XXX and six additional detectives will staff the Unit. (Source of origin from which these detectives will participate is delineated).
  - "The selection criteria for the Unit is based on prior or current homicide experience, a commitment to the mission of the taskforce, and specialized skills including bilingual abilities (at least one Spanish speaker will be required) and "cold case" experience.
- Facilities.
  - This Unit will require a secure office with sufficient space for the assigned detectives, plus storage space for the numerous casebooks that will be in constant transit between City and Divisional archives and the Unit's office. This office will require telephones, computers, fax, and a copy machine.
  - Sufficient vehicles will have to be provided. The investigation of unsolved cases generally requires a greater amount of travel than newly occurring investigations because it is common for witnesses and suspects to move out of the area since the time of the crime. Therefore, the provided vehicles will have to be of sufficient quality to provide reliable transportation to various locales across the State.

- Investigative Priorities.
  - This Unit will have the authority to reopen any unsolved homicide case in the City. However, in light of the $50 million in State grants for DNA processing in sexually motivated homicide cases, these cases will have the top priority.
  - Cases will be reopened based on solvability factors. The Unit will focus on cases with suspect DNA that can be submitted to the Combined Offender DNA Information System (CODIS); cases with latent print evidence that can be submitted to Cal-ID, Western States, or the FBI's automated fingerprint systems; cases with ballistic evidence (shell casings) that can be submitted to Drugfire; cases with modus operandi and/or signature aspects that are sufficiently unique to be submitted to the FBI's Violent Crime Apprehension Program (ViCAP); cases with identified suspects and/or witnesses that could not be located or who were uncooperative at the time of the original crime; and cases where suspects were identified and located, but filings weren't obtained due to the unavailability of evidence processing techniques that have been developed since the time of these crimes.
- Organization/Administration.
  - This Unit will establish and maintain a close working relationship with Scientific Investigation Division (SID) and the Forensic Science Section of the District Attorney's Office. Scientific Investigation Division will designate a criminalist for evidence evaluation and processing; the District Attorney's Office will provide legal advice and support to the taskforce throughout the investigative and prosecution phases.
  - A reporting schedule will be instituted to keep the Department apprised of the efforts of the Unit. It is expected that the first several months will be strictly devoted to research and the identification of those cases with the highest solvability factors. As these cases are identified, the appropriate requests for evidence processing will be submitted. As stated earlier, there will be a priority placed on sexual assault homicides so that full advantage can be taken of the $50 million grant (this grant is only in effect for two more years). It is expected that the application of new forensic techniques will result in numerous cases being solved, however, due to processing delays, it is estimated that suspects will not begin to be identified via the use of these techniques for approximately six months after evidence submissions.
  - This Unit will have the authority to investigate any case no longer being actively pursued by divisional homicide units. If the detective who originally investigated the case is still working for the department, (s)he will be involved in the investigation to the degree necessary for the successful resolution of the case. Any clearances obtained by the taskforce will be credited to the Division that holds the investigative responsibility for the case. Therefore, the official case responsibility for statistical purposes will remain with the division assigned the case at the time the Unit initiates its investigation.
  - The Unit will be the primary duty assignment for the assigned detectives. The Unit will be under the command and control of Robbery-Homicide Division and its sole mission will be the investigation of cold-case homicides.

CASE TRACKING AND CLUE MANAGEMENT SYSTEMS

The decision to implement a cold case squad and to proactively address cold cases necessitates a records system to keep track of the cases and their status. Will you continue to use written or computerized forms currently in use? Is there a need to design new forms? The records system should be able to give an overview of the case such that a supervisor or investigator can see at a glance necessary particulars of the case as well as its status. As cases are solved, the records must indicate their closure so that needless time and effort are not later spent pulling the case from archives only to find that it has been investigated and solved. Also, the ability to retrieve this information and to show the squad's successes may be a significant factor in obtaining additional financial and investigative resources.

In one systematic review of cold cases, a large agency discovered that faulty record keeping in old paper binders had erroneously neglected to record hundreds of cases as solved that were still carried on the books as unsolved. Hundreds of investigator hours were necessitated to separate these cases before it was possible to begin to systematically review unsolved cases. Subsequently, however, after many investigative successes, it was discovered that the records system was not constructed as to allow retrieval of these successfully solved cold cases.

Numerous computer database programs are available. These can be implemented on a computerized system linked within the agency computer network, or standalone systems. Specificity of who is responsible to enter data and to monitor data entry and case status will assist in timely and efficient cold case identification, review, assignment, and updating.

Identifying data, computerized alphabetically and in an accessible and easy-to-use database, may include (when known):

- Victim name and related information
- Date and time of offense
- Date and time of finding of body
- Suspect name and related information
- Names of original investigators
- Case summary of known facts
- Record tracking information by supervisor or investigator on timely basis

EXAMPLE PROTOCOL — COLD CASE SQUAD

The operational protocols vary among agencies. The following protocol is utilized by the San Diego, California, Police Department Homicide Evidence Assessment Team (H.E.A.T.)

H.E.A.T.

Open Case Review Protocol

The Homicide Evidence Assessment Team (H.E.A.T.) has been formed to reinvestigate homicide cases that have been inactivated by the original investigative team. Additionally, we will review cases brought to our attention by investigators who believe a case is workable and solvable. Our course of action in reviewing a case should be:

The case is logged out of the Records Division by the H.E.A.T. custodian of records.

The case is logged into the H.E.A.T. Case Review Log.

The case is assigned to a detective for review. After the case is reviewed by a detective, an Open Case Evaluation form is to be completed and attached to the case (see Figure 11.5). The entire case will be returned to the H.E.A.T. sergeant after the review is completed. Each investigator should keep in mind that evaluating the case for eventual reinvestigation does not equate to immediately investigating the case. A case should not be reopened unless there is ample time to pursue the investigation.

If the case is to be reopened, the reviewing detective may elect to reinvestigate the case. The reinvestigation will be conducted by one or two pairs of investigators after the case is reviewed by each person participating in the investigation.

HOMICIDE
OPEN CASE EVALUATION FORM

CASE # _____

TEAM #_____ TYPE _____

VICTIM(S) _____

DATE/TIME   LOCATION OF
OCCURRED_____ OCCURRENCE _____

SUSPECT(S):

☐   SUSPECT PREVIOUSLY IDENTIFIED   NAME(S):_____
☐   SUSPECT IDENTIFIED BY FORENSIC METHODS
☐   SUSPECT INFORMATION RECEIVED FROM CRIME STOPPERS, ETC.
☐   WARRANT OUTSTANDING
☐   SUSPECT INFORMATION RECEIVED FROM WITNESS

WITNESSES:

☐   WITNESS NEVER CONTACTED   NAME(S):_____
☐   WITNESS NEEDED TO BE RE-INTERVIEWED   NAME(S): _____
☐   PHOTO LINE-UP NEEDED TO BE SHOWN
☐   OTHER _____

FORENSIC EVIDENCE:

☐   LATENT PRINTS TO BE EXAMINED
☐   CAL ID PRINTS ON FILE TO BE CHECKED
☐   DNA EVIDENCE TO BE ANALYZED
☐   DRUGFIRE
☐   PROCESS / ANALYZE EVIDENCE
☐   OTHER_____
      _____

CASE SUMMARY: _____
_____
_____
_____
_____
_____
_____
_____

IN THE OPINION OF THIS EVALUATOR, THIS CASE WARRANTS RE-INVESTIGATION

☐   YES   PRIORITY # _____
☐   NO

NAME:_____   DATE: _____

APPROVED: _____

FIGURE 11.5 H.E.A.T. Team Open Case Evaluation form.

If the case is not to be opened for reinvestigation it will be reviewed by the sergeant. If the sergeant and the investigator agree that there is no possibility of resolving the case, a summary will be written by the sergeant and the case will be returned to Records Division via the H.E.A.T. custodian of records (see Figure 11.6).

H.E.A.T. is made up of one San Diego Police Department sergeant and three San Diego Police Department detectives. One District Attorney Investigator is assigned to the team. Each pair of investigators will work together while reinvestigating the case. The objective of the investigation is to resolve the case through an arrest and prosecution of the suspect or the identification of the suspect, even if there is not enough evidence to support a prosecution.

SAN DIEGO POLICE DEPARTMENT
HOMICIDE EVIDENCE ASSESSMENT TEAM
CASE SUMMARY

INVESTIGATOR:_____DATE ASSIGNED:_____

CASE NUMBER: _____DATE:_____TIME:_____

LOCATION: _____

VICTIM: _____ SUSPECT: _____

WEAPON: _____

EVIDENCE SUMMARY: _____
_____
_____
_____

CASE
SUMMARY:_____
_____
_____
_____
_____
_____
_____
_____
_____
_____
_____
_____
_____
_____
_____
_____
_____
_____
_____
_____
_____
_____
_____
_____
_____
_____
_____
_____
_____

FIGURE 11.6 H.E.A.T. Case Summary form.

All investigative efforts will be documented on a Police Department Investigator's Report. The reports will be individually prepared by the investigator or they can be recorded and submitted to the support staff for typing.

Team Members

The team will be made up of members of the San Diego Police Department Homicide Unit, and the San Diego County District Attorney's investigative staff.

Lieutenant: One of the lieutenants assigned to the Homicide Unit will manage the team. The lieutenant will coordinate liaison with the press and the participating agencies.

Sergeant: One Homicide sergeant will supervise the daily operations of the team.

Investigators: The investigators will consist of three San Diego Police Department Detectives and one District Attorney investigator.

UNSOLVED HOMICIDE EVALUATIONS

Unsolved homicide cases will be reviewed in their entirety including viewing all evidence. Following the review, the case will be given a priority number using the following criteria. This process will be used to determine whether the case warrants reinvestigation.

Priority 1 — Suspect(s) have previously been identified. A warrant of arrest has previously been issued. A suspect has been identified by forensic methods. The cases will be given the highest priority for reinvestigation.

Priority 2 — There are witnesses who can assist in identifying the suspect(s). Information has developed that identifies possible suspect(s). Evidence has been developed that can assist in identifying suspect(s). Initial investigation identifies witnesses who could not be located or need to be reinterviewed. These cases will be reinvestigated.

Priority 3 — Evidence has been preserved, and modern technology, ie,, AFIS, DNA, Drugfire, and vacuum metal deposition, can be utilized to process and analyze evidence. These cases will be reclassified depending on the results of the additional laboratory analysis.

Priority 4 — There are no known witnesses who can assist in identifying the suspect(s). There is no physical evidence that can assist in identifying the suspect(s). There is no physical evidence that can assist in identifying the suspect(s). These cases will not be re-investigated.

STATE AGENCY — COLD CASE SQUAD PROTOCOL

The following standard operating protocol outlines the selection of team members and protocol used in assigning cases to the cold case teams of the Indiana State Police. The agency implemented two investigative teams in 1998 and they continue to operate today. The teams comprise two very experienced detectives and each team operates on opposite ends of the state.

I. PURPOSE
   Establishes guidelines for the selection and utilization of the cold case team personnel.
II. POLICY
   The unlawful taking of a human life should not go unresolved just because of the passage of time. The selection, training, and utilization of detectives assigned to investigate unresolved homicides (cold cases) are outlined in this procedure.
III. PROCEDURE
   A. The investigation of an unresolved homicide could be considered when the investigation has been closed or suspended and enough time has elapsed to assume that new leads will be forthcoming. The term "cold case" should only be used on investigations that have fallen into that category; ideally, when enough time has passed that the perpetrator begins to feel confident enough to talk freely about their involvement. This length of time can be anywhere from 5 years or more.
   B. The careful selection for investigation of an unresolved homicide case is paramount in the team's ability to successfully resolve the case. The following factors shall be considered before a case selection is made:

1. Known cause of death — A thorough, well documented, and photographed autopsy is essential.
2. Witnesses — Witnesses may, over a period of time, begin to relax their fear or loyalty to the perpetrator. The reverse is true when considering a case selection. As an example; if all of the witnesses have died or cannot be found, the chances for a successful conclusion will be greatly diminished.
3. Suspects — Known suspect(s) who had motive or evidence linking them to a homicide, is an additional factor that increases the probabilities for successful conclusion. The former friends or relatives of these suspects may no longer be loyal to them and may be willing to share information now which they would not have had at the time of the crime.
4. Informants — The use of informants in the investigation of any crime is important. In the investigation of cold cases informants are invaluable. It is a rare person who can remain silent forever. Almost without exception, perpetrators will talk during a weak moment. While under the influence of alcohol or during a moment of anger, they will talk, and someone will be listening. Finding these people can make or break investigations.
5. Evidence — The amount and type of evidence is extremely important in the probability of resolution of a cold case. The proper collection and storage of evidence is essential; without such the potential for successful conclusion will be limited.
6. Forensic technologies — New technologies in the identification of human tissues and fluids have made great strides in recent times. If the collection and storage of these types of evidence have been done properly, the use of this type of technology, which was not available when these homicides were committed, greatly increases the chances of successful resolution of the cases.

C. Case Selection Process
   1. Priority will be given to cases contained in the files of the Indiana State Police, however, consideration shall be given to homicide cases from other law enforcement agencies; if asked to do so and the case meets the selection criteria.
   2. Appropriate cold case team/detectives shall review the case files for cases with solvability factors. The selection and review shall be accomplished under the direction and supervision of the regional investigative commander.
   3. During the selection process, consultation with laboratory and evidence personnel is extremely important. The physical evidence is a very important solvability factor. The team must be sure the evidence collected at the time of the homicide has been properly stored, the chain of custody is still intact, and, in cases where there is trace evidence, there is enough for modern laboratory techniques to be utilized.
   4. Case selection requires approval by both the applicable regional investigative commander and the appropriate BCI North/South Operations commander.

D. Organization and Team Selection
   1. Cold case detectives shall be supervised by their respective regional investigative commander. The appropriate BCI North/South Operations commander shall have secondary supervision and shall place cold case detectives into a team concept, wherever appropriate.
   2. When a vacancy exists, the appropriate BCI North/South Operations commander shall notify the appropriate regional investigative commander and shall advertise the vacancy statewide for a minimum of 21 days. Interested personnel shall submit a memorandum, with appropriate endorsements and recommendations, through channels, to the appropriate BCI North/South Operations commander. The appropriate

BCI North/South Operations commander shall, with the approval of the commander of the BCI, accept requests for TDY assignments to each cold case team.

3. Detectives wanting to be assigned to a cold case team must:
   a. Be a detective assigned to BCI
   b. Have extensive experience, training, ability, and interest in homicide investigations
   c. Be a volunteer
   d. Have excellent interview techniques
   e. Have excellent writing and verbal skills
   f. Have patience, diplomacy, and an open mind

E. The recommendations of a detective for a cold case team shall be made by the regional investigative commander, the appropriate BCI North/South Operations commander, and current members of the cold case team having the vacancy, per approval by the BCI commander.

F. The TCY assignment may be terminated, at any time, upon:
   1. Request, in writing, by the assigned detective and approval by the appropriate BCI North/South Operations commander; or
   2. By request by the appropriate BCI North/South Operations commander, CID commander, or BCI commander.

G. Each TDY assignment shall be reviewed on an annual basis, dependent on the date each cold case detective began a TDY assignment. Requests for extensions of assignments to a cold case team may be made by the detective assigned to the team. Extensions of assignment may be granted only with the approval of the appropriate BCI North/South Operations   commander.

H. This procedure is to be used in conjunction with all relevant Department regulations, rules, policies, and procedures.

MEDIA AND COLD CASE SQUADS

Despite the uneasy relationship that has existed on some occasions between the news media and law enforcement, the relationship between news media and cold case squads may be positive for both. When cold cases are solved, the media reports these with favorable publicity for the law enforcement agency. The public *is* interested in these cases. This, in turn, may bring forth witnesses or information for other unsolved cases. In addition, the media may assist by reaching out to reluctant or uncooperative witnesses, or serve as a medium to seek information or offer rewards. In some circumstances, the media has assisted cold case investigations by running stories on anniversaries or other significant dates of cold case homicides.

ADDITIONAL TRAINING AND RESOURCES
FOR COLD CASE SQUADS

Cold case homicide investigative techniques and tactics build upon the experience and expertise of those involved in homicide investigation and the training they have incurred over the years, or decades. Specialized investigation of cold case homicides have been conducted by the NCIS, the Army Criminal Investigation Division, and Air Force Office of Special Investigations. These military-related organizations may be able to assist municipal or other local or state cold case squads when there is a nexus to a military involvement, such as involvement of military personnel as victims or suspects. In addition, the U.S. Marshall's Service operates a number of joint-agency fugitive task forces. Local and state agencies often participate in these efforts, and cold case squads may benefit from this arrangement. Other assistance might be available from the FBI through utilization of its laboratory resources, as well as ViCAP, or direct investigative assistance in some circumstances.

The Vidocq Society is a potential resource to those involved in cold case investigation, whether it be a formal cold case squad or a single cold case investigation. The services and work of this organization will be addressed in Chapter 32.

NORTH AMERICA COLD CASE INVESTIGATION UNITS

In 2000, Senior Special Agent Ray Lundin of the Kansas Bureau of Investigation distributed the results of a nationwide survey of law enforcement agency cold case homicide investigation units. This list was updated in 2005 and is published below with the permission of the Kansas Bureau of Investigation.

Alaska State Troopers
Cold Case Team
5700 East Tudor Road
Anchorage, AK 99507
907-269-5738

Albuquerque Police Department
Criminal Investigation Division
400 Roma NW
Albuquerque, NM 87102
505-768-2436

Anne Arundel County, MD Police Department
Criminal Investigation Division
8495 Veterans Highway
Millersville, MD 21108
410-222-3460

Atlanta Police Department
Cold Case Unit/Homicide
675 Ponce Deleon Ave.
Atlanta, GA 30308
404-730-4557
404-853-4235

Aurora Police Department
15001 E. Alameda Dr.
Aurora, CO 80012
303-739-6102

Austin Police Department
Cold Case Unit
P.O. Box 689001
Austin, TX 78768-9001
512-974-8572

Baltimore City Police Department
Homicide-Cold Case Unit
601 E. Fayette St.
Baltimore, MD 21202
410-396-2121

Baton Rouge Police Department
Cold Case Homicide Unit
704 Mayflower St., Room 100
Baton Rouge, LA 70802
225-389-4869

Boston Police Department
Cold Case Squad
1 Schroeder Plaza
Boston, MA 02120-2014
617-343-5837

Brooklyn Center Police Department
6645 Humboldt Ave North
Brooklyn Center, MN 55430
763-503-3226

Charlotte Police Department
Cold Case Squad
601 East Trade Street
Charlotte, NC 28202
704-336-5108

Chicago Police Department
Central Homicide Evaluation Support
Squad Room 101
1121 South State Street
Chicago, IL 60605
312-747-7157

Cleveland Police Department
Cold Case Homicide Unit
1300 Ontario
Cleveland, OH 44113
216-623-5464

Columbia Police Department
Major Crimes Unit
600 E. Walnut
Columbia, MO 65201
573-874-7414

Columbus Police Department
Unsolved Homicide Case Review Team
120 Marconi Blvd.
Columbus, OH 43215
614-645-4036

Covington Police Department
1929 Madison Ave.
Covington, KY 41014
606-292-2278

Dallas Police Department
Homicide-Cold Case Squad
2014 Main St.
Dallas, TX 75201
214-670-6976

Delaware State Police
Homicide Cold Case Squad
P.O. Box 430
Dover, DE 19903
302-739-5997/739-7850

Des Moines Police Department
Robbery-Homicide-Cold Case Squad
East 1st St. and Court Ave.
Des Moines, IA 50309
515-283-4869

Detroit Police Department
Homicide Section
1300 Beaubien
Detroit, MI 48226
313-596-2266

Federal Bureau of Investigation
Washington Field Office
Cold Case Homicide Squad
Squad CR-2
601 4th St. NW
Washington, DC 20535
202-278-2373

Florida Department of Law Enforcement
SE Florida Cold Case Committee
7265 NW 25th St.
Miami, FL 33122
800-226-3023

Georgetown Division of Police
Criminal Investigations
550 Bourbon St.
Georgetown, KY 40324
502-863-7828

Hartford Police Department
Major Crime Unit Cold Case Squad
50 Jennings Rd.
Hartford, CT 06120
860-527-7300

Hennepin County Sheriff's Department
400 S 4th St, Suite 600
Minneapolis, MN 55415
612-348-5056

Huntington Beach Police Department
Crimes Against Persons Unit
2000 Main St.
Huntington Beach, CA 92648
714-536-5947

Illinois State Police
Investigative Section
1100 Eastport Plaza Dr.
Collinsville, IL 62234
618-346-3670

Indiana State Police
Criminal Investigation Division
IGCN, 100 North Senate Ave.
Indianapolis, IN 46204-2259
317-232-4338
or

Indiana State Police
Cold Case Squad
Indiana State Police Region 1
1550 East 181 Ave.
Lowell IN 46356
219-696-6242
or

Indiana State Police Cold Case Squad
1425 Miami Trail
Bremen, IN 46506
574-546-4900

Indianapolis Police Department
Special Investigations Unit
50 North Alabama St
Indianapolis, IN 46204
317-327-1751

Jackson Police Department
Homicide-Cold Case Unit
P.O. Box 17
Jackson, MS 39205
601-960-1306

Kansas Bureau of Investigation
Cold Case Squad
1620 SW Tyler
Topeka, KS 66612
785-296-8200

Kansas City Police Department
Cold Case Squad
1125 Locust Street
Kansas City, MO 64106
816-234-5330

Los Angeles Police Department, Central Division
Community Law Enforcement and Recovery
  CLEAR-
1 Gateway Plaza
Los Angeles, CA 90012
213-922-3537
* Gang-related murders only*
or

Cold Case Homicide Unit
Robbery-Homicide Division
150 N. Los Angeles St., Rm 503
Los Angeles, CA 90012
213-847-0970

Maryland State Police Support Services Bureau
Criminal Enforcement Command, Special
  Investigations
7175 Columbia Gateway Drive
Columbia, MD 21046
410-290-0050 x 166

Marysville Police Department
316 6th St./P.O. Box 670
Marysville, CA 95901
530-741-6611

Massachusetts State Police
Cold Case Homicide Unit
Route 20
Sturbridge, MA 01566
508-347-4816

Miami Police Department
Homicide-Cold Case Squad
400 NW 2nd Ave.
Miami, FL 33128
305-579-6530

Memphis Police Department
Old Mysteries Homicide Unit
Criminal Justice Center Homicide Office,
  Rm 1121
201 Poplar Ave.
Memphis, TN 38103 901-545-5300

Michigan State Police
Criminal Investigations Division Complex
4000 Collins Rd., P.O. Box 30632
Lansing, MI 48909
517-336-3437
or

Michigan State Police
Second District Headquarters
Second District Cold Case Team
42145 W. 7 Mile Road
Northville, MI 48167
248-380-1020
or

Michigan State Police
Fifth District Headquarters
Fifth District Cold Case Team
108 W. Michigan Ave,
Paw Paw, MI 49079
616-657-6081

Minnesota Department of Public Safety
Bureau of Criminal Apprehension Cold Case
  Homicide Unit
1246 University Ave.
St. Paul, MN 55104-4197
651-642-0560

Missouri Highway Patrol
Support Services Coordinator Violent Crime
  Support Unit
1510 E. Elm
Jefferson City, MO 65102
573-526-6122

Naval Criminal Investigative Services
Investigative Services Cold Case Homicide
  Unit
Washington Navy Yard
716 Sicard St, SE Suite 200 Bldg 111
Washington, DC 20388-5380
360-257-3359

Nebraska State Patrol
Cold Case Squad
P.O. Box 94907
Lincoln, NE 68509
402-471-8637

New Hampshire State Police
Major Crimes-Historical Homicide Section
10 Hazen Dr.
Concord, NH 03305
603-271-2662

New Jersey State Police
Major Crimes-Cold Case Squad
P.O. Box 7068
West Trenton, NJ 08620
609-882-2000 x 2421

New Orleans Police Department
Cold Case Squad
715 South Broad Street
New Orleans, LA 70119
504-826-1300

New York City Police Department
300 Gold Street
Brooklyn, NY 11201
718-834-2777

**North Dakota Bureau of Criminal
Investigation**
P.O. Box 1054
Bismarck, ND 58502-1054
701-328-5500

Oakland Police Department
DNA Cold Case Team
455 7th Street
Oakland, CA 94607
510-238-3821

Omaha Police Department
Homicide-Cold Case Unit
505 South 15 Street
Omaha, NE 68102
402-444-5654

Pawtucket Police Department
121 Roosevelt Ave.
Pawtucket, RI 02860
401-727-9100

Philadelphia Police Department
Homicide Unit Special Investigations Unit Cold
  Case Squad
700 Franklin Square
Philadelphia, PA 19106
215-686-3334

Phoenix Police Department
Cold Case Squad
620 West Washington St
Phoenix, AZ 85003
602-262-6106

Pittsburg Police Department
Cold Case Homicide Unit
202 Penn Circle West
Pittsburg, PA 15206
412-665-4050

Rapid City Police Department
Criminal Investigation Division
300 Kansas City Street
Rapid City, SD 57701
605-394-4134

Richmond Police Department
Cold Case Homicide Task Force
6 North 6 St, Suite 300
Richmond, VA 23219
804-646-6741

San Antonio Police Department
Homicide Unit
214 West Nueva
San Antonio, TX 78207
210-207-7667

San Diego Police Department
Homicide Cold Case Team
1401 Broadway MS 713
San Diego, CA 92101
619-531-2473

South Burlington Police Department
Bureau of Criminal Investigations
575 Dorset Street, Ste. 2
South Burlington, VT 05403
802-846-4182

Tukwila Police Department
Cold Case Unit
6200 Southcenter Blvd
Tukwila, WA 98188
206-433-1821

Tulsa Police Department
Cold Case Unit
600 S. Civic Center
Tulsa, OK 74103
918-596-9135

Washington DC Metro Police Department
Cold Case Unit
300 Indiana NW Rm 3153
Washington, DC 20001
202-727-6027

Washoe County Sheriff's Department
Cold Case Unit
911 Parr Blvd
Reno, NV 89512
775-328-3337

West Virginia State Police
Homicide Unit
406 North Jefferson St.
Lewisburg, WV 24901
304-647-7600

Wisconsin Department of Justice
Division of Criminal Investigations-Special
  Assignments Unit
P.O. Box 7857
Madison, WI 53707-7857
608-266-1671

Canada

Edmonton Police
Historical Homicide Unit
9620 103A-Avenue
Edmonton, AB
Canada T5H 0H7
780-421-3384

Ottawa-Carlton Regional Police Service
Homicide-Cold Case Squad
P.O. Box 9634, Station T
Ottawa, ON
Canada K1G 6H5
613-236-1222 x 2547

Saskatoon Police Service
Major Crimes – Cold Squad
P.O. Box 1728
Saskatoon, SK
Canada S7K 3R6
306-975-1419

RCMP Surrey Satellite Complex
Major Crime Unsolved Homicide Unit
12992-76 Ave
Surrey, BC
Canada V3W 2V6
604-543-4816

Toronto Police Service
Homicide Squad Cold Case
40 College St 3rd Floor
Toronto, ON
Canada M5G 2J3
416-808-7419

Ontario Provincial Police
Cold Case Initiative
777 Memorial Avenue
Orillia, ON
Canada L3V 7V3
705-329-6330

ACKNOWLEDGMENTS

I wish to extend my gratitude to Director Larry Welch of the Kansas Bureau of Investigation for his assistance in providing material for the preparation of this chapter. Director Welch has exemplified the law enforcement professional, and fostered proactive cold case homicide investigations. In 2005, the KBI and other team members participated in the solution of the notorious "BTK" cold cases from the 1970s Wichita, Kansas, area. In addition, I wish to recognize and extend my appreciation to Assistant Director Larry Thomas, Senior Special Agent Ray Lundin, Special Agents Brad Cordts and Katie Schuetz and crime analyst Jeff Muckenthaler of the KBI for their assistance and participation in the preparation of this resource, as well as to acknowledge their role in the solution of this notorious case.

Further, I wish to thank Detective Rick Jackson, Los Angeles Police Department, Cold Case Squad, and Lieutenant Jorge Duran of the San Diego Police Department H.E.A.T. team for providing the material and taking the time and effort to assist in presenting their experience for all of us to learn from. In addition, I wish to acknowledge the ready interest and assistance of Major Larry C. Turner, Commander, Criminal Division, of the Indiana State Police for his professionalism and assistance. Each of these persons has exemplified American law enforcement at its best, and I am grateful to all for their efforts.

SUGGESTED READING

Adams, M. (2003). Cold case squad: Partnering with volunteers to solve old homicide cases. *Subject to Debate* Vol. 17 pp 1, 7). Washington, D.C.: Police executive research forum.

Anonymous. (2003). Los Angeles Sheriff's cold case unit uses old fingerprints in new ways. (February 14, 2003). *Crime Control Digest*. 37(6) p.6.

Blankstein, A. (April 21, 2002). When trail goes cold, homicide unit turns up heat. *Los Angeles Times*. B-3.

Eliopulos, L.N. (2003). *Death Investigator's Handbook: Expanded and Updated Edition*. Boulder, CO. Paladin Press.

Ellis, K. (2004). Kansas city cold case squad solves string of murders. *Subject to Debate*. 18(7), pp. 1, 7.

Gore, W.D. (Winter 2003–2004). A new look at the DA's Bureau of Investigations. *Law Enforcement Quarterly*. V32, pp.16–17.

Markey. J. (2003) New technology and old police work. *FBI Law Enforcement Bulletin*. V72N9. September, 2003.

NIJ. (2002). Using DNA to solve cold cases. (Commission report no. NCJ 194197). Washington D.C.. National Institute of Justice.

Nyberg, R. (1999). Investigations: Cold case squads reactivate old investigations. *Law and Order*, 47(10), pp 127–130.

Nyberg, R. and Jurovics, S. (1993). MUST: A team for unsolved homicides. *FBI Law Enforcement Bulletin.* V63, 3 (March, 1993). P2.

Regini, C.L. (1997). The cold case concept. *FBI Law Enforcement Bulletin.* V66, 8. (August, 1997). p.1, 6.

Smith, C.A. (1999). Tulsa's gray squad solves cold cases. (November, 1999). *Law and Order.* V47, 11. pp.48, 49.

Spraggs, D. (2003). How to open a cold case. *Police Magazine.* (May, 2003). Pp. 28–31.

Turner, R. and Kosa, R. (2003). Cold case squads: Leaving no stone unturned. (Report NCJ 199781). (July 2003). Washington, D.C. Bureau of Justice Assistance.

Wellford, C., and Cronin, J. (2000). Clearing up homicide clearance rates. *National Institute of Justice Journal* (April, 2000). Washington, D.C.

12 The Media in Cold Case Investigation

Richard H. Walton

CONTENTS

INTRODUCTION

Despite the sometimes rancorous relationship between members of law enforcement and the media —misunderstanding on both sides — the news media play an integral role in the function of a free society. The media, through print outlets such as newspaper and magazines and through video and the Internet, inform the public of local, regional, and national news and events. In this manner, they serve to help safeguard the public. Agency news releases, publication of the FBI's Top Ten Wanted fugitive list, and television shows such as "America's Most Wanted" utilize different forms of media to alert the public to wanted persons, and regularly result in the featured fugitives' apprehension as a direct result of public involvement.

Crime and politics are chief among those events that have been regularly reported since news reporting began. The public is fascinated with crime, and this interest has long been noticed by those who report crime, those who investigate crime, and those who study various aspects of crime and public interest. In the investigation of cold case homicides, the media have taken on a new, and valuable, role in their mission to inform and safeguard the public. The media serve as an *information resource* for cold case homicide investigation, and in some instances, may be the only repository of information cold case investigators have when they seek to build a case from scratch. In addition, the media at times may assist in the furtherance of a cold case investigation.

This chapter presents the role of the media in cold case investigation. This role is presented in three major categories. These categories are; (1) information base, (2) generating public interest and assistance, and (3) reporting the successful conclusion, increasing affirmation of agency mission, and enhancing positive public relations.

THE MEDIA AS INFORMATION RESOURCES

During the initial review of a cold case file, and subsequent in-depth familiarization with the case, investigators become immersed in the facts of the case. These facts encompass people, places, dates and times, relationships, and more. Media records with potential information about the crime may include:

- Newspaper reporting at the time of the crime and thereafter
- "Sunday Supplement" and other reviews in subsequent years and decades
- Magazine articles, books, or other literary publications
- Old video clips and, sometimes, movies.

Review of available newspaper and other media reports of the cold case under investigation is suggested during the early stages of a cold case investigation. These accounts may yield information not necessarily found in the case reports. Of importance in this review is to determine what facts and information regarding the case are to be found in the media sources. Among these may be:

- Nature and location of injuries
- Weapon used
- Property taken
- Ingress and egress to the crime scene
- Other information known only to the killer

This information could become an issue later during suspect development or at defense when someone says "Well, I read about it in the papers."

This source may be especially more valuable in older, sketchier, and seemingly uninformative or incomplete case files. In my experience, the older the homicide case, the more detailed and voluminous the written media reporting *may* be. This reporting, however, might have been influenced by a number of other factors at the time, including:

- Victim status — prostitute versus young child of prominent citizen
- Other newsworthy events at the time
- Bizarre or more unusual elements of the crime
- Mystery surrounding the crime, or lack thereof
- Political links or ramifications
- Relationship to other crimes
- Personal or professional interest of the editor
- "Newsworthiness"

Keep in mind that while the media serve as unofficial records of events, they do serve as a record. In this regard, the media may serve as a basis to turn a once unofficial record into the official record. These issues may become a major source of information in those cases in which files are missing or nonexistent, and provide the basis for crime scene reconstruction and identification of those involved in the case as victims, suspects, investigators, etc. Keep in mind, however, that information in media accounts is only as reliable as the sources of information, the interpretation and repetition of the information, and any self-serving motives of those providing information. Just like in a police investigation.

NEWSPAPERS

Print media was the standard for decades of how Americans received their news. In the age before radio, and later television, it was *the* primary news medium. Newspapers were the daily format for news, and magazines and short story booklets or magazine articles also recorded people, stories, and events. In prior decades, it was not unusual for towns and cities to have multiple competing print news media. These operated on a morning daily schedule, a afternoon basis, sometimes a semiweekly or weekly schedule, or variations of these. When newspapers competed with one another, it might not be unusual to find one paper hitting the streets in the morning hours, while the competition came out in the afternoon. Over the past two decades, however, many major dailies have closed their doors. Some have been bought out by other news organizations or merged with other media interests.

For cold case investigators, this is relevant, as a review of both editions may be valuable, as well as the awareness of potential other sources of news reporting. Due to deadlines for reporter's stories, what one newspaper printed in detail might have been only lightly touched by the competitor, which instead perhaps concentrated on an aspect of the story totally neglected by the competition. And that's what reporting was: *competition.*

Then, like now, the media sought to solicit readership and to sell advertising. Crime stories could mean additional sales. On occasion, and in response to intense public interest, newspapers would rush urgent breaking news stories to press — often to "scoop" the competition in editions in additional editions known as *"extras."* These might be exemplified by the word "EXTRA" in color at the top of the first page. The use of this color, as well as the extra edition, were more expensive to produce and featured only the most sensational of cases (see Figure 12.1).

Where to Find Old Newspapers

Historically, newspaper publishers themselves kept back copies of their editions. This served not only as a record of their business, but, in the pre-computer age, as an in-house source of background information on persons, events, places, and other items of report. These repositories of back issues were called the *morgue*. This is *not* to be confused with the coroner's repository of the deceased by the same name.

In the past quarter century, however, some newspapers have eliminated the storage costs and other accompanying problems and issues by getting rid of their original hard copies of back editions. Computerized data systems and other technological advances have eliminated the need to maintain hard copies of daily editions. Decades of back issues took up a lot of space. After copying these to microfilm, many news organizations have simply destroyed the original copies or donated them to universities or research facilities that have room to store them (see Figure 12.2). In some instances, publishers may retain hard copies for a set period of time before copying them to microfilm and destroying or otherwise discarding them.

For cold case investigators seeking to locate back issues of local newspapers, whether original hard copy or microfilm-style copies, there are a number of places to explore. Among these are:

FIGURE 12.1 *Humboldt Standard* EXTRA newspaper 1925. Review of newspapers is necessary to identify witnesses and information not found in the file as well as what information is found in the public domain. Older newspapers may furnish more detail than more recent. (*Humboldt Standard*)

- The local newspaper publishing company (if still in business locally). When this source is contacted, however, keep in mind that good reporters sense stories in the making. If known detectives start asking questions about cold cases, so might a reporter.
- Local library. May possess original or microfilm copies (see Figure 12.3 and Figure 12.4).
- Local college or university. Most often possess microfilm copies, but may have originals.
- Other college or university operated libraries or research facilities.

FIGURE 12.2 Cold case investigator may spend hours reading microfilm, a tactic not encountered in normal homicide investigations. (Author's file)

- Local historical society. May possess older, original newspapers as result of donation by the newspaper publisher.
- State archives or repositories.

What Might Be Found in the Newspapers

"Killed by two savage blows on the forehead, the lifeless body of Mrs. Pearl Martin, 55, was discovered yesterday afternoon lying at the bottom of steps, which connected the Martin garage with the family living quarters at 2926 E Street…Mrs. Hazel Skipper, 16 West Trinity St., on her way to an appointment with Mrs. Martin, discovered the crime and notified police at about 2 p.m. when she looked through the half-open garage doors at the Martin residence."

FIGURE 12.3 Libraries may be a source of a number of investigative aids in cold case investigation, including newspapers, city directories, and telephone books. (Author's file)

FIGURE 12.4 Microfilm homicide report *San Diego Union* front page June 7, 1965. (*The San Diego Union-Tribune*. With permission)

This was the lead story reporting a homicide in the Eureka, California *Humboldt Times* newspaper on December 11, 1946, and reported again in a story on cold case homicides in the *Times-Standard* newspaper in Eureka, California, 58 years later. The information revealed in these few passages is not untypical reporting, even today. Cold case investigators reviewing this case would immediately note that in just these few sentences is found information that:

- Identifies the name of the victim
- Identifies the age of the victim

- Identifies the victim's address
- Identifies the location where the body was found
- Identifies the name of the person who discovered the crime
- Identifies the name of the person reporting the crime
- Reports the manner of death
- Reports the location of potential fatal wounds to the victim
- Describes the scene of the crime
- Reports the date and time the crime was reported to police
- Reports the circumstances by which the victim was discovered

In this and subsequent reports, the newspaper reported that she was the victim of a robbery and that a handgun and approximately $300 in cash and jewelry were reported missing. Thus, information perhaps known only to the suspect was now in the public domain.

Initial and subsequent newspaper reports regularly report information of interest in a cold case investigation. In addition to the aforementioned topics, they not uncommonly provide information that includes:

- Names and addresses of witnesses
- Names and addresses of friends and associates of the victim
- Names and addresses of relatives and co-workers of the victim
- Employment information regarding victim
- Victim's marital status
- Victim's past or ongoing relationships
- Identities of those last known to have seen the victim
- Names of responding law enforcement officers and investigators
- Identities of initial coroner or medical examiner personnel
- Identity as to where the remains were transported
- Other circumstances surrounding discovery of the body
- Victim's activities prior to disappearance or commission of crime
- Reported relationships of victim, including possible suspects
- Suppositions and theories of those who knew the victim
- Other similar crimes in the neighborhood or time span
- Political or time and circumstances potentially relevant to the crime
- Identities of persons of interest
- Statements by friends, associates, and others
- Name of the author of the article
- Description or discussion of the weapon used
- Description of victim injuries
- Description of evidence seen by others
- Discussion of evidence or property seized by law enforcement investigators
- Coroner or medical examiner findings

In some, especially the more notorious or sensational cases, suspects have mailed letters or items belonging to the victim to local news media. In most cases, these have been turned over to the police. Cold case investigators should keep this possibility in mind during interviews and conversations with media representatives. If this has happened, do they still possess any of these items?

Searching the Newspapers

Depending upon the source location, newspaper contents may be indexed or catalogued to allow searching for specific news stories, or they may not be catalogued at all. In either case, investigators

FIGURE 12.5 Library newspaper file index system. Not all libraries have index systems, and, in their absence, the only way to research information about cold cases is to begin with the initial reporting and review subsequent issues. (Author's file)

should query the custodian of the newspapers or files to ascertain what retrieval options exist. The systems are as follows:

- Catalog systems may be indexed by card index files in which articles between a given time period are referenced by type, i.e., "crime," or "murder"; by individual names; or a variety of other methods (see Figure 12.5). Investigators will need to identify what, if any, information retrieval systems exist and to work with the custodian of the newspaper's files to maximize efforts to retrieve all relevant items. In other instances, they might be computerized back to a certain date, which would more readily facilitate item retrieval.
- Non-catalogued. In this situation, the newspapers are usually filed and maintained by year on shelves or stacks, or on microfilm. Investigators will need to know a starting date or period to begin a review. In my experience, homicide cases are usually found within the first few pages, if not the first page, depending upon the time period, size of the newspaper, perceived public interest, and other editing factors. If the date of the homicide is not known and the identity of the victim is, the death certificate may provide a starting date for a newspaper search. These searches will be very time consuming.

Keep in mind that, as the case grew "cold," so did media interest. Stories that once occupied front pages on consecutive issues became smaller references inside the paper, often weeks or months later, and ultimately nothing more than a brief mention that detectives were still following up on leads. As fresh cases overtake ongoing investigations and consume law enforcement resources, the news media experience a similar situation. Their business is to report the news and, for the most part, they do not go back to a story unless there is a "newsy" element. As a consequence, media reporting of a homicide may trail off after a day or two, a week, or a month.

In either case, however, it may be prudent to check newspaper accounts for a month or two afterward for any mention and on anniversaries of crimes.

- Internet. Investigators may search on line for newspaper articles, and some search engines may allow searching for specific news items. My experience in doing this has suggested that searching the local newspaper as well as searching the nearest large city newspaper may prove beneficial. In some instances, expand your search for other large newspapers of national scale. These may include the *Los Angeles Times*, the *Washington Post, New York Times*, and others. Some newspapers, however, do not put stories prior to 2000 on the World Wide Web due to legal concerns addressing copyright and royalty issues for authors of articles. I have not found this to be a uniform practice, however. In addition, local universities or colleges may have research facilities that may assist investigator efforts in this regard.

The Photographic Record

Newspaper reports were, and are, often illustrated with photographs and diagrams or sketches of the scene of the crime (see Figure 12.6). Photos may be of the exterior of the building of a crime scene, interior shots, neighborhood shots, or a combination of these. Additional photos to be found in review of newspapers in the course of a cold case investigation depict:

- Other persons connected to the victim or the crime, often identifying them by name, occupation, and address.
- Weapons
- Scene of the crime
- Persons present within the crime scene

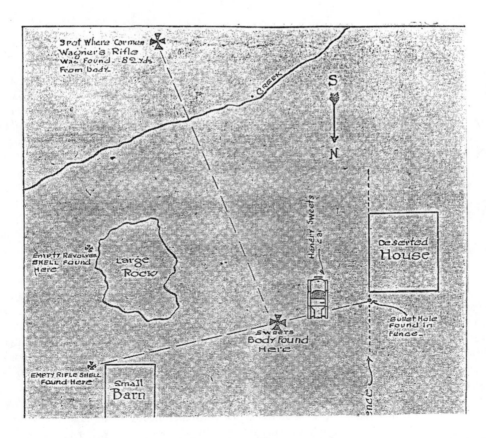

FIGURE 12.6 While perhaps more common many decades ago, media crime scene sketches are to be found in reporting today as well. They can serve to orient the reader. Note the specific distance and orientation of evidence. (*Humboldt Standard*)

- Surroundings of the crime scene
- Potential witnesses or suspects (in crowd scenes)

In the past, private photographers in some jurisdictions, not uncommonly responded to crime scenes to take pictures for the law enforcement agencies. For other purposes, including financial gain, other persons may also have taken photos of the crime scene or related locations or persons or items and sold or otherwise furnished these to the media. During the review of the newspaper photos, cold case investigators may seek to ascertain who *took* the photographs. This source information is usually noted at the bottom of the picture. In cases of private photographers, cold case investigators may seek to locate them to ascertain whether they have other photographs of the case and to attempt to obtain copies. In those instances in which the photographer is found to be dead, attempts may be made to identify the descendants of the photographer or to learn the disposition of photographs remaining in the individual's estate.

In situations where the local photographer was a professional and operated a business, inquiry to determine who bought the business might learn whether the purchaser also bought any photographic collections. Other sources of potential photographs may be local private photograph collections, historical society photograph collections, local or state archives or colleges or university libraries or photo collections.

When reviewing newspaper accounts, it was not uncommon to see a photograph of the victim's face with the article. *Who* furnished the picture? *Where* did it come from?

Keep in mind that reporters' information is only as good as their sources.

FILM AND AUDIO MEDIA

With the growth of television in the 1950s, and later cable news networks in the early 1980s, written media began to be usurped by these media. In decades past, many stations were individually owned and affiliated with major news organizations such as ABC, NBC, or CBS. In later periods, many of these stations began to be bought by other media concerns and it would not be uncommon to find a station in one city owned by a company that owns similar media in other cities and states. Newspaper and film stories and photographs were carried and transmitted nationally and internationally by the Associated Press (AP) and United Press International (UPI). These two organizations also transmitted photos for the newspaper media for many decades.

Local camera crews (often just one reporter and a photographer) recorded information in the field for nightly broadcast. After shooting the event, the crew brought the film back to the studio, where it was edited for broadcast. It was up to the discretion of the editor to preserve and broadcast what suited their purpose. Material that was not broadcast often wound up on the proverbial "cutting-room floor" and was discarded.

Film and video taken in the field is described in the media jargon as "raw material" or "raw footage." Raw material is all the film or footage that was shot, including the snippets that found their way onto the air. This material was normally discarded, unless, perhaps, the case was high profile. Investigators should ask if the station retains any raw footage. However, news media will release only to law enforcement, even under subpoena, material that was aired, and will not normally release unaired footage. This material may be protected under the shield laws that govern media disclosure of sources or other material.

Material that is broadcast is "aired material" or "air cuts." This distinction is important for cold case investigators to understand. Aired material is that portion of the raw material that was broadcast by the medium. This is the material normally retained by the news facility. For cold case investigators, it may be significant to understand that, in older cases, it was not uncommon for news cameras and reporters to conduct an interview with a witness or other person at length and shoot perhaps 20 minutes of footage. However, by the time editing was complete, perhaps 2 minutes was aired, and partial statements — *sound bites* — were broadcast. It would not be unusual for a reporter's 3-minute interview to be reduced to a 15-second sound bite.

As a consequence, for cold case investigators, ease of media review and access to this material is somewhat more difficult. In my opinion, written media no longer report in detail to the degree as was once common. One of the many advantages of assigning senior or veteran investigators to cold case homicide investigation is their grounding in the local community. This experience includes knowledge of media, newspapers, and audio-video, and changes in media ownership or broadcast initials as well as potential personal contacts.

When reviewing and investigating cold cases, do not *assume* anything. This includes assumption that the film media has nothing remaining decades later. You don't know until you inquire, and you might find that local media still possesses film footage many decades old. This was the experience of El Cajon, California, cold case investigators Robert Anderson and Jon Wooddell during their investigation of the 1965 homicide and other crimes committed by serial killer Clyde Wilkerson (discussed in Chapter 4). Investigators discovered that San Diego television station KFMB retained aired footage of their coverage of the case, and the station converted it to videotape and provided it to detectives.

Not uncommonly, news stations may have video footage dating back to their origins. KFMB retained film video dating to the late 1950s and early 1960s. The earliest format was 16mm film, and a transition from film to video began in the 1970s. This format was originally a three-quarter-inch Sony Beta-formatted tape with a different encoding from the Home Beta format. The three-quarter-inch format later changed to a one-half-inch format, and to a mix of one-half-inch Beta and digital. The current trend is to all-digital format.

ELEMENTS OF A NEWSCAST

Depending upon the time period and type of newscast, these elements made up the dissemination of the news event:

- Film or videotape of the event
- Written script of what was aired in the media
- Anchor's script of what was aired regarding the story

Depending upon age, film footage may not have had sound on the same reel. Sound came later with the addition of a sound stripe. Film with audio was sometimes accompanied by a separate sound track containing the reporter's narration of the story. In addition, the media had a "reporter package" where the narration is put on the story and the anchor would make reference to the reporter, whose narration is on one track and field footage is on another.

Further, in stories where there is no reporter in the footage and the anchor speaks over it, there might have been an original reporter, but 3–4 days later they might have pulled the footage from the crime scene or topic and the anchor would now say "Now for an update…" and reuse this footage, imposing later dialogue over earlier footage as the anchor narrated it on air.

Contacting the Media

Any contact with the media offers a potential for making law enforcement's cold case effort public. As with some prosecutors and judges, there are misconceptions about what cold case investigation is and how it is conducted. Cold case investigators can go a long way by educating those in the media about some of the aspects of cold case investigation and how it differs from hot case investigation. Among these differences is maintaining a lack of publicity until the right time. Responsible journalists may understand this and ask that they be notified when the case breaks. This is not unreasonable and may facilitate obtaining the desired footage and information, as well as promoting relations for future cooperation.

Although a personal contact is most desirable, when seeking this information, it is suggested that investigators first approach the station management. Contact may be made with the manager or a "special projects" person. In some instances, the station might request a subpoena. This is one reason a prosecutor should be brought on board as early as possible in the investigation. Keep in mind that the degree and speed of cooperation vary on a case-by-case basis, depending upon station personnel, resources, and policies.

Media Retrieval

Media stations have different filing systems, and, like those in law enforcement, these have changed and evolved over the years and decades. Once-common card files have been replaced by computerized databases, and, on occasion, some stations still maintain both. Before the advent of the computer, card index files, which require a manual search, were common. In some instances, these were later transferred to a computer program, but that program may have become history with software advances and the data may no longer be retrievable. Many stations, as do some law enforcement agencies, maintain offsite storage facilities, and it may require some time and effort on the part of station personnel for them to cross-check records in available databases and to retrieve the material. Remember, the information on card files is only as good as the person who filled it out, and information retrieval may well depend upon the ability to cross-check information between cards.

When contacting media, date of the crime, discovery of the body, or when the story aired is important for their search. Knowing this date allows them to more quickly identify and retrieve the film. Since computers, however, software for newsrooms allows them to search national as well as local stories.

When attempting to locate the film, also try to locate the written script. The *written script* is what is said on the air; it may also include what the reporter *did* during the broadcast of the story, and may include narration and text of the sound bite. The written script is not uncommonly transcribed and filed. If it was read by an anchor, what the anchor says is also in the script. Names in sound bites and scripts may be searchable in databases and, in older instances, card files, depending upon how the story was catalogued by the local station.

Maintenance of scripts may vary from station to station, depending upon their policies, and may be searchable depending upon their filing systems or databases. Usually, however, what is saved is only that which was aired. Also ask if they have still pictures, "stills," from old interviews.

When reviewing older footage, do not be surprised to see camera crews standing in the heart of the crime scene, or officers handling evidence in front of the camera. It happened.

During review of footage, investigators should note what is revealed about people and the scene. In particular:

- Names. Cold case investigators should cross check to be sure that persons interviewed by the media had been interviewed by law enforcement. These investigative statements should be cross-checked to their media accounts.
- Dates and times. These should be compared to the case file and may assist in timeline preparation or enhance or discredit statements of concerned persons.
- Scene and analysis of what the footage shows and comparison with case photos.

Film Degradation or Quality

Film is subject to degradation, depending upon storage conditions and exposure to heat and humidity. Normally, film does not readily show detail like blood spatter and holes unless a zoom lens was used. In addition, film footage is usually not of the quality of later videotape. In certain cases, cold case investigators may wish to have a forensic specialist examine the film for possible enhancement of frames or images. In addition to consultation with local law enforcement or state laboratory personnel, a source of assistance in this area would be the National Law Enforcement and Corrections Technology Center. Further discussion of this organization is found elsewhere in Chapter 32.

MAGAZINES AND OTHER LITERATURE

When reviewing cold cases, keep in mind that these may have been written up in magazines or books. During the course of investigation, officers from the time period of the case, friends or family of the victim, or other witnesses may have knowledge of whether, and when, the story was reported in news magazines or literary magazines or books.

In previous decades, magazines such as *True Detective* and similar works regularly published true-crime stories submitted by law enforcement authors (see Figure 12.7). These reports may detail names, events, and other matters concerning the crime, as well as photographs. It may be prudent to ascertain whether any such publication occurred. Keep in mind that these accounts may be "enhanced" or embellished. When direct knowledge of the existence of a specific article or crime report is not known, cold case investigators may attempt to use Internet resources such as http://www.e-bay.com to identify and locate these articles.

During the course of a cold case investigation, it may prove valuable to ascertain whether any persons connected to, or known to, the original or subsequent investigation authored any published material or unpublished manuscripts. Comparison of what is revealed in this material with the case file may be of interest in the cold case investigation.

FIGURE 12.7 *True Detective*, 1958. This issue carried detailed reporting and pictures to be found nowhere else when cold case investigators revisited the 1957 murders of two El Segundo Police officers in 2003. (Courtesy of the El Segundo Police Department)

```
                    POINTS OF ORIGIN


                          by


                     John L. Orr
```

It flared up much quicker than he expected. He had planted the device only seven minutes earlier and already the paper bag was on fire. The blossoming flames quickly spread to a weathered cardboard box, then began eating away at the side of a discarded sofa next to it. He lowered himself in the driver's seat and squinted through binoculars for a better view. It was a moonless night and the flickering light from the fire looked obscenely out of place, scarring the otherwise serene August evening. Beyond the carport where the fire was burning, he saw the HOLLYWOOD sign lighting up the horizon above the deteriorating city.

FIGURE 12.8 Cold case investigators should inquire if anyone connected with a cold case authored any papers, stories or other literature on the case. This front page of a text authored by former Glendale, California, arson investigator John Orr helped to convict him for setting a series of fires, including one that killed four people. His descriptions of "fictional" events were too close to factual to be considered fictional by investigators, and the jury agreed. He is now serving four life terms. (Courtesy of Special Agent Mike Matassa, ATF)

In one example, a fire of suspicious origin in South Pasadena, California, in 1984 claimed the lives of four persons, including a 2-year-old boy. It was initially ruled "accidental," although some fire investigators did not agree with this conclusion by law enforcement investigators. The fire case was closed and remained this way for over a decade.

Among those involved in the earliest stages of the investigation was Glendale, California, fire department arson investigator John Orr. Orr was considered an expert arson investigator by his peers, and highly respected. In 1998, Orr was convicted of setting the fatal fire, one in a series the esteemed fire marshal had set over the years. During the course of their investigation, investigators discovered that Orr had authored an *unpublished manuscript* detailing people and events in a fatal arson (see Figure 12.8). The revelations contained in this document became a pivotal point during the investigation and ultimate conviction of Orr for the murders. Further detail on this crime and related events is detailed in *Fire Lover*, by author Joseph Wambaugh.

OTHER MEDIA SOURCES FOR INFORMATION

Ever wonder how or where the media obtains information for broadcast today on something that happened years, or decades, ago? Complete with footage and pictures? Go to http://www.footage.net. This website links over 20 archives, including NBC and ABC broadcasting networks (CBS does not participate). Since 1994, this news-footage network has offered the media the ability to rapidly find previous news reports and archival footage. This site links to stock footage houses with access to footage, news reports, and more. After checking with your local media, this may be a good place to start when searching for footage and pictures. Links are provided to numerous sources of historical clips, images, and footage. The following was retrieved from this World Wide Web Site:

- **Global Search**. Search method to locate footage sources from stock, archival and news footage collections.
- **ZAP Request**. When you do not have time to do your own search, a request via this method sends a request to over 50 of the world's largest footage sources.

For further information:

Footage.net
44 East 32nd Street, 8th Floor
New York, NY 10016
212-251-8645
info@footage.net

CASE STUDY

The information contained in the following case history is drawn only from four newspaper accounts and the death certificate. The information presented is retrieved from post-initial-reporting articles in the *Los Angeles Times*, January 5, 1989, and the *San Francisco Chronicle* from July 9, 1991 and May 20 and 21st, 1998. The subject is the still unsolved murder of San Francisco police officer Lester Garnier (see Figure 12.9). The purpose of this is to illustrate the *detailed* information that might be uncovered in a cold case newspaper review and to explore possible avenues of investigation due to the passage of time in light of changes in relationships and technology.

It will appear that there is information in these reports that many investigators would prefer not to see in the press. These reports reflect the depths of investigation and variety of sources utilized in news reporting. By use of this case example, I intend in no manner to criticize,

FIGURE 12.9 San Francisco Police Officer Lester Garnier was murdered in Walnut Creek, California, in 1988. His murder remains unsolved. (Courtesy of Lt. John Hennessey, San Francisco Police Department)

demean, or impugn the character or reputations of the victim or of any personnel involved in the investigation, nor of the law enforcement agencies. In cold case investigation, best results are obtained not by looking back and saying, "Why didn't they do this?" or "Why did they do that?" but rather by objective, systematic study of the facts and evidence and moving forward in a cooperative manner with the objective of solving the case.

What happened in the past is in the past ... move forward.

THE INITIAL INVESTIGATION

The Crime Scene

Police Officer Lester Garnier was found shot to death, slumped behind the wheel of his blue 1984 Corvette, in a parking lot of a shopping mall in Walnut Creek, California, on July 11, 1988. The general location is a suburb of homes and office complexes on the east side of San Francisco Bay.

The vehicle was angled across three spaces near a group of upscale department stores. This was a position that a police lieutenant would later state indicated that he was making a "meet." The same quoted lieutenant stated that the murder had to be work related, as his car was placed so that no one could surprise him.

The victim was found by workers at approximately 7:30 a.m., the vehicle having been reported as having been there all night. The car still had its parking lights on, the doors were unlocked and the driver's window was down. He apparently had no gun or any money with him at the time of his death.

The victim's face was streaked with dry blood and blood stained his long-sleeved white sweatshirt and Levi pants. Victim's badge was inside one of the car's storage compartments.

Upon report of the crime, eight officers from the 78-member Walnut Creek police department, which usually experiences perhaps one murder a year, responded to the scene.

REPORTED WITNESS STATEMENTS

1. A workman in the shopping center reported hearing several gunfire-like noises approximately 11:30 PM but paid no attention as it was near the 4th of July. This witness later observed two women walking in the parking lot area. This may be the same witness as # 3 reported below.

2. Another witness told of seeing a woman exit the passenger's side of Garnier's vehicle. Police used a hypnotist with this witness in an attempt to create a composite drawing of the woman, who was described as being approximately 28 years old, blonde, 5 feet six inches to five feet eight inches, weight approximately 110 pounds. Neither woman had been identified as of July 9, 1991, despite repeated requests by police to the public for information. This may be the same as #4 below.

3. Approximately 11:15 p.m., a man laying carpet at a store near the Ross Dress for Less Parking lot heard what appeared to be two or three gunshots coming from the vicinity of the parking lot. A few minutes later he saw two women walking through the lot. One woman was described as in "... her mid-30s, tall and slender with blond hair below her shoulders." The other was described as being in her 20s and having shoulder-length blond hair and a medium build. The witness stated he observed the taller woman drive away in a faded blue Toyota, while the other drove away in a Toyota or Datsun with white or gray oxidized paint.

4. Another witness reported driving through the parking lot about 11:30 p.m. and observing a "slim, blond woman get out of the passenger's door of Garnier's Corvette. The witness said the woman circled the car and appeared to look in the driver's window before she walked away. None of the women was ever located."

THE INVESTIGATION

These news accounts further reported that, within approximately 3 years of the homicide, the Walnut Creek Police Department had "… interviewed more than 600 persons and traveled hundreds of miles in search of clues." During this, they had used hypnosis on a key witness and also consulted a psychic. In addition, "… every time a similar gun was used in a crime elsewhere," investigators "discussed it" with law enforcement representatives of that agency.

The investigation into Ganier's personal and professional life is reported in the news accounts. The media also stated that investigators had spoken to "several hundred prostitutes" Garnier had arrested in the course of his undercover work. Other information found in these reports includes:

1. Evidence

According to media reports, little physical evidence was recovered at the scene. However, the reporting in these articles indicates that fingerprints and a spent bullet were recovered. According to the media, "Fingerprints in the car didn't produce a suspect."

The news reports further stated that, "… police recovered one copper jacketed bullet from inside Garnier's sweatshirt and tested it against similar guns owned by eight San Francisco police officers, finding no matches. In a report by the *Los Angeles Times* in 1989, the media review suggested deeper elements of the investigation, noting that the "revolvers" of 10 San Francisco police officers had been reportedly checked by Walnut Creek detectives.

In my experience, the media and others have not infrequently, in the past, lumped the term "revolver" as identifying *all* handguns, including semi-automatics, which is not correct. According to the chief of SFPD, this was done "merely to cover all the bases." The chief is further reported as saying he had no knowledge of a police officer as a suspect in this case. By this and other news reports, it was suggested that a strong rift had occurred between the SFPD and the agency of primary jurisdiction, the Walnut Creek police department. Senior officers and investigators of the SFPD are identified and quoted at length in these accounts regarding their lack of participation in the initial investigation.

The *San Francisco Chronicle* in 1991 further reported similarly that, "In addition, they ran innumerable fingerprint checks and test-fired the weapons of eight officers in the San Francisco Police Department who owned guns similar to the murder weapon. In at least one instance, a San Francisco officer submitted to a lie detector test." This brings up the question of why were the guns and fingerprints of fellow officers examined? The answer to this would be found in the review of later news reports.

"Within the San Francisco department, rumors have circulated that an officer killed Garnier and that Walnut Creek did not trust San Francisco police to help find the killer. Some San Francisco officers are angry that their detectives were not summoned to the murder scene immediately." Senior SFPD officers are quoted regarding their perception of the Walnut Creek investigation. In response, Walnut Creek police are reported as responding that they tested the officers' weapons "'to cover potential defense issues at a later time' and that they came up with no ballistic matches." Walnut Creek police were reported as saying the suspect could be, or could not be, a police officer. This area of investigation had not been eliminated.

2. The Victim

Garnier's life was reportedly examined in detail by investigating detectives and published in the press. He was held in high esteem by his colleagues and known as a very cautious man. According to the press, Garnier "… was extremely particular about who he let into his car, but apparently allowed his assailant to get into his vehicle and sit next to him without evidence of a struggle." On the night of the homicide, he apparently left his 9mm and .357 caliber handguns at home.

The media, and investigation, explored his past. Garnier was born in the local Mission District of San Francisco and attended Mission Dolores Elementary School and Riordan High School. Described by a classmate as a "solid B student," the victim was further described as "street smart." After school he would stay around the Boys and Girls Club. Garnier was named Boy of the Year and Regional Boy of the Year, and earned a trip to Washington, D.C. to meet President Ford. Those who knew him said they had never heard anyone say anything bad about him.

Beginning in 1980, Garnier worked for the Broodmoor Police Department, a suburb near San Francisco. He joined the SFPD that same year and spent 4 years as a patrol officer at the Northern Station in the Fillmore District. He arrested three gunmen holding up a restaurant on a main city street in 1981, and in 1983, helped capture an attempted murderer. He was twice decorated for bravery. In 1984, he transferred to the vice unit, and worked there until his own murder. During this time, he had arrested hundreds of prostitutes. Prior to his assignment to the unit, a series of scandals and allegations of corruption had been levied against the SFPD. These were reported in the media as centering on the vice unit amid allegations of officers' using and selling drugs, hiring prostitutes and providing favors to bookies, drug dealers, and pimps.

When he was off duty, Garnier worked three part-time jobs (other accounts state four part-time jobs), and reports indicated that he was further thinking of opening up a small business — a hot dog stand. He bought the Corvette and had a cell phone. The latter was not yet common at that time. Garnier liked nice clothes, worked out, and had dated a number of women.

According to these reports, Garnier purchased a home with a pool in nearby Concord and lived there with his parents shortly before his death. Other reports say he helped his parents purchase the home. He was reportedly a quiet person and did not often speak about his job with his family. He did, as was reported, once say that "There are good policemen and bad policemen, just like anything else."

3. Victim's Movements on the Night of the Homicide

On the night of the homicide, Garnier ate a roast beef dinner with his family and left his home at approximately 8:45 p.m. At approximately 9 p.m., he called his "best friend," the owner of a San Francisco gas station. The two had spoken of going to see the movie *Bull Durham* but Garnier said he was behind schedule and could not make it. His best friend later reported that he tried to call Garnier back but that the phone just kept ringing.

4. The Weapon

The weapon used in the slaying was an AMT .380 caliber semi-automatic pistol. It has never been recovered.

5. Motive

No motive has been identified in this crime.

6. Suspect

No suspect has been identified in this crime.

7. The Wounds

The victim was shot twice at close range, once in the right temple and once in the right side.

8. The Political and Investigative Environment

Not unheard of in hot cases, politics and other elements are thrust into homicide investigations. Cold case investigations are no different. By 1991, according to press reports, police had no reported motive or suspect. The two lead detectives on the case are identified and quoted during the news reports. Detectives reportedly had eliminated motives that included robbery, revenge, a casual pickup, girlfriend, or prostitutes that Garnier had arrested. At this time, police discounted any relationship of this crime to a series of political scandals within San Francisco City Hall. Press reports offer insight into elements that cold case investigators may need to examine in depth for relevance to the murder of Officer Garnier.

Not long before his murder, Officer Garnier was assigned to surveillance duty on a brothel that reportedly specialized in underage girls. This was part of an investigation into the activities of the brothel that led to the indictment of the city's chief administrative officer, a San Francisco police officer, and numerous others for patronizing the brothel. The investigation stemmed from an informant's letter advising of the brothel and a second letter notifying the SFPD of possible officer patronage of the brothel. Later reports of a friend of Office Garnier note that Garnier told his friend he was working on a case that had high-level political ramifications. Subsequently, the brothel was raided on April 30, 1988, but the two named "ringleaders" got away. Officials were later reported as saying the suspects were tipped off in advance of the raid. When one *timelines* the events reflected in news accounts, this was reportedly almost a year after the initial reports of the existence of the brothel, yet just slightly over 2 months *before* Officer Garnier's murder.

Garnier's surveillance activities were reportedly documented in his logs. The newspaper reports detail statements of other "authorities" relating to past "police bachelor parties" attended by officers from other jurisdictions in which young prostitutes were alleged to have attended by invitation of the officer indicted in the brothel case. The indicted officer's lawyer is quoted in the articles suggesting that Garnier may have attended one of these "stag parties" while a reserve officer, and perhaps known some of the girls in the brothel he was staking out. In addition, the indicted officer had previously served as a reserve officer in the same agency as Officer Garnier. According to the press accounts, the SFPD could not verify this information and the former officer "could not be reached for comment." According to the news accounts, the SFPD officer was fired from the force after pleading to one count of unlawful sex with a minor in which he received a suspended sentence, fine, and probation. The city official also pleaded guilty to patronizing the brothel, was fined $100,000, and "performed six months of community service picking up trash in the city." The chief of police at the time of the murder was reported as saying Officer Garnier's murder was not connected to the prostitution ring and in 1998 reportedly said that while he could not recall saying this, assumed it was the result of information from subordinate officers.

The news media often timelines events in accounts of reporting of events, and in this instance, provided summaries detailing, in part, the careers of the dismissed officer and murder victim Garnier as well as other events:

- Garnier served as a reserve officer in 1980. During this period the dismissed officer was employed for a private security service at an apartment complex near Broadmoor, had friends on that force, and may have known Garnier.
- Garnier joined the SFPD in 1980 and the dismissed officer in mid 1982.
- One of the brothel ringleaders attended bachelor parties also attended by members of the Broadmoor Police Department and other agencies. The dismissed officer allegedly invited prostitutes to these parties.
- May, 1987, SFPD received anonymous letter regarding the brothel. A second letter followed 2 months later.
- April 30, 1988 the brothel is raided.
- Capture of one of the brothel-owner suspects in Oklahoma on July 9, 1988.
- Officer Garnier was murdered the next day.
- Presence of a grand jury investigation of a prostitution ring specializing in underage girls.
- Capture of second brothel owner suspect in South Carolina on July 19, 1989, after the case is aired on "America's Most Wanted" television show.

- Walnut Creek police were reported as interviewing a SFPD narcotics officer who had filed an unsuccessful lawsuit alleging that he had been punished for "blowing the whistle" on corruption within the department.
- Early 1998 SFPD reopens an investigation as a result of discovery of an internal memorandum in a vice unit file suggesting the presence of a corrupt officer within the unit about the time Garnier was murdered. The SFPD pledges to follow this investigation to wherever it leads.

According to newspaper reports, police were unable to find any link between the death of Officer Garnier and the prostitution ring. Interestingly enough, the news accounts do not report how well Garnier and the dismissed officer knew each other, and noted that this relationship was one that was being investigated.

These accounts reflect concern and anger by SFPD police officials and investigators about their lack of participation in the initial homicide investigation. This decision not to conduct a formal investigation into the death of one of their "own" is reported as a decision that "… still rankles officers in the department," although it occurred in another agency's jurisdiction. These accounts further suggest that Walnut Creek police "… tried with little success" to establish a link between the murder and allegations of corruption or scandals within the SFPD of the period.

According to press reports in 1998, the FBI confirmed that Walnut Creek investigators had requested the Bureau to reopen an investigation into allegations of corruption involving SFPD officers that had been conducted in the mid 1980s. An FBI agent is quoted as saying that Walnut Creek police were interested in knowing if someone from within the SFPD had been involved in the murder of Officer Garnier. The request had been denied due to lack of new information.

Based upon review of these four newspaper reports only, and assuming the validity as written, cold case investigators would seek to apply the advantages to be gained from exploiting (1) changes in relationships and (2) advanced technology, as discussed in later chapters.

- Changes in technology
  - AFIS. Rerun all fingerprints and utilize updated databanks and techniques. Also run them in other local and state databanks.
  - NIBIN. Input and run the bullet through updated databanks, despite the age of the case. In addition, due to the growth of laboratories in the region, update publicizing this bullet to local crime laboratories and police agencies. The news reports do not indicate that the shell casings were recovered; however, this avenue would be explored also.
- Changes in relationships
  - It appears from the news media reports that hundreds of persons, including those arrested by the victim, were interviewed against a possible background of corruption and a prostitution ring. These included suspects in the brothel investigation as well as friends and co-workers of the victim. Cold case investigators may seek to identify those for re-contact and interview in light of the intervening years and changes in lifestyles or relationships as well as to update information they may have "heard" over the years. Among these would be those close to or associated with named principals, either personal or professional relationships.
  - Reinterview those close to the victim for additional statements after passage of time.

The news accounts further suggest exploration and a review of

- Cell phone records (if obtained) and residence or work telephone records of victim and others. Cell phones were coming of age at this time and were not the compact devices we have today. The carriers have changed many times since this time period and if these records were not obtained during the initial investigation, they may or may not be available now. How the victim came to be where he was when reportedly going to a movie with a friend is of interest. In addition:

- Phone records of the two fugitives and communications before the murder.
- Known associates of the two fugitives just before and after the murder.
- Parallel duty assignments that might have brought victim and the dismissed officer into possible frequent contacts. Reinterview of co-workers, friends, and associates of each.

These ideas are but a few that may be suggested from review of these media reports. A full, in-depth identification and review of all media accounts might provide further detail for possible exploration. This example is used for illustrative purposes only.

MEDIA ASSISTANCE IN COLD CASE INVESTIGATION

Unlike hot homicide investigation, there is no fresh crime scene to which the media responds to begin to take pictures and conduct interviews. The press usually doesn't know when a cold case is reactivated, and does not learn of it until the case is solved and a news conference is called or a news release is generated by the agency. In the course of cold case investigations, investigators may seek to maintain a low profile to further their efforts until the suspect has been identified and taken into custody. The element of surprise may be a consideration in many of these cases.

In some instances, however, and as an investigation progresses, investigators may decide whether to release information to the public. These situations may include:

- Law enforcement efforts to seek new witnesses and tips
- Publishing or running stories on anniversaries of a crime or other significant dates
- Law enforcement attempts to identify property associated with unknown or known victims
- Law enforcement attempts to locate suspects or others

Law enforcement efforts may utilize more proactive methods, depending upon the circumstances of the case. These may include:

- National media or special reenactments of crimes and information wanted such as "America's Most Wanted"
- National law enforcement media resources such as the *FBI Law Enforcement Bulletin*
- Written flyers and posters, widespread or localized
- Local television or radio broadcasts
- Newspaper announcements
- Local magazine or other publications

Consideration of media resources in furtherance of cold case investigation should not be limited to newspapers, radio, or television (see Figure 12.10). Seeking information through other forms of media may include Internet web sites such as:

- Agency World Wide Web site.
- Special focus websites such as http://doenetwork.org. This volunteer organization assists law enforcement concerning unexplained disappearances and unidentified victims from North America, Australia, and Europe. See Chapter 32.

FIGURE 12.10 On June 19, 1991, this young girl apparently answered the doorbell at her family residence in a condominium complex shortly after 9 p.m. A short time later, her family noticed her missing, and saw her shoes by the door. The next morning, her body was found by workers at a nearby business complex, still wearing the pajamas she had worn when she disappeared. She had been hacked to death. A billboard donated by the advertising agency was utilized to seek information about the case. The murder went unsolved. In October, 2003, the DNA Laboratory of the San Diego, California, Police Department discovered a DNA profile match between oral swabs and fingernail material collected from the victim and the DNA profile of a neighbor, a convicted felon. The suspect was convicted and sentenced to death. (Courtesy of Detective Bob Conrad, Chula Vista Police Department)

CASE STUDY

On May 28, 1982, 16-year-old Los Gatos, California, high school student Russell Jordan vanished without a trace. A missing persons report was taken by the Santa Cruz County Sheriff's Office, Jordan's official county of residence. The student disappeared, however, in neighboring Santa Clara County, where he attended school. During the investigation it was discovered that he had cleaned out his high school locker a month before he disappeared, and many presumed the youth was a runaway juvenile. In April, 1995, a transient found some bones in Los Gatos Creek not far from the boy's high school. Determined to assist police, the homeless person picked up some bones and carried them to the front counter of the police department.

Responding officers returned to the scene and conducted a detailed search in which they applied anthropological recovery techniques and recovered more remains. Winter rains and wildlife activity had affected the site, however. The skull and other parts were missing, and could not be located. Among the items recovered, was a distinctive belt buckle. Investigators were aware of the missing juvenile from 13 years before, and believed that this might be the missing boy. The belt buckle was identified as very similar to the one he was last known to be wearing, but could not be considered conclusive proof of identity. The remains were turned over to the county medical examiner. Although the case was treated as a homicide by the police department, they were unable to identify the remains. *Forensic anthropology* examination suggested that the remains were of the same description as the missing boy, but identification was inconclusive.

In late 1999, advances in DNA technology presented the Los Gatos Police Department with the opportunity for further investigative possibility. The remains were sent to the FBI mitochondrial DNA unit. In 2003, this specialized unit of the FBI Laboratory affirmed the identity through *mitochondrial DNA* comparison to the victim's mother.

In March of 2003, the results of the DNA examination were published in the newspapers with a request for information. As a result of this newspaper story, a former classmate of the youth came forward to admit that the missing boy was not a runaway juvenile but in fact had been murdered by another classmate.

Sergeant Tim Morgan and Officer Randy Bishop of the Los Gatos Police Department moved quickly on the investigation. They learned that after Jordan was reported as a runaway, Jordan's friend, Sean Viehweg, had told others that he was not a runaway, and admitted that he had killed the boy. Thus, other *classmates* knew but had kept quiet over the decades. Investigators began to interview others in Jordan's close circle of friends, and as a result, obtained the names of two other classmates with knowledge of the murder. In the course of this investigation, officers of this smaller police agency encountered what many in cold case investigation have discovered is not unusual: the need to travel and the extra unbudgeted expense of this particular investigation.

One of the witnesses to the admission still lived locally, but another now lived many miles away in Eureka, in northern California. Morgan and Bishop located and interviewed the second witness, who admitted to helping Viehweg dispose of the body the day after the murder. As a result, investigators obtained an arrest warrant for Viehweg.

Investigation revealed that Viehweg, now 38 years old, lived near Klamath Falls, a small farming community in southern Oregon. In my experience, it is not unusual that suspects in cold case homicides have often moved out of the state in which they committed their crimes. Viehweg was now married and had a family. In the course of planning their strategy for the investigation, the investigators contacted detectives in the Los Angeles Police Department Cold Case Squad to draw upon their experiences and expertise in this phase of the investigation. This was an excellent tactic on the part of the Los Gatos investigators.

The investigators contacted law enforcement in the jurisdiction where Viehweg now lived, and strategized their investigative plan. In this phase of the investigation, there are no clear-cut rules to define what cold case investigators should do. Each case, and circumstance, is different. Investigators consider the suspect's background and the life he or she has led in the period since the homicide. *Is the suspect a career criminal? Is the suspect a serial killer? Is this the suspect's only crime?* The investigators had checked Viehweg's background. He had served honorably in the military, including duty in Somalia, Panama, the Persian Gulf, and elsewhere for 8 years. Nothing suggested a serious criminal history. Officers were aware, however, that at this phase of the investigation, contact with the suspect offers a number of possible outcomes. These may be (1) fight (2) flight, or (3) or admission or confession.

Individual investigators have different methods that have worked for them, and here is where experience and training pay off. Sgt. Morgan and Officer Bishop, assisted by officers from the local jurisdiction, contacted Viehweg, in a low-key approach at his home. At this initial contact, cold case investigators should note, and record, the *immediate* reaction of a suspect when confronted about the past crime or advised of the investigator's jurisdiction. Observe that reaction and record their *exact* words at this initial confrontation with their past. Viehweg turned "white." He agreed to accompany officers to the local law enforcement facility for an interview and was arrested on May 17, 2003. He ultimately waived extradition to return to California, and offered a defense that he killed the victim when the victim assaulted him with a knife. The suspect subsequently pleaded no contest on December 18, 2003, to one count of voluntary manslaughter. He was sentenced to 6 years in prison.

Identified cold case issues:

- Initial report as missing juvenile
- Knowledge, and silence, by peer group (classmates)
- Recovery of suspected remains but inability to confirm identity
- DNA advances that allow for positive identification of the remains
- News media information and request for information from the public

- Previous silent witness coming forward
- Identification of other witnesses and accomplices
- Suspect's out-of-state residence and arrest by local law enforcement agency from another jurisdiction
- Legal considerations of prosecution as juvenile or adult
- Suspect's lifestyle and law-abiding status since the murder
- Age of the case and lack of witnesses to the act

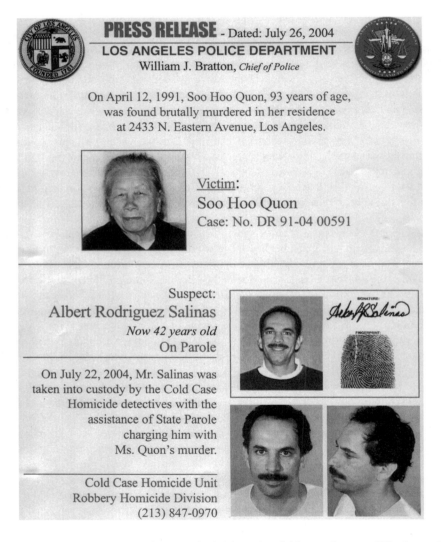

FIGURE 12.11 (See color insert following p. 216.) Cold case homicides are the most difficult to solve. When they are resolved, it is incumbent upon law enforcement to blow its own horn. There can be no better use of resources than to clear an old, unsolved murder. This reassures the public that these victims are not forgotten, and that the law enforcement agency is committed to solving these crimes. In cases involving the member of a minority community that has local media, press releases should be brought to their attention in addition to regular press outlets. In this case, the LAPD solved a 13-year-old homicide of an elderly woman. It was no surprise that the offender was a parolee. (Courtesy of Detective Rick Jackson, Los Angeles Police Department Robbery-Homicide, Cold Case Squad.)

MEDIA AND REPORTING OF SOLVED COLD CASES

Announcement to the public via the news media of the successful conclusion of a cold case investigation serves a number of purposes. Among these are:

- Announces the identification and arrest of an alleged murderer.
- Advises the public that law enforcement has not forgotten these cases, as exemplified by this case solution.
- May stimulate others with knowledge of unsolved homicides to come forward with information.
- Recognizes the role of the dedicated persons and investigators who made this possible.
- Reaffirms the commitment of the police agency to serve and protect the community.

Other Guidelines

Prior to the news release or new conference, the victim's family or other concerned persons should be notified. It would not be unusual for the media to locate and contact relatives of the victim and suspect after the announcement. Efforts to provide victim assistance resources should be made available to victim's family members as soon as possible upon arrest of suspect and prior to news release.

In cold cases where the victim was a member of a minority community, the agency may consider news or press release to be disseminated to any media groups that focus on or are dedicated to that community. As an example, if the victim was a member of a Korean community and that community has a community newspaper or radio or television station, be sure that these entities are notified of the arrest and case developments (see Figure 12.11).

CONCLUSION

Freedom of the press is a hallmark of democracy and a necessary component of our society. The press, like law enforcement, helps to safeguard the public and to expose wrongdoing. For cold case homicide investigations, the press may serve as an information base, providing a record of persons and events sometimes not retained, or found, in the original case file. These records may offer additional avenues of investigation for cold case investigators through reporting of persons, events, and other information pertaining to the crime and related events. In addition, the media may serve to generate public interest and assistance for cold case investigations, and ultimately serves to broadcast the successes of cold case investigations. These successes reflect positively on the law enforcement agency and remind the public, and those who have killed and not yet been caught, that law enforcement does not forget.

ACKNOWLEDGMENTS

I wish to extend my gratitude and appreciation to Mr. David Gotfredson of KFMB in San Diego, California. Mr. Gotfredson is a veteran newsman and editor and contributed much of the material used as a basis in this chapter. In addition, I wish to also thank Mr. David Browning for his material, input, and thoughtful review of this chapter. Mr. Browning is a veteran producer of news and documentaries for CBS News. He has been with this network most of the time since 1966, covering stories such as the RFK assassination, the Manson murders, the Patty Hearst kidnapping and trial, as well as natural disasters, political conventions, and Hollywood frivolities. In the 1990s, he served in the CBS Reports documentary unit, writing and producing the television memoirs of Walter Cronkite and Mike Wallace and has worked in recent years primarily for "60 Minutes" as well as occasional production duties for "48 Hours."

In addition, I wish to express my gratitude and appreciation to Sergeant Tim Morgan and Captain Duino Giordano, now retired, of the Los Gatos, California, Police Department for their in-depth review and discussion of the Viehweg case with me, and for their professional solution to the murder of Russell Jordan.

SUGGESTED READING

Anonymous. The State: Metro Desk. Pg2. (January 5, 1989). *Los Angeles Times*. Los Angeles, California.

Durant, C. Humboldt County's cold cases: Can these crimes be solved? (May 29, 2005). *Times-Standard*. Eureka, California.

Gathright, A. (2003). Others knew of killing, D.A. says: Los Gatos students remained silent about 1982 death. (May 10, 2003). *San Francisco Chronicle*.

Ryan, K. (2003). No contest plea in '82 killing of teen. (December 19, 2003). *San Francisco Chronicle*.

Stannard, M. (2003) Arrest in 1982 Los Gatos Killing: Oregon man accused in death of classmate in high school years. (May 9, 2002) *San Francisco Chronicle*.

Stannard, M.B. (2003). Dad says his son admitted to killing: Self-defense claim in 1982 death of Los Gatos classmante. (May 12, 2003). *San Francisco Chronicle*.

Sward, S. and Wallace, B. (1998). Still no suspect, motive in '88 killing of SF cop: '88 slaying stumps Walnut Creek police. (July 9, 1991 Final Edition) *San Francisco Chronicle*.

Sward, S. and Wallace, B. (1991). New probe of S.F. cop's '88 slaying. (May 20, 1998 Final Edition) *San Francisco Chronicle*.

Sward, S. and Wallace, B. (1991). How trail grew cold in '88 S.F. cop killing. (May 21, 1998 Final Edition) *San Francisco Chronicle*.

Wambaugh, J. (2002). *Fire Lover: A True Story*. New York: Avon books.

Part II

Technology

13 Friction Skin Impressions

Edwardo Palma

CONTENTS

INTRODUCTION

On the surface, fingerprint collection and identification might seem simple, but it should be left up to properly trained specialists qualified to collect, develop, and individualize fingerprint evidence. Fingerprint evidence, which has a long history, is an efficient method of identification if used properly. It has been used successfully to solve many crimes from burglaries to homicides. In some cases, fingerprint evidence is the only evidence connecting the perpetrator to the crime. In other cases, fingerprint evidence is helpful to investigators when it corroborates eyewitness statements or other evidence. Take, for instance, a case in which an eyewitness accuses a certain person in a crime but that suspect adamantly denies involvement; the exclusion of alleged suspects as donors of the fingerprint evidence is just as valuable as identifying the donor. When suspects are eliminated based on fingerprint evidence early in the investigation, the investigators are able to focus their attention and resources elsewhere.

This chapter will enhance the investigator's knowledge of fingerprint evidence from the earliest years of detection methods to the most modern. The information contained will help investigators appreciate the significant advances made between 1980 and 2000 in the area of fingerprint detection. In addition, the more recent use of a valid scientific methodology of fingerprint identification/individualization known as *Ridgeology** will be presented. Ridgeology uses biology, histology, genetics, and embryology as the basis for establishing the individuality or identification of fingerprints.

To allow this chapter to accomplish the goals set out by the book's author, we as investigators need to educate ourselves about advances made in the field of fingerprint evidence. For this to be effective, one must appreciate the rich history of fingerprints and the research and development that have pushed the science of fingerprints into the modern era. The science of DNA has held the limelight in forensic science in recent years, but fingerprints can be differentiated between monozygotic twins, while their DNA profiles cannot be differentiated. In return, fingerprints that lack qualitative and quantitative detail for individualization can be analyzed for DNA content, to obtain a genetic profile of the subject.

MAN'S KNOWLEDGE AND USES OF FINGERPRINTS

China would have to be regarded as the birthplace of man's use of fingerprints. In China, the intentional use of fingerprints dates back centuries from the first use of clay seals to the unmistakable use of ink impressions on legal documents. During the Han Dynasty (202–220 B.C.) clay fingerprint seals were commonly used among officials to sign official documents. In approximately 650 A.D., a law book of Yung-Hwui described the use of fingerprints to officially sign divorce matters between a man and a woman. From this, we can surmise that authentication of the seal had to come from a skilled individual who could read the fingerprint by comparing it to an identical matching impression made in either clay or ink. The use of fingerprints as a signature is proof that the Chinese understood their significance long before the Englishman Sir William Hershel (1858) collected handprints of natives in India and attempted to claim he was the inventor of modern fingerprinting. **The Chinese use of clay fingerprint seals showed that the Chinese understood the significance of fingerprints to establish individuality.

A Chinese crime novel written in the 12th century by Shi-naingan, entitled *The Story of the River Bank,* says "Wu Sung captured two women who had killed his brother … He compelled them to ink their fingers and to record their fingerprints." Undoubtedly the Chinese had advanced fingerprinting to a level of acceptance in criminal matters. This, however, appears to be more a coercion of the two women into a confession rather than a comparison of fingerprints to bloody fingerprints at a murder scene. This is significant, because the West would not see a crime novel with a fingerprint connection until the 19th century, written by well known American novelist Mark Twain.

Twain's novel *Pudd'nhead Wilson* (1893) features a fictional detective who makes use of fingerprints in a criminal proceeding. Pudd'nhead, an attorney, identifies two twins by their fingerprints, and assures the jury he will use them to convict the murderer. This novel was written 2 years after Vucetich's fingerprint classification system was proven practical enough to be placed in service. Juan Vucetich (born Josip Vucetic) (1858–1925), a Croatian-born Argentinean schooled in anthropology, became a police official with the Central Police Department, La Plata, Argentina, where he pioneered the use of fingerprints. Vucetich acknowledged reading about the research of

---

* 1983, New word coined by David R. Ashbaugh of the Royal Canadian Mounted Police used to describe a scientific method of analysis, comparison and evaluation of friction skin incorporating friction ridge detail viewed in three levels of detail for individualization.

** It is documented in the late 19th century that both Henry Faulds and Juan Vucetich knew fingerprints were used in China and Vucetich traveled to China and India to further educate himself on the subject of fingerprints.

FIGURE 13.1 The black lines represent the friction ridges of the fingerprint. The white spaces between the black lines are furrows. The print was recorded with black printer's ink.

another fingerprint pioneer, Sir Francis Galton (1822–1911), in the journal *Revue Scientific*. Vucetich took that research and expanded Galton's ideas to form a working classification system for filing and retrieving fingerprints. He also used the same crime-solving ideas put forward by still another fingerprint pioneer, Henry Faulds (1843–1930), who is given credit for first suggesting the use of fingerprints in a criminal case and writing about it in a letter published in the British scientific journal *Nature* on October 28, 1880.

Dr. Henry Faulds, who studied medicine in Scotland, was sent to Japan as a doctor and evangelist where opened the Tuskiji Hospital in Tokyo. While studying prehistoric pottery shards, he saw that finger marks made before the clay had hardened remained after firing. Later, he observed that bloody finger marks might lead to the scientific identification of criminals by comparison of the papillary ridges especially if a previous record of all 10 finger marks had been taken. He suggested that fingerprints could be used in investigations to eliminate an accused individual, and also to prove identity by comparison of finger marks left at scenes of crimes by the criminal.

Faulds states in a letter published in the scientific journal of that day:

> I have had experience in two such cases, and found useful evidence in these marks. In one case greasy finger marks revealed who had been drinking some rectified spirits. The pattern was unique, and fortunately I had had previously obtained a copy of it. They agreed with microscopic fidelity. In the other case sooty finger marks of a person climbing a white wall were of great use as negative evidence. Other cases might occur in medicolegal investigations, as when only the hands of some mutilated victim were found.

To accomplish this comparison, Faulds suggested that a very small dab of printer's ink could be spread thinly over the surface of a slate or smooth board to record the pattern of the papillary lines of a finger (see Figure 13.1). Although it is now known that China had for centuries practiced what Faulds had suggested in his letter, it was a new discovery to him. He states in his letter, "I have heard since coming to these general conclusions … that the Chinese criminals from early times have been made to give the impressions of their fingers just as we make ours yield their photographs." Faulds, through his own curiosity while studying ancient pottery, rediscovered this practice and became the first European to suggest the practice to the West.

By 1891, Vucetich's inked fingerprint classification system was proven practical enough for identifying repeat criminals to be placed in service in the La Plata Police Department. In 1892, he made the first positive latent fingerprint identification in a murder case. The case was the bloody murder of two young brothers. The mother maintained that an outsider had committed the murders. Vucetich, nonetheless, committed to his ideas about the possibility of identifying a bloody fingerprint, continued to investigate. He discovered that the bloody fingerprint belonged to the mother of the murdered boys, which ultimately led to her confession.

The Argentinean police adopted Vucetich's method of fingerprint classification, which spread to police forces of Spanish-speaking countries around the world. Vucetich personally classified 101 different types of fingerprints based on Sir Francis Galton's incomplete taxonomy of fingerprint patterns. Vucetich went on to identify 23 more felons with his method of classification. On September 1, 1891, his system of fingerprint classification was adopted. However, a decade would pass before Henry De Forrest at the New York Civil Service Commission introduced fingerprints into the U.S. Today there are over 35 million sets of computerized fingerprint records in the FBI's IAFIS.

FINGERPRINT IDENTIFICATION THEN AND NOW

On May 25, 1995, crime scene investigators (CSI) arrived at the house of a prominent Pasadena, California resident to investigate the murder of an 82-year-old female. The Police Department suspected that she had been murdered during the commission of a burglary. At their request, three Los Angeles County Sheriff's Department CSI investigators responded to the murder scene and proceeded to brush black fingerprint powder over all likely surfaces that could possibly retain fingerprints.

Fingerprints recovered from crime scenes in police circles are known as *latent prints*. The word latent is derived from the Latin word meaning "to lie hidden." Black fingerprint powder has a long history of successful use in "bringing out" or making a latent print visible when brushed with a carbon, fiberglass, or camel-hair brush to reveal the hidden fingerprints. It is commonly used on nonporous surfaces such as glass, metal, and finished or painted wood surfaces. Other colors of fingerprint powder have been employed to provide appropriate contrast on particular surfaces.

Shortly after their arrival, the Sheriff's Department personnel were able to recover fingerprints from the suspected entry point. The CSI team, being expert fingerprint examiners themselves, recognized that the fingerprint impressions were not from the victim because the prints recovered showed no signs of skin creases or flattening of fingerprint ridges that an 82-year-old victim would have. The recovered latent prints were crisp and clear, so clear that they warranted a rush to the nearest bureau that operated a computer terminal specifically designed to read fingerprints.

The input into the Automated Fingerprint Identification System (AFIS) would require preparation in the form of photography and other specialized techniques devised in Japan that were introduced into the U.S. in 1983. The Pasadena fingerprint was photographed with Polaroid® film to produce an image of the fingerprint enlarged 5:1. The technician placed a semi-clear Mylar foil over the fingerprint image, tracing the ridgelines of the fingerprint with a pencil. The purpose of this tracing is to remove unwanted background "noise" and provide high-contrast ridgelines for the computer fingerprint scanner. The scanner then converts the image into a digitized signal. Computer software then converts the unique fingerprint characteristics into a string of numbers. AFIS provides a rapid search of the known fingerprint number strings that are unique to that particular fingerprint. However, because of possible distortion in fingerprint characteristics*, the

---

* Distortions to characteristics of fingerprint ridges are caused by many factors, primarily surface to skin deposition pressure and lateral pressure when the skin of the finger makes contact with a receiving surface. Distortions can change the appearance of the print making it unrecognizable when compared to the original. Distortion is more likely to be a cause for failure to individualized fingerprints to the original creator of the fingerprint as opposed to be falsely individualized to another person.

number strings may vary. Consequently, fingerprint experts are required to review and verify all possible fingerprint hits suspected to correspond.

In this case, CSI Bill Leo did a fingerprint comparison to verify the AFIS hit and identified suspect James Edgar Williamson Jr., a step-grandson of the victim, and an arrest warrant was obtained based on the fingerprint evidence found in the vicinity of the point of entry that strongly implicated him. Williamson, upon hearing the news media broadcast, decided to turn himself in at a nearby Orange County fire station.

Without the technology of AFIS, the above case could have easily gone unsolved for many years. When the perpetrator of a crime is not a relative or acquaintance and the death is the outcome of a chance encounter, the chances are increased that the case will eventually turn cold. Fingerprint evidence properly collected and preserved, either by fingerprint powder and lifting tape or by photography, will be available for review for decades.

Millions of fingerprint cards maintained by the FBI have been submitted since 1924, when Congress established the Bureau of Identification to fill the need for a national repository of fingerprint cards, which were then stored and searched using the Henry classification system that originated in England in 1901. Until that time, fingerprint cards were classified, stored, and searched by fingerprint classifiers that require all 10 fingerprints to obtain a classification formula to file the card. Searching a single or partial fingerprint like a latent print was next to impossible. Single fingerprint systems like the Battley single fingerprint system were devised and employed using a 3×5-inch card upon which a rolled and plain impression was placed and then classified. The Battley system used a separate classification glass from the one used for the Henry classification system. The Henry system used a reticle glass with the straight classification line placed over the fingerprint, whereas the Battley system employed a reticle glass with seven concentric rings that was used to obtain the necessary information about each single print. The FBI modified the classification ring so both Henry and Battley classifications could be done with one reticle. The fingerprint information was gleaned from two focal points — the core (center) and the delta. Once the latent print information was classified, the print could be searched through the Battley single fingerprint files.

The FBI gave up on the Battley system and then used the FiveFinger Classification. The left and right hands from a separate fingerprint card were filed separately. A latent fingerprint developed at a crime scene had potential as evidence, but that rested on being able to identify suspects to compare their fingerprints or classify the latent print with a Battley-classifying ring and manually search a single fingerprint file. This action proved to be an expensive task with long hours of searching fingerprint files only to find many prints were never identified.

Two decades of research and development in America, Japan, and Europe and the resulting computer hardware and software were needed to handle the millions of fingerprints stored in static file cabinets. The biggest technological leap forward came when development of computer technology and optical-image storage became sophisticated enough in mid 1980 that a computer could handle large volumes of fingerprint data. In fact, some computer processors and storage devices were specifically built to handle fingerprint data. The only task remaining was to convert fingerprint cards containing inked fingerprints into a digitized format that computers could analyze.

The FBI database is a collection of fingerprint records, many of which are electronically submitted to the FBI from state identification bureaus that, in turn, have received prints from local law enforcement agencies. Latent print examiners have begun to electronically search latent fingerprints against this national fingerprint database, as well as local databases, and many cold fingerprint identifications such as the Williamson case cited above have resulted.

Investigators in cold cases should not assume that because a previous request for a fingerprint check was unproductive, that the same results would be obtained today. The accessibility to larger fingerprint databases has improved, so investigators should re-request fingerprint checks. Investigators should not assume that laboratories have gone through every possible file. They should insist on receiving documentation as to which databases their case prints were checked against, i.e., local city and county, regional or neighboring counties, state and regional or neighboring states, and federal.

With the relatively recent development of terrorist threats to our nation, the Department of Homeland Security is actively checking passenger entry and exit points (land, sea, and air) in the U.S. The previous IDENT AFIS system started by the U.S. Immigration and Naturalization Service has expanded search capabilities and in the first 6 months of 2005 it identified over 200 fugitive felons. Crime scene fingerprints can be checked against the IDENT database of known fingerprints, and fingerprints of wanted fugitives can be earmarked in the database for expeditious notification when a fugitive attempts to either enter or exit the country. The IDENT system has recently been made available to local police agencies.

DERMAL FRICTION SKIN RIDGES: THE LIVING SKIN BEHIND THE FINGERPRINT

The skin that is responsible for leaving finger marks is referred to as friction skin. It is found on the palmar side of the hands and plantar side or soles of the feet, including the phalangeal surfaces of the fingers and the toes of the feet. The first person responsible for calling this dermal skin "friction ridges" was David Hepburn (1895) of Scotland. He recognized that the dermal ridges assisted grasping by creating friction. He named the two larger cushion pads of the palm, the *thenar* (the cushion pad directly under the thumb, and the *hypothenar* (the cushion pad directly under the little finger). The third area in a palm is called the interdigital area, which lies just below the area where the fingers attach to the palm (see Figure 13.2).

Interdigital patterns many times are mistaken for fingerprints. A police officer trained as a fingerprint examiner may not have had formal training on identifying partial palm print impressions, and partial interdigital loop impressions may be mistaken for fingerprints and thus remain unidentified. A qualified friction skin examiner trained on the orientation and recognition of palmprints should reexamine unidentified fingerprints in cold cases. Partial palm prints, especially from the thenar, hypothenar and interdigital areas, are found in as many as 30% to 45% of crime scenes. Therefore, manufacturers of automated fingerprint systems are incorporating palm print databases in AFIS, called Automated Palmprint Identification System (APIS). In many police agencies, the

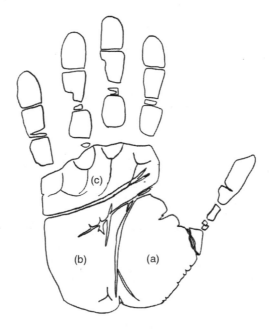

FIGURE 13.2 Outline of the palmar surface of the right hand, (A) indicates the *thenar* cushion area, (B) *hypothenar* cushion area (C) *interdigital* area containing finger-like patterns.

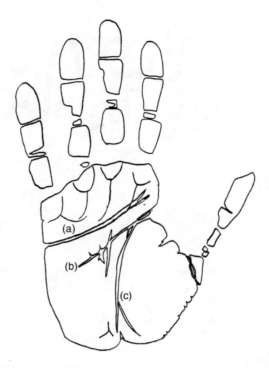

FIGURE 13.3. (a) Distal transverse crease (b) Proximal transverse crease (c) Radial longitudinal crease.

practice of palm print collection is not customary at the time of booking. Recent legislation has been enacted in some states authorizing collection of palm prints along with DNA samples from convicted felons.

In addition to the pads in the palm, other features are visible. When looking at the palm of the hand, flexion creases are noticeable. These are the folds associated with the joints that permit the hand to bend or flex when grasping. Most people have three main flexion creases in the palm (see Figure 13.3). The *radial longitudinal crease* separates the thenar and hypothenar. The *proximal transverse crease* and the *distal transverse crease* split the palm horizontally and can be seen when the fingers are drawn to touch the palm nearest the wrist. The palm surface contains patterns similar to fingerprint patterns, and has large areas of ridges with no patterns. Palmer friction skin is just as identifiable as finger patterns.

BIOLOGY ASPECT OF FRICTION RIDGE SKIN

A specific group of cells, called basal cells, found on the underside top layer of skin called the *epidermis* is responsible for friction skin *uniqueness* and *persistence*. Uniqueness is due to the particular pattern of features in a given area of the friction skin. Distinct ridge features of the skin are randomly created by a burst of basal cells that reach maturity in a fetus at about 24 weeks. Persistency implies that those peculiar features remain the same throughout one's life and are persistent even after death until decomposition totally destroys the skin. The dermis skin is the lower layer of skin that contains blood vessels, nerve endings and perspiration glands. One can get an understanding of the persistency feature of this very important cell layer made up of basal cells by observing what happens when our skin is cut or abraded. Some injuries to the skin do not penetrate the basal layer. A surface injury is noticeable for only about 2 weeks. The area of the skin that was affected by the injury will heal and return to its original appearance. However, when

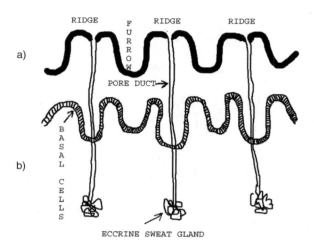

FIGURE 13.4 Friction ridge skin cross section view. (a) epidermis or upper layer of skin; (b) dermis, or lower layer of skin.

the skin is cut more deeply and bleeds, basal cells are destroyed. When the skin heals, it heals with a scar, especially noticeable in the friction skin. Scars in the friction skin lend additional individualizing characteristics to the skin.

In 1684, Nehemiah Grew described sweat pores, epidermal ridges, and their various arrangements in a scientific paper on the subject. Scientists over the years have used developments in biology, embryology, genetics, mathematics, and physics to help describe friction skin and further the science of fingerprints. Recently a *holistic* approach has been used in examination of fingerprints. No longer is the fingerprint identification determined by a threshold number of "points of identity." The holistic approach incorporates a scientific method called *"Ridgeology,"* wherein the fingerprint specialist makes a complete study of the ridgeline structure and shape, down to near microscopic level, for agreement of detail between the latent and known impressions.

Skin gland activity is a natural biological phenomenon where water and salt along with other organic mixtures of amino acids and semisolid fatty acids and proteins are secreted to the skin surface. The *eccrine* gland, the gland found in the tissues of the hands and feet, dispenses moisture (>98%) over the entire skin surface and, most importantly, to the underside of hands and feet. This distribution of moisture is through a series of pore ducts found on the top of friction ridge skin. The simplest touch of this moisture can deposit an outline or pattern of the friction skin on the surface touched (see Figure 13.4). The raised skin can also transfer oils and moisture from one's own body to another surface by touching other areas of the body before touching a surface. *Sebaceous* and *apocrine* glands, associated with hair follicles, secrete oily secretions that contain proteins, carbohydrates, sterols, glycerides, fatty acids, wax ester and squalene. These secretions are easily picked up and transferred by the friction ridge skin of the fingers.

When one looks closely at the friction skin of the hand, two distinct shades of color in the skin are seen. The darker of the two (providing the skin is clean and not contaminated) is actually the furrow. This is the space between the raised ridges. The actual raised ridge is between the darker furrow lines and is more translucent because of the mammalian *epithelium skin,* which is made up of cornified (keratinized) cells that are stratified to make up the *epidermis* layer that forms the ridge structure.*

The basal layer of epithelial stem cells is responsible for the proliferation of epidermal cells, referred to as keratinocytes, which appear as stratified tissue that forms the upper epidermis layer

---

* The outer nonsensitive and nonvascular epithelial layer of the skin that overlies the dermis layer

of skin. These cornified bundles of cells are being pushed up to form the strata layers of the epidermis. Friction ridge skin forms by the 16th week of gestation. The proliferation of cells continues after birth to sustain the permanence of friction ridge structure, and that permanence is one of the bases for friction ridge identification of fingerprint patterns.

The actual individualization of *latent* prints is made possible because of two biological factors. First, as basal stem cells divide proliferating keratinocytes, they move in tandem toward the skin surface by resilient bundles or cables that anchor to cell–cell junctions called *desmosomes*. Thus, desmosomes and basal cells provide the basis for permanence of the friction ridge structure. Second, the eccrine sweat gland distributed over the entire friction skin area exudes perspiration that is 98% water, but also contains organic and inorganic compounds.

The perspiration helps maintain pliable skin that enables precision gripping or power grasping by the hand. Friction ridges are coated with continuous perspiration that exudes from the pore openings located on the top of the ridges. When these ridges contact a surface, either porous (e.g., paper, wood or cardboard) or nonporous (e.g., glass, metal or plastic), an outline of the friction ridge design is transferred to that surface that is typically a partial image of the finger, palm, or both. The same holds true with a bare foot impression.

"Sebum" is waxy oil from the *sebaceous* gland. Sebaceous and apocrine glands are not found on the papillary skin, but rather are associated with hair follicles on other areas of the body. Therefore, the waxy oil found on the friction ridges is considered a natural contaminant from other areas of the body.

Knowing what the constituents are that are found on friction ridges from eccrine secretions or from the sebaceous and apocrine glands assists CSIs in approaching latent print sequential chemical processing of the latent print impressions at crime scenes.

Fingerprint Processes

In the past 2 decades, techniques for development of latent fingerprints have rapidly expanded from the traditional black powder method to more sophisticated fluorescent powders and cyanocrylate (CA) or superglue fuming techniques. The old iodine fuming method has taken a back seat to the CA common superglue method because of the versatility of CA to be stained or powdered for visualization. We have also seen a shift from the use of silver nitrate for detection of salt residue from fingerprints to a more refined mixture called physical developer (PD).

The traditional Ninhydrin Reagent (NIN) for staining amino acids found in latent fingerprints is still the workhorse for processing porous surfaces such as paper; however, chemical advances with amino acid-specific reagents called *ninhydrin analogs* are better suited because of their luminescent selectivity where surface background interference is an issue on porous surfaces.

Lasers and alternate light sources (ALS) or forensic light sources (FLS) capable of delivering monochromatic light are useful as forensic tools. These instruments help extend the visual capability of the human eye to see and record fingerprints that might otherwise be considered to be of no value for identification. Now investigators are routinely developing fingerprints on surfaces previously thought to be incapable of yielding fingerprints.

Investigators can no longer ignore surfaces that have been wet or are wet when encountered. Development of fingerprints exposed to water through condensation or rain can be achieved using small-particle reagent (SPR) that uses molybdenum disulfide powder in a detergent solution, or PD, a salt-silver developer that is used for the detection of fingerprints on paper even if the paper had been wet.

Two Types of Fingerprint Evidence

Before continuing a discussion about fingerprint evidence, we must have an understanding of the two types encountered at crime scenes: V*isible impressions* and *non-visible impressions*.

1. Visible (patent) print impressions.
    a. Friction ridges from the fingers, palms, soles or toes made deliberate with ink or live scan for recording known impressions.
    b. Non-deliberate fingers, palms, soles, or toes contaminated with, for example, blood, paint, grease, grime, etc.
    c. Non-deliberate fingers, palms, soles, or toes depressed or indented into malleable material e.g. wet paint, chewing gum, grease, etc., these impressions are commonly called molded or plastic impressions.
    d. Negative print impression where fingers, palms soles or toes through touch remove material from the surface.
2. Non-visible (latent) impressions – these require a physical or chemical development to make them visible.

FACTORS AFFECTING WHETHER FINGERPRINTS ARE DEPOSITIED ON OR RECOVERED FROM A SURFACE

Not all fingerprints are transferred to a surface, and when there is a transfer, not all fingerprints are usable. Age, gender, occupation, and illnesses may affect whether people will leave fingerprints when they touch a surface. The pressure involved in touching the surface and the amount of moisture on the finger also play a part in whether a usable fingerprint is left. If the receiving surface is dirty, rough, textured, or contoured, the chances are diminished that a usable fingerprint will be left. A fingerprint may appear smudged due to excess perspiration and pressure. It may be that too limited an area of the finger is transferred, so that there are insufficient characteristics to make it useful for individualization.

Environmental conditions after the fingerprint is deposited are critical for the recovery of a good usable print. Heat can affect the constituents by evaporating moisture or hardening fats and waxes in the latent print, leaving the print dry and incapable of absorbing fingerprint powder. Wet conditions can wash away water-soluble constituents like chloride salts and amino acids, thus affecting the chemical reaction of reagents like NIN, 1,8-Diazafluoren-9-one (DFO) and silver nitrate. However, a wet condition may not affect a fingerprint that contains a significant amount of sebaceous secretions. Such a print, once dry, could be developed with fingerprint powder.

Fingerprints deposited on surfaces are delicate. Latent print impressions can easily be accidentally wiped off during processing, or unintentionally damaged or lost by mishandling of evidence. Latent prints can be damaged by an improper processing technique or an improper chemical sequence during the recovery procedure. Latent prints developed without regard to chemical sequencing can limit processing potential of a print, leaving the print faint or overdeveloped and difficult to examine. Following proper processing guidelines during the recovery mode is critical for the successful development of usable latent print impressions.

SURFACES

Whenever fingerprint detection is necessary, the most important element to consider is the type of surface that contains the latent print impression. The type of surface dictates the type of process to use for development and recovery of fingerprints. There are three types of surfaces that all fingerprint technicians recognize. Identifying the surface is the first step in choosing the proper sequences and types of processes to use to develop fingerprints.

1. Nonporous surfaces
2. Porous surfaces
3. Adhesive surfaces

Examples of *nonporous* surfaces:

- Glass
- Metal
- Plastic
- Fired ceramic
- Glossy painted surfaces

Examples of *porous* surfaces:

- Unfinished wood
- Paper
- Cardboard
- Fabric
- Unfired ceramic
- Non-gloss painted surfaces

Adhesive surfaces can be found on many commercial tapes — masking, duct, electrician's, etc. Tapes contain two surfaces; the sticky side and the backing material that can be made of paper, plastic, cloth, or a combination.

SEQUENCING

A sequence in applying enhancement techniques must be considered to optimize fingerprint recovery. Improper application of a fingerprint development process can restrict or limit any further development techniques used later on. It was once thought that the use of powders excluded the use of chemicals, but advances in technology have changed that assumption. For example, an application of black powder on nonporous surfaces could lessen the chances of developing amino acids using NIN, but vacuum metal deposition (VMD) can be used after black powder application because the powder may have not developed prints that the VMD possibly could. There are so many processes available today that processing manuals or guides should be considered before applying any detection method for developing fingerprints.

The suggested sequence for testing a nonporous surface thought to contain fingerprints is:

1. Visual examination of the surface with a strong light in a darkened room.
2. Examination with laser or alternate light source for any inherent fingerprint fluorescence.
3. CA (cyanoacrylate) fuming of the object to form a white crystalline fingerprint.
4. Reexamination with laser or alternate light source for any surface reflectance yielding fingerprints.
5. Dye staining of the polycyanoacrylate.
6. Reexamination with laser or alternate light source for any luminescence yielding fingerprints.
7. For small to medium objects, test surface with a VMD.
8. Visual surface examination with a strong light.
9. Test surface with fingerprint powder*. With conventional powders, reexamination visually with light; utilize laser or alternate light source when fluorescent powders are employed.

The suggested sequence for testing a porous surface is as follows:

1. Visual examination
2. Checking for inherent fluorescence using laser or alternate light source

---

* Conventional or magnetic black or gray powder, or fluorescent powders.

   3. Iodine fuming
   4. DFO
   5. Laser or alternate light source
   6. NIN
   7. Physical developer

ADHESIVE SURFACES

Adhesive surfaces in the past were mostly ignored as a viable surface for fingerprint recovery, so in many homicide cases only the non-adhesive surface would have been tested for fingerprints. Today, fingerprints can be detected with the proper technique on both the adhesive side and the backing material. Developing fingerprints on tape is a relatively simple. Moreover, the approach and selection of powder or chemical should be an experimental exercise on similar tape to learn and understand the kind of results possible. One thing that must be considered is the protection of the adhesive side of the tape while processing the backing, and vice versa. A product called "Un-do"® found at local craft stores can be used to separate or unstick the tape adhesion when the condition is either adhesive-to-adhesive or adhesive-to-surface. As the Un-do solvent is applied, the tape can gently be pulled apart. Once separated, the adhesive is allowed to dry thoroughly before applying a fingerprint development technique. However, the two sides of the tape will require different processing techniques to visualize fingerprints.

Here are some suggestions for sequencing adhesive tape development.

- Non-adhesive side of tape:
   a. Visual examination
   b. Inherent fluorescence, using laser or alternate light source
   c. Cyanoacrylate fuming
   d. Laser or alternate light source
   e. Dyeing of cyanoacrylate
   f. Laser or alternate light source
   g. Vacuum metal deposition (VMD)
   h. Powder

- Adhesive side of tape:
   a. Visual
   b. Inherent fluorescence by laser or alternate light source
   c. Sticky-side powder; alternate black or white (best on black electrical tape) powder; gentian violet
   d. Laser or alternate light source

BLOODY FINGERPRINTS ON POROUS AND NONPOROUS SURFACES

When testing bloodstained impressions on *nonporous* surfaces, the practice in the past was to photograph visible bloody fingerprint impressions then dust with black fingerprint powder before lifting with tape. Today, powdering practices have shifted to chemicals that react with the protein in blood residue, generally producing a bright purple color. An advantage to chemicals over powder dusting is brighter development and finer detail enhancement of the friction skin pattern. In the past, NIN was used (to react with the amino acids in the blood) for enhancing bloody prints. Blood detection chemicals were also used, but they were usually the carcinogenic benzidine-type chemicals that are not advisable for use. Investigators examining cold case evidence that may have been previously tested for blood should practice personal safety by utilizing latex gloves and other safety equipment when examining evidence in cold cases that might have been exposed to carcinogens.

To preserve and enhance friction ridge detail of bloody fingerprints the following protein enhancement chemicals are suggested:

- Amido black
- Coomassie brilliant blue
- Crowle's double stain
- Aqueous leucocrystal violet
- Fuchsin red (Hungarian red)
- Benzoxanthene yellow

The above chemical reagents are excellent choices because bloody impressions can be fixed before staining. Detection is carried out in a lighted environment and basic forensic photography techniques can be used in the collection and preservation (as opposed to the use of luminol or fluorescein in a darkened room). These stains provide an advantage over heme-reactive chemicals, in that the resulting friction ridge detail will be sharper. However, if the application is to detect traces of bloody fingerprints on *dark surfaces* and for subsequent DNA testing, Bergeron (2003) suggested using a methanol-based suspension of titanium dioxide. Other heme-reacting chemicals are:

- Fluorescein
- Phenolphthalein
- Leucomalachite
- Tetramethybenzidine
- Luminol

Keep in mind that other latent print impressions may have been deposited on the nonporous surface as well. Cyanoacrylate preprocessing can preserve latent prints that might otherwise be destroyed by the protein staining technique. Research has shown that cyanoacrylate preprocessing is best followed by amido black when applying a sequential technique for developing bloody fingerprint impressions and latent fingerprints on nonporous surfaces.

STANDARD FINGERPRINT DETECTION AND RECOVERY TECHNIQUES

Visual technique enhanced with oblique light#*: Deposits of latent fingerprints reflect light. Examining a surface with oblique light can reveal the location of fingerprints.

Photography#: Latent fingerprints can be photographed at times without any pretreatment of powders or chemicals.

Ultraviolet Light (UV)#: Ultraviolet light and some inexpensive LED blue lights are useful for observations of reflection or absorption of wet and dry bloody fingerprints. UV light also can be used to observe fluorescence of special powders and chemicals used to treat fingerprints.

Cyanoacrylate (CA)**: Cyanoacrylate is the active ingredient in "superglue." Its fumes are attracted to the moisture of fingerprints. Research has shown that various heating methods for fuming CA work well. However, CA fumes are irritating to the mucus membrane and must be contained in a fuming chamber or tank. The chamber must be aired out before retrieving objects containing fingerprints. Developed fingerprints can be dye stained and photographed, and then powdered for lifting.

---

* Fingerprint detection techniques suffixed with # symbol have been used 25 or more years.
** Fingerprint detection techniques suffixed with * symbol were increasingly used for the observation, detection or enhancement of fingerprint traces within the last 10 or more years.

Dye Stains

- **Rhodamine 6G***: Widely used dye for staining latent prints developed with CA. UV light can be used to visualize the fluorescence.
- **Ardrox***: A yellow oily fluorescent chemical used to dye stain CA-fumed fingerprints. Can be applied full strength or diluted, then rinsed with tap water. The surface must be thoroughly dry before view with UV light or special blue lights.
- **Basic Yellow***: A brilliant yellow dye stain applied after CA.

Powders

- **Fingerprint Powders#**: Powders adhere to both water and fatty deposits of fingerprints. The choice of powder depends on the surface condition and color. Some specialized powders have fluorescent properties that can be used with UV light or special blue lights. Prints are photographed or lifted with tape.
- **Small Particle Reagent (SPR)***: The active ingredient is molybdenum disulfide particles that adhere to fatty components of latent prints. This method is useful for detecting fingerprints on wet surfaces.

Adhesive Reagents

- **Sticky-Side Powder *(SSP)**: This material adheres to the fingerprint on the adhesive side of tape. This is a wet process where the powder is painted on the adhesive side of tape and rinsed with tap water to reveal fingerprints. Various tapes respond differently to this process so testing should be carried out on similar tape before proceeding with actual evidence.
- **Gentian Violet (Crystal Violet)***: This is a fat-soluble stain that can develop fingerprints on adhesive tape surfaces. The prints are stained dark purple against the light background tape.
- **Iodine#**: Iodine is a temporary development process for fingerprints. Iodine fumes react with fatty deposits to produce a yellow-brown reaction that dissipates over time, making the prints no longer visible. Developed fingerprints must be photographed before they dissipate. Porous and nonporous surfaces can be fumed.
- **Ninhydrin# (NIN)**: This is used to recover fingerprints on porous surfaces. NIN reacts with amino acids in a latent print. Depending on the composition of the print, the developing time could be from a few minutes to several days. Heat and humidity can be used to accelerate the process, so that developing time can be reduced to a few minutes. Prints must be photographed.
- **Silver Nitrate#**: This chemical reacts with sodium chloride in the skin secretions, developing fingerprints on porous surfaces. Reactions must be photographed to recover fingerprints before background discoloration occurs.

Blood Reagents

- **Leucocrystal Violet (LCV)***: This presumptive test for blood is highly sensitive for developing visible and invisible blood trace fingerprints. It is applied by spraying non porous surfaces and some porous surfaces containing traces of bloody prints. Prints must be photographed to be recovered.
- **NIN#**: Reacts with amino acids in blood. The non-accelerated method should be used. Fingerprints must be photographed to be recovered.
- **Ruthenium Tetroxide (RTX)***: Modified RTX is a simple and rapid application. Surfaces can be fumed, dipped, or sprayed to reveal sebaceous fingerprints. Prints must be photographed to be recovered. However, on some surfaces, prints can be lifted with lifting tape and transferred to a backing card.

Prints from Human Skin

Human skin is a difficult surface for the development of fingerprints. Environmental conditions and body temperature are critical and must be controlled as soon as the body is discovered. Most attempts to develop fingerprints on human skin are not successful. However, they should be tried. The following techniques are simple and rapid for the detection of latent print on human skin.

- **Iodine/Silverplate Transfer#**: First, iodine fumes are directed over the suspected area using a fuming wand, which requires blowing one's breath through the tube to warm the iodine crystals. The crystals sublime to a gaseous state. Fumes turn yellowish-brown in contact with sebaceous latent prints. A silver-plated small metal sheet is then gently pressed against the surface for a few seconds. The plate is then exposed to UV light or sunlight. When conditions are right, a dark fingerprint image appears. The plate must immediately be removed from the light and the print image photographed.
- **CA#**: The body is tented and fumed with cyanoacrylate. Powder or a dye stain is applied to enhance fingerprints for viewing.
- **Ruthenium Tetroxide (RTX)***: The skin surface is fumed with an apparatus that consists of a small glass jar with an inlet tube and an exit tube. Fumes are directed from the exit tube to the surface suspected of containing latent prints. Sebaceous prints present under the right conditions develop a light gray color. Fingerprints are recorded photographically. Lifting with fingerprint tape can sometimes be employed. However, background skin surface texture can interfere, making some lifts unacceptable for comparisons.

SOPHISTICATED FINGERPRINT DETECTION AND RECOVERY TECHNIQUES

Specialized Light Sources Designed for Forensic Use

- **Light Amplification by Stimulated Emission of Radiation (LASER)**: Since the late 1970s, lasers have been in limited use for the detection of forensic evidence. Four types of lasers have been employed: The argon ion; the Nd:YAG; the copper vapor; and the tunable dye laser. Those in the blue-green bandwidth are most popular. Some laser equipment requires dedicated electrical power and a cooling system to keep it within operating temperatures, so portability is eliminated. The Nd:YAG laser is a pulsating laser that has portability, but the pulse is annoying while examining fingerprints.
- **Alternate Light Sources or Forensic Light Sources (ALS/FLS)**: High-intensity white-light lamps fitted with filters capable of selecting a monochromatic band of light in bandwidths from UV radiation through to the red end of the visible spectrum. These specialized light sources are well suited for crime scene use due to their portability. Although the ALS/FLS does not have the light intensity that a laser has, with proper use it can be just as effective.

Digital Photography

Digital photography is rapidly replacing traditional silver-based film. Detail image information not discernible to the human eye can be controlled by computer keyboard inputs to enhance its visibility. Developed latent fingerprints can be captured with digital cameras or flatbed scanners and then processed using digital enhancement software. Most popular among fingerprint specialists is Adobe® software. Off-the-shelf software can mimic darkroom photography techniques that are common among fingerprint specialists. Some specialized routines like Fast Fourier Transform (FFT) are useful to remove repeating background patterns, thereby effectively bringing out the obscured detail of a fingerprint. In 1995, this technique was used in a murder case in Washington State to enhance a palm print in blood on a bedsheet that was processed with amido black. The technician

FIGURE 13.5 Fingerprint on newspaper that was digitally enhanced to suppress the black type letters.

suppressed the fabric background using FFT, enhancing the palm print. The palm print was later identified as the suspect's (State of Washington v. Eric Hayden (1998).

Figure 13.5 and Figure 13.6 demonstrate an example of the sophistication of digital imaging. A fingerprint was detected using NIN on a newspaper. The black ink type visually interfered with the analysis of the fingerprint. The black ink was suppressed using digital imaging, resulting in sufficient ridge detail for AFIS entry.

Other Development Methods

- **Liquid Iodine#**: Iodine/benzoflavone can be used as fine spray reagent at the crime scene on both porous and nonporous surfaces. Latent prints appear as dark blue impressions.
- **Vacuum CA***: Vacuum chambers develop fingerprints more evenly because the glue fumes distribute throughout the chamber. After fuming, luminescent stains are recommended. This technique is best for firearms. Plastic baggies are also processed in this way.
- **Special Fluorescent Powders Requiring UV or FLS/ALS***: Fluorescent powders work well on dark or multicolored nonporous surfaces.
  - *Fluorescent dyes requiring FLS/ALS**: Rhodamine 6G, basic yellow 40, basic red 28, RAM, 4-(dicyanomethylene) DCM, NBD-chloride, Rose Bengal, Radiant Orange and Styryl 7. Many other luminescent dyes have been used experimentally as cyanoacrylate stains.

FIGURE 13.6 Original fingerprint on newspaper.

- **1, 8 Diazafluorenone (DFO)***: This is a fluorescing NIN analog that can develop more fingerprints than NIN itself. This chemical is an excellent choice when reviewing porous evidence such as paper in cold cases.
- **Physical Developer (PD)***: This chemical is a silver-based developer that is excellent for processing items exposed to water. In the review of cold case homicide evidence, PD is another good choice for evidence previously exposed to iodine and ninhydrin.

Blood Reagents*

- **Amido Black**: A dye that stains proteins present in blood but will not detect normal residue of latent prints. Amido black can be used on porous and nonporous surfaces. It is useful on older bloody fingerprints that have been dry for some time. Amido black is not to be used on heavily bloodstained items. DNA analysis is possible even after application of amido black on both porous and nonporous surfaces.
- **Coomassie Blue**: This is a dye that binds to protein in bloody fingerprints. The darker blue color is proportionate to the amount of protein found in the blood residue.
- **Crowle's Double Stain**: This reagent is sensitive to blood but is least effective for DNA recovery from porous items.
- **MultiMetal Deposition (MMD)***: (physical developer modified with colloidal gold) This reagent can be used on many types of wet or dry porous and nonporous surfaces. Even fingerprints on older evidence items have been recovered with this technique, but

on porous items such as paper, conventional NIN and DFO are preferred, as is CA for nonporous surfaces.

- **Vacuum Metal Deposition (VMD)***: (At times can reveal fingerprints when other techniques have not.) This process deposits thin layers of gold and zinc through a process known as vacuum-coating technology to reveal prints either as positive or negative images. VMD has had success in developing prints on evidence that is several years old where other techniques failed to reveal any prints whatsoever.
- **Osmium Tetroxide (OsO₄)#**: This reagent is similar to iodine in that it reacts with the oils and fatty substances in latent prints. Unlike iodine fuming, the coloration of the print is permanent when using OsO_4. It has many disadvantages as a practical latent print development technique: it is expensive, it has explosive qualities, and the vapors are highly poisonous.
- **Autoradiography#**: This was an experimental technique. Latent print residues treated with radioactive aqueous solutions were placed in direct contact with photographic film or ordinary x-ray plates. This technique might have been used in highly specialized laboratories.
- **X-ray#**: Latent prints were dusted with lead powder then x-rayed. This technique could have been used on currency and bank checks or porous surfaces that have multicolored designed background that made it difficult to see prints developed with conventional techniques.

CONCLUSION

In this chapter, the investigator working cold cases has been given some background information on the history of fingerprints, the biology of friction ridge skin, and the myriad techniques that can be applied to develop fingerprints on various surfaces. Investigators should realize that fingerprint techniques are constantly changing and improving. New chemical formulations and instrumentation is being researched. Whatever the method or technique used to develop latent residues left behind by fingers or palms in the past, cases can be reexamined with improved fingerprint applications such as vacuum metal deposition or physical developer.

When to use one method over another or in what sequence depends on the surface involved and on the environment to which the surface was exposed. Each method or technique is capable of producing results, but there may be one technique that is more suited than the others for a given surface and environmental conditions.

REFERENCES

Alfonso, L., and Fuchs, Elaine, Stem cells of the skin epithelium, 2003, PNAS, vol. 100, supp. 1. [Online] http://WWW.pnas.org/cgi/content/full/100/suppl_1/11830.

Ashbaugh, David R., Palmar flexion crease identification, *Journal of Forensic Identification, JFI*, 41 (4), 1991 pp. 255272.

Ashbaugh, David R., *Quantitative-Qualitative Friction Ridge Analysis: An Introduction to Basic and Advanced Ridgeology*, 1999, Boca Raton, CRC Press.

Baxes, Gregory A., *Digital Image Processing: Principles and Applications*, 1994, New York, John Wiley & Sons, Inc.

Bridges, B. C., *Practical Fingerprinting*, 1942, Funk & Wagnalls Company.

Champod, Christophe, Lennard, C.J., and Milutin, P.M.M. *Fingerprints and Other Ridge Skin Impressions*, 2004, Boca Raton, CRC Press.

Cowger, James F., *Friction Ridge Skin: Comparison and Identification of Fingerprints*, 1983, New York, Elsevier Science.

Everse, K.E. and Menzel, E.R., Blood Print Detection by Fluorescence, Center for Forensic Studies, Texas Tech University, National Science Foundation, Grant CHE 83 13527.

Faulds, Henry, On the skinfurrows of the hand, *1880, Nature,* [reprinted] 1999, Minutia p. 89.

Fregeau, C.J., Germain, O., Fourney, R.M., Fingerprint enhancement revisited and the effects of blood enhancement chemicals on subsequent profiler plus fluorescent short tandem repeat DNA analysis of fresh and aged bloody fingerprints. *Journal of Forensic Science,* 2000 Mar: 45(2):354–80.

Lee, Henry C. and Gaensslen, R.E., *Advances in Fingerprint Technology,* 1st ed.1991, New York, Elsevier, p.21.

Lee, Henry C. and Gaensslen, R.E., *Advances in Fingerprint Technology,* 2nd ed., 2001, Boca Raton, CRC Press.

May, Dr. Julia, 2002. Hand across the water: Hand imagery in the Aboriginal Australian and Puebloan artistic traditions. Lecture presented at University of Virginia. *The Kluge Ruhe Aboriginal Art Circular,* vol. 5, no. 1.

Media Cybernetics Reference Manual, Image Pro Plus, 1993, Media Cybernetics, Inc.

Moenssens, Andre A., *Fingerprint Techniques,* 1971, Chilton, 174193.

Margot, P. and Lennard, C., *Fingerprint Detection Techniques,* 1994, Université de Lausanne.

Olsen, Robert. Sr., *Scott's Fingerprint Mechanics,* 1978, Charles C. Thomas.

http:/encyclopedia.thefreedictionary.com/juan+vuceich

http://www.reason.com/rb/rb022002.shtml

FBI Laboratory, Processing Guide for Developing Latent Prints, 2001,U.S. Department of Justice, Federal Bureau of Investigations, Washington, D.C.

Russ, John C., *The Image Processing Handbook, 2nd ed.,* 1995, Boca Raton, CRC Press, Inc.

Anonymous (1995). Latent prints identifying suspects within hours. *The Print,* (Nov/Dec. pg. 11, 6).

Scene of Crime Handbook of Fingerprint Development Techniques, abridged from Manual of Fingerprint Development Techniques, Home Office, Scientific Research and Development Branch, 1988, London, U.K.

Tillett, L. Scott, FBI fingerprints go digital, Federal Computer Week, http:// www.fcw.com. Accessed August, 1999.

Wertheim, Pat, Inked major case prints, *Journal of Forensic Identification,* 49 (5) 1999, 468.

14 Automated Fingerprint Identification Systems

Peter D. Komarinski

CONTENTS

INTRODUCTION

Unsolved cases may not have been solved for several reasons. The evidence collected at the crime scene did not point to a suspect, the crime outstripped the resources of the investigating agency, an avalanche of new cases prevented further development of leads on this case, or perhaps the physical evidence itself was not sufficiently complete to be of much use in making identification. As a result, the case went cold.

In addition to a review of the details of a cold case, there is a review of the physical evidence collected at the crime scene. Is that evidence still available? Is it still usable? Does it remain "of value?" In touching the crime scene did the perpetrator leave a finger image that was captured by the evidence technicians? Is that latent finger image still available? This section addresses that latent print left at the crime scene by the perpetrator and the information that can be retrieved from it today, information that might not have been retrieved during the original investigation. The significant difference between then and now is the proliferation of and generational improvement of Automated Fingerprint Identification Systems, i.e., AFIS systems.

BASIC LATENT PRINT IDENTIFICATION PRACTICES

In the past, the primary method of making a latent print identification relied on the ability of a latent print examiner to physically compare a relatively short list of fingerprint cards (referred to as Tenprint cards since they contain all 10 finger images as well as the plain impressions at the bottom of the card) against the latent print found at a crime scene (see Figure 14.1).

This might involve a review of a few dozen cards of known felons. If there was no match, no identification was made. Another method of making identifications rested on the use of elimination prints, in which the finger images of the persons who had legitimate access to the crime scene (e.g., homeowner at a burglary) were compared against the latent print. This was a relatively simple

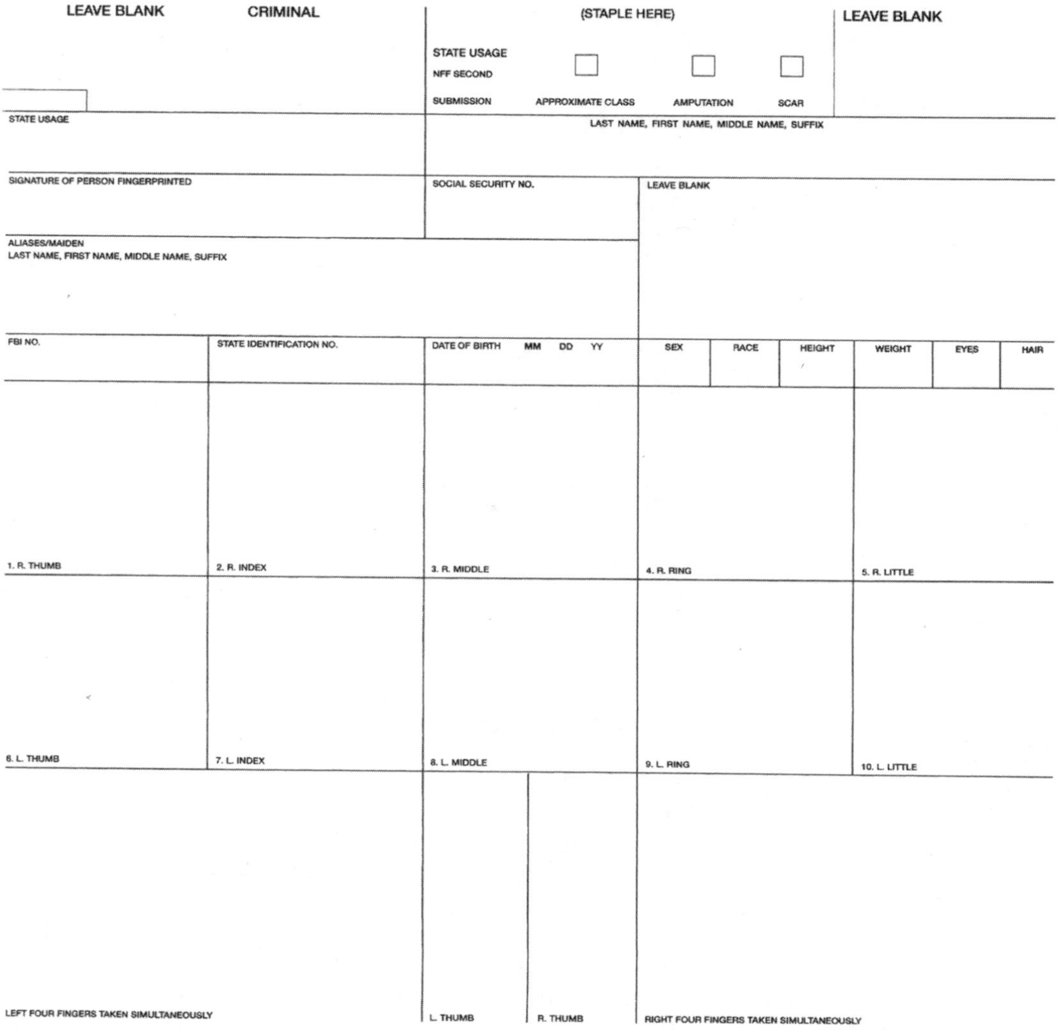

LEAVE BLANK	CRIMINAL		(STAPLE HERE)			LEAVE BLANK

STATE USAGE
NFF SECOND
SUBMISSION   APPROXIMATE CLASS   AMPUTATION   SCAR

STATE USAGE

LAST NAME, FIRST NAME, MIDDLE NAME, SUFFIX

SIGNATURE OF PERSON FINGERPRINTED   SOCIAL SECURITY NO.   LEAVE BLANK

ALIASES/MAIDEN
LAST NAME, FIRST NAME, MIDDLE NAME, SUFFIX

FBI NO.	STATE IDENTIFICATION NO.	DATE OF BIRTH MM DD YY	SEX	RACE	HEIGHT	WEIGHT	EYES	HAIR

1. R. THUMB	2. R. INDEX	3. R. MIDDLE	4. R. RING	5. R. LITTLE

6. L. THUMB	7. L. INDEX	8. L. MIDDLE	9. L. RING	10. L. LITTLE

LEFT FOUR FINGERS TAKEN SIMULTANEOUSLY	L. THUMB	R. THUMB	RIGHT FOUR FINGERS TAKEN SIMULTANEOUSLY

FIGURE 14.1 Tenprint card. (Author's File)

process because the victim could be printed and the prints compared with the latent print. The third method was to compare suspect prints with the latent print found at the crime scene. A suspect would be fingerprinted and the images on the Tenprint card compared with the latent print image(s). Generally speaking, if they matched, there would be an arrest, case closed. All of this depends on the expertise and experience of the latent print examiner and the resources available.

This basic system worked, and continues to work, in many agencies. However, the process contains many assumptions and limitations. The first assumption is that the latent print found at the crime scene is "of value," that it contains sufficient ridge detail and image characteristics to effect a positive identification. Second, it assumes that the perpetrator has previously been fingerprinted and that the Tenprint record is in the identification area for comparison. Third, it assumes that the latent print examiner has sufficient time and expertise to review each finger image in the record file to make a reasonable comparison against the latent print from the crime scene. This is a manual system of latent print comparison. There is no automation required, and the most advanced piece of equipment is the examiner's reticle (see Figure 14.2). It is also a very limited application

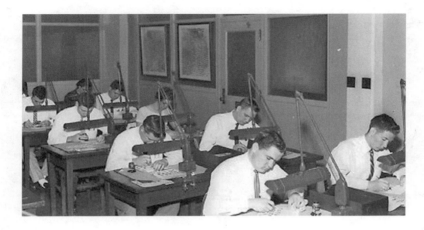

FIGURE 14.2 Examiners still use the reticle as they did in the past. Note the reticle on the desk in the left foreground in this historical photo of FBI examiners. (Courtesy of FBI.)

because it compares the latent print only against the images immediately available in the Tenprint card file.

Many agencies have moved forward in their identification processes and now use some form of AFIS. Computer technology, advanced software, unparalleled reliability, and immense databases have combined to bring to the latent print examiner the ability to make identifications that were not possible before. The latent print examiner may now be able to bring to the investigator the identity of the person whose latent prints were found at the crime scene. This new information might close the case.

FINGERPRINT IDENTIFICATION SYSTEMS

Every agency has a records section for storing information. These records include case files, fingerprint (i.e., Tenprint) cards and perhaps criminal histories. Many larger agencies and most states have a fingerprint identification system that has been operational for years. These agencies are the repositories for both the physical Tenprint card as well as the criminal history associated with that record. Because there are so many variants of identification agencies, this discussion describes the operation through a single state agency that serves as the repository for all the criminal justice agencies within the state.

When a person was arrested and fingerprinted, the fingerprint card was sent to the identification agency to determine whether the person had a criminal record or any outstanding warrants or wants. The textual information along with the characteristics of the 10 finger images was searched against the existing list of records. If there was a match, the rap sheet containing the criminal history was sent to the inquiring agency. If there was no match, a record was created with a unique number (commonly referred to as a State Identification Number or SID) and the information was returned to the inquiring agency.

Because identification agencies have been in operation for over 100 years, there have been many changes in the process and procedures. Prior to the age of electronics, this was an almost entirely manual process that required the arresting officer to ink the 10 fingers and roll them onto the Tenprint card. Descriptive information was written into the boxes of the card and the card mailed to the state identification agency. Once there, the Tenprint card would be given to an examiner who would classify each of the finger images and assign pattern type and classification based on prescribed rules, usually the Henry classification system. The card would then be taken through a

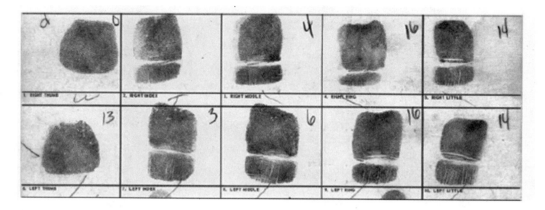

FIGURE 14.3 Prior to the age of electronics, the 10 fingers would be inked and rolled onto the Tenprint card.

lengthy process to visually compare the images against Tenprint records that had the same pattern classification (see Figure 14.3). The results of this search were mailed back to the inquiring agency.

This manual process, which required several days, if not weeks, from booking to response, remained relatively unchanged until the 1970s, when computers were introduced. Computers provided a better, faster, and less expensive method of retaining and retrieving textual information. Coupled with improvements in communications such as telephone systems and fax machines, the process for identifying an individual and providing a rap sheet improved both in quality and timeliness. While these improvements were under way, there was also an increase in the number of records being processed as the identifying agencies grew and provided background checks and rapsheets for increasingly greater numbers of people.

On the heels of the improvements to the Tenprint or identification process, a secondary benefit to the investigator was the availability of more prints to search against. As part of a booking process, the arrestee was typically fingerprinted three times: One card was usually sent to the FBI, the state identification agency, and the local sheriff's office or police agency records section. This local record would be used by the latent print examiner at the police department to immediately compare against a latent print found at a crime scene.

This process of identification continued into the 1980s when government leaders realized that the time spent to process the increasing volume of Tenprint cards was no longer acceptable. Individuals were being released without the benefit of a background check because it took too long. As state agencies began to get bogged down, so did the FBI. The thousands of file cabinets housing millions of fingerprint cards continued to grow.

The solution to the problem was to automate the identification process. Wherever and whenever possible, manual steps in the process were to be replaced with automated electronic transactions. The federal government made millions of dollars available to states and units of local governments in a program called the National Criminal History Improvement Project, or NCHIP. The goal of these efforts was to automate the fingerprint identification process, to make an AFIS.

AFIS SYSTEMS

AFIS systems have provided an increasingly important tool for investigators. The number of Tenprint identifications made with the assistance of AFIS technology is in the tens of millions. The number of latent print identifications is in the tens of thousands. The majority of identifications made with finger images are made with AFIS systems.

The AFIS system is commonly linked to a Computerized Criminal History or CCH, which stores information about the subject's history such as previous arrests or fingerprintable events such as a job application. The subject's CCH file information is increased with each new event. In its simplest form, an AFIS system has three elements:

1. Identification parameters — e.g., SID, and other data linking the record to an individual.
2. Image data
3. Minutiae that contain the friction ridge detail and image characteristics

A key element that distinguishes AFIS systems from previous identification systems is the ability to capture, store, and search on finger images. While the automation of textual information has been around for many years, it is only within the past 20 years that the finger image and characteristics have been converted into an electronic format useful for searching. The AFIS technology that was in use at the time of the crime may have been upgraded, with more accuracy and a larger database of fingerprint records.

AFIS systems incorporate many components that are common in every system, regardless of vendor. Among these are coders, matchers, and storage databases. *Coders* are an element of the image capture process during which the finger image is digitized (think of it as digitally photographed). As part of this process the coders examine the unique image characteristics such as a friction ridge ending, a split or bifurcation, island as well as the direction of the ridge flow, and the finger pattern. These unique points are referred to as *minutiae*. It is these minutiae that are used in AFIS searches by another device called a *matcher*.

As its name implies, the matcher compares the minutiae from a recent submission against minutiae records in its database to determine if any record in the database matches. If a Tenprint match occurs, there is a high degree of probability, now usually in excess of 99%. This degree of accuracy is due to several factors, including the use of two or more finger images to effect the search.

LATENT PRINT APPLICATIONS OF AFIS

With so many Tenprint records on the AFIS database, it becomes apparent that there are many opportunities to exploit the powers of AFIS systems to make latent print identifications. The examiners are no longer limited by the physical space required to house the Tenprint cards of known felons. The database with these records can be tens, hundreds, even thousands of miles away from the AFIS terminal and examiner. More importantly, these examiners can use the power of AFIS technology to search an entire database, millions of records, tens of millions of images, in just a few minutes.

Popular television shows that refer to the use of AFIS systems frequently, and mistakenly, state that the system made a "hit," i.e., the s*ystem* made the latent print identification. AFIS merely produced a *list of candidates* in order of probability. The latent print examiner, with years of training and experience, made the identification. AFIS narrowed the list of candidates from several million to one, two, or none.

This example might help explain the AFIS concept. Think of all the Tenprint cards stored in the cabinets in Figure 14.4 Multiply that number by 10 because there are 10 fingers per card. (Actually, there are usually 20 finger images, as each finger is captured individually, then repeated in groups on the bottom of the card.)

If an examiner were to compare the latent print in question with every image on every card in every file cabinet, the process could take years. By searching the minutiae of these records, AFIS can complete the search in minutes and present a list of only the most likely candidates to the latent print examiner.

FIGURE 14.4 Cabinets full of Tenprint cards.

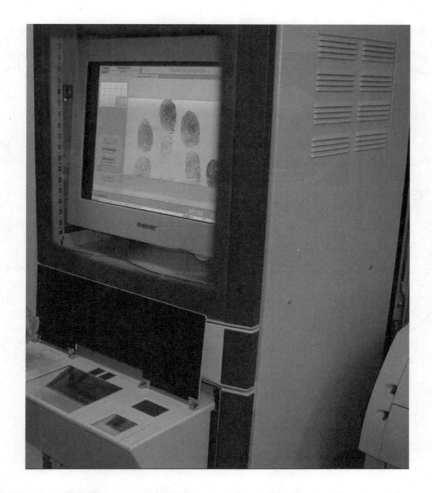

FIGURE 14.5 A Livescan device electronically captures finger images at a defined resolution.

While it is convenient to think of AFIS processing as a completely automated process, it begins and ends with *people*. At the initial enrollment where the Tenprint record is created, a person either rolled inked fingers onto a Tenprint card, or rolled the fingers onto a glass platen of a Livescan device (see Figure 14.5). A Livescan device electronically captures finger images at a defined resolution, similar to a very high-end scanner. The data fields either on the paper or electronic Tenprint records are completed by a person.

People are responsible for the care and maintenance of the AFIS system, and in the case of latent print identification practices, a person makes the final determination as to whether the latent print in question matches the image on the AFIS database. The latent print examiner, in addition to the skills required to make a comparison and identification or non-identification decision, also has to know how to operate the AFIS system; how to launch a search, review candidate lists and exercise the AFIS system to produce the most likely candidate. Unlike the Tenprint examiner who has 10 usually clear images to search with (actually 20 if the 10 plain or flat impressions are included), the latent print examiner has only the latent print found at a crime scene. The rolled Tenprint finger images may contain up to 150 unique minutiae points for the Tenprint examiner to work with. The latent print examiner may have fewer than 10. Even with these constraints, both examiners are able to do their jobs with remarkable accuracy.

AFIS Search Options

Many AFIS systems provide the latent print examiner with three opportunities for searching. These searches are:

1. The Latent to Tenprint (LT/TP) in which the latent print is searched against all 10 finger images within a defined database. If there is no identification, the latent print image can be saved in the Unsolved Latent file for subsequent searching.
2. The Tenprint to Unsolved Latent (TP/UL) in which the minutiae from new Tenprint records are automatically matched against those latent prints that were not previously identified.
3. Unsolved Latent to Unsolved Latent (LT/LT) in which no identification has been made, but the unsolved database is searched to determine if prints from the same person have been found at another crime scene. This information can help detectives from different departments share information because they are looking for the same suspect.

In addition to these three types of searches, other databases can be searched. If the search of the local AFIS database does not result in a match, the state or FBI database can be searched. This can be somewhat time consuming, but worth the investment of resources.

Given this background of how the latent print components of AFIS systems work, coupled with the myriad of choices for making a latent print search on the system and the various types of searches that can be made, as well as the hierarchy of searches, cold case investigators can see the relevance and value of AFIS in cold cases that contain latent prints. With this understanding of how AFIS systems work, the investigator is better equipped to use the power of AFIS to make an identification and perhaps close a case.

Further AFIS Application to Cold Cases

In reviewing the evidence, the investigator might inquire as to whether the latent print was searched on an AFIS system. If so, what system, when, by whom, and what is the current status i.e., is it in the unsolved latent (UL) print file?

The investigator might further ask if the print was searched on any other AFIS system, such as the FBI's IAFIS. If so, the same questions apply. If not, why not?

If the latent print has been searched in the past, search it again. And again. And again. As with any system that involves people and technology, there are always improvements. People get better at their jobs; systems get better with newer software and hardware. AFIS systems do not remain static. They get better, faster, bigger, and more accurate. Perhaps the reason no identification was made on the first search was because of the limitations of the earlier AFIS systems. The new systems have better coders that can extract minutiae more accurately and completely than before. A blurred minutiae point on the latent print image that could not be identified a few years ago by the coder might be more apparent with newer technology. This crucial bit of data may lead to identification. Further, people become better at what they do. The skill set of the latent print examiner who originally searched the latent print on AFIS may have improved along with a better understanding of how to get the most out of the system.

In addition to better coders, the matching algorithms have improved. Latent print examiners are presented with fewer, but better candidates on their searches than in the past. Ask any latent print examiners who have searched latent prints on a new or upgraded system and they will tell you that the results are impressive. It is not unusual to make an identification on a record that was present at the time of the original search, but failed to hit. Better coders, better matchers and a recoded and expanded database all contribute to making more identifications.

Cold case investigators should be aware that a search of the current database may produce an identification for a record that was *not* present at the time of the original search. Conversely, there may now be multiple image records of the same person. This might provide additional opportunities for identification that were not available at the time of the original search.

In addition to the processes within the AFIS environment, there are *imaging tools* that can aid the latent print examiner in teasing out the best latent print image possible. These tools do not enhance the latent print, but rather may change the background so that the image and image characteristics are clearer. Think of two latent prints that overlie each other. Imaging technology can hide either of the two images without enhancing or adding to either image. A latent print on a red background can be more apparent when the red is masked. The same applies to a latent on a patterned background.

While the earlier AFIS systems were limited to a single database, many vendors now offer access to the FBI's IAFIS 48 million record criminal database as a feature of their newer systems. The latent print images, after completing a search of the local and state AFIS databases, can be searched again without the need to recapture or redigitize the latent print. This saves time and resources.

Unfortunately, not every latent print has been searched through an AFIS system. Many latent prints remain in in files and are never searched on AFIS. The reasons for this are many, but may include a lack of understanding of AFIS or the skills required to be an AFIS operator or latent print examiner. There is always someone available at a local, state, or federal level who will assist, however. Another problem has been that many latent prints do not continue to be searched until all reasonable options are tried. In some cases, if no identification is made based upon the local database, no further searches are conducted.

AN EXAMPLE OF AFIS AND COLD CASES

An example of the improvements to AFIS and the resultant increase in the number of latent print identifications may help. The New York State Division of Criminal Justice Services is the state repository for all fingerprints cards in New York. Whether the arrest took place in Manhattan or Manhasset, Buffalo or Binghamton, there is a record at DCJS.

DCJS began its AFIS program in the mid 1980s. By the late 1990s the system was due for a major upgrade. Under the direction of Deputy Commissioners Clyde DeWeese and Daniel Foro, DCJS, along with it vendor Sagem Morpho, embarked on a massive plan to replace the entire system. Virtually every piece of hardware and software would be replaced. Staff would have to be trained on the new system. All components would have to be tested individually, and then assembled as a system before replacing the existing AFIS system. The change, or "cutover," from the old to the new system would have to be seamless and completed within a matter of hours.

Elements of the improved system included new coders, matchers, and storage devices. Records in the Unsolved Latent file would have to be transferred to the new system, and the entire 5,000,000-record database recoded. After months of testing, planning, and analyses, the new system was installed. The benefits in speed, accuracy, and throughput were noticed immediately.

With a database that was recoded using the latest coding algorithms to identify minutiae and ridge characteristics, more true minutiae were identified. Better matchers resulted in a more accurate list of candidates. The imagestorage devices such as the Random Array of Independent Drives (RAIDS) could produce the images on demand.

With the assistance of AFIS managers such as Jack Meagher and Dick Higgins of DCJS and Sgt. Ken Calvey, Commanding Officer of the NYPD Latent Print Unit, I assembled a list of all cases in the Unsolved Latent file, sorted by examiner and crime type. This list, built with the assistance of Sagem staff such as Jim Ware, contained cases that were searched before the system upgrade. The lists were distributed to every latent print examiner who had a case on the UL file and each examiner was individually instructed on the purpose and suggested approaches to using the list. The cases on the list would be searched at intervals after the new latent prints had been searched.

The results were immediate. As they began to re-search their old cases, examiners found they were making hits on candidates that were not identified in the past. In addition, the number of identifications on new cases was also improving. Due to the improvements in the system, the number of identifications doubled. Further discussion of this can be found in my new book *Automated Fingerprint Identification Systems* by Peter Komarinski.

Does AFIS work on cold cases? Absolutely.

CONCLUSION

If the Cold Case contains a latent fingerprint, it must be searched on AFIS systems. Failure in the past to make an identification on this piece of evidence has little bearing on the likelihood for making an identification today. Better technology, better tools, and better-trained staff can all contribute to making the identification that can lead to an arrest, conviction and closure. Keep searching.

ACKNOWLEDGMENT

Richard H. Walton wishes to acknowledge and extend his gratitude to Peter Komarinski for his contribution of this chapter. Mr. Komarinski is the principal consultant of Komarinski & Associates, LLC, a biometric consulting firm in Rotterdam, New York. Chair of the AFIS Committee of the International Association for Identification (IAI), Mr. Komarinski holds a Master's Degree in Criminal Justice from State University of New York. He began his service in criminal justice over 30 years ago and has served in a variety of positions including the McKay Commission, which investigated the Attica prison uprising.

Mr. Komarinski has served as a research analyst with a medium-size law enforcement agency as well as a criminal justice program analyst and research analyst for a state correctional oversight agency and research specialist for the state criminal justice planning agency. Mr. Komarinski retired from the New York State Division of Criminal Justice Services as manager of the Statewide Automated Fingerprint Identification System (SAFIS). He has written extensively and is the author of *Automated Fingerprint Identification Systems (AFIS)* published in January, 2005, by Elsevier/Academic Press.

15 From Serology to DNA in Cold Case Investigations

Michael J. Grubb

CONTENTS

INTRODUCTION

DNA is arguably the most valuable tool of the cold case investigator. Thousands of criminal cases have been solved across the country through the use of this powerful tool. It is the basis for genetic variation in all living things, responsible for passing on genetic traits from generation to generation. Nearly all the cells in the human body have a nucleus, each of which is packed with the full complement of chromosomes inherited from the individual's parents. The chromosomes are composed of DNA and protein. Different sequential combinations of four basic building blocks of DNA (the nucleotide bases guanine, adenine, thymine, and cytosine) result in the remarkable variation we see in humans, other animals, and plants. The variation is so great that each person's DNA is unique, with the exception of identical twins.

DEVELOPMENTS IN DNA SCIENCE AS USED IN FORENSIC SCIENCE

DNA was first applied as an investigative tool in crime investigation in the U.S. in about 1986 (see Figure 15.1). Two different types of DNA analysis were available then, and which method was

FIGURE 15.1 DNA Laboratory. Criminalist prepares evidence samples for DNA analysis. (Courtesy of Mike Grubb)

applied to evidence depended on the sample size and the capabilities of the laboratory. Restriction fragment length polymorphism (RFLP) was a tremendously time-intensive method, and a full profile took as long as 2 months to develop. A bloodstain of approximately one-quarter inch in diameter was necessary to obtain a profile. In sex crimes cases, thousands of sperm cells were necessary in the sample being tested in order to obtain an RFLP profile. Cases with relatively few sperm recovered did not yield a result. Even with these limitations, some states began developing statewide felon DNA databases using RFLP, and dozens of cases were solved in this way. The advantage of RFLP was that it was very discriminating, typically giving DNA profile frequencies in the "one in several million" to "one in several billion" range.

At the same time, polymerase chain reaction (PCR) DNA typing became available (see Figure 15.2). The PCR method had an important advantage over RFLP. An amplification process was used to replicate certain parts of the DNA present, so that very small samples could be used to develop significant genetic information. However, when the PCR method was first applied, it was limited in its discriminating power as it encompassed a single genetic locus, which was able to divide the population into approximately 20 subgroups. That locus was referred to as DQA1. It was very useful for those cases where sample was limited or somewhat degraded. In about 1994, the value of PCR DNA typing was increased with the addition of "Polymarker," five additional DNA loci that increased the discriminating power of PCR-based DNA typing. With DQA1 and Polymarker, crime laboratories still had the advantage of being able to analyze very small samples, but now had a typing result that would yield a DNA profile frequency of "one in several thousand." This was extremely useful in casework with possible suspects, but the population frequency information with DQA1/Polymarker was not sufficiently discriminating to make it useful for large-scale databasing.

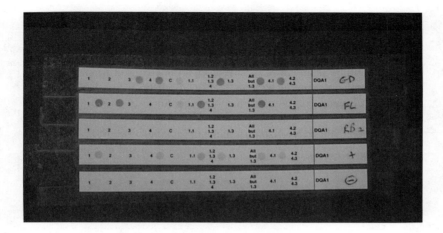

FIGURE 15.2 DQ Alpha PCR DNA Analysis. Between 1986 and 2000, the "dot blot" method pictured here was used for analysis of DNA. "DQ Alpha" and "Polymarker" PCR-based DNA analysis was performed using this technique. (Courtesy of Mike Grubb)

In the late 1990s, the technology to analyze short tandem repeat (STR) DNA using PCR technology became available. Spaced along the strands of DNA that are coiled in the nucleus of the cell are sections that code for certain biological traits or functions; these areas are known as genes. There is also a considerable amount of DNA between the genes that doesn't have a known purpose (it doesn't code for any biological trait). It has been shown that much of this DNA between the genes has a repeating pattern of nucleotide bases. The number of repeats in a given stretch of DNA is an inherited trait, varies widely from person to person, and is the basis for STR DNA profiling. STR DNA testing gives the criminalist the ability to analyze up to 16 regions of DNA, resulting in statistical power even greater than was possible with RFLP. The advent of STRs gave the crime labs the ultimate tool — a PCR-based system (so very small samples can be analyzed), with the power of individualization necessary for nationwide databasing of DNA profiles of convicted felons and casework samples. Using STRs, a typical laboratory report will provide frequency calculations in the trillions or quadrillions (a report might state, for example, "this DNA profile occurs in one person in every eight quadrillion" — this number represents approximately a million times the population of the planet). Because of the rarity of a given DNA profile, when a match is established between a casework sample and a person, many experts believe it is now possible to state the sample (bloodstain, semen stain, etc.) originated from that person, barring the existence of an identical twin (see Figure 15.3).

The states in the late 1980s and 1990s with RFLP-based databases converted those databases to STRs by reanalyzing the samples. STRs is now the standard DNA analysis method accepted nationwide. An agreed-upon set of 13 DNA loci (loci is the plural of locus, meaning the position on a given chromosome) are uniformly tested and constitute the basis for state and national databases. The databases are part of a system called CODIS, which allows DNA profiles of convicted offenders and evidence samples from unsolved crimes to be entered into a computer and compared electronically.

CODIS — THE COMBINED DNA INDEX SYSTEM

CODIS has three levels, local (LDIS), state (SDIS) and national (NDIS). At the local level, a crime laboratory will input DNA profiles obtained from evidence items. Only crime laboratories accredited by the American Society of Crime Laboratory Directors/Laboratory Accreditation Board (ASCLD/LAB) or the National Forensic Science Technology Center (NFSTC) may input data into

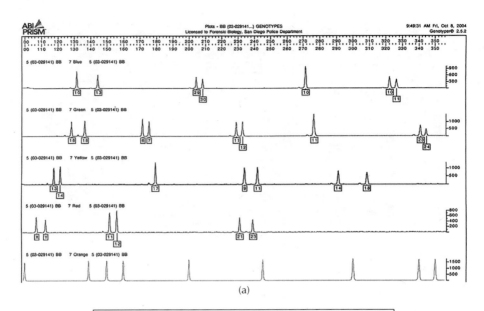

(a)

Identifiler™ analysis of crime scene sample	
Locus	Profile uploaded to CODIS database
D8S1179	10, 13
D21S11	29, 30
D7S820	10
CSF1PO	10, 11
D3S1358	16, 18
THO1	6, 7
D13S317	11, 12
D16S539	11
D2S1338	23, 24
D19S433	13, 14
vWA	17
TPOX	9, 11
D18S51	14, 18
Amelogenin	X, Y
D5S818	11, 12
FGA	21, 23

(b)

FIGURE 15.3 STR DNA Profile. The Short Tandem Repeat (STR) analysis of a sample using capillary electrophoresis results in a series of peaks on a printout, indicating the presence of certain DNA alleles (a). This information is translated into a numerical sequence (b) that is then uploaded as a DNA profile into CODIS. The CODIS software then searches the database for the same numerical sequence, indicating a match. (Courtesy of Mike Grubb)

CODIS. For each state, the felon DNA database resides at a single laboratory. That laboratory will also receive uploaded unsolved-case DNA profiles from local crime laboratories, which will be searched against all felons who have been profiled and entered into the CODIS system. The profile will also be searched against all other unsolved-case-evidence DNA profiles (forensic unknowns) in the state CODIS system. Three things may result: (1) the evidence DNA profile may match a convicted offender in the state's database; (2) the evidence profile may match against another evidence profile, thereby linking two cases together; or (3) no matching profiles will be found.

The state uploads its convicted felon and forensic unknowns to NDIS periodically so that the searches are expanded to the national level. Many "hits" have been obtained between an evidence sample (forensic unknown) from one state matching a convicted offender in another state's database. To date (2004), there are over 1.7 million DNA profiles of offenders in the NDIS system, and over 79,000 forensic unknowns from casework samples. Over 20,000 cases have been solved or aided nationwide with the assistance of the CODIS/NDIS systems.

Even though a forensic unknown may not hit against a known felon the first time it is searched, it remains in the system, so that if the assailant in the case is entered into the CODIS database at a later time, that felon's sample will "hit" against the forensic unknown entered previously.

There is a general movement nationwide to increase the scope of the felon DNA databases. The classes of felonies that qualify for inclusion in the database vary from state to state. A few states include only DNA profiles of convicted sex crime felons and violent felons. Most states are moving toward inclusion of all felons, and some include felony arrestees. The widening scope of felon DNA database statutes is driven by results from states that include burglars and drug offenders in CODIS. They are obtaining a remarkably high number of hits against sex crime evidence profiles.

Within the "local database" consisting of evidence profiles developed in their casework, many crime laboratories include legally obtained DNA profiles of suspects. It is possible, then, that a laboratory could determine the perpetrator of a crime by use of this local database, even though the suspect has not been convicted of a felony. Suspect profiles, however, cannot be uploaded into SDIS or NDIS. Suspect searches are restricted to the local level.

CODIS has value beyond matching a convicted felon with an evidence DNA profile. The sample may match with another evidence sample, or "forensic unknown," previously loaded into the system. Thus, it is common to establish sex crime series based on DNA profiles, even though the M.O. may not have led the investigators to suspect the same perpetrator. This also alerts investigators from multiple jurisdictions that they are looking for the same individual, and they can compare investigative leads. Linking multiple sex offenses can have the potential of building a case against a suspect that cannot be built on any single case in the series. With the solution of any one of the cases in the series, the entire series of cases can be solved.

CODIS also has a missing persons index containing both STR (when possible) and mitochondrial DNA types from unidentified human remains. In an attempt to identify the remains, these DNA profiles can be compared against relatives of missing persons.

Mitochondrial DNA

In some samples, such as bone, hair, teeth, or samples that have suffered environmental insult, sufficient nuclear DNA may not be available. Mitochondrial DNA (mtDNA) can be analyzed in these samples. The mitochondria of cells are structures found in the cytoplasm of the cells as opposed to in the nucleus. The mitochondria produce most of the energy needed by the cell to function. Many cells have only a single nucleus but contain a multitude of mitochondria, making mitochondrial DNA analysis more sensitive than STR typing. Mitochondrial DNA types are different from and are not as discriminating as STR DNA profiling results, and cannot provide the rare DNA profile frequencies that we see in an STR report. Mitochondrial DNA results are reported in terms of frequencies typically on the order of one in several hundred. A mitochondrial DNA type is searched against the mtDNA database maintained by the FBI, to determine the observed frequency of that type. Mitochondrial DNA types are passed on to an offspring through the egg and not the sperm, so a person's mitochondrial DNA type will be the same as his or her mother's type.

Most public crime laboratories are currently using either the FBI laboratory or private consulting laboratories for mitochondrial DNA work. Mitochondrial DNA typing is used less frequently than STR profiling, is technically challenging, and is a relatively expensive process. To date it has been more cost-effective for public crime laboratories to send this work out than to try to complete it themselves.

Y CHROMOSOME STR ANALYSIS

Within the complement of 23 pairs of chromosomes in each nucleated cell, females possess two "X" chromosomes, and males possess an "X" and a "Y" chromosome. Laboratories are just starting to work with Y-chromosome STRs. These are STR loci that are on the Y chromosome only, so they are specific to the male and are particularly useful when a mixture of male and female body fluids are present that cannot be sufficiently separated by differential extraction. An example would be a case of oral copulation of a female victim by a male. The male assailant's DNA is present in the cellular component of his saliva, and would be transferred to the vaginal area of the victim. However, when the sample collected is a vaginal swab, the victim's DNA will overwhelm in quantity the DNA present as a result of the male's saliva. Many laboratories cannot even detect the DNA from the saliva in such a case. However, the male assailant's epithelial cells will be specifically targeted in the Y STR procedure. There will be no contribution from the female victim, as she possesses no Y chromosome. This technique allows the DNA laboratory to specifically amplify the genetic information from the Y chromosomes that were contributed by the male assailant, even when there is an overwhelming amount of DNA present from the female victim.

SAMPLE STORAGE AND DEGRADATION

DNA in biological samples can be detected and profiled for many years on stains kept either frozen or in a dry room temperature condition. Evidence-bearing biological stains maintained at room temperature should be kept in paper packaging. If plastic packaging is used at room temperature, trapped moisture encourages the growth of bacteria and problems may be encountered in DNA profiling. Exposure of biological samples to sunlight, heat or moisture can rapidly lead to DNA degradation and the failure to obtain DNA profiles.

IMPORTANCE OF DNA TO THE COLD CASE INVESTIGATOR

The investigator will be wise to focus on the potential for the existence of probative biological evidence that can be DNA profiled. It is also wise for the investigator to make use of crime laboratory personnel to discuss any physical evidence that exists and to develop a "plan of attack" regarding its analysis. The criminalist will often have insight into potential evidence value that the investigator overlooked.

When the cold case investigator encounters a case where RFLP or DQA1/Polymarker technology was used in DNA analysis, the evidence may need to be reanalyzed using STRs. In addition, many samples that were insufficient for RFLP profiling years ago may be sufficient for STR analysis now.

It should also be realized that there has been a change in the way investigators think about biological evidence with the advent of STR DNA profiling. Samples that were never previously considered suitable are more often now being looked at as a possible source of DNA information. For example, a baseball cap can be tested for the DNA of the habitual wearer. A gearshift knob can be swabbed and a DNA profile can be obtained for a recent driver. A licked envelope, cigarette

Evidence	Possible location of DNA on the evidence	Source of DNA
Baseball bat or similar weapon	Handle, end	Sweat, skin, blood, tissue
Hat, bandanna, or mask	Inside	Sweat, hair, dandruff
Eyeglasses	Nose or ear pieces, lens	Sweat, skin
Facial tissue, cotton swab	Surface area	Mucus, blood, sweat, semen, ear wax
Dirty laundry	Surface area	Blood, sweat, semen
Toothpick	Tips	Saliva
Used cigarette	Cigarette butt	Saliva
Stamp or envelope	Licked area	Saliva
Tape or ligature	Inside/outside surface	Skin, sweat
Bottle, can, or glass	Sides, mouthpiece	Saliva, sweat
Used condom	Inside/outside surface	Semen, vaginal, or rectal cells
Blanket, pillow, sheet	Surface area	Sweat, hair, semen, urine, saliva
"Through and through" bullet	Outside surface	Blood, tissue
Bite mark	Person's skin or clothing	Saliva
Fingernail, partial fingernail	Scrapings	Blood, sweat, tissue

FIGURE 15.4 Identifying DNA Evidence. This figure indicates some of the places from which DNA might be recovered and which may be found during the course of a cold case homicide investigation. (Reprinted with permission of the National Institute of Justice).

butt, chewed piece of gum, saliva left on the rim of a drinking glass — all are very suitable sources of DNA. Evidence that may have been originally overlooked when DNA was a newer science can still be revisited if the evidence items have been properly maintained (see Figure 15.4 and Figure 15.5).

DNA can also be used to establish a familial relationship, when necessary. If the investigator is faced with a bloodstain and there is no known DNA sample for comparison from the suspected source, it is possible to use DNA samples from the parents or children of the suspected source to solve the question. If, in fact, the stain originated from a parent or child of the person being tested, then the DNA laboratory will be able to show that with a very high degree of likelihood. One half of the DNA characteristics found in a biological sample result from a maternal contribution, and the other half from a paternal contribution. It is also possible to use known DNA samples from

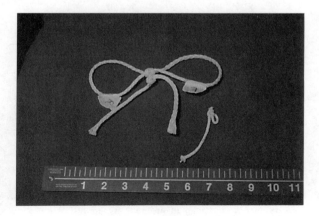

FIGURE 15.5 Ligature. Ligatures may offer a source of DNA from both suspect and victim. (Courtesy of Sgt. Bill Holmes, San Diego Police Department)

siblings of the suspected source to show a familial relationship when those are the only samples available.

CASE EXAMPLE OF THE USE OF DNA ON A COLD CASE —THE KEEVER/SELLERS HOMICIDES

Nine-year-old Jonathan Sellers and his friend, 13-year-old Charlie Keever, rode their bicycles on a path by a river in south San Diego in 1993. Their bodies were found the next day in a makeshift enclosure in some brush. Jonathan Sellers body was hanging from a branch. Charlie Keever's body was close by. The usual biological samples were collected at autopsy, including oral and anal swabs. Samples of these swabs were extracted and searched for spermatozoa soon after the crime, but no spermatozoa were found. Other evidence collected from the crime scene included cigarette butts that had been stubbed out into the ground in the vicinity of the bodies (see Figure 15.6).

In 2001, a reanalysis of the case was attempted, as the new STR DNA technology had been brought on line, and it would now be possible to check any DNA profile obtained against a database of about 80,000 (at that time) felons in the California State felon DNA database. A more effective

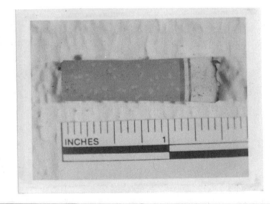

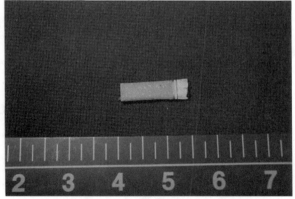

FIGURE 15.6 Cigarette butts as a source of DNA. Cigarette butts recovered at crime scenes may offer a source of suspect DNA. When found in the review of cold case homicide evidence, these should be profiled utilizing advanced DNA techniques. In 1993, at the time of this crime, older DNA technology led to a DQAlpha/Polymarker DNA type, but that was insufficient for identification of a suspect using CODIS. Reanalysis of these recovered cigarette butts and other evidence using STR DNA technology in 2001 identified a suspect profile in the brutal murders of two young boys. (Courtesy of Sgt. Bill Holmes, San Diego Police Department)

method of extraction of spermatozoa from swabs was used, resulting in the finding of spermatozoa in the oral swab from one of the boys. An STR profile was developed, and matched a sex felon serving a 70-year term for a violent rape he had committed in San Diego several months after the Keever and Sellers homicides.

DNA profiles from the cigarette butts at the scene also matched the suspect, Scott Erskine. At trial, Erskine did not deny having killed the boys, and he was convicted of two counts of first degree murder. This conviction resulted in large part from the tenacity of San Diego Police Detective Sergeant Bill Holmes, enhanced by advances in technology and the teamwork with the Crime Lab.

SEROLOGY

Prior to the use of DNA to discriminate biological samples from different individuals, the science of identification of body fluids in the crime laboratory was known as "serology." Serology Units once existed in laboratories where the DNA Units now stand. Serology now refers largely to the work done in "screening" evidence items for biological stains, and identifying those stains as blood, semen, saliva, etc. Serology Units in crime laboratories applied limited genetic marker testing of antigens, enzymes, and proteins as a means of distinguishing biological samples from different individuals. In the vast majority of crime laboratories now, serology refers to the steps prior to DNA extraction and profiling.

It is strongly recommended that the cold case investigator obtain the assistance of a criminalist when reviewing serology reports. It is difficult for an untrained investigator to discern all of the important information in these reports.

IDENTIFICATION OF BIOLOGICAL STAINS

Blood has been identified in stains via color tests for decades. Phenolphthalin, benzidine, tetramethyl benzidine (TMB), and ortho-tolidine are examples of some of these "presumptive" color tests. When a stain looks like a bloodstain and gives a positive presumptive test, the analyst may "presume" it is a bloodstain, and would normally then undertake further analysis of the stain to determine species origin, etc. Another presumptive test for blood sometimes used as a spray reagent is leuco-malachite green (LMG). LMG is used when blood is suspected to have been cleaned up from a surface, or to help develop faint bloody shoeprints on a light-colored carpet or floor. Luminol is also used as a presumptive test for blood, for example on dark surfaces or dark carpets where visualization of blood is very difficult. Luminol causes the faint bloodstains to *luminesce* in the dark when the reagent is sprayed onto the surface.

The next step would be to identify the stain as of human origin or of some other species' origin. This was accomplished by a "*preciptin*" test, reacting bloodstains against anti-human protein antiserum, as well as against *antisera* to other species. Several papers were published as early as 1901 regarding immunological differentiation of human blood from animal blood. The preciptin tests as used in crime laboratories were often performed by a "*gel diffusion*" test, where an extract of the questioned bloodstain was allowed to diffuse out into a gel medium and react with anti-human antiserum placed in an adjacent well in the gel. A white preciptin band of antigen-antibody reaction in the gel between the questioned stain and the anti-human antiserum was indicative of the presence of human proteins in the questioned sample. Another means of conducting the species test was through the use of "*crossover electrophoresis*." Rather than allowing the antigens and antibodies to diffuse together, in crossover electrophoresis they were forced into each other by means of an electrical current running through the gel. In many crime laboratories, human blood is now identified with the use of a one-step "*card*" technique that detects trace levels of human hemoglobin.

Semen is identified by the microscopic identification of the presence of spermatozoa. In the absence of spermatozoa (for example, in cases involving vasectomized men), semen can still be identified through the identification of the semen-specific protein P30 in the stain. The enzyme acid phosphatase has also been used for decades as an indicator of the presence of semen. When a stain reacts positively for the presence of acid phosphatase, and the reaction is strong and relatively rapid, the analyst has good reason to suspect the stain contains semen. The finding of acid phosphatase alone, however, in the absence of spermatozoa or P30, is not conclusive proof of the presence of semen. Semen is now commonly identified using a one-step "card" technique that detects trace amounts of the P30 protein.

Saliva is indicated by the presence of the enzyme amylase in the stain. Amylase is found in high concentrations in saliva, and at lower concentrations in other body fluids. Reports often talk about the "possible presence of saliva," or perhaps only an "elevated level of amylase" in a particular sample. These hints at the possible presence of saliva may be worth pursuing. This is represented in Figure 15.7.

GEORGE B TELLEVIK,
Chief

STATE OF WASHINGTON

WASHINGTON STATE PATROL

2nd Floor Public Safety Bldg., 610 3rd Avenue • Seattle, Washington 98104-1820 • (206) 464-7038 • (SCAN) 576-7038

CRIME LABORATORY REPORT

Agency: Seattle Police Department

Laboratory No. 193-05823

Suspect: Not Listed

Agency Case No. 93-304200

Victim: Mia Zapata

Officer: Detective Allan R. Lima

__Evidence Examined:__

Item 20: Sealed envelope containing a liquid blood sample from "Mia Zapata."

Item 21: Sealed bag containing samples recovered from the body of "Mia Zapata", including oral, anal and vaginal swabs, vaginal wash, swabs from the right and left nipples, and a control swab from the breast.

Item 28: Sealed bag containing a pair of black cutoff jeans.

Item 29: Sealed bag containing a pair of black underpants.

__Procedures and Results:__

The blood sample from Mia Zapata was typed and was found to be ABO type O, and Lewis type Le^{a-b+}, which indicates that she is a secretor. A secretor is an individual whose ABO blood group is expressed in other body fluids such as saliva, vaginal secretions, etc.

The vaginal, oral and anal swabs were examined for spermatozoa and P30 (a semen-specific protein) with negative results. The vaginal wash was examined for spermatozoa, with negative results. Amylase (an enzyme found in high levels in saliva) was found to be elevated in the vaginal swabs. This indicates the possible presence of saliva in this sample. Moderate levels of amylase were detected on the swabs from the nipples.

Secreted H(O) antigens were detected in the vaginal swab sample. No secreted ABO antigens were detected in the swabs from the nipples.

September 14, 1993

Michael J. Grubb, Supervising Forensic Scientist

(a)

FIGURE 15.7 Serology Report. These reports may be found in pre-DNA unsolved cases. It is strongly recommended that investigators seek the assistance of qualified laboratory personnel to review these reports. It is difficult for an untrained investigator to discern all of the important information in these reports. (Courtesy of Mike Grubb)

Laboratory Number: 193-05823
Agency: Seattle Police Department
Agency Number: 93-304200
Suspect: Not Listed
Victim: Mia Zapata
Officer: Detective Allan R. Lima

The underpants and cutoff jeans were examined for the presence of acid phosphatase, an enzyme found in high levels in semen and in lower levels in other body fluids. No acid phosphatase was detected on these garments. Three hairs were recovered from the cutoff jeans, and were repackaged with that garment.

Conclusions:

No semen was found on the vaginal, oral or anal swabs, vaginal wash, or on the underpants or cutoff jeans.

Saliva may be present in the vaginal swab, but no ABO antigens foreign to Mia Zapata were detected in that sample. No blood group substances were detected on the swabs from the nipples.

Michael J. Grubb, Supervising Forensic Scientist   September 14, 1993

(b)

FIGURE 15.7 (Continued).

GENETIC MARKERS

The value of genetic markers is in their ability to provide information as to whether a bloodstain or semen stain *could have* originated from a particular individual. Prior to about 1973 (this year varies from lab to lab), most reports will describe the identification of stains as to the body-fluid type. The only genetic marker (genetic characteristics that allow us to distinguish one person's biological material from another's) in use in the crime laboratory prior to the early 1970s was the ABO system of blood grouping. Liquid blood and bloodstains were typed based on the detection of "antigens" on the red blood cell surfaces. The population could be subdivided into four groups: A; B; AB; and O. The typing of bloodstains in the ABO system extends as far back as the discovery of the existence of ABO blood groups, to 1901 and work done by Landsteiner.

Semen and saliva stains could also be typed in the ABO system, but only if the donor of the stain was a "*secretor.*" Approximately 75% of the general population are secretors. These individuals secrete their ABO blood type into their other body fluids, such as semen, saliva, and vaginal secretions. Those that do not secrete these substances are referred to as non-secretors. ABO typing is generally not possible on a semen or saliva stain from a non-secretor.

In the mid 1970s, crime laboratories were busily trying to add genetic markers to their repertoire. These genetic markers were protein and enzyme markers. For example, phosphoglucomutase (PGM), erythrocyte acid phosphatase (EAP), esterase D (EsD), and adenylate kinase (AK) are enzymes found in the blood that are polymorphic –that is, they are found in different forms in different people. They are referred to as genetic markers because they are inherited from one's parents, and they are passed from generation to generation in predictable patterns. See Table 15.1 for a more complete listing of these protein and enzyme genetic markers, and their approximate distributions in the population.

Some of these enzyme markers were also of value for other biological materials. Semen could be typed in the ABO/Secretor system, as well as for the commonly used polymorphic enzyme systems PGM/PGM subtyping, Peptidase A, and rarely others. Hairs could be typed in the PGM and EsD systems.

In those cases where the laboratory was fortunate enough to obtain typing results in several genetic marker systems, the significance of the match between the evidence sample and the known

TABLE 15.1
Population Frequencies for the Various Genetic Marker Systems (%)

ABO System (Caucasians in San Francisco Bay Area)

A	41
B	11
AB	3
O	45

Secretor system (Caucasians in Michigan)

Secretor	75
Non-secretor	25

PGM (phosphoglucomutase) — (Caucasians in California)

1	59
2	5
2–1	36

PGM subtyping — (Caucasians)

1+1+	40
1+1–	18
1–1–	2
2+1+	21
2+1–	4
2–1+	7
2–1–	2
2+2+	3
2+2–	2
2–2–	1

AK (adenylate kinase) — (Caucasians in California)

1	93
2–1	7
2	less than 1

ADA (adenosine deaminase) — (Caucasians in California and Hawaii)

1	90
2–1	10
2	less than 1

EsD (esterase D) — (Caucasians in California)

1	80
2–1	19
2	1

EAP (erythrocyte acid phosphatase) — (Caucasians in California)

A	11
B	39
BA	42
CB	4
CB	3
C	less than 1

TABLE 15.1(Continued)
Population Frequencies for the Various Genetic Marker Systems (%)

GLO (glyoxalase) — (Caucasians in Michigan)

1	20
2–1	52
2	28

Note: Frequencies are from Gaensslen, R.E, Sourcebook in Forensic Serology, Immunology and Biochemistry, U.S. Dept. of Justice, National Institute of Justice, 1983, with the exception of PGM subtyping frequencies, which are from Gaensslen, Bell and Lee, Distributions of Genetic Markers in United States Populations: II. Isoenzyme Systems, *Journal of Forensic Sciences*, Vol. 32, No. 5, Sept. 1987, pp 1348–1381. Frequencies rounded to the nearest whole number.

sample of the suspect or victim was determined by a frequency calculation. For example, a bloodstain on a suspect's shirt is typed as ABO type B, PGM type 2-1, EsD type 2-1, and EAP type BA. This combination of genetic markers would have significance if the victim's control blood sample was shown to have the same genetic marker profile, and the suspect's own blood was different. Beyond being able to say that the blood on the suspect's shirt is not the suspect's own blood, and could be from the victim, we can attach a significance to this by calculating the frequency with which this combination of genetic markers occurs in the population. ABO type B occurs in 11% of the population. PGM type 2-1 occurs in 36% of the population, EsD type 2-1 occurs in 19% of the population, and AP type BA occurs in 42% of the population. To calculate the frequency of a person with this combination of genetic markers, we can multiply their individual frequencies ($.11 \times .36 \times .19 \times .42 = .003$). Individuals with this combination of genetic markers constitute only 0.3 % of the population, or 3 in 1000. This would have been considered an outstanding result in the pre-DNA serology laboratory.

Masking of Genetic Markers

A limiting factor in the serology lab's ability to give useful information to the investigator in the pre-DNA years was the phenomenon of "*masking*." In sexual assault cases, the biological samples were usually mixed on swabs and clothing stains. When results were obtained for genetic markers on these swabs and stains, the victim's types would have to be subtracted out before stating any conclusions about the genetic markers contributed by the assailant. For example, the following is a typical set of case findings:

- Vaginal swab: A and H* antigens found, PGM 2-1 found. Suspect: ABO type A, secretor, PGM type 2-1.
- Victim: ABO type A, secretor, PGM type 1.

Although the findings on the swab perfectly correspond to the suspect in the case (type A, secretor, PGM 2-1, a combination found in about 11% of the population, the conclusion has to be couched in conservative terms. Some of the genetic markers could have come from the victim in this case, so the report would properly state: "The A and H antigens found in the vaginal swab

---

* (ABO type A secretors would normally secrete both A and H(O) antigens into their saliva, semen, vaginal secretions, etc.)

may have been contributed by the victim herself. The victim could not, however, be the source of the PGM "2" band. Therefore, the semen is from an individual of either PGM type 2-1 or 2. This includes approximately 41% of the male population." This was a very common pre-DNA problem. The advent of DNA testing allowed the examiner to separate sperm DNA from non-sperm DNA. A clean and separate profile can be obtained from each contributor.

The ABO, secretor, and protein and enzyme typing systems were what the crime labs had to work with until the advent of DNA typing in the late 1980s. Many crime labs continued to conduct non-DNA genetic markers into the 1990s.

What a Serology Report Says and Doesn't Say

A serology report is distinguished from a DNA report not only by the *methods* applied to the evidence, but also by the *significance* of the findings. The most informative serology report will indicate whether and where blood, semen, or other biological materials were found on evidence items, and will indicate whether genetic marker testing of samples of that biological material *is indicative of* the stain originating from the victim or suspect. The percentage of the population that shares the particular genetic combination is often given in a serology report. For example, the conclusion of the serology report might state: "The bloodstain on the suspect's shirt has genetic markers indicating that the suspect could not be the source of the blood. Based on the genetic markers found, the victim could be the source of the blood on the suspect's shirt. This combination of types occurs in approximately 6% of the Caucasian population, 4% of the Black population, and 3% of the Hispanic population." The percentages in the report gives the reader a sense of the significance of the match between the victim's known blood and the questioned stain on the suspect.

The report does not positively identify the source (victim, suspect, etc.) of the biological material. This is where a DNA report is significantly different. Some laboratories are now comfortable identifying an individual as the source of a sample (barring the existence of an identical twin) based on the astronomical population frequencies in DNA reports.

COLD CASE EXAMPLE OF USE OF A DATED SEROLOGY REPORT — THE MIA ZAPATA CASE

In July of 1993, a rising female rock star in Seattle was sexually assaulted, strangled, and left in the street. No semen was found in vaginal swabs or on the victim's clothing. The Medical Examiner, however, noted marks on the victim's breasts that appeared to be faint bitemarks (see Figure 15.8). Moistened swabs were used to collect any possible saliva that was present.

A subsequent crime laboratory report discussed "moderate levels of amylase" having been found on the breast swabs (see Figure 15.7). Amylase was also found in the vaginal swab. ABO/Secretor typing of the swabs at that time gave no result other than the victim's own ABO type.

Nine years later, cold case detectives in Seattle were reviewing the case and raised the question of attempting a DNA profile of the possible saliva present on the vaginal swab and breast swabs. The vaginal swab posed a technical problem, as there was no way to separate the cellular material from the victim's vaginal secretions from any cellular material from the saliva. However, the breast swabs gave a DNA profile foreign to the victim. The profile was searched against the National DNA Identification System (NDIS) and a hit was obtained against Jesus Mezquia, a 48-year-old Cuban fisherman living in Florida. Further investigation showed that Mezquia had been in Seattle at about the time of the Zapata murder. When questioned by detectives, he denied knowing or ever being in contact with the victim. This statement was useful to the prosecutors at trial, since Mezquia had removed any innocent means of his DNA being on the victim's body. The jury found him guilty of first degree murder.

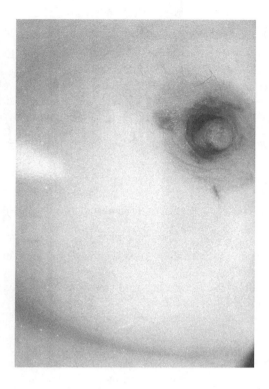

FIGURE 15.8 Bite mark DNA evidence. In older cases in which bite marks were evident or suspected during the investigation, cold case investigators should seek to determine whether any swabs were taken of the suspected bite mark. While bite mark identification is more interpretive, DNA analysis of these is far more definitive for investigation and suspect identification purposes.

THE COLD CASE INVESTIGATOR'S CLUES FROM A SEROLOGY REPORT

- The existence of a serology report in a cold case investigation indicates that biological evidence was an issue when the case was looked at previously, and the results or conclusions listed in the report will tell the investigator whether there are or were biological materials (blood, semen, saliva, etc.) present on evidence items in the case. There may also be an indication in the serology report as to how much of the stain sample was consumed in the previous analysis, and how much may still exist as evidence in the case.
- The investigator should realize that it might be prudent to follow up on apparent exclusions based on serology. What may have appeared to be an exclusion of an individual based on dated genetic marker testing should be followed up with DNA profiling. The now-antiquated methods of genetic marker testing (such as ABO typing of bloodstains or semen stains) were more problematic and more likely to result in an error than DNA profiling.

SEROLOGY AND DNA ADVANCES WITH TIME

Prior to the early 1970s

- Bloodstains were typed in the ABO system only
- Semen and saliva stains were typed in the ABO/Secretor systems only

Early 1970s through late 1980s

- Bloodstains were typed in the ABO, PGM, PGMsubtype, EAP, EsD, AK, ADA, and Hp systems (and occasionally others).
- Semen stains were typed in the ABO/Secretor systems, as well as in some of the isoenzyme systems such as PGM, PGMsubtype, and Esterase D.
- Saliva stains were still typed in the ABO/Secretor systems.

Late 1980s through 2000

- RFLP (Restriction fragment length polymorphism) was introduced as a DNA analysis method.
- Bloodstains, semen stains and other biological material was DNA profiled using RFLP DNA technology.
- Relatively large stains were needed to achieve DNA profile results.
- RFLP results were very discriminating, resulting in frequency statistics commonly in the billions.
- PCR (Polymerase chain reaction) was introduced as a DNA analysis method suitable for small samples.
- Bloodstains, semen stains and other biological materials were DNA typed using PCR-based methods.
- The PCR systems in use were DQ alpha and Polymarker.
- Using DQ alpha alone, the population was broken down into only about 20 different types.
- Adding Polymarker made the results much more discriminating.

Since 2000

- All forms of biological evidence have been DNA profiled using a PCR-based method known as STRs (Short Tandem Repeats). This is the current state of the art for DNA profiling.
- Using 13 genetic loci, this system distinguishes between all individuals other than identical twins.

TABLE 15.2
Serology vs. DNA

Serology-Then	DNA-Now
Sample size needed	
Bloodstain, 1/4-inch diameter	Bloodstain 1/32-inch diameter
Semen stain, 1/2 inch diameter	Extremely small semen stain, containing only about 50 sperm cells
Discriminating Power	
Lucky to get "1 in 100" frequencies	Reports indicate astronomical frequencies such as "1 in 5 quadrillion"
Degradation with Time	
Many of the protein and enzyme genetic markers would deteriorate in a matter of weeks in a stain at room temperature	DNA is much more stable than the protein and enzyme genetic markers A DNA profile can be obtained from stains that are years old, even when kept at room temperature

- Results are reported in terms of frequencies typically on the order of one in trillions or quadrillions.
- For some evidence that doesn't lend itself to STR profiling (such as hair shafts and some bone evidence), mitochondrial DNA can be typed (see DNA chapter).

ACKNOWLEDGMENT

Richard H. Walton wishes to express his gratitude to Michael J. Grubb, Crime Laboratory Manager for the San Diego, California, Police Department for his authorship of this chapter. In addition, he has given much of his time and energy in reviewing and offering positive suggestions for other segments of this book. Mr. Grubb obtained his B.S. degree from University of California at Berkeley in 1975 and began his forensic career at the Institute of Forensic Sciences in Oakland, California, the same year.

Michael J. Grubb wishes to thank Patrick O'Donnell, Ph.D., supervisor of the DNA Unit of the San Diego Police Crime Lab for his discussion, input and review, which has greatly contributed to this chapter, as well as Brian Burritt for his contribution on CODIS.

SUGGESTED READING

Gaensslen, R.E., Sourcebook in Forensic Serology, Immunology, and Biochemistry, U.S. Dept. of Justice, National Institute of Justice, 1983, p. 222.

16 Mitochondrial DNA Examination of Cold Case Crime Scene Hairs

Terry Melton

CONTENTS

INTRODUCTION

Many cold cases have been reopened in hopes that DNA profiling of evidentiary material might strengthen a case against an existing but weak suspect or identify new leads and new suspects. "Cold hits" are made when nuclear DNA (STR) profiles of semen, blood, or saliva crime scene samples are linked to convicted felon DNA profiles that are stored in the national DNA database (CODIS). Even when actual evidence-to-felon hits are not obtained, intercase hits between crime scene samples can be useful in investigating serial crimes, where a single unknown perpetrator has left biological material at multiple scenes. No other single technology has been more valuable to cold case investigators than nuclear DNA profiling.

A lesser-known form of DNA testing, however, also is being used for cold case investigation. In the 1990s, mitochondrial DNA (mtDNA) analysis was introduced for samples that had traditionally been unsatisfactory for STR profiling. The earliest use of mtDNA analysis was for the identification of human skeletal remains that contained insufficient or degraded nuclear DNA, but sufficient mitochondrial DNA to aid in matching an individual to his or her maternal relatives. Since 1993, the Armed Forces DNA Identification Laboratory in Rockville, Maryland, has been using mtDNA to return the skeletal remains of military dead to their families. Identification of missing persons is also aided by this technology. A cutting from a skeletal sample is analyzed, and, in the event of a match, the mtDNA profile of the bone will be the same as the profile of a mother, sibling, or other maternal relative of the individual.

DNA is difficult to recover from very small or environmentally challenged samples. It is degraded or destroyed by heat, moisture, acidity, and fungal or bacterial overgrowth, and its preservation is aided by cold arid conditions. While nuclear DNA is present in only two copies per

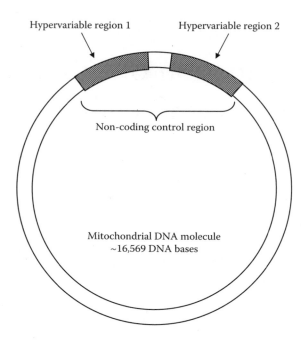

FIGURE 16.1 Schematic diagram of the circular mtDNA molecule, which contains double stranded DNA that is 16,569 DNA bases long. Forensic analysis examines the order of the DNA bases in two hypervariable regions that characterizes a maternal lineage.

cell, the small circular mtDNA molecule (Figure 16.1) is present in hundreds to thousands of copies per cell and is therefore a naturally abundant DNA molecule.

Though all DNA breaks down over time, this natural abundance means that usually enough copies of mtDNA remain for capture and analysis by the forensic laboratory when nuclear DNA is gone. During the 1990s, forensic scientists learned that, while naturally shed human hair roots do not contain sufficient nuclear DNA for routine STR typing, they contain abundant mtDNA. An additional valuable discovery was that shed hair fragments of all kinds with no root are just as useful for this type of testing as hairs with naturally shed roots (some hairs with large, fresh, plucked roots or follicular sheath material can be successfully tested for STRs) (see Figure 16.2). Today, the ability to perform mtDNA analysis on virtually any hair is a bonus technique in the investigation of criminal cases. In addition to head and pubic hairs, body hairs, eyelashes, nose hair, and eyebrow hair are excellent candidates for mtDNA analysis.

Mitochondrial DNA was first used in the courtroom by the FBI to aid in the conviction of a suspect charged with the 1996 rape and murder of a young child in Tennessee. In this case, a pubic hair found in the victim's throat could not be excluded as having come from defendant William Ware. Since that case, hundreds of cases have been examined using mtDNA analysis, and dozens have successfully been tried in the courtroom. A sizeable body of peer-reviewed scientific literature on the forensic use of mtDNA is available, and courtroom admissibility hearings, while still under way in some jurisdictions, have uniformly allowed its courtroom introduction throughout the United States.

ADVANTAGES AND LIMITATIONS OF MTDNA ANALYSIS

A nuclear DNA match of the 13 core STR loci permits little doubt that a questioned sample has come from a known individual, except when identical twins must be discriminated. However, because mtDNA is maternally inherited, all of a woman's offspring, her siblings, her mother, and other maternal relatives will have the same mtDNA profile (see Figure 16.3). Mitochondrial DNA,

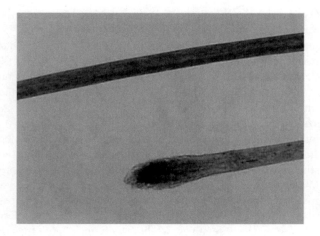

FIGURE 16.2 Photograph of hair shaft (top) and naturally shed hair root (bottom). These are the kinds of hair samples that are analyzed for mtDNA. (Houck/West Virginia University)

therefore, is not a unique identifier in the way that nuclear DNA is, and the test's conclusion can be only whether a known individual is excluded as the donor of the questioned sample. In testimony, a mtDNA forensic examiner will state whether the known individual (and his or her maternal relatives) could or could not have deposited a crime scene hair, but can never state unequivocally that a hair came from a particular person. In fact, because we lose track of our distant maternal relatives, we must assume that an apparently unrelated individual may have the same type we have; this means that exclusionary testing of the victim, victim's partner, victim's non-maternal relatives, and alternative suspects is often necessary when mtDNA analysis is used.

Because an mtDNA type is found in maternally related individuals, it is unlikely that a felon database, such as the national CODIS system, will ever be developed for mtDNA cold-hit searching. Because of this, in any given case, investigators must develop a list of potential donors to be compared with the analyzed questioned hairs, such as victims and suspects, their relatives, and even elimination samples for crime scene personnel. The probative value of the questioned hair

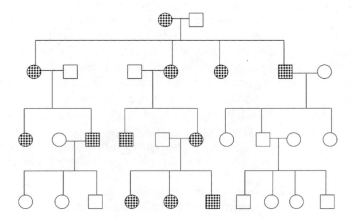

FIGURE 16.3 Pedigree chart showing the maternal inheritance of mtDNA. Women are circles and men are squares. The individuals with the pattern have the same mtDNA type, and can all be traced maternally to the woman in the top line. Note that men inherit their mother's mtDNA type, but do not pass it on to their children.

will dictate the range of known samples that should be considered for comparison to the questioned samples.

While non-uniqueness is a limitation, there are thousands of different mtDNA types, and the relative population frequency of almost any type is low. In most cases, at least 99% of the population will be excluded as contributors and the pool of random individuals who could have contributed the sample is small (less than 1%). In many cases, well over 99.9% of the population can be excluded. The inability to use mtDNA in quite the same way as nuclear DNA highlights its value as a "part of the puzzle," meaning that mtDNA almost always supplements other information in the theory of the crime and that evidence tested by this method would rarely be the only evidence.

An advantage, however, of mtDNA use is that if a victim is missing (no-body homicide), a single maternal relative may donate the mtDNA reference sample to compare to suspected crime scene victim hairs. When a suspect is long deceased, missing, or unavailable for other reasons, his or her maternal relative may provide the mtDNA reference sample for comparison to crime scene samples. Alternatively, exhumed skeletal remains such as teeth, femurs, or ribs from individuals who have no known living maternal relatives, while usually unsuitable for nuclear DNA analysis, are almost always satisfactory for mtDNA use as known reference samples, although collection is more difficult and costly.

CRIME SCENE HAIRS

A recent development in the area of post-conviction relief is the mtDNA re-examination of shed crime scene hairs previously examined by a trace examiner using only a microscope. In a number of older cases, exonerations or new trials have been won when mtDNA analysis of a hair has proven without any doubt that a convicted offender could not have left the hair in question. In these cases, during trial, a trace examiner had testified that the hair "matched" the defendant and the jury weighed this limited testimony heavily. A recent study by the FBI, however, showed that such microscopic evaluations, in their highly experienced trace evidence examiner's hands, resulted in false positives about 11% of the time when the match was tested using mtDNA analysis. Similarly, false negatives also occur: that is, hairs that might have shed light on a case were discounted by the examiner because the microscopic evaluation showed no visual "match" between an individual and a crime scene hair. Because the range of physical variation in hair samples from a single individual is vast, it is conceivable that physical differences of color, diameter, and structure between hairs from widely diverse locations of the body could be wrongly interpreted.

The knowledge that false negatives and false positives may occur with hair microscopy provides an opportunity for the cold case investigator. By reexamining old records, laboratory and expert reports, stored evidence, and transcribed testimony from interviews, depositions, hearings, and trials, the investigator may locate previously slide-mounted hairs, loose hairs on clothing or in envelopes or paperfolds, or other crime scene material that was previously discounted on the basis that either "one can't do anything with shed hairs or hairs with no root" or "the trace examiner said there was no match." These sample hairs can open up new avenues for consideration of alternative or weak suspects who might have left them at the crime scene. Similarly, crime scene hairs could help place a victim in probative relevant locations.

Because no hair root is necessary for mtDNA analysis, many previously discounted smaller and fragmented hairs have recently become valuable pieces of evidence. Examples are hair that is:

- Under a victim's fingernails or in the victim's hand
- Trapped in a cracked windshield in a vehicular homicide (can place individuals in certain seats)
- Superimposed on blood or other liquids at the crime scene
- Pubic hair in a sexual assault where the perpetrator has worn a condom
- Recovered from wrappings on the body or the body bag

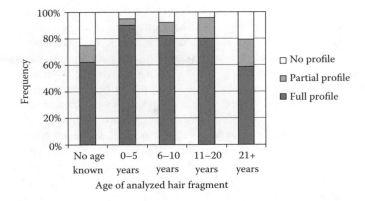

FIGURE 16.4 Older hairs (analyzed many years after a crime) typically are more difficult to analyze than younger hairs, however, almost 80% of hairs in their third decade after collection yield partial or full mtDNA profiles. (from Melton et al. (2005) Forensic mitochondrial DNA analysis of 691 casework hairs. *Journal of Forensic Sciences* 50:73-80)

- Recovered at autopsy
- Stuck on the murder weapon, tape bindings, or ligatures
- Collected from probative locations on clothing (inside underwear)
- In the mouth, throat, vagina or rectum
- In a discarded mask or abandoned getaway vehicle
- Adhering to bumper or undercarriage of a hit-and-run vehicle
- From the suspect's vehicle (trunk or passenger seat)
- In the mechanism or tape of an explosive device

In any case, hair samples as small as 2 mm can be used for mtDNA analysis and eventual comparison to known individuals. Hair as old as 4 decades has been successfully tested, and it is unknown what the most extreme age for successful testing might be. In general, scientists have observed that full or partial mtDNA profiles can be obtained most successfully on recently shed hairs, but that hairs over 21 years of age provide partial or full profiles in almost 80% of cases. With this information, cold cases dating back to the 1960s are candidates for re-examination (see Figure 16.4).

In the event that crime scene hairs are located for examination and analysis, several steps leading up to the actual mtDNA analysis itself will be helpful. While following standard chain-of-custody protocols, an investigator should plan for a brief microscopic evaluation by a qualified hair microscopist. The hair can be measured and photographed, and if a sizeable plucked root with follicular or sheath material is determined to exist, nuclear (STR) DNA testing can be attempted. Hairs can be slide-mounted for comparison with other hairs in the case. Rather than comparing the questioned hairs to exemplar (known) hairs from reference individuals in the case, which, as stated above, can lead to false positives or false negatives, a microscopist can classify or group questioned hairs according to their general appearances, which then allows the selection of one or two hairs from each group for mtDNA analysis. On rare occasions, an exclusion of an individual might be obtained without DNA analysis because the physical differences between questioned and known hairs are extreme, but this is an exceptional occurrence. In general, the hairs selected for mtDNA analysis should have substantial probative value to the case, as the expense of testing usually will mean that a limited number of hairs can be analyzed.

Determining the probative value of a questioned hair can be critical to a case. Unlike semen or blood, which is often present due to criminal activity such as sexual or physical assault, hairs may simply be deposited from an individual who has been innocently present before, during, or after the crime has occurred. By themselves, hairs are not indicators of any specific activity, especially since humans naturally lose 75–100 head hairs per day. Exceptions to this are forcibly removed hairs such as those yanked out during a struggle, or pubic hairs, which are not shed onto floors or furniture as often as head hairs. The STR DNA match rate to suspects or victims when semen or blood is present is known to be about 70%; this is because semen and blood are often present as a result of the crime. However, the mtDNA match rate with hairs is significantly lower: about 50%. This is because hairs are everywhere in our environment and may simply collect on clothing, shoes, floors, and furniture and be unrelated to crime scene activity.

Because maternal relatives share the same mtDNA profile, using mtDNA analysis to investigate a within-family crime is not useful, for example, when one sibling has allegedly been murdered by another. Hairs found at the scene will be uninformative as to the correct donor based on mtDNA analysis. However, all probative hairs should be collected, for if the theory of the crime later is determined to be incorrect, and a non-family member becomes a suspect, the hairs may become useful evidence.

Hairs found on the floor of a public restroom will be less valuable to the theory of the crime than non-victim hairs found inside the victim's clothing at that location. Because mtDNA is not a unique identifier, linking a hair from clothing to a suspect is more powerful than linking a hair from the floor to that suspect, since an argument can always be made that the hair was contributed by someone unrelated to the case who just happened to have the same profile as the suspect.

THE ANALYTICAL PROCESS

An mtDNA analysis begins when DNA is extracted from biological material, such as a tooth, blood sample, or hair. Extraction is the most critical stage of the analysis, because the DNA that is authentic to the sample is being purified away from all other biological materials in the sample, and laboratory personnel are concerned with the integrity and cleanliness of the sample, laboratory environment, equipment, and chemical reagents. Typically, a laboratory carefully cleans a hair shaft in an ultrasonic water bath, and then grinds the hair into a sterile solution (see Figure 16.5). This solution is treated with chemicals to separate the DNA into a new sterile tube.

A process called the polymerase chain reaction (PCR) is then used to amplify or create many copies of the two hypervariable portions of the non-coding region of the mtDNA molecule, using

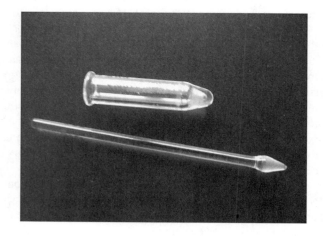

FIGURE 16.5 The mini glass grinder that is used to break up a hair into a chemical solution during the DNA extraction stage. The grinder is effectively a mortar and pestle in which the two pieces are machined to fit perfectly together for grinding. (Kontes Glass Co., Vineland, New Jersey)

flanking primers (Figure 16.1). This region contains the mtDNA sequence information: the exact order of the As, Cs, Gs, and Ts that characterize that sample. Primers are small bits of DNA that identify and adhere to the ends of the region one wishes to PCR amplify, therefore targeting a region for amplification and subsequent analysis.

Care is taken to eliminate the introduction of exogenous (contaminant) DNA during both the extraction and amplification steps via methods such as the use of prepackaged sterile equipment and reagents, aerosol-resistant barrier pipette tips, gloves, masks, and lab coats, separation of pre- and post-amplification areas in the lab using dedicated reagents for each, ultraviolet irradiation of equipment, and autoclaving of tubes and reagent stocks. Questioned samples are processed at different times from known reference samples and they are usually processed in different laboratory rooms.

When adequate amounts of PCR product are amplified to provide all the necessary information about the two hypervariable regions, sequencing reactions are performed. These chemical reactions use each PCR product as a template to create a new complementary strand of DNA in which some of the As, Ts, Cs, and Gs (DNA bases) that make up the DNA sequence are labeled with dye. The DNA strands created in this stage are then separated according to size by an automated sequencing machine that uses a laser to "read" the sequence, or order, of the DNA bases. Where possible, the sequences of both hypervariable regions are determined on both strands of the double-stranded DNA molecule, with sufficient redundancy to confirm the DNA bases (A, C, G, T) that characterize that particular sample.

At least two forensic analysts independently assemble the sequence and agree on the final DNA sequence that has been obtained. The entire process is then repeated with a known sample, usually blood or saliva collected from a known individual. The sequences from both samples, each about 780 bases long, are compared to determine whether they match. The analysts assess the results of the analysis and determine whether any portions of it need to be repeated.

Finally, in the event of an inclusion, or match, the Scientific Working Group on DNA Analysis Methods (SWGDAM) mtDNA database, which is maintained by the FBI, is searched for the mitochondrial sequence that has been observed for the samples. The analysts can then report the number of observations of this type based on the nucleotide positions that have been read. The number of times that a type or profile has previously been observed is used to calculate a simple statistic which guides understanding of both the court and trier of fact about the significance of the match. It is important that a mtDNA analyst state clearly, both in a final report and in testimony, that an individual and his or her maternal relatives cannot be excluded as the donor of a questioned hair. With this statement of a "match," the analyst may qualify the statement with additional information such as "We are 95% confident that the true frequency of this type in North American populations does not exceed 0.06%." In other words, the analyst does not try to state that the profile is unique but is saying that there is 95% confidence that at least 99.94% of North Americans will not have the type in question.

MITOCHONDRIAL DNA COLD CASES

LORI ROSCETTI HOMICIDE

Lori Roscetti, a medical student in Chicago, was abducted, raped, and murdered in 1986. Four Chicago gang members were arrested for the crime, tried, and convicted in 1988. A review of the case evidence some years later by defense attorneys revealed the presence of numerous undetected semen stains on the victim's raincoat as well as three unanalyzed hairs. STR typing of the semen stains eliminated all the original convicted men and the victim's boyfriend as donors of the semen. Mitochondrial DNA analysis of the three questioned hairs also eliminated all the original convicted men. The convictions of these four gang members were vacated in 2001.

Within 1 month of the exonerations and release, another individual came forward to report that his brother and an accomplice might have committed the Roscetti murder. Because the informant and his brother were maternally related, the informant donated a sample for mtDNA comparison with the questioned hairs. This comparison revealed that the informant and his brother were not excluded as the donor of one questioned crime scene hair. The accomplice's mother also donated a sample for mtDNA analysis. The results of this comparison showed that she and her son were not excluded as the donor of a second questioned crime scene hair. Based on this preliminary and suggestive mtDNA testing, court orders were obtained to procure blood samples from the two new suspects. STR typing of their blood samples revealed that the new suspects were likely donors of the semen stains on the victim's raincoat. Both suspects were arrested, and charged, and later confessed to the murder of Lori Roscetti.

TERRORIST STORAGE LOCKER

Armenian nationalists rented a locker in the Cleveland area during the 1970s for the storage of guns and explosives. Rental fees on the locker were not paid in 1996, which triggered an opening and investigation of the locker by authorities, including The Bureau of Alcohol, Tobacco, and Firearms once munitions were discovered. Several evidentiary hair fragments were collected from a coat and moving blankets inside the locker. Mitochondrial DNA analysis of these fragments in 1999 matched their profile to that of the leader of the terrorist group, Mourad Topalian. Topalian was arrested, charged, convicted and sentenced to 37 months in prison in 2000. An "ancient" mtDNA analysis was necessary for the hairs, because their mtDNA was minimal and degraded after exposure to the heat of the storage facility over many years. This slightly more specialized approach allows abundant but degraded DNA, such as mtDNA in 25-year-old hairs, to be captured in smaller fragments.

WILLIAM GREGORY EXONERATION

This 1992 cold case remains open. William Gregory, an African-American, was arrested, charged, and sentenced for the attempted rape of a Caucasian woman in his apartment complex after the victim identified him in a suspect lineup. There was no other evidence in the case except for six "Negroid" head hairs discovered in pantyhose used as a mask at the crime scene. The pantyhose had been washed and hung in the victim's bathroom prior to the crime. At the 1993 trial a hair microscopist stated that the hairs could have come from Gregory, and this testimony was helpful to the prosecution. Gregory maintained his innocence even though he was offered a lesser sentence in exchange for a guilty plea. Mitochondrial DNA testing was performed in 2000; the six hairs shared the same mtDNA profile but had a different mtDNA profile from that of Gregory. He was released from prison shortly after testing. The questioned hairs also did not match the victim. The case remains unsolved and no new suspect has been identified. This case was the first U.S. case in which mtDNA aided an exoneration.

CONCLUSION

Mitochondrial DNA analysis may supplement other tools used in cold case investigations, especially when probative hairs are discovered in old crime scene evidence collections. Until 1996, when the FBI started using mtDNA analysis, the only science routinely being applied to shed hairs was descriptive microscopy, a science prone to bias due to its subjective nature. While microscopy still has a valuable role to play in the evaluation of questioned hair evidence, it should no longer be used without confirmatory mtDNA analysis. Hairs that are candidates for analysis can be of any age and size, and do not need any root material.

While mtDNA matches provide limited statistical power due to the maternal inheritance pattern, when no other analytical process is available, they can provide compelling supportive data that can aid the trier of fact just as any circumstantial evidence can. For example, when pubic hairs are found at a sexual assault scene in the absence of semen, investigators are likely to invest in mtDNA analysis of this very valuable evidentiary specimen. In most cases when a match is obtained, it is possible to eliminate well over 99% of the general population as contributors of a specific hair, with the exception of maternal relatives. With the availability of mtDNA analysis of questioned hair evidence, cold cases may be reopened with the knowledge that a validated scientific process can be applied to valuable forensic evidence of previously limited value.

Robert H. Walton wishes to express gratitude and appreciation to Terry Melton, Ph.D., for her authorship of this chapter. Dr. Melton received her M.S. and Ph.D. in genetics from Penn State University in State College. She is the president and CEO of Mitotyping Technologies, a private company specializing in performing mtDNA analyses for agencies in the criminal justice system across North America. Dr. Melton possesses a strong research background in the study of mtDNA and has published and presented on this subject to numerous forensic and law enforcement venues.

SUGGESTED READING

Holland, M.M. and Parsons, T.J. (1999) Mitochondrial DNA sequence analysis: Validation and use for forensic casework. *Forensic Science Review* 11:21–50.

Isenberg, A.R. and Moore, J.M. (1999) Mitochondrial DNA analysis at the FBI Laboratory. Forensic Science Communications 1(2), www.fbi.gov/hq/lab/fsc/backissu/july1999/dnalist.htm.

Melton, T., Dimick, G., Higgins, B., Lindstrom, L., and Nelson, K. (2005) Forensic mitochondrial DNA analysis of 691 casework hairs. *Journal of Forensic Sciences* 50:73–80.

17 DNA as a Witness

Zach Gaskin

CONTENTS

INTRODUCTION

As scientists learn more about the secrets that are held within our genetic code, we find ourselves searching for answers to questions about the physical characteristics of the persons involved at the crime scene. Some of the questions that are typically asked of eyewitnesses are beginning to be addressed by analyzing the DNA specimens found at the scene of the crime. You may have asked your laboratory the question, "Can this DNA sample tell me anything about my suspect, such as race, eye color, or sex?" The STR test currently used as the standard for human identification can tell you what the sex of donor is, but what about race and eye color? Advances stemming from the completion of the human genome project are emerging and one such advancement has significance to the modern criminal investigation.

RACE AND DNA

The term "race" is politically charged and has many connotations. Some believe that there is one race, the human race. Others define people subjectively into multiple categories. Therefore, to describe the differences that are apparent between population groups and the blending of population groups, the more accurate and technical term for measuring the racial differences among humans is "bio-geographical ancestry" or BGA. The term BGA ignores geopolitical boundaries or country borders and recent historical prejudices. The term speaks to the biological differences that we all have, based on the historical makeup of our families. To visualize the dynamics of your family influence on your BGA, you have to look back only a few generations.

In Figure 17.1, the shades represent the different genetic material or DNA types of your family members and how they are passed down to you. If the square parent on the left was African American and the circle parent on the right was Caucasian, you would expect the child to be roughly half African American and half Caucasian.

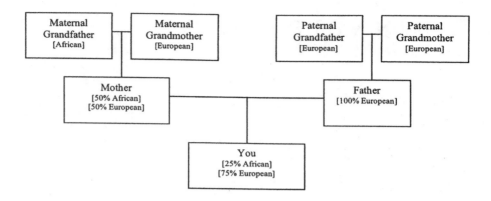

FIGURE 17.1 Pedigree chart. A family pedigree illustrating the DNA inherited from each family member. (Zach Gaskin)

Figure 17.1 is a basic pedigree showing the way we inherit DNA from our parents and grandparents. This simplified illustration of heredity allows us to see that a child will inherit half of his/her DNA from the mother and half from the father. Also, this means that each grandparent will have contributed a quarter of the DNA to the grandchild. In Figure 17.1, the maternal grandfather is African and the other three grandparents are European. The resulting grandchild will have a genetic makeup that is one quarter African and three quarters European.

In 2003, a new type of DNA test was developed for defining an individual's BGA strictly from his or her DNA. This investigative tool allows the detective to paint a picture of the person who left DNA at the crime scene by determining the percentages of European, East Asian, Native American, and Sub-Saharan African. Having this DNA technology available is like placing an eyewitness at every crime scene where DNA is left behind, describing generally the visual characteristics of the perpetrator or victim. For that, the test was aptly named "DNAWitness™."

A Good Witness is Hard to Find

Finding an eyewitness in a cold case may be nearly impossible, especially when many years have passed. Persons linked to the case have moved on or died, and the evidence may degrade to the point where it may not be useful. One of the best investigative tools available to detectives is the national database of registered offenders referred to as CODIS. When DNA is identified in a cold case and a usable STR profile can be explored using CODIS, you might solve the case right away with a "hit" or match with a registered offender. When a match can't be made, your DNA sample becomes another "forensic unknown" in the database and you may be back to square one. Previously, DNA that had been tested was considered nonprobative without a database match and typically was placed in storage in the event that a suspect might later be identified. Investigators now have the option to perform a BGA test and provide some information to a stalled investigation. With DNAWitness, you can get a sense of who suspects are by knowing what they generally look like (see Figure 17.2).

Starting Smart with BGA

While most agencies have limited budgets, the efficiency provided by BGA testing can also have a significant impact on the resources allocated to cold cases. Even with grant funding available, the money saved by starting with reliable information about the ancestry profile of the DNA donor makes for an intelligent and streamlined investigation.

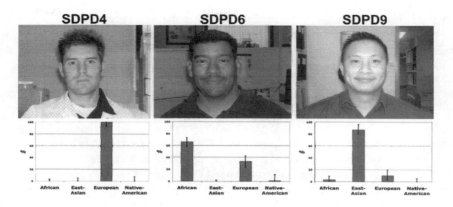

FIGURE 17.2 Results from DNA Witness™ test. (Zach Gaskin)

The information gained from BGA testing in a cold case investigation can help streamline the investigation. Understanding the type of person should be included in the investigation based on the BGA results can affect the questioning of witnesses and the searching of leads. A false lead indicating an African American male as a possible suspect can easily be ruled out if the BGA profile is 90% European and 10% East Asian. Depending on the size and scope of the investigation, this could have a profound impact on the workload and resources of the investigation.

The time saved for an investigation may be the most beneficial aspect of the DNAWitness™ test. Even though the investigation is of a cold case, the time spent by the investigators is precious because every moment chasing a false lead is time not being spent on the next investigation. The level of efficiency in an investigation is paramount and can have an influence on future victims if the case is either solved or goes unsolved for too long. By freeing time for new investigations you effectively are impacting the lives of citizens.

While most agencies have limited budgets, the efficiency that is provided by DNAWitness can also have a significant impact on the resources allocated to cold cases. Even with grant money available, the money saved by starting with reliable information about the ancestry profile of the DNA donor makes for an intelligent and streamlined investigation.

Case Study: Twenty Years in the Wrong Direction

In 1984, a young Caucasian girl living in a rural county in Florida was found raped and murdered. When interviewed, a few friends indicated that she had been hanging around with a new group of people and that each of the men in the group was Caucasian. At the time of the murder, DNA testing was in its infancy, but detectives collected samples from the woman's body and had them tested against the blood samples from the young woman's new friends. Each man was found to be excluded. Many years later, the DNA from the body of the victim was put into the CODIS database with no success and the case was, once again, at a standstill. With no other information, the case became cold and was eventually assigned to a newly formed cold case squad in late 2003. The investigative agency decided that determining the bio-geographical ancestry (BGA) might prove useful. A test for BGA was performed on the unknown DNA and it determined that the donor of the DNA was someone who was 96% Sub-Saharan African. This result ruled out any further investigation necessary of any persons of interest who happened to be Caucasian. The new cold case squad detective indicated that "all along from the beginning of the investigation her killer was thought to be Caucasian." When the investigator was asked why she thought the original detectives became so focused on Caucasians, she said that "at the time of the murder, the population makeup of the county was primarily Caucasian and the information about her new group of friends most likely led the investigators down that path." This BGA profile was a shock to the investigator, who indicated that, around the time that the victim was found, there had been an African American man who had been convicted of sexual assault, but he was not seen as a potential suspect 20 years ago. This case remains unsolved, but the investigation has completely changed direction and the investigator now has a better focus on potential suspects.

Investigations and So-Called "Expert" Opinions on Race

There are many reasons that an investigation heads off in the wrong direction with regards to the race of the suspect or victim. In cold cases where the body of a victim has never been identified, there may be opinions about the race of the victim from several sources.

The crime lab may produce an STR profile and calculate the random match probability. This statistical calculation is usually performed on three possible racial classifications; Caucasian, African American, and Hispanic. The numbers for the three groups found in the crime lab report do not indicate the most likely racial group of the donor of the DNA, they simply indicate how likely it is to pick a random person who would have the same profile as your victim or suspect.

The crime lab can also report on evidence, such as hair, that may confuse the issue when it comes to race. The crime lab will not likely tell you the definite race of your perpetrator from hair evidence, but report on the findings of the evidence that was presented to them. If hairs from the scene are reported to be both Caucasoid and Negroid then you are left with the same questions about who your suspect really is. If only one racial group is indicated, you have to keep an open mind as to how that hair was transferred to the crime scene.

Medical examiners can be persuaded to offer an opinion about the race of a victim when the body cannot be identified by traditional means. It is not always obvious when certain body parts are missing or the body is heavily degraded. The opinion offered may seem harmless, but the emphasis placed on the opinion is what can lead the investigation in the wrong direction.

Psychological profilers may also offer an opinion on race based on a pattern of behavior. Just as we are all different at the genetic level but have similarities, so are criminals and the crimes they commit. Just because most serial killers or snipers are Caucasian does not mean that all serial killers and snipers are Caucasian. Once again, it is not the information that the profiler reports but the level of focus placed on a potentially faulty piece of information.

Detectives have the task of interpreting all of the expert opinions and creating a path to a successful resolution. Along with the experts, detectives also have to take into account information from nonexpert witnesses, evidence, the demographic of the location where the victim was found and their own intuition. When it comes to determining race using expert opinions and gut feelings, there is a high likelihood that the assumptions may be incorrect. The implications of being wrong about your victim or suspect can be the pitfall that prevents you from closing the case.

Painting a Picture with DNA

It is not always easy to visualize what the BGA profile is telling you, so a photographic database of mug shots was assembled and is constantly expanding to include individuals at all possible ratios of BGA. This photographic database allows the investigator to see the faces of individuals who have BGA profiles similar to the profile found from the unknown DNA. The photo database illustrates the level of variation in appearance at a given BGA profile and what type of person is definitely not included. For instance, the difference between a person with 50% African and 75% African may be slight or significant, but without the photos it is left to the imagination of the detective.

The database also contains information about each individual's parents and grandparents as to their country of origin and how they self-report their ethnic identity. This can be helpful in cases where infants are the victims. Information about the possible scenarios for how the parents may appear can provide a logical starting point. In a case where a baby had been found dead shortly after birth, the DNAWitness test provided a profile that was primarily Sub-Saharan African. When the investigator was asked how this might impact his investigation, he replied, "You eliminated two thirds of the parents that needed to be interviewed."

THE ULTIMATE INVESTIGATION USING DNA

As DNA is better understood, so too will be the investigative power of DNA. Currently, we can match a suspect to a crime with DNA through good old-fashioned detective work and link a suspect to a crime through a national DNA database. BGA tests such as DNAWitness allow us another level of investigative success. Although DNAWitness can aid a cold case investigation, the real power of the test may prove to be in its use in the first few days of an investigation. Imagine if every crime scene involving DNA could give you a BGA profile. How might that impact your investigation? How might that BGA profile shape the mode of the modern criminal investigation?

ACKNOWLEDGMENT

Richard H. Walton wishes to extend his appreciation to Zach Gaskin for his authorship and contribution of this chapter. Mr. Gaskin is currently CEO of United Forensics, Inc., a forensic DNA analysis laboratory specializing in the complete investigative DNA solution and innovative forensic research. His previous employment was as the technical director of forensics for DNAPrint Genomics, where he oversaw all forensic research, product development, and operations. Prior to his position at DNAPrint, Mr. Gaskin was a criminalist for the San Diego Police Department and the Florida Department of Law Enforcement Crime Laboratories.

18 Combined DNA Index System (CODIS)

Richard H. Walton

CONTENTS

HISTORY

Recognition of the value of DNA as a means of individual identification in the late 1980s led to the FBI's establishment of the COmbined DNA Index System (CODIS) in 1990. The system initially began as a pilot project and served 14 states and local laboratories. In 1994, Congress passed Public Law 103-322, the DNA Identification Act (42 U.S.C.§14132). This act formalized the FBI's authority to establish a national DNA index for law enforcement, and to establish DNA indexes for persons convicted of crimes, samples recovered from crime scenes, and samples recovered from unidentified human remains. On October 13, 1998, the FBI announced the operation of the National DNA Index System (NDIS).

HOW CODIS IS USED

CODIS is a collaborative effort among local, state, and federal law enforcement agencies. It is similar to the Integrated Automated Fingerprint Identification System (IAFIS), also operated by the FBI. Just as fingerprints from crime scenes are run through a computer system in search of a known individual with matching prints on file, CODIS allows a DNA profile found at a crime scene to be entered into a computer database in search of an individual with that DNA profile. The individuals in this database are offenders who have given a DNA sample after being convicted of a qualifying offense. Law enforcement is thus able to identify or link possible suspects when no prior knowledge of the suspect existed.

Many in law enforcement contend that DNA is the most significant advance in criminal identification since fingerprints. The importance of this investigative tool in cold case homicide investigation cannot be overstated. In the past, jurisdictions tended to act independently in homicide investigations, failing to realize or admit that another jurisdiction might hold the key to solving their case. DNA and the CODIS system force the issue, bringing together the scene and offender.

System Design and Structure

The CODIS system utilizes a three-tier structure to input and access DNA profile data. The three levels are local (LDIS), state (SDIS), and national (NDIS). The local level contains profiles of forensic samples developed through casework. Also in the local database are the DNA profiles of suspects who gave samples for comparison in their respective cases. From the local level, DNA profiles from casework evidence (called forensic unknowns) are uploaded to the SDIS. Local suspect DNA profiles have not generally been uploaded to SDIS, as the state DNA database laboratories have been adding only convicted offender profiles as per state law. There are variations, state to state, in the classifications of the offenders who populate the databases. For example, one state might include only sex felons and violent felons. Another state might also include convicted robbers and burglars. When a match is achieved locally between a forensic unknown and the submitted known DNA sample from a suspect on the case, the forensic unknown is uploaded to SDIS. In this way it is possible to match to other forensic unknowns statewide, thereby solving additional crimes that occurred in other jurisdictions (see Figure 18.1).

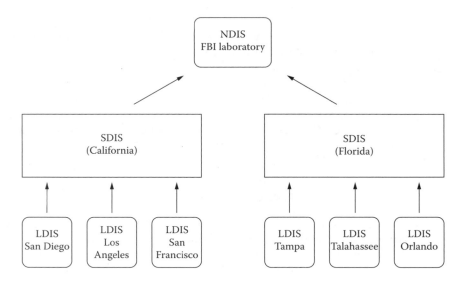

FIGURE 18.1 CODIS utilizes a three-tiered system. DNA profile information originates at the local DNA Index System (LDIS) and can be uploaded to the State (SDIS) DNA Index System. Ultimately these DNA profiles can be uploaded to the National DNA Index System (NDIS) operated by the FBI Laboratory. (Author's drawing)

If no match is achieved when a forensic unknown profile is uploaded to SDIS, the profile will then be uploaded to NDIS for comparison to a national index of crimes and known offenders. NDIS is in essence a network of all the state DNA databases (see Table 18.1). If no match is achieved the first time a forensic unknown is searched against the SDIS or NDIS databases, the sample will be searched again periodically against those databases automatically, without any further effort on the part of the local laboratory or investigator. In this way, if an offender sample is entered well after the entry of the forensic unknown, a "hit" will be achieved. The separate databases are further described as follows:

- **LDIS.** Local DNA CODIS laboratory. Casework samples such as semen stains are examined, DNA extracted, profiled, then entered into the local database. Suspect's DNA profile would also be loaded into the local database. Cases may be solved locally if a forensic unknown matches a suspect profile.
- **SDIS.** State DNA CODIS laboratory. Convicted-offender samples are analyzed and the DNA profiles are entered into SDIS. These profiles are compared against the forensic unknowns from casework that are uploaded by the local crime laboratories. The forensic unknowns are also compared against other forensic unknowns in the database. When forensic unknowns from multiple cases exhibit the same DNA profile (a case-to-case match), a crime series has been established.
- **NDIS.** National DNA CODIS laboratory. This is the final level of the CODIS system and serves as a repository for DNA profiles submitted by participating states. After submission and comparison at the local and state levels, a profile is entered into this national database and compared with a national index of forensic unknowns as well as convicted offenders. As a result, NDIS allows states to exchange DNA profiles and to perform interstate comparisons of DNA profiles.

Under the law establishing the NDIS, only the following types of DNA data may be stored in this national index administered by the Director of the FBI. These are:

- DNA identification records of persons convicted of crimes
- Analyses of DNA samples recovered from crime scenes
- Analyses of DNA samples recovered from unidentified human remains
- Analyses of DNA samples voluntarily contributed by relatives of missing persons

SOFTWARE

CODIS is a software system developed by the FBI that blends computer technology and forensic science into a valuable means for solving violent crimes. It is an automated DNA information processing and telecommunications system that supports LDIS, SDIS, and NDIS. This system allows *public* forensic laboratories throughout the U.S. to exchange and compare DNA profiles electronically.

Criminal justice laboratories in the U.S. are linked by the Criminal Justice Information Services Wide Area Network (CJIS WAN) operated by the FBI. This system offers a secure Internet style of connectivity, and is accessible only by authorized terminals within participating laboratories. LDIS and SDIS participants provide their own computer systems, and the FBI provides and installs CODIS software in these laboratories. In addition, the FBI provides free training and user support to any state and local law enforcement laboratories performing DNA analysis. CODIS is currently installed in more than 100 laboratories.

Private laboratories do not have access to the CODIS database, and those that develop DNA profiles would send those profiles back to the client laboratory for entering into CODIS.

SOURCES OF DNA PROFILES

Since the inception of NDIS and a number of successful case resolutions, many states have expanded the scope of their initial DNA database legislation. Some states initially required only those convicted of felony sex offenses to provide a specimen, while other states prescribed an expanded list of those qualifying to provide samples. Some states have expanded their qualifying offenses in order to increase their DNA database. A few states have included misdemeanors, and some states have begun collecting DNA samples from suspects as well as convicted offenders. Due to the changing nature of individual state requirements and mandates, cold case investigators should consult their local crime laboratory, state criminal justice laboratory or attorney general for current status and requirements.

THE INDEXES

Forensic Index

This index contains DNA profiles from crime scene evidence. Matches made between profiles in the Forensic Index can link crime scenes to one another. Based upon a match that extends across political boundaries, police in those jurisdictions will learn of their common interest in a serial offender, and can then coordinate their respective investigations and share information and leads they developed independently. As of February 2006, this index contained 126,315 profiles.

Offender Index

This index contains DNA profiles of individuals convicted of sex-related offenses and other violent crimes, and some states include robbery, burglary, and drug felonies. Some states include some misdemeanors and suspect samples. As of February 2006, this index contained 2,826,505 profiles.

NATIONAL MISSING PERSONS DNA INDEX

Similar and parallel to the CODIS forensic unknown and offender database is a DNA database of missing persons. The National Missing Persons DNA Database was initially outlined in 1996 but not funded by Congress until 1999. Its goal is to match found unidentified human remains to DNA profiles of missing persons. DNA profiles representing these missing persons may have come from the individual's dentures, or hair from a hairbrush, or some other "secondary standard" that individual left behind. In the absence of a reliable secondary DNA standard representing that individual, the DNA profiles of close relatives (parents, children, and siblings) of the missing person can be entered into the database. STR DNA information will be used if possible, but mitochondrial DNA will also be used in the missing persons database. If the only sample recovered (from found remains) is weathered bone, it is likely that the only result obtained will be a mitochondrial DNA type.

UNIDENTIFIED HUMAN REMAINS INDEX

Typically, when human remains are found, the local investigator will attempt to determine whether there is a matching local case that explains the remains. When no clear matching case is obvious, a portion of the remains (usually a section of long bone, such as femur) is sent to the state database laboratory that is handling found remains and missing persons. This laboratory will attempt STR DNA profiling as well as mitochondrial DNA typing. Just as convicted offender and forensic

TABLE 18.1
NDIS Search Table

INDEX	Forensic	Convicted Offender	Missing Person	Unidentified Human Remains	Relatives of Missing Persons
Forensic	•	•	•	•	
Convicted Offender	•		•	•	
Missing Person	•	•		•	
Unidentified Human Remains	•	•	•	•	•
Relatives of Missing Persons				•	

Note: This table demonstrates the search sequences that automatically occur when a DNA profile is entered into NDIS. As is shown, unidentified human remains are checked against all indexes.

unknowns are uploaded to search against a national database, there is a national database containing DNA information relating to missing persons and found human remains. Details of the process are shown in Table 18.1.

THE PROCESS INVOLVED IN A "HIT"

After first checking against the local DNA database, the local laboratory uses their CODIS computer to upload a "forensic unknown" to the state DNA database. The forensic unknown is a DNA profile obtained from an item of evidence in a criminal case. That uploaded DNA profile is compared against the existing offender index and the forensic index at the state level.

If a "hit" is made between the forensic unknown and an offender in the database, the state laboratory contacts the local laboratory to inform them of the potential match. Usually, the state lab will reprofile the offender's known sample, to ensure that no sample switching occurred. At that point a written "hit report" is sent from the state laboratory to the local laboratory, providing additional information that includes case number, victim's name, and the name and criminal ID number of the offender. Detectives at the local level would then be in a position to evaluate the evidence against the offender in this cold hit case. The hit report is considered probable cause to obtain a search warrant to obtain a new reference sample from the identified individual. Law enforcement investigators subsequently collect a fresh DNA sample from the identified convicted offender and this sample is forwarded to the local laboratory to confirm the DNA profile.

ACKNOWLEDGMENTS

I wish to express my gratitude to Mike Grubb, Crime Lab Manager for the San Diego, California, Police Department for his input and review that have so contributed to this chapter. In addition, I wish to acknowledge and express my thanks to Deputy District Attorney Rock Harmon of the Alameda County, California, District Attorney's Office for providing the information and giving generously of his time to assist in the preparation of Figure 18.2. Mr. Harmon is a veteran prosecutor and advocate for cold case homicide review and reactivation of these cases and an accomplished prosecutor in this specialty arena.

Investigating a cold hit
Case-to-offender

1. CODIS makes a "Hit" and matches a scene to a known offender or another scene. A *cold case report* is issued.
2. Holders of the offender profile retypes original sample to confirm validity.
3. Investigators from the agency providing the crime scene evidence are furnished the name of the suspect as well as the agency submitting the offender's name to CODIS.
4. Locate named suspect and identify custody status.
   - In custody? If so, where?
   - Out of custody? Where is suspect at present?
5. Locate case file.
   - Review case investigation
   - Review, identify, and inspect evidence to determine additional testing. Consider need for additional testing prior to interview. For example, if hit is on vaginal swab and victim's panties are down around her ankles, have panties examined to see if sperm present in crotch. No sperm in crotch makes sperm in vagina more material. Information like this is critical to know for the interview.
     - o Suggested priority of evidence in a review:
       1. Swabs
       2. Clothing
       3. Bedding
6. Research criminal history of the suspect through old case files.
   - Identify past record of arrests through rap sheet and other sources.
   - Attempt to place suspect in area of offense at time of crime through agency records, drivers license, traffic violations, utilities, etc.
   - Consider possibility of suspect for other unsolved crimes both near and more distant from offense identified by CODIS return.
7. Prepare to interview suspect.
   - Identify and contact detectives, probation and parole officers, and others who have interviewed suspect in the past. What works, what doesn't.
8. Search warrant for new reference sample, a secondary DNA sample. Be prepared to interview suspect at time of search.
9. Interview suspect and attempt to obtain admissions or confession.
   - If suspect refuses to provide a sample yet denies the act, that is indicative of consciousness of guilt at trial. In most jurisdictions, a refusal can be used to compel a sample. Follow state law, department practices and policies, and advice of prosecutor.
10. Typing of new offender sample and comparison to evidence from scene.
11. Post-interview follow-up investigation.
12. Charging of case.

FIGURE 18.2 Investigating a Cold Hit Flow Chart.

SUGGESTED READING

NIJ Special Report: *Using DNA to Solve Cold Cases.* July, 2002.

"The FBI's DNA & Databasing Initiatives: Nuclear DNA Analysis, Mitochondrial DNA Analysis, CODIS. FBI Laboratory Division (October 2000).

Federal Bureau of Investigation. National DNA Index System Press Release October 13, 1998.

Butler, J.M. (2003). Forensic DNA typing: Biology & technology behind STR markers. California: San Diego.

Eliopulos, L.N. (2003). Death investigators handbook: Expanded and updated edition. Boulder, Colorado. Paladin Press.

19 National Integrated Ballistic Information Network (NIBIN)

Richard H. Walton

CONTENTS

Every firearm has individual characteristics that are as unique to it as fingerprints are to human beings. When a firearm is fired, it transfers these characteristics, in the form of microscopic scratches and indentations, to the projectile and cartridge cases fired in it. The barrel of the firearm marks the projectile traveling through it and the breech mechanism marks the expended cartridge case. Efforts to match firearms to fired cartridge cases and bullets are found in criminal cases going back to the beginning of the 20th century, and the forensic application of technology to this field began in earnest in the 1920s.

When bullets or cartridge cases are recovered during a criminal investigation, firearms examiners can use these marks for comparison to determine whether they were fired in or from a suspect's firearm. Similarly, if the firearm is recovered at the scene, test firing the weapon creates exemplar bullets and cartridge casings for future comparison. Bullets and cartridge cases found at one crime scene can also be compared with those found at another to link the crimes (see Figure 19.1).

In the past, this has been a tedious and time-consuming process. Each item was compared piece by piece with a large number, usually maintained only by the particular agency. A successful match depended upon the skill and expertise of a qualified firearms examiner. Only when investigators had reason to believe the firearm, casings or bullets may be involved in another case, possibly in another jurisdiction, were these then compared to that separate case. No means of automatic comparison existed. This manual process was hindered by limited available resources and time constraints, making matches less likely. This began to change in the 1990s.

CEASEFIRE, DRUGFIRE, Bulletproof, and NIBIN

In 1992, the Bureau of Alcohol, Tobacco and Firearms (ATF), a Federal law enforcement agency, developed and began to implement CEASEFIRE. This was an enforcement program aimed at addressing firearms-related violence in the wake of the spike in homicide rates of the 1980s and early 1990s. In the beginning, the plan sought to enter into a national computer system all data

FIGURE 19.1 Rounds expended in semi-automatic firearms account for the majority of cartridge casings recovered at crime scenes. (Author's photo)

obtained from firearms seized as a result of investigation by ATF personnel. In addition, local and state law enforcement could utilize this system to enter and retrieve information for investigative purposes related to their own firearms-related criminal investigations. As a result, this system would serve as a central database for all data on firearms used in crimes.

In January 1993, the ATF viewed a presentation from Forensic Technology, Incorporated, (FTI) of a new system that allowed firearms examiners to rapidly examine large numbers of fired bullets. This system, known as *Bulletproof*, allowed data sharing among terminals, thus permitting tracking of mobile criminals. As a result, the ATF leased equipment from the firm and began exploring other uses for this technology. Between 1993 and 1994, ATF financed CEASEFIRE, a private initiative, in Washington, D.C., and Atlanta, Georgia. This pilot program was a spin-off from the ATF program Achilles. Achilles was a nationwide program, active in 21 sites, that had been implemented as a vehicle for enforcing provisions of the Armed Career Criminal and Comprehensive Crime Control Acts. CEASEFIRE provided comprehensive and focused investigative assistance through integration of ATF investigative expertise with new state-of-the-art technology. In 1995, ATF formulated a set of principles for expansion of ballistic imaging technology sites and utilization of these resources by local law enforcement.

During the previous period, however, the FBI had implemented a computerized ballistic imaging system of its own, DRUGFIRE. Some agencies opted for the ATF system and some opted for DRUGFIRE. There was a glitch, however. The two systems were *incompatible* and did not speak to each other. Data entered into one system could not be utilized in the other. As a result, two different systems that could not be linked together were beginning to appear and spread in the nation's law enforcement forensic community. An independent evaluation of the Bulletproof and DRUGFIRE systems ensued.

Both ballistic imaging systems use computer-searching capabilities to match recovered crime scene evidence against information stored in a computer database. The review found that processing casings and projectiles on a common versatile platform would offer the best solution to a need for ballistic imaging requirements. As a result of this review, FTI developed Brasscatcher (see Figure 19.2).

This development provided a platform that could evaluate both projectiles and cartridge casings. This new system was referred to as the "Integrated Ballistics Identification System," or "IBIS." IBIS was composed of Bulletproof and Brasscatcher. IBIS provided for the first time a platform for evaluating both projectiles and cartridge casings on the same system.

In January 1996, ATF and the FBI acknowledged a need for interoperability. In June of that year, the National Institute of Standards and Technology (NIST) issued a report to define minimal specifications for this interoperability. The report provided the manufacturers of IBIS and Drugfire with specifications to make hardware and software modifications to their systems to achieve interoperability. In May 1997, ATF and the FBI entered into an agreement. In the NIBIN Concept

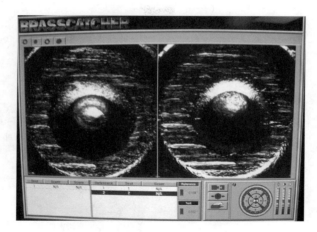

FIGURE 19.2 Brass Catcher monitor screen. Ballistic imaging systems use computer-searching capabilities to match recovered crime scene evidence against information stored in a computer database. (Courtesy of Mike Grubb, San Diego Police Department Crime Lab)

Paper, each pledged to make no modifications to existing systems that would exacerbate the differences in the technology. From this agreement arose the term "National Integrated Ballistics Information Network. (NIBIN)." As a part of this agreement, ATF agreed to stop referring to its ballistic imaging program as CEASEFIRE, and the FBI agreed to stop using the term DRUGFIRE for its program.

The NIBIN Board was created to unify Federal efforts to deploy ballistics imaging technology. The three-member board comprises one member each from ATF and FBI, and a member from the state and local law enforcement communities. Each agency continued to operate its own system, however. By the summer of 1999, after extensive testing and research by NIST into the potential for interoperability, the NIBIN Board made the decision to pursue the single network goal through interagency cooperation and joint deployment of only one system. In December, 1999, ATF and FBI signed a Memorandum of Understanding (MOU) delineating each agency's role in the creation of the NIBIN network. As a result, ATF was responsible for field operations, including purchase of equipment and training of users, and the FBI for providing a communications network.

In February, 2000, ATF completed its strategic plan to support the "rollout," the change from DRUGFIRE to NIBIN. The plan included the creation and staffing of the NIBIN branch as part of the Firearms Programs Division of the ATF, to support NIBIN operations. It also became clear that it would be necessary to enable information sharing among more sites in the same region, necessitating the creation of regional servers capable of correlating and storing more data and of communicating with more sites than under the previous hub configuration. FTI began developing a regional server to meet this need. Criteria were established to evaluate agencies for participation, including population served, firearms-related crime, and number of firearms recovered.

SETUP AND DESIGN

NIBIN setup has occurred on a regional basis. The initial design system divided the nation into 16 regional multi-state regions, with every major population center having access to integrated ballistic imaging technology (see Figure 19.3).

ATF purchases IBIS equipment for deployment to law enforcement agencies and contracts with FTI to train users from the approved site. This deployment is the result of the agency participating

NIBIN Regions

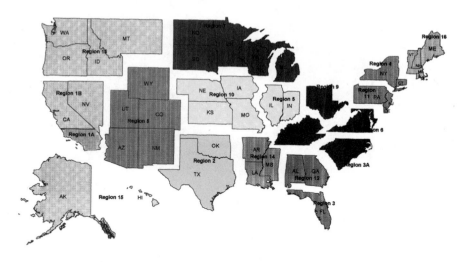

FIGURE 19.3 NIBIN Regional Map. (Courtesy of ATF)

in an MOU and meeting established criteria. ATF ensures that the equipment is properly installed and that personnel are trained and qualified. Thereafter, ATF provides for regular updates and service, as well as administering the network by which it communicates. It also monitors use statistics to ensure that the equipment is being used to its maximum effectiveness. In turn, the partner agency agrees to support the program by:

- Providing adequate staff and resources
- Entering as much crime gun evidence as possible into their IBIS systems
- Sharing evidence and intelligence information with other law enforcement agencies
- Abiding by ATF regulations for system use

By law, the NIBIN program is expressly *restricted to* the ballistic imaging of data associated with *crime guns*. Ballistics systems deployed to Federal, state, or local authorities *cannot* be used to capture or store images acquired at the point of manufacture, importation, or sale, or any other data associated with such images. This includes information about the purchaser, the firearm type, model, caliber, gauge, serial number, or the date of manufacture.

These units are connected together into the NIBIN. This network allows firearms technicians to acquire, digitize, and compare markings made by a firearm on bullets and cartridge cases. By this, the system minimizes the amount of non-matching evidence that firearms examiners must inspect to discover a match.

Practically speaking, it has been observed by system users and detectives that firearms used for criminal purposes tend to travel in certain "corridors," such as along the eastern seaboard or along the west coast. These regional corridors, or partitions, are automatically checked. Routine checks are *not* made on a national search, however.

It is important for investigators to work with the lab, and to give them information so they know which region to search.

FIGURE 19.4 An Individual Data Acquisition Station (DAS) comprises a computer and microscope that allow for either acquisition or image evaluation. Individual stations are linked to a Regional Server, where images are stored and bullet or cartridge case correlation requests are sent. (Author's file)

EQUIPMENT AND NETWORKING

Four different types of IBIS equipment make up the NIBIN network:

1. Regional Server. The central data repository for the region, where all images are stored and bullet or cartridge case correlation requests are executed.
2. DAS Remote. Data Acquisition Station (DAS). This is the main unit of the IBIS system, comprising a microscope and a computer unit that will allow for either acquisition or image evaluation. DAS Remotes are linked via a local area network (LAN) to a Regional Server, where the images are stored and bullet/cartridge case correlation requests are sent (see Figure 19.4).
3. RBI. A portable cartridge case system which permits on-site capture of fired cartridge cases for immediate transmission to a central IBIS location for processing and comparison.
4. Matchpoint. A desktop computer connected via LAN to a DAS Remote, serving as an additional workspace for the analysis of images.

How It Works

IBIS technology was designed for operation by a firearms examiner or technician, with or without extensive previous experience using a computer. A firearms examiner or technician may be trained to enter the markings from crime scene bullets and cartridge cases. In addition to demographic information such as crime, date, and other information, each record contains images of the bullet or cartridge case.

For a cartridge case, images correlated include (if present):

- **Breech face.** These marks are the result of final finishing in the manufacturing process. The breech face is the largest surface for marks.
- **Firing pin.** Examination can be made on rimfire cartridge cases. Differences in firing pin shapes and sizes assist in finding a match.

FIGURE 19.5 Fired Bullet. Images of the land impressions offer the most accurate and dependable potential for a match. The land impression is the narrower image in the center, and the groove impression the wider impression on each side of the land impression. (Courtesy of Mike Grubb, San Diego Police Department Crime Lab)

- **Ejector.** The ejector mark is caused when the fired cartridge case contacts a projection of metal in the breech of the firearm. The purpose of the ejector is to direct the fired cartridge case out of the firearm.

For a bullet, images of the **land impressions** are stored. Markings on this engraved portion of the bullet after it leaves the barrel offers the most accurate and dependable potential for a match (see Figure 19.5).

If the image has been captured by a DAS Remote, the data is then sent from the DAS Remote to the regional server for storage and correlation against other images in the regional database. Correlation results, a selection of images with very high correlation scores, are then sent back to the DAS Remote.

The IBIS comparison analysis does *not* positively match bullets or cartridge cases fired from the same weapon. This *must* be done by a firearms examiner. The system produces a short list of potential candidates for the match, those that exhibit a high correlation of similar characteristics. When an image looks as though a possible match could exist, the firearms examiner examines the original specimen(s) on a comparison microscope.

To use NIBIN, examiners or technicians enter bullet or casing evidence into the IBIS unit. The images are correlated against earlier entries. Searches may be made against evidence from the same jurisdiction, neighboring jurisdictions, or eventually jurisdictions across the country. Search results alert firearms examiners to possible matches. The examiners then compare the original evidence to confirm a "hit."

"Hit" Defined

A "hit" is defined as a linkage of two different crime investigations by the user of the NIBIN technology, where previously there had been *no known connection* between the investigations. A hit is a linkage between cases, not individual pieces of evidence. Multiple bullets or casings may be entered as part of the same case record. In this event, each discovered linkage to an additional case constitutes a hit. Other NIBIN linkages derived by investigative leads, hunches, or previously identified laboratory examinations are not "hits" according to this definition.

A hit must be confirmed by a firearms examiner examining the actual specimens under a microscope.

Key to the success of this program is input of data — cartridge cases and expended projectiles — from participating agencies. Similar to that of AFIS databanks and CODIS, it is important for law enforcement personnel to understand the importance of *resubmitting* shooting evidence for inclusion and search against the database. Since the beginning of the program, ATF has encouraged use of the following priority order for entering evidence into NIBIN:

1. Bullets and cartridge case evidence from crimes where no firearm has been recovered.
2. Test fires from firearms seized during criminal activities or search warrants.

The ATF has determined that the higher the ratio of physical evidence (i.e., bullets and cartridge cases) to test fires, the more successful a laboratory can be in linking unsolved shooting cases. Certain calibers make up the vast majority of those firearms used in crimes. These are:

- .25 auto
- .32 auto
- .380 auto
- 9mm
- .38/357
- 10mm/40 S&W
- .45 auto

By and large, these cartridge cases are recovered from a crime scene when they are expended from *semi-automatic* weapons (the 9mm and .45 can be found in and fired from fully automatic weapons). Bullets, cartridge cases, and firearm test fires from other types of weapons may be entered into the system as well.

When multiple cartridge cases are found at the scene, all should be identified to make sure each was fired from the same weapon.

Each ATF field office has one or more special agents designated as NIBIN coordinators. These coordinators work with receiving police departments and laboratories for equipment acquisition, installation and operation as well as coordinating investigative efforts.

ORGANIZATION AND HISTORY OF ATF

The forerunner of the ATF was historically the tax-collecting, enforcement, and regulatory branch of the U.S. Treasury Department. This agency derives its authority from Congress and cannot enact laws nor amend laws. The passage of the National Firearms Act in 1934 and the Federal Firearms Act 4 years later involved taxation of regulated weapons (ie., machine guns). This taxation was assimilated with tobacco tax collection under the auspices of the Bureau of Internal Revenue until the early 1950s. In a 1952 reorganization, this bureau became the Internal Revenue Service (IRS), and firearms and tobacco taxation was delegated to the Alcohol and Tobacco Tax Division. This lasted until passage of the 1968 Gun Control Act, which added explosives regulation to the body. In addition, this act now required serial numbers be affixed to all firearms. The 1970 Organized Crime Control Act solidified ATF explosives authority, and the 1982 Anti-Arson Act gave ATF responsibility for investigation of commercial arson.

On July 1, 1972, the agency became a more autonomous unit within the Treasury Department and separated from the more revenue-collecting mission of the IRS. Since 9/11, the organization is now under the auspices of the U.S. Department of Justice, and is commonly known again as ATF.

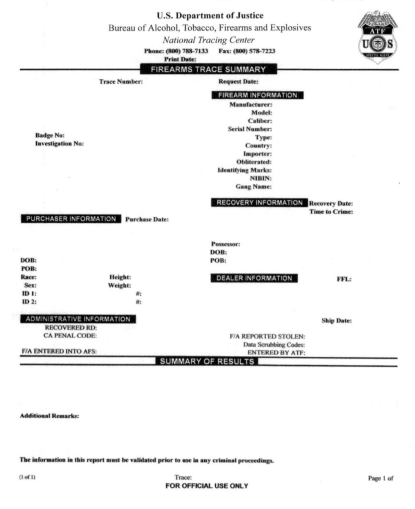

FIGURE 19.6 A separate report is generated for each individual firearm subjected to a trace investigation.

Further ATF Cold Case Resources

Cold case investigators have conducted investigations in which they have sought to locate the firearms records of dealers who are no longer in business. If the name of the dealer is known, or becomes known, it is suggested that investigators attempt to contact the dealer for a statement, copies of records, and any other pertinent information that might be generated. In cases where the name of the dealer is unknown, but the make and serial number are recorded in the file (as in the case of a recovered weapon at some point during the investigation), ATF may possess records pertinent to the investigation. Licensed firearms dealers, importers, or manufacturers who discontinue business are required to forward their business records to the ATF (see Figure 19.6).

National Firearms Tracing Center

- Traces the origins and ownership of recovered firearms used in crimes. This database information, which derives from recovered and traced firearms, is available to federal, state, and local law enforcement or foreign law enforcement authorities.
- Is the main repository of all the records of federal firearms dealers who are no longer in business. A firearms trace may provide information, as shown in Figure 19.6.

The National Firearms Tracing Center is the main repository of all records of federal firearms dealers who are no longer in business.

National Tracing Center
ATF/Records Center
244 Needy Road
Martinsburg, WV 25401
1-800-788-7133, ext. 1590

National Licensing Center

The National Licensing Center is responsible for licensing all manufacturers, importers, dealers, and collectors of firearms in the U.S. The center's firearms records system provides the means to trace firearms and explosives.

National Licensing Center
2600 Century Parkway NE
Suite 400
Atlanta, GA 30345
404-417-2750/1-866-662-2750
nlc@atf.gov

ACKNOWLEDGMENTS

I wish to thank ATF Supervising Special Agent Lisa Kincaid for providing me much of the material used in the preparation of this segment. SA Kincaid, a veteran investigator with the agency, was instrumental in setting up the NIBIN system in a region stretching from Texas to Guam, including Southern California. In addition, I wish to extend my gratitude to Supervising Criminalist Richard Grzybowski at the ATF laboratory in Walnut Creek, California, for his explanations and insight into the practical implementation and utilization of the NIBIN system and ATF resources. Further, I wish to extend my thanks to Mr. James Stam, IBIS supervisor of the firearms unit and Mr. Eugene LaChimia, criminalist, at the San Diego, California, Police Department laboratory, for their interest, expertise, and assistance in the compilation of this chapter.

Part III

Investigative Tools

20 Forensic Anthropology In Cold Cases

Madeleine Hinkes

CONTENTS

INTRODUCTION

Such is the nature of cold cases that the body may not be immediately available for autopsy and analysis. Someone disappears; weeks, months, even years later, remains are found. They may be decomposed, incomplete, skeletonized, ravaged by animals, or otherwise unrecognizable. Who is this person? How and when did he or she die? These are questions that need answers, for legal and humanitarian reasons. Now is the time to call in a forensic anthropologist, an individual uniquely qualified to assist in the recovery and identification of human remains.

Anthropology is the study of the human species. Cultural anthropologists examine human behavior in all its infinite variety around the world. Biological (or physical) anthropologists study humans as biological creatures and have built a rich tradition of research in human growth and development, physiological adaptations, genetics, anthropometry (measurement of body segments), and human variation.

Forensic anthropologists are a subset of biological anthropologists who bring their training and experience to medicolegal problems, such as human identification. These individuals are well trained in human anatomy and osteology, as well as archaeological field techniques. They specialize in studying remains that have lost the soft tissue components relied on for traditional identification and analysis. Those who make a profession out of studying the human skeleton know that each person's skeleton has certain identifying features that can be interpreted by someone who knows how to read the clues.

Forensic anthropologists are usually found in anthropology departments at colleges and universities, often within the law enforcement jurisdiction. It is important to distinguish between a physical and a forensic anthropologist. Both may know bones, but only a forensic anthropologist is also skilled in evidence collection, report preparation, and court testimony. A forensic anthropologist knows how to function as a member of a medicolegal team, working with homicide investigators, medical examiners, attorneys, and crime lab personnel. The best place to find one is in the listing of the American Board of Forensic Anthropology (www.csuchico.edu/anth/ABFA/). The Board comprises Ph.D.-level forensic anthropologists who have attained the requisite level of skill and experience to pass an intensive 8-hour examination and are now board certified.

SEARCH AND RECOVERY

Remains pertinent to a cold case investigation are sometimes found accidentally; hikers come across a body, the family dog brings home a human bone. At other times, a search for remains is actively undertaken in response to a tip or other source of information. In either case, the forensic anthropologist can provide invaluable assistance by adapting archaeological techniques to the special needs of a criminal investigation — recover the remains and preserve the evidence. This expert can also distinguish between human and nonhuman bone, determine which body parts are accounted for, and estimate postmortem interval based on contextual information.

A surface find can be localized or scattered with the effects of decomposition and scavenger activity. Rather than pick up each portion as found, it is better to mark each portion with a pin flag, in order to get an overview of the distribution. This overview may reveal useful patterns in interpretation of the scene. The search area should be expanded until no more remains are found, using trained dogs if necessary. It is crucial to thoroughly document the scene with photographs and verify the location and distances with good maps and GPS. As remains are bagged, the bags should be labeled to correlate with the position of the remains on the map.

Locating clandestine graves can be difficult, and a variety of techniques are used depending on finances and the availability of personnel and specialized equipment. The simplest method is a foot search of the suspicious area. Investigators walk an area in a systematic fashion, looking for surface irregularities, inconsistencies in vegetation patterns or soil compaction, or for animal signs (e.g., a bone in or near a packrat nest). Trained dogs, a soil probe, or a metal detector can be used.

Remote sensing techniques such as aerial photography or infrared scanner (thermal) imagery might be useful, giving a "bird's-eye view" of vegetation differences that might signal a gravesite. When no surface traces can be noted, a variety of geophysical methods such as soil resistivity, electromagnetic survey, and ground-penetrating radar is available to detect a gravesite. The common feature of the techniques is that manmade signals are sent into the earth to detect subsurface structural or chemical anomalies. Aerated soil is less dense and shows a different pattern of conductivity. All of these techniques require special equipment and trained personnel. A good discussion of all these methods can be found in Killam (1990).

Necrosearch International is a nonprofit organization founded in 1991 to assist law enforcement agencies by providing training and onsite investigations. The organization provides personnel and equipment in the areas of, to name a few, botany, cadaver dogs, entomology, geophysics, and remote sensing (www.necrosearch.org). Jackson (2002) tells the interesting story of how the organization came into being, with much information useful to investigators.

Some jurisdictions have their own specialized response and recovery teams. One such team is the Los Angeles County Special Operations Response Team (SORT). Team members, including archaeologists and criminalists, assist in search and recovery and also present skeletal recovery workshops.

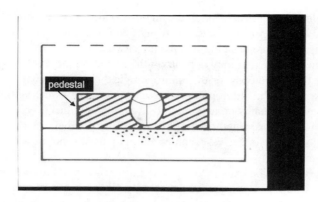

FIGURE 20.1 An archaeological pedestal. (Burns 1999:192)

Once a grave has been located, it is excavated. A grave is a crime scene. It is a potential source of evidence, and must be handled with care by trained personnel. Recovery takes time and should not be rushed or performed under adverse conditions, such as darkness or heavy rain. The discussion here presents general guidelines only; more detailed methodologies can be found in Morse et al. (1983) and Burns (1999), but no book can substitute for field training.

Excavation tools include shovels, trowels, brushes, bamboo or wooden picks for close work near remains, and buckets to haul soil to a screen for sifting (1/8-inch mesh is recommended). Photo or video documentation is essential. Initially, surface vegetation and leaf litter are removed, watching for any bits of evidence. After establishing a reference datum point, preferably with GPS, the area is staked out and mapped. Once the grave outline is defined, soil is removed in shallow layers and sifted. It is important to work horizontally, shovel scraping rather than digging to minimize damage to the remains. When the body is reached, it is photographed, and its position evaluated. If the remains are fairly intact, wrapped, or otherwise contained, recovery is less complicated; the remains can be lifted out as a whole. If the grave is shallow, recovery personnel should dig down carefully to expose the remains in their entirety. A deeper grave necessitates that the remains be pedestaled in order to have room to work and to be able to see what is going on (Figure 20.1).

As the remains are exposed, they are photographed and described in place. Disinterment involves the body parts themselves, and possibly loose finger or toenails, hair, teeth, and personal effects. The anthropologist can inventory the remains to see what is present. Excavation of the grave should continue down to sterile soil, sifting the soil beneath the body. Any insects can be saved for examination by an entomologist. The remains are then wrapped and labeled and prepared for transport back to the medical examiner's office. The final step is to clean up the site.

In some cases, cemetery exhumation might be required in order to reexamine the remains. Burial might have been in an above-ground crypt or subsurface grave. Cemetery personnel will have the skill and equipment to exhume these remains, under the watchful eye of the investigator. The closed container should be transported to the medical examiner's office for opening and examination under controlled conditions.

ANALYSIS

However the remains are recovered, whatever condition the remains are in, the forensic anthropologist follows the same basic analytical steps. The completeness and condition of the remains may affect the quality and quantity of determinations which can be made, but even incomplete or fragmentary remains can yield useful information to a person trained in their analysis. A good forensic anthropologist is equally comfortable with fleshed, decomposed, and skeletonized remains. Our main request of the investigator is to *let us help with the recovery*, if possible, and show us all the remains, rather than just bringing us a bone or two.

The timing of the initial exam may depend on the medical examiner. He or she may want the anthropologist there for the autopsy, or the anthropological exam can take place after the autopsy. If the remains are skeletal, the anthropological exam may serve as the autopsy. In any case, the first step is to lay out the remains in anatomic position and document the inventory on paper and photographically. Most forensic anthropologists prefer to do their own photo documentation. Because it may be years before a case comes to trial, these photos will serve to refresh the anthropologist's memory.

Any clothing present can be examined for sizing information as well as to ensure that no body parts are still in the clothing. Radiographs are usually taken as part of the autopsy protocol, but the anthropologist might request additional shots. Any nonhuman bones can be segregated. Evidence for commingling, in the form of duplicate bones, incompatible size or maturation stage, is noted. At this time, the anthropologist might perform a preliminary assessment of sex, age, and race, which will be reassessed after more detailed analysis.

Adherent soft tissue may need to be removed to facilitate osteological analysis, a process known as maceration. This is usually accomplished by soaking bones in hot water and mild powdered laundry detergent on a hot plate. Periodically, the murky water is poured off, and the soft tissue is gently scraped or pulled from the bone. This process may take hours or days to complete. A final soak in hot water and sudsy ammonia serves to degrease and deodorize the bones (Fenton et al. 2003). The use of bleach is not recommended, as it can damage some delicate bone structures. If there is an anatomical specimen preparation facility nearby, as at a medical school, they may have a beetle colony for rapid defleshing.

Bones are reconstructed as deemed necessary for analysis. This is especially useful for severe cranial trauma. Clean bone fragments are slowly glued together, using an acetone-soluble glue such as Duco™ and placing the reconstructed fragments in a sandbox to dry. This is a time-consuming process, but the results can pay off remarkably by defining entrance or exit gunshot wounds or a central focus of blunt force trauma.

At this point, a general biological profile can be constructed, including sex, age, biological ancestry, and stature. Features unique to an individual, such as skeletal anomalies, pathologies, or traumata can be assessed. The discussion that follows is not a how-to manual, but rather an illustration of what assistance a forensic anthropologist can offer. For detailed methodology, refer to Maples and France 1999; Buikstra and Ubelaker 1994; Burns 1999; Iscan and Kennedy 1989; Krogman and Iscan 1986; Rathbun and Buikstra 1984; Reichs 1986, 1998; Stewart 1979; Byers 2002.

BIOLOGICAL PROFILE

Sex

If the remains are fleshed, determination of sex is fairly straightforward. Skeletonized remains require the skills of a forensic anthropologist. The pelvis is the most dimorphic area of the skeleton, the female's being shaped for childbearing. This results in a long pubis, broad sciatic notch, and wide subpubic angle. Details and side-by-side comparisons can be found in an osteology book such as White (2000). An experienced forensic anthropologist can correctly estimate sex from the pelvis 95-98% of the time.

If a pelvis is absent, the cranium also contains many dimorphic features, though not as definitive as the pelvis. Areas to look at include the forehead, chin, and the back of the skull. There are metric and statistical techniques that can be used in the determination of sex (Giles 1970), but caution is advised. A female of a large-bodied northern European population and a male of a small-bodied southeast Asian population might be difficult to distinguish. Cranial sex can be correctly estimated 80-85% of the time.

Males in general have larger bodies and heavier bones than females, and this is reflected in joint size and areas of muscle attachment. Again, an understanding of inherent population variability is necessary. Simply looking at pictures in a book or taking measurements without understanding the morphology behind them will not suffice.

Children's (subadult) skeletons are much less dimorphic until puberty, and any assessment of sex should be offered with caution. When subadult remains are discovered, it is best to search the lists of missing boys and girls.

Age

Age estimates are based on the development, maturation, and subsequent degeneration of the human frame, and are well within the purview of the forensic anthropologist. Growth and development of teeth and bones proceeds at a fairly predictable pace, so it is usually not too difficult to estimate the biological age of a growing child within a narrow range, using tables developed on modern children around the world (Ubelaker 1989).

Fetal age is assessed using the measured lengths of the long bones and an inventory of centers of ossification, the beginnings of the bones themselves. To the untrained eye, these centers might not even appear to be bone. For infants and older children, the anthropologist relies on dental calcification and eruption, long-bone growth, and epiphyseal development and closure at the growth plates (Scheuer & Black 2000).

For adults, after bone and tooth development have been completed, a few areas of the skeleton are particularly useful. These include the pubic symphysis (Suchey and Katz 1986; Brooks and Suchey 1990), auricular surface of the ilium (Lovejoy et al. 1985), and costochondral junctions (Iscan et al. 1984). If only the cranium is present, the stage of suture closure can yield a general age estimate (Meindl and Lovejoy 1985).

Degenerative changes are also taken into account, such as changes in weight-bearing joints of the legs and lower back. However, these are not age specific and may be hastened by heavy or repetitive physical activity during life.

Microscopic changes in long-bone cortex and dental enamel can also be used to estimate age, but the techniques are complicated and best left to anthropologists who specialize in them (Kerley 1970; Kerley and Ubelaker 1978; Maples 1978; Stout 1988).

Accuracy of age estimation depends on the abundance of remains and the experience of the anthropologist. The estimated age range reflects individual variation. Precision diminishes with increasing age of the deceased.

Ancestry

Biological ancestry, or race, can be extremely difficult to evaluate in skeletal remains because living populations have few clear distinguishing features, and most of those are soft-tissue features. Nevertheless, certain morphological features of the cranium, face, and teeth may serve to distinguish among European, African, and Asian or Native American ancestry (Gill and Rhine 1990). These features include length of the cranium, breadth of the face, projection of the jaws, and morphology of the nasal root. The assessment is complicated by admixture, or generations of mixing among the basic groups. An appreciation of human variability, the hallmark of biological anthropology, is necessary, along with a measure of caution. The investigator also needs to realize that biological race may not exactly reflect an individual's self-identification into a particular group. Metric and statistical techniques are also available, and may be useful in backing up visual determinations (Giles and Elliot 1962).

The Forensic Anthropology Data Bank at the University of Tennessee provides a valuable research tool in its ongoing collection of biological data on documented forensic cases. Reference groups include American White, American Black, Mexican-American, South Japanese, and American Indians, among others. Measurements taken at specific landmarks on unknown crania (or other bones) can be compared statistically with the database using the FORDISC program (Jantz and Moore-Jansen 1988; Moore-Jansen et al. 1994); version 3.0 has just been released (web.utk.edu/~anthrop/FACdatabank.html). The comparison may facilitate evaluation of biological ancestry.

In the absence of a skull, racial determinations are very difficult and should be expressed with the appropriate degree of uncertainty.

Stature

Stature (height) is calculated using the measured length of a long bone (one of six bones in the arm or leg) in the sex-and-race-appropriate equations. These are a series of regression formulae developed in the 1950s to predict stature based on the measured length of a long bone (Trotter 1970). These equations are being refined in the Forensic Anthropology Data Bank to account for secular trends in modern populations and interpopulational variation.

Weight is very difficult to estimate from skeletal remains, but associated clothing may give some clues. A heavy individual may show increased degeneration at the weight-bearing joints. Body build (or skeletal robusticity) is to evaluate using the development of areas of muscle attachment.

Handedness can often be inferred based on asymmetric development of shoulder joints and arm bones, with the dominant side being larger or longer.

Skeletal Anomalies

Every person's skeleton is unique, due to aspects of genetics, growth and development, health, nutrition, and lifestyle. This fact is repeatedly brought home to the forensic anthropologist at each analysis, and, if antemortem information is available, some of these anomalies may prove useful for identification. Examples of some anomalies include: different number of vertebrae in each segment of the spine, 11 or 13 pairs of ribs instead of the usual 12, accessory bones or articular facets, and a variety of discrete (nonmetric) traits such as a metopic suture (Berry and Berry 1967; Finnegan 1978). A sternal aperture (Figure 20.2) with its location near the heart, might be mistaken for a gunshot wound. In reality, it is a developmental defect resulting from incomplete fusion of the distal segments of the growing sternum (Barnes 1994). It can be distinguished from a gunshot wound by its smooth, even edges and lack of any other tissue damage.

Antemortem Trauma and Disease

Many people break bones during their lifetimes due to falls, vehicular accidents, or physical altercations. Generally, the younger you are, the more quickly and completely the fractures will mend. Years later, the only evidence of the fracture may be a slight surface irregularity on the bone. Other times, the deformity is more marked. Orthopedic pins, joint prostheses, or other surgical interventions may be in place. Skeletal evidence for child abuse may be apparent in multiple fractures in various stages of healing (Harris et al. 1996; Kerley 1978; Walker et al. 1997).

A variety of diseases can affect bones, including vitamin deficiencies, tuberculosis, malignancies and metastases, infections, and metabolic disorders (Ortner and Putschar 2003). Nutritional or age-related osteoporosis may be noted. While the specific pathogen might not be identifiable, the anthropologist can provide an accurate description of bony changes that may facilitate a differential diagnosis.

A feature known as parturition scars or birth scars can sometimes be seen on the female pelvis as shallow depressions on the dorsal surfaces of the pubic bones near the symphyseal

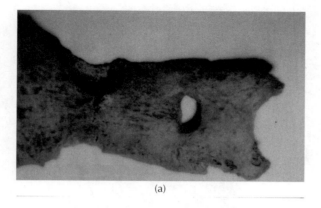

(a)

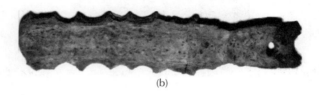

(b)

FIGURE 20.2 Sternal aperture. (a) View of the sternum; (b) Closeup of sternal aperture. (Courtesy of Madeleine Hinkes)

border (Stewart 1970; Suchey et al.1979). While presence of these dorsal pits is strongly suggestive of a full-term pregnancy, the number or size of the pits is only weakly correlated with the number of pregnancies.

PERIMORTEM TRAUMA

While it is the legal responsibility of the medical examiner or coroner to determine cause and manner of death, the forensic anthropologist can often provide useful information based on an examination of bone (Rathbun and Buikstra 1984; Reichs 1986, 1998; Byers 2002). "Perimortem" trauma is that occurring at or around the time of death, thus showing no evidence of healing. Anthropologists are often called to testify on issues of trauma, even when soft tissue is present.

Interpretation of this trauma depends on an understanding of soft tissue and the mechanical properties of bone as a living tissue and how it responds to sharp force, blunt force, or projectile trauma. Bone fragments may need to be reconstructed. Radiography may be helpful. Magnification of the wound may provide details of the tool marks. A casual stroll through the tool aisle of a hardware store reveals a stunning array of objects that can be used to inflict damage on a human body.

Blunt force trauma results from a blow with a wide-edged instrument and is indicated by depressed fractures and radiating fracture lines. It may be possible to determine the instrument, number of blows, sequence, and directionality (Galloway 1999; Rich et al. 2005). Massive blunt force trauma can result from vehicular or aircraft accidents.

A fractured hyoid bone is often cited as proof of manual strangulation, but its presence or absence is not definitive evidence. Ubelaker (1992) reports that 34% of manual strangulation victims show a fractured hyoid. It is actually the thyroid cartilage that is most likely to be fractured in all types of strangulation.

FIGURE 20.3 Incised marks on neck vertebra resulting from an attempt to behead the victim with a knife. (Courtesy of Madeleine Hinkes)

Sharp force trauma results from an implement with a narrow edge or point (cutting, chopping, stabbing). The resulting incised marks are often noted on ribs or vertebrae (Figure 20.3). Cut marks and saw marks can be molded, using dental products, for more detailed analysis of the blade characteristics.

Cut marks in areas of the skeleton that are normally protected within a joint, such as the head of the femur or the trochlea of the humerus, may represent dismemberment marks (Figure 20.4).

Projectile trauma most commonly results from firearms. It might be possible to determine the type of firearm, caliber, direction of travel, and sequence of wounds. Few anthropologists have expertise with the weapons themselves; instead, their expertise lies in a detailed description of the characteristics of the bone defects.

POSTMORTEM CHANGES

Numerous factors, many of which are part of the natural taphonomic processes, can affect human remains (Haglund & Sorg 1997, 2002). Taphonomy is the study of the processes that affect human remains from death until recovery. Bones exposed on the ground surface can show weathering, breakage, disarticulation, and scattering. Small bones can be incorporated into packrat nests. The marks left by animal teeth (punch marks or crushing from carnivore teeth, parallel grooves from rodent gnawing) can, at first glance, simulate trauma or toolmarks (Figure 20.5). Magnification and a trained eye are useful in distinguishing real trauma from "pseudotrauma."

Buried remains are not entirely protected. Although sheltered from most animal activity, buried remains can be damaged or deteriorated by groundwater, acidic soil, or ground pressure.

The recovery process itself might damage bones if not handled properly. Careless use of excavating tools or rough handling and inadequate packaging might break bones. These recent marks can be distinguished by differences in bone color at the new cut or break.

If the remains are burned, a determination must be made as to whether the burning occurred in the perimortem or postmortem interval. Bones burned when dry show a particular pattern of cracking and longitudinal splitting. This situation might occur as a result of a ground fire sweeping

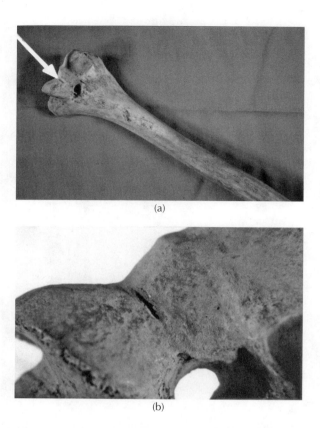

(a)

(b)

FIGURE 20.4 Dismemberment marks. (a) View of the humerus; (b) Closeup of cut mark on trochlea. (Courtesy of Madeleine Hinkes)

over an area where skeletal remains are exposed on the surface. In contrast, bones that are burned "green" (i.e., having a high moisture content) show curvilinear or transverse cracking and warping due the moisture's being pulled out in firing (Figure 20.6). This pattern indicates an individual who died in or shortly before the fire and may be a significant factor in covering up a homicide.

FIGURE 20.5 Marks left by rodent teeth. Parallel grooves on right parietal bone. (Courtesy of Madeleine Hinkes)

FIGURE 20.6 Comparison of bone burned green and dry. (Top) bone burned green (fresh); (bottom) bone burned dry. (Courtesy of Madeleine Hinkes)

Bone fractures due to trauma will need to be distinguished from bone fractures due to burning. The pattern of burning may be affected by soft tissue: parts of the body protected by a heavy muscle layer may burn less than bones close to the skin surface.

Extremely hot fires (>800°C) or fires of long duration can cremate a body. The resulting cremains are usually brittle small fragments. Only the smallest bones (carpals, phalanges) may still be intact, making it extremely difficult to assess biological parameters. Some anthropologists are called in on civil cases to analyze cremains from a funeral home in an attempt to determine whether they are, in fact, the remains of the deceased (Maples and Browning 1994; Correia 1997; Ubelaker 1989). All burned remains require very careful handling to prevent further damage.

ESTIMATION OF POSTMORTEM INTERVAL

The ease of estimating postmortem interval diminishes with increasing time since death. Usually, by the time an anthropologist is called in on the case, the remains are well along the path of decomposition, and postmortem interval is measured in weeks, months, or years, rather than hours.

The pace of decomposition is affected by ecological factors such as temperature, humidity, elevation, and shade. Remains can become skeletonized in as little as 2 weeks in the desert summer, or may retain soft tissue for years if buried or wrapped in some way. Cold temperatures, burial, or immersion in water slows decomposition, while heat accelerates the process.

The Anthropological Research Facility at the University of Tennessee, Knoxville, (commonly known as "The Body Farm") has devoted years to the study of decomposition of human remains under a variety of circumstances (Rodriguez and Bass 1983, 1985; Bass 2003). Their timeline works well in similar environments but does not have universal applicability. In the Southwest, for example, human bodies often pass through a dry mummification stage that is rarely seen in the Southeast (Galloway et al. 1989). It makes sense for the investigator to consult the local experts first.

Insects are a reliable line of evidence in the estimation of postmortem interval. Although anthropologists are not entomologists, we have seen enough insects in association with bodies in different stages of decomposition to have a feel for the insect successions. The anthropologist will also notice plant growth around, or possibly invading, the remains, which may help to set the upper or lower limits of postmortem interval. Another line of evidence comes from clothing or other materials in the grave or around the remains, which deteriorate at different rates (Morse et al. 1983).

A new, specialized area of research involves chemical analysis of the soil under the body, specifically the volatile fatty acids contained in the fluids of decomposition (Vass et al. 1992; Bass 2003). This technique looks promising for the future of time-since-death estimations.

IDENTIFICATION

Identification of decomposed, fragmentary, incomplete, or skeletonized remains is not a simple process, but it is crucial to the investigation. Success depends on the nature of the remains and the quality of antemortem records.

A positive identification results from a combination of anatomic detail sufficiently unique to provide convincing proof. It results from matching postmortem and antemortem biology, through fingerprints, radiographs, or serology including DNA. A probable identification is supported by all available evidence, but that evidence is insufficient for a positive identification, due to inadequate records or remains. Usually there is good circumstantial information to support this level of identification. At a much lower level of certainty is a consistent identification; the antemortem and postmortem information match, but there are no individualizing features. An exclusionary identification is possible when everyone else from an incident has been identified and no antemortem data for the last individual are inconsistent with the remains.

After a long postmortem interval, fingerprints and visual recognition will not be possible. Personal effects may be available, but these should provide a starting point for an identification, not an endpoint

The postmortem examination may yield medical and surgical history of the deceased, along with tissues for serology and toxicology. If teeth or dental structures are present, a dental exam is performed by a qualified forensic odontologist. Even if no restorations are noted, an antemortem–postmortem match could be made on the anatomy of the dental root, pulp chamber, or alveolar bone. DNA can be extracted from tooth roots.

If the case is cold because the remains are found long after death, bones and teeth may be the only sources of data for identification. Biological information can be determined from the remains, as described earlier, but these data are rarely specific enough for a positive identification. If antemortem radiographs are available, along with the corresponding remains, a match can be attempted. Besides dental x-rays, individuals might have had a sinus series, chest x-rays, or bone density studies. The anthropologist needs to address a specific issue: are these antemortem and postmortem structures radiographically identical because they are the same in most people or because these are, in fact, films of the same individual? Some research in a documented skeletal collection may be necessary to prove the point (Scammell 1991). These days, more films are from

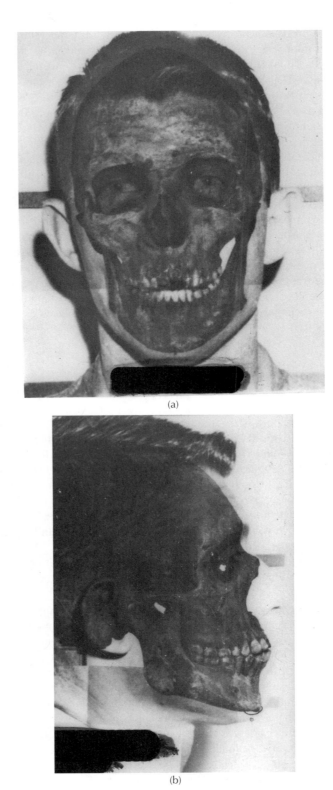

(a)

(b)

FIGURE 20.7 Superimposed skull. (a) Front view; (b) side view. (Courtesy of Madeleine Hinkes)

CT scans or MRIs, so anthropologists are learning to read these films too (Rogers 2002). Poor antemortem film quality can often be enhanced through digitization or enlargement (Fitzpatrick et al.1996).

DNA can often be recovered from skeletal remains, but there may be degradation problems. The Central Identification Laboratory in Hawaii (CILHI) has achieved good results with skeletal DNA extracted more than 30 years after death.

Facial reconstructions or approximations, either two- or three dimensional, can be accomplished as a means to develop leads. These techniques put a face on a skull, so that the reconstruction can be published in the hope that someone will recognize it. This recognition does not make a positive identification. The technique requires artistic skill beyond the capabilities of most anthropologists, but their demographic data are useful to the artist (Taylor 2001; Iscan and Helmer 1993).

Skull/photo superimposition is a technique using video or still cameras to compare the morphology of the skull with an antemortem photograph. This necessitates a good idea of whose remains these might be. The skull should be reasonably intact and should be placed in the same perspective as the photograph. It is a fairly straightforward process to compare points of concordance between bony landmarks and overlying soft tissue, such as the bridge of the nose, the distance between the eyes, and the most forward point of the chin (Austin-Smith and Maples 1994; Helmer et al. 1989). If two photographs are used (for example, a frontal and side view), the possibility of error is greatly reduced (Figure 20.7). This technique was used successfully in the identification process of the Romanov family (Maples and Browning 1994) and of Joseph Mengele (Helmer 1987).

CASE STUDY — CRYSTAL'S STORY

On January 12, 1965, Crystal Smith died. Her stepmother Marie found the 30-month-old girl on the floor of her bedroom, unconscious and convulsing. She was rushed to the hospital, and brain damage was suspected.

Her death was attributed to post-traumatic cerebral hemorrhage. The medical examiner noted nearly 36 recent bruises on the child's body. Her stepmother told authorities that Crystal's weak ankles gave her trouble walking, and that she had recently fallen off a swing. The paternal grandmother suspected something worse, but no charges were brought.

In January 2003, Crystal's case was reopened by two detectives from the El Cajon, California, Police Department Cold homicide Unit, Detectives Richard Rouleau and Jim Ferguson. The detectives thought this was a homicide, but the District Attorney needed more evidence to prosecute. The detectives interviewed family and friends and found Marie living in Casa Grande, Arizona, with Crystal's father.

In June 2003, Crystal's small pink casket was exhumed from a San Diego mausoleum, and a second autopsy was performed. Areas of bruising were still visible on the dried scalp tissue. This autopsy revealed that Crystal's cranial trauma was due to a blow to the head, not a fall. The medical examiner found no brain abnormality. The anthropologist found no evidence of a bone abnormality in the feet or ankles that would have made Crystal "clumsy."

The detectives believed that Marie had been responsible for the child's death 38 years before. On December 16, detectives went to Marie's home with a warrant for her arrest. She was now 66 years old. Also present was her natural daughter, aged 44. As the daughter went to answer the door, she heard a gunshot. Detectives found Marie bleeding from a head wound, with a .22 pistol at her side.

The outcome took everyone by surprise, since there had never been mention of a gun. Although Marie never confessed, the prosecutor and detectives considered the case closed. In January 2004, Crystal was re-interred in the mausoleum (Soto 2004). This cold case was resolved through the hard work and cooperation of many different agencies and investigators.

ACKNOWLEDGMENT

Richard H. Walton wishes to express gratitude to Madeleine Hinkes, Ph.D, for her authorship and contribution of this chapter. Madeleine J. Hinkes received her Ph.D. in Anthropology from the University of Arizona. Upon graduation, she spent 7 years working at the U.S. Army Central Identification Lab in Hawaii. She currently teaches anthropology at San Diego Mesa College and serves as the forensic anthropology consultant for San Diego and Imperial Counties in southern California. Her research interests are skeletal biology and human variation. Dr. Hinkes is a fellow of the American Academy of Forensic Sciences and a Diplomate of the American Board of Forensic Anthropology. She serves on the Board of Directors for the Forensic Specialties Accreditation Board and the Ellis Kerley Forensic Sciences Foundation.

REFERENCES

Austin-Smith, D. and W.R. Maples. The reliability of skull/photograph superimposition in individual identification. *Journal of Forensic Sciences* 39(2):446–455, 1994.

Barnes, E. *Developmental Defects of the Axial Skeleton in Paleopathology.* University Press of Colorado, Niwot, CO, 1994.

Bass, W.M. and J. Jefferson. *Death's Acre.* G.P. Putnam's Sons, New York, 2003.

Berry, A.C. and R.J. Berry. Epigenetic variation in the human cranium. *Journal of Anatomy* 101:361–379, 1967.

Brooks, S.T. and J.M. Suchey. Skeletal age determination based on the os pubis: A comparison of the Acsadi-Nemeskeri and Suchey-Brooks methods. *Human Evolution* 5(3):227–238, 1990.

Buikstra, J.B. and D.H. Ubelaker. Standards for Data Collection from Human Skeletal Remains. Arkansas Archeological Survey Research Series No. 44, 1994.

Burns, K.R. *Forensic Anthropology Training Manual.* Prentice Hall, Upper Saddle River, NJ, 1999.

Byers, S.N. *Introduction to Forensic Anthropology.* Allyn and Bacon, Boston, MA, 2002.

Correia, P.M.M. Fire modification of bone: A review of the literature. In Haglund, W.D. and M.H. Sorg (Eds.) *Forensic Taphonomy.* CRC Press, Boca Raton FL, 1997.

Fenton, T.W., W.H. Birkby, and J. Cornelison. A fast and safe non-bleaching method for forensic skeletal preparation. *Journal of Forensic Sciences* 48(1):274–276, 2003.

Finnegan, M. Non-metric variation of the infracranial skeleton. *Journal of Anatomy* 125:23–37, 1978.

Fitzpatrick, J.J. et al. Optical and digital techniques for enhancing radiographic anatomy for identification of human remains. *Journal of Forensic Sciences* 41(6):947–59, 1996.

Galloway, A, (Ed.) *Broken Bones: Anthropological Analysis of Blunt Force Trauma.* Charles C. Thomas, Springfield IL, 1999.

Galloway, A, W.H. Birkby, A.M. Jones, T.E. Henry, and B.O. Parks. Decay rates of human remains in an arid environment. *Journal of Forensic Sciences* 34:607–616, 1989.

Giles, E. Discriminant function sexing of the human skeleton. In *Personal Identification in Mass Disasters,* T.D. Stewart (Ed.), pp. 99–110, Smithsonian Institution, Washington, DC, 1970

Giles, E. and O. Elliot. Race identification from cranial measurements. *Journal of Forensic Sciences* 7:147–57, 1962.

Gill, G.W. and S. Rhine (Eds.) Skeletal Attribution of Race. Maxwell Museum of Anthropology Anthropological Papers No. 4, Albuquerque NM, 1990.

Haglund, W.D. and M.H. Sorg (Eds.) *Forensic Taphonomy.* CRC Press, Boca Raton FL, 1997.

Haglund, W.D. and M.H. Sorg (Eds.) *Advances in Forensic Taphonomy.* CRC Press, Boca Raton FL, 2002.

Harris, V.J., M.A. Lorand, J.J. Fitzpatrick, and D.K. Sofer. *Radiographic Atlas of Child Abuse.* Igaku-Shoin Medical Publishers, New York, 1996.

Helmer, R. Identification of the cadaver remains of Josef Mengele. *Journal of Forensic Sciences* 32(6): 1622–1644, 1987.

Helmer, R.P., J.B. Schimmler, and J. Rieger. On the conclusiveness of skull identification via the video superimposition technique. *Canadian Society of Forensic Sciences Journal* 22:177–94, 1989.

Iscan, M.Y., S.R. Loth, and R.K. Wright. Age estimation from the rib by phase analysis: White males. *Journal of Forensic Sciences* 29:1094–1104, 1984.

Iscan, M.Y. and R.P. Helmer (Eds.) *Forensic Analysis of the Skull*. Wiley-Liss, New York, 1993.

Iscan, M.Y. and K.A.R. Kennedy (Eds.) *Reconstruction of Life from the Skeleton*. Alan R. Liss, Inc., New York, 1989.

Jackson, S. *No Stone Unturned: The True Story of Necrosearch International*. Kensington Books, New York, 2002.

Jantz, R.L. and P.H. Moore-Jansen. A Data Base for Forensic Anthropology: Structure, Content and Analysis: Report of Investigation 47. Department of Anthropology, University of Tennessee, Knoxville, 1988.

Kerley, E.R. Estimation of Skeletal Age: After About Age 30. In *Personal Identification in Mass Disasters*, T.D. Stewart (Ed.), pp. 57–70, Smithsonian Institution, Washington, DC, 1970.

Kerley, E.R. The identification of battered-infant skeletons. *Journal of Forensic Sciences* 23(1):163–168, 1978.

Kerley, E.R. and D.H. Ubelaker. Revisions in the microscopic method of estimating age at death in human cortical bone. *American Journal of Physical Anthropology* 49:545–46, 1978.

Killam, E.W. *The Detection of Human Remains*. Charles C Thomas, Springfield IL, 1990.

Krogman, W.M. and M.Y. Iscan. *The Human Skeleton in Forensic Medicine*. Charles C. Thomas, Springfield IL, 1986.

Lovejoy, C.O., R.S. Meindl, T.R. Pryzbeck, and R. Mensforth. Chronological metamorphosis of the auricular surface of the ilium. *American Journal of Physical Anthropology* 68:15–28, 1985.

Maples, W.R. An improved technique using dental histology for the estimation of adult age. *Journal of Forensic Sciences* 23:764–770. 1978.

Maples, W.R. and D.L. France. Forensic Anthropology. In Caplan, Y.H. and R.S. Frank (Eds.) *Medicolegal Death Investigation: Treatises in the Forensic Sciences,* pp. 229–248. Forensic Sciences Foundation Press, Colorado Springs CO, 1999.

Maples, W.R. and M. Browning. *Dead Men Do Tell Tales*. Doubleday, New York, 1994.

Meindl, R.S. and C.O. Lovejoy. Ectocranial suture closure. *American Journal of Physical Anthropology* 68:57–66, 1985.

Moore-Jansen, P.H., S.D. Ousley, and R.L. Jantz. Data Collection Procedures for Forensic Skeletal Material. Report of Investigations No. 48, University of Tennessee Department of Anthropology, Knoxville, 1994.

Morse, D., J. Duncan, and J. Stoutamire (Eds.) Handbook of Forensic Archaeology and Anthropology. Florida State University Foundation, Inc., Tallahassee FL, 1983.

Ortner, D.J. and W.G.J. Putschar. *Identification of Pathological Conditions in Human Skeletal Remains (2nd ed.)*. Academic Press, San Diego CA, 2003.

Rathbun, T.A. and J.E. Buikstra (Eds.) *Human Identification*. Charles C. Thomas, Springfield IL, 1984.

Reichs, K.J. (Ed.) *Forensic Osteology*. Charles C Thomas, Springfield IL, 1986.

Reichs, K.J. (Ed.) *Forensic Osteology: Advances in the Identification of Human Remains*. 2nd ed. Charles C. Thomas, Springfield IL, 1998.

Rich, J., D.E. Dean, and R. H. Powers. *Forensic Medicine of the Lower Extremity*. Humana Press, Totowa, NJ, 2005.

Rodriguez, W.C. and W.M. Bass. Insect activity and its relationship to decay rates of human cadavers in East Tennessee. *Journal of Forensic Sciences* 28:423–432, 1983.

Rodriguez, W.C. and W.M. Bass. Decomposition of buried bodies and methods that may aid in their location. *Journal of Forensic Sciences* 30:836–852, 1985.

Rogers, L.F. *Radiology of Skeletal Trauma (3rd ed.)*. Churchill Livingstone, NY, 2002.

Scammell, H. *Mortal Remains*. Harper Collins, New York, 1991.

Scheuer, L. and S. Black. *Developmental Juvenile Osteology*. Academic Press, San Diego CA, 2000.

Stewart, T.D. Identification of the Scars of Parturition in the Skeletal Remains of Females. In *Personal Identification in Mass Disasters*, T.D. Stewart (Ed.), pp. 127-135, Smithsonian Institution, Washington, DC, 1970.

Stewart, T.D. *Essentials of Forensic Anthropology*. Charles C Thomas, Springfield IL, 1979.

Stout, S.D. The Use of Histomorphology to Estimate Age. *Journal of Forensic Science* 33:121–5, 1988.

Suchey, J.M., D.V. Wiseley, R.F. Green, and T.T. Noguchi. Analysis of dorsal pitting in the os pubis in an extensive sample of modern American females. *American Journal of Physical Anthropology* 51:517–540, 1979.

Suchey, J.M. and D. Katz. Skeletal age standards derived from an extensive multiracial sample of modern Americans. *American Journal of Physical Anthropology* 69:269, 1986.

Soto, Onell R., After Nearly 40 Years, A Murder Case Is Closed. *San Diego Union-Tribune* July 18, 2004, page A1, A20.

Taylor, K.T. *Forensic Art and Illustration.* CRC Press, Boca Raton FL, 2001.

Trotter, M. Estimation of Stature from Intact Limb Bones. In *Personal Identification in Mass Disasters*, T.D. Stewart (Ed.), pp. 127–135, Smithsonian Institution, Washington, DC, 1970.

Ubelaker, D.H. Human Skeletal Remains: Excavation, Analysis, Interpretation. Taraxacum Manuals on Archeology, Washington DC, 1989 (2nd ed.).

Ubelaker, D.H. Hyoid fracture and strangulation. *Journal of Forensic* Science 37(5):1216–1222, 1992.

Vass, A.A., W.M. Bass, J.D. Wolt, J.E. Foss, and J.T. Ammons. Time since death determinations of human cadavers using soil solution. *Journal of Forensic Sciences* 37:1236–1253, 1992.

Walker, P.L., D.C. Cook, and P.M. Lambert. Skeletal evidence for child abuse: A physical anthropological perspective. *Journal of Forensic Sciences* 42(2):196–207, 1997.

White, T.D. *Human Osteology* (2nd ed.), Academic Press, Inc., New York NY, 2000.

21 Forensic Dentistry in Cold Case Homicide Investigation

Norman D. Sperber

CONTENTS

INTRODUCTION

Cold cases are solved using a variety of means and methods. Modern technological developments are a leading factor, especially in the area of genetics (DNA). The discipline of forensic odontology (forensic dentistry) can assist cold case homicide investigators in a variety of situations. This chapter presents the practical use of forensic odontology in cold case homicide investigation through its use in the identification process and the role of bitemark analysis.

DENTAL IDENTIFICATION

Since approximately 1980, several advances have occurred in this field. The states of California and Washington developed data processing that linked missing persons' *dental* information with that of unidentified deceased individuals, including unidentified living persons. Comparisons with *reported missing individuals* eliminated the necessity for impractical, expensive, and complex procedures that would have required the entry of dental information from *all* living persons. Following California's success in the positive identification of dozens of individuals employing a central clearing house supervised by the Department of Justice Sacramento, the U.S. government requested that I develop a computerized dental identification system through National Crime

Information Center (N.C.I.C.) for the identification of human remains. Dr. Irvin Sopher (1976) has excellently addressed the rationale for dental identification as follows:

> The individuality or specificity of the dentition is based upon the multiple points of comparison inherent in a variable combination of events, which alter the status of a given set of thirty-two teeth, each comprising five anatomic surfaces. Such events include (1) hereditary, congenital, or developmental alterations; (2) acquired, natural, or traumatic alterations; (3) the presence or absence in multiple combinations of one, many, or most of the thirty-two units; and (4) the combinations and permutations in the variable construction, constitution, and morphology of a various array of restorable procedures, materials, and prosthetic devices employed by the dental profession. In addition, the innumerable features of the dental and jaw structure, as revealed by the roentgenogram, further enhance the criterion of individuality. The instance where chronologic age exercises a role in the identification, the added dimension of time and its effect on the teeth is introduced as a measurable criterion.

> More concisely put, the presence of 160 available dental surfaces (32 teeth times 5 surfaces) subject to alteration by decay and restoration, the latter process including numerous materials of varying shape and size, as well as the innumerable combinations of one or more missing teeth at variable locations, impart uniqueness or specificity to the dental medium.

> Indeed, a basic premise of dental identification is that no two mouths are identical. Theoretically, this may represent a true statement; however, in actuality the reliability of this statement depends upon the number of points of specificity available for the comparison between the ante-mortem and the post-mortem data in any particular case. The greater the number of quantitative and qualitative points of comparison, the more reliable is the comparison and the more nearly one approaches the axiom. Computer models have shown that there are more than 2.5 million possibilities in charting the human mouth. Much effort is currently being expended in evaluating the efficacy of computerized dental charts as a means of classifying mass identification data."

COLD CASE IDENTIFICATION OF UNKNOWN PERSONS THROUGH DENTAL X-RAYS

Positive identification of an individual, who cannot be recognized by the usual means such as viewing the body, fingerprints, tattoos, personal possessions, or identification papers, is often successfully accomplished through dental means. The dentition (teeth, soft tissue, and the supporting bone) is unique for every individual. This identification can be accomplished years, even decades, after death (Figure 21.1).

Dental records are usually considered to mean x-rays and written records. Because written records are sometimes inaccurate, most experts in the field will agree that x-rays are by far the most important and reliable method as they readily demonstrate the morphology (shape) of existing restorations (fillings) or crowns, fixed bridges, root canal procedures and missing teeth (see Figure 21.2). In addition, forensic dentists can observe the shape of the roots, the shape of the crowns (portion of tooth above the gingival (gum), the relationship of the roots to anatomical landmarks such as the maxillary sinus and to adjacent teeth. These relationships become exceptionally important when an individual has not required dental procedures. In some states, labeling of removable full and partial dentures is required. However, an unmarked denture found near a body can be linked to it if the forensic dentist is convinced that the denture "fits" in all respects. This facet can be determined if little or no decomposition has occurred.

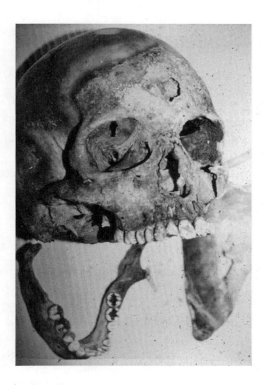

FIGURE 21.1 This homicide victim was discovered in a cistern. Postmortem x-rays were made and compared with the dental x-rays of a female missing for almost 10 years. Examination of the skull revealed that an erosive liquid was applied in an attempt to thwart identification. Segments of bone covering the roots had been destroyed during this process. It was also observed that extensive areas of the skull were etched, a condition not normally seen in skulls similarly exposed to the elements.

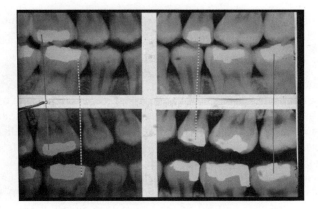

FIGURE 21.2 Antemortem and postmortem X-rays. Upon inspection of the comparison x-rays, it is possible to see similarities between the antemortem films (top) and the postmortem films (bottom). The white areas represent dental restorative materials (amalgam). Some of the postmortem x-rays reveal amalgam restorations not seen in the antemortem films, a fact that indicates the restorations were completed before the victim's death. A suspect was eventually identified, tried, and convicted for the murder.

If the identification of the decedent is unknown in a cold case investigation, several steps can be considered by the investigator(s):

- Have dental records been created (especially full mouth x-rays)?
- What agency (federal, state or local) has custody of said x-rays?
- If this evidence has not been collected, is exhumation of the body possible or has the body been cremated?
- If the dental x-rays exist, has the information therein been distributed to local, state, or federal systems?
- Have there been recent submissions or inquiries to agencies listed above?
- Are there existing antemortem x-rays in the possession of investigators?
- If antemortem and postmortem records are available, has a certified forensic dentist compared them? A list of such individuals is available online by visiting the website of the American Board of Forensic Odontology.

Thus, when case circumstances are such that investigators have an unknown victim with dentition (teeth present):

- a. Check with your State Coroner's Office or State Medical Examiner's Office if there is such an agency.
- b. In California, check with the Department of Justice's Missing, Unidentified Person's System (MUPS), which includes the Unidentified Persons System (UPS) and the Missing Person System (MPS). Its telephone number is 916-227-3290.
- c. FBI/NCIC (dental files)

Possible Sources for Antemortem X-rays

- Prisons or jails
- Union sources if the employment of the individual is known
- Federal sources (National Crime Information Center)
- Private dental sources
- Dental specialists such as oral surgeons, prosthodontists, or periodontists

NCIC MISSING PERSON AND UNIDENTIFIED PERSON FILE

Cold case investigations may be stalled, often for years, due to the inability to recover the body and learn what it can tell us. Cases that begin as a missing persons report not uncommonly become a homicide case, but until the body is located, the case may languish in a state of limbo. Sadly, this is all too common for reported missing children. Not infrequently, bodies or their parts may repose in the medical examiner's office in one jurisdiction and other parts from the same body in the coroner's office in another jurisdiction.

In an effort to unite information between those agencies that recover unidentified bodies or body parts and those agencies that hold missing persons reports, the NCIC has set up a system for data entry by these agencies in efforts to obtain a match between the two databases. This may offer a significant resource to cold case investigators. However, investigators are reminded that the information in the computer is only as reliable and accurate as it was entered into the data system. The system is not perfect. If information is miscoded on the entry forms, or if erroneous information due to error on the part of the person filling out the forms occurs, a match between these two databases may not occur.

U.S. Department of Justice
Federal Bureau of Investigation

National Crime Information Center (NCIC)

Missing Person File

Data Collection Entry Guide

Agency Case Number

For Official Use Only

FIGURE 21.3 National Crime Information Center (NCIC) Missing Person File. This packet contains forms to submit missing person information to the NCIC to be cross-checked against the Unidentified Person File. Dental information requested should be filled out by a trained dentist.

NCIC Missing Person File

This file inputs data through a Missing Persons Packet. Entry of a missing person into this index is accomplished by the completion of a form and its submission to NCIC by the responsible agency (Figure 21.3, Figure 21.4). This packet seeks information that includes:

- Initial report completed by the reporting officer and entered into NCIC immediately.
- Personal descriptors. Information completed by parent or legal guardian, next of kin, and returned to the police agency that completed the initial report.
- Jewelry description.
- Medical/optical information.
- Medical release forms.

In addition, a list of personal descriptors is offered to investigators to further define a missing person. These descriptors include:

- Artificial body parts and legs
- Eye disorders

I-694 (Rev. 10-12-94)

MISSING PERSON REPORT
FOR NCIC RECORD ENTRY

Date

Message Key (See definitions on page 1) (MKE)	Reporting Agency	(ORI)	Name of Missing Person	(NAM)

Message Key (MKE): Disability (EMD), Endangered (EME), Involuntary (EMI), Juvenile (EMJ), Victim (EMV), Caution

Sex (SEX)	Race (RAC)	Place of Birth (POB)	Date of Birth (DOB)	Date of Emancipation (DOE)

Sex: Male (M), Female (F). Race: Asian or Pacific Islander (A), Black (B), American Indian/Alaskan Native (I), Unknown (U), White (W)

Height (HGT)	Weight (WGT)	Eye Color (EYE)	Hair Color (HAI)	FBI Number (FBI)

Eye Color: Black (BLK), Blue (BLU), Brown (BRO), Gray (GRY), Green (GRN), Hazel (HAZ), Maroon (MAR), Multicolored (MUL), Pink (PNK), Unknown (XXX)

Hair Color: Black (BLK), Blonde/Strawberry (BLN), Red/Auburn (RED), Sandy (SDY), Brown (BRO), Gray/Partially Gray (GRY), White (WHI), Unknown (XXX)

Skin Tone (SKN): Albino (ALB), Black (BLK), Dark (DRK), Dk Brown (DBR), Fair (FAR), Light (LGT), Lt Brown (LBR), Medium (MED), Med Brown (MBR), Olive (OLV), Ruddy (RUD), Sallow (SAL), Yellow (YEL)

Scars, marks, tattoos, and other characteristics (SMT) (See check list)

Fingerprint Classification* (FPC)

Other Identifying Numbers (MNU)	Social Security Number (SOC)	Operator's License Number (OLN)	Operator's License State (OLS)	Operator's License Year of Expiration (OLY)

Missing Person (MNP): Missing Person (MP), Catastrophe Victim (DV)	Date of Last Contact (DLC)	Originating Agency Case Number (OCA)	Miscellaneous (MIS) Include build, handedness, any illness or diseases, clothing description, hair description, etc.

Miscellaneous Information

Below is a list of clothing and personal effects. Please indicate those items the missing person was last seen wearing. Include style, type, size, color, condition, labels, or laundry markings. (MIS)

Item	Style/Type	Size	Color	Markings	Item	Style/Type	Size	Color	Markings
Head Gear					Shoes/Boots/Sneakers				
Scarf/Tie/Gloves					Underwear				
Coat/Jacket/Vest					Bra/Girdle/Slip				
Sweater					Stockings/Pantyhose				
Shirt/Blouse					Wallet/Purse				
Pants/Skirt					Money				
Belts/Suspenders					Glasses				
Socks					Other				

LICENSE PLATE AND VEHICLE INFORMATION

License Plate Number (LIC)	State (LIS)	Year Expires (LIY)	License Plate Type (LIT)

Vehicle Identification Number (VIN)	Year (VYR)	Make (VMA)	Model (VMO)	Style (VST)	Color (VCO)

Does the missing person have corrected vision? (SMT): Yes, No, Glasses, Con Lenses

Has missing person ever donated blood? No, Yes Where?

Has the missing person ever been fingerprinted? No, Yes If so by whom?

Blood Type (BLT): A Positive (APOS), A Negative (ANEG), A Unknown (AUNK), B Positive (BPOS), B Negative (BNEG), B Unknown (BUNK), AB Positive (ABPOS), AB Negative (ABNEG), AB Unknown (ABUNK), O Positive (OPOS), O Negative (ONEG), O Unknown (OUNK)

Circumcision (CRC): Was (C), Was not (N), Unknown (U)

Footprints Available (FPA): Yes (Y), No (N)

Body X-Rays (BXR): Full (F), None (N), Partial (P)

Corrective Vision Prescription (VRX)	Jewelry Type (See check list) (JWT)	Jewelry Description (JWL)

Aliases	Reporting Agency Telephone Number	Reporting Officer

Complainant's Name	Complainant's Address	Complainant's Telephone Number

Relationship of Complainant to Missing Person	Missing Person's Address	Missing Person's Occupation (MIS)

NCIC Number (NIC)	Places missing person frequented (MIS)

Close friends/relatives	Possible destination (MIS)

Investigating Officer and Telephone Number (MIS)	Complainant's Signature	Date

* Submit fingerprints to the FBI CJIS Division .10th and Pennsylvania Ave., Washington D.C. 20537

FIGURE 21.4 Missing Person Report for NCIC Record Entry. This information may be filled out by law enforcement upon taking a missing person report.

- Deafness
- Deformities
- Fractured bones
- Medical devices
- Missing body parts/organs
- Moles
- Needle or "track" marks
- Other physical characteristics
- Scars, Marks, tattoos

- Skin discolorations
- Medical condition and diseases
- Drugs of abuse
- Therapeutic drugs

Dental History Information

Dental characteristics are a significant feature in the Missing Persons File. A packet of forms detailing requested information is provided by NCIC for data entry. The information supplied in this packet is designed to be completed by a *dentist* familiar with the missing person as his or her patient or as a previous patient. The dental report is extremely comprehensive and was designed for entry into the NCIC for comparison with dental data of unidentified individuals. This format has changed over the years, however. While information sought through these descriptors is best supplied by a trained dentist, in some instances these forms have been filled out by the patrol officer taking a missing person's report or by investigators. The result has been less than satisfactory in many instances. Certainly, a law enforcement officer, unless he or she is a dentist, should not fill out dental forms. In addition to patient information, information sought includes

- Date of last patient treatment.
- Charting dentist contact information.
- Are X-rays available?
- Date last X-rays were taken.
- Are dental models available?
- Are photographs of teeth available?
- Are all 32 teeth present without decay, restoration or any unusual characteristics?
- Tooth restoration including caries and types of fillings and crowns and combinations.
- Dentures/partial dentures and replacement teeth.
- Other forensic odontological descriptors.

NCIC Unidentified Person File

The Unidentified Person Packet is used for initial and immediate data entry into the NCIC system (Figure 21.5, Figure 21.6, and Figure 21.7). Criteria for entry into the NCIC Unidentified Person File identifies:

- Unidentified deceased. Any unidentified deceased person and/or body parts when a body has been dismembered.
- Unidentified living person. A living person of any age who is unable to ascertain his/her identity. This can include those with amnesia, victims, infants, etc. There may be consent issues involved in this category.
- Unidentified catastrophe victim. Any unidentified victim or body parts dismembered as a result of a disaster.

Antemortem Personal descriptors in this file include those designed to correspond to the Missing Persons system, for example:

- Artificial body parts and aids
- Eye disorders
- Deafness
- Deformities
- Fractured bones

U.S. Department of Justice
Federal Bureau of Investigation

National Crime Information Center (NCIC)

Unidentified Person File

Data Collection Entry Guide

Agency Case Number

For Official Use Only

FIGURE 21.5 National Crime Information Center (NCIC) Unidentified Person File. This file contains information that is automatically checked against the Missing Persons database.

- Medical devices
- Missing body parts/organs
- Moles
- Needle "track" marks
- Other physical characteristics
- Scars
- Tattoos
- Skin discoloration
- Medical conditions and diseases
- Drugs of abuse
- Therapeutic drugs
- Jewelry type
- Optic information

Dental Information
- Coroner's Case number
- Charting dentist's name and address.
- X-rays available?

1-695 (Rev. 10-12-94)

UNIDENTIFIED PERSON REPORT
FOR NCIC RECORD ENTRY

Date _____

Message Key (see definitions on page 1) (MKE)	Reporting Agency	(ORI)	Body Parts Status	(BPS)
☐ Unidentified Deceased (EUD) ☐ Unidentified Living (EUL) ☐ Unidentified Catastrophe Victim (EUV)			☐ Complete Body (ALL)　☐ Complete Skeleton (SKL)	

Body Parts Status (if incomplete body or skeleton, see body diagram for coding corresponding parts) (BPS)

1　2　3　4　5　6　7　8　9　10　11　12　13　14

N - Not Recovered　　R - Recovered　　S - Skeletal

Sex (SEX)	Race (RAC)	Estimated Year of Birth Range (EYB)
☐ Male (M) ☐ Female (F) ☐ Unknown (U)	☐ Asian/Pacific Islander (A) ☐ Black (B) ☐ American Indian/Alaskan Native (I) ☐ White (W) ☐ Unknown (U)	☐☐☐☐ - ☐☐☐☐

Estimated Date of Death (EDD)	Date Body Found (DBF)	Approximate Height Range (HGT)	Approximate Weight Range (WGT)
		☐☐☐ - ☐☐☐	☐☐☐ - ☐☐☐

Eye Color (EYE)		Hair Color (HAI)	
☐ Brown (BRO)　☐ Hazel (HAZ) ☐ Black (BLK)　☐ Gray (GRY)　☐ Maroon (MAR) ☐ Blue (BLU)　☐ Green (GRN)　☐ Multicolored (MUL) ☐ Pink (PNK)　☐ Unknown (XXX)		☐ Brown (BRO)　☐ Sandy (SDY) ☐ Black (BLK)　☐ Gray/Partially Gray (GRY)　☐ White (WHS) ☐ Blonde/Strawberry (BLN)　☐ Red/Auburn (RED)　☐ Unknown (XXX)	

Scars, Marks, Tattoos, and Other Characteristics (SMT)
(See attached Personal Descriptors check list)

Fingerprint Classification* (FPC)

1　2　3　4　5　6　7　8　9　10　11　12　13　14　15　16　17　18　19　20

Reporting Agency's Case Number (OCA)

Miscellaneous (MIS)
Information such as build, clothing description, handedness, weather conditions at the time of death, place where the body was found, etc. should be included. If additional space is needed, attach additional sheet.**

Below is a list of clothing and personal effects. Please indicate those items that have been found with the person or body. Include style, type, size, color, condition, etc.

Item	Style/Type	Size	Color	Markings	Item	Style/Type	Size	Color	Markings
Head Gear					Shoes/Boots/Sneakers				
Scarf/Tie/Gloves					Underwear				
Coat/Jacket/Vest					Bra/Girdle/Slip				
Sweater					Stockings/Pantyhose				
Shirt/Blouse					Wallet/Purse				
Pants/Skirt					Money				
Belt/Suspenders					Glasses				
Socks					Other				
Other					Other				

Blood Type (BLT)		Circumcision (CRC)	Footprints Available (FPA)
☐ A Positive (APOS)　☐ B Positive (BPOS)　☐ AB Positive (ABPOS)　☐ O Positive (OPOS) ☐ A Negative (ANEG)　☐ B Negative (BNEG)　☐ AB Negative (ABNEG)　☐ O Negative (ONEG) ☐ A Unknown (AUNK)　☐ B Unknown (BUNK)　☐ AB Unknown (ABUNK)　☐ O Unknown (OUNK)		☐ Was (C)　☐ Unknown (U) ☐ Was not (N)	☐ Yes (Y)　☐ No (N)

Body X-Rays Available (BXR)	Corrective Vision Prescription	(VRX)
☐ Full (F)　☐ Partial (P)　☐ None (N)		

Manner of Death (CDA)	Cause of Death (CDA)
☐ Accidental (A)　☐ Natural Causes (N) ☐ Homicide (H)　☐ Suicide (S)　☐ Unknown (U)	

Jewelry Type (See check list) (JWT)	Jewelry Description (JWL)

Medical Examiner/Coroner Agency Name and Case Number (MAN)	Medical Examiner/Coroner Locality (MAL)	Medical Examiner/Coroner Telephone Number (MAT)

NCIC Number (NIC)	Investigating Officer and Telephone Number (MIS)

* If fingerprints are available submit a copy to the FBI CJIS Division ,10th and Pennsylvania Ave., Washington D.C. 20537
** All dental information should be recorded on the dental report and entered in NCIC as a supplemental record

FIGURE 21.6 NCIC Unidentified Person Report for NCIC Entry. This file contains information that is automatically checked against the Missing Persons file.

- Date last X-rays taken.
- Dental models available?
- Photographs of teeth available?
- Whether all 32 teeth are present without decay, restoration or any unusual characteristics.
- Tooth restoration including caries and types of fillings and crowns and restorations.
- Dentures/partial dentures and replacement teeth.
- Other forensic odontological descriptors.

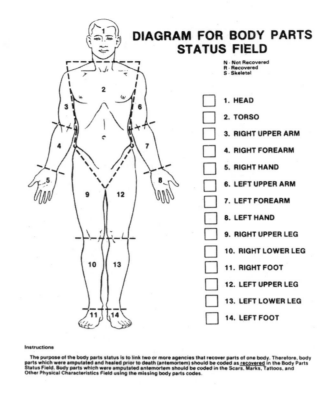

DIAGRAM FOR BODY PARTS STATUS FIELD

N - Not Recovered
R - Recovered
S - Skeletal

1. HEAD
2. TORSO
3. RIGHT UPPER ARM
4. RIGHT FOREARM
5. RIGHT HAND
6. LEFT UPPER ARM
7. LEFT FOREARM
8. LEFT HAND
9. RIGHT UPPER LEG
10. RIGHT LOWER LEG
11. RIGHT FOOT
12. LEFT UPPER LEG
13. LEFT LOWER LEG
14. LEFT FOOT

Instructions

The purpose of the body parts status is to link two or more agencies that recover parts of one body. Therefore, body parts which were amputated and healed prior to death (antemortem) should be coded as recovered in the Body Parts Status Field. Body parts which were amputated antemortem should be coded in the Scars, Marks, Tattoos, and Other Physical Characteristics Field using the missing body parts codes.

FIGURE 21.7 The purpose of the body parts status is to link two or more agencies that recover parts of one body.

BITEMARKS ON VICTIMS OR PERPETRATORS

Bitemark evidence in felony crimes such as homicide, child abuse, and sex crimes has been recognized by the courts in numerous jurisdictions for several decades. When properly preserved and protected, these marks can provide an important link between victim and assailant. While bitemarks on victims are seemingly the most common encountered during law enforcement investigations, equally incriminating may be those inflicted by the victim on the assailant.

Analysis of bitemarks on perpetrators and victims is one of the responsibilities of modern forensic dentistry. Bite mark analysis is more *interpretive* and less objective than, for example, toxicology or DNA procedures. In fact, several cases of positive comparisons logged by a number of odontologists have been reversed by DNA analysis. I have urged odontologists for years to employ standard odontology procedures with caution. There have been far too many criticisms of existing procedures in legal literature. Bitemark analysis has been termed a "junk science." Some experts in the field believe that it is not a science at all, especially when lesions occurring during resuscitative attempts by medical personnel have been falsely identified as bitemarks. The field of odontology has always urged the collection of saliva for DNA analysis. Unfortunately, for one reason or another, this important procedure is not undertaken and valuable accurate genetic evidence is lost. The forensic odontologist may not be called by the investigators early in the case.

Not uncommonly, case or file review will reveal the presence of bitemarks on either the victim or a suspect. Investigators should consider:

- Were swabbings of the alleged bitemark accomplished?
  - What swabbing procedure was used?
  - Have these swabbing been located?
  - Is there an original serology report?
  - Have the swabbings been re-examined?
  - What were the results?
- Is clothing that was over the bitemark available for DNA testing?
- If DNA results were obtained, were they entered into CODIS?
- Were salivary specimens secured from victim or suspect?
- If photographs are available, were they examined by a certified forensic dentist?

In the circumstances listed above, cold case investigators should consult with a qualified forensic odontologist.

BITEMARK PHOTOGRAPHY

A number of issues may confront cold case investigators when reviewing past photographs of purported bitemarks (Figure 21.8). These photographs may be valuable evidence, but a number of factors can affect their usefulness and reliability. Film type and camera angle might be important considerations in evaluating the reliability of these photographs. In reviewing, investigators should consider:

- How long after the crime were the photographs taken?
- What was the distance from camera to the bitemark?
- Is this record sufficiently documented?
  - Date
  - Time
  - Photographer
- Are there both black and white and color photos available? Black and white photographs cannot differentiate between e.g., freckles and an actual bitemark.
- At what camera angles were the photographs taken? Right angle photography eliminates distortion.
- Were the photographs taken before or after the autopsy?
- Was a ruler or scale placed next to the alleged bitemark during photography? (other objects such as blood pressure cuff or a wrist watch strap may be used if they are close to the lesion and if they are obtainable).
- Who took the photographs?
  - Is this photographer still available?
  - Does the photographer have any notes, records, or other photographs?

If the photography is distorted, a forensic dentist may be able to use a computer program to eliminate this problem.

BITEMARK IMPRESSIONS

Similar considerations as to conditions of swabbings or photography should be considered when reviewing bitemark impressions. In addition, cold case investigators need to know:

- Were they taken by a forensic odontologist, dentist, or experienced lab technician?
- What materials were used?
- What procedures were used or followed during this process?

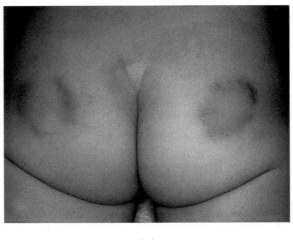

(a)

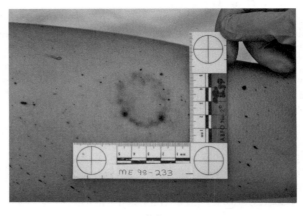

(b)

FIGURE 21.8 (See color insert following p. 216.) (a) The photograph illustrates the difference between diffuse (bluffy) bitemarks on the left and right buttocks of a young victim; (b) illustrates the well defined marks (rectangular images) of the lower incisors seen on the inner thigh of a homicide victim. Note the American Board of Forensic Odontology (ABFO) No. 2 ruler. A flexible rule such as a tape measure is less reliable due to distortion that may have been introduced on curved surfaces. This ruler was designed by the ABFO to render an image measurement in a 1:1 ratio or lifesize proportion. Although measurement scale is in centimeters and millimeters, the L-shaped instrument is one inch wide on both legs of the ruler.

It is also important to point out that in some cases, toothmarks have been found in objects such as chewing gum, apples, and cheese. In one case I investigated, toothmarks of the driver were found on the steering wheel of his truck. In another case, toothmarks of the victim were found in the weather stripping of the suspect's vehicle. The victim explained that she bit the weather stripping to leave a trace of her as she was being sexually assaulted.

Standard procedures in evaluating bitemark cases:

• Orienting photographs
• Swab for DNA evidence

- Close-up photography
- Impressions of bitemark if perforations are noted

EXHUMATIONS OF EMBALMED BODIES WITH BITEMARKS

At autopsies, photographs of suspected bitemarks are usually taken by pathologists. On occasion, these bitemark lesions may not be recognized at the time of autopsy. If this is the case, an exhumation may yield better photographic images with proximating rulers in place. It should be understood that the embalming process is not always effective and that the lesion may not be as obvious or objective as the original autopsy photographs might have been had they been photographed at that time. I was able to secure photographic images of an embalmed decedent that were eventually used in a homicide trial in California.

Qualified forensic dentists can be located through the American Board of Forensic Odontology at http://www.ABFO.org or the American Academy of Forensic Sciences at P.O. Box 669, Colorado Springs, CO 80901. 719-636-1100; http://www.aafs.org.

ACKNOWLEDGMENT

Richard H. Walton wishes to extend appreciation and gratitude to Dr. Norman D. "Skip" Sperber for his authorship of this chapter. Dr. Sperber has been repeatedly acknowledged as perhaps the world's leading forensic odontologist, and his leadership efforts in this field have contributed greatly to the betterment of the forensic and law enforcement spectrum for over 50 years. Prior to his graduation from New York University College of Dentistry in 1954, Dr. Sperber worked for the New York Chief Medical Examiner's Office in New York City. After passing his board exams in New York and California, he practiced in his field and served 10 years as a dental officer in the U.S. Navy. In 1963, Dr. Sperber was appointed the forensic dentist for the San Diego County, California, Coroner's Office (later Medical Examiner), and has served continually since.

Dr. Sperber has instructed law enforcement officers in aspects of forensic dentistry for over 30 years. In 1983, he attended and completed, on his own time, the San Diego Police and Sheriff's Reserve Academy, and became a reserve police officer.

Dr. Sperber helped devise the first civilian dental identification computer system in the U.S. in 1978, one used extensively to identify over 100 of 144 victims from a mid-air collision over San Diego the following year. As a result of a U.S. Congressional appointment, he devised the first national dental identification system in the history of the U.S., the dental section of the NCIC computer relating unidentified persons data to missing persons data. He continues today as a consultant in that capacity. He has testified in over 215 trials, including the first U.S. Courts Martial bitemark case, and as a primary forensic bitemark expert in the cases against Ted Bundy and Jeffrey Dahmer.

Dr. Sperber has served as director of the American Board of Forensic Odontology, as well as chair positions and other duties and accomplishments. He has served as vice president of the American Academy of Forensic Sciences (AAFS) and as chair of the Odontology Section of this highly respected organization. In 2000, he and a co-dentist were named the first Distinguished Fellows from the dental section of the AAFS. He was one of three dentists to design the first state system (California) for body identification and continues to the present as chief forensic dentist for the California Department of Justice's statewide identification system.

BIBLIOGRAPHY

Sperber, N.D., D.D.S. (1981). Bitemark evidence in crimes against persons. FBI Law Enforcement Bulletin. (July, 1981). Washington, D.C.
Sopher, I.M. (1976). Forensic Dentistry. Thomas Publishing Springfield, IL.

22 Forensic Exhumation

Richard H. Walton

CONTENTS

INTRODUCTION

For the purposes of this book, a forensic exhumation is the legally sanctioned act or process of disinterring or digging up a previously lawfully buried human body for law enforcement associated forensic purposes. This form of exhumation may be undertaken at the direction of a court order, or, in some cases, may result from consent by those persons with standing to give such sanction. These would usually include close family members. A forensic exhumation is normally conducted at the grave site within a cemetery or in a mausoleum under the auspices of law enforcement, forensic personnel, medical examiner or coroner personnel, and cemetery representatives. During a forensic exhumation, the search for evidence is usually more specifically focused and this focus underlies the legal procedure preceding and governing the exhumation process.

CONSIDERATIONS IN THE EXHUMATION PROCESS

This act is differentiated from the recovery of the remains of an otherwise buried person, as would be exemplified by a forensic excavation or body recovery of a crime victim from its burial location. During such an excavation, the excavation site is treated as a crime scene and appropriate recording and photographic record is conducted. During the course of an excavation, investigation is usually in a more general stage and the search for evidence is a primary factor among investigative considerations.

WHY CONDUCT A FORENSIC EXHUMATION?

With the increased use of DNA as an investigative tool, a forensic exhumation is becoming a more commonplace procedure in the criminal investigation process. Modern technology and advanced criminal investigation methods have enhanced the application of this technique to make it a viable procedure under some circumstances during the investigation process (Figure 22.1).

A forensic exhumation may be utilized by cold case homicide investigators for purposes of:

- Obtaining biological material for mitochondrial or nuclear DNA testing to aid in identification of the remains.
- Obtaining biological material for use in mitochondrial DNA (mtDNA) testing to determine DNA profiles of those related to the deceased.
- Exclusion of persons of interest.
- Investigation purposes to determine whether injuries were compatible with witness statements or other case investigation information.
- Anthropological or medical examination to support or disaffirm a proposed defense version of events as to how injuries were received.
- Secondary autopsy.
- Forensic odontological purposes, including identification.

FIGURE 22.1 Forensic exhumation. Tree roots and minimal remains. The condition of the remains will be unknown until the casket is opened. In this example, few remains have been found due to severe decomposition. Note the tree roots throughout the casket. (Courtesy of Connie Milton, San Diego County Sheriff's Department)

The Death Certificate

The death certificate is a legal document that contains important information for use in consideration of a forensic exhumation (Figure 22.2). Information to be found on this document may include:

- Disposition of Remains. This would indicate whether the remains were buried, cremated, or other information. As in any other investigation, however, investigate and confirm any reported disposition.
- Date of disposition of the remains.
- Name and address of the cemetery or crematory.
- Name and address of attending physician.
- Name and license number of embalmer, if applicable.
- Name of funeral director or person acting on their behalf.

When reviewing the death certificate, it is suggested that a check be made with the registrar to ascertain whether any supplemental amendments to the death certificate were subsequently added. Further discussion of the death certificate can be found in Chapter 9.

Disposition of Human Remains

What happens to the body after death and the autopsy may become a significant issue in cold case homicide investigations. A number of possible dispositions of the physical remains are:

- Cremation. The remains are burned in a crematorium and (if properly conducted) reduced to ashes. These remains become known as cremains. Cremains may be scattered at sea or on private property with any appropriate health or other permits. In addition, some churches have a separate interment area known as a "niche" for cremains. Remains or cremated remains can also be buried in some veterans cemeteries. Examinations including DNA, toxicology, and similar testing cannot normally be conducted upon remains in this condition.
- Burial in ground without embalming.
- Burial in ground after embalming.
- Entombment in mausoleum/crypt (embalming is normally required by cemetery).
- Burial at sea.

Investigative Considerations

Cold case investigators may be faced with a number of issues when considering a forensic exhumation. Among these may be:

- What is the purpose of the exhumation? A primary consideration in the decision to conduct a forensic exhumation is to establish the specific information that such an exhumation will provide cold case investigators. For example, are samples sought for DNA testing or for anthropological examination?
- Are the remains to be removed or examined on site? This will assist in the determination of whether the remains are to be removed from the grave and the necessity for proper transportation equipment, or whether the necessary requirements can be accomplished on-site and without the necessity to remove the remains.

When investigators determine that exhumation of remains is necessary for investigation purposes, there are a number of preliminary issues to be considered. Among these are:

- Confirm the physical location of the human remains. This would include the name and address of the cemetery or mausoleum, and the plot or grave number, if applicable.

CERTIFICATE OF DEATH
STATE OF CALIFORNIA
USE BLACK INK ONLY / NO ERASURES, WHITEOUTS OR ALTERATIONS
VS-11 (REV 1/03)

STATE FILE NUMBER	LOCAL REGISTRATION NUMBER

DECEDENT'S PERSONAL DATA

| 1. NAME OF DECEDENT --- FIRST (Given) | 2. MIDDLE | 3. LAST (Family) | |

| AKA. ALSO KNOWN AS --- Include full AKA (FIRST, MIDDLE, LAST) | 4. DATE OF BIRTH mm/dd/ccyy | 5. AGE Yrs. | IF UNDER ONE YEAR Months / Days | IF UNDER 24 HOURS Hours / Minutes | 6. SEX |

| 9. BIRTH STATE/FOREIGN COUNTRY | 10. SOCIAL SECURITY NUMBER | 11. EVER IN U.S. ARMED FORCES? ☐ YES ☐ NO ☐ UNK | 12. MARITAL STATUS (at Time of Death) | 7. DATE OF DEATH mm/dd/ccyy | 8. HOUR (24 Hours) |

| 13. EDUCATION --- Highest Level/Degree (see worksheet on back) | 14/15. WAS DECEDENT SPANISH/HISPANIC/LATINO? (If yes, see worksheet on back.) ☐ YES ☐ NO | 16. DECEDENT'S RACE --- Up to 3 races may be listed (see worksheet on back) |

| 17. USUAL OCCUPATION --- Type of work for most of life. DO NOT USE RETIRED | 18. KIND OF BUSINESS OR INDUSTRY (e.g., grocery store, road construction, employment agency, etc.) | 19. YEARS IN OCCUPATION |

USUAL RESIDENCE

| 20. DECEDENT'S RESIDENCE (Street and number or location) |

| 21. CITY | 22. COUNTY/PROVINCE | 23. ZIP CODE | 24. YEARS IN COUNTY | 25. STATE/FOREIGN COUNTRY |

INFORMANT

| 26. INFORMANT'S NAME, RELATIONSHIP | 27. INFORMANT'S MAILING ADDRESS (Street and number or rural route number, city or town, state, ZIP) |

SPOUSE AND PARENT INFORMATION

| 28. NAME OF SURVIVING SPOUSE --- FIRST | 29. MIDDLE | 30. LAST (Maiden Name) | |

| 31. NAME OF FATHER --- FIRST | 32. MIDDLE | 33. LAST | 34. BIRTH STATE |

| 35. NAME OF MOTHER --- FIRST | 36. MIDDLE | 37. LAST (Maiden) | 38. BIRTH STATE |

FUNERAL DIRECTOR/ LOCAL REGISTRAR

| 39. DISPOSITION DATE mm/dd/ccyy | 40. PLACE OF FINAL DISPOSITION | |

| 41. TYPE OF DISPOSITION(S) | 42. SIGNATURE OF EMBALMER | 43. LICENSE NUMBER |

| 44. NAME OF FUNERAL ESTABLISHMENT | 45. LICENSE NUMBER | 46. SIGNATURE OF LOCAL REGISTRAR | 47. DATE mm/dd/ccyy |

PLACE OF DEATH

| 101. PLACE OF DEATH | 102. IF HOSPITAL, SPECIFY ONE ☐ IP ☐ ER/OP ☐ DOA | 103. IF OTHER THAN HOSPITAL, SPECIFY ONE ☐ Hospice ☐ Nursing Home/LTC ☐ Decedent's Home ☐ Other |

| 104. COUNTY | 105. FACILITY ADDRESS OR LOCATION WHERE FOUND (Street and number or location) | 106. CITY |

CAUSE OF DEATH

107. CAUSE OF DEATH	Enter the chain of events --- diseases, injuries, or complications --- that directly caused death. DO NOT enter terminal events such as cardiac arrest, respiratory arrest, or ventricular fibrillation without showing the etiology. DO NOT ABBREVIATE.	Time Interval Between Onset and Death	108. DEATH REPORTED TO CORONER? ☐ YES ☐ NO REFERRAL NUMBER
IMMEDIATE CAUSE (Final disease or condition resulting in death) → (A)		(AT)	
Sequentially, list conditions, if any, leading to cause on Line A. Enter UNDERLYING CAUSE (disease or injury that initiated the events resulting in death) LAST (B)		(BT)	109. BIOPSY PERFORMED? ☐ YES ☐ NO
(C)		(CT)	110. AUTOPSY PERFORMED? ☐ YES ☐ NO
(D)		(DT)	111. USED IN DETERMINING CAUSE? ☐ YES ☐ NO

| 112. OTHER SIGNIFICANT CONDITIONS CONTRIBUTING TO DEATH BUT NOT RESULTING IN THE UNDERLYING CAUSE GIVEN IN 107 |

| 113. WAS OPERATION PERFORMED FOR ANY CONDITION IN ITEM 107 OR 112? (If yes, list type of operation and date.) | 113A. IF FEMALE, PREGNANT IN LAST YEAR? ☐ YES ☐ NO ☐ UNK |

PHYSICIAN'S CERTIFICATION

| 114. I CERTIFY THAT TO THE BEST OF MY KNOWLEDGE DEATH OCCURRED AT THE HOUR, DATE, AND PLACE STATED FROM THE CAUSES STATED. Decedent Attended Since / Decedent Last Seen Alive (A) mm/dd/ccyy (B) mm/dd/ccyy | 115. SIGNATURE AND TITLE OF CERTIFIER | 116. LICENSE NUMBER | 117. DATE mm/dd/ccyy |
| | 118. TYPE ATTENDING PHYSICIAN'S NAME, MAILING ADDRESS, ZIP CODE | | |

CORONER'S USE ONLY

| 119. I CERTIFY THAT IN MY OPINION DEATH OCCURRED AT THE HOUR, DATE, AND PLACE STATED FROM THE CAUSES STATED. MANNER OF DEATH ☐ Natural ☐ Accident ☐ Homicide ☐ Suicide ☐ Pending Investigation ☐ Could not be determined | 120. INJURED AT WORK? ☐ YES ☐ NO ☐ UNK | 121. INJURY DATE mm/dd/ccyy | 122. HOUR (24 Hours) |

| 123. PLACE OF INJURY (e.g., home, construction site, wooded area, etc.) |

| 124. DESCRIBE HOW INJURY OCCURRED (Events which resulted in injury) |

| 125. LOCATION OF INJURY (Street and number, or location, and city, and ZIP) |

| 126. SIGNATURE OF CORONER / DEPUTY CORONER | 127. DATE mm/dd/ccyy | 128. TYPE NAME, TITLE OF CORONER / DEPUTY CORONER |

| STATE REGISTRAR | A | B | C | D | E | | FAX AUTH. # | CENSUS TRACT |

FIGURE 22.2 Death Certificate. (Author's file)

Confirmation of the location of the remains should be made as post-interment actions may have resulted in removal and other disposition of the remains that are not reflected in the initial investigation or records available to investigators. In some cases, family members may have disinterred the remains for reburial at another location at a later date. This information may be available from the cemetery or from city or county health department.

- Determine what treatments were applied to the remains.
  - Embalmed?
  - Cremated?
  - Buried without embalming?

VISIT THE CEMETERY AND GRAVE LOCATION

Prior to an exhumation, cold case investigators may seek to visit the cemetery and grave location, and to meet with representatives of the cemetery. Investigators may seek to review cemetery records if these records are available, although a court order may be necessary. Most burial requirements are regulated at the state level, and these vary from state to state. Similarly, recordkeeping systems and retention policies may also vary.

Depending on age, remaining paper records may be in the format of the whole file, or could be a book summary or card file only. During this review, investigators should seek to identify:

- Names in these records that are not found in the case investigation file.
- Who paid for the funeral and/or burial expenses.
- *Visitor's Log.* This document is normally returned to the family at the conclusion of services, and cold case investigators may ask family members for this log for investigative review. This document could be reviewed with selected family members to identify friends, associates, or other relations to the victim.
- *Arrangement Sheets.* These list relatives down to grandchildren, and include information from family members for death certificate, planning of services, etc.
- Type of burial container. Was it a metal coffin or a wood coffin? A vault is a concrete enclosure into which is placed the coffin. This in turn is covered by a concrete lid. This may factor into preservation of the remains after passage of time and soil and moisture conditions. In addition, coffins may have gaskets or seals. Lesser expensive coffins, whether metal or wood, may lack these seals and this may affect preservation of remains.
- Any permits for burial or other disposition, including transfer of remains.
- Copies of any checks written for cemetery services.
- Copies of any worksheets.
- Logs of family conversations, i.e., any problems or other concerns.
- *Removal Sheet.* This is the form cemetery personnel fill out when they pick up the body for transport to the cemetery. This will contain vital information, including social security number, when deceased was last seen by physician, name of primary physician, time of death, next of kin, and personal effects on the body if brought in.
- *Hospital Sheet.* Vital information from hospital containing much of the same information as the Removal Sheet. This serves as a double check for the Removal Sheet.
- *Clothing Sheet.* Clothing brought in by family for dressing the deceased.
- Name of the "Case Arranger." This is the cemetery person who oversees the interment process. It may be beneficial to inquire if any photographs were taken, or whether there was media coverage at the time of the service.
- Name of the Funeral Director. This person handles the funeral as set up per the Case Arranger.

APPLICATION AND PERMIT FOR DISPOSITION OF HUMAN REMAINS

USE BLACK INK ONLY — MAKE NO ERASURES, WHITEOUTS OR OTHER ALTERATIONS

1A. NAME OF DECEDENT—FIRST (GIVEN)	1B. MIDDLE	1C. LAST (FAMILY)	2. DATE OF BIRTH MONTH, DAY, YEAR	3. DATE OF DEATH MONTH, DAY, YEAR	4. SEX

5A. CITY OF DEATH	5B. COUNTY OF DEATH — OUTSIDE CALIF., ENTER STATE	6. NAME, RELATIONSHIP, FULL MAILING ADDRESS AND ZIP CODE OF INFORMANT

7A. TYPED NAME AND ADDRESS OF CALIFORNIA - FUNERAL DIRECTOR OR PERSON ACTING AS SUCH	7B. CALIF. LICENSE NUMBER — IF APPLICABLE

8A. SIGNATURE OF APPLICANT—Person taking permit | 8B. DATE SIGNED

ACKNOWLEDGEMENT OF APPLICANT — I hereby acknowledge as applicant that the proposed disposition stated herein is one of the dispositions authorized by Section 103055 of the Health and Safety Code, and was authorized pursuant to Section 7100 of the Health and Safety Code. ▶

PERMIT

AUTHORIZATION OF LOCAL REGISTRAR

ANY CHANGE IN DISPOSITION REQUIRES A NEW PERMIT TO SHOW FINAL DISPOSITION

THIS PERMIT IS ISSUED IN ACCORDANCE WITH PROVISIONS OF THE CALIFORNIA HEALTH AND SAFETY CODE AND IS THE AUTHORITY FOR THE DISPOSITION SPECIFIED IN THIS PERMIT. NOTE: THIS PERMIT GIVES NO RIGHT OF DISPOSAL OUTSIDE OF CALIFORNIA

9A. AMOUNT OF FEE PAID	9B. DATE PERMIT ISSUED	9C. SIGNATURE OF LOCAL REGISTRAR ISSUING PERMIT ▶

9D. ADDRESS OF REGISTRAR OF DISTRICT OF DEATH — IF DEATH OCCURRED IN CALIFORNIA	9E. ADDRESS OF REGISTRAR OF DISTRICT OF DISPOSITION — IF DISPOSITION IS TO OCCUR IN ANOTHER DISTRICT IN CALIFORNIA

10. AUTHORIZED DISPOSITION(S) CHECK APPLICABLE ITEMS | **FOR CORONER'S USE ONLY**

- A. BURIAL (INCLUDES ENTOMBMENT)
- B. CREMATION
- C. DISPOSITION OF CREMATED REMAINS OTHER THAN IN A CEMETERY
- D. SCIENTIFIC USE
- E. TEMPORARY ENVAULTMENT
- F. DISINTERMENT
- G. SHIP IN TO CALIFORNIA
- D. TRANSIT TO OUTSIDE OF CALIFORNIA
- I. DISPOSITION PENDING — REMAINS LOCATED AT (Name and Address)

COMPLETE ALL APPLICABLE ITEMS

BURIAL	11A. NAME AND ADDRESS OF CALIFORNIA CEMETERY	11B. DATE BURIED	11C. SIGNATURE OF PERSON IN CHARGE OF BURIAL ▶
CREMATION	12A. NAME AND ADDRESS OF CALIFORNIA CREMATORY	12B. DATE CREMATED	12C. SIGNATURE OF PERSON IN CHARGE OF CREMATION ▶
SCIENTIFIC USE	13A. NAME AND ADDRESS OF CALIFORNIA FACILITY RECEIVING REMAINS	13B. DATE RECEIVED	13C. SIGNATURE OF PERSON IN CHARGE OF FACILITY ▶
TRANSIT	14A. NAME AND ADDRESS IN RECEIVING STATE OR COUNTRY WHERE REMAINS OR CREMATED REMAINS ARE TO BE SHIPPED	14B. DATE SHIPPED	14C. ADDRESS AND SIGNATURE OF PERSON IN CHARGE OF PLACING WITH THE CARRIER ▶
SCATTERING/BURIAL AT SEA OR DISPOSITION OTHER THAN IN A CEMETERY	15A. ADDRESS, NEAREST POINT ON SHORELINE, OR OTHER DESCRIPTION SUFFICIENT TO IDENTIFY FINAL PLACE AND CA DISTRICT OF DISPOSITION. IF BURIAL AT SEA, ONLY ENTER LATITUDE AND LONGITUDE	15B. DATE OF DISPOSITION	15C. SIGNATURE OF PERSON IN CHARGE OF DISPOSITION ▶ / 15D. LICENSE NUMBER OF CREMATED REMAINS DISPOSER — IF APPLICABLE

COPY 1 OF THE PERMIT ACCOMPANIES THE REMAINS TO THE STATED PLACE OF DISPOSITION. THE PERSON IN CHARGE OF DISPOSITION IS RESPONSIBLE FOR COMPLETING AND FORWARDING THE PERMIT WITHIN 10 DAYS OF DISPOSITION TO THE REGISTRAR OF THE DISTRICT IN WHICH DISPOSITION OCCURRED OR THE DISTRICT NEAREST THE POINT WHERE THE CREMATED REMAINS WERE SCATTERED AT SEA. THE LOCAL REGISTRAR MAY DESTROY ANY ORIGINAL OR DUPLICATE PERMIT AFTER ONE YEAR FROM ISSUE DATE.

COPY 1   STATE OF CALIFORNIA, DEPARTMENT OF HEALTH SERVICES, OFFICE OF STATE REGISTRAR   VS9 (REV. 3/03)

FIGURE 22.3 Forensic exhumation and disinterrment may require permits as well as a separate permit to re-inter the remains. (Author's file)

- Other persons who are involved in arrangements and interment. Some institutions have a "Super Director" who handles both mortuary and cemetery aspects, but this varies from place to place.
- *Embalming Report.* This report describes the physical condition and review of the body and its preparation for interment.

By meeting with cemetery personnel, investigators might establish a single liaison person, someone with the authority to get things done. Keep in mind that cemetery personnel may be sensitive to the image or negative publicity aspects of disinterment procedures. In addition, they may have concerns regarding publicity, security, etc. Any disinterment is usually done in view of the visiting public or ongoing interment services, and investigators should be cognizant of these concerns.

When meeting with these representatives, cold case investigators should seek to identify specific permits, procedures, or other costs associated with disinterment and re-interment (see Figure 22.3). Among the permits that may be required are:

- City exhumation permit.
- County health department exhumation permit.

FIGURE 22.4 Backhoe. Depending upon burial circumstances, specialized equipment may be necessary for ease of exhumation. Check with the cemetery prior to exhumation to determine the necessity for any specialized equipment. (Courtesy of Connie Milton, San Diego County Sheriff's Department)

- Separate re-interment permit.
- Other permits or fees.
- An exhumation may require use of cemetery personnel and specialized equipment, including backhoes (see Figure 22.4). Investigators should inquire whether the cemetery will absorb the cost of the disinterment and re-interment, or whether the law enforcement agency will be responsible for these costs (and these costs must be approved *before* you start digging). In some cases, the cemetery may absorb the costs of the procedures when ordered to do so by court order, but will charge when requested to do so by consent of family member.

Observations at the Grave

- Soil moisture and drainage. Is the grave in a swampy location where water accumulates or is it in a location that has good drainage?
- Water-table level. Swampy?
- Vegetation. Are there trees or tree roots crowding the grave location?
- Soil conditions. Is the gravesite collapsed or does it appear flat and level?
- Any other obstacles that may inhibit or complicate the exhumation process?

DRAFTING THE REQUEST FOR A FORENSIC EXHUMATION

This is a process with significant legal considerations that should be accomplished with the support and assistance of a deputy district attorney or similar counterpart. A representative of this office may wish to be present at the exhumation. The specific format can vary, depending upon local rules and procedures, but a good rule of thumb when considering drafting a request for an exhumation and an application for a court order is to think of it as an affidavit in support for a search warrant. As such, the purpose is to lay out for the magistrate what you want to do, where you want to do it, and why you want to do it. This would include:

- Name of affiant.
- Position or title of affiant.

- Location where property (remains) is sought.
- Reason for affiant's belief that the property (remains) sought is at the subject location.
- Persons authorized or permitted to take part in the exhumation procedure, sampling, or forensic examination and testing procedures.
- Description of property sought. This may indicate the actions to be taken at the exhumation, including whether the remains are to be examined on scene or removed to another location. If the remains are to be removed to another location, this should be spelled out in the affidavit, including who is to take custody of the remains, where they are specifically to be removed to, and the purpose to which the remains will be subjected, i.e., forensic anthropological examination, removal of biological matter for DNA testing purposes, etc.
- Re-interment considerations.
- Statement of probable cause. This is the narrative that explains to the judge the history of the case and why this exhumation is necessary. This would include:
- A summary of the initial investigation, including names, dates, and events.
- A summary of any follow-up investigations after the initial investigation.
- A summary of the re-activation of the case, including names, dates, and events leading to the request for an order for exhumation
- Why the exhumation is necessary. This would include description of what examinations, if any, were previously conducted upon the remains, and why the proposed examinations are to be conducted at this time (i.e., advances in DNA technology, etc). If necessary, investigators may also wish to include a discussion of the technology to educate the magistrate in this area.
- Other information as dictated by specific case factors or legal considerations.
- Date of affidavit.
- Signature of affiant.

THE COURT ORDER

A court order should be issued by the court with jurisdiction to do so, preferably a Superior Court. The order would be issued in the name of the People of the State, similar to that of a search warrant. Included within a court order for exhumation would be (see Figure 22.5):

- Name of the body to be exhumed.
- Name of cemetery, memorial park, or other location from which body is to be exhumed.
- Specific location, including street address and plot or gravesite identifying number from which body is to be exhumed.
- Specifically define who (i.e., representative of Medical Examiner's Office) will take a part of the remains graveside, or, if necessary, orders that the remains, or parts thereof, be transported to a specific location (i.e., Medical Examiner's Office, crime laboratory, or other location described by address) for the needed examination (and DNA testing, if applicable).
- upon completion of examination and testing, orders the remains of (name of body) to be re-interred at the identified cemetery at its original location.

The Exhumation

- Normally, the removal of the earth above the coffin is accomplished by heavy equipment or by laborers using hand tools.
- Specialized equipment may be required to remove a cement cap overlying the top of the vault or coffin, if present.

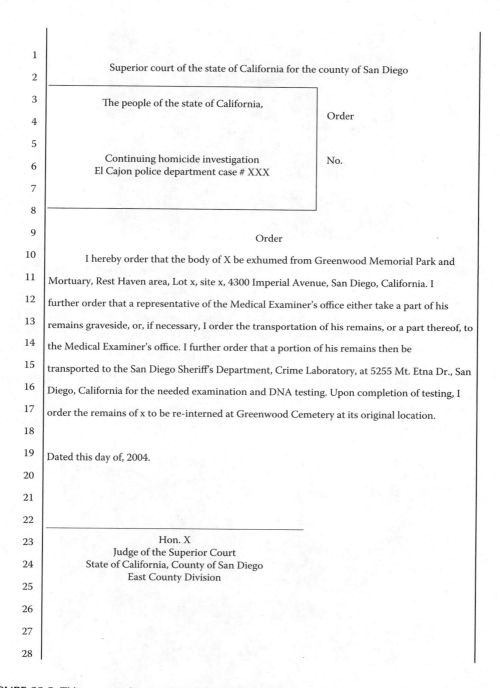

1

2 Superior court of the state of California for the county of San Diego

3   The people of the state of California,

4   Order

5

6   Continuing homicide investigation   No.
           El Cajon police department case # XXX

7

8

9   Order

10   I hereby order that the body of X be exhumed from Greenwood Memorial Park and

11 Mortuary, Rest Haven area, Lot x, site x, 4300 Imperial Avenue, San Diego, California. I

12 further order that a representative of the Medical Examiner's office either take a part of his

13 remains graveside, or, if necessary, I order the transportation of his remains, or a part thereof, to

14 the Medical Examiner's office. I further order that a portion of his remains then be

15 transported to the San Diego Sheriff's Department, Crime Laboratory, at 5255 Mt. Etna Dr., San

16 Diego, California for the needed examination and DNA testing. Upon completion of testing, I

17 order the remains of x to be re-interned at Greenwood Cemetery at its original location.

18

19 Dated this day of, 2004.

20

21

22

23   Hon. X
                    Judge of the Superior Court
24   State of California, County of San Diego
                      East County Division
25

26

27

28

FIGURE 22.5 This court order mandates that the body be removed from a described location under the auspices of a representative of the Medical Examiner's Office, or that a portion of the remains be removed and transported to the sheriff's department crime laboratory. The order further states that, upon completion of the examination, the remains be reinterred at the original location. (Courtesy of Deputy District Attorney Dan Lamborn, San Diego County District Attorney's Office)

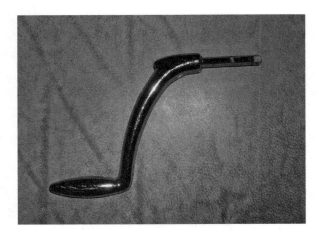

FIGURE 22.6 A coffin key may be necessary to open a locked coffin. This universal tool may be available from the cemetery. (Courtesy of Daniel Williams)

- Arrangements for opening the coffin should be negotiated and understood between law enforcement personnel and cemetery personnel. Knowledge of burial container type is of importance, as in some cases, a coffin key may be required to unlock the casket . (Figure 22.6). This is a universal tool used to secure casket lids.
- Assure that all properly equipped and authorized personnel are present at the appointed time and place, and understand their role.
  - Medical examiner's or coroner's representative to physically handle the remains.
  - Are the remains to be removed fully, or samples to be taken at the gravesite? (Figure 22.7)

FIGURE 22.7 An exhumation should be conducted with dignity. A forensic exhumation and transportation of the remains for forensic purposes constitute a solemn procedure necessitating respect by all parties. In the "Boulder Jane Doe" case, a local mortuary donated the services of a hearse to respectfully transport her remains for processing. (Courtesy of Detective Steve Ainsworth, Boulder County, Colorado, Sheriff's Office)

Recording the Exhumation

Record names of all persons present.

Make a photographic record.

Prepare written reports in accordance with standard reporting procedures, including date, time, and other information detailing the exhumation process.

Note any unusual conditions or observations encountered during the exhumation.

The Embalming Process

For many homicide investigators, knowledge or involvement in the disposition of the remains post autopsy are minimal. The embalming process is essentially a preservation and disinfection procedure applied to the body after the autopsy and prior to interment. This procedure results in additional trauma and alteration of the body, and may be of significant importance to later cold case investigators. It is usually accomplished in three steps.

Step One. The body is positioned and the features are set. This stage includes eye and mouth closure. The mouth is wired or sewn shut, eye caps are set under the eyes and hands are set properly. Factors included in this process include the amount of trauma, cause, and manner of death. Different scenarios require different fluid mixtures.

Step 2. An incision is made above the clavicle and the carotid artery is raised and a small incision is made in the jugular vein. A canula from the embalming machine (Figure 22.8) is placed into the incision and embalming fluid is injected into the body through the carotid while at the same time blood is drained out thru the vein. About 3 gallons of fluid, a formaldehyde and water mix, is usually put into body. The body is bathed, cleansed, and massaged for even distribution of the fluid.

FIGURE 22.8 Embalming Machine. (Courtesy of Daniel Williams)

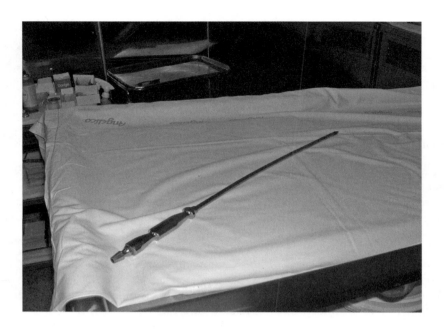

FIGURE 22.9 Trocar. (Courtesy of Daniel Williams)

Step 3. The third stage in this process occurs when a trocar is inserted into the abdomen approximately two fingers above the navel. This is a long instrument hooked up to an aspirator (see Figure 22.9). The main internal organs, including heart, lungs, liver, and intestines are aspirated and full-strength cavity fluid is injected into the cavity for preservation and disinfection. Once this is done, incisions are sewn and sealed and the body is cleansed. Head hair is washed, the body is bathed and dried, the hair is dried and ready for dressing and application of appropriate cosmetics.

During the embalming process, not all blood is drained out and some remains with fluid. Embalming and burial practices vary, and embalming is not required by law in some states.

In addition, embalming may bring out bruises not necessarily noticed during previous examinations. After embalming, bitemarks may remain visible, although there may be a lesser chance for their survival in an unembalmed body.

The Embalming Report

This report records information about the body at time of receipt by the embalmer and the procedures and processes subsequently utilized (Figure 22.10 and Figure 22.11). In addition to recording the date and case number, it will further report:

- Identification of the Deceased
  - Name
  - Gender
  - Age
  - Eye and Hair Color
  - Estimated Height and Weight

IDENTIFICATION:

Embalming Report

Date: _____   Case Number: _____

Deceased Name: _____   I.D. Tag Present: No ☐ Yes ☐

Gender: _____ Age: _____   Estimated Weight: _____   Estimated Height: _____

Color of Eyes: _____   Color of Hair: _____   Beard/Mustache? No ☐ Yes ☐

Place of Death: _____   Date of Death: _____   Time: 0:00 AM

Removed From: _____   Date Removed: _____   Time: _____

Removed By: _____   Personal Effects? No ☐ Yes ☐ See HMIS

Elapsed Time between Death and Embalming _____

Receiving Location: Greenwood Memorial Park & Mortuary

CONDITION OF DECEASED PRIOR TO EMBALMING DECEASED:

☐ Normal   ☐ Emaciated   ☐ Lividity   ☐ Purge   ☐ Jaundice
☐ Edema   ☐ Skin Slip   ☐ Pacemaker   ☐ Tissue Gas   ☐ Rigor Mortis   ☐ IV Leakage
☐ Organ Donor (skin) (eyes) (bone) (internal organs)
☐ Autopsy (full) (thoracic) (abdominal) (cranial)

Mutilations Present: _____

Discolorations: _____

Identifying Marks: _____

* Use Anatomic Outline Chart To Indicate Body Areas affected and general comments

Deceased Refrigerated? No ☐ Yes ☐ How Long? _____

DISINFECTION:

☐ Eyes   ☐ Other body orifices   ☐ Body orifices packed
☐ Nose   ☐ Deceased bathed with antiseptic soap
☐ Mouth   ☐ Hair Washed

POSING FEATURES:

Mouth Closure: ☐ Suture   Mouth Shaping: ☐ Natural   Eye Closure: ☐ Cotton
               ☐ Needle Injector   ☐ Dentures   ☐ Eye Caps
               ☐ Other   ☐ Mouth Former   ☐ Stay Cream
                                                ☐ Other   ☐ Donor

EMBALMING TECHNIQUE:

Arteries Injected: Veins Drained:

Carotid	☐ Right	☐ Left	Iliac	☐ Right	☐ Left	Jugular	☐ Right	☐ Left
Subclavian	☐ Right	☐ Left	Femoral	☐ Right	☐ Left	Axillary	☐ Right	☐ Left
Axillary	☐ Right	☐ Left	Radial	☐ Right	☐ Left	Iliac	☐ Right	☐ Left
Brachial	☐ Right	☐ Left	Ulnar	☐ Right	☐ Left	Femoral	☐ Right	☐ Left

Injection Pressure: _____ lbs.   Rate of Flow: ☐ slight ☐ ¼ ☐ ½ ☐ Full

Injection Method: Drainage Method:
☐ Intermittent ☐ Continuous   ☐ Intermittent ☐ Continuous ☐ Restricted ☐ Heart Tap

Condition of Arteries: _____   Drainage Received: _____

FLUID DILUTIONS: ### BRAND OF FLUID & TOTAL CONCENTRATE USED:

Pre/Co injection: _____ Oz. _____ Gal.; Index _____   Pre/Co Injection: _____ Oz. ____

1st Injection: _____ Oz. _____ Gal.; Index _____   Arterial: _____ Oz. ____

2nd Injection: _____ Oz. _____ Gal.; Index _____   Humectant: _____ Oz. ____

3rd Injection: _____ Oz. _____ Gal.; Index _____   Dye: _____ Oz. ____

                                                   Other: _____ Oz. ____

CAVITY TREATMENT:

☐ Hydro Aspirator   ☐ Trocar Button
☐ Electric Aspirator   ☐ Suture

Condition of Abdominal Area: _____

Total Cavity Chemical Used: Oz.: _____   Index: _____   Fluid Name: _____

Were Cavities Treated Immediately Following Arterial Injection? ☐ Yes ☐ If No, How Long? _____

Total Cavity Chemical Used (Autopsy): Oz.: _____ Index: _____ Fluid Name: _____

Total Cavity Chemical Used (Viscera): Oz.: _____ Index: _____ Fluid Name: _____

Chemical Powder: ☐ Yes ☐ No

FIGURE 22.10 This report provides information about post-autopsy processing of the remains. (Courtesy of Daniel Williams)

- Date of Death
- Place of Death
- Date Removed
- Removed From
- Removed By

ANATOMIC OUTLINE CHART

Deceased Name————————————————— Case #—————————————————

Please indicate on chart all identifying scars, incisions, tattoos, and special body characteristics

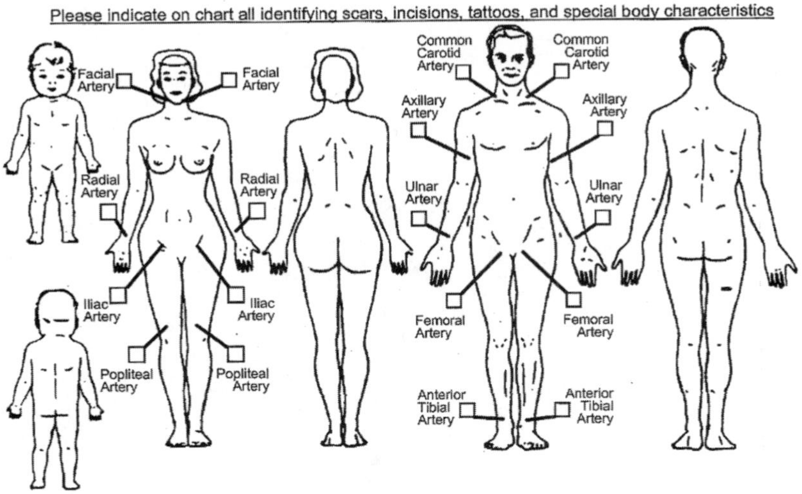

1-Embalming Incision	11-Jaundice	21-Amputation	31-Livor Mortis
2-Trocar Entry	12-Pacemaker Removed? Yes/No	22-Birthmark	32-Mutilation
3-Discoloration	13-Purge	23-Burn	33-Odor
4-Autopsy Incision	14-Emaciation	24-Cast	34-Tissue Donations
5-Catheter/IV	15-Open Sores	25-Decomposition	35-Tracheotomy
6-Skin Slip	16-Organ Donation Trauma	26-Decubitus Ulcers	36-Traumatic Wound
7-Edema	17-Surgical Incision	27-Dehydration	37-Tumor
8-Catheter Urinary	18-Surgical Staples	28-Ecchymosis (no swelling)	38————
9-Gas	19-Tattoo	29-Hematoma (swollen)	39————
10-Scar	20-Rigor Mortis	30-IV Leak	40————

Plastic Garments Used: Yes —— No——   Type Used:_____

Dry Chemicals Used: Yes —— No ——   Type Used: ———————— Quantity Used: —————

ADDITIONAL REMARKS AND COMMENTS CONCERNING CASE:

_____

_____

_____

Embalmer's Signature ———————————————— License #————— Date—————

Provisional Embalmer's/Apprentice's Signature ——————— License #————— Date—————

Dressed by Signature ————————————————————— Date—————

Casketed By Signature ———————————————————— Date—————

Cosmetized by Signature ———————————————————— Date—————

FIGURE 22.11 This portion of the embalming report provides further information about procedures affecting the remains. (Courtesy of Daniel Williams)

- Personal Effects
- Elapsed Time Between Death and Embalming
- Receiving Location
- Condition of Deceased Prior To Embalming
  - Normal

- Edema
- Emaciated
- Skin Slip
- Lividity
- Pacemaker
- Purge
- Tissue Gas
- Jaundice
- Rigor Mortis
- IV Leakage
- Organ Donor
- Autopsy
- Mutilations Present
- Discolorations
- Identifying Marks
- Was Deceased Refrigerated

Disinfection treatments, posing features, and embalming techniques will be further reported and described in detail. Note that additional information may include:

- Plastic garments used (yes/no) and type
- Dry chemicals used (yes/no) and type
- Embalmer's signature and license number and date
- Provisional embalmer's/apprentice's signature and date
- Dressed by signature and date
- Casketed by signature and date
- Cosmetized by signature and date

Finding Usable DNA

The ability to extract usable DNA after burial is dependent upon numerous factors. These factors may include:

- Degradation due to severe deterioration of all biological matter. Such deterioration may be brought about through:
  - Extreme or long-term moisture.
  - Extreme or long-term heat.
  - Soil conditions.
  - Severe physical decomposition prior to burial.
  - Degree of severity of decomposition after burial (Figure 22.12).

Desirable locations for successful retrieval of DNA after burial include bone, teeth, fingernails, and toenails (Figure 22.13).

Bone and teeth require significant additional processing prior to DNA analysis. Fingernails or toenails may assist in expediting DNA analysis. Hair is often a source of last resort for successful DNA retrieval. The embalming process should not interfere with the ability to extract viable DNA, especially when the primary samples used for DNA analysis from exhumed remains are bone, teeth, fingernails or toenails. The embalming fluid is not going to enter these samples to any

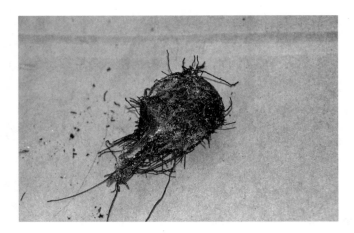

FIGURE 22.12 This portion of the femur removed during a forensic exhumation from unembalmed remains illustrates a concern for degradation of DNA, as very little bone material remains. Note the roots. (Courtesy of Connie Milton, San Diego County Sheriff's Department)

significant degree. In addition, deep muscle tissues, if present, may also provide successful DNA results (Figure 22.14).

Figures 22.15 and 22.16 illustrate the conditions that investigators may encounter due to differences in burial containers and embalming.

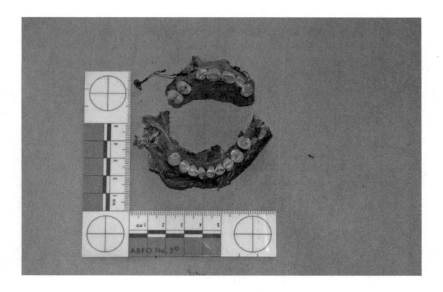

FIGURE 22.13 The pulp within teeth may offer a remaining source of DNA. Teeth and bone, however, require significant additional processing by the laboratory in order to attempt to extract DNA. (Courtesy of Connie Milton, San Diego County Sheriff's Department)

FIGURE 22.14 This femur from an embalmed body was removed during a forensic exhumation and was a good source of DNA. (Courtesy of Connie Milton, San Diego County Sheriff's Department)

FIGURE 22.15 This figure illustrates remains exhumed after 30 years. The person was embalmed and buried in a metal casket.

FIGURE 22.16 This female was not embalmed and was buried in a wooden coffin. (Courtesy of Connie Milton, San Diego County Sheriff's Department)

CASE STUDY: "BOULDER JANE DOE"

In April 1954, while hiking near Boulder, Colorado, two college students discovered the nude body of a 19–20-year-old female. A pathologist later concluded that the victim had been alive when thrown down an almost 30-foot embankment into Boulder Creek. She suffered a skull fracture and numerous broken bones, and, when found, had been ravaged by animals. No identifying features except for an appendectomy scar were discovered, and she had no fillings in her teeth that might offer assistance for dental records at the time.

News of the discovery and lack of identity of this person became a major story for the Boulder and Denver newspapers. These records preserved in-depth details about the victim, the circumstances, and names of those involved in the discovery and investigation. A local pathologist performed an autopsy, and the Coroner held a *Coroner's Inquest* that ultimately concluded that the victim died "… from shock caused by severe beating by person or persons unknown, with felonious intent."

Ultimately, no clothing or murder weapon was found, and she was listed as simply "unidentified woman." According to Boulder-area historian and newspaper columnist, Silvia Pettem, local towns-people, in the spirit of the Mountain West, took up a collection to buy her a plot in the Columbia Cemetery and marked her final resting place with a granite marker (Figure 22.17). The casket was donated by a local mortuary and a Catholic priest donated his time for the funeral service. Unfortunately, she is one of an unknown number of "John" and "Jane Does" whose cases have long gone unsolved.

For nearly a decade, Silvia Pettem had been interested in the case and had compiled newspaper accounts of it. In the course of her research, she utilized original newspaper narrative descriptions and photographs of the crime scene to relocate the homicide location from almost 50 years before (Figure 22.18 and Figure 22.19).

FIGURE 22.17 Boulder Jane Doe headstone. (Courtesy of Detective Steve Ainsworth, Boulder County Sheriff's Office, Boulder, Colorado)

In September, 2003, knowing of the advances in forensic technology, Pettem approached the Boulder County Sheriff's Office and inquired whether it would be possible for the body to be exhumed and possibly identified. A search of the sheriff's files found no remaining records or evidence (not unusual after such a length of time in many jurisdictions although it was suspected that this and other cases had been removed several decades before by a disgruntled official), and investigators began reconstructing the cold case homicide almost from scratch.

They discovered that the pathologist who conducted the original autopsy, one of only a few surviving original persons in this case, was still alive. At age 85, he still retained his copy of his autopsy report. In addition, the investigators discovered the *Coroner's Inquest report*. These documents, coupled with appropriate interviews and detailed newspaper accounts became the basis for the reactivation of this cold case homicide.

The *news media* picked up the case, and donations to defray the costs of exhumation and forensic analysis were donated by the community. Ms. Pettem learned of the services of the Vidocq Society from the Department of Justice and made inquiry of this organization for possible assistance in the investigation. Forensic specialists associated with the Vidocq Society responded to assist the local authorities, and the body was exhumed. The following is the affidavit that became the basis for a court order for the exhumation.

FIGURE 22.18 The original site as it appeared in the April 9, 1954 edition of the *Rocky Mountain News*. This caption reported "Jim "James" Andes (left) and Wayne Swanson pointing out the rock where they found the nude battered body of a young girl. The two Colorado University freshmen from Illinois found the body during a warm-afternoon hike along Boulder Creek. Note the rock formation and water level. At this time, the region had been in a lengthy drought. (Reprinted with the permission of *Rocky Mountain News*.)

FIGURE 22.19 Historian-journalist Silvia Pettem based her search on detailed newspaper accounts that reported the location as 300 yards from a known location along a described roadway. In her quest, Ms. Pettem consulted highway maintenance records and learned that the last major improvement on this gravel road occurred when it was regraded in 1953, 1 year before the crime. She located the river site, and then used original newspaper photographs to compare rock formations then and now. (Courtesy of Silvia Pettem)

AFFIDAVIT FOR SEARCH WARRANT

The affiant is Detective Steven G. Ainsworth, a duly commissioned officer of the Boulder County Sheriff's Office. The affiant has been in law enforcement continuously since 1977 and has investigated in excess of 350 death of all manners, including homicides. The affiant also is a certified death investigator certified through the Colorado Coroner's Association, and has attended numerous courses on death investigation, including homicides. The affiant, being duly sworn, deposes and states:

On October 2, 2003, I met with Detective Lieutenant Phil West, a duly commissioned officer of the Boulder County Sheriff's Office, and Silvia Pettem, a local author. Pettem had newspaper articles detailing an apparent homicide of a female whose body was found 300 feet east of Boulder Falls in the creek bed of Boulder Creek, in Boulder Canyon, County of Boulder, State of Colorado. The female's nude body was found by two CU students on April 8, 1954, according to the newspaper accounts. Also, according to newspaper accounts, the pathologist who performed the autopsy, Dr. Freburn L. James, said the victim had been dead from three to seven days. The accounts were photocopies printed in *The Denver Post, The Rocky Mountain News*, and *The Boulder Daily Camera*. The case was never solved and the victim remains unidentified. Pettem's reasoning for giving us this information was to determine if there was a possibility that the victim could be identified and a possible suspect identified through technological advances which have been made since 1954. Pettem told us, and newspaper accounts bear out the fact that the victim was buried on April 22, 1954 at the Columbia Cemetery bounded by Pleasant and College Streets on the north and south respectively, and Ninth and Eighth Streets on the east and west sides, in the City of Boulder, County of Boulder, State of Colorado. Additionally, I found a *Record Of Funeral*, serial number 7896 generated by Howe Mortuary of Boulder which details the expenses and arrangements for the funeral of "Unidentified Murdered Girl" buried on April 22, 1954. The cemetery indicated on the form is "Columbia."

Pettem also produced a photocopy of a handwritten verdict of a coroner's inquest which is attached to and incorporated herein by reference. The inquest verdict, across the top of which is handwritten "Verdict of Jury", was that the death of the unidentified woman was due to shock "caused by a severe beating by person or persons unknown, with felonious intent." I obtained a copy of the unidentified victim's death certificate from the Boulder County Coroner's Office, issued by the State of Colorado. It states the victim's death was a homicide, "caused by shock and exposure to fracture of skull, fracture of left arm, fracture of 4 ribs left, multiple abrasions." It also states the injuries occurred "near Boulder, Boulder County, Colo." and was signed on April 21, 1954 by George W Howe, Coroner.

Lt. West, Pettem, and I went to the Colorado State Archives to attempt to locate Boulder County Sheriff reports and/or Boulder County Coroner reports which document the homicide, but were unable to locate any. We later went to Columbia Cemetery and Pettem showed us the unidentified victim's grave, which is marked with a black granite headstone with the inscription:

> JANE DOE
> APRIL 1954
> AGE ABOUT
> 20 YEARS.

I noted that the graves on either side, both of which were interred several years later, were sunken, indicating their caskets had broken and collapsed. The Jane Doe grave was relatively even with the surrounding soil, indicating that it had probably not collapsed.

On October 7, 2003, I spoke with Dr. Mike Dobersen, the Arapahoe County Coroner. I know Dr. Dobersen personally and know that he is a board certified forensic pathologist. I asked Dr. Dobersen if he has had any experience with exhuming a body. For the purposes of conducting forensic testing and he told me he has done seven or eight exhumations for that purpose. I asked him if he had an opinion to a reasonable degree of medical certainty if DNA samples would be available and a facial reconstruction would be possible in a body which has been buried for 49 years, as has "Jane Doe". He said one of his exhumations was on a body which had been buried for twenty years and there certainly was enough material in that case. He said that, even if the casket had collapsed over the past forty nine years, the compaction should have been at a slow enough rate as to not crush the skull, enabling a successful reconstruction. Dr. Dobersen also said that mitochondrial DNA would be obtainable from the pulp of a tooth and possibly from the hair and a DNA profile would be obtainable for comparison to a known sample for positive identification purposes.

On October 22, 2003, I went to Howe Mortuary-Boulder and spoke with the owner, Danielle Vandiver about this case. I asked if she could determine from the *Record of Funeral* in what type of casket Jane Doe was buried. She looked at the record and said she did not know but it was probably a cloth covered fiberboard one, as one of the newspaper accounts described it as gray cloth covered. I then showed her a photograph of the graveside service which showed the casket and she said it was a metal one. I also checked Howe's records from that time period and finally found the 1954 records combined in the 1955 file. I found an envelope containing flower cards which were sent to the funeral by several people in the community. There were no other records in the file.

On October 29, 2003, I checked the City of Boulder website and found an interactive site of the Columbia Cemetery. I had previously learned that Columbia is not an active cemetery and is adminis-tered by the City of Boulder Parks Department. I found that, on that website there is an index where one enters the name of the deceased and is able to access location information as well as a photo of the grave. I selected the Js, then "Jane Doe", which took me to a file with a photo of the small granite headstone I had seen personally. It gave the official location as Section B, Lot 015, Grave 3NE. It also brings up a map of the entire cemetery which shows where the queried grave is located. I noted the spot indicated on the map was where I had personally been and had seen the Jane Doe grave.

In researching leads sheets generated in the original case, I found that several reports of missing women had not been properly followed up by today's standards, in that more can be done to determine if the missing person reported is, in fact Jane Doe. I also found at least two entries on the *Doe Network* website of missing women whose physical descriptions and the time of disappearance match Jane Doe. The *Doe Network* is a website dedicated to finding leads in missing persons cases and cases where a body is unidentified. These leads can be narrowed further by characteristics unique to the Jane Doe case, then DNA compared from the old cases to Jane Doe's DNA.

The affiant believes sufficient probable cause has been shown to believe the offense of Murder in the First Degree, contrary to CRS 40-2-1 and 40-2-3, was committed between April 1, 1954 and April 5, 1954 at or about the Boulder Falls area of Boulder Canyon Drive, County of Boulder, State of Colorado by a person or persons unknown.

The affiant further believes that there is specific physical evidence which is located in the plot know as the Jane Doe gravesite, Section B, Lot 015, Grave 3NE at Columbia Cemetery located at Ninth and College Streets, City of Boulder, County of Boulder, State of Colorado, which could be of great assistance in identifying the victim and furthering the criminal investigation of her murder, to wit:

1. The physical remains of Jane Doe
2. Trace evidence

The affiant therefore requests the court issue a warrant authorizing the search of the above named location and seizing the above named evidence from that location at this time.

_____

AFFIANT

Subscribed in my presence and sworn to before me this_____ day of _____, 2003, County of Boulder, State of Colorado

_____

JUDGE

FIGURE 22.20 A forensic exhumation may involve a variety of tools to access the site for further exhumation. (Courtesy of Detective Steve Ainsworth, Boulder County, Colorado, Sheriff's Office)

On February 4, 2004, a World Wide Web page, http://boulderjanedoe.com was launched by Silvia Pettem to solicit information and provide investigative assistance relating to this case.

On June 8, 2004, the exhumation process began. The event was filmed by a camera crew from "America's Most Wanted." Sheriff's personnel and Boulder County forensic anthropologist Beth Conour were assisted and supervised by forensic pathologist Dr. Richard Froede; Dr. Walter Birkby, a forensic anthropologist; and Dr. Robert Goldberg, a medical doctor. A backhoe was used for initial earth movement, but the process soon became a forensic anthropological "dig" (Figures 22.20–22.23).

Fifty years of water and earth movement had caused substantial deterioration of the coffin and disturbance of the remains, and it took 2 days to complete the forensic exhumation.

The recovered bones were released to Dr. Birkby and transported to his Human Identification Laboratory in Tucson, Arizona (see Figure 22.24 and Figure 22.25).

Luck can be a solvability factor in cold case homicide investigation. Due to the publicity, a subject came forward a few months later with a magazine photo that had been taken of the victim while she lay in the morgue (see Figure 22.26). It had reportedly been taken by a university student who worked in the morgue at the time, and published in an "off-campus sex magazine." The photo provided investigators with the only known photo remaining from the original period. Subsequently, other photos surfaced anonymously, but were believed to have been taken by a local newspaper editor at the request of the mortuary.

Re-autopsy, as could be conducted, confirmed the original injuries and identified an additional injury not noted in the coroner's report. The right patella had been fractured, an injury consistent with being struck by a moving automobile. Investigation by Ms. Pettem involved locating an automobile museum and recording measurements of period automobiles. The injuries were consistent with the location of bumper heights found during her investigation. It was subsequently theorized that "Jane Doe" had been struck elsewhere by a vehicle and thrown into the ditch. A simulated reconstruction, utilizing a dummy of approximately the victim's height and weight, resulted in abrasion patterns and a landing position consistent with this theory and manner of disposal.

FIGURE 22.21 Forensic anthropologist Beth Conour of the Boulder County, Colorado, Coroner's Office spent many hours tediously removing dirt to gain access to "Jane Doe." Forensic anthropology work is not always glamorous and conducted inside a laboratory setting. (Courtesy of Detective Steve Ainsworth, Boulder County, Colorado, Sheriff's Office)

FIGURE 22.22 Once the dirt and other material are removed, recovery is a slow process using simple hand tools. Here the hair and remains are recovered. (Courtesy of Detective Steve Ainsworth, Boulder County, Colorado, Sheriff's Office)

FIGURE 22.23 In their attempt to begin the identification process, working slowly and carefully, the forensic recovery team uncovered the sought-after remains. (Courtesy of Detective Steve Ainsworth, Boulder County, Colorado, Sheriff's Office)

The skull was reconstructed by Dr. Birkby (see Figure 22.27), and ultimately it and a leg bone were sent to the anthropology laboratory at Michigan State University. This laboratory specializes in identification of human remains and possesses extensive forensic capability. Here, the skull was photographed and a DNA sample was obtained from the leg bone. Using photo superimposition techniques, two women missing during the approximate time period were excluded from further consideration. In one case, that of a missing teenager abducted in December of 1953 from Canada, similarities between "Jane Doe" and the Canadian victim were striking, and the investigation

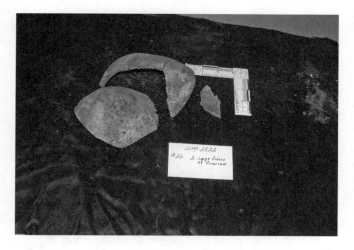

FIGURE 22.24 Pieces of skull cap. (Courtesy of Detective Steve Ainsworth, Boulder County, Colorado, Sheriff's Office)

FIGURE 22.25 Due to water conditions and earth movement, the coffin had collapsed. The skull bones were recovered in large and small pieces. Many hours of analysis and reconstruction were to follow. (Courtesy of Detective Steve Ainsworth, Boulder County, Colorado, Sheriff's Office)

FIGURE 22.26 Because of the new publicity, a citizen came forward with a photograph of the victim taken in the county morgue in 1954. Not uncommonly, photos in cold cases surface as a result of media publicity and word of mouth during these investigations. (Name withheld at owner's request)

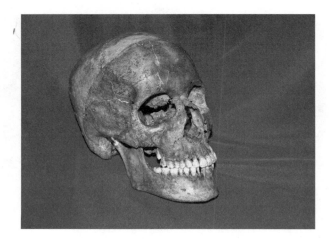

FIGURE 22.27 Reconstruction of the many small skull fragments by forensic experts began to put a "face" back on "Boulder Jane Doe." (Courtesy of Detective Steve Ainsworth, Boulder County, Colorado, Sheriff's Office)

became international in scope. Further investigation included comparison of mitochondrial testing of hair from "Jane Doe" with that of the Canadian victim's family (her brother was now a homicide detective) as well as attempts to recover latent prints through "superglue" from books and other memorabilia that once belonged to the victim of this abduction and were still in possession of her family. One rolled fingerprint from "Jane Doe" had been recovered, as the others were destroyed by animal action. It had been retained until 1993 when it was reportedly destroyed by the FBI.

The skull was sent to forensic sculptor and co-founder of the Vidocq Society Frank Bender for reconstruction of the victim's facial features (see Figure 22.28). Mr. Bender has been highly

FIGURE 22.28 The reconstructed skull was forwarded to Vidocq Society founder and forensic sculptor Frank Bender. Bender's uncanny ability to reconstruct lifelike features from a skull or to age-enhance fugitives has resulted in numerous identifications and fugitive apprehensions. The Boulder County Sheriff's Office unveiled the bust with a press conference that sought media exposure of the case in hopes that someone might recognize the likeness and come forward with information that will help identify "Boulder Jane Doe." (Courtesy of Frank Bender, V.S.M)

successful in reconstructing features of unidentified deceased persons and of age-enhancing fugitives. His works have appeared on "America's Most Wanted" and on June 13th, 2005, the Boulder County Sheriff's Office and Frank Bender unveiled a reconstructed likeness of "Jane Doe." Local and national news media gave the case widespread publicity. As a result, numerous persons called in with possible information that "Jane Doe" was a missing relative. The investigation, including use of DNA, has continued.

SIGNIFICANT COLD CASE ISSUES

This case represents a significant number of the cold case investigation techniques and situational circumstances discussed throughout this book. Among these are:

- Extensive (50-year) cold case period
- Newspapers used as source of case information ultimately contributing as an official record of events when agency records no longer exist
- Newspaper photos and descriptions used to rediscover original crime scene
- Identification of living original case participants (pathologist) and recovery of vital documents
- Discovery and recovery of Coroner's Inquest report
- Use of death certificate as official record of homicide and source of investigative information
- Disappearance of original law enforcement agency case file
- Lack of remaining physical evidence
- Use of State Archives for records search
- Inquiry and inspection of mortuary/funeral home records
  - Identification and utilization of mortuary records
  - Identification of casket material to evaluate potential for continued existence of remains
  - Commingling of records
- Visit to grave scene and recording of observations
- Investigative use of the Doe Network in course of identification of remains
- Referral to the Vidocq Society for forensic and other assistance
- Forensic exhumation of victim's remains
  - Affidavit for search warrant to recover specific physical evidence from an unsolved homicide utilizing newspaper records in combination with independent investigation and recovery of few remaining official records
  - Application of forensic anthropology methods
- Utilization of advanced technology for identification purposes, including
  - MtDNA testing
  - Nuclear DNA testing
  - Potential for advanced fingerprint lifting capability using "Superglue"
  - Forensic reconstruction and use of photographic superimposition techniques
- Locating period automobiles through museum resources for potential reconstruction purposes
- Reconstruction and simulation of theorized events yielding substantiating suggestion of event sequence
- Forensic artistry constructing an image of the victim based upon anthropological features for media usage
- Media Role and publicity
  - Internet web page dedicated to this specific "Jane Doe" case
  - Use of Doe Network for possible identification purposes

- Citizen comes forward with only known original photograph of victim
- Local and national news coverage
- Additional photos surface, apparently taken by newspaper photographer
- Determination that suspect in Canadian disappearance was excluded by polygraph examination and other investigation circa 1953.
- International scope of local case

ACKNOWLEDGMENTS

I wish to extend my appreciation to Criminalist Connie Milton of the San Diego County, California, Sheriff's Department Crime Lab. Her experiences and expertise in the exhumation process and DNA processing have greatly contributed to this chapter. In addition, I wish to thank Agent Jon Wooddell of the El Cajon, California, Police Department and Officer Robert Anderson of the Murrietta, California, Police Department, for sharing their experiences and expertise in the exhumation process. I also wish to acknowledge the great contribution and assistance provided by Mr. Dan Lamborn, Supervising Deputy District Attorney of the San Diego County, California, District Attorney's Office, Cold Case Investigation Unit for his thoughtful input and review. Further, I wish to acknowledge and thank Mr. Daniel Williams, Mortuary Manager of the Greenwood Cemetery and Memorial Park, San Diego, California, for his professional expertise and contribution to this segment.

In addition, I wish to acknowledge and extend my gratitude to Detective Steve Ainsworth and Lieutenant Phil West of the Boulder County, Colorado, Sheriff's Department for their assistance in the preparation of the Jane Doe case study. As do Agents Anderson and Wooddell, Detective Ainsworth represents the tenacity and personal and professional determination that so exemplify cold case investigators. In addition, I wish to recognize and acknowledge the efforts of Silvia Pettem for dedication on behalf of this and all other "Does" whose murders or disappearances have remained unsolved. Further, this case exemplifies the spirit of the Vidocq Society and its members, who contribute in a voluntary manner so much to finding the answer to unsolved cases.

This case study was prepared based upon review of official documents and detailed interviews with Detective Ainsworth and Silvia Pettem, and from articles prepared by Ms. Pettem in the Summer, 2004, issue of *The Vidocq Society Journal,* and by Dr. Golberg and Lt. West in the Fall issue of this journal.

BIBLIOGRAPHY

Goldberg, R. and West, P. (2004) Boulder Colorado's Jane Doe: Part II. *Vidocq Society Journal.* (Fall, 2004). 15/4. pp 1-4.

Pettem, S. (2004). Vidocq Expertise and the reopening of the case of Boulder's Jane Doe Homicide. *Vidocq Society Journal.* (Summer, 2004). 15/3. pp 8-11.

http://boulderjanedoe.com

http://doenetwork.us

23 Criminal Investigative Analysis In Cold Case Investigations

Sharon Pagaling Hagan

CONTENTS

In solving a problem of this sort, the grand thing is to be able to reason backward. That is a very useful accomplishment, and a very easy one, but people do not practice it much. In the everyday affairs of life it is more useful to reason forward, and so the other comes to be neglected...Let me see if I can make it clearer. Most people, if you describe a train of events to them, will tell you what the result would be. They can put those events together in their minds, and argue from them that something will come to pass. There are few people, however, who, if you told them a result, would be able to evolve from their own inner consciousness what the steps were which led up to that result. This power is what I mean when I talk of reasoning backward, or analytically.

Sherlock Holmes
From A Study in Scarlet, *by Sir Arthur Conan Doyle*

Homicide cases often remain unsolved because pertinent information or evidence was either over-looked or misinterpreted. Upon close inspection and analysis of an unsolved case, investigators sometimes discover that theories originally pursued regarding the motive, the manner in which the crime was committed, and the primary suspect(s) are inconsistent with the crime scene, the physical and/or trace evidence, and wound pathology. These common pitfalls are magnified with the passage of time.

The purpose of this chapter is to provide investigators with an introduction to the analysis of a cold homicide from a behavioral perspective. The degree to which an investigator understands human behavior and is able to apply such understanding to a crime scene is directly related to his or her ability to be successful in homicide investigation. Unfortunately, over time, homicide investigation has become increasingly focused upon forensic analysis of trace and biological evidence to solve cases, while the behavioral component has been neglected.

Criminal investigative analysis is a behavioral analytic process that integrates information regarding the victim, the initial crime scene investigation, physical and trace evidence, wound patterns, toxicological examination results, geographical information (including demographics and crime patterns), witness accounts, and an indirect personality assessment of any potential suspects.

Investigators tasked with a cold homicide investigation can benefit from the process of criminal investigative analysis in:

- Organizing old case files
- Prioritizing cases based upon solvability factors
- Identifying elements of the original investigation that require follow-up
- Providing new focus to the investigation by integrating a prediction of human behavior with the most recent advancements in forensic science

HISTORICAL PERSPECTIVE

Criminal investigative analysis is an investigative tool developed by the Federal Bureau of Investigation's Behavioral Science Unit. During the 1970s, special agents assigned to the unit believed that a detailed understanding of the behaviors exhibited by an offender during the commission of a violent crime could assist investigators in the identification, investigation, and successful prosecution of the subject. The agents began conducting research on violent offenders to identify commonalities and behavioral patterns that could assist police investigators in the detection of such offenders.

Robert Ressler, Ann Burgess and John Douglas provided an early example of such research in *Sexual Homicide* (1988), which compiled information obtained from interviews and background investigations of 36 sexual killers. Ressler and Douglas identified commonalities shared by the offenders, including the habitual use of violent pornography from an early age, dysfunctional relationships with their parents, and social isolation from peers. Although their study gathered data from a relatively small number of subjects, the information offered clinicians and criminal justice professionals insight into the behavioral traits, personality characteristics, and patterns of social interaction that might assist the criminal justice system in the identification and management of such individuals.

Although criminal investigative analysis, commonly termed "psychological" or "criminal profiling," has received much attention from the media and has been popularized in television, movies, and books, the potential benefits of this investigative tool continue to be misunderstood. The most common misconception is that criminal profiling is identical to criminal investigative analysis; in fact, profiling is only one element of criminal investigative analysis. A behavioral profile, or description of an unidentified offender's personality and lifestyle, may assist investigators in the identification of an offender by narrowing the focus of an investigation to a more restricted pool of potential suspects. A profile may be particularly useful in cases in which a potential suspect is not identified during the initial investigation, because the profile can then be used to reevaluate those people who have already been contacted that bear similarity to the profile. However, while such a description may be useful to investigators during their search for the offender, profiles have rarely if ever led to the actual identification of an offender. Further, "profiling" information is not admissible in court to prove the guilt or innocence of a defendant.*

Criminal investigative analysis refers to a range of functions related to the behavioral analysis of violent crimes, and the perpetrators who commit such crimes. The types of analytical services available to investigators and prosecutors include:

- Crime scene analysis and reconstruction
- Indirect personality assessment
- Threat assessment
- Interview and interrogation strategies
- Crime linkage analysis
- Equivocal death investigation
- Trial and cross-examination strategy
- Expert testimony**

Criminal investigative analysis is currently conducted by a small group of highly skilled crime analysts who are trained in numerous disciplines including the psychology of persons who commit violent crimes, forensic science disciplines such as DNA analysis, comparative analysis, trace evidence, toxicology, bloodstain interpretation, wound pathology, threat assessment, interview and interrogation, crime scene analysis, and crime scene reconstruction. These analysts, who are sworn or retired law enforcement professionals, have completed a structured training and certification program under the supervision of the International Criminal Investigative Analysis Fellowship (ICIAF). Investigative assistance and expertise is available from members of the ICIAF to requesting investigators or prosecutors within the U.S., Canada, Australia, and several European countries, often at no expense to the requesting agency.

INVESTIGATIVE ROLE

Criminal investigative analysis can assist investigators to organize existing case materials, identify "good" cold cases, prioritize cases based upon solvability factors, and identify issues that require additional investigative follow-up. Although advances in forensic science have enabled law enforcement agencies to solve crimes through biological evidence that identifies the perpetrator, investigators still need help to accurately interpret crime scenes that reveal such evidence.

Investigators who are confronted with the task of reactivating an unsolved homicide investigation typically face a variety of challenges resulting from the passage of time. Such challenges include the retirement or death of the original investigators, missing or deteriorated physical evidence, misplaced or lost case notes, incomplete or partial case files, poor documentation of previous investigative efforts, photographs that are of poor quality or insufficient quantity, and the death or unknown location of key witnesses.

A thorough and fresh evaluation of the case by newly assigned detectives who have no prior commitment or loyalty to the theories that were originally developed regarding the motive or responsible person(s) has proven instrumental in solving many cold homicides. However, recontacting and establishing a positive relationship with the original investigators can be helpful. It is essential that the newly assigned investigators not criticize the original investigation or point out any investigative errors that may have been identified by reactivation of the investigation. The

---

* Testimony regarding behavioral profiles of offenders who commit various types of crimes has been ruled to be potentially prejudicial and/or of limited probative value in the determination of the facts relevant to a specific crime or defendant.
** Expert testimony has been allowed regarding crime scene analysis, crime scene reconstruction and staging.

original investigators may have saved their investigative notes, know the whereabouts of missing case materials, or recall information pertinent to the crime that was not documented in reports.

The passage of time has also proven beneficial to the successful resolution of many unsolved homicide cases by offering investigators the opportunity to reinterview potential witnesses, persons associated with the victim and any potential suspects for pertinent information that developed after the initial investigation was concluded. Likewise, deteriorated relationships may allow investigators to access information withheld by witnesses who were originally motivated by loyalty or fear.

INVESTIGATIVE MATERIALS

Ideally, before a comprehensive analysis of the crime is initiated, investigators should compile as much of the following materials as possible:

- Complete historical information regarding the victim(s)
- Natural/candid photographs of victim(s) in life
- Initial and follow-up investigative reports
- Media accounts, including newspaper clippings, videotapes of television news, etc.
- Geographical information, including map(s), crime rates, and similar crimes committed during that period of time
- Narrative description(s) of crime scene(s)
- Photographs of crime scene(s)
- Photographs of decedent(s) at scene
- Crime scene diagram(s)
- Laboratory reports and analyses
- Autopsy report(s), diagrams and photographs

VICTIMOLOGY

Criminal investigative analysis begins with an in-depth study of the victim's personality and lifestyle. To this end, a thorough background investigation of the victim is essential to shed light on such questions that may help focus the investigation. For example: Why was it "necessary" for this particular person to die? Did someone perceive him or her as an obstacle? What was his or her risk level of becoming the victim of a violent crime? Was the victim "specifically selected" by the offender, or was his or her interaction with the offender the result of opportunity and circumstance? Did the geographic location where the crime was committed affect the victim's risk level? Was the victim "security conscious," or did he or she feel comfortable leaving windows and doors unlocked? Did lifestyle place the victim in contact with persons who potentially posed a physical threat? Had he or she previously been the victim of violent crime or expressed concern regarding his or her safety? Had the victim ever discussed how he or she planned to defend him- or herself if he or she were threatened or assaulted? What was the victim's medical and psychological history? Was the victim involved in any high-risk behaviors such as drug or alcohol abuse, domestic violence, extramarital sexual encounters, sexual deviation(s) or criminal enterprise?

Experience has shown that most homicides are the result of interpersonal conflict, and the offender can be found in the victim's family, social network or work environment. Homicides that are motivated by interpersonal conflict are an attempt by perpetrators to "solve a problem" they are experiencing with the victims. As such, consideration of any potential problems and conflicts that may have either been present in the victim's personal life, or perceived as a problem or conflict by a potential offender, is often effective in narrowing the search for the perpetrator. Experience has shown that, with the passage of time, persons who had close personal relationships with the victim become more willing to divulge sensitive or unflattering information regarding a victim's lifestyle and activities.

Investigators should make every effort to obtain an understanding of the victim's background, personality, lifestyle and interpersonal relationships, with particular attention to compilation of a detailed timeline of the victim's activities and contacts with other persons during the last 72 hours of life. Investigators should produce a detailed timeline of everyone the victim had contact with during this 72-hour window that precedes the murder, including telephone conversations and written messages. In most cases, the decision to commit a murder is made within a relatively short period of time prior to initiation of the assault. As a result, the perpetrator can typically be found within the group of persons who had contact with the victim within the last few days, hours, and sometimes minutes that preceded the murder.

GEOGRAPHIC INFORMATION

Information regarding the geographic location, accessibility, and the area surrounding the crime scene(s) is important to the analysis. How and where did the offender encounter the victim? What types of crimes were common to the area during that period of time, and were there any crimes that bore resemblance to the behaviors the offender displayed during the murder of the victim? Information should be accumulated regarding traffic patterns, accessibility to and from major thoroughfares, lighting conditions, and environmental factors including weather. Was the victim vulnerable to an assault by a stranger, or could the victim have only been contacted in that particular location, at that particular time, by someone familiar?

Geographic analysis can assist in narrowing the search for an offender responsible for a crime or a series of crimes that involve multiple locations. If possible, investigators should consult with a geographic profiler to identify the most probable area in which the offender might be found. Because offenders can often be found a short distance from the crime scene, a less formal technique involves marking the areas on a map that approximates a half-mile radius around each location, and then concentrating the search for the offender in any areas that overlap and are therefore geographically common to the scenes.

CRIME SCENE ANALYSIS

Crime scenes depict the final outcome of the behavioral interaction between the offender(s) and the victim(s). Unfortunately, this simple truth is complicated by the fact that the locations are typically not sterile environments prior to initiation of the murder and therefore contain various evidence items not related to the crime. Consequently, to most effectively filter out such misleading items and identify only those pertinent to the homicide investigation, investigators must make a concerted effort to determine the preexisting condition of the crime scene. As specific information is often unavailable regarding the condition of the crime location on a particular day and time, investigators may be limited to whatever information they can obtain regarding the "normal" appearance of the scene. This process is essential because many homicide investigators rely heavily upon forensic examination of biological and physical evidence recovered from the scene to identify the perpetrator. Scientific testing of items that are not associated with the murder, and that erroneously identify innocent persons, will confuse the investigation and may even exonerate the responsible party.

Physical evidence from a crime scene is the product of behaviors that were exhibited by an offender(s) and victim(s). A crime scene (cs) may be represented by the equation: $cs = o$ (offender) $+ v$ (victim). Analysis of a crime scene from this perspective encourages investigators to more fully consider the contribution the victim's behavior likely had on the crime scene, which is essential to avoid the all-too-frequent error of attributing the scene solely to behaviors exhibited by the offender. Further, analysis from this perspective allows investigators to acquire an accurate assessment of the manner in which the offender behaved by acquainting themselves with the victim's personality and behavioral patterns, and "subtracting," so to speak, the victim's behavior from the crime scene. This concept can be represented thus: $o = cs - v$. Theoretically, once the victim's behavior is subtracted from the scene, the behavioral evidence that remains can more appropriately be attributed to the offender. The following case description illustrates the importance of understanding the "preexisting" condition of the crime scene, as well as the behavioral patterns of the victim.

CASE STUDY

Investigators responded to a single-family residence located in a new housing development at approximately noon on a weekday regarding the homicide of a 38-year-old pregnant female. The victim's husband told detectives he had discovered his wife's body several minutes earlier when he came home to drive her to a counseling appointment. The residence was in significant disarray. Furniture was knocked over, drawers were emptied, and the contents scattered. A waterbed had been punctured and was leaking onto the carpet, and a large entertainment center situated in the living room had been overturned. Many household items, including several televisions, the dining room chairs, and the contents of the kitchen cabinets and refrigerator, were strewn about the back yard. All of the upholstered living room furniture had been cut and were heavily stained with the victim's blood. A blood trail led from the living room into the master bathroom. The victim was located in the bathtub in the master bathroom, under a plastic jug that was partially filled with coins, and a laundry hamper. The body was in a semi-seated position, and the victim was wearing a bra, panties, dress, and wristwatch. Although there was no water in the bathtub, a bloody ring rimmed the tub and blood spatter was visible on the adjacent wall. Chemical burns were present over portions of the right side of the victim's body and both shoulders, her hair appeared to have been bleached, and a small portion of her hair had been shaved above her right forehead. Barber shears, scissors, tweezers, and a bloodstained towel were found beneath her body. A racial slur was written on the bathroom mirror in toothpaste. The victim's cause of death was manual strangulation, but she had also suffered five stab wounds to her right back and buttocks and blunt force trauma to her head, left breast, face, and left leg. She suffered fractures to her nose and two ribs, had many bruises and abrasions to her arms and legs, and no evidence of defense-style injuries. During the course of the investigation, detectives learned the victim had a volatile temper and on a previous occasion had slashed the furniture after becoming angry. The couple had a history of domestic violence and had argued repeatedly during the preceding days. According to a female friend of the victim who had visited the residence on the morning of the murder, the victim had admitted causing nearly all of the damage to the home after her husband left for work. Interviews of the couple's neighbors revealed the victim's husband had arrived at the residence approximately 15 minutes prior to the time he had given to the investigators. He was subsequently arrested and convicted of the murders of his wife and unborn child.

As illustrated by this case, essential information regarding the behavioral sequence that occurred during the crime, the probable motive for the crime, the type of relationship the victim likely had with the perpetrator, and the type of person most likely to have committed the crime can be garnered through analysis of the crime scene and victimology. This information can also be useful during the interview or interrogation of suspects, and by prosecutors to distinguish between planned and impulsive homicides.

Information regarding the sequence of behaviors that occurred at the scene can be obtained through careful consideration and integration of the crime scene characteristics with the physical evidence. These characteristics may include, but are not limited to:

- The amount of risk the offender accepted to commit the crime
- The manner in which the offender approached the victim
- The size of the crime scene

- Bloodstain patterns
- Items taken or left behind
- Positioning and disposition of the body
- Wound patterns
- Indications of post-mortem activity at the crime scene
- Indications of sexual activity

Some murders involve multiple crime scenes that may include a point of abduction, initial assault, murder, body storage, and body- and evidence-disposal sites. When multiple crime scenes are involved, it is typically more difficult for investigators to locate pertinent physical evidence and information regarding the behavioral interaction of the offender and the victim.

OFFENDER RISK

The offender determines the time, place, and circumstances under which the murder occurs. Because the offender is in control of these factors, investigators can learn a great deal by examining the environmental factors (location, time, lighting conditions, and traffic patterns in the area where the crime occurred), and assessing the amount of risk the offender was willing to accept to commit the crime.

Regardless of the time or location an offender selects for the murder, he or she cannot be absolutely certain of not being seen by witnesses. An offender might reduce that risk by altering his or her appearance or by committing the murder during late night or early morning hours. In general, however, the anxiety an offender has regarding the possibility of being seen by witnesses depends on several factors: the type of relationship the offender has with the victim; the extent to which he or she "belongs" at the location where the crime will occur; and the number of potential witnesses the offender believes will likely be present in the vicinity when the crime is committed.

An offender who has a close personal relationship with his or her victim often has less concern about being seen by other persons while either with the victim or at the location. An offender who "belongs" at a location, because he or she resides, works, or frequently visits the area, is often unconcerned that his or her presence at the scene will be noticed and considered unusual by potential witnesses. Persons who have a legitimate reason for being in the area (for example, service workers) are often not reported to investigators during the neighborhood canvasses that are typically conducted in the hours immediately following discovery of the victim's body and during the subsequent investigation. Potential witnesses are not usually asked questions regarding *all persons* seen in the area, but rather are primarily focused on persons who were perceived as being somehow *unusual*.

Offenders who are strangers to their victims and do not frequent the area where the crime occurs also tend to be less concerned that other persons will be able to accurately identify them to law enforcement as potential suspects. These offenders are often careful not to return to the area of the crime in order to avoid being recognized.

Another type of risk offenders likely consider both before and after commission of the murder is the likelihood they will eventually be identified as the person responsible for the victim's death. Criminally sophisticated offenders may take precautions to either reduce or eliminate physical and trace evidence from the scene by wearing gloves, using condoms, cleaning the crime scene after the murder, and removing items from the scene they believe might reveal their identity. However, given the dramatic strides in forensic science, even the most knowledgeable and criminally sophisticated offenders can no longer be confident they did not leave potentially incriminating evidence at the scene.

Prior to the commission of a planned homicide, and frequently during the commission of a more spontaneous killing, offenders consider the likelihood they will be interrupted by unexpected persons or events. Unexpected visitors, the premature arrival of other residents to the location, mail delivery, or even incoming unanswered telephone calls may sharply curtail the amount of time the offender is willing to spend at the scene. Offenders may take precautions to reduce the number of potential interruptions, including familiarizing themselves with the victim's schedule and routine behaviors, unplugging or disabling telephones and extinguishing all interior and exterior lights.

If the murder involved prior planning, offenders may have taken precautions to facilitate their escape from the scene in order to avoid being apprehended. In these instances, offenders may plan their escape route, prop windows and doors open, and position a vehicle, bicycle, or other means of transportation in a location that is out of view but easily accessible.

METHOD OF APPROACH

Analysis of the manner in which an offender likely gained access to his or her victim often supplies investigators with valuable insight regarding the offender's perception of his or her own talents and weaknesses, as well as identification of behaviors he or she is willing to exhibit. Although homicide scenes frequently lack conclusive evidence regarding the exact manner in which an offender was able to access a victim, criminal justice professionals are frequently able to accurately theorize the method that was employed through an analysis of the crime scene, the victim's personality, lifestyle, and circumstances, and the "process of elimination."

Hazelwood and Warren (2001) suggest sexually motivated offenders use three methods to approach victims: the con, the blitz and the surprise. Offenders who are confident in the strength and persuasiveness of their interpersonal skills prefer the con approach. These offenders attempt to literally talk their victims into positions of vulnerability or persuade them to accompany them to locations that afford the offenders a sufficient degree of privacy to perpetrate the crime. The blitz-style approach is the immediate application of debilitating force to incapacitate and render victims incapable of physical resistance. Offenders who select the surprise approach use their physical strength to quickly gain control of the victim. Offenders who are more confident of their physical prowess than their social skills prefer the surprise approach. The correct identification of the method of approach an offender uses during the commission of a violent crime can help identify and facilitate the interview and prosecution of the perpetrator.

Few crime scenes exhibit evidence of forced entry. Because most homicides are the result of interpersonal conflict, it is common for victims to have admitted offenders to the location or willingly spent time with them immediately before the murder. Knowledge of the victim's habits is often helpful in determining whether other persons would have had access to the crime scene location, whether the victim routinely left doors or windows open or unlocked, or would have answered the door to an unexpected visitor or stranger.

SIZE OF THE CRIME SCENE

A crime scene littered with overturned furniture is behaviorally quite different from a small, contained scene that is limited to the location of body. Expanded crime scenes may result from several scenarios, including recognition by the victim that the offender posed a significant threat prior to initiation of the assault; a substantial attempt by the victim to defend him- or herself; an inability by an offender to effectively control a victim during an assault; or the possibility there was an escalation of violence from a verbal argument to a physical assault. Expanded crime scenes are also more likely to be found in homicides that were not carefully planned by the offender, and in cases where the victims and the offenders were of comparable size and strength. Conversely, smaller, more contained scenes are more likely to be found in premeditated murders or cases where the offender was either significantly larger or stronger than the victim, or was able to exert and maintain effective control of the victim throughout the assault.

BLOODSTAIN PATTERNS AND DEPOSITS

Accurate analysis of the bloodstain patterns and deposits found at the crime scene may provide police investigators with extremely valuable information regarding the physical movements of the offender and victim during the murder. Conversely, misinterpretation of bloodstain patterns may cause a homicide to remain unsolved. Analysis of bloodstain patterns from an unsolved homicide depends upon the quality and quantity of photographs taken of the crime scene.

It is important when inferring behavior from bloodstain patterns to differentiate between blood from the victim and blood from the offender. In some cases, careful analysis has enabled investigators to discover that blood previously assumed to have come from the victim was actually deposited by the perpetrator. Investigators are encouraged to seek an informed opinion regarding any blood deposits associated with an unsolved murder in order to obtain an enhanced understanding of the behaviors that likely occurred at the scene.

ITEMS TAKEN OR LEFT BEHIND

Did the offender use items he found at the scene to facilitate the murder, or did the offender bring all of the items to the scene for the specific purpose of perpetrating the crime? What, if anything, is missing from the scene? Were any items left at the scene that do not belong?

There are several possible explanations as to why an offender may have utilized items available at the crime scene, such as knives and heavy objects as weapons, or clothing items as bindings. These include: (1) a murder that involved little or no prior planning; (2) a murder in which the offender was familiar with the location where the crime was committed and was confident the items could be found there; or (3) the offender was not willing to risk being found in possession of weapons, tools, or binding materials as he or she approached or left the crime scene.

Offenders who choose to bring specific objects to the scene may do so because they are routinely in possession of the item (e.g., a pocket knife, handgun), the crime involves a significant degree of prior planning, or the items utilized by the offenders are of special significance to them.

Offenders who are criminally sophisticated — or who are forensically knowledgeable — are careful not to leave transportable items behind that could lead to their identification. Homicides committed by such offenders may show evidence that they attempted to "clean up" prior to departing the scene, and any incriminating evidence was taken and discarded a safe distance away. In contrast, offenders who utilize weapons, bindings, or other items that have special meaning or significance (e.g., linked to their sexual fantasy), are often unwilling to discard them and choose to retain possession of them so they can use them again. In these instances, investigators are often able to recover the items from the offender's possessions months or even years after the crime was committed.

POSITIONING AND DISPOSITION OF THE BODY

The manner in which the victim's body was left often provides investigators with valuable information regarding the relationship, if any, the offender had with the victim, the emotional state of the offender immediately following the murder, and any logistical problems that the offender perceived following the murder.

Offenders can choose among numerous options once they are satisfied the victims are dead. They may choose to leave the body at the crime scene without any further manipulation, transport it to another location, conceal or cover it, or, in rare instances, a perpetrator may position and "display" the body in a manner that will likely be particularly provocative or shocking to the person who finds the body.

In most instances, offenders are anxious to distance themselves from the crime scene and the victim's body shortly after the commission of the murder. They are aware that continued association with the victim's body increases their risk of being discovered. Consequently, only offenders who have serious mental impairments are driven by a specific need (usually sexual), or believe they must alter the death scene somehow in order to avoid detection will remain in contact with the body.

Offenders who are confident that other persons are not aware of their association with the victim are more likely to leave the body at the crime scene. However, offenders who had a close personal relationship with the victim, or who believed their association with the victim near the time of death was witnessed or known by others, may attempt to transport or conceal the body in hopes of either delaying or preventing discovery of the murder.

The amount of time and contact an offender has with the victim's body following the murder is a function, at least in part, of the offender's personality and ability to function under pressure. Offenders who had a close personal relationship with the victim or who cannot tolerate touching a deceased person may have more difficulty controlling their emotions sufficiently in order to move or manipulate the deceased. Crime scenes sometimes reflect evidence that offenders "changed their minds," and aborted an attempt to move or transport the victim's body.

The offender's ability to transport the victim's body is influenced by such factors as physical strength, access to a vehicle, and sufficient opportunity. Disposition of the body is influenced by the physical strength of the offender, a significant disparity in size between the victim and the offender, the physical layout of the murder scene, the degree of privacy the murder scene affords the offender, and the offender's ability to easily and covertly access an appropriate means of transportation. For instance, did the residence where the crime was committed have an attached garage, or could the vehicle be parked only in an open area in view of potential witnesses? How many persons were present and active in the area during the time immediately following the murder? Was there any indication the offender remained at the murder scene for an extended period after the death, waiting for nightfall? Were window coverings manipulated, did the offender engage in extensive clean-up, or did the offender eat, sleep, launder clothing, or bathe at the crime scene?

CAUSE OF DEATH AND WOUND PATTERNS

Significant information regarding the sequence of events at the crime scene is available by examination and assessment of the victim's wounds. Factors that are often relevant to the behavioral analysis of a murder include: the presence of blunt force trauma, the presence or absence of defense-style injuries, identification of patterned injuries, analysis of the lethality of multiple wounds, estimation of the time period during which the wounds were inflicted, the cause of death, and postmortem activity. It is essential that the wounds be considered within the context of the scene, and background information regarding the victim's personality, history of drug and alcohol use, medical history, and lifestyle. In some instances, a thorough analysis may reveal that the death was not the result of homicide. This is illustrated by the following case, which was initially suspected to be a homicide.

Case Study

A 20-year-old male college student resided in a private room on the second floor of a fraternity house, which was located in a low-crime-rate area. He was academically successful, had an active social life, a steady girlfriend, and a positive relationship with his family. He had a minor criminal history resulting from several incidents during which he had been drinking alcoholic beverages. He had no reported enemies, and no history of physical or psychological problems. Shortly before his death, his parents said he had been anxious regarding his course of study, and had suffered bouts of insomnia. Two fraternity-house roommates told investigators they last saw him at approximately 1 a.m. when he retired to his room, following a quiet evening of television. During the next 2 days, his roommates said they knocked on the deceased's door and called his name; however, when they got no answer, assumed he was visiting friends.

His roommates obtained a key to to the young man's room from the company that managed the house and discovered the deceased in bed, partially covered by a comforter. The room was dark, music was playing, and the deceased was wearing earplugs. Bloodstains were apparent on three walls, the rug, desk, and bedding. His shirt, shorts, and sock bottoms were bloodstained. His shirt had numerous defects that corresponded to numerous of his 25 stab wounds and four incised wounds to his face, scalp, neck, chest, and wrists. He had also suffered fatal stab wounds to his chest that penetrated both lungs and his heart, a fatal 4-inch-deep incised wound across his neck, and moderately deep horizontal incised wounds to both wrists. There was no evidence of blunt-force trauma, broken bones, torture, bindings, or sexual assault. Several minor abrasions and cuts were found on the fingers of his right hand, but there was no indication of defense-style injuries. A toxicological examination revealed no traces of alcohol or drugs. A bloodstained knife was found on the bed and all of the fingerprints on the knife were matched to the decedent. There was no indication of forced entry or a struggle involving a second person. None of the deceased's roommates reported hearing any sounds emanating from the young man's bedroom or finding any evidence that an intruder had been present in the house.

Analysis of the deceased's wounds revealed that all of the stab wounds were uniform and had no jagged edges (which would be consistent with a struggle); many were superficial and all of the wounds were located within his own reach. Although stabbing is the least common method of suicide, experience has shown that suicide cannot be eliminated from consideration based upon the severity of the wounds. Because the deceased had no history of suicidal ideation, his family and friends, as well as numerous investigators, were reluctant to accept a finding of suicide. However, an integrative analysis of his personality, wounds, and the physical evidence brought perspective to the case and convinced all parties he had committed suicide.

Detectives involved in a cold homicide investigation should carefully review the postmortem medical examination report and photographs, and consult with a forensic pathologist to obtain a thorough understanding of the victim's wounds, the manner and mode of death, and an estimate of the length of time the victim could have remained ambulatory before succumbing to such wounds. Investigators are often reluctant to thoroughly review the autopsy report and photographs because they have little or no training in wound pathology and find the medical terminology used in the autopsy report difficult to understand. Consequently, after determining the victim's cause of death, they do not adequately consider the implications of any other injuries.

Minor injuries, such as bruising to the victim's face, are important to the analysis of a homicide because they may indicate that an escalation of violence occurred. Murders motivated by interpersonal conflict often begin as verbal arguments that escalate to physical assaults. The possibility that the victim exchanged blows with the offender should be considered. The presence of defense-style injuries or bruising to the victim's body are also consistent with the possibility that an argument and physical struggle preceded the murder. Recognition of these types of wounds may be an indication the offender did not originally approach the victim with the intent to kill. In such cases, the offender may have had a personal but problematic relationship with his or her victim, and may have rationalized the murder as justifiable.

Offenders intent on ensuring the victim's death often inflict multiple potentially fatal injuries. Infliction of serious injury that does not cause immediate death may motivate the offender to resort to another mode of attack (e.g., manual strangulation followed by a gunshot wound; a gunshot wound followed by throat slashing; stomping of the abdominal region followed by stabbing injuries). A pathologist is usually able to estimate the amount of time necessary for the victim to succumb to each of the potentially fatal injuries. The following case summary is an example of a homicide that involved multiple fatal injuries.

CASE STUDY

A 22-year old female was last seen entering her apartment with her 2-year-old child at approximately 1 a.m. after playing cards at her female next-door neighbor's apartment. Residents in the complex told investigators they had been awakened several hours later by loud noises, including voices arguing, a baby crying and several loud "thumps." The victim was found dead in her locked apartment approximately 36 hours later, when the apartment manager went to the apartment to investigate the source of water leaking into the unit immediately below.

Evidence at the scene indicated a struggle had occurred in the living room, the victim's body had been dragged into the bedroom, and then partially covered with newspaper. She was dressed in her normal sleeping attire; however, her bra had been pushed up, exposing her right breast. The child was unharmed. The victim's cause of death was listed as internal hemorrhage due to blunt force trauma to her abdomen. A patterned bruise was faintly visible on the victim's abdomen. She suffered blunt force injury to her head and neck and all of the injuries were consistent with stomping and kicking injuries. She had numerous bruises on her face, left knee and left elbow. She had facial suffusion, conjunctival hemorrhages, and scalp edema caused by mechanical compression of her neck. The victim also had a stab wound to her neck that occurred prior to death, and five additional stab wounds to her abdomen that were inflicted between the perimortem and postmortem states. There were no injuries to the victim's hands, no evidence of binding, or sexual assault. The victim had a trace amount of alcohol in her system, but no drugs were found. A knife stained with the victim's blood was found stored with other knives in a butcher block on the kitchen counter. After a prolonged investigation, the boyfriend of the victim's next-door neighbor was eventually identified as the perpetrator. He told investigators he had gone to the victim's apartment for sexual purposes. She had refused him and he became enraged. He admitted taking the victim's door key, returning to her apartment the day following the murder and turning the water on in order to ensure the safety of the child.

Analysis of this case provided investigators with valuable information regarding the sequence of events that led up to the victim's death. The analysis was used to narrow the focus of the investigation to persons who were known to the victim, and later provided investigators with information that was useful during the interview and subsequent prosecution of the offender.

SEXUAL ACTIVITY

A thorough understanding of the crime scene is necessary before investigators can efficiently search for and identify trace evidence left by an offender. While some crime scenes contain obvious indications the offender had sexual contact with the victim close to the time of the murder, evidence of sexual activity is often difficult to identify. Various types of sexual activity may occur during a homicide, including masturbation by the offender onto the victim's body, oral copulation, penile vaginal penetration or penetration with a foreign object. Sexual activity may occur prior to, during, or following the victim's death.

Sexual activity by the offender can offer investigators an opportunity to identify the perpetrator of an unsolved homicide. Although it is relatively common for sexually motivated offenders to experience sexual dysfunction, recent advances in forensic science have enabled scientists to identify and retest extremely small deposits of trace evidence. In cold case investigations, detectives should request that forensic scientists review all physical evidence to determine the utility of conducting further laboratory tests for identifiable material. Items that have been previously analyzed using older less sensitive or discriminating forensic techniques, or evidence not previously analyzed, should be carefully evaluated.

Experience has shown that serology DNA test results are often misinterpreted. Even experienced investigators are prone to misinterpreting the conclusions drawn from test results. For instance, are the test results consistent with sexual contact? Are any of the samples tested inconsistent with the victim? How many donors contributed to the sample(s) that were tested? Was the victim's consensual sexual partner(s) excluded? Have all potentially relevant samples been tested? Investigators should consult with forensic scientists to thoroughly review all of the biological and trace evidence associated with the crime to gain a thorough understanding of the meaning of the test results and determine whether further testing is feasible.

The following case was submitted for analysis to determine whether the victim's death was the result of sexual misadventure, as the defendant claimed, or homicide.

CASE STUDY

The 55-year-old male victim was a successful businessman, lived alone, and was openly homo-sexual. He drank excessively and frequented several local bars, where he flashed significant amounts of money and enjoyed giving others the impression he was wealthy. The victim was described as security conscious and routinely locked his doors and windows. His neighbor said the residence had appeared secure at 5:30 p.m., however, at 7:45 p.m., the garage door was standing open and the victim's car was gone. When she was unable to contact the victim by telephone, the neighbor called the police.

The police entered the residence through an unlocked garage door that led into the kitchen and observed an empty liquor bottle on the table. The telephone had been unplugged. The victim's nude body was lying on his bed in the unlit master bedroom. An electrical cord had been wrapped around the victim's neck five times and the lamp to which it was attached was hanging down toward the floor. Minor lacerations were visible on the victim's face, chin, and chest. Semen that did not match the victim's DNA profile was recovered from his chest and a towel that was lying near the corner of the bed. His DNA and the unidentified DNA profile were recovered from an empty glass on the bedside table. A dresser drawer had been overturned near the foot of the bed, and several items were missing from the residence, including the victim's vehicle, a briefcase, a gold ring, a jewelry box, and his wallet, which contained his identification and credit cards. The vehicle was recovered the following day in a residential area where it had been abandoned, and bloodhounds led investigators from the vehicle to a nearby bus stop. A latent fingerprint was located on the base of the lamp. The fingerprint was matched to a young married man approximately 1 year later following his arrest for theft.

The analysis integrated information regarding the victim's lifestyle and sexual habits with the wound patterns and physical evidence found at the scene. Investigation of the victim's behavioral patterns showed that he had no history of using ligatures or other devices to restrict his breathing during sexual activity, and no information was found to indicate he had any suicidal intent. The wound patterns found on the victim's face, chin, and chest were consistent with the base of the lamp that was found attached to his neck, suggesting that the item had likely not been applied with the victim's consent. The prosecutors used the analysis to effectively refute the defendant's claim of consensual sexual misadventure, and the defendant was convicted of murder.

STAGED CRIME SCENES

The Crime Classification Manual defines staging as the alteration of the death scene to either direct the investigation away from the perpetrator or to protect the deceased or his or her family from potential embarrassment (Douglas, Burgess, Burgess & Ressler, 1992). In homicides, staging involves a variety of behaviors that might be exhibited at the scene following a death, including alteration of the scene so that it appears to have been financially or sexually motivated, or reporting the victim to law enforcement authorities as a missing person. When a death scene is staged, it is nearly always accomplished by a person who had a close personal relationship to the deceased.

One of the most common instances in which staging is encountered is in a domestic homicide in which a spouse is murdered at the family residence. In these cases, perpetrators are aware that if the spouse's body is discovered at the unaltered scene, they will immediately become the primary suspect. The perpetrators will therefore attempt to rearrange the scene to suggest an alternative motive for the crime, provide misleading statements to investigators, or clean the scene, hide the body, and report the victim as a missing person.

Staged scenes are often recognizable because the circumstances surrounding the victim's death or disappearance are inconsistent with the physical evidence and victimology. Domestic homicides are typically committed by offenders who are criminally inexperienced and who are therefore unaware of the appearance of a genuine crime scene. Their inexperience, combined with the likelihood that they attempted to alter the crime scene while agitated or in a highly emotional state, inhibit their ability to think clearly. As a result, individuals who stage scenes often make unintended errors, termed "red flags," that reveal that the scene is inconsistent with an actual burglary, sexual assault, kidnapping or missing person case (Douglas et al., 1992).

Criminal investigative analysts can assist investigators and prosecutors in the identification of the sometimes-minute inconsistencies reflected in the scene or in problematic statements made to the investigators. The case example that follows illustrates numerous crime scene indicators often found in a staged domestic homicide.

Case Study

The victim was an attractive, physically fit middle-aged woman who resided with her husband of 30 years. Their home was located in an upscale neighborhood that had a low rate of violent crime. The victim had many friends, was socially active, and was a part-time teacher. On the day of her death, the victim taught a morning class, then purchased coffee and a pastry before returning to her residence to prepare for an afternoon lesson. At approximately 1:40 p.m., the victim's husband returned to the residence in the company of two of the couple's friends and found the front door standing open. He found the victim's body lying head first near the bottom of the basement stairs fully dressed, with the exception of one of her shoes, which was recovered on a step above her body. After summoning his companions and asking them to telephone for help, the victim's husband pulled her body onto the cement basement floor and attempted resuscitation. Emergency personnel who responded to the scene were unable to revive the victim and she was pronounced dead at the scene.

The victim's husband tearfully told investigators he had warned the victim the shoes she had been wearing that day were not appropriate for the basement stairs and that she had slipped before. There was no sign of forced entry, however, the couple was not security conscious and had often left doors and windows unlocked. None of the neighbors reported seeing any strangers in the area, heard any dogs barking or heard loud voices or screams in the time period during which the victim died. There was no evidence of ransacking or theft, although many items of value were openly displayed. Examination of the residence with luminol revealed the presence of blood on a kitchen chair, on the kitchen floor through the main hallway to the area at the top of the basement stairs and bloody drag marks on the last seven steps in the basement. Blood had been cleaned from the kitchen floor, the hallway, and the area at the top of the basement stairs, and the blood was matched to the victim. The postmortem examination revealed the victim's cause of death was massive head injury and manual strangulation. She suffered multiple lacerations to the back of her head, her skull was fractured, and she had numerous bruises and lacerations to her forehead, left cheek, eyes, lips, and jaw line. She had defense-style injuries to her left arm and wrist. During the investigation, detectives discovered the victim's husband had uncharacteristically removed vegetation from a back gate, making it operational, several days before her death. A financial investigation revealed the couple had depleted most of their financial assets during the preceding several years. A search of the vehicle operated by the victim's husband produced a shirt and shoes stained with the victim's blood, which had been hidden beneath the driver's seat. Analyses of his cellular telephone records were inconsistent with the locations he claimed to have visited during the time his wife was killed.

To obtain a better understanding of this murder, the assigned investigators requested the assistance of a criminal investigative analyst shortly after this crime was committed. Following a careful review of the victimology, physical evidence, witness statements, and wound pathology, the analyst prepared a detailed written report that delineated the "red flags" that were present in the crime scene. During the trial of the victim's husband, the prosecutor consulted with the analyst during cross-examination of the defendant and utilized the report to effectively describe the elements of staging during his closing statement to the jury.

EVALUATION OF EYEWITNESS EVIDENCE

Detectives involved in cold homicide investigations often rely heavily upon the accuracy of eyewitness accounts, particularly in cases with no physical or biological evidence.

Since the 1970s, researchers have been studying the causes of eyewitness errors (Loftus, 1979). The unreliability of eyewitness accounts and identifications has been dramatically illustrated by recent court cases in which DNA evidence exonerated individuals wrongfully convicted of violent crimes. These wrongful convictions were found to have been based almost exclusively on testimony from eyewitnesses who remained convinced that their identifications were accurate. Despite the fallibility of such evidence, testimony from eyewitnesses is often perceived as the most compelling trial evidence.

Misconceptions regarding the manner in which human memory functions and the factors that influence an eyewitness's ability to accurately make an identification are common not only in the general population, but throughout the criminal justice system. Historically, criminal investigators have routinely relied upon statements from witnesses to develop investigative leads, identify perpetrators, and exonerate the innocent. Additionally, criminal prosecutions have frequently been based exclusively upon identifications by individuals who claim to have seen either the victim or suspect engaged in normal noncriminal behaviors prior to the commission of the crime. DNA evidence, on the other hand, is often difficult for jurors to understand (Ainsworth, 1998).

Despite belief to the contrary, the identification process does not operate like a videotape recording system. Scientific research has shown that several cognitive processes are involved in "identification memory," which enables someone to accurately select a person from a photographic or live presentation. These processes, which consist of encoding, storage, and retrieval operate separately, but each is essential to the identification process. Identification memory is a complicated process that is vulnerable to alteration by numerous factors, including the nature of the instructions given to the eyewitness regarding identification, the amount of time between the witnessed event and identification, the presentation format, the emotional state of the eyewitness, environmental factors such as lighting and duration of the event, and the degree of familiarity the eyewitness had with the potential suspect. As a result, memories are vulnerable to change by internal and external conditions, interactions with other persons, and exposure to additional information.

One of the most prevalent techniques used within the criminal justice system to evaluate the accuracy of eyewitness statements is an assessment of the level of confidence the witness reports. Although it has been popularly assumed that confidence is predictive of accuracy, researchers have found a relatively weak correlation, which would likely be functionally worthless in real-life settings (Wells and Loftus, 1984; and Sporer, 1995). Recent findings have revealed that a witness's confidence level is affected by factors unrelated to accuracy, such as receiving affirmative feedback, which confirms the accuracy of their identification (Wells and Bradfield, 1998, 1999). This finding has important implications for homicide investigations. It is common for investigators to solicit a self-confidence rating from witnesses regarding the accuracy of their identification, and to use their confidence level as a basis for prioritization of leads. Investigators and prosecutors also use the witness's confidence level to make a determination of whether there is sufficient probable cause to make an arrest or file charges.

Another misperception is that an eyewitness who was highly emotional at the time of the event is a more reliable and accurate witness. It is assumed that a witness or victim will not forget a person they saw during a violent or threatening encounter and that human memory regarding this type of event is essentially unaffected by the passage of time. Researchers have determined that high levels of stress actually interfere with a person's ability to encode information, and that people who are only moderately aroused are more likely to make accurate identifications (Christianson, 1992; Deffenbacher, 1983).

The role that familiarity plays in accurate identification is another issue that is frequently misunderstood. Higher rates of misidentification have been found with persons who had previously been seen than for total strangers; however, higher confidence ratings were reported in identifications of persons rated as familiar (Read, 1994). Researchers believe witnesses are often unable to distinguish between two or more memories, possibly because they perceive them to be similar in quality, content, or characteristics. Accurate identification requires that the person recall the exact context in which they saw the person, and not base identification on exposure to media accounts, viewing mug shots, or conversations with other persons (Reed, 2004). This finding has significant implications during assessment of statements from neighbors or persons who regularly saw the person they identified, and for identifications that followed publicity of the crime. Research by Shapiro and Penrod (1986) found that the only characteristic predictive of identification accuracy was distinctiveness of appearance.

Detectives should carefully review the procedures utilized and the circumstances under which eyewitnesses made identifications. Close scrutiny should be given to any witnesses who became more confident over time regarding the accuracy of their report or who reported details or events they could not have witnessed due to distance, impaired eyesight, insufficient lighting or position; or reported new details or modification of their account following exposure to other witnesses or media coverage.

Witnesses who were young children at the time of the event require special consideration. Criminal justice professionals should review *Children Who Witness Homicide and Other Violent Crimes* (Boychuk-Spears, 2002), for recommendations regarding appropriate interviewing procedures and analyses of statements given by children.

Unfortunately, procedures utilized by police investigators regarding eyewitness identifications have not comprehensively integrated the findings of psychological researchers. Although a collaboration of researchers and criminal justice professionals in 1999 produced the U.S. Department of Justice's publication Eyewitness Evidence: A Guide for Law Enforcement, their recommendations regarding double-blind testing and sequential presentation format have not been commonly adopted (Wells, Malpass, Lindsay, Fisher, Turtle and Fulero, 2000).

CONCLUSION

Criminal investigative analysis is a valuable tool that can bring fresh focus to the investigation of a cold case by providing a comprehensive understanding of the manner in which the crime was committed. The technique integrates information regarding the victim, the initial crime scene investigation, physical and trace evidence, wound patterns, toxicological examination results, geography, witness accounts, and an indirect personality assessment of potential suspects. This comprehensive analysis process can serve as a means of organizing numerous sources of investigative information from a cold case file that might otherwise remain dormant for many years. The passage of time is both an enemy and an ally with regard to a cold homicide case. New insights spawned by a comprehensive analysis of the case are possible through integration of all available information, including behavioral analysis of the interaction of the victim and offender, forensic evidence, and a determination of the feasibility of conducting scientific tests on evidentiary items that may have been overlooked or misinterpreted. Criminal investigative analysis is available to investigators and prosecutors upon their request from members of the International Criminal Investigative Analysis Fellowship (ICIAF).

ACKNOWLEDGMENTS

Richard H. Walton wishes to express gratitude and appreciation to Sharon Pagaling Hagan for her authorship and contribution of this chapter. Sharon Pagaling Hagan is a retired Special Agent Supervisor of the California Department of Justice's Violent Crime Profiling Unit. She has studied criminal investigative profiling and crime scene analysis in conjunction with the International Criminal Investigative Analysis Fellowship and the FBI's National Center for the Analysis of Violent Crime. She has consulted and provided investigative assistance to law enforcement agencies and prosecutors throughout California and nationally regarding homicide, sexual assault, threat assessment, and child abduction cases. She has provided training for thousands of criminal justice professionals and has appeared as an expert witness in state and federal courts. She received her undergraduate degree from California State University, Sacramento, and is pending completion of graduate study in psychology.

In addition, Ms. Pagaling Hagan wishes to acknowledge and extend her gratitude to Dr. Kim Rossmo, Bruce Moran, Gregg McCrary, Dr. David Stubbins, Jill Spriggs, Marla Moura, Mark McKinley, and Laurie Jasienczyk for their contributions and review of this chapter.

REFERENCES

Ainsworth, P.B. (1998). *Psychology, Law and Eyewitness Testimony.* West Sussex, England: John Wiley & Sons, Inc.

Boychuk-Spears, T. (2002). Children who witness homicide and other violent crimes (pp. 91–115). San Diego, CA: Specialized Training Services.

Christianson, S.A. (1992). Emotional stress and eyewitness memory: A critical review. *Psychological Bulletin, 112*, 284–309.

Deffenbacher, K. (1983). The influence of arousal on reliability of testimony. In S.M.A. Lloyd-Bostock and B.R. Clifford (Eds.), *Evaluating Witness Evidence: Recent Psychological Research and New Perspectives* (pp. 235–251). Chichester, England: Wiley.

Douglas, J.E., Burgess, A.W., Burgess, A.G. and Ressler, R.K. (1992). *Crime Classification Manual* (pp. 249–258). New York: Lexington Books.

Hazelwood, R.R. and Burgess, A.W. (2001). The behavioral-oriented interview of rape victims: The key to profiling. In Hazelwood, R.R. and Burgess, A.W. (Eds.), *Practical Aspects of Rape Investigation: A Multidisciplinary Approach*, Second Edition, (pp. 118–119). Boca Raton, FL: CRC Press.

Read, J.D. (1994). Understanding bystander misidentifications: The role of familiarity and contextual knowledge. In D.F. Ross, J.D. Read, and M.P. Toglia (Eds.), *Adult Eyewitness Testimony: Current Trends and Developments* (pp. 56–79). New York: Cambridge University Press.

Reed, S.K. (2004). *Cognition: Theory and Applications* (pp. 111–115). Belmont, CA: Wadsworth/Thomson Learning.

Ressler, R.K., Burgess, A.W. and Douglas, J.E. (1988). *Sexual Homicide: Patterns and Motives.* New York: Lexington Books.

Sporer, S., Penrod, S., Read, D., and Cutler, B.L. (1995). Choosing, confidence and accuracy: A meta-analysis of the confidence-accuracy relation in eyewitness identification studies. *Psychological Bulletin, 118*, 315–327.

Technical Working Group for Eyewitness Evidence (1999). Eyewitness evidence: A guide for law enforcement (Booklet). Washington, DC: United States Department of Justice, Office of Justice Programs.

Wells, G.L. and Bradfield, A.L. (1998). Good, you identified the suspect: Feedback to eyewitnesses distorts their reports of the witnessing experience. *Journal of Applied Psychology, 83*, 360–376.

Wells, G.L. and Bradfield, A.L. (1999). Distortions in eyewitnesses' recollections: Can the post identification feedback effect be moderated? *Psychological Science, 10*, 138–144.

Wells, G.L. and Loftus, E.F. (1984). *Eyewitness Testimony: Psychological Perspectives.* Cambridge, MA: Cambridge University Press.

Wells, G.L., Malpass, R.S., Lindsay, R.C.L., Fisher, R.P., Turtle, J.W. and Fulero, S. (2000). From the lab to the police station. *American Psychologist, 55 (6)*, 581–598.

24 Warming up with Wiretaps

Robert P. Hickey

CONTENTS

The wiretap is an underutilized and overfeared tool in the investigation of cold homicides. The purpose of this chapter is to demystify the use of wiretaps and to suggest how and when to use them to solve cold case homicides. While wiretaps or, more accurately put, *electronic intercepts,* require substantial resources, they should not be overlooked because of the fear of the unknown, instead, they should be thought of as a glorified search warrant that requires additional executive approval and often a fairly significant commitment of resources. Most jurisdictions require approval from the presiding judge, police chief, sheriff, or agency head and the district attorney, or attorney general. Significant resources are required to monitor the "lines" and complement the intercept with surveillance and proactive investigative methods commonly referred to as "tickling the wire." That said, the payoff can be immense. When nearly all else fails, a wiretap can be the best chance to capture the suspect's conversations about the murder or its coverup.

The San Diego Police Department and District Attorney's Office has used wiretaps in cold homicide investigations to establish a "target's" motive to commit the murder, to record a target crafting a bogus alibi, to catch targets planning additional murders and to prosecute people close to the killers in order to leverage them into cooperating in a murder investigation. The Los Angeles Police Department and District Attorney's Office used a wiretap after 20 years to put the final pieces of a puzzle together in a successful murder prosecution.

WHAT IS A WIRETAP?

A wiretap is an order from a judge authorizing a law enforcement agency to intercept wire, electronic digital pager, or electronic cellular telephone communications. This includes common telephone conversations over a hard line, cellular phone or cellular phone with a "walkie-talkie" feature, and text messages to or from a pager or telephone.

Wiretaps and the resources to run them are available in most jurisdictions.

Wiretaps are available under federal jurisdiction and in most states. Check Figure 24.1 to see which states have a statute authorizing wiretaps and note the frequency, or infrequency, of wiretap orders granted in a particular jurisdiction in 2004 to gauge whether it will take a pioneer-like effort to get a wiretap application through the process.

Wiretaps are usually available only in investigations of certain serious crimes listed in the authorizing statute. I am unaware of a state wiretap statute that does not include murder as a qualifying crime but check for this or other limits specific to the jurisdiction before investing any time or effort into obtaining a wiretap order.

The next question is the availability of a "wire room" or facility where the telecommunications company can send the data and where law enforcement can receive, monitor, and collect the conversations or text messages. Few city or county agencies have these facilities, but most local FBI and DEA offices have modern wire rooms and are usually willing to make their assets available to local law enforcement. Contacting the FBI's Violent Crimes Task Force responsible for the jurisdiction is the best first move to find a wire room and to get technical advice. Federal agencies are particularly helpful if the murder, suspect, or investigation has a tie to narcotics activity.

Finally, make sure your agency has, or another agency can provide, qualified agents or officers to monitor the intercept. Wiretap statutes typically require that the intercepts be monitored by people with specific qualifications. Check the statute and check with the prosecutor's office.

APPLICATION TO COLD HOMICIDES

Wiretaps can be useful in warming up a cold homicide; however, the status of the investigation and circumstances of the crime must be appropriate. For instance, you would not expect to gain anything from a wiretap for a murder committed by a lone perpetrator without an accomplice after the fact, and without a person to whom the perpetrator has confessed or to whom the perpetrator would be expected to confess. Much more promising are murders involving multiple perpetrators, subjects who helped the killer plan the offense, subjects who provided weapons or information to the killer, subjects who helped the killer conceal the crime or murder weapon, or subjects in whom the killer has confided about the killing.

The San Diego Police Department proved these points with three wiretaps against several Blood street gang members in 2003. The target Blood gang was at war with a rival Blood gang that resulted in at least a half-dozen murders and over 50 shootings. Gang Detectives John Davis and Ron Newquist worked sources to develop probable cause to instigate wiretaps against several key gang members, which solved two shootings and sent 10 violent gang members to prison.

Multiple Perpetrators

The possibilities of obtaining incriminatory conversations among subjects who committed a murder together is a great foundation for obtaining a wiretap and either jumpstarting or putting a cold case over the top. Even after many years, you could expect fellow killers to talk about their crime or evasion of arrest, particularly if one is a "weak link" or less culpable. In fact, the passage of time could help by wearing on the conscience of one of the perpetrators. The trick is finding probable cause to believe that the subjects would be discussing the crime after several or many years. Tips

	State/Jurisdiction	Wiretap Statute (Yes/No)	Statute	Number of Orders (2004)
1	Federal	Yes	18:2510 – 2520	730
2	Alabama	No	-	-
3	Alaska	Yes	12.37	0
4	Arizona	Yes	ARS 13-3010 – 13-3018	10
5	Arkansas	No	-	-
6	California	Yes	Penal code sections 629.50-629.98	180
7	Colorado	Yes	16-15-102	0
8	Connecticut	Yes	54-41a – 54-41t	0
9	Delaware	Yes	11 Del.C.Chap.24	4
10	District of Columbia	Yes	23-541 – 23-556	0
11	Florida	Yes	934.01 – 934.10	72
12	Georgia	Yes	16-11-64	33
13	Hawaii	Yes	803-41 – 803-48	0
14	Idaho	Yes	18-6701 – 18-6710	0
15	Illinois	Yes	720 ILCS Sec.5/108B	21
16	Indiana	Yes	35-33.5-3-1	0
17	Iowa	Yes	808B.1 – 808B.9	0
18	Kansas	Yes	22-2514–22-2516	0
19	Kentucky	No	-	-
20	Louisiana	Yes	Act No. 121 3B No.233 15:1308(A)(2)	0
21	Maine	Yes	15 M.R.S.A. sec 709 et seq.	0
22	Maryland	Yes	10-401 – 10-411	34
23	Massachusetts	Yes	272:99	23
24	Michigan	No	-	-
25	Minnesota	Yes	626A.01 – 626A.21	1
26	Mississippi	Yes	41-29-501	3
27	Missouri	Yes	33-542.400 – 542.424	0
28	Montana	No	-	-
29	Nebraska	Yes	86-290 – 86-294	0
30	Nevada	Yes	179.0410 – 179.515, NRS 200.620	8
31	New Hampshire	Yes	570-A:1 – A:11	13
32	New Jersey	Yes	2A-156A-1 – 156A-34	144
33	New Mexico	Yes	30-12-2 – 30-12-11	0
34	New York	Yes	CPL Article 700	347
35	North Carolina	Yes	N.C.G.S.15A-286	0
36	North Dakota	Yes	29-29.2	0
37	Ohio	Yes	2933.51 – 2933.66	1
38	Oklahoma	Yes	13 O.S.176.1 – 176.14	16
39	Oregon	Yes	ORS 133.721 – 133.739	0
40	Pennsylvania	Yes	18 Pa.C.S. sec 5701-5728	32
41	Rhode Island	Yes	12-5.1-1 – 12-5.1-16	0
42	South Carolina	Yes	SC code section 17-30-10 et seq.	0
43	South Dakota	Yes	23A – 35A	0
44	Tennessee	Yes	40-6-301 – 40-6-311	36
45	Texas	Yes	Crim.Proc.Sec. 18.20	0
46	Utah	Yes	77-23a-1 – 77-23a-16	0
47	Vermont	No	-	-
48	Virginia	Yes	19.2-61	0
49	Washington	Yes	9.73	0
50	West Virginia	Yes	62-1D-11	0
51	Wisconsin	Yes	968.27 – 968.33	2
52	Wyoming	Yes	7-3-701 – 7-3-712	0

*Administrative office of the United States Courts 2004 Wiretap Report Table1, April 2005

FIGURE 24.1 Code Section Chart. (Courtesy of Robert Hickey)

from a family member or friend to whom one of the perpetrators confessed, or evidence that the killers are still in constant contact are helpful facts, but you still may need to engage in proactive measures to both obtain probable cause to get the intercept and to gain incriminatory conversations during the wiretap. Such techniques are up to the investigator's imagination and some suggestions will be discussed below.

Gang murders almost always involve multiple perpetrators. During the wiretap investigation mentioned above, San Diego Police Detective John Davis, the affiant, proved that members of criminal enterprises talk to each other over the phone to plan their crimes. In the transcript excerpt below, the police capture one Blood gang member (Caller) calling another (Target) to get firearms (called "footballs," "thing things," "thangs," "Jesses," "candles" or "candle lights" as code) in order to commit a revenge shooting. The Blood gang members just learned that one of their associates had been murdered at a mall by a Crip gang member (see Figure 24.2).

Caller:	Hey man, you here or you there?
Target:	Uh, I'm here.
Caller:	I'm gonna snatch up some candle lights.
....	
Target:	Niggas get any word back on your boy?
Caller:	We just seen that motherfucker on the news man.
....	
Target:	What the fuck they sayin?
Caller:	Blood he's dead right there he dead in front of the mall, dead, homie
	shotgunned down homie, baby mama crying.
....	
Target:	Blood you can't get, you can't get that thing, thing?
Caller:	Uh, shit, yeah!
Target:	Yeah, I'm gonna probably need that.

FIGURE 24.2 Transcript, part one. (Courtesy of Robert Hickey)

The target then called his girlfriend at her apartment where he had hidden firearms (see Figure 24.3).

Target:	What's up?
Girlfriend:	What's up?
Target:	The homie wants to come over there.
Girlfriend:	Who?
Target:	He about to get that uh, thang.
Girlfriend:	Okay.
Target:	Uh, he'll call me when he get over there.
Girlfriend:	Okay, alright.
Target:	You know that, don't give 'em that, don't give 'em that them new
	footballs, give 'em that old ass....ball.
Girlfriend:	Yep, okay.
Target:	That one that uh...old ass football.
Girlfriend:	Okay.

FIGURE 24.3 Transcript, part two. (Courtesy of Robert Hickey)

The gang member called the target back and exclaimed that "somebody gotta lay down," meaning be killed, and asked for more firearms (see Figure 24.4).

Caller:	Fuck it, somebody gotta lay down, fuck all that bullshit!
Target:	Hey what's with it?
Caller:	Hey mother fucker, I need that second thing thing too.
Target:	Alright.
Caller:	If it's bool (cool) with you I mean.
Target:	Yeah.

FIGURE 24.4 Transcript, part three. (Courtesy of Robert Hickey)

The San Diego Police Department prevented a shooting by catching four gang members leaving the target's girlfriend's apartment complex with the firearms. The target and the four who picked up the guns were convicted of conspiracy to commit a drive-by shooting, and the girlfriend pled guilty to aiding a criminal street gang. While Detective Davis's wiretap did not directly solve the cold homicides, it did help break the back of a criminal street gang and create leverage over suspects linked to the murders.

Accomplices Before or After the Fact

Even if your target committed the murder alone, look to see if you have a subject who in any way helped the target. Did someone supply the murder weapon with or without knowledge of its intended use? Did someone tell the killer where to find the victim with or without knowledge of the killer's intent? Did someone help the killer dispose of the body? Did someone help the killer get rid of the weapon with or without knowledge of the murder? Your target could be expected to speak with anyone fitting the above description under the proper circumstances.

Consider the scenario above where the target's girlfriend supplied firearms to gang members to be used in a shooting. If the gang members went on to commit a shooting, the police could easily have provoked additional calls between the girlfriend (who kept the firearms at her apartment) and the target or the target and the shooters.

Persons in Whom the Killer Has or May Confide

Oftentimes cold homicides are revived when a "source" close to the killer comes forward with information based upon his or her observations of the killer or statements made by the killer. Obviously, you would first consider employing the new source, if cooperative, to place recorded consensual "pretext" calls to the killer — no wiretap needed. But consider if the source is not cooperative (e.g., an anonymous tipster who you have identified), or if you learn about the source's information from a third party (e.g., "my sister told me her ex-husband killed someone in a robbery, but she won't work with you because he's the father of her children"). It is not difficult to think of ways to manipulate even an uncooperative or unknowing source into eliciting incriminatory statements from the killer.

Would it not be possible to use someone like a sibling or spouse to unwittingly gain an incriminatory statement from your killer? With the right pressure you could expect the source to call the killer and question him or her about the murder.

The police may not need to manipulate the players in the gang or criminal enterprise scenario. During another wiretap involving the same investigation discussed above, the San Diego Police Detective Ron Newquist proved that members of criminal enterprises talk to each other about their past crimes for one reason or another. In the transcript excerpt below (see Figure 24.5), the police captured one Blood gang member (Caller) confessing to anther gang member (Target) about shooting a member of a rival Blood gang set called "the South." Caller was worried because his victim was related to a famous deceased member of the rival gang and the shooter heard that the rival gang was after him. Notice how both speakers often replace the letter "c" with the letter "b" to avoid using the first letter of the name of their most traditional and hated rivals, the Crips. The term "Ru" is short for Piru, derived from a street in Los Angeles, which is another name for Blood gang members. The police had no problem determining which shooting Caller was confessing to because he gave his victim's moniker, "Lil Gansta Ern." This is dynamite evidence and solved a shooting for which the police previously had no suspects.

Caller:	Them niggas wanna get me, Blood.
Target:	Who?
Caller:	South niggas.
....	
Target:	Who told you this, brackin Blood?
Caller:	Uh - somebody from the South told me this, Blood.
Target:	Yeah
Caller:	Yeah, Blood. Them niggas, they just wanna get me because - South - Blood - Them niggas got pull in the set. They found out. Okay - "Lil Gangsta Ern" right?
Target:	Yeah
Caller:	Blood - when they took the thing out, Blood, they saw "Blood-Blood" got hit with a "9" in the arm.
Target:	Uh-huh.
....	
Caller:	Blood, "Big Homie" said, before Gangsta Ern died, they will always watch over Blood because Gangsta Ern is such a little rider, or whatever, right?
Target:	Uh huh.
Caller:	Blood. I don't know how they found out, Blood. They found out it was me. They know about Rich. They not trippin off of Rich cause Little Rich shot at em with a .38.
Target:	Uh-huh.
Caller:	They wanna come get me, Blood. They wanna put the smash down. You know what I'm sayin?
Target:	Uh huh.
....	
Caller:	They said, Blood - And they know my name, Blood. They know about Rich. They not trippin off of Rich cause all Rich did was shoot at em, Blood. They found out, Blood. About me, Blood. . .
Target:	Oh, brazy. Hold on, Ru.

FIGURE 24.5 Transcript, part four. (Courtesy of Robert Hickey)

Criminals are also known to brag. During the same wire, Detective Newquist captured yet another Blood gang member (Target 2) confessing to shooting a rival (see Figure 24.6). Note how the other gang member (Caller 2) is enthusiastic about getting involved in shootings himself. Again, the police had no problem determining which shooting "Target 2" was confessing to because he gave a time frame for the shooting and the location of the victim's gunshot wound to the stomach or, as the shooter called it, the "yomach."

Again, dynamite evidence that solved a shooting.

Target2:	You hear what I did?
Caller2:	When?
Target2:	Couple nights ago.
Caller2:	You did that?
Target2:	Yeah.
Caller2:	On who? No, no, no, no. Uh - he 'K'd" (killed)?
Target2:	Na, I didn't. Hit him in the yomach.
Caller2:	Oh. Hey - hey - hey -
Target2:	Yeah - yeah -
Caller2:	Blood. You need to do that for me, blood. That's the only way I'm gonna get these chips, homie. On some real shit. And when it come down to that riding-type shit, blood, it's gonna be me and you on the late night logo.
Target2:	Yeah.

FIGURE 24.6 Transcript, part five. (Courtesy of Robert Hickey)

BUILDING A WIRETAP AFFIDAVIT

States derive the power to authorize wiretaps through the federal wiretap statute so they follow similar requirements. Most statutes require that the affidavit: demonstrate that all other investigative techniques have been exhausted to the point that a wiretap is necessary to build a prosecutable case, identify a target subject and target telephone, and establish probable cause to believe that the target phone will be used by a subject to discuss a qualifying target offense. Check the applicable statute, but expect to meet these requirements.

EXHAUSTION OF OTHER LAW ENFORCEMENT TECHNIQUES AND NECESSITY

All jurisdictions require in some form and to some degree that the affidavit contain an explanation regarding why a wiretap is needed. In other words, you must lay out what evidence you have, what investigative techniques you have tried and why other techniques not yet attempted would not likely succeed. Explain why a wiretap is necessary to make the case or to lead the investigation toward a prosecutable case. Look no further than the other traditional techniques discussed in this text to get an idea of other techniques you must discount as sufficient to make a prosecutable case.

The affidavit should detail why the following tools are or were insufficient to meet your investigative goals: undercover police officers, confidential informants, surveillance, search warrants, pen registers and phone tolls, grand jury subpoenas and immunity, trash searches, mail cover requests, closed circuit television monitoring, consensual recordings or "pretext calls," financial investigations, and, if you have used prior wiretaps, why they did not meet the objectives of the investigation.

THE TARGET TELEPHONE

The affidavit must identify a target telephone. The phone number can come from any lawful source such as informants, a tip, subpoenaed records, or pretext calls. Use a search warrant or administrative subpoena to obtain subscriber information such as the provider telecommunications company, the person who "owns" the number, and how long the line has been in service and the billing address. If the person who owns or primarily uses the phone is not the suspect, explain how the subscriber is connected to the suspect. Depending on the jurisdiction the target telephone need not be the killer's, but could be someone who witnessed the crime, an accomplice, or someone with whom the killer is expected to speak.

Some jurisdiction may require, and I recommend, that you obtain call or toll records or "pen registers" for the phone beforehand. (Identifying the parties the target speaks with regularly will help you monitor and manipulate the parties during the intercept.) Most of this process is getting easier with the spread of cellular phones and digital cable phone lines.

THE TARGET SUBJECT

The target subject or person you expect to use the phone to discuss the murder should be named if known or otherwise described as closely as possible. If you can identify the target, provide information such as residence, occupation, and criminal history. If not, describe the target by his or her relationship to the target phone and other parties to the murder. Describe how and why there is probable cause to believe this person is linked to the murder. This will be the meat of the probable cause supporting the intercept.

Relationship Between the Target, the Phone and the Crime

The affidavit must include language explaining why you believe the target's conversations will be captured on the target telephone and that at least one conversation will be related to the murder or coverup. Consider the following questions. Has a source reported that he or she spoke to the killer about the murder over the telephone? Has a source reported that a third party spoke to the killer about the murder over the telephone? Can you demonstrate through records or witnesses that this is a telephone the target uses or calls frequently? Many of these questions will be answered through the investigation but others will require the investigator's opinions about criminal behavior. Be sure to articulate the foundation for those opinions in the affidavit. In a cold homicide you will need to explain why, after years, you expect the target to speak about the murder at all. If necessary, lay out your plans to "tickle the wire" and get the target talking, without revealing tactical details that could compromise future investigations.

Some jurisdictions or agencies, including the U.S. Department of Justice, require what is commonly referred to as a "dirty call," meaning evidence of a specific call by the target subject on the target telephone about criminal activity. Check the statute and seek the advice of the prosecuting agency to determine if and to what extent you must meet this requirement.

Additional Approval and Procedural Requirements

As mentioned earlier, wiretaps require approval from the top level of every agency involved. That could mean the presiding judge, police chief, sheriff, or agency head and the district attorney or attorney general. Involve the prosecuting attorney's office as soon as you begin to consider seeking a wiretap. The prosecutor's office may have policies in place as to when and how they will seek a wiretap. I recommend providing a draft of the affidavit to the appropriate judge ahead of time so he or she will be knowledgeable about the wiretap before you seek his or her approval.

You must also make advanced contact with the telecommunications company to assure the intercept is in place as soon as possible after the judge signs the orders.

Once the wiretap is in place, follow the recording and reporting requirements specific to your jurisdiction. These will include the "minimization" process (monitoring and recording only "pertinent" calls), the manner in which the intercepted calls are recorded (digital or tape) and how they are sealed, and the requirements for how to report the status of the intercept to the authorizing judge.

"TICKLING THE WIRE" — TIPS TO WARM UP A COLD CASE DURING A WIRETAP

Because this is a cold case, you will most likely need to engage in proactive methods of investigation to provoke the target into making incriminatory statements over the telephone. The tactics are limited only by the law and your imagination. Sensitivity in your approach is the key. A blunt frontal attack on the target is more likely to lead to no statement rather than a confession. Find a "dupe." Approach people you know the target speaks to over the phone. Think of co-killers, accomplices, family members, the sources who helped you create probable cause for the intercept. If it makes sense to discuss the murder with the dupe, do not necessarily mention the target — maybe describe the target to the extent that the dupe will know who you are talking about. If you need to discuss the target with the dupe do not necessarily mention the murder — maybe ask general questions about the target around the time of the murder. Get the dupe and the target talking about the investigation over the phone and continue to "tickle." This is the fun part.

CASE STUDY

On March 17, 1983, Dr. Stephen Graham reported his wife, Elaine Graham, missing. She was last seen that morning driving her 1971 yellow Volkswagen when she left her 2-year-old daughter at the babysitter's house and drove toward the California State University Northridge (CSUN) campus near Los Angeles to attend classes. Elaine Graham was 29 years old when she disappeared.

THE INITIAL INVESTIGATION

On March 23, the Santa Ana Police Department found Graham's vehicle parked in the customer parking lot at the Fashion Square Mall in Santa Ana. The doors were unlocked. Police impounded the car.

Based on the unusual circumstances, Detectives Paul Tippin and Leroy Orozco from the Los Angeles Police Department's Robbery-Homicide Division assumed investigative responsibility. Detectives found a baby's car seat on the front passenger seat and Graham's schoolbooks on the rear seat. Although there were no obvious signs of foul play, they noted the driver's seat was positioned for a person much larger than for someone Elaine Graham's size.

Detectives further discovered that a Santa Ana Police sergeant had observed Graham's vehicle parked at the same location on March 18 between 2:00 a.m. and 4:00 a.m.

Detectives conducted numerous interviews and investigated several potential leads, following up on calls from concerned citizens and anonymous sources.

On July 7, detectives received a telephone call from an anonymous source. This citizen stated that an individual named Jay Marr might have been responsible for Elaine Graham's disappearance. The unidentified caller further stated that Marr was in custody in Orange County. Upon researching this information, detectives learned Marr's true name was Edmond Jay Marr. The Westminster Police Department had arrested Marr for robbery on April 23, 1983, and at the time of his arrest, Marr was armed with a .45 caliber semi-automatic handgun and money that was taken during the commission of the crime. In addition to the weapon, officers recovered Marr's black Samsonite bag. The bag contained Marr's personal belongings, including an Explorer MM III knife secured in a leather sheath. The weapon had a 5-inch double-sided blade and a black handle.

Detectives learned that Marr's mother, Francis Marr, lived approximately two blocks away from the CSUN campus. Detectives further discovered that Marr's sister, Kathleen Marr, lived in the city of Orange, about half a mile from where the victim's vehicle was found and 56 miles from the CSUN campus.

On July 11, 1983, detectives interviewed Francis Marr. She said that her son had been in and out of trouble throughout his childhood and teens, and had entered the U.S. Army in July 1981. He had been arrested for robbery and smoked marijuana. Mrs. Marr recalled that on March 16, 1983, she had telephoned the Fort Irwin military base to check on Edmond only to learn that her son had been discharged from the military. During the early afternoon hours of that same day, Edmond unexpectedly arrived at her residence. He stayed the night and on the following morning, Mrs. Marr told him that he had to leave. She indicated that after leaving her apartment, Edmond went to his sister's residence in the city of Orange.

Mrs. Marr stated that she became aware of Elaine Graham's disappearance from the media publicity and posters being distributed around the CSUN campus. She and her daughter discussed the possibility of Edmond's involvement in Elaine Graham's disappearance. Reasons for their concerns included (1) Edmond was upset at being discharged from the army; (2) on March 16, 1983, he unexpectedly arrived at his mother's residence, which was near the CSUN campus; (3) on March 17, 1983, the day of Elaine Graham's disappearance, Edmond traveled from the Northridge area to the city of Orange, arriving at his sister's residence in the late afternoon hours; (4) Elaine Graham's vehicle was recovered within walking distance of Kathleen Marr's residence; (5) Edmond did not have a vehicle of his own; and (6) Edmond had a history of violent behavior.

Frances Marr told detectives that approximately 1 week after Elaine Graham's disappearance, Edmond returned to her residence. She told him that he could not live with her. Edmond was angry and left, stating that he was going to live with the Smith (name changed) family.

On July 12, 1983, detectives interviewed Kathleen Marr. She told them that on March 16, 1983 she received a telephone call from her brother, Edmond. He told her that he would be coming to visit; however, he did not say when he would be arriving. The next day, Edmond arrived at her apartment at approximately 5:30 p.m. and told his sister he took a bus to get there. That evening, Kathleen, her roommate (Edward X), and Marr went to a party, where, Kathleen stated, her brother acted very withdrawn. During the party, Edmond told her that he was carrying a gun, but she did not see the weapon. When asked why he had the gun, Edmond stated that he carried it for self protection or to help someone in trouble, such as a rape victim.

Kathleen described her brother as a violent person who felt superior to women. He smoked marijuana and liked different types of drugs. She indicated that Edmond was a loner who frequently left during the day and returned late at night. On the occasions that Kathleen allowed him to drive her vehicle, she noticed that he always moved the seat back.

Before Marr entered the military, he dated Amber X. Edmond confided to Kathleen that when he would get mad at Amber he would sexually abuse her. Amber X refused to be interviewed. On March 18, 1983, Edmond left Kathleen's residence and told her he was moving to San Diego with some friends to become a mercenary. She stated that she spoke to him via telephone while he was detained for robbery. During one conversation, Kathleen asked Edmond if he had done anything else and he told her that he had committed other robberies.

Detectives also interviewed Bradley and Gary Smith (name changed). The Smith family lived a few blocks south of the CSUN campus. Bradley Smith stated that he had been Marr's close friend for many years. Marr used marijuana, LSD, and PCP. Bradley stated that he returned to his parent's home in Northridge after being away for his spring quarter at college in 1983. When he arrived, he found that Marr had recently moved into the home. During his stay, Marr purchased a large quantity of marijuana and indicated that he planned to sell the narcotics at the Fort Irwin military base in Barstow. Marr possessed a .45 caliber handgun and he practiced shooting the weapon in an area that is the entrance into Brown's Canyon. Bradley was surprised when detectives informed him about Marr's robbery arrest, but added that he knew Marr was capable of committing a crime of this nature.

Gary Smith told detectives that he and Marr first met in high school and had been friends for approximately 10 years. He described Marr has a loner who did not have many friends. While in high school, Gary introduced Marr to the Brown's Canyon area. They frequently went there together to hike. Marr told him that after he was discharged from the military he went to his mother's residence, but she would not allow him to live there. He then stayed a few days at his sister's residence before finally moving into the Smith home. Gary also added that Marr was very familiar with the CSUN campus and would cut through the campus when traveling between his mother's residence and the Smith residence.

Detectives continued investigating Marr's background for possible connections to Elaine Graham, but found no nexus. Detectives learned that Marr had previously worked at a children's hospital for approximately 2 years before he enlisted in the Army. The hospital is located approximately one-quarter mile from the Santa Ana Fashion Mall and is midway along the route between the mall and Kathleen Marr's residence. On September 1, 1983, detectives interviewed Marr while he was in custody. Marr informed detectives that he had been discharged from the service in the middle of March and subsequently moved into his mother's residence for 2 to 3 weeks. He recalled spending a weekend at his sister's residence during April and stated that he had gone to a party with her. Marr said he used the RTD bus line to get to his sister's residence. After moving out of his mother's residence, he moved in with the Smith family, which was located just southeast of the CSUN campus. Marr admitted that he had been on the campus grounds since the time of his discharge, recalling he had met some girls in the library. After reviewing a photograph of Elaine Graham, Marr denied ever seeing her before.

He admitted that he had driven a car to his sister's house and when he did he took a route directly by the Santa Ana Fashion Mall, where the victim's vehicle was discovered. Marr stated that he arrived at his mother's and sister's sometime during the last week of March or the first week of April 1983.

On November 27, 1983, two citizens discovered skeletal remains in a wash located in Brown's Canyon area. Officers responded to the location, secured the immediate area, and notified the Los Angeles County Coroner's Office.

On November 28, 1983, detectives and the Coroner's Office responded to Brown's Canyon. Doctor J. Wallace Graham of the Coroner's Office examined the skeletal remains and compared the teeth to Elaine Graham's dental charts. He determined the remains were those of Elaine Graham. In addition to the doctor's identification, identical clothing listed on the Elaine Graham's Missing Persons report was found at the scene. The clothing found included a long-sleeved, dark blue plaid shirt, and a white or gray long-sleeved sweatshirt. These articles of clothing were turned inside out, with the sweatshirt being inside of the shirt. The buttons of the blue shirt were still fastened, giving the impression the garments had been pulled off Graham at the same time. A pair of blue jeans was found less than a foot above the two shirts.

The location where Elaine Graham's skeletal remains were found was a remote area approximately one eighth of a mile from Brown's Canyon Road. They were not visible from the road. All the remains, including the skull, were found with her clothing and clog-style shoes within an approximate 5-yard radius. The walk from the road to the recovery site was mostly uphill and over a small wash that was difficult to traverse. The detectives concluded that the clothing and clogs being found at the exact location of the skeletal remains dismissed the possibility of Elaine Graham's body being thrown or pushed from the cliff above. Due to the steep terrain leading up to the remains, it appeared likely that the victim was led up the hill to the location, as opposed to someone carrying her there. These facts supported the detectives' theory that Elaine Graham was taken to that area by a suspect and subsequently murdered there.

On November 29, 1983, Dr. William E. Sherry, a Los Angeles County Deputy Medical Examiner, analyzed the remains that were collected from the crime scene. Dr. Sherry noted a defect in the anterior aspect of the lower thoracic vertebra, which was consistent with having been made by a sharp-edged instrument (see Figure 24.7). Therefore, the cause of death was attributed to be a stab wound to the chest and abdomen. It was Dr. Sherry's opinion that a stab wound inflicted to that portion of the vertebra would most likely have perforated the aorta.

Upon learning Dr. Sherry's medical findings, detectives recalled that a double-edged knife had been recovered from Marr's personal belongings after his Westminster robbery arrest (see Figure 24.8). On December 14, 1983, detectives contacted Westminster Police Department and were informed that Marr's property was still in their possession. The evidence was recovered and transferred to the custody of the Los Angeles Police Department.

On December 19, 1983, Scientific Investigation Division (SID) Criminalist Greg Matheson examined the knife and tote bag that was found within Marr's black Samsonite bag. He found

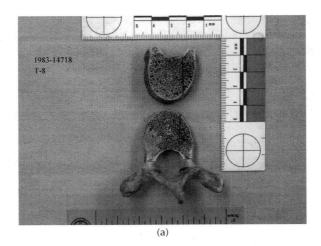

(a)

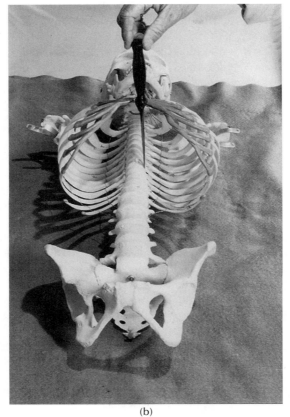

(b)

FIGURE 24.7 Vertebrae showing cut. (Courtesy of Detective Tim Marcia, Los Angeles Police Department)

human blood beneath the knife's hilt and on the tote bag. Using conventional serology typing methods, he determined that the blood from the knife hilt was type A. This matched Elaine Graham's blood type and did not match Marr's type O blood. The biological sample from the tote bag was of insufficient quantity for typing.

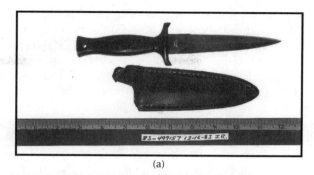

(a)

(b)

FIGURE 24.8 Knife found in suspect's bag. (Courtesy of Detective Tim Marcia, Los Angeles Police Department)

Although there was probable cause to believe Edmond Jay Marr was responsible for the murder of Elaine Graham, Los Angeles County District Attorney's Office requested additional investigation on September 14, 1984. The case remained unsolved.

REOPENING THE INVESTIGATION IN 2002

By 2002, Detective Paul Tippin had retired from the LAPD and was now a District Attorney Investigator with Orange County, California, District Attorney's Office. He had never forgotten this case and was keenly aware that changes in technology might now allow it to be solved. In April, he requested that cold case investigators reopen the investigation. Not long before, the LAPD had started a cold case unit, and Detective Tim Marcia and his partner, Detective Rick Jackson, picked up the file.

They requested that the Serology Unit of the Los Angeles Police Department's SID reexamine the biological evidence recovered during the original investigation. Because of the quantity of sample needed during the blood typing process commonly used in 1983, all of the known blood had been used.

In December, SID Criminalist Nick Sanchez reexamined an area beneath the knife's hilt and detected a trace amount of human blood. He used polymerase chain reaction (PCR) testing to isolate DNA extracts. The DNA profile revealed that it was Elaine Graham's blood.

On November 21, 2002, Detectives Marcia and Jackson interviewed a previously identified witness, Robert B. During 1983, Robert B. and Edmond Marr were in the United States Army together. In early February, 1983, Robert B. purchased a .22 caliber handgun. About 3 weeks later he sold the weapon to Marr. Additionally, Robert B. stated that he owned a survival-type boot knife and that when he sold the gun to Marr, Marr said he liked the knife. Robert B. described the knife as being approximately 7 inches long with a double-edged blade and a steel handle. A short time later, Robert B. saw Edmond Marr carrying the same type of knife. Robert B. identified the knife found in Marr's property as being the same type of knife he and Marr owned. Robert B.'s *timeline* indicated that Marr purchased the knife between approximately March 9 and March 16, 1983.

Detectives Jackson and Marcia crafted an investigative strategy aimed at putting the case over the top. They knew that Marr's mother and sister provided information about Marr when interviewed in 1983. Jackson and Marcia expected they and other family and friends might have learned more over the last 20 years. Although Frances Marr and Kathleen Marr were cooperative during the original investigation, the detectives believed that attitudes and alliances might have changed over 2 decades. It was reasonable to assume that Edmond Marr and his family members might have mended their previous differences and were currently in contact with one another.

Rather than contact them directly, the detectives thought their best chance to gain honest information was with a wiretap. The detectives obtained wiretaps for phones used by Marr, his mother, his sister, and a friend who resided with Marr.

To "tickle" the wire, the LAPD orchestrated an article about Ms. Graham's murder in the *Los Angeles Times* naming Marr as a suspect. They also anonymously mailed a copy of the article to Marr.

The day the article appeared in the paper, the wiretap captured a call between two of Marr's relatives, Frances Marr ("FM") and Edward Cardona ("EC") wherein Cardona acknowledged that Marr admitted to taking Ms. Graham's VW from the college parking lot. This was in direct conflict to what Marr told the police in 1983, when he had denied ever seeing the car before. Figure 24.9 displays a portion of that call.

EC: I even asked him point blank, I think about ten years ago. Did you do it?

FM: You asked him?

EC: I asked him point blank –

FM: You

EC: I said, hey fella, you know between you and me. I don't care about nobody else –

FM: Uh huh.

EC: Did you do this?

FM: Uh huh.

EC: No, I didn't do that. He said, I – I - you know me- I was – you know I - I was – I think he said he was going through a parking lot. He had been some place. He was tired of walking and he didn't have no money for bus fare, and he said he was looking to get in a car. Steal a car, so you know – he was going through the parking lot, he said and so he saw a Volkswagen with the keys in it.

FM: Uh huh.

EC: So he said he got into it. He said, man I got keys. I got a car. It's a Volkswagen – you know – it's a long – long way and all.

FM: So he did take the car huh?

EC: Yeah. He said he took the car. . .

FIGURE 24.9 Transcript of phone call part one. (Courtesy of Robert Hickey)

PD : Did he ever confess this murder to you?

IS : He tried to and I said I don't want to know nothing. Don't tell me anything. I don't want to be an accessory before the fact.

PD : Yeah – after the fact.

IS : And Patrick, if ever – ever I needed you - I needed you now.

PD : Yeah.

IS : What did you want when you called?

PD : I just wanted to call and see how you were doing.

....

PD : – was it a male or a female that he killed?

IS : Female.

PD : Oh female?

IS : Yeah.

PD : A woman.

IS : It was some kind of a – some kind of a – you know – that eh – eh – you know – one of these crazy things – you know – like – like what – ah – ah – a ritual or something like that.

FIGURE 24.10 Transcript of phone call part two. (Courtesy of Robert Hickey)

On February 10, 2003, Marr was arrested at the residence that he shared with Irving Silverman. Following the arrest, police executed a search warrant at his home. Even after 20 years, the detectives recovered several incriminating pieces of evidence.

Among the items seized was a document from 1994 in Marr's handwriting. In the document, Marr wrote about being part of a cult while stationed at Fort Irwin. He wrote about breaking away from the cult by having to kill someone.

In a second document, also from 1994, Marr wrote about a message that he received during a dream about women being the anti-Christ. This same document also referred to the demonic cult that he was involved with at Fort Irwin. He also wrote that "during my life there were crimes committed I don't want to remember."

On the evening of Marr's arrest, the intercept captured a call between two of Marr's friends, Irving Silverman ("IS") and Patrick Dillon ("PD"), which exposed what amounted to a confession by Marr (see Figure 24.10).

Because of this call, detectives interviewed Silverman and were able to gain even more incriminatory information that Marr had admitted to Silverman, including "ritualistic killing" information that was known only to the murderer.

Given the dogged work of Detectives Tippen, Jackson, and Marcia, and Deputy District Attorney John Lewin, Marr pled guilty to second degree murder with a knife and was sentenced to 16 years to life in prison on April 5, 2005.

SUMMARY

As shown by the success in the San Diego and Los Angeles County examples, wiretaps can help solve cold case homicides and create prosecutable cases. The process may be foreign to some but it is not unreasonably burdensome. It may just be your last, best chance.

Here is a basic chronology of how to approach a wiretap once your department thinks it has the need to seek one:

- Find the relevant statute in your jurisdiction to learn particular probable cause requirements and monitoring and reporting requirements.
- Determine which county or state has jurisdiction (typically where the hard line is located or, if a cellular phone, where the calls originate or where the phone is located).
- Contact the prosecuting authority.
- Find a "wire room" (you may need to work with the local office of the FBI or DEA).
- Find authorized officers or agents to monitor the wire.
- Determine the strategy and resources needed to monitor and "tickle the wire."
- Subpoena phone-record and toll information (if necessary or wanted).
- Determine which judge can sign and authorize the intercept.
- Draft the affidavit and submit to the prosecuting authority.
- Contact the telecommunication company.
- Provide a draft of the affidavit and sample orders to the judge.
- Draft instruction and schedule for wire monitors.
- Finalize the affidavit and orders and submit them to the judge.
- Once signed, deliver or fax the orders to the telecommunications company.

Richard H. Walton would like to extend gratitude and appreciation to Robert Hickey for his authorship and contribution of this chapter. Mr. Hickey has been a Deputy District Attorney in San Diego County, California for almost 10 years and is currently assigned to the Gang Prosecution Unit. Mr. Hickey graduated from the University of San Diego School of Law in 1994 and also practiced law at a large international law firm for a year and a half. He was the first San Diego prosecutor to use state wiretaps in cold case homicides and gang-violence investigations and has overseen more than seven wiretaps. He has also worked with investigators to bring five cold case homicides to prosecution and is a recipient of the prestigious FBI Director's Award.

In addition, I wish to acknowledge and thank Detectives Tim Marcia and Rick Jackson of the LAPD Cold Case Team for their enthusiastic cooperation in providing the extensive material used in preparing the case study. District Attorney Investigator Paul Tippin is to be commended for his tenacity and perseverance in the pursuit of justice, one that is echoed by Detectives Marcia and Jackson, and that exemplifies the best in law enforcement and cold case investigation.

25 Bloodstain Pattern Analysis in Homicide Cold Case Investigations

Tom Bevel

CONTENTS

INTRODUCTION

The chronology of a homicide that goes unsolved for several years may be classified as still active, but often goes from a proactive investigation to a reactive investigation. This means that work is completed on the case only when new leads come in. The unsolved case is shoved back in priorities to allow more investigative time for recent cases with greater solvability factors. At some point, the unsolved case is sent to a cold case unit if the agency has one.

Investigating homicide cold cases usually requires looking at three different areas. The first is relationship oriented. People involved in the case may now be willing to talk to the investigators due to divorce, deaths, or other changed relationships. The second area is new technology oriented, where we need only identify what new forensic techniques or tools are available today that were not available at the time of the crime; DNA is the most common new forensic discipline used in cold case investigations. The third area is to ensure that all available forensic disciplines were originally used. For some crimes, we simply need to use all of the forensic tools that were in place at the time, but, for whatever reason, were never applied in the case in question. One forensic tool that has often been overlooked in past cases is bloodstain pattern analysis (BPA). Crimes of violence frequently produce bloodstains which, when properly studied, will aid in reconstructing the occurrences that took place to produce the patterns found at the scene, on victims or suspects, and on their clothing. This discipline adds another investigative tool for determining what happened, how it occurred, who was or was not involved, number of blows struck, which hand was used to deliver the blows in a beating and the position of the victim and suspect during the attack and subsequent movement (Bevel, 1992). One of the best properties of blood spatters is that they will always appear in a manner that is consistent with the events that produced them. Even in staged crime scenes where blood is used to set up the scene, the bloodstains will look consistent with the staging event that produced them.

While BPA has a long history of use in violent crime investigations, the value of this discipline is still today often overlooked in many investigations. Thus, it is not too surprising that BPA may not have been applied to many older case investigations.

A Brief History of Bloodstain Pattern Analysis

Studies and research in BPA, as a forensic discipline, are documented in several European countries in the late 1800s. As far back as 1220–1235, Germanic law in the *Sachsenspiegel* dealt with the raising of the "hue and cry" and the necessity of proving one's innocence when a criminal was caught in the act or caught with blood on his or her hands. (Bevel and Gardner, 2002) Today, we would all recognize the importance of identifying that the substance on the person's hands is blood, whether it is animal or human and whether it is the victim's blood. From its early day application of little in-depth analysis, the BPA discipline has grown dramatically to where today it can reveal a vast amount of information about what happened during and after the crime.

An early application of BPA in police investigations was documented in 1875 in Denver, Colorado. Sheriff David J. Cook used bloodstain interpretation to reconstruct the violent killing of four Italian musicians on October 21, 1875. When the suspects were caught several days later, they were found to still have dried blood stains on their undershirts. The suspects confessed to the crime and confirmed Sheriff Cook's theory of the murders. Due to the confessions, the reconstruction, based partly on BPA, did not get used at trial. (Adair, 1999)

One of the early judicial uses of BPA in America was in the case of *State of California v. Jack Ryan* in 1925. Dr. Ernst A. Victors, M.D. and Edward Oscar Heinrich (sometimes called the Wizard of Berkeley or the American Sherlock Holmes) combined forces and used BPA to identify blood spatter locations and direction of travel on the coat of Jack Ryan, who was accused of killing Henry Sweet and Carmen Wagner. This case is discussed in the Introduction.

Another early and renowned court case in which BPA was admitted in American courts was the *State of Ohio v. Samuel Sheppard* in 1955. This was in the form of an affidavit by Dr. Paul Kirk explaining his analysis of the crime scene, which included BPA. Due to Dr. Kirk's analysis having been recorded in an affidavit, his reasoning and logic are explained in detail and is quite fascinating reading for anyone interested in BPA or crime scene reconstruction. Dr. Kirk's affidavit can be obtained from many different sources to include the internet.

Methodology of BPA in Homicide Cold Cases

Unique to cold case investigations is that the investigator no longer has the ability to personally view the crime scene, as it has long ago been processed and released. The cold case investigator has to depend on what others have done long before the analyst became involved in the case. The quality of the crime scene documentation, collection, and preservation of physical evidence dictates the quality and extent to which the BPA expert can go in their analysis and opinions. Some of the items needed for an analysis include the following:

- Investigative reports by responding officers
- Investigative reports by detectives
- CSI reports on scene processing and evidence collection
- Witness or accused statements, interviews, or depositions
- Autopsy protocol

- Photographs of the crime scene, autopsy, and physical evidence
- Lab reports from serology, DNA, firearms, fingerprints, toxicology, etc.
- Crime scene diagrams
- Reports by EMTs
- All physical evidence that is still available

When the case is assigned to a cold case unit or investigator, the assigned investigator has to read the complete case file to understand what has been done, needs to be done, or redone. In this process, the investigator will evaluate the reports, photographs, and evidence to understand all the minute details of the events that encompass the crime and original investigation. In this process, the investigator continually attempts to understand what events or actions by the attacker and to the victim took place during and immediately after the time of the crime. The investigator will compare the physical evidence analysis against statements given by witnesses or the accused. This is often referred to as a *statement analysis*. This involves comparing the statements against the physical evidence, looking for areas that can be supported by the physical evidence or refuted by it.

The same process followed by the case investigator applies equally to the BPA expert. Bloodstain pattern analysis should always be viewed in a holistic approach and never in a vacuum all by itself. This means that the opinions coming from the bloodstain analysis should be compared against all the other information and evidence. If the BPA opinions are supported and corroborated by other case information and evidence outside of BPA, then it makes the foundation for the BPA opinions even stronger. If the other information or physical evidence is in disagreement with the BPA analysis, then this is a "red flag" that should cause analysts to reanalyze their opinions and attempt to reconcile why there is disagreement. This practice is similar to the "audit" used in crime scene analysis and reconstruction. (Adair, 1999)

The *investigative reports* by responding officers and detectives will give an overview of the entire case and investigation. These reports will furnish needed information about the victim, who called the crime into dispatch, when and where the victim was found, and any additional witness information. This will help acquaint the analyst with the crime, crime scene, its layout and the victim's position as found before examination and transport.

The *CSI reports* on scene processing and evidence collection give an understanding of the scene layout, the size and measurements between items of evidence, and the location in the scene where each item was found. From this information, the analyst is able to identify evidence relationships and the interpretive value between items of related evidence.

The *witness or suspect statements*, interviews, or depositions are used after the bloodstain patterns are identified and analyzed. The statements are tested against the bloodstain patterns and other physical evidence to identify consistencies or inconsistencies in the statements.

The *autopsy protocol* will assist in identifying the type and location of wounds. This will assist in supporting or refuting opinions related to the type of blood staining. For example, if some blood patterns appear to be from an arterial spurt, there should be a wound to the victim's body that will produce such a gush of blood volume. Absent a breached artery on the victim, you may need to look at other possibilities. If blood spatter is believed to be from expectorate, then blood should be found in the mouth or nose of the victim. Identifying types of wounding mechanism such as knives, firearms, or blunt force instrument should be compared against the expected type of blood spatter or castoff stains from each type of weapon and subsequent wound. The autopsy protocol will also address the clothing worn by the victim and what effect they may have on blood patterns or the possible blocking of blood patterns.

Next to bloodstained evidence such as a weapon or suspect clothing that is still in custody, photographs of the crime scene, autopsy, and physical evidence are the most important documentation for the bloodstain pattern analyst. Once all the photographs are in hand, they should be divided into groups. The divisions might include: (1) outside and approach to the scene, (2) the victim at the scene, (3) the victim at autopsy, (4) the room or area where the victim was found,

(5) evidence, (6) suspects, and (7) any other division that is logical. Once the photographs are in logical groups, each one should be sequentially numbered. During the analysis, as important points are shown in the photographs, your notes should also include the number of the photograph so that it can easily be retrieved when needed at a later time.

Another important aspect, the first provided by *in situ* photographs, is the ability to see how the bloodstains on the victim and his or her clothes appeared before the victim was disturbed by the various investigators and transportation to the hospital or morgue. Because we can never collect evidence without losing a portion of its meaning, photographs help to separate "investigative transfer," which is accidentally altered evidence during the collection or processing of the scene and body movement versus actual evidence from the crime itself. Predictably, with movement the still wet blood will create additional bloodstained areas and may disturb or alter existing stains as well as add additional stains. It is important for the analyst to distinguish between stains associated with the crime and those that are created by processing, movement and transportation by the investigators. Equally important is the ability to recognize when this distinction can not be made. In this instance little to no value can be placed on such stains in forming your opinions.

The autopsy photographs will assist in identifying the type, number and location of bleeding wounds. This information will be correlated to bloodstain patterns found at the scene and items of evidence from the scene.

Photographs of victim, his or her clothing and the surrounding area where the victim was found are very important in identifying what type of blood spatter is found or is expected to be present. This will later be contrasted against any blood spatter found on other evidence such as the weapon, suspect, or suspect's clothing. If there is impact spatter from a blunt trauma beating on the suspect's clothing then there should be consistent blood spatter on and around the victim.

The *lab reports* from serology, DNA, firearms, fingerprints, toxicology, etc. will identify that the suspected blood is or is not in fact blood and to whom it belongs. Firearms will identify which bullets were fired from which weapons and fingerprints will identify who created the latent prints found at the scene or on the evidence collected and if any of the prints were made in blood. Also important is whether there are any identifiable prints or DNA that have not been identified as belonging to anyone.

The *crime scene diagrams* will be an invaluable aid in locating where within the scene items of evidence were located as well as an understanding of the physical confines of the scene. Scene photographs tend to always make the area photographed look larger than it really is. Comparing the photographs to the crime scene diagrams will help to understand the spatial relationships as well as place what area within the scene certain photographs are taken of and from what angle and direction.

The *reports by EMTs* will assist in identifying how the EMTs entered the scene, what they touched, how they first observed the victim, and how they moved the victim. Of critical importance is the question of blood in the mouth or nose of the victim upon the EMTs first arrival. Photographs of the victim's mouth or nose may show blood that came after movement of the body during lifesaving attempts or during the medical examiner's or investigator's examination of the body. It is important to also question the first responders, police, firefighters or EMTs as to what they noted about blood in the mouth or nose of the victim before the body was moved.

Examine all physical evidence that is still available. While you want to consider what others in the original investigation found, documented, and reported on the physical evidence, you also need to personally examine the physical evidence. This is to verify that what others reported is still there and to ensure that evidence important to BPA was not omitted due to a lack of BPA knowledge or was simply missed. The more items you can personally exam versus taking someone else's description of what is there, the better. In a cold case, visiting the crime scene may not be an option that is still available. If the scene can still be visited, even if it has long ago been released by law enforcement, make every effort to view the physical site of the crime. At the very least, this will give the investigator an understanding and feel for the spatial relationships within the scene. On multiple occasions, I have visited an old crime scene and was able to find bloodstain patterns reported by the first investigators *still in place*. On several cases, I was able to find blood patterns not reported or that were missed by the first investigators. Some of these blood patterns were crucial in forming a foundation as to what could be opined about the events during the crime.

IDENTIFYING EXPECTORATE BLOOD SPATTER

As blood is shed, stains will be found in areas consistent with what has actually occurred to produce the stains. The geometry and direction of travel of these stains will also be consistent with the event that produced them. This allows BPA to assist in understanding the blood-producing events and ultimately in identifying what is consistent or inconsistent in the statements that are considered to have caused the spatter. If the statement by the accused person is that he or she received blood on his or her clothing from moving and performing CPR on the victim, then the investigator will go through a check list to support or refute this statement or identify that insufficient information does not allow an opinion to be formed. If victim is breathing, he or she may be expelling blood out of the mouth or nose, which will break up the blood and project it on surrounding areas. This usually occurs when the victim is trying to clear blood from the air passages to allow easier breathing. First, check any physical evidence that would indicate that the victim had evidence of blood in the air passage:

1. Check with the first responders to the scene; did they observe blood in the mouth or nose of the victim before the victim was moved?
2. Next check the autopsy report. Is there evidence that blood was aspirated? (Aspirated refers to breathing in as opposed to expectorate, which is breathing out.) Evidence that there was blood aspiration is consistent with breathing by the victim after wounding.
3. Study the photographs of the victim to determine if you are able to see blood in or surrounding the mouth or nose.
4. Check on the clothing of the accused and the victim to see if they were collected in the original investigation.
5. If this clothing is still available, analyze it for spatter the correct size and location consistent with expectorate blood coughed out while trying to clear the victim's airway or forced out from CPR. Look for lighter-in-color spatter due to the blood's being mixed with saliva or mucus. Look for bubble rings where air was mixed with blood projected from the mouth or nose producing bubbles that then burst, leaving bubble rings in the blood spatter. Look for an elevated level of amylase, a digestive enzyme that occurs at a much reduced level in blood than in saliva.

If the first responders report no blood in the mouth or nose, and the autopsy indicates there was no blood aspiration and these are consistent with the photographs of the victim at the scene, then expectorate blood can be eliminated as a mechanism that produced any spatter that may be on the clothing in question. Having eliminated expectorate blood as the mechanism directs the analyst to some other event producing the spatter found on the clothing of the accused. The elimination of expectorate may refute the statement of the accused as to how the blood spatter got on his or her clothing. Obviously, if the physical evidence supports and is consistent with expectorate blood produced from CPR or the victim coughing up blood onto the clothing of the accused, this supports the witness statement and is equally helpful information that may in fact assist in eliminating this person as a possible suspect. There will also be cases in which the analyst is not able to eliminate either possibility of expectorate spatter or spatter from the impacts consistent with the attack. This is exactly how it should be reported, that both are equally possible.

CHEMICAL ENHANCEMENTS

The application of any chemical enhancements should always be one of the last steps to be taken on the analysis of physical evidence. The addition of any fluid dilutes any substances such as blood that may be present on the area being processed. Before any chemical application, ensure that all other processing has been completed and that documentation of the evidence, such as close-up photographs with proper scales of reference, has been completed.

If the case indicates that no blood was found at the scene and the possibility exists that a cleanup took place before the original investigators arrived, then the use of blood chemical enhancements may be needed. Chemicals such as Luminol, Fluorescein, Blue Star™; TMB (tetramethylbenzidine); LMG (Leucomalachite Green); LCV (Liquid Crystal Violet); or Amido black, work very well with old and diluted blood even many years later. These or other chemical enhancements can be applied to suspected scenes, clothing, or other items of evidence in search for the presence of blood that will not be visible to the unaided eye. Any of the chemical enhancements are only presumptive for blood, and additional confirmatory tests will be needed. With the ever increasing sensitivity of confirmatory tests, even minute amounts of blood may be identified as blood, human or animal, and, if human, whose blood it is. Establishing that the scene or other evidence was cleaned and that it was the victim's blood that was found, are great clues in directing the new investigation, as someone not living at the location of the murder would have little to gain in cleaning the scene.

The application of any chemical enhancement, when looking for small traces of blood, should be done by a trained analyst who is aware of the many false positives and the safety precautions that should be taken when using such chemicals. A trained analyst will also be able to take the timed photographic exposures required to properly document their findings and to take the most promising samples for confirmatory tests. Further discussion of this topic can be found in Chapter 26.

A METHODOLOGY FOR EXAMINING CLOTHING AND OTHER PHYSICAL EVIDENCE

The first step in looking for blood spatter on clothing or other evidence is viewing the article with a good light source and some type of magnification. Then, using the knowledge of the events that took place and the type of bleeding wounds that were present, predict what type of spatter would result. This often requires the analyst to mentally reenact events and actions to identify where blood spatter would go onto the clothing. In some cases, this may also require a physical reenactment to properly visualize relationships between body movement, clothing, and other issues. Look in the expected locations for the type of blood staining that would result from movement and actions involved in the crime. In one case where this methodology was employed, my mental reenactment directed me to look inside the cuff of a white dress shirt. Directional spatter was found high up inside the cuff. While others had examined the shirt and found spatter and directional stains on the outside of the shirt cuff, they were too few in number, and thus the opinion was inconclusive about what occurred to produce them. However, there was enough spatter when both the inside and outside of the cuff were viewed together. Thus, an opinion could be given as to the events that would be consistent in producing them. In any mental or physical reenactment be sure to consider what witnesses said they did, such as rendering CPR. Also consider other known actions that occurred during the crime such as the attack on the victim. Both possibilities should be given equal consideration in searching for the predicted type and location of possible blood staining. If no bloodstains are found, remember the axiom written by Dr. Carl Sagan that states, "Absence of evidence is not evidence of absence." (Sagan, 1977) The original quote was not directed toward forensic science, but its meaning works well for science and the discipline of BPA. In forensic science as it relates to BPA, if there are no bloodstains, all you can say is that there is an absence of bloodstains, and be very careful about taking your opinion further. You can always say much more about the possibilities when there are bloodstains present than when none are found.

Dark-colored clothing poses quite a challenge to find and document small to mist-sized spatter. After the visual exam with good lighting and magnification, examine the clothing with a microscope from 10X to 60X magnification. Two additional techniques to consider are the night vision setting on a video camera and infrared photography. Many of the newer video cameras can view objects and film them in near-zero light levels. When blood spatters are present on dark clothing the video camera's night vision tends to create a visible contrast between the dark clothing and the dark spatter. This will direct you to the suspected spatter locations and allows testing with a presumptive and further lab testing if the presumptive is positive. Another photographic method is to use infrared (IR) film. This method also gives a contrast between the dark clothing and the blood spatter and documents what is found. Presumptive and further lab testing, if the presumptive is positive, is still required.

Any chemical enhancement on clothing should always be the last resort. The application of any chemical further dilutes any blood that may be present and more dilution makes confirmation tests more difficult or impossible.

APPLYING THE SCIENTIFIC METHOD TO YOUR ANALYSIS

Many bloodstain patterns have more than one mechanism or event that is capable of creating the patterns. An example is expectorated spatter versus backspatter from a gunshot. Both are capable of producing mist-sized spatter. As a result, the analyst often has to consider different, viable mechanisms that might have created the pattern in question. The best methodology to use, in identifying which event is the best explanation to account for the pattern, is the scientific method. An example of the steps taken in this process is shown in Figure 25.1

If after applying the scientific method to multiple viable possibilities and finding that none of the possibilities can be eliminated, the answer is that each mechanism is possible. However, the goal is to identify which of the possible mechanisms is the best explanation. This can only be done by proving each of the hypotheses wrong. When you are unable to prove one hypothesis wrong then this hypothesis becomes the best explanation. The best explanation has to be supported with and by the facts in the case.

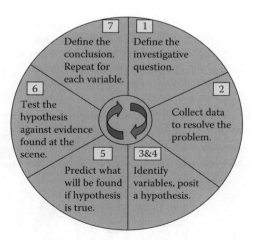

FIGURE 25.1 The scientific method is shown in a clockwise-moving circle process. This method encourages the analyst to adequately consider all viable actions that could explain the question being analyzed. This method is referred to as a self-correcting circle process that leads to the best explanation, and often leads to additional questions.

CASE ANALYSIS EXAMPLES

CASE 1

A case example of applying the scientific process has multiple mist-sized bloodstains and blood, human tissue, bone, or hair on the lower center of a suspect's T-shirt. The subject wearing the shirt is the husband of the adult female victim and father to the two juvenile victims. When the husband drove up to his garage and opened the garage overhead door he observed his wife supine on the garage floor beside the open passenger door of their two-door older Ford Bronco. After checking his wife and determining that she was dead from a gunshot to her head, the subject looked into the rear of the vehicle. His daughter was sitting in the right rear passenger's seat; seatbelted in and slumped over to her left. The daughter also appeared to be dead from a gunshot wound to the head. The subject next looked to his son, who was slumped part way over the left rear passenger's seat and shot one time in the upper left side. Believing his son might be alive; the subject lifted him out of the vehicle, laid him on the ground next to the boy's mother and performed CPR on him. The subject then called police.

One of the investigative questions in this case is: How did the spatter and bone fragment get on the front of the subject's T-shirt (Figure 25.2 and Figure 25.3)? Viable ways the spatter and bone fragment could have gotten on the shirt include:

1. Back spatter from gunshot to victim
2. Expectorate from doing CPR to victim
3. A hand slap into blood
4. Rehydrating spatter by contact with the wet T-shirt and then transferring to shirt

Possibilities number one and two were offered by the prosecution, and possibilities three and four were offered by the defense. Each of the identified possibilities are formed into a hypothesis and tested, trying to prove each false as shown below.

1. Hypothesis (H)-1 *The spatter is from backspatter that occurred when the juvenile female was shot.* I would predict that:

- There will be spatter consistent in size and location surrounding the victim of the gunshot.
- The spatter and bone on the shirt will be identified to this victim.
- This area of the T-shirt would be exposed and in proximity at the time of the shooting.
- The spatter will be driven into the weave of the T-shirt.
- The spatter will not be diluted from rehydrating.

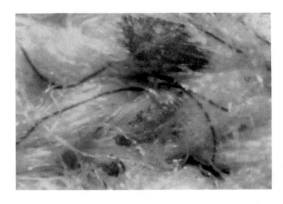

FIGURE 25.2 This close-up photograph shows one of the blood spatters on the front of the husband's T-shirt.

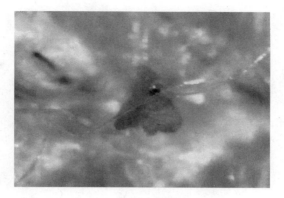

FIGURE 25.3 Shows the human tissue on the front of the husband's T-shirt.

All of the above predictions are compared against the physical evidence and lab reports and are consistent with the spatter in question. The juvenile female in the right rear of the vehicle has mist-sized spatter consistent with back spatter from a gunshot above her on the roll bar and headliner and to her right on the window glass and hard plastic side molding. The entire mist-sized spatter pattern area is consistent with her head gunshot while she is sitting in the right rear seat. The mist-sized spatter on the T-shirt of the accused is identified through DNA to belong to the juvenile female. The spatter on the T-shirt is driven into the weave consistent with projected back spatter. *H-1 is not proved false.*

2. H-2 *The spatter is from performing CPR on the juvenile male victim.* I would predict that:

- The spatter will be identified to the juvenile male victim as the accused stated he did CPR on him.
- There is evidence on and around the juvenile victim consistent with the size of the misting stains on the T-shirt.
- This victim will have a wound to bone capable of creating the bone fragment found on the T-shirt.

In testing the predictions, the blood spatter and bone were identified through DNA as coming from the female and not the male victim. *H-2 is proved false.*

3. H-3 *The spatter is from a hand slap into blood.* I would predict that:

- There will be evidence that the accused got the juvenile female's blood on his hand.
- The blood-covered hand was held in an orientation and location capable of producing a vertical, linear, spatter pattern onto the front lower center of the T-shirt.

In testing the predictions against the physical evidence at the scene and the statements, the accused stated that he did not touch the female victim. He further stated that he did not enter into the rear seat area where this victim was located.

A hand orientated to produce a similar linear pattern from a hand slap in front of the tee shirt while wearing the shirt is very difficult to position. Such a position would require an effort to accomplish and thus would be a purposeful act and highly improbable in this case. The subject did not give a statement about blood on his hand or any statement about a hand slap. *H-3 was proved false.*

4. H-4 *The spatter is from the wet T-shirt contacting and rehydrating spatter and transferring the rehydrated spatter onto the tee shirt.* I would predict that:

- There will be evidence that spatter at the scene from a gunshot was rehydrated and transferred.
- There is a location in the vehicle and around the juvenile female victim that would allow the T-shirt to come into contact with the spatter in a straight in and straight out movement with little to no lateral movement.
- Recreating like spatter and transfer will be possible by experimentation under like conditions.
- The accused will state that he was in the area around the juvenile female victim.
- The blood transfer onto the wet T-shirt will produce diluted stains and there will be lateral movement observed.

Experiments under like conditions were not able to create similar spatter by re-hydrating spatter and then transferring them to a wet tee shirt. The accused stated that he did not enter into the area where the juvenile victim was located. In experiments, the spatter that was rehydrated and then transferred to the wet T-shirt was visibly diluted and showed lateral movement. *H-4 was proved false.*

Hypothesis H-1 is the best explanation for the mist-sized spatter to the front lower center T-shirt of the accused. The spatter is consistent with backspatter from a gunshot into the juvenile female's head and consistent with spatter found around her in the vehicle. The bone fragment is also consistent with the gunshot to the victim's head when the T-shirt was present at the time of the shooting.

CASE 2

A husband returning from work found his wife dead on the master bathroom floor. Upon rolling her from her right side to her back, her head hit into a pool of blood on the floor, creating spatter. The husband then jumped over the victim to the floor on her right side. From her right side the husband preformed CPR on his wife. He held his wife's head and it slipped out of his hand and hit into a pool of blood on the floor, producing a second spatter event. The husband's right shirt sleeve cuff had soaked blood, directional spatter, and transfers on the outside of the cuff (Figure 25.4 and Figure 25.5). There were not enough stains to allow an opinion as to what produced them.

In applying the scientific method, mental and physical reenactments, I predicted what type of bloodstains would be produced in doing CPR and predicted where they would be found. Upon examining

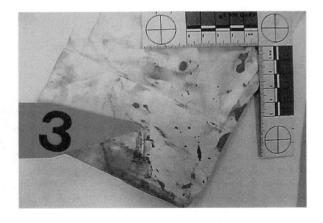

FIGURE 25.4 Bloodstains on the outside cuff of the suspect's dress shirt.

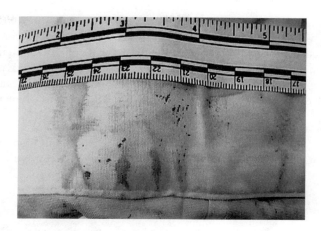

FIGURE 25.5 The inside of the dress shirt cuff. Considering both the inside and outside of the cuff in concert, there are enough spatters to form an opinion as to what actions occurred to produce these stains.

the shirt, no such spatters were found. In also mentally and physically reenacting how the victim's wounds were created, I predicted what type of spatter would be created and where it would be found. The multiple blunt trauma blows to the victim's head would produce spatter and directional spatter to the outside of the long sleeve cuff and possibly to the inside of the cuff. The outside did contain such spatter, but not enough to form an opinion. In examining the inside of the same cuff, additional directional spatter was found some distance up into the cuff. With the spatter on both the outside and the inside of the cuff, taken in concert, there was enough to offer an opinion. Possible ways the spatter could have been created on both the outside and the inside of the right cuff included: (1) CPR, (2) head hitting into pool of blood on floor, and (3) impact blows to the victim's head. In applying the scientific method to consider the possible ways this spatter could be created, three hypotheses were formed:

1. H-1 *Performing CPR created spatter onto both outside and inside of the right cuff.* I would predict that:

- The victim's mouth and nose will have blood in them. There will be consistent spatter around the victim's mouth and upper torso consistent with spatter on the shirt cuff.
- The shirt cuff and forearm will be held in an alignment allowing spatter to get onto the inside and outside of the shirt cuff.
- I would look for bubble rings and spatter that is lighter in color as it is mixed with saliva.

H-1 is tested against the above predictions and is proved false as there is not consistent spatter around the victim's mouth or upper torso. There is neither blood in her mouth and no bubble rings nor lighter in color spatter. A consistent alignment with the cuff and forearm is not impossible, but it is improbable. *H-1 is proved false.*

2. H-2 *The victim's head impacting into the blood pool on the floor created spatter onto both the outside and inside of the right shirt cuff.* I would predict that spatter created from the victim's head hitting into a blood pool on the floor will require the cuff and forearm to align parallel with the floor and in front of the impact. H-2 is tested against the above predictions and is proved false as the alignment from rolling her onto her back or from dropping her head into a pool of blood will not allow the correct alignment of the cuff and forearm. *H-2 is proved false.*

3. H-3 *Impacts to the victim's skull created spatter onto the inside and outside of the shirt's right cuff.* I would predict that the cuff and forearm would be in a correct alignment to get directional spatter onto both the inside and outside of the right cuff. H-3 is tested against the above predictions and is not proved false. As the other possibilities, H-1 and H-2, were eliminated or highly improbable, then the best explanation that remains is H-3, spatter created at the time the victim was struck with a blunt instrument to her head.

H-3 is tested against the above predictions and is *not* proved false.

As the other possibilities, H-1 and H-2, were eliminated or highly improbable, then the best explanation that remains is H-3, spatter created at the time the victim was struck with a blunt instrument to her head.

CASE 3

In another case, for 7 years the husband was ruled a hero for shooting an intruder who was attacking his wife with a hammer. According to the husband, after hearing a strange noise he retrieved a .45 caliber handgun from his bedroom and ran down a hallway toward the dining area. He saw his wife in a fetal position on the floor with the intruder behind her, beating her head with a hammer. The husband stated that the intruder was facing toward the husband as the husband was running down the hallway. The husband shot the intruder in the head and the man fell backwards onto the carpet, landing supine on the floor. The husband continued running up to the man, straddled him, and shot him in the head at close range as the man lay on the carpeted floor. A study of the photographs indicated two areas with blood evidence that caused concern. The first contained both spatter and cast-off bloodstains on the wall beside the female victim's right shoulder and directional cast-off on the ceiling traveling toward the wall with the spatter on it (see Figure 25.6 and Figure 25.7).

In considering where the female's body was found and where her blood pool on the carpet was located, in conjunction with the husband's statement of the intruder facing toward the husband as the husband ran down the hallway, you are able to predict how the bloodstains should appear. The cast-off blood and impact spatter should be found extending along the wall and not extended from the floor to the ceiling. The spatter and cast-off blood were not consistent with the position described by the husband. It was consistent with the intruder facing toward the wall and not facing down the hallway. But, if the intruder is facing the wall, the bullet trajectory into the intruder's head becomes

FIGURE 25.6 The wall above, below, and around the light switch has both spatter and cast-off bloodstains. The likely position to create consistent stains is facing the wall at a 90-degree angle; however, this position would not allow the correct bullet trajectory into the intruder's head. The position described by the husband would rotate the intruder 45 degrees, placing the intruder's right shoulder toward the wall with the spatter. This position would allow a correct bullet trajectory, but would not allow the correct position to create the spatter and cast-off stains.

FIGURE 25.7 There are two separate blood pools in the carpet. According to the husband's statement, there should only be one. Having two separate blood pools indicates that the intruder's body was in one area long enough to form a pool, then in a separate area also long enough to form a blood pool. The distance between the two pools is consistent with rolling the person over from front to back.

inconsistent. The second area of concern was two different blood pools from the intruder as his body lay on the carpeted floor as shown in Figure 25.7.

The husband stated that, after the first shot, the man fell over backward onto the carpet and onto his back. The husband continued running up to the intruder and shot him again in the head at close range. The husband stated he did not move the intruder. The first responders stated that they only moved the intruder from the carpet up to a gurney for transport out of the scene. They were sure they did not move or roll the intruder over to create a second pool of blood. A study of the photographs of the intruder at the scene indicated that the passive blood flows and blood transfer on his forehead were consistent with his being rolled from face-down onto his back. This would explain how two different blood pools were created. Again, this was not consistent with the actions stated by the husband.

In the above case, the clothing of all three of the involved people was still available for analysis. DNA examinations that had not been conducted in the original investigation were completed for the second investigation. This revealed that the type, location, and direction of the blood spatter on each of the participants' clothing was consistent with the husband killing his wife with the hammer and in shooting the reported intruder. The intruder had been lured to the scene by the husband in a premeditated plan to get rid of his wife and to put the blame on the reported intruder. A lot of additional information was used in the successful prosecution of the husband at trial. The BPA evidence was used in concert with the additional information to assist in explaining what events took place during the commission of the two murders.

SUMMARY

Bloodstain pattern analysis is one of the forensic disciplines that should be considered in the reinvestigation of any homicide cold case. As the above case examples demonstrate, BPA can greatly assist in identifying what events took place during the commission of a crime as well as provide the best explanation as to how questioned bloodspatter was produced onto items of evidence such as the suspect's clothing. Of equal importance is the verification of the statements being consistent with the physical evidence and bloodstain pattern analysis. It is just as beneficial for the investigation to verify statements as true as it is to identify false statements, as both will assist in directing the investigation.

Richard H. Walton wishes to recognize and thank Captain Tom Bevel for his valuable contribution to this book with this chapter.

Captain Tom Bevel (Ret.), served 27 years with the Oklahoma City, Oklahoma Police Department. He is the coauthor of the text book *Bloodstain Pattern Analysis with an Introduction to Crime Scene Reconstruction*, now in its second edition. Captain Bevel has been a consultant in questioned death cases in 46 U.S. States and nine foreign countries. He is a Distinguished Member of both the International Association of Bloodstain Pattern Analyst and The Association for Crime Scene Reconstruction. He has been a case consultant for the U.S. Inspector General, U.S. Justice Department, Federal Bureau of Investigation and several U.S. Attorney General Offices. Captain Bevel is a graduate of the Scenes of Crime Officers Course, Metropolitan Police Academy, Hendon, England and the Medical Legal course at London Medical College. Cases he has consulted on have been presented on New Detectives, Medical Detectives, 20/20, Biography, 60 Minutes, 48 Hours, and Court TV.

REFERENCE

Bevel, T., A Basic Overview of Bloodstain Pattern Analysis, Southern Police Institute, University of Louisville, Homicide Investigation Handout, 1992.

Bevel, T. and Gardner, R.M., *Bloodstain Pattern Analysis – With an Introduction to Crime Scene Reconstruction*, 2nd ed., CRC Press, Boca Raton, Fl., 2002, p 6,7.

Adair, T., Recognition of Bloodstain Evidence in Historical Denver, Colorado, *International Association of Bloodstain Pattern Analysts NEWS*. December 1999, Volume 15, Number 3.

Sagan, Carl, *Dragons of Eden*, Ballantine Press, 1977, p 7.

26 Luminol

Rod Englert

CONTENTS

INTRODUCTION

Luminol is a presumptive test for the presence of blood. It does not identify the source of the blood, rather it suggests that a suspect pattern or stain may originate with blood-based compounds. While luminol is a law enforcement tool often utilized during the investigation of fresh homicides, it is a very useful instrument in cold case homicide investigation. Interestingly enough, while some law enforcement agencies have used this tool extensively, others have not heard of it. This chapter presents the practical use and value of luminol in cold case investigations.

COMPOSITION AND BACKGROUND

The chemical name of luminol is 3-Aminophthalhydrazide. It is a very sensitive chemical compound. Luminol can detect, thus illuminate, one part blood in one million. This is analogized to one drop of blood in 999,999 drops of water. A luminol test is predicated on the fact that certain hemoglobin derivatives significantly enhance the chemical luminescence exhibited by luminol when it oxidizes in an alkaline solution. The effective use of luminol as a compound is dependent upon the proper mixture of the compounds and appropriate application. Luminol is not a confirmatory test for blood. When applied to a surface suspected of containing blood, it gives off a blue-green luminescence whose presence only presumes that the suspect material providing luminescence may be blood. Once a suspected pattern is revealed, further confirmatory testing is required. The spraying of luminol does not impede further confirmatory testing or DNA typing.

    Luminol was reportedly first synthesized in Germany in 1902 and underwent further refinement and investigation in the succeeding decades. It was not until the late 1920s, however, that the compound was named luminol, producer of light. During the late 1930s, applications of luminol indicated the presence of blood in water, both clean and soapy, and in sewage. The presence of blood was also detected following application of a spray mixture on paper, fabrics, and iron pipes that had been exposed to the elements for 3 years. The test for the detection of blood works better on old blood stains, as opposed to fresh blood. The blood needs to degrade for some time prior to giving a stronger luminescence.

The forensic use of luminol was first proposed in 1937. A luminol reagent was sprayed on a test pattern of blood that had been allowed to dry for 2 weeks and exposed to the elements. When the luminol reagent was sprayed onto the blood, all bloodstained areas exhibited a blue light for 10 to 15 minutes. These early experiments also reported that, while the luminescence disappeared, it would reappear with a fresh application. This is analogous to the drying and cracking of old paint that has been exposed to the elements.

The reaction of luminol on aged bloodstains is more pronounced due to the oxidation process that has occurred during the intervening time period. That older, dried blood exhibits a stronger luminescence than fresh blood holds true today. In 1942, the luminol test was further recommended for use in forensic blood detection. Further investigative experimentation continued into the 1970s, when its forensic application became somewhat more common.

Usage of Luminol

Some Misconceptions

As a presumptive test, luminol *presumes* the luminescence may be blood. Through its application, luminol *illuminates* the patterns resulting from the suspected substance.

Confirmation of the suspected stains, however, must be accomplished by other lab tests such as DNA, which can provide the donor. The legal and scientific use of luminol has been accepted in some states, and sparingly in others. A few states disallow the use of the tool because of misinformed reasons, which include the following:

- It is carcinogenic.
  - *It is not reported to be carcinogenic.*
- It cannot be properly photographed.
  - *It can be photographed.*
- Spraying of luminol will create patterns not previously present.
  - *It does not produce false patterns, but if over-sprayed, will create a false background.*
- Luminol will destroy potential for subsequent DNA examination.
  - *DNA testing and other confirmatory tests are not affected by the use of luminol.*

Common Uses of Luminol

The most common uses of luminol in cold case homicide investigations may include:

- **Examination of evidence** — Use of luminol in this instance may include articles or evidence containing suspected blood not yet visible to the unaided eye. These may include clothing, weapons, and other articles. Luminol may be especially useful if evidence has been stored without exposure to the elements or other degrading circumstances.
- **Examination of a suspected homicide scene** — Use of luminol in this instance can be exemplified by instances in which investigators seek to determine whether a homicide may have occurred at a particular location. This might be in response to informant information, admissions, confessions, or other investigative activity. Luminol may be used to cover large crime scenes in fresh or cold case homicides, thus producing the original pattern. While luminol can be used on outdoor crime scenes within a short period after the offense, it can also be used on indoor crime scenes even after a lengthy period

of time has passed. Its use in cold case homicide investigation is most effective when applied to areas that have been protected from the elements, including:

- Vehicle interiors, including dashboards, floor mats, and other coverings such as seats, trunk carpet, and so forth
- Floor surfaces of homes, offices, storage facilities, and similar structures including concrete slabs, wood floors, and rugs or carpets
- Cracks and crevices in floors and walls, in areas in which suspected cleaning has occurred
- Wall surfaces
- Furniture

In addition, luminol may also illuminate:

- Blood tracks
- Drag marks
- Hand impressions
- Swipes
- Bloodspatter impacts

Application and Use

Luminol is prepared at the scene or in the laboratory by a qualified, experienced analyst. When mixed with distilled water, premeasured quantities of sodium perborate and sodium carbonate must be shaken well before application. The solution is applied as an aerosol mist from a spray container. Prior to application, however, a controlled sample of known blood must be sprayed to test the mixture. Luminol has minimal shelf life and should be applied immediately after it is mixed. The longer the time span between its mixture and application, the weaker the reaction of luminescence. Practically speaking, degradation could begin to occur within 24 hours. A fresh amount should be prepared for each day's use.

The application of luminol involves a number of procedures. These include:

- Identification of suspect exhibit areas to be treated and examined
- Mixture and application of luminol
- Observation of the pattern resulting from the application of luminol
- Photographing the resulting pattern
- Documentation of the examination

To facilitate and reveal the luminescence, application is most often accomplished under darkened conditions. The analyst does not concentrate on the luminescence, but rather on the pattern that cannot be seen with the naked eye. While many objects will glow, a pattern will not be present on items such as metal rivets on a pair of jeans, cleansers used to clean toilet bowls and bathroom sinks, certain plant material with iron in the pulp, as well as some other substrates.

Many cases involve gunshots where the perpetrator is so close to the victim when shots are fired that blood spatters back toward the shooter in specks so small that the naked eye cannot detect them (see Figure 26.1). A pattern is created, however (see Figure 26.2), and when the analyst discovers the pattern with luminol, a representative sample must be taken for DNA analysis.

In cold case homicide investigation, an advantage of luminol is that it gives off a *more intense* luminescence when applied to *aged* blood stains. This does not mean, however, one can determine the age of the bloodstains from the intense chemical luminescence that occurs from older blood.

Luminol does not inhibit followup testing for DNA and other confirmatory tests. Chemicals used in the cleaning of any suspected items of evidence may give a false positive reaction

FIGURE 26.1 In a case where a husband shot his wife, this photo illustrates the distribution of blood from high velocity impact spatter from the wife onto the husband's shirt. (Courtesy of Rod Englert)

with what appears to be a blood pattern of significance. Additional DNA testing is necessary to confirm the presence of blood before giving an opinion about the pattern.

Photography

The utilization of luminol necessitates the proper photography and documentation of its application. It is recommended that this should be undertaken by those experienced in this technique. Experiments in the early 1970s identified means and methods to obtain good photographic records of bloodstains as revealed by application of luminol, and this was recommended for adoption as a standard practice.

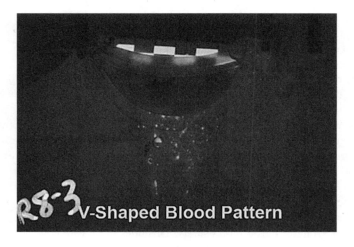

FIGURE 26.2 Application of luminol on the T-shirt shown in Figure 26.1 revealed the "V"-shaped pattern created by an outer garment worn over the T-shirt in Figure 26.1 above. (Courtesy of Rod Englert)

FIGURE 26.3 Overspray of luminol on car door. (Courtesy of Rod Englert)

Luminol is very difficult to photograph, as this process must occur under conditions of little or no light. Photography of a luminol application without expensive commercial photographic equipment requires patience and skill, utilizing a cable release to operate an open shutter. The trick is knowing when to *close* the shutter, for if it is closed too soon the picture is gone. You only get *one* good chance to obtain a good photograph as a documentation record, because the spraying of luminol may distort or change the original pattern, dependent upon the surface of what the blood is on. As an example, if luminol is sprayed on the metal of a car door, the suspected pattern will run and create another type of pattern not representative of the original crime scene (see Figure 26.3). This also illustrates the necessity of using more than one camera during the application and photographic process, as chances are increased that one of the cameras will capture the image.

During photography, it is important to provide enough lighting to ensure that one captures the luminescence as well as the subject being photographed. Whether it be a light switch, a piece of furniture, or article of clothing, the jurors can not only see what you describe as a blood transfer on a switch when it is presented in court, they can also observe the glowing pattern around the light switch.

Excluded Surfaces and False Positives

A disadvantage to luminol addresses its application on certain surfaces. These include those metals with copper salts. Bronze and brass, and similar alloys containing copper, may give a false reaction. These materials are often found on locks, door handles, and other similar materials. Other materials that may produce a false positive reading include:

- Grease and oils with trace amounts of copper
- Some cleaning materials
- Certain plant matter and vegetables, including horseradish, turnips, potatoes, onions, apples, apricots, and blackberries
- Some paints
- Some ceramic tiles and grouts
- Certain body materials including bone marrow, brain tissue, spinal fluid, intestinal and lung tissue, as well as leukocytes and mucous

Post-Incident Cleaning

During the intervening time period since commission of the offense and investigative response and detection, suspects may clean their clothing. Luminol may still be effective despite the passage of time. Patterns may be revealed despite washings of cloth, depending on the number of times the clothes are washed, soap used, and how well it was washed. Dry cleaning, however, pretty much eliminates the patterns that might be illuminated by the use of luminol.

CASE STUDY

In 1992, a family of four in Southern California was found murdered. The young mother and her three children each had been shot in the head as they lay asleep in their separate beds. The father was missing at the time, but 1 week later was found dead in his vehicle. The cause of his death was determined to be cyanide poisoning. The case was investigated by detectives and the answer to what occurred lay in a piece of evidence taken during a search of the residence. That piece of evidence was a maroon-colored bathrobe (see Figure 26.4).

The jurisdiction investigating the five deaths came under attack by the media for being unable to resolve the case. The case attracted international attention that involved Interpol, the CIA, and the victims' family in another country. In 1995, the bathrobe removed from the home of the victims was treated with luminol. The results were positive, and revealed that family members donated the blood patterns on the robe. DNA tests were subsequently conducted on the areas that luminesced, revealing patterns resembling backspatter of blood from gunshot in the form of high-velocity mist. When the family members' blood was projected onto the sleeve and chest area of the dark red (blood-colored) housecoat, the DNA results told the story. The father had been observed wearing the bathrobe around the time of the murders by the housekeeper who went to the residence on her

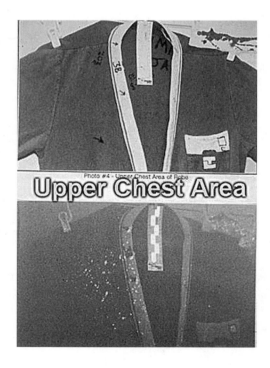

FIGURE 26.4 (See color insert following p. 216.) The house coat in natural light (top). The same house coat (bottom) after application of luminol revealing blood spatter on the upper chest area. (Courtesy of Rod Englert)

day off. The evidence left no doubt that the father had killed each member of the family prior to committing suicide because of heavy debt and possibly other reasons that will never be known.

CONCLUSION

Luminol is a viable tool to allow law enforcement to determine the possible presence of human blood on evidence or at a scene, or to illuminate blood-based impressions left as a result of the criminal act. When applied by a competent professional and properly photographed, luminol preserves a record for the court and the jury to see. Luminol may illuminate that which was not known previously during an investigation, and as a result, help provide answers and contribute to the solution of cold case homicides.

ACKNOWLEDGMENTS

Richard H. Walton would like to express gratitude and appreciation to Rod Englert for his authorship and contribution of this chapter. Mr. Englert retired in 1995 as Chief Deputy and Commander of the Operations Division of the Multnomah County Sheriff's Office in Portland, Oregon, after 40 years in law enforcement. He began his career with the Downey, California, Police Department after graduation from the Los Angeles Police Academy. He joined the Multnomah County Sheriff's Department in 1969 and spent a large portion of his career working major crimes, narcotics, and homicide. He has qualified as a court expert in homicide in 26 states, and has conducted over 520 lectures and training seminars on managing criminal investigations, solving unresolved homicides, bloodspatter interpretation and crime scene reconstruction in the U.S., Canada, Europe, and Russia. He obtained his bachelor's degree in Police Administration from California State University at Los Angles and was president of the 159th session of the FBI National Academy. In addition to membership in the International Homicide Investigator's Association and numerous state homicide investigator associations, he is a Fellow, Distinguished Member, Past President, and Chairman of the Board of the Association of Crime Scene Reconstructionists; a Fellow of the American Academy of Forensic Sciences, and Past President of the International Association of Blood Pattern Analysts. In addition, he has received the Lecturer of Merit and Distinguished Faculty Award from the National College of District Attorneys.

BIBLIOGRAPHY

Grispino, R.J. (1990). The Effect of Luminol on the Serological Analysis of Dried Human Bloodstains. *Crime Laboratory Digest*. Vol. 17, No. 1.

Gross, A.N., Harris, K.A., Kaldun, G.I. The Effect of Luminol in Presumptive Tests and DNA Analysis Using Polymerase Chain Reaction. *Journal of Forensic Sciences*. 1999.

Hesskew, D. (1997). Focus: Police Science, Luminol. *Law and Order Magazine*. November 1991.

Laux, Dale L. The Effects of Luminol on the Subsequent Analysis of Bloodstains. *Journal of Forensic Sciences*. Vol. 36, No. 5. September 1991.

Laux, Dale L., The Detection of Blood using Luminol. *In Principles of Bloodstain Pattern Analysis: Theory and Practice*. S.H. James, P.E. Kish, and T.P. Sutton, Eds. Boca Raton: CRC Press, 2005.

Montpetit, D.A. A Novel Approach to Obtaining Reliable PCR Results from Luminol Treated Bloodstains. *Forensic Science*. 2000.

REFERENCE

Yeshion, Ted. Florida Department of Law Enforcement (Ret.). Conversations, lesson handouts and workbooks on Presumptive Tests and Luminol.

27 Forensic Document Examination

Paul R. Edholm, Jr.

CONTENTS

THE FORENSIC DOCUMENT EXAMINER

A forensic document examiner is usually an expert who makes a close and critical study of any material or portion of a questioned document such as handwriting or hand printing, examination of ink, paper, photocopying, typewriting, etc. Various methods of these types of examinations may include:

- Visual
- Microscopic

- Ultraviolet or Infrared
- Chemical

Individuals who enter this profession may work in a laboratory under the direction of a forensic document examiner or they may attend courses in document examination. Both must apprentice for a period of at least 2 years. To be qualified as a document examiner one must appear in court and testify as to one's training and expertise. Then, it is up to the judge whether he or she believes one is qualified to testify as an expert.

Form Blindness Test

The Form Blindness Test was developed by Albert S. Osborn and was published in his 1910 book entitled *Questioned Documents*. This test focuses on the perception of handwriting forms and tries to establish whether certain people can see minute differences in form. The test is often given to ascertain whether a person has the aptitude to become a document examiner.

Graphologists

Often times, graphologists testify as document examiners or handwriting analysts. They are often allowed to testify in court because they have received some training and have expertise in stating what the inference of character is from a person's handwriting. The theory here is that graphology is an expression of personality, and the graphologist believes that systematic analysis of the way words and letters are formed reveal traits of personality.

> Most forensic document examiners do not subscribe to graphology as its status is often discredited or disqualified in court.

Copybook Writing

Copybook writing is the first basic writing taught in school. Obviously, handprinted capital letters are taught first, and then handprinted lower-case letters. Finally, cursive handwriting is taught. There are several different types of handwriting systems taught in this country, and all over the world. As soon as we as individual writers feel comfortable in our writing without having to think how to form each stroke of each individual letter, we begin to express our individuality. We may copy the handwriting of a parent, friend or teacher. If a person is a member of a gang, another gang member's handwriting might be imitated. However, while your handwriting may not seem highly individualized, it is individual to you and to you alone.

Graphic Maturity

About the time that average writers graduate from high school, they have experimented with various types of handwriting or signatures and will have eliminated the juvenile characteristics or traits from their handwriting and thereby attained graphic maturity. From this point on in their lives, their handwriting will probably not change.

Obtaining Handwriting Exemplars

Obtaining a handwriting exemplar is not a violation of the 4th, 5th, or 6th Amendment to the Constitution. If the court orders that a handwriting exemplar be produced for the court, it can hold the subject in contempt if he or she provides only disguised handwriting where the most conspicuous features are changed. The jury can infer guilt if the subject or defendant refuses to give a handwriting exemplar, because the examination of that exemplar can either prove or disprove the subject's innocence or guilt.

Someone who is familiar with a person's handwriting, such as a spouse or co-worker, can testify to the example's ownership. This is a significant aspect of forensic document examination in cold case homicide investigation. For example, in a cold case where the physician was deceased, cases have been successfully prosecuted in which the doctor's nurse could testify that the hand-writing was that of her former employer.

- When a subject or defendant is asked to produce a sample of handwriting, you can instruct him or her to:
  - Write faster or slower.
  - Write smaller or larger.
  - Write with a backhand or forehand slant.
  - Write with the opposite hand.
  - Write in cursive handwriting or hand printing.

You should try to make the subject or defendant comfortable when obtaining handwriting exemplars, but try to duplicate the conditions under which the questioned document was written, i.e., sitting or standing.

- What you should not do when obtaining handwriting exemplars:
  - Do not show the questioned document to the subject.
  - Do not advise the subject to write material that you have written or typed on the exemplar form.
  - Do not show or tell subjects how to make letter forms, instead tell them to "do the best you can."
  - Do not have subjects combine cursive handwriting and hand printing exemplars on one page. Have them write and print separately on separate exemplars.

If the subject first objects to giving a handwriting exemplar, but then decides to, get the questioned material right away. He or she may balk at doing as much handwriting as you want and you might not be able to obtain the questioned material later.

CUSTODIAN OF RECORDS

Under certain circumstances, a company's custodian of records or other qualified witness may be called upon to testify as to acts, conditions, or events as indicated in their business records. Such testimony is useful for proving bank account transactions, fraudulent charges made on credit cards, etc. However, these witnesses must meet certain preliminary requirements concerning their knowledge of the method in which the business records were made and kept.

Listed below is a list of preliminary questions to ask the custodian of records:

- *What is your job title?* Also ask if they have ever qualified as a custodian of records. Some companies do not have anyone specifically designated as such, but have accountants, comptrollers, or fraud investigators who serve the same role.
- *Are you familiar with the manner and method in which records are maintained at your company?* These might be financial, employment, or what-have-you; choose the one that is germane to your case.
- *How was this particular record prepared and is it maintained on your computer?* Refer him or her to the document or transaction in question and ask him or her to pull up that record on the computer screen.
- *Was this record made in the normal course of business?*

- *Was this record made at or near the time of the event in question?* If it is a credit card case for instance, was the charge recorded in the records at or near the time the charge was made?
- Then ask about the specific incident (charge, deposit, withdrawal, etc.)

After you have covered all of the above issues, write a report of the entire interview with the custodian of records so that you can show that the Evidence Code Sections have been met and the records can be admitted into a court of law.

Classes of Specimens

1. *Collected or Undictated*: This consists of writing executed from day to day in the normal course of business, social or personal affairs.
2. *Requested or Dictated*: This consists of material written at the request of an attorney, judge, or investigator for the sole purpose of comparison with questioned documents. See Figure 27.1 for a partial list of sources of handwriting specimens.

With collected or undictated records, the principal points to consider are:

- The amount of writing available
- Similarity of subject matter
- Relative dates of questioned and known writing
- Conditions under which the specimens were prepared (plenty of time, done in haste, etc.)
- Type of writing instrument
- Type of paper

With requested or dictated standards, the principal points to consider are:

- The material must be dictated with no help with spelling, punctuation or grammar.
- Dictated text must have the same words, phrases, and letter combinations, and should be repeated.
- There should be an adequate amount of writing.
- Same type of writing instrument.
- Same type of paper.
- Dictation should include a rest period.

Terminology Regarding Signatures

- *Spurious Signature* — a fraudulent freehand signature with no apparent attempt at simulation.
- *Simulated Signature* — a fraudulent signature that was executed purely by simulation (also known as freehand or imitated signature). This signature is usually drawn.
- *Photocopy* — a reproduction of a signature made by any office copying system. *Note: The signature is not an inked signature, but is made up of a series of toner dots.*
- *Traced Forgery Signature* — a fraudulent signature executed by following the outline of a genuine signature by one of the following:
  - *Transmitted Light* — the original is viewed with a light source behind the document allowing the forger to trace it onto a spurious document.
  - *Indented Outline* — the original is traced over, which causes an indented outline in the copy beneath. This indented outline is then covered with a suitable ink stroke.

101 SOURCES OF HANDWRITING SPECIMENS

1.	Account books	52.	Leases, real property
2.	Affidavits	53.	Letters
3.	Assignments	54.	Library card applications
4.	Autographs	55.	Light company applications
5.	Automobile insurance applications	56.	Life insurance applications
6.	Automobile license applications	57.	Loan applications
7.	Automobile title certificates	58.	Mail orders
8.	Bank deposit slips	59.	Manuscripts
9.	Bank safe deposit entry slips	60.	Marriage records
10.	Bank savings withdrawal slips	61.	Membership cards
11.	Bank signature cards	62.	Memoranda of all kinds
12.	Bank statements, receipts for	63.	Military papers
13.	Bible entries	64.	Mortgages
14.	Bills of sale	65.	Newspaper advertisement copy
15.	Bonds	66.	Occupational writings
16.	Books, signatures of owner in	67.	Package receipts
17.	Building "after hours" registers	68.	Parents signatures on report cards
18.	Business license applications	69.	Partnership papers
19.	Charity pledges	70.	Pawn tickets
20.	Check book stubs	71.	Passports
21.	Checks, including endorsements	72.	Payroll receipts
22.	Church pledges	73.	Pension applications
23.	Convention registration books	74.	Permit applications
24.	Contracts	75.	Petitions, referendum, etc.
25.	Cooking recipes	76.	Photograph albums
26.	Corporation papers	77.	Pleadings
27.	Criminal records	78.	Postal cards
28.	Credit applications	79.	Probate court papers
29.	Credit cards	80.	Promissory notes
30.	Deeds	81.	Property damage reports
31.	Deeds of trust	82.	Receipts for rent, etc.
32.	Depositions	83.	Registered mail return receipts
33.	Diaries	84.	Releases of mortgages
34.	Dog license applications	85.	Rental contracts for equipment
35.	Drafts	86.	Reports
36.	Drive-it-yourself applications	87.	Retail store sales slips
37.	Drivers licenses and applications	88.	School and college papers
38.	Druggists' poison registers	89.	Social security cards and papers
39.	Employment applications	90.	Sport and game score cards
40.	Envelopes	91.	Stock certificates, endorsements on
41.	Fishing licenses	92.	Surety bond applications
42.	Funeral attendance registers	93.	Tax estimates and returns
43.	Gas service applications	94.	Telegram copy
44.	Gasoline mileage records	95.	Telephone service applications
45.	Gate records at defense plants	96.	Time sheets
46.	Greeting cards, Christmas, etc.	97.	Traffic tickets
47.	Hospital entry applications, etc.	98.	Voting registration records
48.	Hotel and motel guest register	99.	Water company service applications
49.	Hunting license	100.	Wills
50.	Identification cards	101.	Workmen's compensation papers
51.	Inventories		

FIGURE 27.1 101 Sources of Handwriting Specimens. This is a starting point if you don't know where to obtain collected specimens.

- *Carbon* — such a spurious document can be produced with the aid of carbon paper. It is first traced over the original signature using carbon paper between the legitimate and spurious documents. This spurious carbon signature is then covered with a suitable ink stroke (usually felt tip pen covers up more of the carbon outline).

Forensic Document Terminology

- *Baseline* — a real or imaginary line upon which writing rests. It can be straight, curved or diagonal.
- *Cursive Writing* — writing in which individual letters of words are generally joined.
- *Hand Printing* — any disconnected style of writing in which each letter is individually executed.

- *Disguised Writing* — deliberately altered writing with the intention of changing established characteristics. Usually what is changed the most is:
  - Size
  - Slant
  - Capital letters
  - Hesitation, patching, slowly drawn strokes
  - Writing with the opposite hand
- *Forgery* — a non-genuine document issued with the intent to defraud; a spurious document or fraudulent signature
- *Individual Characteristic* — one which is highly personal or peculiar and is unlikely to occur in other instances
- *Initial Stroke* — a stroke leading into the first letter of a word
- *Terminal Stroke* — the final stroke associated with the ending letter of a word
- *Line Quality* — refers to how smoothly curved strokes are executed; results from such factors as speed, rhythm, and smoothness of movement
- *Model signature* — a genuine signature used as a sample to prepare a simulated or traced forgery
- *Pen Lift* — interruption of a written line (usually in cursive writing) by temporarily removing the writing instrument from the document
- *Pen Pressure* — the force with which the pen contacts the paper (if heavy, may cause indentations on the page beneath)
- *Ratio or Proportion* — the ratio between the sizes of the tall letters such as "l and t" and all capitals, and the short letters such as "a, e, i, o, u"
- *Retouching* — retracing or altering a defective portion of a written stroke (such as to make it look more like the model signature)
- *Slant* — angle or inclination of the vertical axis of letters or numerals that deviates from 90 degrees vertical
- *Spacing* — distances between individual letters in a word or between words; usually expressed in letter widths rather than absolute distances
- *Traced Forgery* — a fraudulent signature executed by following the outline of genuine writing (or a model signature) with a writing instrument
- *Tremor* — the condition of a written line usually portrayed by irregular, shaky strokes that lack smooth and continuous direction in the curved portion of the stroke
- *Variation* — there are numerous variations within our own handwriting:
  - No individual ever writes the same twice.
  - No two people write exactly the same way.
  - We introduce variation within our own writing each time we write.
  - Variation is inherent; we are not machines.
  - Once you see exactness something is wrong; it may be traced.

HANDWRITING CHARACTERISTICS

Handwriting is identifiable because individual characteristics are assimilated into it, whether consciously or unconsciously.

Individual characteristics are considered in terms of:

- *Letter size* — capital letters compared with lower case letters.
- *Ratio* — the ratio between the tall letters (such as l, t and all capitals) and the short letters a, e, i, o, and u) tends to remain constant.
- *Connecting stroke* (in cursive writing, not printing) is the connecting stroke that allows the writer to proceed without having to lift the pen from the paper.

- Pen Lifts, Gaps, and Hesitations
  - Pen lifts may be in the wrong place in a spurious signature.
  - A gap within a word is identifiable due to its location or width.
  - Hesitation is the momentary stopping of the pen. It may be caused by a forger who is unfamiliar with the writing style of the person whose signature he or she is forging.
- *Letter Spacing* — is measured in terms of letter width, not millimeters or inches.
- *Slant* — slant of letters from 90 degrees vertical, one of the most obvious features
- *Line Quality* — good line quality is characterized by the fact that it is freely and naturally written. Poor line quality of the simulated forgery is caused by shifting the eye from the model to that being forged.
- *Alignment* — alignment to the baseline (a real or imaginary line upon which writing sits) rests with the letters themselves and deviations from the baseline
- *Punctuation and Other Markings* — punctuation marks such as the "i" dots and "t" crossings can identify the writer.

Note: It would be highly unlikely that suspects would remember all of these aspects when trying to forge the victims' signatures while at the same time trying to suppress their own writing.

IDENTIFICATION OF HANDWRITING

The system of writing is composed of three factors:

1. Copy book — the way we are taught to write.
   - The three major systems taught today in the U.S. exhibit no significant differences. They are: (1) Zaner-Blosser; (2) Palmer; (3) Mills.
2. The individualization each person puts into it based on departure from the copy book.
3. One's physical and mental condition at the time of the writing.

Characteristics of Handwriting

- Letter Form
- Skill (important when dealing with forgeries)
- Letter height relationships are important
- Slant is usually pretty constant

People vary in their ability to write. Some are quite skillful and it would be uncharacteristic to find an awkward handwriting sample written by the same person, or, if the writers were not skillful, it would be difficult for them to improve their handwriting.

It is difficult to identify the writing of adolescents. There are a lot of similarities. They are more interested in getting the point across than in pretty writing.

Letter Slant and Size

A protractor or a transparent rule with 1/8" increments is used to measure the slant from vertical to the size of letters (which should be compared in letter size, not actual inches).

Obliterations

By examination under infrared radiation, it may be possible to decipher the original writing that was obliterated by scribbling over it. This is possible only if the overlying ink does not absorb infrared radiation and the covered entry reflects it. If the same ink was used in both the original and overwriting, then this technique will be of no value.

Oftentimes, backlighting may be useful.

When liquid paper is used to cover writing, acetone used on the reverse side of the page should make it visible. One might have to spray a solvent (such as Radio Shack Component Cooler®) on the back side, which temporarily makes the obliterated writing visible. Then the writing can be photographed.

However, it may be an obliteration with a bank stamp (such as on a canceled check). If the stamp is red, a red filter is used. The filter drops out that color and the signature is visible with no obliteration.

EXAMINATION OF PAPER UNDER ULTRAVIOLET AND INFRARED LIGHT

UV light can be used to check the fluorescence of the paper's color. Some components in the papers may fluoresce. IR excitation may help determine the luminescence.

Fluorescence Analysis Cabinet

This unit is used as a darkroom for applications which require high-contrast fluorescence analysis. It provides long-wavelength UV irradiance (between 320 and 400 NM (nanometers) and short-wavelength UV irradiance (between 180 and 280) NM. Certain inks will absorb light under the UV light source and fluoresce. When paper fibers are disturbed by erasure, UV light can show the disruption. Papers manufactured by different companies will fluoresce differently based on fiber, filler and sizing.

Folds in a Document

First, determine whether the writing was done before or after the fold, as folding disturbs the paper fibers, which results in absorption and the spreading of the ink (see Figure 27.2). If writing was done before the paper is folded, then ink spreading does not occur. However, if the writing is done after the fold with a ballpoint pen, that ink oftentimes skips across the fold, leaving a deposit of excess ink.

Watermarks

Watermarks are probably the best way to identify quality paper (not copier paper), and can be used to identify the approximate date of manufacture. Watermarks are impressed into the paper by a

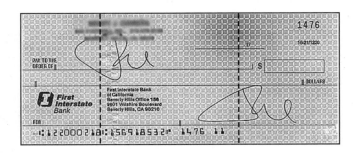

FIGURE 27.2 Folds in a document. Was the writing done before or after the fold? Folding disturbs the paper fibers, resulting in the absorption and spreading of the ink. If writing was done before paper is folded, ink spreading does not occur. Ballpoint ink often just skips across the fold, leaving a deposit of excess ink.

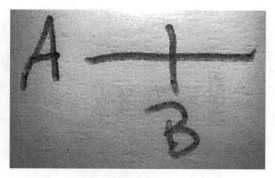

FIGURE 27.3 Line crossings. A visual exam may be deceptive, as a dark line intersecting with a lighter line will always appear to be on top. Line crossings are affected by the type of writing instrument, ink, writing material, and the age of the writing. Which line was written first, A or B? The answer is provided in the bottom photo, taken at 60X magnification. The top photo was taken at 10X.

"dandy roll" (a cylinder with wire gauze), which creates the impression over the paper pulp. They are identified by using oblique light, a light table, or ultraviolet light. "Lockwood-Post's Directory of the Pulp Paper and Allied Trades" lists the various watermarks and contact information.

Sequence of Line Crossings

Many document problems can be solved by determining the sequence of line crossings (see Figure 27.3):

- Is the writing in the proper sequence?
- Was material added at a later date?
- A visual examination is often deceptive, as a darker line intersecting with a lighter line will always appear to be on top.
- Line crossings are affected by the type of writing instrument, ink, and age of the document.
- Oftentimes, the sequence of line crossings can be determined with enlarged photographs.
- A technique using lift tape may be able to determine which line was written first.

Indented Writing

This refers to the indentation on paper that was *beneath* the original document when it was executed. Deciphering indented writing can be accomplished by *oblique light*, which creates a shadow; however, this method is extremely limited, or *chemical staining* with iodine fumes to make the writing legible; however, this method damages the document. One method that should *never* be used is drawing over the impression with a pencil.

FIGURE 27.4 This check contains physical erasures on the white background. The payee and the amount have been changed and overwritten. The signature has been overwritten as well. As you can see from the lower right hand corner, the check was cashed.

The most successful method of examination is the *ESDA or Electrostatic Detection Apparatus,* which is used to detect indented writing up to several pages beneath the original document. In this method, the indented document is placed on top of a vacuum plate and covered with plastic film. The vacuum is then turned on. A corona unit is held above the document and toner powder is applied. The surface is charged and the indented image becomes visible because the image obtained is the result of a negatively charged film repelling the negatively charged toner.

To save the image, you can photograph it or cover it with a transparent adhesive sheet. Excessive handling can affect the results of this process.

Erased Writing

There are two categories of erasure (see Figure 27.4):

1. Physical: the result of rubber eraser, which damages the paper fibers. Whether the erasure can be restored depends on the extent of the damage.
2. Chemical: such as ink eradicator, which sometimes can be made legible by using infrared or ultraviolet light.

Several methods, including oblique lighting, reflected light, and transmitted light are used to detect erased writing. Various photographic methods can also be used, including ultraviolet and or infrared.

Chemical methods of detecting erased writing are based on variables that include the type of eraser, type of paper, pressure used to make the erasure, storage conditions, and the passage of time. A powdered mixture that adheres to the roughened surface of the paper can be used. This technique should only be used with the permission of the person requesting the examination.

Obtaining Fingerprints from Documents

The most common method is a chemical process called *Ninhydrin,* an amino acid reagent that can be applied to porous surfaces in a variety of solutions to develop latent finger and palm prints.

Before this process is attempted, the document — front and back with a scale included — should be photographed (see Figure 27.5). This is done because the ink often bleeds, making the document unusable for any later comparison. The document will have purple stains on it — often the fingerprints you are looking for, but it is important to preserve those documents in plastic to avoid contaminating your own clothing. This stuff will not come out.

Another method is *iodine fuming*, a process that is popular on thermal paper, which is adversely affected by ninhydrin.

FIGURE 27.5 If you are going to process a check in Ninhydrin for fingerprints, photograph it first front and back.

Fax Copies

The quality of facsimile-transmitted documents does not allow for adequate examination because of the reproduction's notched or stepped effect (see Figure 27.6). Image quality is affected by the type of printing process of the fax machine itself, its resolution and setting. Another consideration is whether you are looking at tremor in the handwriting or telephone line interference. The original or at least first-generation photocopies are required for any subsequent examination.

Check Washing

A washed check is one that has been dipped in one of a number of solvents to remove the handwriting on it (see Figure 27.7). Following the solvent, like a photographic print in a darkroom, the process must be fixed or set. The check is then dried, and a new payee, date, and amounts are affixed.

Viewing washed checks under UV light oftentimes provides more detail and contrast to an area that is not visible under normal lighting conditions. UV light often causes certain types of ink to

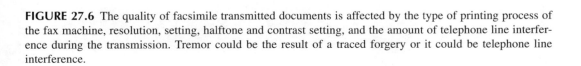

FIGURE 27.6 The quality of facsimile transmitted documents is affected by the type of printing process of the fax machine, resolution, setting, halftone and contrast setting, and the amount of telephone line interference during the transmission. Tremor could be the result of a traced forgery or it could be telephone line interference.

FIGURE 27.7 A washed check is dipped in acetone (nail polish remover or a number of other solvents), and the handwritten ink is removed. The check is then dipped in household bleach to fix (or set) it. The check is then dried and a new payee, date, and amount are affixed. This check was originally made payable to Southern California Gas Company in the amount of $27.73 on January 2, 1993.

fluoresce. Only one type of ink, the kind in gel pens, is "counterfeit proof" to solvents or any other type of chemical used in check washing.

Frank Abagnale of "Catch Me If You Can" fame, who now consults for law enforcement and other companies so that this type of thing can't happen again, has tested over 1,500 pens. He recommends the Uni-Ball Gel Impact pen, which sells for about $2.00. This pen is impervious to check washing.

PRESERVING QUESTIONED DOCUMENTS

Careful handling of these documents prior to their submission to a document examiner is of extreme importance. The person handling them should mark them inconspicuously on the reverse. Keep these documents in protective envelopes (archival quality is best), and do not fold, staple or unstaple, or write over them on another piece of paper such as a Post-It note, causing an indentation. Protect the documents from strong light, as some are light sensitive.

ACKNOWLEDGMENT

Richard H. Walton wishes to thank Paul Edholm, forensic document examiner, for his authorship of this chapter. Mr. Edholm served approximately 27 years with the Beverly Hills, California Police Department. He worked as a detective and forensic document examiner prior to his retirement. Mr. Edholm is a member of the International Association for Identification (Questioned Document Section) and is a Fellow and a Board Certified Forensic Document Examiner by the American Board of Forensic Examiners. He has taught master's level courses at National University and Advanced Officer Courses in the area of Handwriting for the Orange County, California, Sheriff's Department. He began qualifying as an expert in questioned document examination in 1985 and has so qualified in Superior, Federal, and Civil Courts. He has also been court appointed as a questioned-document expert by the Superior Court in California and has served as guest speaker in the field of questioned document examination for various police departments and public/private organizations.

28 Forensic Art in Cold Cases

Karen T. Taylor

CONTENTS

INTRODUCTION TO FORENSIC ART

By their nature, cold cases may require that investigators delve into their most creative processes. Perhaps that *might* include a little forensic art. The combination of *art and science* or even *art and investigation* could sound incongruous. Yet elements of forensic art have proven to be a valuable tool for resolution of many long-term unsolved cases. During my years as a forensic artist at the Texas Department of Public Safety and now as a freelancer, requests for my investigative-related art have often been linked to cold cases. Inherently, many forensic art processes are done as a "last resort," usually after more traditional investigative methods have been unsuccessful. This chapter synopsizes some of the methods to aid investigators that are described more expansively in my textbook *Forensic Art and Illustration* (Taylor, 2001). Suggestions are offered here for ways in which creative use of forensic art might enhance various types of cold case investigations.

This chapter will enable you to:

- **Understand the basic techniques of forensic art.**
- **Consider whether a forensic art technique might be useful in your investigation.**
- **Identify what the forensic artist needs from the investigator.**
- **Select a qualified forensic artist.**

SCOPE OF FORENSIC ART

Forensic art is any art that is of a forensic nature; that is, art used in conjunction with legal procedures. A working definition of **forensic art is any art that aids in the identification, apprehension, or conviction of criminal offenders, or that aids in the location of victims or identification of unknown deceased persons.**

Many law enforcement officers have come to know the power of forensic art. They have seen a composite drawing lead to the perpetrator they seek, or a facial reconstruction help reveal the identity of a homicide victim. Age progressions help officers recover abducted children and locate fugitives who have been at large for many years. Many have witnessed the profound impact and clarity that forensic art can bring to court proceedings.

While not every forensic art attempt is successful and not every cold case lends itself to the use of forensic art, this work does contribute significantly in many criminal investigations. The increasing options for image enhancement and modification that computers allow mean this role is likely to escalate in the future. **It is incumbent upon all who bear the responsibilities of criminal investigations and prosecutions to understand more about forensic art.**

FOUR CATEGORIES OF FORENSIC ART METHODS

1. **Composite Imagery.** Graphic images made up from the combination of individually described component parts (may include full body drawings or object/evidence drawings). Composite images are likely the most familiar type of forensic art. A composite image enables officers and the public to better focus on a suspect's appearance based on the witness's description rather than on a potentially erroneous image in their own minds derived solely from a verbal or written description. The term composite is sometimes mistakenly used to describe child age progressions, fugitive updates, postmortem images, or facial reconstructions. **But composite images refer specifically to images produced with the assistance of witness input,** not those based on photographs or skulls. **Composites may be hand-drawn, hand-assembled, or computer-aided.**
2. **Image Modification and Image Identification.** Methods of manipulation, enhancement, comparison, and categorization of photographic images. Most criminal investigations

include use of photographic images of various types. These may be crime scene photos, morgue photos, victim injury photos, suspect mugshots, surveillance images and others. Review of facial or other images by a forensic artist may result in a needed boost to a cold case. This could involve assessment, comparison, and sometimes enhancement or modification. It is logical that forensic artists, who are usually also "facial identification specialists," become involved in these procedures. **Child age progressions or fugitive updates are examples of image modification that require knowledge of craniofacial growth and aging respectively.** Such appearance updates encourage the viewer to visualize a present-day likeness of a given face rather than an outdated image. **Photo-to-photo or video-to-photo comparisons are examples of image identification that also require a solid foundation in anatomical knowledge of the face.**

3. **Demonstrative Evidence.** Visual information for case presentation in court as trial displays. Art for court presentation aids both judge and jury in the visualization and understanding of complex crime scenes and events. Certain forensic artists specialize exclusively in demonstrative evidence preparation. These displays may be two- or three-dimensional or computer-generated. Skillfully prepared trial displays may be particularly important in the presentation of resolved cold cases. In addition to clarifying the past events of the crime itself, the investigator and prosecutor may also need to explain the long-term course of the investigation. (It is not within the scope of this chapter to cover preparation of trial displays, because an entire book could be written on that topic alone.)

4. **Facial Reconstruction and Postmortem Identification Aids.** Methods to aid in the identification of human physical remains in various conditions. Artwork in this category is intended to provide a link between an unidentified person and the records needed to positively identify him or her. This is especially significant because an unidentified body likely means a murder unsolved and a murderer walking free. *In cold cases, identification of the victim is sometimes the critical first step for all the investigative pieces to fall into place.* **Postmortem imagery is a method of forensic art done when bodies are in good enough condition for the artist to develop a reasonable facial likeness based on morgue or crime scene photographs or by viewing the actual body.** For aid in the identification of semi-skeletal or skeletal remains, **facial reconstruction from the skull may be done two-dimensionally by drawing or three-dimensionally by sculpting.** Ideally, the artist and anthropologist collaborate to construct the facial features of the unknown individual on the basis of the underlying cranial structure. In some skeletal cases, a team-approach method of **superimposition comparison may be used for assessing the likelihood of a match between a skull and a missing person's facial photograph.** While not generally considered a means of positive identification, a reasonable congruence between skull and photo would point to the next logical step, such as DNA comparison. The superimposition comparison method may be indicated when few antemortem records for a missing person exist.

COMPOSITE IMAGERY IN COLD CASES

CIRCUMSTANCES FOR DOING COMPOSITE IMAGES

Normally, the request for a composite image is made soon after a major crime has occurred and police have a witness they believe capable of providing a good description of the perpetrator. **In cold case investigations, you may consider the potential usefulness of producing *new* composite images. These might be totally new or re-dos of old composites.** Development of full-body images or object or evidence drawings may also be undertaken.

PROCEDURAL CONSIDERATIONS FOR THE COMPOSITE INTERVIEW

Overall Significance of the Composite Interview

To prepare a high-quality composite image, the interview is everything. The skill and care taken to interview individuals for the purpose of developing composite images, whether by hand-drawn, mechanically assembled, or computer-generated methods, cannot be overemphasized. **For new or revised composites in cold cases, it is advisable that only the most skilled and experienced composite artists and interviewers be used.**

Any artist or software technician who produces composites must have a solid grasp of the **processes by which our minds encode memories** and the **effects of trauma on memory.** Essential too, is a working **knowledge of facial anatomy,** particularly as it relates to our abilities to recognize faces. The psychological and medicolegal literature provides a wealth of studies and articles about cognition and perception, memory and trauma, victimology, facial recognition, eyewitness identification, and interviewing methods.

Many researchers in the psychological literature describe **a three-stage memory process: the acquisition stage, the retention stage, and the retrieval stage.**

In *Forensic Art and Illustration*, the method of cognitive interviewing is presented as a recommended approach to optimum memory retrieval for successful composite interviews. A **composite-specific method of interviewing** is described in which cognitive interviewing is incorporated with **use of reference cues** in the form of facial photographs to trigger recognition ability and augment recall.

Other Interview and Memory Factors...FACE FACTS

Numerous other factors may have significance in the interview and composite generation process as well as the recognition and identification processes. Composites should be prepared with these concepts in mind. Understanding them may help determine the wisdom or appropriateness of new or revised composites. I like to call them *face facts.*

- **We encode faces in memory *as a whole.*** The single most important factor for attaining likeness and individuality in composites, thus hopefully triggering recognition, is proportion or layout. I call this capturing the *gestalt* of a face. By this I mean that the image of the face as a whole is more important, and probably more recognizable, than any of its individual parts. We encode faces into memory holistically rather than as individual component parts.
- **We place more importance on some features than others for recognition.** Hair is usually remembered and described most frequently from memory, followed by eyes and eyebrows, nose, and general facial structure. By contrast, the cheeks, mouth, and forehead seem less important for recognition. While encoding of a face in memory is usually done as an overall "grasp," when looking at certain faces, we may quickly focus our attention on odd features such as huge ears, crooked noses, or crossed eyes. Good examples would be the face (and nose) of comedian Bob Hope and the face (and birthmark) of former Soviet Premier Mikhail Gorbachev.
- **We tend to place more importance on the upper half of the face in memory.** Psychological studies indicate this, as does my case experience drawing thousands of composites.
- **Memories of faces come back in flickering, elusive glimpses**, not like photographs you can hold at will in your mind. Sketch artists must understand this and work to assist the witness in bringing back the needed information again and again throughout the drawing process.

- **We can *recognize* more than we can *recall*.** This fact makes a strong case for the use by composite artists of an interview methodology that integrates both cognitive interviewing for free recall and use of photo references as triggers to recognition. This usually promotes optimum use of memory for faces. Recall is a *verbally conveyed* skill, so the mental processing of a *visual* image can be difficult in words alone. Using visual photographic cues may make the task easier.
- **All faces are *not* created equal.** Studies have shown that some faces are simply easier to describe and recognize than others. Faces that are either particularly attractive or unattractive seem to better capture our attention. This appears to suggest that distinctiveness rather than typicality is what makes faces more recognizable.
- **All witnesses are *not* created equal.** In a perfect world of forensic art, every witness would observe the suspect under excellent conditions for the needed period of time, and be able to describe the face in exquisite detail. Of course, this does not happen. To further complicate matters, studies have determined that a witness who appears to be giving a good description, may, in fact, not be as good at recognizing. The witness may simply be *fluent* or *confident* in describing a face, yet the description may turn out to be less than accurate. This may mean that other witnesses, disregarded in the early stages of an investigation because of a perceived lack of confidence, might be worth reinterviewing.

REINTERVIEWING WITNESSES

Certainly the reinterviewing of witnesses is a well known means of generating new or additional information in a case. Surprisingly, it is sometimes possible to reinterview witnesses and develop useful composites even after the passage of a lot of time. However, potential candidates for reinterviewing should be carefully assessed.

For an event to be encoded into memory, it must first be perceived and experienced. **In general, witnesses who have experienced trauma in association with the event may have a stronger memory, though this is by no means a hard and fast rule.**

Simple physical and environmental obstacles inherent in the event, or so-called situational factors, should be considered when assessing a witness. Such commonsense things as:

- **Duration of View.** The longer a person has to look at something, the better his or her memory will be.
- **Point of View.** The primary point of view by the witness should dictate the view of the facial drawing done by the composite artist.
- **Obstructions to View.** Any object that interferes with the witness's sight of the subject can pose serious difficulty.
- **Lighting conditions.** The artist must determine the lighting conditions under which the target suspect's face was seen.
- **Distance from subject.** Subjects viewed at closer distances are better perceived that those viewed at long distances.
- **Movement or Motion.** Motion can diminish the time that the witness is allowed to view the face, and blurring of features may occur.
- **Time Since Event**

A number of researchers have assessed the effects of time elapsed in relation to the retrieval aspect of memory. They have attempted to define variables based on both accuracy of verbal descriptions and facial identification success. Results have varied according to the type of material studied, such as visual vs. verbal, and according to the form of the memory test.

As a *very* general guideline, it is better to do composite interviews with less traumatized victims or witnesses promptly after an event. "Promptly" may mean an hour, a day, or a week.

Severely traumatized victims may require more time to regain their bearings and be emotionally ready to do a composite interview. Most people benefit from, at minimum, a night's sleep and a sort of "regrouping" period after a traumatic event. The time required for trauma victims to be prepared to do a composite interview may vary considerably from days to many weeks or even longer, depending on their physical and emotional injuries.

It is important to acknowledge that memories held regarding a situation of severe trauma may be lifelong and quite vivid. This may be described as **extended retention.** Most people, when asked to recall their circumstances upon hearing of certain tragedies, find that their memories were quite clear. Where were you when you found out that President Kennedy had been assassinated? Or that Princess Diana had died? Or on September 11, 2001?

This extended retention may benefit the cold case investigator. Witnesses who were unavailable for composite interviews in the early stages of an investigation because they were too traumatized or perhaps too young, might actually be able to do a sketch later in time. It should be remembered, however, that such a sketch would be potentially viewed with greater scrutiny in court if it led to a perpetrator. The best use of a sketch like this might be quietly rather than in a public release, a judgment call that must be made case to case.

When assessing individuals for potential reinterviews, the investigator should also consider other victim or witness factors. Clearly, the degree of involvement by the victim or witness may have a marked effect on his or her abilities during the acquisition stage of memory and on ability to convey information after the crime has occurred. Witnesses tend to fall into three categories with regard to involvement in an event: active, passive, or inactive.

Active witnesses may be actual victims of crime, or close observers who have felt personally threatened. **Passive witnesses** are usually impartial observers who view an incident from a safe distance and feel no personal threat. **Inactive witnesses** generally have no knowledge that a crime has taken place or that something they have seen may be significant.

Witnesses who are actively or passively involved usually have better recollection of an event than those who are merely bystanders. All of these issues are highly complex and **it is recommended that input from a qualified mental health professional be sought in circumstances where there is any doubt about potential psychological harm to a crime victim.**

Other victim or witness factors may relate to perceptions of individual witnesses due to their age, race, sex, or personal experience or prejudices. For example, for each of us, our own age affects how we describe the age of others, as does our physical build, our skin color, and so on. The witness's use of drugs or alcohol or any other handicaps due to deficiencies in eyesight, hearing, or mental faculties may also come into play.

Redoing preexisting composites should only be done after careful consideration of the potential ramifications. These days, we see more and more that new images are released at the direction of media entities or even bereaved victim family members. I know that certain forensic artists actually *encourage* victim family members to go outside of law enforcement to commission composites if they are unsatisfied. I consider this an unethical practice that can actually jeopardize investigations. Certainly, the existence of multiple composite images creates a prime opportunity for defense attorneys to question the drawings in trial, possibly developing reasonable doubt. In addition, who will check out tips from composites not authorized by police?

The potential upside of new composite images is that they can be used as tools to generate new interest in an old investigation. If there is a new witness who has not done a composite in the past, it is not the same sort of complicated matter as redoing existing images. On rare occasions, there are situations where there was a problem with the preparation of a drawing and a witness is simply not satisfied with the original composite. Investigators might ask another artist to attempt to produce an image that will be more acceptable and accurate to the witness. In this case, the preparation of a new composite would be reasonable.

We tend to think composites and other graphic images are produced only for the purpose of release to the media and exposure to the general public. However, **in some instances, it may be**

FIGURE 28.1 Composite drawing by KTT of suspect as described by a sexual assault victim (left) and photo of the subject identified (right). (Courtesy of Karen T. Taylor)

useful to reserve the composite information for limited distribution to a targeted area or group of people. It may also be produced strictly for the quiet use of the investigator to generate new leads.

COMPOSITE DRAWING EXAMPLES

Figure 28.1 shows a composite sketch based on the description of a victim of sexual assault. While the sketch was prepared fairly close to the time of the event, it was not given much distribution. Later, the subject was arrested on an unrelated auto-theft charge. Vehicle- theft investigators happened to notice a resemblance to the sketch that had been circulated around the police agency. This led to the subject's being charged and convicted of the sexual assault.

Figure 28.2 shows a composite sketch drawn from the description of a young victim of aggravated sexual assault. This witness had seen her husband brutally murdered in her presence as

FIGURE 28.2 Composite drawing by KTT of suspect as described by a victim in a sexual assault/homicide case (left) and photo of the subject identified (right) with bandanna added.

he prayed for her safety. The likeness is notable even though the drawing was not prepared until many months after the event occurred. It was a key feature in the prosecution of the offender.

TYPES OF COMPOSITE SYSTEMS

Composite images may be produced by hand in the form of sketches, by hand-assembly kits, or by use of computer-based composite systems. **The quality of the interview process and the knowledge of both memory function and anatomy are far more important than the choice of method.**

A particularly notable phenomenon is the benefit of "sketch quality" versus "photographic quality" in the production of composite images. My friend Tom Macris, a highly successful police artist formerly with the San Jose, California Police Department, addresses this point in his paper "Composite Art: General Principles for Man and Machine":

> Sketch quality in a composite has always offered one key advantage over photo detail. This advantage is that when viewing a completed composite sketch, one is forced to apply a very fruitful margin for interpretation. The accomplished police artist knows how the addition of superfluous detail is an overkill which defeats the purpose of the composite.
>
> In a photographic composite, when such precise details are included and visually totaled, they may result in a product which precisely suggests an absolute identity. This tempts the viewer to interpret what the composite is trying to say very narrowly, thereby leaving many potential stones unturned in the investigation. It is as if twentieth century man, raised on the precise nature of photographic images, maintains a knee-jerk response to expect all photographic images to be precise representations of the subject. This misleading quality is compounded by the fact that much of the detail or subtlety was not even initially requested by the witness. It simply (and unnecessarily) came with the image. (Macris, 1987)

It is my opinion that choice of a composite system, if other than hand-drawn sketches are to be used, should involve careful consideration of this "sketch quality" versus "photo quality" phenomenon. Also important in product selection is the effectiveness of the tools for easy modification that a given system contains. There should be high-quality, flexible graphic tools capable of producing various adjustments as needed.

A good system should allow the production of:

- Both male and female faces
- Faces of any age group
- Faces of any racial, ancestral, or ethnic group
- Facial hair as needed
- Assorted headgear and eyewear
- Basic facial expressions

DRAWINGS OTHER THAN THE FACE

It is possible that a thorough case review might trigger ideas for other drawings that might be useful to the cold case investigation. Witness statements might include descriptions of items in words alone. Basically, most anything that a witness can describe, a good forensic artist can draw.

Such drawings could depict:

- Full body
- Unique body parts
- Vehicles, including aircraft and marinecraft; vehicle interiors; logos of vehicle manufacturers; bumper stickers or decals; exterior painted designs
- Details of interiors of locations
- Weapons

- Articles of clothing or footwear; printing on T-shirts; printing or logos on ballcaps, footwear, or clothing brands; other clothing details; monograms; jewelry; or watches; and eyeglasses
- Unusual or personalized drug paraphernalia
- Gang- or organized-group-related insignias
- Tattoos, moles, scars, or deformities

On several occasions, I have sketched physical body parts or unique characteristics of perpetrators, usually sex offenders, that victims were able to describe in great detail. When such traits appear on a suspect, the evidence can be very damaging, particularly when the specific trait would not be observable while the person was clothed.

CONSIDERATIONS FOR THE INVESTIGATOR

- Are there any witnesses who could be interviewed or reinterviewed to provide descriptions of faces?
- What were the physical situational factors and circumstances of the viewing?
- Were the witnesses actively, passively, or inactively involved in the event? What is their current psychological state?
- Would it be useful to have drawings of other items as part of the investigation?
- Should these images be distributed widely or used only for investigative purposes?

WHAT THE ARTIST NEEDS

- Enough insight into the investigation to properly interview the witness
- Some background information about the witness
- Ideally, experience in complex interviews

IMAGE MODIFICATION: CHILD AGE PROGRESSION IN COLD CASES

CIRCUMSTANCES FOR DOING CHILD AGE PROGRESSION

As parents know, children change and grow so quickly that photographs taken of them become out of date after a very short period of time. In the cases of missing and abducted children, the need for an "up-to-date" look of the child is critical. **Child age progression, either hand drawn or computer generated, helps provide a more current and effective facial image for distribution of case information regarding a missing child.**

There are no hard rules about the timeframes in which child age progressions can be done. However, some forensic artists decline cases of children who fall into an age group so young that no growth data exists to aid in prediction of the face. Others rely more heavily on genetic trends and facial patterns influenced by heredity and will attempt any case for which there are family photographs.

It is likely that the best child age progressions are based on a balance of genetic prediction of likeness combined with quantifiable growth data. And hopefully, new growth data sets are being developed all the time to aid with this work.

The odds are also better for cases in which there are excellent photos from which to work.

PROCEDURAL CONSIDERATIONS FOR CHILD AGE PROGRESSION

Choice of Method for Child Age Progressions

Effective child age progressions have been done by hand-drawn methods, on computer, or using a combination of both. Because of the volume of work done at the National Center for Missing and

Exploited Children, the computer-generated method is best known. Forensic artists may specialize in one method or another or may offer various approaches, depending on the particular case needs.

Importance of Artist's Knowledge

As previously stated with regard to composite images, it matters less whether an image is hand drawn or computer generated than that the artist is a skilled interviewer with knowledge of facial anatomy. With child age progressions, the same logic applies with regard to foundational knowledge of how faces grow and mature.

Neither the most technically skilled computer technician nor the finest portrait artist can produce high quality child age progressions without an understanding of craniofacial growth. The importance of this knowledge cannot be overemphasized.

Artists must understand that there are certain growth trends that effect growth on all our faces and then incorporate these with specific elements observed within an individual family. The very obvious proportional change in the *amount* of lower face is one of the most fundamental aspects of facial growth. Over time, young children's faces grow downward and forward. There is usually a strong retention of a "look" in the eye area as we grow. Childhood expressions may last a lifetime.

The forensic artist who attempts child age progressions must also have a general understanding of the **eruption patterns of the teeth.** Lack of attention to the teeth can produce a very incorrect or even distorted look in a finished updated image.

Also beneficial is reliable background information on the child regarding health or possible lifestyle. These factors aid the artist in determining whether to make the child appear more or less robust or healthy looking in the age progression. Any insights about habitual expressions or behaviors might also be subtly incorporated.

Forensic Art and Illustration offers a series of photographs showing growth in the same face from age 18 months to age 25, accompanied by an explanation of the anatomical dynamics involved.

Photographs for Child Age Progression

The quality of available photographs may also play a significant part in the determination of which method to use. If the photographs are of high quality and the required angles of view are available, then the logical choice would be a computer application. If the photographs are inferior and cannot be scanned effectively, a hand-drawn facial image might be the better choice, using the photographs just for reference input. Video images may be of such low resolution that they cannot be effectively used as stills; in such cases, they should be used only for the insights they afford into the child's appearance.

As preparation for a child age progression, you should attempt to get the best quality photographs available. It is beneficial to have multiple photos of the child in various views, particularly those taken near the time of disappearance.

Artists who use a computer approach must collect, sort by age, and store photographs of various unrelated children to incorporate into their child age progressions as needed. For example, a hairstyle or shirt collar may be pulled from the photo of any child of appropriate age, sex, and ancestry. School photographs of children are ideal for this purpose.

Good quality photographs of family members from both sides may be beneficial for assessing and gathering facial details. A child's face should be carefully studied and compared with any available family photographs. There may actually be a resemblance of specific features to grandparents or other relatives that is stronger than resemblance to parents.

Ideally, facial photographs of parents or siblings are in the same angle of view as the target photo of the missing child that will be scanned and updated. **Photos of parents and siblings at the age to which the child's face will be progressed are most beneficial.** Of course, in cases of parental abduction, family photographs from the abducting parent's side may be unavailable.

FIGURE 28.3 Hand-drawn age progression by KTT based on photograph of a male child at 2 1/2 years of age (upper left), projecting the appearance to 18 years of age (upper right), photo of the young man when located at age 18 (lower left), and age progression with facial hair added (lower right). (Courtesy of Karen T. Taylor)

Child Age Progression Case Example

Figure 28.3 shows a hand-drawn age progression based on photographs of a male child at 2 1/2 years of age, projecting the appearance to 18 years. After his location, photographs of the boy at age 18 were compared with the age progression, adding facial hair to resemble his own.

Considerations for the Investigator

- Would a child age progression benefit this investigation?
- Do good quality photographs of the child exist? How many? What facial views?
- Are there available photographs of the parents? Siblings? Grandparents or other close relatives?
- Are there any known habits or expressions that might aid in the age progression process?
- How about health or lifestyle factors?

What the Artist Needs

- Enough insight into the investigation to properly prepare the child age progression
- Some background information about the child and his or her family

- Knowledge of craniofacial growth
- The best available photographs of the child in multiple views
- Photographs of family members, particularly at the age to which the target child will be advanced

IMAGE MODIFICATION: ADULT AGE PROGRESSION IN COLD CASES

CIRCUMSTANCES FOR DOING ADULT AGE PROGRESSION

Adult age progression may be done in circumstances where an "updated" image might lead to new case information or even case resolution. Either innocent missing persons or sought-after fugitives may be age progressed, though the fugitive updates are far more commonly done. **Both the terms "adult age progression" and "fugitive updates" are used, depending on the status of the target individual.**

Adult age progression, either hand drawn or computer-generated, helps provide a more current and effective facial image for distribution of case information regarding a missing adult or fugitive.

An age-old problem in the corrections aspect of law enforcement is the reality that incarcerated prisoners sometimes escape. The concept of "updating" the appearance of long-term missing fugitives has gained popularity in the last 2 decades or so. In the U.S. and several other countries, the medium of television has encouraged the production of age progressed images of adult individuals to augment stories of sought-after criminals, usually fugitives. Adult age progression is sometimes done as part of the investigative effort to locate long-term absent adults who are classified as missing persons.

Most cases in which adult age progressions or fugitive updates are done involve high-profile criminals or missing persons sought by members of law enforcement for many years. The most logical circumstances for use of the method include cases in which there are at least fairly good photographs available of the subject, even though they are out of date.

There is no specified time frame after which updates should be done, though common sense dictates that enough time should have passed for significant aging to have occurred. In addition, it may be especially beneficial to produce updates when investigators have gained intelligence information regarding the person's current appearance to include such things as weight changes, and hair or facial hair changes.

In some cases, the production of an age progression is precipitated by an event such as an upcoming anniversary of a major crime or a planned media story about the crime. **The age progression can encourage renewed interest in the investigation and hopefully generate new leads.**

PROCEDURAL CONSIDERATIONS FOR ADULT AGE PROGRESSION

Choice of Method for Adult Age Progressions

Effective adult age progressions have been done by hand-drawn methods, on computer, or using a combination of both. They have also been done sculpturally, as was the well-documented case of fugitive John List by forensic artist Frank Bender.

The most significant factor is the artist's foundation in anatomical knowledge about the face, not the type of method used.

Importance of Artist's Knowledge

As with all other aspects of forensic art, the artist should carefully study and assess each case individually rather than assume that every person will have precisely the same indications of age on the face. A sound understanding of the physical mechanics of the facial aging process helps to promote reasonable judgments and predictions.

Neither the most technically skilled computer technician nor the finest portrait artist can produce high quality adult age progressions without an understanding of craniofacial aging. The importance of this knowledge cannot be overemphasized.

Throughout our lives, the changes that occur in our faces are influenced by genetics, environment, and lifestyle. Forensic artists who attempt to project the advanced appearance of faces must first study the facial morphology of the target face, assess genetic predisposition to the extent possible, and learn what they can about the possible environment and lifestyle of the person.

The cold case investigator should search out and provide any reliable background information on the target person regarding health and lifestyle factors. This helps the artist determine the relative harshness or mildness with which the face should be aged. For example, the face of a health-conscious person should be aged differently from the face of a known drug abuser or alcoholic. Smoking and inclination toward sun exposure should also be considerations.

Forensic Art and Illustration gives detailed decade-by-decade information as a resource for artists who employ this method, along with a reference gallery of photographs for additional guidance.

Knowledge about the creation of facial expressions and their role in the development of wrinkles is important for the artist. Expressions may contribute to a certain "look" throughout life. While this "lifelong look" does not absolutely hold true for all people, it is true for a large number of them. Therefore, the maintenance of the "look" should be a goal of adult age progressions. This nebulous quality is what allows us to recognize childhood and adolescent friends as adults when we see them at class reunions.

Photographs for Adult Age Progression

When investigators have spent many years searching for a particular fugitive, they generally develop a thick file of information on their subject. This usually includes multiple photographs. It is beneficial and wise to review any available photographs of a subject to be aged. Certainly, we all have different looks in different photographs taken under different circumstances — and photographs can be very deceiving. Most people hate to think that they really look like their driver's license photograph.

The more photographs made available to the forensic artist for assessment, the better. Even if a frontal view is to be developed, oblique or lateral views should be studied if provided in the case file.

As with the projection of craniofacial growth in child age progressions, **the process of projecting age may be made more accurate if the artist has access to photographs of family members.** It is sometimes possible to discern a trend or tendency within a family that can be incorporated into the age progression. Predictably, fugitives' families may not be cooperative in providing photographs of family members. Law enforcement officers may, however, have access to photos such as those in driver's license or arrest records. High school or college yearbooks may also be a source.

Depending upon the age of the target subject, parents' photos or siblings' photos can be assessed. I have found older siblings' photos to be particularly useful.

FUGITIVE UPDATE CASE EXAMPLE

Figure 28.4 shows the case of Virgilio Paz Romero. A Cuban national, Paz was a part of a conspiracy in the political assassination of former Chilean ambassador Orlondo Letelier and a young aide. The murders, resulting from a car bomb in a busy area of Washington, D.C. in 1976, led to strained relations between the U.S. and Chile for over a decade. The fugitive update was prepared from very poor quality photocopies of a photo of Paz from years earlier. He was captured after 15 years at large, 3 days after the updated drawing aired on "America's Most Wanted" in 1991. At the time

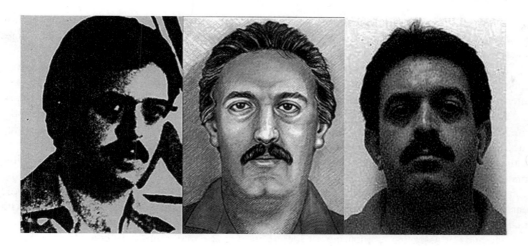

FIGURE 28.4 (See color insert following p. 216.) Virgilio Paz Romero in poor-quality photocopy (left), fugitive update by KTT (center) and after capture (right). (Courtesy of Karen T. Taylor)

of his capture, he was considered one of the most wanted men in the world. There was a lot of teasing because I chose to draw him with a red shirt and he was apprehended wearing an identical red shirt.

CONSIDERATIONS FOR THE INVESTIGATOR

- Would it be useful to have an updated facial image of a primary person in the case?
- Are there good quality photos of that person? How many?
- What about photos of members of his or her family? Are they obtainable?
- Are there any known health or lifestyle factors that might be helpful in the age progression process?
- Are there any characteristic facial expressions attributable to the person? Do photos of the expressions exist or are there associates who could describe them?

WHAT THE ARTIST NEEDS

- Enough insight into the investigation to properly prepare the adult age progression
- Some background information about the subject and his or her family
- Knowledge of craniofacial aging and expressions
- The best available photographs of the subject in multiple views
- Photographs of family members, particularly at the age to which the target subject will be advanced

IMAGE IDENTIFICATION IN COLD CASES

CIRCUMSTANCES FOR DOING IMAGE IDENTIFICATION

In today's investigative world, there are many occasions in which it would be beneficial to know the identity of a particular facial image or whether two faces are one and the same. We are photographed and videotaped in many aspects of our lives and these images often enter into criminal investigations. This will likely escalate in the years ahead.

Because of the nature of their work, forensic artists are often considered "facial identification specialists." Over time, I began to be asked more and more to give opinions regarding facial images even when no drawing was needed.

In recent years, I have been asked to assess photographs of people believed to be fugitives, missing children, long-lost relatives, missing-in-action war veterans, celebrities caught topless, literary figures, historical personages from presidents to outlaws of the Wild West, and many others.

I do not relish this role, since it is often one of very little certainty, a lot of speculation, and a great risk of being totally wrong. For these reasons, I rarely give a specific or firm opinion regarding arbitrary face-to-face comparisons. A phrase I use is, "I find nothing to indicate it is not the person," rather than "it is the person." I believe the former is a far more appropriate response for a possible match, considering the nature and limitations of such comparisons.

Yet with all this said, there are times when the "eye" of a forensic artist may offer the cold case investigator some valuable insights. I try to offer any insights that are reasonable, always with many caveats about the limited nature of face-to-face comparisons.

Methods of assessing, comparing, or identifying facial photographs vary considerably. In this chapter, I address only those done artistically rather than those done by computer means. **By whatever method an image is assessed, the most important factor once again is a solid foundation in anatomical knowledge of the face.**

As a state police forensic artist in Texas, my job duties would routinely include the visual assessment and comparison of facial images. Crime analysts and officers request assistance in determining whether two images could actually be the same person. Fraud cases in which individuals have multiple forms of identification in different names are always prevalent. Fugitive case investigators sometimes ask that known mug photos are compared with surveillance photographs of individuals they believe might be the subjects they seek. Sadly, on occasion, I am asked to review child pornography, comparing faces shown with the facial photos of missing children.

In all of these cases, my evaluations are made almost solely by just looking at the photos. **The anatomical morphological traits of faces are compared with one another, strictly on a visual basis. This approach may prove accurate if the evaluator is skilled and experienced, but it is far from scientific or definitive.**

As part of certain investigations, I have been asked to simply review photographs to see if there might be something that I see that others have missed. A few years ago, I was presented with crime scene photographs from a 2-year-old unsolved homicide case. In this murder of a senior citizen, police believed that they were seeking a lone assailant. Upon study of the photos, I could readily see and define three distinctly different sets of footprints, which changed the course of the investigation. I can't claim to fully understand why some of us have better **pattern-recognition** cognitive abilities than others, but it does seem to be the case. So, at times, there are real advantages to a "fresh look" at an unsolved cold case, especially with an "artist's eye."

PROCEDURAL CONSIDERATIONS FOR IMAGE IDENTIFICATION

Face-to-face comparisons can be approached in different ways. Sometimes an anatomical morphological evaluation is made. In other instances, a more electronic, technology-based assessment is made. There may be benefit to a team approach that makes use of the expertise of multiple individuals. For example, a comparison of two facial images might involve:

- Bony cranial structure assessment by an anthropologist
- Facial feature comparison by a forensic artist, an anatomist, or even a plastic surgeon
- Dental assessment and comparison by a dental specialist or forensic odontologist
- Evaluation of the effects of lighting and exposure in the photograph by a photographer or digital imaging specialist.

Forensic Art and Illustration includes suggested guidelines for simple evaluation and comparison of facial photographs and a discussion of the factors to consider. This is meant for use in investigative-related assessment of the facial characteristics to determine the *possibility* that certain photos may or may not depict the same individual. **This approach is not appropriate or legally valid for determination of a positive identification.**

A methodical step-by-step approach is recommended for evaluation. Multiple factors must be considered when reviewing facial images. Some fundamental concerns are the angle of view and the age of the subject in the image. Some elements of the facial "look" are simply natural, such as weight change or expression, while others may be intentional alterations of appearance. It can be helpful to assess the primary factors first and then consider other aspects and features one at a time.

In certain rare instances, an experienced facial identification specialist, anatomist, or anthropologist may give an opinion as to a match. However, **such visual assessment comparisons may be useful tools to eliminate an individual as a possible match or simply may indicate that further investigation is warranted.**

IMAGE IDENTIFICATION CASE EXAMPLE

Image identification may involve face-to-face comparison of photos or other images, or it may be related to developing some type of forensic art to aid with identifying a subject captured on a surveillance system. Figure 28.5 shows a person sought in a homicide case that involved the

FIGURE 28.5 Surveillance image of suspect in a homicide case (top) from which a facial drawing was prepared by KTT (lower left) and the subject identified (lower right). (Courtesy of Karen T. Taylor)

brutal murder of an elderly man on Christmas Day. Texas Rangers located a surveillance image of the suspect's face and wanted to improve its quality for distribution. Video, photographic, and electronic methods of enhancement proved unsuccessful, so I was asked to do a drawing of the person in the still frame. With some speculation, the frontal drawing was produced, but there was no identification for several years. Subsequently, the case was presented on "America's Most Wanted," and a tip was called in from across the U.S., leading to the positive identification of the murderer through comparison of his fingerprints to latent prints from the crime scene. An important lesson learned from this case is that no matter how accurate a forensic art image might be, *it must be seen by the right person for it to prove successful.* Sometimes it's just a matter of luck or serendipity.

CONSIDERATIONS FOR THE INVESTIGATOR

- Who might be the best person for the job of comparison? A forensic artist? An anthropologist? An anatomist? A dental specialist? A photographer? A digital imaging or video specialist? Or *all* of them?
- What are the potential sources for comparison photos? High school year books? 50 state DL checks for name or alias names?

WHAT THE ARTIST NEEDS

- Enough insight into the investigation to properly do the face-to-face assessment
- Some background information about the subject and his/her lifestyle
- Knowledge of craniofacial anatomy
- The best available photographs of the subject in multiple views

POSTMORTEM IMAGERY IN COLD CASES

CIRCUMSTANCES FOR DOING POSTMORTEM DRAWING OR IMAGERY

Postmortem drawing or imagery is a method of forensic art done when bodies are in good enough condition for the artist to develop a reasonable likeness based on morgue or crime scene photographs or by viewing the actual body. If the art is developed by hand sketching, it is generally called *postmortem drawing.* If it is done by means of computer-assisted graphics, it is referred to as *postmortem imagery.*

The primary purpose of postmortem drawing is to attach a name to the body as a result of someone viewing the facial image, so that medical records of a missing person can be compared with the body and lead to a legally valid positive identification. I often refer to my role as forensic artist as being the "middle man." The artwork is intended to provide a link between an unidentified person and the records needed to positively identify him or her.

It is the re-animation of the face from a photograph taken after death that is one of the most difficult but necessary aspects of postmortem drawing. Adding that look of "life" is a difficult-to-describe, intangible action that the forensic artist must learn to accomplish.

Forensic artists are usually requested to do postmortem drawings in cases that fall into two broad categories. The first group includes unidentified deceased persons whose photographs are inappropriate for media distribution or viewing by possible family members because of trauma or postmortem effects on the face. The second group includes unidentified deceased individuals who have been buried for a period of time before personal identification has taken place and only photographs remain.

Postmortem drawings may be done in cases of various types of death and to depict faces in different postmortem stages. **For the cold case investigator, the unidentified person likely would** be a victim of homicide or unnatural death, but could also be a long-term unidentified individual who died of apparent natural causes.

Cases in Which Postmortem Drawing Is Used

- Suicides, natural deaths, or homicides
- Traffic fatalities
- Blunt- or sharp-trauma fatalities
- Gunshot wound fatalities
- Drowning or boating accidents
- Some other transportation disasters
- Non-extensive conflagrations or fires
- Other miscellaneous types of homicidal violence

Cases in Which Postmortem Drawing Is Generally Not Used

- Extensive conflagrations
- Explosions
- Air Disasters

PROCEDURAL CONSIDERATIONS FOR DOING POSTMORTEM DRAWING OR IMAGERY

Choice of Method for Postmortem Drawing or Imagery

If good quality facial photographs are available of the deceased, it may be preferable to do computer-based facial images, using tools in software to "clean up" the areas of damage to the face. If the photos are of poorer quality, taken at less than ideal angles with poor lighting, a hand-drawn approach is probably indicated.

Importance of Artist's Knowledge

Forensic art is a field that merges artistic skills with academic knowledge about a number of subjects. If an artist is to attempt unidentified deceased cases, there must be yet another entire new body of anatomical knowledge skills acquired. **The benefit of collaboration between the artist and scientist cannot be underestimated in forensic art, particularly in unidentified deceased cases.**

Photography for Postmortem Drawing or Imagery

A primary difficulty in postmortem drawing cases is the lack of access to the body for viewing or photography. If a body is available for viewing by the artist, this is recommended. Although not a pleasant experience, the act of personally viewing the body may provide insights into the facial appearance not possible from photos alone.

Ideally, postmortem photographs are taken in **frontal and lateral views** including a scale or ruler with attention paid to avoiding distortion. The **scale** should be placed perpendicular to the camera lens so that it can be accurately read. If the jaw is hanging, it should be raised into as normal a position as possible.

In some jurisdictions, it may be possible to request that additional photographs be made for the artist's purposes. **More than likely, in cold cases, the photographs already taken will be the only ones available.** The odds are that the body has been long buried before the artist ever receives the request to do a postmortem drawing.

Depending upon the available material in the case file, the artist may benefit from access to **full-body photographs** in addition to facial ones. This gives a sense of body weight and body style, useful information for determining facial fullness. Full-length figure drawings depicting the clothing and appropriate body style may also be done. Photos **of specific body details** such as the hands, any scars, marks, or tattoos, or other unique traits may also form the basis for drawings. When photographs are inappropriate for public viewing, drawings can be prepared of most any other needed features. Examples might be tattoo drawings based on photos of decomposing skin or clothing details based on tattered soiled garments found with the body. I have also drawn hands with jewelry in the correct placement as found on the body, including nail shapes and nail-polish color.

Photographs of the **dentition**, particularly if there are unique traits, may be used to draw the mouth in a slightly open fashion to reveal the teeth. With good photographs, the teeth can be drawn very specifically. Artists with computer imaging skills may import the actual teeth images from morgue photos and incorporate them into their postmortem facial depictions. In fact, the teeth may be the most reliable trait in cases of decomposed faces, since they are not subject to easy change, as are the soft tissues.

When I receive cases with poor quality photographs, I must decide if the face represented in the photographs is in good enough condition for me to develop a reasonable facsimile in drawing form. I also factor into my decisions the thought that my drawing may be the only opportunity that this person ever has to be identified and laid to rest. **If the photographs do not provide adequate information or the condition of the body is too bad, the postmortem drawing should not be attempted.**

Scientific Input for Postmortem Drawing or Imagery

In an ideal situation, the artist would have full access to discussions with the forensic pathologist or other scientific specialists who examine the body. This is not often the case. It is very important for the artist to receive copies of the autopsy or other scientific reports such as odontological or anthropological information. Typically, the artist might need clarification of such things as correspondence of body weight to facial fullness, or distinction between postmortem changes and antemortem traits. In photographs, insect bites may be difficult to distinguish from small moles.

In *Forensic Art and Illustration*, there is information about postmortem changes that affect the face to aid the artist with re-animation of the face in the forensic artwork. Methods for use of dental information and photos are described so that the artist might better correct for the common slack-jawed position after death. There are specific palpebral changes that often occur in the eye area that must also be understood.

For me, postmortem drawing is probably the most difficult type of forensic art, or at least the type about which I feel most tentative. I am far more comfortable with a totally skeletonized case in which I have the skull to study.

Postmortem Drawing Case Examples

Figure 28.6 shows a case in which an oblique angle morgue photo was used to develop a postmortem drawing approximately 2 years after the deceased body was found. She had been sexually assaulted, stabbed, beaten in the head with a claw hammer and dumped from a bridge. The murder victim was identified and her assailant was subsequently tied to a series of murders.

Figure 28.7 shows a poster from an unidentified deceased case in which the full figure has been drawn. I used photographs of clothing and jewelry items found with the remains to prepare the drawing. An effort was also made, based on the scientific reports, to depict the petite stature and short-legged body style.

Considerations for the Investigator

- Would a postmortem drawing or image be useful in the case?
- What sort of photographs are available of the deceased? From the crime scene? From the morgue? Full-body photos? Detail photos? Photos of the teeth?

FIGURE 28.6 Oblique morgue photograph of unidentified homicide victim (left), postmortem drawing by KTT drawn by rotating the face (center), and life photo (right). (Courtesy of Karen T. Taylor)

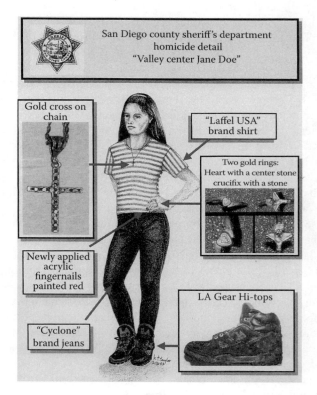

FIGURE 28.7 (See color insert following p. 216.) Drawing of full body by KTT on a poster used to show clothing, jewelry, and body style of an unidentified deceased victim of homicide. (Courtesy of San Diego County Sheriff's Department)

- Are there photos of associated items like clothing, hats, jewelry, dentures?
- Is the body too decomposed for postmortem imagery from photos alone?
- Was sufficient information recorded at autopsy (if the body is buried) to confirm identity if a name surfaces from the forensic art? Dental records? Radiographs? DNA specimen?
- Should the tissue be removed to provide the artist with a cleaned skull for reconstruction? Cost? Potential ramifications?

WHAT THE ARTIST NEEDS

- Enough information about the investigation to properly prepare the postmortem drawing
- Both crime scene photographs and autopsy photographs if available
- Specimens or good photos of available items like hair, dentures, eyeglasses, clothing, hats
- Access to autopsy or other scientific reports
- Knowledge of taphonomic changes that affect the face such as rigor mortis, livor mortis, autolysis, putrefaction, insect and animal activity

TWO-DIMENSIONAL FACIAL RECONSTRUCTION IN COLD CASES

CIRCUMSTANCES FOR DOING TWO-DIMENSIONAL FACIAL RECONSTRUCTION

The technique of two-dimensional facial reconstruction from the skull is a method of forensic art used to aid in identifying skeletal remains. The artist and anthropologist collaborate to construct the facial features of the unknown individual on the basis of the underlying cranial structure.

We automatically think of all of the various scientific methods of identifying bodies today that we have seen used so often on television: fingerprint comparisons, radiograph and dental comparisons, and DNA. Yet the simple fact is that these are all comparative methods, which means that there must first be records in order for them to be compared with a body.

Again, I characterize my forensic artist role as that of "middle man." Ideally, my **artwork provides the needed connection between an unidentified deceased person and the records needed to identify that person.** Placing an item of forensic art in the public media or in police publications may generate a lead or tip that results in a possible name attached to the body. Then science can do its job of comparing the body to a missing person's records and positively identifying the body by any of various available means.

For the cold case detective, the identification of the murder victim may be the most critical step needed to get the investigation started. This is particularly true because statistics indicate that so many victims of homicide died at the hands of a close associate. **Establishing the identity of the victim may lead to all of the pieces of the investigative puzzle coming together.**

Law enforcement agencies and medical examiners are regularly presented with difficult cases of unidentified victims of homicide or unexplained death. It is their statutory and moral obligation to make every attempt to identify these individuals. There are numerous reasons to identify bodies. Doing a representation of an individual's visage may be the only hope of ever identifying that person. For every life, there is someone somewhere who cares. Missing persons who are never located or identified may leave behind complicated legal issues such as inheritances and other business matters. Especially significant is the knowledge that an **unidentified body likely means a murder unsolved and a murderer walking free.**

Due to situational and climatic factors, human remains may be found in a great variety of physical conditions. When bodies are severely damaged or in advanced stages of decompositional change, postmortem drawings may not be possible. In instances of semi-skeletal or totally skeletonized remains, a method of reconstructing the face from the skull may be necessary.

PROCEDURAL CONSIDERATIONS FOR DOING TWO-DIMENSIONAL FACIAL RECONSTRUCTION

Choice of Method for Facial Reconstruction

Both two-and three-dimensional facial reconstruction methods have proven successful, but some cases may be better done by either one or the other method. The artist may prefer one procedure or have greater skill in a particular artistic approach.

Extremely fragile skulls, either forensic or historical cases, might not be strong enough to bear the weight of clay for a sculptural reconstruction. In such cases, particularly if the damage is in the facial area, a two-dimensional approach may be taken.

Three-dimensional reconstruction offers the advantage of viewing and photographing the sculpture in multiple views. In addition, actual items recovered at the scene with the skeletal body, such as eyeglasses, jewelry, or clothing, can sometimes be placed directly on the finished sculpture. These days, technology even allows that the forensic sculpture can be scanned and placed on web sites, showing it in a rotating or 360-degree fashion.

A plus with the drawing approach is that it is somewhat less expensive, and the skull is left uncovered so that it is available for other types of analyses to be conducted. With the drawing approach it is also easy to alter the hair, facial hair, or eye color using matte acetate overlays, without purchasing wigs or prosthetic eyes. It is also simple to scan a drawn facial reconstruction into graphics software and manipulate the hair or facial hair, add glasses, and so forth.

On several occasions, I have been asked to prepare reconstructed faces on available radiographs or x-rays in cases where the body has been buried, but I decline to do this for several reasons. My two-dimensional technique is based on certain formulae applied to life-size undistorted photographs of a skull using discernible bony landmarks. In a radiograph, it cannot be assumed that the image is life size, because most equipment produces a variable enlargement factor of an indeterminate percentage. The use of calculations would therefore be incorrect. Further, **from a radiograph alone, it is not possible to accurately locate many of the bony landmarks needed for reconstruction.**

In some cases, it is possible to do methods of facial reconstruction based on **damaged or incomplete skulls.** However, such restoration can prove very challenging and is not a job for the inexperienced.

Importance of Artist's Knowledge

As emphasized in all other sections of this chapter, the artist must have the appropriate anatomical and technique knowledge base to enter into each type of forensic art. Just because artists draw effective composites, it does not mean that they can do unidentified deceased cases without training specifically for that area. An entirely new set of skills and knowledge is needed for facial reconstruction.

The artist must gain enough understanding of technical and anatomical language to communicate with scientific professionals and interpret their reports.

Forensic Art and Illustration includes a chapter on Skull Protection and Preparation for Reconstruction, co-authored by Betty Pat. Gatliff and myself. We outline specific procedures that should be followed to prepare a skull for reconstruction, whether the forensic art project will be done two dimensionally or three dimensionally. It is critical that care be taken to protect the integrity of the skull as an item of evidence, and to ensure appropriate transferal from person to person or "chain of custody." Equally important is physical protection of the skull, because certain parts are extremely fragile.

Occasionally, it is necessary to restore missing or incomplete areas of the skull before reconstruction is attempted. Guidance for this is also included in the above-mentioned chapter.

My book also includes in-depth chapters on Two-Dimensional Facial Reconstruction from the Skull and Three-Dimensional Facial Reconstruction on the Skull. Included are step-by-step procedures for each method along with hundreds of illustrations and photographs.

The artist should receive a cleaned, uncontaminated skull, transferred using the evidence transferal procedures for the particular jurisdiction. It is important that the teeth be carefully attended to and inventoried.

Scientific Input for Facial Reconstruction

Again, the benefit of collaboration between the artist and scientist cannot be over-emphasized in forensic art, particularly in unidentified deceased cases.

Before the artist attempts any skull restoration or facial reconstruction, as much information as possible should be gathered concerning a particular case. Various scientific specialists may need to be consulted, particularly a skilled **physical or forensic anthropologist.** Only through anthropological evaluation to determine age, sex, and ancestry can the artist select the appropriate tissue depth data as preparation for rebuilding a face on the skull.

It may be **important that specimens of the teeth or areas of bone be removed for the DNA retrieval before the artist is given the skull**. The investigator should determine whether any needed specimens should be taken, to ensure that there is no contamination from cements or other artistic materials potentially used by the forensic artist, or even by handling of the skull by the artist.

The dentition of the skull should always be considered to be an extremely important element for identification. If reconstruction will be done, the investigator should attempt to retrieve all available teeth for the artist to use. The evaluation and input of a trained dental professional is particularly helpful to the artist who does facial reconstruction.

Photography for Two-Dimensional Facial Reconstruction

Photography is an integral part of the two-dimensional facial reconstruction process and must be done very precisely. The procedure that I developed in the mid 1980s requires that tissue-depth markers first be cut and glued to the skull. Then, frontal and lateral photographs are made with the skull in an orientation called the Frankfort Horizontal. The needed photography method is outlined specifically in *Forensic Art and Illustration*.

Some officers have requested that I do two-dimensional facial reconstruction from photographs that they have taken of a skull. I decline to do this because of the need for precision photography with the tissue depth markers in place.

Two-Dimensional Facial Reconstruction Examples

Figure 28.8 shows a case in which two-dimensional facial reconstruction led to the identity of a young female homicide victim. Most of the teeth were recovered with the remains, along with a hair specimen. These were provided to me by the investigator for inclusion in the drawing.

Figure 28.9 is a homicide case in which only the cranium and upper teeth were recovered. With anthropological input, I was able to approximate the mandible and develop two-dimensional reconstruction drawings that aided in the victim's identification.

Considerations for the Investigator

- Will the unidentified body have to be exhumed to perform this procedure? Is the burial location known?
- Will it be possible to get the skull cleaned for transferal to the artist?
- Have all available teeth been recovered and provided with the skull?
- Are there any hair specimens, glasses, dentures, items of clothing, hats, or other artifacts that the artist should see?
- Have all the necessary specimens of teeth or bone for potential DNA use been obtained before the skull goes to the artist?

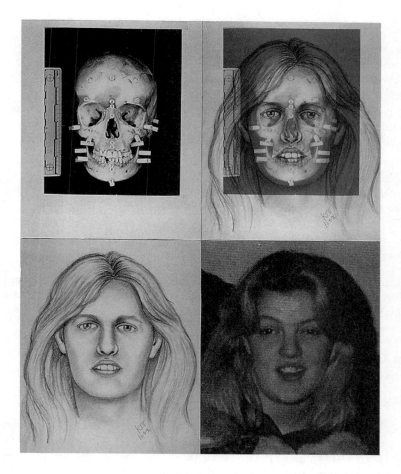

FIGURE 28.8 Skull (upper left), two-dimensional facial reconstruction by KTT with skull visible beneath (upper right), two-dimensional facial reconstruction (lower left), and victim identified (lower right). (Courtesy of Karen T. Taylor)

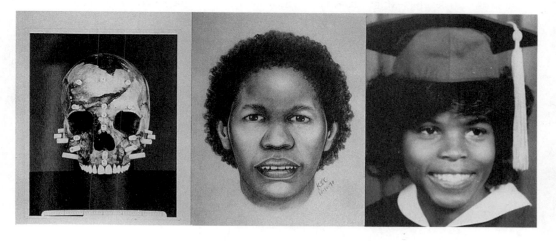

FIGURE 28.9 Skull with missing mandible (left), two-dimensional facial reconstruction by KTT (center), and victim identified (right). (Courtesy of Karen T. Taylor)

WHAT THE ARTIST NEEDS

- Enough information about the investigation to properly prepare the facial reconstruction
- Cleaned, uncontaminated skull
- Input from a qualified anthropologist and dental specialist if possible
- Access to autopsy or other scientific reports
- Any available photos from the scene that show the body or its accoutrements
- Specimens or good photos of available items like hair, dentures, glasses, clothing, hats
- Knowledge of taphonomic changes that affect the face
- Knowledge of bony to soft tissue correspondences.

THREE-DIMENSIONAL FACIAL RECONSTRUCTION IN COLD CASES

CIRCUMSTANCES FOR DOING THREE-DIMENSIONAL FACIAL RECONSTRUCTION

Facial sculpture, synonymous with facial or skull reconstruction, restoration, approximation, and reproduction, is a method of forensic art used to help identify skeletal remains. The artist and anthropologist collaborate to construct the facial features of the unknown individual on the basis of the underlying cranial structure.

PROCEDURAL CONSIDERATIONS FOR DOING THREE-DIMENSIONAL FACIAL RECONSTRUCTION

Choice of Method for Facial Reconstruction

See the discussion in the section on two-dimensional facial reconstruction to help determine whether a drawn or sculptural approach is best for your case.

In the area of forensic sculpture or three-dimensional facial reconstruction, there are two primary approaches: the **anatomical method** and the **tissue-depth method**.

Generally, in the anatomical method of facial reconstruction, muscles are defined individually to flesh out the face, and tissue-depth data are not utilized. The anatomical method is associated originally with the Russians and is most commonly used in England. It is also preferred by museum preparators who develop exhibits based on ancient skulls. Due to the nature of the method, it tends to be more time consuming.

The tissue-depth method involves use of data gained in anthropological studies as a guide for building up to the facial surfaces. It is considered the "American Method" and is the approach most commonly used in law enforcement cases. Generally, it is faster to do than the anatomical method.

It is my belief that the most advantageous method for law enforcement use is probably a combination of both the anatomical approach and the tissue-depth approach that I call the **combination method**.

Importance of Artist's Knowledge

See the discussion in the section on two-dimensional facial reconstruction.

Scientific Input for Three-Dimensional Facial Reconstruction

See the discussion in the section on two-dimensional facial reconstruction.

Photography for Three-Dimensional Facial Reconstruction

The photography of the finished forensic sculpture may be simple or elaborate, but it should be distortion free. The usual five views that are shot are frontal, oblique left, lateral left, oblique right, and lateral right.

Take care to light the sculpture in such a way that the morphological details are shown, not diminished. While dramatic lighting may be desirable in portrait photography, the goal here is to convey information rather than to flatter. A backdrop that is solid in color and neutral will also help emphasize the face. Soft, diffuse lighting is preferable.

With forensic reconstructions, it is usually relatively simple to generate media attention, if desired. Members of the media find the sculpted face of a homicide victim an interesting subject. While beneficial and necessary for distribution of the facial replica, such interviews should be carefully controlled. **Caution should be taken by the investigator to control the facial views given to the media to ensure that they don't simply use distorted photos shot for their dramatic appeal, rather than for maximum definition of the face.**

When using digital cameras, particular attention should be paid to preventing distortions. Use of a tripod helps prevent upward or downward angles because they distort the features. The sculpted face should be photographed very straight on or in direct profile.

THREE-DIMENSIONAL FACIAL RECONSTRUCTION EXAMPLE

Figure 28.10 shows the profile view of a three-dimensional facial reconstruction done over an unidentified skull by forensic sculptor Betty Pat. Gatliff. It is placed alongside a photo of the subsequently identified victim for comparison.

CONSIDERATIONS FOR THE INVESTIGATOR

- Will the unidentified body have to be exhumed to perform this procedure? Is the burial location known?
- Will it be possible to get the skull cleaned for transferal to the artist?
- Have all available teeth been recovered and provided with the skull?

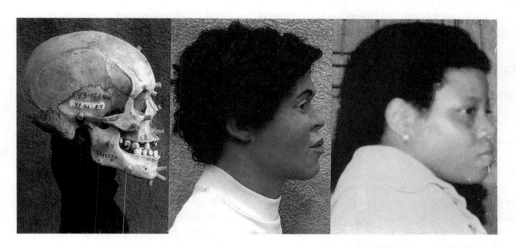

FIGURE 28.10 Skull (left), three-dimensional facial reconstruction by Betty Pat. Gatliff (center), and victim identified (right). (Courtesy of Betty Pat. Gatliff and Karen T. Taylor)

- Are there any hair specimens, glasses, dentures, items of clothing, hats, or other artifacts that the artist should see?
- Have all the necessary specimens of teeth or bone for potential DNA use been obtained before the skull goes to the artist?

WHAT THE ARTIST NEEDS

- Enough information about the investigation to properly prepare the facial reconstruction
- Cleaned, uncontaminated skull, sturdy enough to bear the weight of the clay sculpture
- Input from a qualified anthropologist and dental specialist if possible
- Access to autopsy or other scientific reports
- Any available photos from the scene that show the body or its accoutrements
- Specimens or good photos of available items like hair, dentures, glasses, clothing, hats
- Knowledge of taphonomic changes that affect the face
- Knowledge of bony to soft tissue correspondences
- Sculpture skills

SUPERIMPOSITION COMPARISON IN COLD CASES

CIRCUMSTANCES FOR DOING SUPERIMPOSITION COMPARISON

In one other method that I will include in brief, the artist can act as part of a team of facial identification specialists.

When semi-skeletal or skeletal bodies are found and investigators have no idea at all as to the identity of the deceased, a method of facial reconstruction is indicated. However, **there are some cases in which crime analysts or investigators have suspicions that the body might be a certain missing person.** If there are no dental or other antemortem records for comparison, a method of superimposition comparison might be helpful, especially if good photographs of the missing person exist.

A practical factor is that superimposition comparisons may save investigative dollars in the long run. The procedure may quickly eliminate a possible missing person as a match for the unidentified deceased. Or, it may be a strong indicator that the next step, perhaps time-consuming or pricey tests, would be warranted.

While not generally considered a means of positive identification, a reasonable congruence between skull and photo would point to the next logical step such as DNA comparison.

PROCEDURAL CONSIDERATIONS FOR DOING SUPERIMPOSITION COMPARISON

Superimpositions have actually been done for over 100 years and have recently developed into a more technologically useful tool for assessing identification of unknown skeletal remains. These techniques fall into three general categories: **photographic, video** and **computer-aided**. It is likely that each technique has unique advantages and disadvantages.

Undoubtedly, further technological advances in computer digitization and photographic enhancement will yield a degree of accuracy not yet obtainable by today's methodology.[3]

Forensic Art and Illustration includes a chapter by forensic anthropologist Dr. David Glassman on Methods of Superimposition. The chapter discusses the critical variables necessary to develop an accurate comparison, and describes the video superimposition procedure and subsequent analysis technique. Also specified is the type of video equipment needed.

Essentially, superimposition comparisons focus on orientation and scale. The skull must be placed so that it is in the same orientation and at the same scale as the face in the photograph used for comparison. This is far easier said than done. Dr. Glassman and I have worked on many cases, primarily using the video approach.

The artist is often the member of the team tasked with achieving the correct orientation, using experience and skill gained through other forensic art tasks. Usually the science part of this art/science task is a forensic anthropologist. At times, other team members might be a pathologist, an anatomist, an odontologist, dentist, orthodontist, or others. There should also be photographic and video specialists.

Once the correct scale and orientation are achieved through trial and error, then the critical variables may be assessed. These include, but are not limited to, positioning, size, distortion, features to be used for comparison and the defining limits for concluding a possible match or exclusion.

In general, **the comparison is more effective and has greater odds for accuracy if several views of the missing person's face are available.** Photographs from various angles should be overlaid if possible, reorienting the skull with each new photo. Straight frontal views and profile views are the simplest to position. Oblique views are more complicated and may result in inaccurate interpretation.

When recovered with a skull, the anterior or frontal teeth can be very useful as part of the superimposition process. If the investigator can find smiling photographs of the missing person and they reveal the teeth clearly, this is an added plus.

Skeletal remains do not need to be complete to be useful in superimposition comparisons. Missing mandible cases or those with areas of damage can be used.

It is important to note that, while the artist may be a valuable member of the team, the scientist should make any judgment calls regarding identity of the deceased. The artist is not qualified to do this.

VIDEO SUPERIMPOSITION COMPARISON EXAMPLE

Figure 28.11 shows a case of superimposition comparison done jointly by Dr. David Glassman and myself. The skull was quite fragmentary and had to be reassembled. Then, we were able to overlay it with photos of a missing person known to have disappeared from the general area where the remains were found. Time-since-death estimations and physical parameters from Dr. Glassman's report were also consistent, though there were no antemortem dental records available. Using video equipment, we established a congruence that indicated further investigation in this direction was appropriate, ultimately leading to his positive identification.

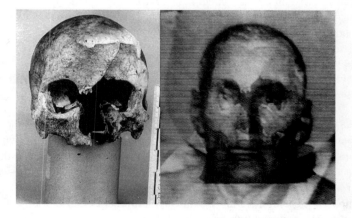

FIGURE 28.11 Superimposition comparison by KTT and forensic anthropologist David Glassman, Ph.D. of a fractured cranium (left) and a photographic image (right). (Courtesy of Karen T. Taylor)

CONSIDERATIONS FOR THE INVESTIGATOR

- Do circumstances in a missing person's investigation correlate with the circumstances of the skeletal recovery? Time frame? General location?
- Do physical details of the missing person correlate with the skeletal body? Age? Race? Sex? Clothing? Other?
- Are photographs of the missing person available? Multiple views? Teeth showing?
- Will the unidentified body have to be exhumed to perform this procedure? Is the burial location known?
- Have all available teeth been recovered and provided with the skull?
- What specialists can be assembled as a team for the superimposition comparison? A forensic artist? An anthropologist? An anatomist? A dental specialist? A photography specialist? A video specialist?
- Is the needed imaging equipment available?

WHAT THE ARTIST NEEDS

- Enough information about the investigation to properly assist with the superimposition procedure
- Knowledge of craniofacial anatomy
- Working environment within a team of qualified science professionals
- Assistance of photographic or video experts with knowledge of the superimposition process
- Video equipment that includes two cameras, a monitor, and an image-mixing capability
- Skull, with mandible in place and front teeth accurately affixed in the sockets, if available
- Photographs of the missing person for comparison, preferably multiple facial angles

QUALIFICATIONS OF THE FORENSIC ARTIST

TRAINING AND EDUCATION

To aid in your selection and hiring of an artist practitioner, you should have some understanding of the training and qualifications of forensic artists. This might also help to guide the training for individuals within your agency who have demonstrated an aptitude for this work.

The forensic art field does not have a specific set of educational requirements or defined career paths. Many forensic artists today are capable of performing a wide spectrum of art functions to assist in criminal investigations and case presentations. However, some artists specialize almost exclusively in one aspect of forensic art such as composite imagery, facial reconstruction from skulls, or child age progression.

Most police agencies in the U.S. utilize a forensic artist on an "as-needed" basis, using either someone on staff in another capacity or hiring a freelancer. Certain agencies employ a full-time artist, but such instances are rare and usually occur in federal or state agencies or in very large cities.

Practitioners in this business tend to enter the field from various directions. Many are police officers who began doing forensic art out of necessity on cases within their own agencies. Others are civilian employees working within police agencies who demonstrated artistic talent and were recruited by detectives to help with their investigations. Some are trained artists who contract with law enforcement agencies on a freelance basis.

Depending upon which forensic art specialty practitioners choose, their education should be geared accordingly, with the intention being to "fill the gaps" of their own previous training and experience. For example, experienced police officers who have spent many years conducting interviews and testifying in court may require additional art training. Civilian artists, whether employed in law enforcement or freelancers, must learn about functioning within the proper restraints of the laws of the jurisdiction within which they work.

Training for artists should also facilitate the specific area of forensic art to be done. Anyone who prepares composite images should have training in interview techniques and sensitivity to crime victims. Serious composite artists should consider this an area for career-long improvement. Such artists can never have too much knowledge about memory-enhancing interview techniques, and they should feel compelled to constantly read literature involving research in this area.

Those artists who work with image modification, particularly by computer methods, should seek training and expertise in softwares that allow the manipulations and enhancements they require. Image modifications such as age progressions that project growth in a child's face require study of the complex patterns of craniofacial growth. Age progressions of the faces of long-term missing fugitives require knowledge of facial aging. Both types of age progressions can be enhanced by an understanding of human dentition and the associated patterns of dental eruption in children as well as modifications that occur in the forms around the mouth with aging and dental attrition.

Artists who prepare demonstrative evidence or trial displays must have a wide array of skills. This field has become so multifaceted that many have chosen to specialize in a particular category. Displays can be hand drawn, graphic art, photographic, computer-assisted, three-dimensional or animated. They can be as simple as an enlargement of two side-by-side fingerprints for comparison or as complex as elaborately animated reenactments of an event.

Those who do postmortem imagery or facial reconstruction from the skull must delve into an entirely different base of learning. Postmortem drawings require a working knowledge of taphonomic changes that occur with death and their effects on the face. Facial reconstructionists work very closely with physical or forensic anthropologists and often gain knowledge in that field that directly benefits their work. Trained medical illustrators are "naturals" for going into facial reconstruction because of their strong foundation in facial anatomy.

Methods of superimposition comparison of skulls to photographs of missing persons are generally best approached as a team effort. The forensic artist, as one member of the team, provides knowledge of the morphological structures of the face that aids in the orientation of the skull into the correct position for overlay comparisons. The scientifically trained experts make the assessments that can lead to identification.

Again, the benefit of collaboration between the artist and scientist cannot be underestimated in forensic art, particularly in unidentified deceased cases.

EXPERIENCE

It is worth emphasizing that forensic art is extremely experience based. Investigators are encouraged to utilize the skills of artists who are experienced in identification-specific work rather than just portrait or other arts. **Because artwork in cold cases may be complex, the skills of experienced artists are ideal.** On the other hand, if no funds for an experienced artist are available, maybe a talented volunteer beginner might be worth a shot.

As with any other profession, it is always advisable to check an artist's credentials, experience, and references. Ask to see a portfolio of drawings and sculptures to assess basic art skills. Ask to view photographs of previous forensic art cases, especially if you are hiring a freelancer. Ask about solved cases and be prepared to verify any claims of previous "hits." Consider the training needed for the specific task you need. Are you choosing the best artist for the job? Has he or she had the training needed to do the work?

CERTIFICATION

There is a certification program for forensic artists within the International Association for Identification. This is the only existing certification process under the auspices of a professional organization and involves a testing procedure and peer review.

Some artists attend a workshop and receive a "certificate" upon completion of the course. Such a certificate is a "certificate of attendance," and means only that the person attended the workshop for the required time. The certificate may be important documentation of the hours of training received, useful in court testimony or when applying for certification. However, a **"certificate of attendance" is not a "certification."**

Fee Structure

Salaries and fees in the forensic art field vary tremendously throughout the U.S. and Canada. There is also variation in the ways in which jobs are assigned and valued. As with any field, experience and demonstrated success bring higher fees. Only a handful of artists are full-time employees with law enforcement agencies. Freelance or contract employees may charge by the job or by the hour.

DEALINGS BETWEEN THE ARTIST AND THE INVESTIGATOR

Important aspects of artist/investigator interaction include:

- Good communication
- Proper evidence transferrals when needed
- Possible use of NDAs or non-disclosure agreements, if necessary, with a freelancer

It is my hope that the contents of this chapter will aid cold case investigators to have greater understanding and insight into my field, and encourage them to consider use of forensic art methods. It has been said the pen is mightier than the sword. If used correctly, so is the pencil.

ACKNOWLEDGMENT

Richard H. Walton wishes to extend appreciation to Karen T. Taylor for her gracious contribution and authorship of this chapter. Karen Taylor is considered by many to be one of America's leading forensic artists. Ms. Taylor attended the School of Fine Arts at the University of Texas and the Chelsea School of Fine Arts in London, where she was also a freelance portrait sculptor for Madame Tussaud's Wax Museum. She worked as a forensic artist for 18 years for the Texas Department of Public Safety in Austin, Texas. Her crime-fighting work for law enforcement agencies and FOX television's "America's Most Wanted" has involved a variety of art services to aid in the apprehension and conviction of criminals or further efforts to identify unknown deceased persons.

In addition, her work has been featured on FOX, ABC, CBS, CNN, Court TV, the Discovery Channel, the History Channel, Telemundo and the BBC. The popular CBS drama "CSI" created a forensic artist character based on Ms. Taylor, and her hands and artwork have appeared on the show.

The successes of her forensic art have led to Taylor's being named among "Texas Women of the Century." She has served as a forensic art instructor at the FBI National Academy and other law enforcement academies, universities, and medical schools in the U.S. and Canada, and now devotes her in-depth knowledge of the human face to the training of fine artists. She is the author of *Forensic Art and Illustration*, and the upcoming work, *Understanding the Human Face*. www.karentaylor.com

REFERENCES

Taylor, K.T., *Forensic Art and Illustration*. Boca Raton: CRC Press, 2001.
Macris, T. F., "Composite art, general principles for man and machine," *Identification News,* August, 1987.
Glassman, D.M., Methods of superimposition, in *Forensic Art and Illustration*, Taylor, K.T. Boca Raton: CRC Press, 2001.

29 Cold Case Polygraph

Paul Redden

CONTENTS

INTRODUCTION

The polygraph, more commonly referred to as the lie detector, is another excellent tool available to the cold case investigator that cannot be overlooked or forgotten. In cold case homicide investigations, the polygraph can play a valuable role in assisting and assessing a person's knowledge of or involvement in a case under investigation. In addition, review of cold case files may reveal that subjects involved in the unsolved case had been polygraphed in decades past (see Figure 29.1). Have an examiner review the polygraph charts. Techniques and equipment have changed. Do not assume that the examiner will agree on the earlier conclusions. If subjects are available, and are possible suspects or might have valuable information for your investigation, they should probably be retested. The revived investigation could have produced some new information and questions that now need to be addressed. Sometimes individuals will take a private polygraph examination. Again, do not assume the results are accurate. The information provided to the examiner about the case came from the individual who was tested and could have been inaccurate, which would have played a significant role in the results of the test. The private polygraph examiner will be happy to produce his polygraph file for your review as long as it does not violate any attorney–client privilege.

Role of the Polygraph

There are several things to take into consideration when deciding to use the polygraph in a cold case investigation. Remember, the polygraph is an *aid* to the investigator and should never be considered a substitute or a shortcut to a thorough investigation. The polygraph can be used not only to determine a suspect's involvement in a crime but can also assist in verifying witness

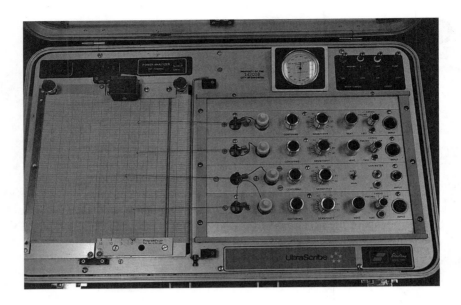

FIGURE 29.1 Old-style analog polygraph.

information or knowledge in a particular crime. Although polygraph results are generally inadmissible in court, the information obtained or statements made to the examiner are. This can also play an important role in pointing the investigation in the right direction.

SELECTION AND QUALIFICATIONS OF POLYGRAPH EXAMINER

If an agency does not have its own polygraph examiner, several things need to be considered in selecting a polygraph examiner. First and foremost, did the examiner receive training at an approved polygraph school? The American Polygraph Association (APA) or the American Association of Police Polygraphists (AAPP) can provide information concerning approved or recognized polygraph schools. Successful completion of an approved polygraph school is a requirement to become a member APA, AAPP or a State Polygraph Association.

Limitations on Examination

Prior to scheduling the polygraph examination, the investigator should be aware of conditions that might prohibit the examination. Persons with physical disabilities, severe heart conditions, pregnancy, or severe psychological disorders are examples of people who may not be suitable for a polygraph examination. Additionally, people who are intoxicated or under the influence of drugs should not be tested. Ideally, the subject should be well rested and nourished. If subjects are taking prescribed medication, they should continue to take their medication as prescribed. The polygraph examiner has the final decision as to whether subjects are suitable for an examination.

Prior to the Examination

The investigator should not interrogate the subject prior to the polygraph examination and should stop all questioning once the subject has agreed to submit to the exam. Continued questioning could have a serious impact on the results of the exam. In addition:

- Do not attempt to explain the polygraph to the subject.
- Do not go into detail about what questions the examiner will ask.

- Never suggest to the subject that the examiner will ask only questions about the investigation.
- Tell subjects that the examiner will explain the entire process and they will be given the opportunity to ask the examiner any questions about the polygraph procedure.

In deciding to use the polygraph in an investigation, think about what there is to gain from the examination. There is a lot of information that is important for the investigation, but in a polygraph examination, target the questions to the most important piece of information that the subject may possess or have knowledge about. There are only three or four relevant questions that can be asked in a polygraph examination, so consider what is the most important question to be answered.

A conference with the investigator and polygraph examiner is extremely necessary prior to the polygraph examination. The investigator needs to discuss all of the case facts with the examiner and should not withhold any information that could assist the examiner during the exam. Remember, the subject could be the perpetrator, and it is imperative that the examiner be aware of all the case facts and information. If subjects think that the examiner is misinformed or uniformed, they will try to use that to their advantage, which could play a role in gaining or losing a confession or valuable information that could assist you in the investigation.

If investigators can observe the polygraph, I encourage them to watch the entire examination. Information often surfaces that they may not be aware of and that can be of assistance in the investigation. If they are there to hear it, they can start using that information immediately. Also, the examiner may need help from the investigator to clarify issues or to ask questions about some of the information that has surfaced during the interview of the subject.

It is my opinion that all polygraph examinations should at least be tape recorded. This protects all involved and may later be extremely valuable in replaying what was said in the polygraph room during the examination. Video taping is even better, as it provides a visual reference to all of the subject's behavior during the examination. Computerized polygraph equipment is capable of digitally recording both audio and video of the examination. The computerized equipment is portable and allows for webcam audio/video recording in virtually any situation (see Figure 29.2).

FIGURE 29.2 Computerized polygraph.

THE EXAMINATION PROCESS

The polygraph is conducted on a voluntary basis. No one can be forced to take a polygraph exam, and it cannot be rushed. A properly conduced examination will last a minimum of 90 minutes and could take several hours to cover a complex case. The examination consists of several different phases, more commonly referred to as pre-test, testing, and post-test phases.

Pre-Test Phase

During this phase, or pre-test interview, the examiner gathers personal information about the subject's background. The examiner will explain how the polygraph works. What components will be physically attached to the subject and what each component is recording, as well as a description of the psycho-physiological aspect of lying, will be explained to subject, who will be given the opportunity to explain what he or she knows about the crime under investigation and will give his or her version of what he or she knows or the role he or she played in the crime under investigation.

The examiner is looking for any changes in the original statement made to the investigator or any additional information that may not have been previously disclosed. This is an interview phase and the examiner will not challenge the subject but will ask questions to clarify any questions that might arise. The examiner will then formulate the questions that will be asked of the subject in the polygraph examination. All of the questions are first reviewed with the subject.

During this review, the individual will be asked to explain the meaning and his or her understanding of the relevant questions that are going to be asked. The examiner does this to make sure he or she understands what is going to be asked in the examination and to ensure the questions have the same meaning to both the examiner and the subject.

Test Phase

This is the actual polygraph examination. The examiner will attach the components to the subject. The components consist of two pneumo tubes, an expandable tube that measures respiration. One goes around the chest and one goes around the stomach. The galvanic skin response (GSR) plates are attached to the fingers and measure the skin response, and the cardio cuff goes around the arm and measures the pulse rate, increases or decreases in blood pressure, and the strength of the heart beat. All of the components are measured simultaneously on the polygraph chart. Subjects will be instructed to remain completely still during the exam and to answer the questions only with a yes or no answer, as previously reviewed. The examiner will adjust the instrument to the subject's physiological level and administer the examination. There is an approximate 25-second time period from one question to the next. This allows time for the subject to react to and recover from any question that poses a threat to their well-being.

There are several types of exams that the examiner can use. Each type of examination has a specific purpose:

- The **S-K-Y** exam, containing three relevant questions, is used to help determine suspicion, knowledge, personal involvement, or lesser involvement in the crime under investigation.
- A **YOU** phase exam contains two or three relevant questions. It is used to determine a specific role in the crime, i.e., "Did you fire the shot that resulted in the death of John Doe?"
- An **Exploratory** exam contains three or four relevant questions and is used to determine the different roles a subject might have committed, i.e., "Did you drive the getaway car? Were you the lookout man?" etc.

- The **Peak of Tension** exam can be used to determine specific knowledge that only the perpetrator should know, i.e., "If you shot John Doe, did you use a .22, .38, .45 ...?" etc. This must be an item of information that is known only to the individual and the investigators and has not been publicly disclosed.

Upon conclusion of the polygraph examination the examiner will probably advise the subject of the results of the examination. The examiner may first ask for a quality control of the charts from another examiner, if readily available, before advising the subject of the findings (see Figure 29.3).

Post Test Phase

The Post Test Phase follows the completion of the examination after the examiner has reached a conclusion. If the subject does not appear to be attempting deception to the relevant questions, he or she will probably be advised that he or she does not appear to be involved in the crime under

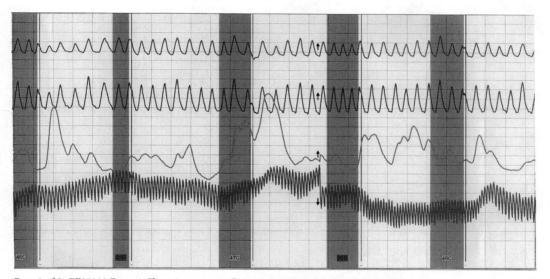

Page 1 of 3 PF11111 Exam 1 Chart 1

		Gain settings:	P2	P1	GS	CA	AU
Subject:		Recorded: Start	5.0	6.6	2.5	3.0	–
Examiner: Paul Redden		Recorded: End	5.0	6.6	3.5	2.1	–
Date: 11/5/1998		Printed: Start	5.0	5.5	1.8	2.8	–
View size: Normal		Printed: End	5.0	5.5	2.8	1.9	–

Time start: 2:42:06 am   Recorded electrodermal: Automatic
End: 2:46:25 am Duration: 04:19   Printed electrodermal: Automatic
Cuff pressure start: 76
End: 79487 (zone)

(a)

FIGURE 29.3 (a) An example of a truthful chart. Numbers 46C, 47C, and 48C are comparison questions. 33R and 35R are the Relevant Questions. They ask, "Did you do the crime?" The subject's blood pressure (red) and the GSR (Green) shows subject is reacting to comparison questions and is therefore considered innocent of the crime under investigation; (b) is a deceptive homicide chart. Blood pressure increases, there is a significant rise in the GSR as well as suppressed cycles in the breathing on the Relevant Questions (33R and 35R). This is an example of a person who is being deceptive as to relevant issues in a crime under investigation.

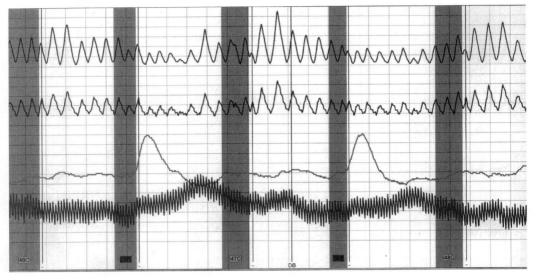

Page 1 of 3 PF11111 Exam 1 Chart 1
Subject:
Examiner: Paul Redden
Date: 11/5/1996
View size: Normal
Time start: 5:04:40 pm
End: 5:08:38 pm Duration: 03:58
Cuff pressure start: 71 End: 66
187 Chart 3 E1 (zone)

Gain settings: P2 P1 GS CAAU
Recorded: Start 5.0 6.0 4.0 2.0 –
Recorded: End   5.0 6.0 5.0 2.0 –
Printed: Start   6.0 7.0 5.0 2.2 –
Printed: End   6.0 7.0 6.0 2.2 –
Recorded electrodermal: Automatic
Printed electrodermal: Automatic

(b)

FIGURE 29.3 (Continued).

investigation. If the individual appears to be attempting deception to the relevant questions, however, the examiner will begin the interrogation process.

The subject being tested will be told that he or she has failed the polygraph examination with regard to the relevant questions, and be given the opportunity to explain his or her reactions. The examiner will confront the individual with his or her reactions and attempt to resolve the issue under investigation. Any statements or confessions the subject makes are admissible. A trained and qualified polygraph examiner will usually not give up very easily at this point. The examiner knows that the subject has failed the test and is probably involved in the crime under investigation.

The examiner wants to verify the reactions that have been collected on the polygraph charts and the subject will be given the opportunity to explain his or her involvement in the crime and the reason the incident occurred. If the subject confesses, the examiner should bring in the investigator and have the subject repeat his or her role to the investigator. Often, additional details of the crime remain to be resolved and the investigator needs to know what the subject has revealed.

EFFECT OF TIME ON COLD CASE POLYGRAPH

I do not think that time produces a significant problem in the use of the polygraph. Short of a medical problem or physical injury people remember significant things that have occurred in their lives. The individual still does not want to get caught and that fear of detection of deception will continue to produce reactions in a polygraph examination.

CONCLUSION

The polygraph is an excellent investigative tool available to the investigator. I encourage its use in cold case homicide investigations. Discuss its capabilities with the examiner. Information obtained in a polygraph examination frequently plays an important role in assisting the investigator and steering the investigation in the right direction.

ACKNOWLEDGMENT

Richard H. Walton wishes to thank Paul Redden for his authorship of this chapter. Mr. Redden, who is a polygraph examiner for the San Diego, California, Police Department, began his law enforcement career in 1969. In 1981, he graduated from the Backster School of Lie Detection and became a polygraph examiner for the San Diego Police Department in 1985. He has administered over 7000 polygraph examinations. He is a certified instructor for the Lafayette Computerized Polygraph and instructs at the school of lie detection from which he graduated. He has taught polygraph examiners throughout Mexico, and the National Police of Bulgaria. In 2003, he was selected Outstanding Polygraph Examiner of the year by the California Polygraph Examiners Association and the Region 1 Outstanding Polygraph Examiner of the year for the American Association of Police Polygraphists at their annual seminar in 2004 in Vancouver, British Columbia.

30 Geographic Profiling in Cold Case Investigations

D. Kim Rossmo

CONTENTS

INTRODUCTION

Cold case detectives are time travelers. They face problems of faded memories, missing witnesses, retired police officers, misplaced evidence, and altered crime scenes. Their criminal investigative expertise must be combined with historical research skills. By definition, cold cases are the hardest because they are the unsolved ones. But, while these investigations are challenging, they do have certain advantages. A cold case detective brings a fresh perspective and a different way of thinking to the investigation, free of any original problematic mindsets and organizational pressures (Rossmo, 2005). Witnesses, accomplices, and family and friends of the offender are sometimes more willing to talk to police with the passage of time, and advances in forensic techniques and behavioral analysis allow the application of new investigative methodologies originally unavailable to investigators.

Many unsolved rapes and murders are stranger crimes. Most homicides are cleared for the simple reason that people are typically killed by someone they know. If there is no relationship between the offender and the victim, the crime is usually much more difficult to solve. Stranger crimes, however, may be part of a larger series. The investigation of serial crime, while a complex and information-intensive task, is actually easier in some respects than single stranger crimes. Special techniques for analyzing intercrime patterns become available to detectives in such cases. Every crime in the pattern can be considered a piece in a jigsaw puzzle. The more pieces, the more information; the more information, the more detailed the overall picture.

Cold case detectives investigating the 1995 shooting of a Baskin-Robbins restaurant owner in Laguna Beach, California, were stymied until they connected the murder to three other Orange County robberies. Identifying a series allowed the robberies to be analyzed as a pattern, rather than as isolated crimes. Each case file contained separate witness descriptions of the offender, in particular, information about a tattoo on his neck. One victim reported the tattoo was a word, a second remembered some of the letters, and a third recalled it was in script writing (L. Velarde, personal communication, May 21, 2005). Detectives Dan Lowrey and Bob Romaine used this integrated description to search a computer database of known gang members. They found Gilberto Corrales Garcia, a violent convicted felon and heavily tattooed former gang member (Welborn, 2003). Garcia was convicted of the murder in 2003, and is currently serving a life sentence with no possibility of parole.

The application of scientific studies of criminal behavior has led to the development of several serial crime investigative techniques, including linkage analysis systems, behavioral (psychological) profiling, geographic profiling, and crime-specific statistical databases. Geographic profiling is a criminal investigative methodology that analyzes crime locations to determine the most likely area of offender residence. Under the appropriate circumstances, it can be a useful tool in cold case investigations.

In this chapter, we first consider the nature of the criminal investigative process. Next, we discuss linkage analysis, an important step in the investigation of stranger serial crime. Then, we examine geographic profiling and its associated investigative strategies. Finally, we present a historic case example.

CRIMINAL INVESTIGATIVE PROCESS

A criminal investigation can be divided into two essential tasks: (1) finding offenders; and (2) proving their guilt. Both tasks must be completed for a crime to be solved. These requirements are not chronologically ordered. Detectives may know who the offender is, but still lack sufficient evidence to prove their guilt.* Conversely, they may be able to prove guilt, but not know the offender's identity. The first situation was the one facing investigators in the 2002 murder of Laci Peterson. Detectives believed strongly that her husband, Scot Peterson, had killed her and her unborn child. Their job was to prove the case in court. The second situation describes the case of

---

* The establishment of guilt is not a police prerogative, and can only be done by a judge or jury. The police therefore never legally "know" who committed a crime before trial. In some cases, however, investigators become convinced a particular person committed the crime, and consequently focus their investigative efforts on collecting evidence against that individual – not on finding other suspects. Theoretically, the evidence collection process should confirm or refute the police theory.

TABLE 30.1
The Criminal Investigative Process

Collect Suspects		Prioritize	Evaluate	Direct/Indirect Evidence
Public	*Databases*	Physical Description	Opportunity	Witness
Tips	Criminal Records	Behavior	Motive	
Witnesses	Police Files	General	Means	
Informants	DMV	Specific	Modus Operandi	
Friends	Other Agencies	Geography	Composite Sketch	Confession
Family		General	Video	
Neighbors		Specific	Alibi	
			Suspect Interview	
			Interviews of Family, Friends, and Neighbors	Physical Evidence

*Header spanning Collect Suspects, Prioritize, Evaluate: **Find Offender**. Header spanning Direct/Indirect Evidence: **Prove Guilt**.*

the Baton Rouge serial murders that occurred from 2001 to 2003. Police had recovered DNA evidence from the crime scenes, so once the offender was identified, his guilt could be established. Of course, sometimes investigators do not know who committed the crime, and could not prove their guilt even if they did. Such cases have a low chance of being solved.

Establishing guilt can be accomplished in one of only three ways: (1) a confession; (2) a witness; or (3) physical evidence (Klockars and Mastrofski, 1991). The task of finding an offender involves collecting, prioritizing, and evaluating suspects. Table 30.1 provides a schematic of the criminal investigative process. It is a simplification of the tasks facing "whodunit" criminal investigations. It does not include every possible investigative approach, and some of the categories overlap. Within these limitations, however, the table provides a framework for strategy development and progress assessment (Rossmo, 2004).

The investigative process is based upon information – its proper collection, analysis, and sharing. The Rand study of the criminal investigation process found the information that led to solved crimes most likely came from the public, then from patrol officers, and third, from detectives (Chaiken, Greenwood, and Petersilia, 1991). This underlines the importance of effective channels of communication between the police and the community, and within the police organization. But not all information has the same value, and investigators must be wary of "static" or "noise" — useless or misleading information. And because investigative efforts can produce hundreds and even thousands of potential suspects, difficulties with information overload often develop. This is the classic needle-in-the-haystack situation. Information management problems are sometimes the reason an investigation ends up as a cold case file.

Linkage Analysis

When FBI Special Agent Clarice Starling finds a Black Witch Moth (*Erebus odora*) chrysalis lodged in the throat of serial killer Buffalo Bill's latest victim, a connection is soon made to another murder. But real crimes, unlike those in Thomas Harris' popular novel *Silence of the Lambs* (1988), are often much more difficult to link. "Prostitute strangled, dumped at the side of the road, no physical evidence," is a depressingly familiar crime scene description.

Establishing which offenses belong to a series is an important and essential task in the investigation of serial crime. This process is known as linkage analysis or comparative case analysis. Realizing the extent of the crime pattern helps determine the appropriate level of police response, facilitates information sharing among investigators and jurisdictions, outlines case similarities, and identifies common suspects. If and when the case is solved, additional crimes are cleared and the court delivers a more appropriate sentence (including dangerous offender or habitual felon designations). Knowing all the pieces of the puzzle allows a comprehensive picture of the offender to be formed and prevents linkage blindness from occurring.

The three main methods used by police investigators to link crimes prior to an offender's apprehension are: (1) physical evidence; (2) offender description; and (3) crime scene behavior. Each method has its strengths and weaknesses. It is not uncommon for a series of crimes to be connected together through a combination of these means.

Physical Evidence

Physical evidence provides the most certain means of linking crimes, though evidence of a type suitable for doing so may not be present in every case. One of the more powerful forensic methods, DNA profiling, has been heralded as the most revolutionary technology in the field of criminal investigation since the development of the Henry System for fingerprinting (Bigbee, Tanton, and Ferrara, 1989; Gaudette, 1990; Kelly, Rankin, and Wink, 1987). As blood, semen, hair, and skin contain DNA, the potential for ascertaining and verifying links in cases of violent and sexual crimes is significant. The establishment of centralized indices to facilitate computerized searches and comparisons is a necessary step in realizing this potential (Miller, 1991).

The FBI's National DNA Index System (NDIS) became operational in 1998 (Weedn and Hicks, 1998). Designed for the compatible storage and comparison of DNA records, the Combined DNA Index System (CODIS) consists of two investigative indices – the forensic index, for unsolved crimes; and the convicted offender index, for known felons. As of April 2005, there are 106,050 forensic profiles, and 2,337,224 convicted offender profiles in NDIS. CODIS has produced over 21,800 hits, and assisted in more than 23,700 investigations.

One of the important functions of such a system is the establishment of crime series (Brown, 1994). For example, DNA pattern matching linked 18 unknown suspect serial cases together in Minnesota, eventually helping to solve them by matching specimens of two offenders to the crime scenes. Such results are common in Britain, where a DNA database has been in existence for some time ("DNA profiling," 1995). It has been responsible for thousands of "hits" – defined as a match between crime scenes or between crime scene and offender. Canada has now also established a national DNA data bank.

Automated fingerprint identification systems (AFIS) allow comparisons and matches that sheer volume would have previously precluded (Sparrow, 1994). Programs such as the Integrated Ballistics Identification System (IBIS), networked into the joint ATF/FBI National Integrated Ballistic Information Network (NIBIN), link crimes committed with firearms through computerized comparisons of microscopic bullet striation patterns and shell casing marks (Dees, 1994; Strandberg, 1994; see also Di Maio, 1985). The British Shoeprint Image Capture and Retrieval System (SICAR) is a national database that connects crime scenes through the geometrical shapes associated with stored images of footprint evidence.

Offender Description

Descriptions of offenders have provided a common and long-used method of linking crimes. Mugshot books, while still in existence, are being replaced by computerized photographic databases that allow for certain physical description parameters to be used to narrow the search. But this is all predicated upon the assumption that there was a witness to the crime. There may not be one in the case of murder or arson. Even in a sexual assault, the victim must see, remember, and accurately recall (acquisition, retention, and retrieval) the offender's description. The ability for investigators to obtain an accurate physical description depends upon such factors as lighting conditions, whether the offender was masked, if the attack was from the rear, and the level of victim trauma, stress, fright, alcohol use, forgetfulness, and cooperation (see Thomas et al., 2004).

Individual physical appearance is also subject to modification. Weight changes slowly, hair more quickly, and clothing daily. Even more stable descriptors such as age, race, height, and build will be viewed subjectively by different victims. Ted Bundy, for example, was able to vary his description, as can be seen from his photographs and police wanted posters (Michaud and Aynesworth, 1983; Winn and Merrill, 1979).

The prevalence of video cameras has enhanced the ability of police to use offender descriptions. Most banks and financial institutions, and many businesses, transportation centers, and building lobby areas have been outfitted with video cameras. CCTV (closed circuit television) coverage of city centers, parking lots, and other public places is now common in Britain. Police agencies make routine use of the photographs and videotape from these cameras to assist in their investigations.

Automated recognition systems for digital facial images now exist and are used for both comparison and identification purposes (Mardia, et al., 1996). Distance and angle measurements are taken between certain facial points (e.g., from lower point of the ear to nose tip, the tangent to chin tip and nose tip, etc.) for both anterior (front) and profile (side) views. Horizontal and vertical landmarks are calculated to produce a mathematical "profile" of the face. This landmark-based data then provides the means of determining correlations between facial images.

These systems can be connected to video cameras placed within airport terminals and used to scan customs and immigration lines. A match with an image in the facial database alerts officials to the possible presence of a person of interest, such as a criminal, missing person, fugitive, abducted child, or terrorist. Police investigators have also used computerized facial recognition systems to assess the probability that two robbers captured on bank cameras are, in fact, the same person. These methods increase the value of offender image data and echo the early work of Alphonse Bertillon in criminal identification through body measurement.

Crime Scene Behavior

The behavioral analysis of crime scenes provides a third, and rapidly developing, methodology for offense comparison. Linking crimes behaviorally requires comparing similarities versus differences for both related and unrelated crimes (see Robertson and Vignaux, 1995). Like crimes should show more similarities than differences, and unlike crimes, more differences than similarities. These comparisons are usually assessed in terms of proximity in time and space between offenses, comparable modus operandi (M.O.), and the presence of signature.

Crimes that take place close together in space and time are obviously more likely to be connected than those separated by significant distance and occurring years apart. This is not to say that some offenders do not travel great distances, change residence, or interrupt their criminal activity for personal, employment, or institutional reasons. It means only that geographic and temporal factors affect the probability of offense linkage, with those more proximate more likely to be connected (Bennell and Canter, 2002).

M.O. involves the mechanics of the crime, and can be broken down into three chronologically ordered stages comprising the methods used by an offender to: (1) hunt (find and attack the victim); (2) commit the crime; and (3) escape from the scene. These three stages can be further subdivided into offensive (what is done to accomplish the crime) and defensive (what is done to avoid identification or apprehension) actions (Rossmo, 2000). The matrix in Table 30.2 illustrates M.O. behavior.

Modus operandi is not constant, but rather varies and changes for a variety of reasons. Like all human behavior, it is subject to individual deviation and random fluctuations. M.O. is responsive to environmental influences, such as victim reaction, the physical conditions of a crime setting, and ongoing police activities and media attention. Displacement may result from police activities, and can take the form of changes in the spatial, temporal, target, tactical, or functional characteristics

---

TABLE 30.2
Modus Operandi Matrix

Action/Stage	Hunt	Crime	Escape
Offensive			
Defensive			

---

of the crimes (Gabor, 1978; Reppetto, 1976). Over time, an offender's M.O. often evolves as the result of education, maturity, and experience; fantasy progression and development can also occur.

Unlike M.O., "signature" is constant, though certain aspects of its expression may evolve and refine over time (Keppel, 1995). Signature is defined as behavior that goes beyond the actions needed to commit the crime; it is a fantasy-based ritual or combination of rituals that represents a unique and personal expression of the offender (Douglas and Munn, 1992). When present, it provides a useful method for establishing links between crimes and can indicate certain underlying needs of the offender.

Staging is another consideration when examining crime scene behavior (Douglas and Munn, 1992). Staging occurs when the crime scene is purposely altered. This is usually done by the offender in an attempt to mislead the police and typically involves a criminal who knew the victim and hopes to create a convincing alternative scenario. Crime scenes have also been changed by family members to protect the victim from embarrassment (e.g., in cases of autoerotic fatalities).

The reality, however, is that the ability of the police to link serial crimes is limited. Establishing offense connections is often a difficult exercise, especially so in busy urban environments characterized by high levels of crime. The backdrop of other similar offenses can interfere with the process, and such "background noise" can make it difficult to know who is responsible for what. Consistency and constancy are not characteristics of many criminal offenders, and when an analysis does indicate that certain crimes are connected, the links are usually referred to in terms of probabilities rather than certainties. This is made all the more difficult when multiple offenders are involved.

A further complication is that the links might be between different incident types. In the case of a serial rapist who breaks into apartments to attack women, for example, police must review not just other rapes and attempts, but also sexual assaults, residential burglaries, and prowlings. Correctly establishing a serial criminal's pattern can involve analyzing hundreds or even thousands of crimes.

The major response to these problems has been the establishment of computer systems containing centralized investigative information networks. The idea of a national computer database to link murders originated with Pierce Brooks, a retired captain of detectives in the Los Angeles Police Department (LAPD) homicide unit (Brooks, 1984; Howlett, Hanfland, and Ressler, 1986). During his investigation of California serial killer Harvey Glatman in the late 1950s, Brooks found he had to resort to combing various newspaper files to locate murders that might fit the pattern from outside LAPD's jurisdiction (Newton, 1998).

Brooks' efforts led to the establishment of the Violent Criminal Apprehension Program (VICAP), which became operational in 1985 under the auspices of the FBI's National Center for the Analysis of Violent Crime (NCAVC). VICAP uses a standardized form containing a series of behaviorally oriented questions concerning the crime, victim, and offender that allows for computerized matching of similar cases from a national database. Several states have also developed their own computerized crime linkage systems, some of which feed into VICAP (Cryan, 1988; Collins et al., 1998; Keppel and Weis, 1993a, 1993b).

The Canadian Violent Crime Linkage Analysis System (ViCLAS), developed by the RCMP for murder and sexual assault cases, went national in 1995 (Johnson, 1994). Since then, ViCLAS has achieved international recognition and has now been adopted for use by several European countries, Australia, and certain American states (Collins et al., 1998). In the U.K., the Serious Crime Analysis Section (SCAS), National Crime Faculty, is mandated to conduct comparative case analysis for murders, rapes, and abductions.

A major difficulty with computerized linkage systems is low reporting rates. This causes a serious data shortage problem because case matches are an exponential function of reporting level (Rossmo, 2000). For example, if only 50% of the crimes are entered, then only 25% of the potential linkages can be identified; with a 20% reporting rate, the linkage ability drops to 4%. It is paradoxical that some police officers, who typically possess little faith in offender rehabilitation, fail to see the value in a comprehensive criminal tracking system.

One of the common reasons quoted for failure to report cases is the time it takes an investigator to complete the input forms, which can involve over 150 questions. Therefore, the choice of behaviors used in the analysis is critical. Both discrimination and utility are important. Certain offender actions are so common (e.g., vaginal intercourse) as to be poor discriminators. Other behaviors are so rare (e.g., the offender writes on the victim's body) that they are unlikely to be encountered. Crime linkage is a holistic process and the questions must also provide a full understanding of events. System designers need to balance the requirement for parsimony with the necessity for a comprehensive assessment of crime scene behavior.

An underlying assumption of linkage systems is that the analyzed behaviors are more or less consistent across offenses. An examination of child abduction murders in the U.S. showed that victim gender and use of bindings were the most important and consistent linkage variables (Hanfland, Keppel, and Weis, 1997). Offender speech forms have been found to be consistent and useful in connecting rape cases (Dale and Davies, 1994), and the London Metropolitan Police Sexual Assault Index analyses verbal themes as part of the process of linking crimes (Copson, 1993). But FBI research on 108 serial rapists determined that 58% of the 119 behavioral variables they examined reflected zero or minimal consistency across crimes (Warren, Reboussin, and Hazelwood, 1995). Alone, such questions make a poor basis for a case linkage system; together, they may point to common underlying fantasies or behavioral themes.

The true strength of these systems therefore lies in their ability to make concurrent comparisons among multiple variables. A study of British serial rapists found that 28% of the offenders took steps to prevent their faces from being seen by the victims (Davies and Dale, 1995). In the FBI research, it was noted that 70% of rape contact sites occurred indoors and 60% within the victim's home (Warren et al., 1995). These are not powerful discriminators separately, but assuming independence between questions, they can be combined in powerful ways. A burglary rapist who covers his face might only represent 17% of the offender population. Additional matching variables can help narrow the investigative focus.

The process of recognition – whether it be of faces, scenes, automobiles, voices, architecture – is based less on individual elements than on the relationships among them. Humans are much better than serial-processing computers at image and complex pattern recognition. As of today, most computerized case linkage systems are only designed to manage and search through large volumes of information, leaving the ultimate determination of case association to the analyst. As the volume of information collected by these databases increases, the need for expert system support becomes more crucial.

Grubin, Kelly, and Ayis (1996) caution that because of "the softer and more fluid substance of behavioral 'evidence' ... [the process of linking crimes] must be based on scientific principles rather than on a combination of intuition, experience and theory" (pp. 12, 20). They summarize the practical problems in using offender behavior to link crimes as follows: (1) consistent but common behaviors; (2) consistent but uncommon behaviors; (3) preciseness of behavior description; (4) behavior influenced by victim response; (5) weighting and relative importance of behaviors; (6) variation in behavior consistency; (7) evolution of behavior; and (8) interpretation of behaviors.

The idea that linked crimes should be interconnected provides one simple method for pattern determination. If crime A shows similarities to crime B, and crime B shows similarities to crime C, then crime C should also show similarities to crime A (Rossmo, 2000). If this is the case, then the probability of these crimes' being connected increases. The results from the case variable matrix can then be plotted in a case linkage chart, which depicts the strength of association, in terms of the behavior variables of interest, between the different crimes. The proper selection and phrasing of crime scene behaviors (variables) are important parts of this analysis.

In summary, crime linkage methods can be outlined as follows:

- Physical evidence
- Offender description
- Crime scene behavior
  - Proximity in time and place
  - M.O.
    - Find and attack the victim.
    - Commit the crime.
    - Escape from the scene.
  - Signature

GEOGRAPHIC PROFILING

Geographic profiling is an investigative methodology that uses the locations of a connected series of crimes to determine the most probable area of offender residence (Rossmo, 2000). It is typically applied in cases of serial murder, rape, arson, robbery, and bombing, though it can be used in single crimes that involve multiple scenes or other significant geographic characteristics. Geographic profiling was developed from research conducted at Simon Fraser University's School of Criminology. Crime Pattern Theory, developed by Professors Paul Brantingham and Patricia Brantingham, provides the conceptual basis for geographic profiling (Brantingham and Brantingham, 1981, 1984, 1993). Crime Pattern Theory states crime locations are not distributed in space randomly, but rather are influenced by the features and road networks of the physical environment. An understanding of these patterns provides a means for determining the most probable area of offender residence.

A mathematical representation of this understanding was encoded in the Criminal Geographic Targeting (CGT) computer algorithm. The CGT model is used to produce jeopardy surfaces – three-dimensional probability surfaces – that outline the most probable area of offender residence. These are displayed through color geoprofile maps that provide a focus for investigative efforts (see Figure 30.1 and Figure 30.2).

While geographic profiling can be used as the basis for several investigative strategies, it is important to stress it cannot solve crimes. Its purpose is to help manage the large volume of information typically generated in major crime investigations. Geographic profiling should be regarded as one of several tools available to detectives, and is best employed in conjunction with other police methods. Address information is an element of most record systems, and geographic

FIGURE 30.1 (See color insert following p. 216.) Jeopardy Surface: Armed Robbery Series, Vancouver, BC.

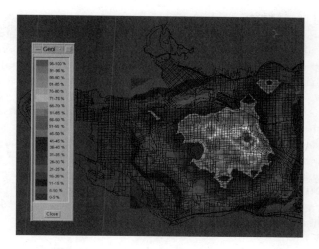

FIGURE 30.2 (See color insert following p. 216.) Geo Profile: Armed Robbery Series, Vancouver, BC.

profiling can be applied in a variety of contexts as a powerful decision support tool. Geographic crime patterns are clues that, when properly decoded, point in the direction of the offender.

For example, in the investigation of a series of over 20 rapes from 1988 to 1996 in St. Louis, Missouri, Detective Mark Kennedy employed both psychological and geographic profiling to prioritize a list of some 90 suspects for DNA testing. In addition to a residential focus, the geoprofile drew attention to the St. Louis State Hospital, and to what appeared to be likely commuting routes used by the offender. When the Southside Rapist was identified through DNA testing subsequent to a burglary arrest, it was found that he had moved several times during the crime series. The geoprofile identified his residential area during his most active rape period – one home was in the top 2% (0.4 mi²), and the other, across the street from the St. Louis State Hospital, in the top 5.6% (1.2 mi²) of the hunting area. The offender, 43-year-old Dennis Rabbitt, pled guilty in January 2000 to 49 counts of rape, sodomy, and burglary, and received five consecutive life terms.

The knowledge gained through research and experience of how and where criminal predators hunt for victims has both practical and theoretical implications. Geographic profiling is now an investigative support service offered to law enforcement agencies in cases of both violent and property crime. It has been used in criminal investigations in Canada, the U.S., the U.K., Europe, Africa, the Middle East, and Australia.

GeoProfiling Considerations

The ability to identify the existence of a serial offender is the starting point of the process. The extent and accuracy of the linkage analysis is important, as the greater the number of crimes, the more accurate the geographic profile. But, providing there is no spatial bias and not too many locations are missed, unlinked crimes are not a critical problem. The CGT algorithm is also quite robust and its results are not significantly affected by the mistaken inclusion of an unconnected crime; generally, at least 90% of the information should be accurate.

While primarily empirical, geographic profiling has both quantitative (objective) and qualitative (subjective) components. The objective component uses a series of geostatistical techniques and quantitative measures, such as the CGT program, to analyze and interpret the point pattern formed by target sites. Because the validity of these measures depends upon number of locations, they are inappropriate for smaller crime series. The subjective component of geographic profiling is based upon the reconstruction and interpretation of the offender's mental map (Homant and Kennedy,

1998). A behavioral (psychological) profile is not a necessary precursor for a geographic profile, but the insights it provides into offender personality, behavior, and lifestyle are useful, particularly in cases involving only a few locations. A geographic profile, in turn, helps refine a psychological profile, focus its application, and increase its utility. The two types of profiles optimize each other and act in tandem to assist investigators in developing a "picture" of the person responsible for the crimes in question.

In 1996, the RCMP investigated a series of 14 arsons of house carports in Burnaby, British Columbia, and requested psychological and geographic profiles. When a suspect who closely matched both profiles came to the attention of the investigator, he carefully focused on him, initiating surveillance and then interviewing strategies. The offender confessed. He closely matched the behavioral profile, and lived just across the street from the highest part of the geoprofile, in 0.6% of the hunting area (0.02 mi^2).

Many different crime factors and environmental elements are considered in the construction and interpretation of a geographic profile. The most relevant ones include:

- Crime locations – offense locations and times are the most important data in a geographic profile. Also significant are the number and type of crime sites.
- Offender type – the type and number of offender(s) affect crime geography. If multiple criminals living apart are involved, the geoprofile will focus on the dominant one's residence. Large amorphous gangs may not be suitable for geographic profiling because of changing group composition. Psychological profiling assists in interpreting offender behavior by providing information on personality, background, and level of organization.
- Hunting style – criminal hunting methods (used to search for, and then attack, victims or targets) influence crime site patterns. An offender's hunting style, therefore, is an important consideration in geographic profiling (see the following section for a more detailed discussion on criminal hunting methods).
- Target backcloth – constrained or patchy target backcloths limit the degree of offender choice and may influence the importance of certain crime site types for the profile.
- Arterial roads and highways – people, including criminals, do not travel as the crow flies. Not only must they follow street layouts, but they are most likely to travel along major arterial routes, freeways, or highways. Crimes often cluster around freeway exits and entrances.
- Bus stops and rapid transit stations – offenders without vehicles may use public transit or travel along bicycle and jogging paths. The locations of these routes and stops are important considerations.
- Physical and psychological boundaries – people are constrained by physical boundaries such as rivers, oceans, lakes, ravines, and highways. Psychological boundaries also influence movement. For example, a criminal of low socioeconomic status may avoid an upper class area, or a black offender might not wish to go into a white neighborhood.
- Zoning and land use – zoning (e.g., residential, commercial, industrial) and land use (e.g., stores, bars, businesses, transportation centers, major facilities, government buildings, military institutions) provide keys as to why someone might be in a particular area. Police in Britain conduct site surveys and location inventories in the area surrounding a crime to help identify what might have brought an offender to a particular location. Similarly, information about the peak area in a geoprofile provides insight into a criminal's anchor point, and zoning classification helps determine if this is a residence or workplace. For example, the geographic profile for a series of bank robberies occurring just after noon fell on a commercially zoned area of the city. The time and location factors correctly suggested an offender who was committing the crimes during his lunch break. The anchor point for his crimes – and the focus of the geoprofile – was therefore his work site, not his home.

- Neighborhood demographics – some sex offenders prefer victims of a certain racial or ethnic group. These groups may be more common in certain neighborhoods than in others, affecting spatial crime patterns.
- Victim routine activities – the patterns of routine victim movements may provide insights as to how the offender is searching for targets.
- Singularities – single offenses that do not appear to fit the overall pattern of the crime series are often a source of important clues, so are worthy of careful review.
- Displacement – media coverage or uniformed police presence can cause spatial displacement, affecting the locations of subsequent crime sites. The geographic profile has to compensate for any displacement issues.

CRIMINAL HUNTING METHODS

The hunting process can be broken down into two components: (1) the search for a suitable victim; and (2) the method of attack. The first component influences selection of victim encounter sites, and the second, body-dump or victim-release sites. A criminal hunting typology can be produced by combining these search and attack elements.

The following four victim search methods have been identified for violent predatory crime:

1. Hunter – an offender who sets out specifically to search for a victim, basing the search from his or her residence.
2. Poacher – an offender who sets out specifically to search for a victim, basing the search from an activity site other than his or her residence, or who commutes or travels to another city during the victim search process.
3. Troller – an offender who, while involved in other non-predatory activities, opportunistically encounters a victim.
4. Trapper –offenders who have an occupation or position where potential victims come to them (e.g., nursing), or by means of subterfuge, entice victims into a home or other location they control (e.g., by placing want ads).

The following three victim attack methods have been identified:

1. Raptor – an offender who attacks a victim upon encounter.
2. Stalker – an offender who, upon encounter, follows a victim, and then attacks at a different location and later time.
3. Ambusher – an offender who attacks a victim after he or she has been enticed to a location, such as a residence or workplace, controlled by the offender.

Hunters are those offenders who specifically set out from their residence to look for victims, searching through areas in their awareness space they believe contain suitable targets. This is the most commonly used method of criminal predators. Westley Allan Dodd, a serial killer executed for the murder of three children in the state of Washington, wrote in his diary, "Now ready for my second day of the hunt.... Will start at about 10 a.m. and take a lunch so I don't have to return home." He was worried, however, that if he murdered a child in the park through which he was searching, he'd lose his "hunting ground for up to two to three months" (Westfall, 1992, p. 59). The crimes of a hunter are generally confined to the offender's city of residence. Conversely, poachers travel outside of their home city, or operate from an activity site other than their residence in the search for targets. While the differentiation between poacher and hunter can be difficult, there are certain indicators that help in the assessment process (see following section).

Trollers are opportunistic offenders who do not specifically search for victims, but rather encounter them during the course of other, usually routine activities. Their crimes are often spontaneous, but many sexual predators fantasize and plan their crimes in advance so they are ready and prepared when an opportunity presents itself (premeditated opportunism).

Trappers have an occupation or position that results in potential victims coming to them (e.g., nurse, hospital orderly, etc.). They also entice victims into their home or other location they control by means of subterfuge. This may be done through entertaining suitors, placing want ads, or taking in boarders. Black widows, "angels of death," and custodial killers are all forms of trappers, and most female serial murderers fall into this category (Hickey, 1986; Segrave, 1992).

Raptors, upon encountering a victim, attack almost immediately. This is the most common method used by criminal predators. Stalkers follow and watch their targets, moving into the victim's activity space, waiting for an opportune moment to strike. The attack, murder, or body-dump sites of stalkers are thus more strongly influenced by their victims' activity spaces. Jon Berry Simonis, the Ski Mask Rapist, attacked women in Florida, Georgia, North Carolina, Ohio, Michigan, Wisconsin, Mississippi, Louisiana, Texas, Oklahoma, and California from 1978 to 1981, becoming progressively more violent before he was eventually arrested by the Louisiana State Police. Simon sometimes stalked his victims, and through his work at a hospital, had access to victims' medical records, including their addresses, marital, and work details (Michaud and Hazelwood, 1998).

Ambushers attack victims they have brought or drawn into their "web" – someplace where the killers have a great deal of control, most often their homes or workplaces. The bodies are usually hidden somewhere on the offender's property.* While victim encounter sites in such cases may provide sufficient spatial information for analysis, many ambushers select marginalized individuals whose disappearances are rarely linked, even when missing person reports are made to the police.

This hunting typology resembles that for burglars proposed by Bennett and Wright (1984), which includes planners, searchers, and opportunists. Surprisingly, it is also remarkably similar to Schaller's (1972) description of hunting methods used by lions in the Serengeti, where he observed ambushing, stalking, driving (direct attack), and unexpected (opportunistic) kills. Offenders may employ different hunting methods, but they usually adopt and stay with one, or at the most two approaches. For example, while trolling is not a primary criminal search technique, it is part of many offenders' repertoires.

Criminal target patterns are determined by offender activity space, hunting method, and victim backcloth. Hunting style is therefore helpful in determining which crime locations are the best predictors of an offender's anchor point under different circumstances. Another purpose of this typology is the identification of those situations where an analysis of the relationship between offender activity space and crime location geography is appropriate. This allows for the elimination of those cases where such an analysis is either impossible or redundant. Poachers, for example, who live in one city and commit their crimes in another, may not reside within their hunting area. Stalkers, whose crime locations are driven more by the activity spaces of their victims than by their own, produce more complex target patterns requiring different analytic methods.

Poacher Indicators

The following factors are indicators of possible offender poaching (also known as commuting). They should be considered in relationship to each other, and within the context of the specific details of the crime series.

Target Area

- The crimes occur in a very small area (a few square blocks).
- There is a specific but rare target/victim type, or a patchy target backcloth.
- The crimes occur in the central business district or a nonresidential area.

---

* This is probably because ambushers are often also trappers, and the latter rarely exhibit significant mobility.

- The crimes occur in wealthy neighborhoods (unlikely areas of offender residence), or neighborhoods with demographics (race/ethnicity/age) inconsistent with the offender's.
- The crimes occur along a major thoroughfare or highway.
- Alternative anchor point possibilities exist (e.g., drug market, freeway exit, metro stop, etc.).

Criminal/Crimes

- Spatial displacement has occurred (as a result of increased police presence or target hardening in the offender's neighborhood).
- There are only a few crimes in the series (less than five); by chance, an offender who is not actually a poacher/commuter may appear to be one if he or she has committed only a few crimes.
- The travel pattern of the crimes shows a definite directional trend.
- The offender is a professional criminal (e.g., a traveling bank robber, high-end burglar, gypsy, etc.).
- The offender is a stalker who follows his or her victims from a fishing hole or trap line, or else uses a nongeographic-based hunting method (e.g., finding targets from notices of estate sales in newspapers, or by reading luggage nametags at airports, etc.).
- Poaching/commuting is suggested by previous experience with local crime patterns.*

CRIME LOCATIONS

Crime locations are the basis of a geographic profile, and a given murder can involve separate encounter, attack, murder, and body-dump sites. But other locations that are not crime sites per se may also be connected to an offense. Examples of such locations include credit or bank card use, mailings, telephone calls, vehicle rentals or drops, witness sightings, and found property or evidence sites. In these cases, it may be possible to geographically profile a single crime, depending upon the number and types of locations.

In October 1995, two teenaged girls in the municipality of Abbotsford, British Columbia, were attacked on the street at night by a man with a baseball bat. One victim was murdered and dumped in the Vedder Canal, some 20 miles away; the other was left for dead, but somehow managed to revive and make her way to a nearby hospital. A few days later the Abbotsford Killer began a series of bizarre actions starting with several taunting 911 telephone calls. He then stole and defaced his murder victim's gravestone and dumped it in the parking lot of a local radio station. Finally, he threw a note wrapped around a wrench through a house window; in the note he admitted to other sexual assaults. These actions provided 13 different sites for the geographic profile. He was eventually caught through a local-based strategy initiated by the Abbotsford Police Department. His residence was in the top 7.7% of the geoprofile (0.6 mi^2).

A geoprofile may result in two peak areas, an indication the offender has more than one anchor point. Manley Eng, responsible for a series of arsons in Saanich and Victoria, British Columbia, left a crime pattern that resulted in dual peaks – one that contained his residence, and the other his probation office. Information regarding land use, zoning, and area characteristics helps interpret such outcomes. Examples of multiple anchor points include:

- Residence and work sites
- Residence and social or family sites

---

* For an analysis of differences in crime scene behaviors between commuter and marauder patterns in U.S. serial rapists, see Chapter 6 (pp. 201-235) of Warren et al. (1995).

- Present and previous residences
- Two or more offenders living apart

Between 1994 and 1998 the Mardi Gra Bomber was responsible for a total of 36 explosive devices, most in the Greater London area (Cooper, 1999). These were mailed or delivered to locations near bank machines, supermarkets, payphones, businesses, and residences. Scotland Yard requested a geographic profile from the Vancouver Police Department. Even though the targets and delivery methods varied, the underlying spatial pattern of the crimes was consistent. The resulting geoprofile had two high probability regions, a primary area around Chiswick in west London, and a secondary peak in southeast London. When police detectives arrested two elderly brothers, it turned out they lived in Chiswick, and their family resided in southeast London. The geoprofile identified the convicted offender's home in the top 3.4% (9.1 mi^2) of the hunting area.

Questions

Investigators may benefit from a geographic perspective on their crimes, independent of a formal profile. It is not just what offenders do, but also what they do not do, that is of interest. Some specific questions worth considering include:

- Locations
  - What are the location types connected to this crime or crime series?
  - Where are these locations? Map them.
  - What are the distances and travel times between them?
- Time
  - When did the crimes occur (date, time, and weekday)?
  - What was the weather?
  - How much time was there between crimes?
- Site Selection
  - How are the crime locations accessed?
  - What else is in the general area?
  - How might the offender have known of these locations?
  - What purpose did the crime locations serve?
- Target Backcloth
  - Where is the target group (and where is it not)?
  - How much control did the offender have over the choice of crime locations?
  - Has displacement (in space or time) occurred?
- Hunting
  - What hunting method did the offender use?
  - Why these sites and not others?
  - What was the offender's likely transportation?

The Rigel Computer System

Rigel is a computerized geographic profiling workstation based on the patented CGT algorithm. It incorporates an analytic engine, GIS capability, database management, and powerful visualization tools. Crime locations, which are broken down by type (e.g., victim encounter, murder, and body-dump sites for a homicide), provide the input and are entered by the optional means of street address, latitude and longitude, or digitization. This reflects the realities of policing in which crimes can happen anywhere – houses, parking lots, back alleys, highways, parks, rivers, mountain ravines, and so on. Latitude and longitude coordinates can be determined from a handheld GPS that reads the user's position from a satellite fix.

Scenarios, wherein crime locations are weighted based upon certain theoretical and methodological principles, are next created and examined. Output is a geoprofile, a color map showing the most likely area of offender residence. Suspect addresses can be evaluated according to their position on the geoprofile (expressed as a hit score percentage on a z-score histogram), allowing the prioritization of known criminals, registered sex offenders, task force tips, and other information.

Rigel was developed by Environmental Criminology Research Inc. (ECRI) of Vancouver, British Columbia (www.ecricanada.com). This provides the computing power for the 1,000,000 or so calculations of the CGT algorithm a typical analysis requires. Geoprofiles and jeopardy surfaces can be rotated and visually manipulated in a variety of ways, facilitating their interpretation. Orthodigital photographs may be overlaid on the peak geoprofile area, assisting the user in viewing land use within the region of interest. Large databases, including sex offender registries, major case management programs, and crime linkage systems (e.g., ViCLAS, VICAP, etc.), can be searched and their entries prioritized by address. *Rigel* is designed to enable law enforcement agencies to geographically optimize their limited resources. It is the main tool used in geographic profiling.

INVESTIGATIVE STRATEGIES AND TACTICS

Certain police strategies and tactics can be more effectively and efficiently conducted with a geographic profile. While specific applications are best determined by the investigators responsible for the case in question, suggested approaches are presented below. The development of these strategies has been an interactive process involving detectives, profilers, and academics. Case examples are used to illustrate these strategies, but it should be made clear that the crimes were not solved by geographic profiling; they were resolved by the assigned investigators. Profiling plays a support role, the importance of which can vary, and it is only one of many techniques in the investigator's repertoire.

While the most common anchor point is the offender's residence, some cases involve other bases of criminal activity. Clifford Olson used body-dump locations near Agassiz Mountain Prison where he had once been incarcerated. John Collins hunted in the area around Eastern Michigan University, where he was a student and summer employee. Aileen Wuornos based her "hitchhooking" from truck stops and freeway entrances in the town of Wildwood. Inmate records, enrollment and employee registries, and field checks were all potentially useful sources of investigative information in these cases. As important as residence is in structuring activity space, the value of business and institutional records should not be overlooked.

Suspect Prioritization

The geographic profile, in conjunction with a behavioral profile, can help focus follow-up investigative work. The problem in many serial violent crime investigations is one of too many suspects rather than too few. Profiling can help reassess and prioritize hundreds or even thousands of suspects, leads, and tips.

The South Side Rapist in Lafayette, Louisiana, committed a series of 14 burglary rapes from 1984 to 1995. Detective McCullan Gallien refused to close the file, and requested a geographic profile that resulted in the identification of a neighborhood not previously considered by investigators. This was used as the basis for suspect and tip prioritization (there were approximately 1,000 suspects and 2,000 tips). One tip involved a sergeant with the Lafayette Parish Sheriff's Department who fit the FBI's psychological profile and lived in the peak area of the geoprofile at the time of the crimes. DNA obtained from a cigarette butt discarded by the suspect matched samples from the crime scenes. The offender confessed, pled guilty, and was sentenced to life in prison. The geoprofile located the rapist's address in the top 2.2% (0.5 mi²) of the hunting area.

Police Information Systems

Additional investigative leads might be obtained from information contained in various computerized police dispatch and record systems (Rebscher and Rohrer, 1991). Offender profile details and case specifics can help further focus the search. Police agencies with computerized records containing description, address, and M.O. of local offenders can also use profiling information, including probable area of residence, as the basis for developing search criteria. Many departments maintain files for parolees and specific types of criminals (Pilant, 1994; Skogan and Antunes, 1979). Sex offenders often have nuisance crimes (e.g., loitering, trespassing, peeping, etc.) in their backgrounds, and the locations of their past offenses may overlap with the present ones.

Task Force Management

Task force operations formed to investigate a specific series of crimes often collect and collate their information in some form of computerized major case management system, such as the British HOLMES or FBI Rapid Start programs (Federal Bureau of Investigation, 1996; U.S. Department of Justice, 1991). Cases suffering from information overload will benefit from the prioritization of data and the application of correlation analysis (Keppel and Birnes, 1995). Geographic profiling can assist in these tasks through the ranking of street addresses, zip or postal codes, and telephone number (NNXs) areas.

This process may also be linked to information available in CD-ROM telephone directory databases listing residential and business names, telephone numbers, addresses, zip or postal codes, business headings, and standard industrial classification (SIC) codes. The details of the specific task force computer database software, including information fields, search time, number of records, and correlational abilities, determine the most appropriate form the geographic profile should take to maximize its usefulness to the police investigation.

Sex Offender Registries

Violent-sex-offender registries are a useful information source for geographic profiling in cases of serial sex crimes. By providing a list of addresses of known sex criminals, these registries can be used with a geographic profile to help prioritize suspects. The U.S. Violent Crime Control and Law Enforcement Act of 1994 "requires states to enact statutes or regulations which require those determined to be sexually violent predators or who are convicted of sexually violent offenses to register with appropriate state law enforcement agencies for ten years after release from prison," or risk the reduction of Federal grant money (U.S. Department of Justice, 1994).

Sex offender registries are powerful tools for monitoring and controlling criminal predators who, unfortunately, are more prevalent than is commonly believed. Washington State established the first such registry, and according to the Seattle Police Department Special Assault Unit, in May of 1995 the City of Seattle had a total of 859 registered sex offenders, an average of 10 per square mile. This figure does not include the 20% of released sex offenders who fail to register.

Government and Business Databases

Databanks are often geographically based, and parole and probation offices, mental health outpatient clinics, social services offices, schools, and other agencies located in prioritized areas can also provide information of value (it has been estimated that approximately 85% of all records contain an address). Several commercial companies (e.g., Seisint, Lexis Nexis, Choicepoint, etc.) offer law enforcement agencies the ability to search multiple personal information databases. Their systems (e.g., Accurint, Autotrack, etc.) use proprietary data mining algorithms to sample and select megaquantities of data bits electronically, and assign them to individual profiles.

A partial listing of the information sources tapped into by these systems includes:

- Public records, such as bankruptcies, tax liens and judgments, professional licenses, boat/aircraft ownership, vehicle registrations and driver's licenses in some states, workers compensation appeals, state/local civil and criminal court filings, federal civil and criminal court filings, dog licenses, tax assessments, real property ownership, and others.
- Commercial records, such as magazine subscriptions, warranty card information, utility bills, credit headers (uses name/address/birth date/social security number, etc., from debtor identification data rather than actual creditworthiness data), telephone listings, unlisted phone numbers (most often obtained from people calling toll-free numbers, thereby inadvertently providing their home telephone number), and others.

In 2001, a serial rapist in Fort Collins, Colorado, assaulted seven women after breaking into their apartments. When investigators submitted a DNA sample from one of the crime scenes to a national databank, a match was found to a crime series 1,750 miles away in Philadelphia (Gibbons, McCoy, and Fish, 2001). The Center City Rapist had preyed on women in the Rittenhouse Square area of Philadelphia from 1997 to 1999, raping five victims and strangling another. He then disappeared, until reappearing in Fort Collins 2 years later. Detectives used commercial database services to develop lists of individuals who lived in Philadelphia from 1997 to 1999, and in Fort Collins in 2001. A geographic profile prepared for the Philadelphia Police Department helped narrow down the specific zip codes used in the search. The two lists were cross-referenced to identify individuals who appeared in both, resulting in more than 1100 names. Follow-up investigation by detectives led to the arrest of Troy Graves. He pled guilty to both sets of crimes, and was sentenced to life imprisonment in 2002 (Dale, 2002).

Motor Vehicle Registrations

A geographic profile can be integrated with suspect vehicle and offender descriptions to search registered motor vehicle and driver's licence files, contained in state or provincial computer record systems. This is often done by first using the geoprofile to prioritize zip or postal codes most likely associated with the offender's residence. The description and geographic parameters act as a linear program to produce a small set of records containing the appropriate data. This strategy results in areas of manageable size for major police investigations.

For example, a new red station wagon driven by a tall white middle-aged male with dark hair may seem to be somewhat vague information. But the description actually contains several parameters: (1) vehicle style – station wagon; (2) vehicle color – red; and (3) vehicle year range – last 5 years. Further focus can be obtained from the various driver descriptors (e.g., sex, race, age range, height, hair color, etc.), though the assumption that the driver is the vehicle's registered owner may be incorrect. These parameters can narrow down hundreds of thousands of records to a few dozen vehicles or drivers when combined with a prioritized list of zip or postal codes. This is sufficient discrimination to allow detailed police follow-up.

A case involving a violent child-sex offender illustrates this point. The geoprofile was first used to prioritize the postal codes for the neighborhood wherein the crimes had occurred. Planning and zoning maps were then studied to eliminate industrial, commercial, and other nonresidential areas. Socioeconomic and demographic census data were also consulted to adjust the priority of those neighborhoods inconsistent with the socioeconomic status of the offender as suggested by the behavioral profile.

The final list of postal codes, ranked by priority of probability, could then be used to conduct a computer search of the provincial motor vehicle department records, which contain postal codes as part of the address associated with the vehicle registered owner and driver's licence files. Suspect vehicle and offender descriptions had been developed by detectives, and this information was combined with the geographic data to effectively focus the search.

Bloodings

During a sexual murder or rape investigation, British police may conduct large-scale DNA testing of all men from the area of the crime ("How the DNA 'Database," 1995). The first such case was the Narborough Murder Enquiry, when "all unalibied male residents in the villages between the ages of seventeen and thirty-four years would be asked to submit blood and saliva samples voluntarily in order to 'eliminate them' as suspects in the footpath murders" (Wambaugh, 1989, pp. 220–221). Close to 4,000 men from the villages of Narborough, Littlethorpe, and Enderby were tested during the investigation.

Considerable police resources and laboratory costs are involved in such "bloodings"; therefore, British police follow intelligence-led DNA screens in which individuals are prioritized based on proximity to crime scene, criminal record, age, and other relevant criteria (National Crime Faculty, 1996; Rossmo, Davies, and Patrick, 2004). In cases of serial crime, geographic profiling can further refine the selection process through targeting by address, or zip or postal code, resulting in more efficient and systematic testing procedures. U.S. and Canadian police are also using this strategy. The Baton Rouge serial murders and the Wichita BTK Strangler investigations both conducted large-scale DNA suspect testing. Geographic profiles had been prepared for investigators in both cases. When 11 sexual assaults occurred in just over 1 month in Mississauga, Ontario, Peel Regional Police detectives collected 312 suspects. Combining the geographic and behavioral profiles with description and interview information, detectives prioritized the suspects into groups and obtained DNA samples from the most probable individuals. The offender was identified in the first lot. He resided within the top 2.2% (0.03 mi^2) of the area under consideration.

Peak-of-Tension Polygraphy

In presumed homicides with known suspects but no bodies, polygraphists have had success in narrowing down the search area for the victim's remains through peak-of-tension (POT) tests (Hagmaier, 1990; see also Cunliffe and Piazza, 1980; Raskin, 1989). POT polygraphy involves monitoring a subject's reaction to photographs, objects, or maps, as opposed to answering verbal questions. A deceptive response to queries concerning the type of location where the victim's body was hidden (e.g., cave, lake, marsh, field, forest, etc.) can help focus a search. Because POT tests often involve maps or area photographs, their usefulness is enhanced when results are combined with a geographic profile.

Missing Bodies

In certain missing person cases that are suspected homicides, geographic profiling can help determine probable body-dump site areas. In November 1993, a teenage boy was found shot dead in his car outside St. Antoine, New Brunswick. His girlfriend was missing, and presumed kidnapped. The murderer was identified through rifle ballistics but disappeared before be could be arrested. After unsuccessfully pursuing various leads and tips, the RCMP began to theorize that the missing female victim had been killed and the offender had committed suicide. Two searches by police and military teams of the rural Bouctouche region failed to find evidence of either body. A geographic profile was then requested. Employing techniques of path analysis, journey-to-crime estimates, and time-distance-speed calculations, the geoprofile outlined two prioritized search areas. A third search effort later located effects of the offender in a river under a railway trestle, and the body of the female victim in a field; the former was found in the highest prioritized area of the geoprofile, and the latter in the second highest.

Austin Ripper

Twenty years after the end of the Civil War, Austin, Texas, was plagued by a series of horrific axe murders (Corcoran, 2000; Hollandsworth, 2000; Humphrey, 1985; Plohetski, 2004; Saylor, 2000). From New Year's Eve 1884 to Christmas Eve 1885, eight people were killed in the capital city of 23,000. The victims were predominantly black females, cooks and maids, taken from their homes at night and "outraged" (to use the newspaper vernacular of the time). The serial killer operated with impunity, not so surprising considering that at any one time there were only four police officers on duty. The media used monikers such as the Austin Ripper, the Austin Axe Murderer, or the Austin Servant Girl Annihilator.* Like Jack the Ripper, his later and more famous cousin, the Austin murderer, was never caught and the case remains unsolved.

"Bloody Work. A Fearful Midnight Murder on West Pecan – Mystery and Crime."**

The first attack occurred on Wednesday morning, early New Year's Eve, December 31, 1884, at 901 West Pecan (now Sixth) Street. Mollie Smith, a mulatto female, worked for Mr. W.K. Hall, and lived in a small apartment at the rear of his house, just back of the kitchen. Sometime between 3:00 a.m. and 4:00 a.m. she was dragged outside, assaulted, and murdered with an axe. She was found behind a small outhouse, 50 steps from the room where she slept. Her boyfriend, Walter Spencer, was also attacked and injured. There was a trail of bare footprints in the fresh snow that led from the murder scene to Shoal Creek, a block away.

"The Foul Fiends.... Another deed of Deviltry in the Crimson Catalogue of Crime."

The next victim was Eliza Shelly, a black female, who lived in a small one-room cabin on the property of Dr. L.B. Johnson, 302 East Cypress (now Third) Street, at San Jacinto Boulevard. The Central Railway line ran in front of the house on the Cypress Street side. Shelly's cabin was some 40 or 50 steps to the rear of Dr. Johnson's neat cottage, separated by a high fence with a connecting gate. An alley ran behind the cabin. Around 6:00 a.m., Thursday, May 7, 1885, Shelly was found murdered in her cabin, her head nearly cleaved in two. The weapon used was possibly a hatchet. Bare footprints were found at the crime scene.

"More Butchery. Another Colored Woman Terribly Stabbed by an Unknown Fiend.... When Will it End?"

Irene Cross, another black female, was attacked on Saturday, May 23, 1885, shortly after midnight. She lived in the yard of Mrs. Whittman, 1737 San Jacinto Boulevard, at Linden (now Seventeenth) Street, across from Scholz's Beer Garden. The murder weapon was apparently a knife. Cross's arm was nearly chopped in two, and her head was cut as if she had been scalped. Her nephew claimed to have seen the assailant. "He said that the intruder was a 'big, chunky negro man, barefooted and with his pants rolled up.' He had on a brown hat and a ragged coat."

"An Atrocious Crime.... One of the Most Horrible Occurrences on Record."

The fourth victim was Mary Ramey, an 11-year-old black girl who lived with her mother, Rebecca Ramey, in the kitchen of the premises of Mr. V.O. Weed, 300 East Cedar (now Fourth) Street, at San Jacinto Boulevard. Sometime between 4:00 a.m. and 5:00 a.m. on Sunday, August 30, 1885, the killer dragged Mary from the kitchen where she was sleeping with her mother to a washhouse outside. Rebecca had been "sandbagged" (knocked unconscious). Mary was "ravished," and an iron pin driven through her ear and into her brain. The ground was damp and the killer's

---

* This name was given to the killer by the writer O. Henry (William Sydney Porter), who was residing in Austin at the time of the murders.

** The quotations in this section are from the *Austin Statesman*.

bare footprints could easily be seen. They went in and out of the backyard, through the alley gate, and into the alley. Bloodhounds followed the trail, which ended at some nearby stables.

"Slain Servants. Monday Morning's Horrible Butchery."

On Monday morning, September 28, 1885, a double murder occurred. Gracie Vance and Orange Washington lived common-law in a small wooden shanty at 2408 West San Marcos (now Guadalupe) Street, catty-corner from the new University of Texas campus. Between 1:00 a.m. and 2:00 a.m., the killer entered the shanty and hit Washington on the skull with an axe, killing him; he was the only male victim in the series. Vance was dragged 75 yards from her room to just back of some stables where she was raped and murdered, "her head almost beaten into a jelly." Two other women, Lucinda Boddy and Patsie Gibson, asleep in the shanty at the time, were also attacked and injured. Vance, Washington, Boddy, and Gibson were all black. A man was seen running toward "Nigger Town." Tracks from the crime scene disappeared in a creek.

"The Demons Have Transferred Their Thirst for Blood to White People!"

Austin's citizens were shocked by the events of Christmas Eve 1885. The killer struck twice in one night, and for the first time his victims were white. Sometime before 11:30 p.m. on Thursday, December 24, 1885, Susan Hancock, "one of the most refined ladies in Austin," was dragged out of her house at 203 East Water (now First) Street, in the neighborhood of German-town. She was found dead in the back yard by her husband, Mr. William H. Hancock, her head split open by an axe.

"The Monsters in Human Shape Who Have Been Doing the Devil's Bidding."

An hour later, Friday morning, at 12:30 a.m., December 25, 1885, Eula Phillips became the second victim of the night. Her nude body was found outside her home, a "dozen squares away" (0.7 miles, a 15-minute walk from the Hancock House). Phillips lived at 302 West Hickory (now Eighth) Street, at Lavaca Street, on the same property as the parents of her husband, James Phillips, Jr. Her forehead had been bashed in with the butt end of an axe. James was also attacked and injured, though the couple's baby boy was not harmed. A bloody trail showed Eula was dragged from her house onto the gallery, through the back yard, across another gallery that connected her house with her husband's parent's house, then into another backyard to some outbuildings. She "had been outraged and most brutally maltreated." Tracks led from the crime scene to Shoal Creek.

Two attacks in the same night and both against white women – predictably, the community reacted with fear and outrage. A half-dozen black men were arrested on mere suspicion immediately following these murders. During 1885, a total of 400 people, mainly black men, were arrested and "severely examined" by police. One man was tried, but ultimately acquitted. Things became complicated, however, when it was discovered that Eula Phillips worked in May Tobin's house of assignation, at 103 Congress Avenue, as a "*nymph du pave*" – a prostitute. Was the killer one of her customers? The theories were as varied as they were speculative. Then, just as mysteriously as they began, the murders stopped. The crimes were never solved.

The Austin Ripper case is now 120 years old, and the murderer is long dead. It is a historical, not a cold case. What can a geographic profile tell us after so much time? At a minimum, it allows us to reassess what is already known, and perhaps provides a geographic perspective on the cast of characters and places.* The following locations of importance are in the peak area of the geoprofile for the Austin Ripper case:

---

* A similar analysis was done on the murder locations of Jack the Ripper in Whitechapel, England, with interesting results (see Rossmo, 2000).

- May Tobin's brothel, 103 Congress Avenue.
- Guy Town, a racially mixed district of prostitution, gambling, and saloons, located roughly between Colorado Avenue on the east and Guadalupe Street on the west, and Live Oak (now Second) on the south and Cedar (now Fourth) Street on the north.
- Pearl House, 221 Congress Avenue. Maurice, a Malay cook employed in 1885 at the Pearl House, disappeared in January 1886. He was presumed by some to be the Austin Ripper.
- Union Depot, 100 block West Cypress (now Third) Street. It is possible the killer worked at the train station, or traveled into the city by train.

While the crimes of the Austin Ripper are likely to remain forever a mystery, it is interesting to imagine what detectives might have accomplished given modern forensic and behavioral analysis techniques.

CONCLUSION

Geographic profiling can provide cold case investigators with a compass for prioritizing suspects and managing information. It is an appropriate technique in cases of serial crime, or those involving multiple locations. Geographic profiling cannot directly solve a crime, but it is a valuable addition to the detective's toolbox. The challenges of cold cases necessitate a comprehensive set of investigative strategies. The use of geography strikes a chord with practitioners, a resonance explained by the old police truism: "When all else fails, return to the scene" (Barrett, 1990, p. 90).

ACKNOWLEDGMENT

Richard H. Walton wishes to extend gratitude and appreciation to Dr. Kim Rossmo for authoring and contributing this chapter. D. Kim Rossmo is a research professor and the director of the Center for Geospatial Intelligence and Investigation (GII) in the Department of Criminal Justice at Texas State University. Formerly, he was a management consultant with the Bureau of Alcohol, Tobacco, Firearms and Explosives (ATF), the Director of Research for the Police Foundation, and the Detective Inspector in charge of the Vancouver Police Department's Geographic Profiling Section. Over the course of his 21-year policing career, he worked assignments in organized crime intelligence, emergency response, patrol, crime prevention, and community liaison. He holds a Ph.D. (Simon Fraser University) in criminology, and has researched and published in the areas of policing, offender profiling, and environmental criminology. He is a member of the International Association of Chiefs of Police (IACP) Advisory Committee for Police Investigative Operations, the International Criminal Investigative Analysis Fellowship, and the South Carolina Research Authority Integrated Solutions Group Advisory Board. He is also an Adjunct Professor at Simon Fraser University and sits on the editorial board for the international journal *Homicide Studies*.

REFERENCES

Barrett, G.M. (1990). Serial murder: A study in psychological analysis, prediction, and profiling. Unpublished master's thesis, University of Louisville, Louisville, KY.

Bennell, C., and Canter, D.V. (2002). Linking commercial burglaries by *modus operandi*: Tests using regression and ROC analysis. *Science and Justice, 42*, 153–164.

Bennett, T., and Wright, R.T. (1984). *Burglars on Burglary: Prevention and the Offender*. Aldershot, Hants: Gower.

Bigbee, D., Tanton, R.L., and Ferrara, P.B. (1989, October). Implementation of DNA analysis in American crime laboratories. *The Police Chief*, pp. 86–89.

Brantingham, P.J., and Brantingham, P.L. (Eds.). (1981). *Environmental Criminology*. Beverly Hills: Sage.

Brantingham, P.J., and Brantingham, P.L. (1984). *Patterns in Crime*. New York: Macmillan.

Brantingham, P.L., and Brantingham, P.J. (1981). Notes on the geometry on crime. In P.J. Brantingham and P.L. Brantingham (Eds.), *Environmental Criminology* (pp. 27–54). Beverly Hills: Sage.

Brantingham, P.L., and Brantingham, P.J. (1993). Environment, routine and situation: Toward a pattern theory of crime. In R.V. Clarke and M. Felson (Eds.), *Routine Activity and Rational Choice* (pp. 259–294). New Brunswick, NJ: Transaction.

Brooks, P.R. (1984, November). VICAP. Lecture presented at Washington Criminal Justice Training Center seminar, Seattle, WA.

Brooks, P.R., Devine, M.J., Green, T.J., Hart, B.L., and Moore, M.D. (1987, June). Serial murder: A criminal justice response. *The Police Chief*, pp. 40–44.

Brooks, P.R., Devine, M.J., Green, T.J., Hart, B.L., and Moore, M.D. (1988). Multi-Agency Investigative Team Manual. Washington, DC: National Institute of Justice.

Brown, J.R. (1994, March). DNA analysis: A significant tool for law enforcement. The *Police Chief*, pp. 51–52.

Chaiken, J.M., Greenwood, P.W., and Petersilia, J. (1991). The Rand study of detectives. In C.B. Klockars and S.D. Mastrofski (Eds.), *Thinking about police: Contemporary Readings* (2nd ed.) (pp. 170–187). New York: McGraw-Hill.

Clarke, R.V., and Felson, M. (Eds.). (1993). *Routine Activity and Rational Choice*. New Brunswick, NJ: Transaction.

Collins, P.I., Johnson, G.F., Choy, A., Davidson, K.T., and MacKay, R.E. (1998). Advances in violent crime analysis and law enforcement: The Canadian Violent Crime Linkage Analysis System. *Journal of Government Information*, 25, 277–284.

Connelly, M. (2005, May 23). Old, but never totally cold. *Los Angeles Times*, p. A1.

Cooper, S. (1999). *Welcome to the Mardi Gra Experience*. London: Blake Publishing.

Copson, G. (1993, May). Offender profiling. Presentation to the Association of Chief Police Officers Crime Sub-Committee on Offender Profiling, London, England.

Corcoran, M. (2000, April 11). Rediscovering Austin's Jack the Ripper. *Austin American-Statesman*.

Cryan, M.P. (1988). Halt program joins VICAP in hunting serial criminals. *Trooper Magazine*, (May/June), 8–9.

Cunliffe, F., and Piazza, P.B. (1980). *Criminalistics and Scientific Investigation*. Englewood Cliffs, NJ: Prentice-Hall.

Dale, A., and Davies, A. (1994). Developments in the analysis of rapists speech. Unpublished manuscript, Police Research Group, Home Office Police Department, London.

Dale, M. (2002, May 31). Airman pleads guilty to Philadelphia killing, rapes. *The Daily Camera*.

Davies, A., and Dale, A. (1995). Locating the stranger rapist (Special Interest Series: Paper 3). London: Police Research Group, Home Office Police Department.

Dees, T.M. (1994, March). Automation of forensic ballistics. *Law Enforcement Technology*, pp. 44, 47.

Dees, T.M. (2004, December). Making the invisible become visible. *Law Enforcement Technology*, pp. 28–30.

Di Maio, V.J.M. (1985). *Gunshot Wounds: Practical Aspects of Firearms, Ballistics, and Forensic Techniques*. Boca Raton, FL: CRC Press.

DNA profiling. (1995, January). *DNA Database*, p. 2.

Douglas, J.E., and Munn, C. (1992). Violent crime scene analysis: Modus operandi, signature, and staging. *FBI Law Enforcement Bulletin*, 61(2), 1–10.

Federal Bureau of Investigation. (1996). Rapid Start Information Management System: Reference Guide. Washington, DC: Author.

Gabor, T. (1978). Crime displacement: The literature and strategies for its investigation. *Crime and Justice*, 6, 100–106.

Gaudette, B.D. (1990). DNA typing: A new service to Canadian police. *RCMP Gazette*, 52(4), 1–7.

Gibbons, T.J. Jr., McCoy, C.R., and Fish, L. (2001, September 18). DNA links Center City rapist to Col. assaults. *Philadelphia Inquirer*.

Green, T.J., and Whitmore, J.E. (1993, June). VICAP's role in multiagency serial murder investigations. *The Police Chief*, pp. 38–45.

Grubin, D., Kelly, P., and Ayis, A. (1996). Linking serious sexual assaults. Unpublished manuscript, Police Research Group, Home Office Police Department, London.

Grubin, D., Kelly, P., and Ayis, A. (1997). Linking serious sexual assaults. Draft briefing note, Police Research Group, Home Office Police Department, London.

Hagmaier, B. (1990, September). Ted Bundy, a case study. Lecture presented at the FBI National Academy retraining session, Bellingham, WA.

Hanfland, K.A., Keppel, R.D., and Weis, J.G. (1997). Case management for missing children homicide investigation. Seattle: Washington State Office of the Attorney General.

Harris, T. (1988). *Silence of the Lambs.* New York: St. Martin's Paperbacks.

Hazelwood, R.R. (1995). Analyzing the rape and profiling the offender. In R.R. Hazelwood and A.W. Burgess (Eds.), *Practical Aspects of Rape Investigation: A Multidisciplinary Approach* (2nd ed.) (pp. 155–181). Boca Raton, FL: CRC Press.

Hickey, E.W. (1986). The female serial murderer 1800-1986. *Journal of Police and Criminal Psychology, 2*(2), 72–81.

Hollandsworth, S. (2000, July). Capital murder. *Texas Monthly,* pp. 106-111, 131–134.

Homant, R.J., and Kennedy, D.B. (1998). Psychological aspects of crime scene profiling: Validity research. *Criminal Justice and Behavior, 25,* 319–343.

How the DNA 'Database' and 'Caseworking' Units will function! (1995, February). *DNA Database,* p. 2.

Howlett, J.B., Hanfland, K.A., and Ressler, R.K. (1986). The Violent Criminal Apprehension Program – VICAP: A progress report. *FBI Law Enforcement Bulletin, 55*(12), 14–22.

Humphrey, D.C. (1985). *Austin: An Illustrated History.* Northridge, CA: Windsor Publications.

Johnson, G. (1994). ViCLAS: Violent Crime Linkage Analysis System. *RCMP Gazette, 56*(10), 9–13.

Kelly, K.F., Rankin, J.J., and Wink, R.C. (1987). Method and applications of DNA fingerprinting: A guide for the non-scientist. *The Criminal Law Review,* 105–110.

Keppel, R.D. (1995). Signature murders: A report of several related cases. *Journal of Forensic Sciences, 40,* 670–674.

Keppel, R.D., and Birnes, W. J. (1995). *The Riverman: Ted Bundy and I Hunt for the Green River Killer.* New York: Simon and Schuster.

Keppel, R.D., and Birnes, W.J. (1997). *Signature Killers.* New York: Simon and Schuster.

Keppel, R.D., and Weis, J.G. (1993a). HITS: Catching criminals in the Northwest. *FBI Law Enforcement Bulletin, 62*(4), 14–19.

Keppel, R.D., and Weis, J.G. (1993b). Improving the investigation of violent crime: The Homicide Investigation and Tracking System (NIJ Publication No. NCJ 141761). Washington, DC: U.S. Government Printing Office.

Keppel, R.D., and Weis, J.G. (1994). Time and distance as solvability factors in murder cases. *Journal of Forensic Sciences, 39,* 386–401.

Klockars, C.B., and Mastrofski, S.D. (Eds.). (1991). *Thinking about Police: Contemporary Readings* (2nd ed.). New York: McGraw-Hill.

Kube, E., and Störzer, H.U. (Eds.). (1991). *Police Research in the Federal Republic of Germany: 15 Years Research within the "Bundeskriminalamt."* Berlin: Springer-Verlag.

Mardia, K.V., Coombes, A., Kirkbride, J., Linney, A., and Bowie, J. L. (1996). On statistical problems with face identification from photographs. *Journal of Applied Statistics, 23,* 655–675.

Michaud, S.G., and Aynesworth, H. (1983). *The Only Living Witness.* New York: Penguin Books.

Michaud, S.G., and Hazelwood, R.R. (1998). *The Evil That Men Do: FBI Profiler Roy Hazelwood's Journey into the Minds of Sexual Predators.* New York: St. Martin's Press.

Miller, J.V. (1991). The FBI's forensic DNA analysis program. *FBI Law Enforcement Bulletin, 60*(7), 11–15.

National Crime Faculty. (1996). Intelligence led DNA screening: A guide for investigating officers. Bramshill: Author.

Newton, M. (1998). *Rope: The Twisted Life and Crimes of Harvey Glatman.* New York: Simon and Schuster.

Pilant, L. (1994, January). Information management. *The Police Chief,* pp. 30-38, 42–47.

Plohetski, T. (2004, October 31). On a killer's trail. *Austin American-Statesman,* pp. A1–A12–A13.

Raskin, D.C. (Ed.). (1989). *Psychological Methods in Criminal Investigation and Evidence.* New York: Springer.

Rebscher, E., and Rohrer, F. (1991). Police information retrieval systems and the role of electronic data processing. In E. Kube and H.U. Störzer (Eds.), *Police Research in the Federal Republic of Germany: 15 Years Research within the "Bundeskriminalamt"* (pp. 241–251). Berlin: Springer-Verlag.

Reppetto, T.A. (1976). Crime prevention and the displacement phenomenon. *Crime and Delinquency, 22,* 168–169.

Ressler, R.K., Burgess, A.W., and Douglas, J.E. (1988). *Sexual Homicide: Patterns and Motives.* Lexington, MA: Lexington Books.

Robertson, B., and Vignaux, G.A. (1995). *Interpreting Evidence: Evaluating Forensic Evidence in the Court-room*. Chichester: John Wiley and Sons.

Rossmo, D.K. (2000). *Geographic Profiling*. Boca Raton, FL: CRC Press.

Rossmo, D.K. (2004). Geographic profiling as problem solving for serial crime. In Q.C. Thurman and J.D. Jamieson (Eds.), *Police Problem Solving* (pp. 121–131). Cincinnati: Anderson Publishing.

Rossmo, D.K. (2005). Criminal investigative failures. Unpublished manuscript, Texas State University, Department of Criminal Justice, San Marcos, TX.

Rossmo, D.K., Davies, A., and Patrick, M. (2004). Exploring the Geo-Demographic And Distance Relationships Between Stranger Rapists and Their Offences (Special Interest Series: Paper 16). London: Research, Development and Statistics Directorate, Home Office.

Saylor, S. (2000). *A Twist at the End*. New York: St. Martin's Press.

Schaller, G.B. (1972). *The Serengeti Lion: A Study of Predator-Prey Relations*. Chicago: University of Chicago Press.

Segrave, K. (1992). *Women Serial and Mass Murderers: A Worldwide Reference, 1580 through 1990*. Jefferson, NC: McFarland.

Skogan, W.G., and Antunes, G.E. (1979). Information, apprehension, and deterrence: Exploring the limits of police productivity. *Journal of Criminal Justice*, 7, 217–241.

Sparrow, M.K. (1994, April). Measuring AFIS matcher accuracy. *The Police Chief*, pp. 147–151.

Strandberg, K.W. (1994, April). FBI's "Drugfire." *Law Enforcement Technology*, pp. 50–51.

Thomas, N., Aitken, C., Lucy, D., and Feist, A. (2004). Predicting the accuracy of stranger rape victims' statements (Special Interest Series: Paper 15). London: Research, Development and Statistics Directorate, Home Office.

U.S. Department of Justice. (1991). Serial Murder Investigation System Conference (Federal Bureau of Investigation). Washington, DC: U.S. Government Printing Office.

U.S. Department of Justice. (1994, October 3). Violent Crime Control and Law Enforcement Act of 1994 (Fact Sheet No. NCJ-FS000067). Washington, DC: U.S. Government Printing Office.

Using DNA to solve cold cases. (2002). NIJ Special Report (NIJ Publication No. NCJ-194197). Washington, DC: U.S. Government Printing Office.

Wambaugh, J. (1989). *The Blooding*. New York: Bantam Books.

Warren, J.I., Reboussin, R., and Hazelwood, R.R. (1995). The geographic and temporal sequencing of serial rape (Federal Bureau of Investigation). Washington, DC: U.S. Government Printing Office.

Weedn, V.W., and Hicks, J.W. (1998). The unrealized potential of DNA testing (NIJ Publication No. NCJ-170596). Washington, DC: U.S. Government Printing Office.

Welborn, L. (2003, December 4). Trial nears end in '95 slaying. *The Orange County Register*, p. A1.

Westfall, B. (1992). Westley Allan Dodd. *Police*, *16*(7), 58–60, 84.

Winn, S. and Merrill, D. (1979). *Ted Bundy: The Killer Next Door*. New York: Bantam Books.

31 "El Segundo"

Richard H. Walton

CONTENTS

INTRODUCTION

The following case history illustrates the methods and techniques that resulted in the identification and apprehension of a suspect in 2003 for the murders of two California police officers in 1957. Many of these means and techniques have been addressed throughout this textbook.

THE CRIMES

At approximately midnight on July 21, 1957, two teenage couples were parked in a lover's lane area near Van Ness Avenue between Imperial Highway and El Segundo Boulevard in the city of Hawthorne, California, an incorporated city in the Los Angeles area. The occupants were two boys, ages 16 and 17, and two girls, both age 15. A suspect, later described as a male, white adult, approximately 25-30 years old, 6'- 6'2, 190 lbs., with light brown hair (combed back with pompadour in the front), receding hairline and wearing a plaid or checkered sport shirt, light red and white in color, and khaki pants, appeared at the right rear window of their metallic blue 1949 Ford sedan (see Figure 31.1).*

The suspect was holding a chrome-plated revolver and stated, "Pay attention. This is a robbery. All I want is your money. I won't hurt you." He had a sharp, clear voice and distinct Southern drawl, and was later described as being of athletic build with broad shoulders and slim waist. The victims would describe him as "extremely polite."

The suspect removed a roll of adhesive tape from his pocket, cut it into short strips with his knife, and placed these strips across the eyes and mouths of the four teenagers. He then proceeded to remove the shirts of both of the male victims and tore them into strips. The suspect then bound their hands behind them, and began to rob the victims of their personal property. After removing a wristwatch from the wrist of one of the females, he used a flashlight, which he had in his possession, and rifled through a purse belonging to one of the female victims, stealing a billfold and miscellaneous items of identification. He then removed a wristwatch from one of the male victims and stole his billfold, containing $15-$20.

The suspect forced the two male victims to lie on the rear floor of the vehicle, and one of the female victims to lie on the rear seat. Entering the driver's side of the vehicle, the suspect sat alongside the other female victim. He started the vehicle and drove a short distance to a more remote location in a nearby oilfield before parking again. The suspect exited the vehicle and ordered the girl in the back seat to lie back. He then walked back around to the front passenger side of the car. He opened the car door, approached the female victim seated in the front seat and began undressing her. He removed her brassiere and began fondling her breasts. He then tied her hands

FIGURE 31.1 Sideview of victims' 1949 Ford, which was stolen by suspect and later recovered abandoned after the murder of the two officers.

---

* All photos Courtesy of Los Angeles County Sheriff's Department unless otherwise noted. These original crime scene photos originated with the investigation conducted by the Los Angeles County Sheriff's Department and the El Segundo Police Department. These have been subsequently enhanced by the Felony Trial Support Division of the Los Angeles County District Attorney's Office.

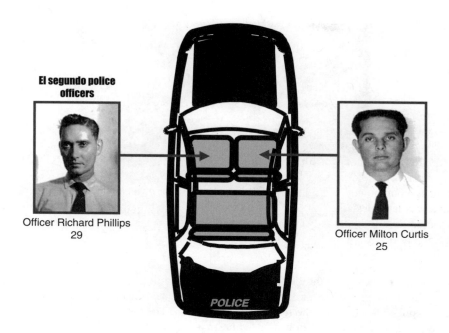

El segundo police officers

Officer Richard Phillips
29

Officer Milton Curtis
25

POLICE

FIGURE 31.2 Victim officer positions. Graphical representation of victim officer positions at time of the murders. Such figures aid in understanding the crime and events, as well as informing others during precharging or jury phases. (Courtesy of Los Angeles D.A.)

behind her back with the brassiere, removed her clothing, and then forcibly raped her on the front seat of the car. He did not rape the girl in the back seat. At the conclusion of the rape, the suspect forced all four of the teenage victims from the car, removed the bindings from their wrists, and forced them all to disrobe. The suspect reentered the vehicle and drove away from the scene, abandoning the victims in this desolate area.

At this time, the crimes had occurred in the jurisdiction of the Hawthorne Police Department. As a result, there was a time lag between receipt of the report of this crime and the notification of other regional law enforcement agencies by teletype or landline. Different agencies operated on different radio frequencies, and as a result, there was a void in interagency communication.

At approximately 1:25 a.m., the suspect was driving the stolen 1949 Ford westbound on Rosecrans Avenue at Sepulveda Boulevard in the city of El Segundo, a bedroom city bordering what is now Los Angeles International Airport. At the time, it was a semi-rural location noted for its oil refineries. The suspect ran a red light at this intersection and was stopped for the traffic violation by patrolling El Segundo police officers Richard Phillips, 29, and Milton Curtis, 25. According to witnesses, the suspect got out of his car and walked toward the radio car, which was stopped directly behind the unreported stolen vehicle. At this time, and as reconstructed by investigators, Officer Phillips was driving the patrol unit and Officer Curtis occupied the right front passenger seat (see Figure 31.2).

Officer Curtis requested a record check on the vehicle via police radio. At this time, the radio transmission was broadcast to a base unit at the El Segundo Police Department, and a record check was then made by a secondary call from the dispatcher to the Los Angeles Police Department's central communication headquarters. (Such organizational procedures in cold cases should be identified by subsequent cold case investigators when reconstructing events, often decades later.)

A second El Segundo police unit arrived at the scene shortly after the record check was transmitted. This police unit was occupied by two other El Segundo police officers, Charles Porter and James Gilbert. Officer Gilbert, riding as passenger, observed Officer Phillips talking to the

FIGURE 31.3 Unit #35 at time of the murders.

suspect, standing to the rear of the 1949 Ford. Both Officer Phillips and the suspect were illuminated by the headlights of the police unit. Officer Curtis was seated in the front passenger seat of the police unit, apparently awaiting the requested information. The backup officers got a good look at the suspect, and later described him as a white male approximately 23 years old, 6'-6'1", full rounded face, short brown hair parted on the side.

Officer Phillips waived Officers Porter and Gilbert on, signaling that everything was all right with the traffic stop. Believing that the stop and the situation were under control, Officers Porter and Gilbert drove away from the scene. The time was approximately 1:27 a.m. Approximately 1 minute later, Officers Porter and Gilbert heard a radio transmission from Officer Phillips requesting an ambulance to the scene of the traffic stop. They immediately returned and found both officers. Officer Curtis was lying on the front seat of the patrol unit, and had been shot three times. Officer Phillips, shot three times in the back, was seen leaning into the passenger side of the radio car with one foot outside the right front passenger door. The 1949 Ford was no longer at the location. Both officers subsequently died as a result of the gunshot wounds, shot from a .22 caliber firearm (see Figure 31.3).

The stolen vehicle was located approximately four blocks west of the shooting scene. There were three bullet strikes to the rear of the vehicle. An examination of Officer Phillips' .38 Special service revolver, found in the dirt at the scene, revealed that he had fired six rounds from his gun at the fleeing suspect/vehicle as it left the scene. Although three bullet impacts were found on the abandoned Ford, only two projectiles were recovered (see Figure 31.4). It was theorized that the suspect might have been hit by one of the bullets. An extensive search was made by "an excess of 500 volunteer officers from all over Southern California" for the suspect, with negative results. It appeared he escaped through the neighboring community of Manhattan Beach by hopping fences and crossing backyards and alleys, as witnesses reported someone running through their backyards.

THE INITIAL INVESTIGATION

Homicide investigators from the Los Angeles County Sheriff's Department (LASD) responded to assist the El Segundo Police Department in the investigation. In the ensuing years, many detectives would travel thousands of miles across the nation in pursuit of leads in this case, and thousands of hours would be spent examining potential forensic evidence.

LASD Identification Deputy Howard Speaks responded to the locations. He processed the crime scene, compiling a photographic record and conducting fingerprint investigations of the patrol car and recovered suspect vehicle. During this process, Deputy Speaks recovered two partial fingerprints from the steering wheel of the 1949 Ford. An additional fingerprint was obtained from a chrome strip (see Figure 31.5).

FIGURE 31.4 Stolen 1949 Ford as it was found after the murder of the officers. Three bullet impacts were located in the vehicle, and investigators theorized that the suspect may have been hit by one bullet. When Mason was arrested in 2003, he had a scar on his right shoulder from one of the officer's .38 Special bullets. Many departments eventually adopted higher-power sidearms such as the .357 Magnum in the 1960s and later. (Courtesy of Los Angeles D.A.)

Deputy Speaks subsequently performed a feat of identification work that was exemplary by 1957 standards. He examined the partial fingerprints and determined them to be different areas of the same finger. With the assistance of the department's photographic unit, these two separate latents were photographed, which resulted in a more complete and clear latent fingerprint. The victim's

FIGURE 31.5 Recovered partial latent fingerprints. LASD Deputy Howard Speaks located two partial prints on the steering wheel, and determined that they were of the same finger. This print was believed to be the suspect's print as the victim's prints were eliminated as the source of the latent print. (Courtesy of Los Angeles D.A.)

fingerprints were eliminated as the source of this recovered print. No matches were made, however, and the prints were therefore believed to belong to the unidentified suspect. In the days before computers and AFIS systems, this was a manual process. During the ensuing decades, more than 1000 person's prints were compared against these. The latent prints were also checked against local, state and FBI fingerprint files but no suspect was ever linked to the fingerprint.

Typically, latent lifts were developed using powder, and then lifted using lift tape. With the passage of time, older tape deteriorates and may separate from the fingerprint card the print was deposited on. As a result, they become of no value for comparison purposes. Fortunately, this was not the case here. By photographing the lifts, Speaks preserved the prints since by 2000, most of the originals had deteriorated to where they were no longer identifiable or useful (see Figure 31.6). The victims of the robbery and rape were able to assist investigators with a description of the suspect, however, and subsequent composite sketches were compiled by an LASD artist (see Figure 31.7).

Much of the victim's clothing and other property were recovered inside the stolen vehicle, but one man's watch and one woman's watch were missing. Based on information and descriptions provided by the young victims, as well as Officers Gilbert and Porter, investigators disseminated a nationwide bulletin (see Figure 31.8 and Figure 31.9).

The first major break in the case occurred by chance, however, with an apparently unrelated incident in a neighboring police jurisdiction. In March 1960, a homeowner who lived approximately 1/4 mile from where the suspect vehicle was abandoned contacted the Manhattan Beach Police Department, a jurisdiction bordering El Segundo. The homeowner stated that in August 1957, his mother had found a Tower brand men's watch in his back yard near an alley. The watch band was broken, so she had it repaired and gave it to her son, who was still wearing it.

In April 1959, the homeowner found the frame of a .22 caliber Harrington and Richardson revolver in the weeds in his yard not far from where the watch had been discovered. The weapon's cylinder was missing, but he had put it in the garage to keep it away from children.

Most recently, he had found the cylinder of the weapon between the rear yard and alleyway of his home, and then decided to notify police. In 2002, the witness was still alive and resided in the same residence. Upon examination, the cylinder contained six expended shell casings, one live cartridge and two empty chambers (see Figure 31.10).

The ammunition recovered inside the cylinder was consistent with the ammunition used to kill the police officers. Realizing the potential of what these gun pieces might mean, Manhattan Beach officers contacted the El Segundo department, and a thorough police search of the area was conducted. This search yielded the cylinder pin to the weapon, and a ladies' watchband and case. The two watches were positively identified as those stolen from the rape and robbery victims prior to the murder of the El Segundo police officers. Personnel from the Los Angeles County Sheriff's Department Crime Lab examined the gun and determined that it was a match to the projectiles recovered from the murdered officers. They now had the weapon used in the murders (see Figure 31.11).

The serial number on this 9-shot .22 caliber revolver provided investigators with a solid lead in the investigation. A trace of this firearm's serial number revealed that it was purchased from a Sears Roebuck and Company store in Shreveport, Louisiana on July 18, 1957. This was three days prior to the murder of the two police officers. Due to the very short timeframe between the purchase of the weapon and the murders, investigators now believed that this individual, or a person using his name, was responsible for the murders. Investigators immediately traveled to Shreveport to continue the investigation, assisted by the FBI and local authorities.

Investigators located and interviewed the young clerk who sold the gun to the purchaser. He remembered the transaction and the individual well. They learned that the gun had been purchased by a male who went by the name "G.D. Wilson" and gave his address as 2831 NW 37th Avenue, Miami, Florida. The subject spoke with a distinct drawl, but not a Louisiana accent. In the original reports, the clerk recalled the subject as possibly wearing khaki pants, but could provide no further information at the time, according to original reports. By now, the original sales slip had been destroyed. Investigators took "...the ledger record of the sale of the gun ... to a photographer and

SHERIFF'S DEPT. LOS ANGELES

FIGURE 31.6 Composite print. In an exemplary feat of identification and technical skill, Deputy Speaks was able to photograph the partial prints and carefully combine these two partial prints to form one composite print. This fingerprint was checked against thousands of persons in the ensuing investigation. Ultimately, with the advent of automated fingerprint identification systems, this single print was traced all the way across the nation from Los Angeles to South Carolina and was matched to Gerald Mason.

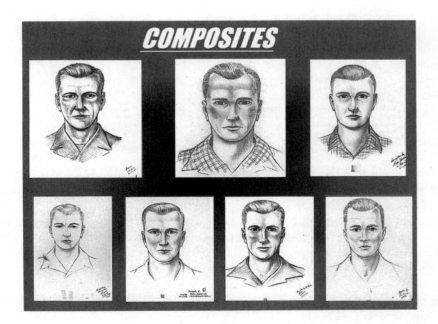

FIGURE 31.7 Composite sketches. After the murders, the four teenagers and two back-up officers provided information to a sheriff's artist. Each appears very similar, and the artist then drew a composite picture from these individual representations. When Mason was identified and arrested, they were remarkably close to Mason. (Courtesy of Los Angeles D.A.)

Murderer of Police Officers !
WANTED
Also Wanted for Rape, Robbery, Kidnapping and Auto Theft

MODUS OPERANDI: At approximately 11:45 PM-7-21-57, four teen-age victims, (2 Girls & 2 Boys) were parked on a "Lovers Lane" when suspect approached carrying a chrome plated .22 caliber revolver, 2" to 4" barrel, a small flashlight and a roll of 1 inch adhesive tape.

Suspect forced victims to tape their own mouths and eyes with strips of tape which he cut from the roll with a pocket knife. He then tied the male victim's arms behind them, with pieces torn from their shirts and then robbed the victims of their wallets and wrist watches. Suspect then raped one of the girls while the two boys and the other girl were forced to lie down in the back of the car. He then forced all the victims to disrobe, after which he drove away with their car with their clothing on the rear seat, leaving them nude.

Approximately twenty minutes later at 1:29 AM - 7-22-57, suspect murdered two police officers when he was stopped for a minor traffic violation while driving the stolen car.

During Robbery - Rape & Kidnapping suspect was very polite, used no profanity and at times was apologetic for his actions. Several times he used the expression "fella" or "fellas". He also referred to police as "policemen." Suspect's opening statement was, "This is a robbery. All I want is your money. I won't hurt you." Suspect spent considerable time with the victims before the rape and at times seemed to be indecisive as to his next moves.

The recovered slugs are .22 caliber, short or longs with a right hand twist, 6 lands and grooves. It is possible that they were fired from a .22 caliber Harrington & Richardson revolver, 2" or 4" barrel.

DESCRIPTION: WM, 25 to 30 years old, 190 lbs., 6' to 6'2", light brown hair, combed back in pompadour style, parted on left side, has receding hairline both sides of forehead; medium complexion with clear skin; sharp clear voice with a slight drawl; muscular build with broad shoulders and slim·waist; was dressed in khaki trousers with short·sleeved sports shirt with red and white squared check pattern, worn outside the trousers.

This print was found in the stolen car and is believed to belong to the suspect. All known persons who had access to the stolen car have been eliminated.

NOTE: The above print is a composite made from two lifts. This print is most likely a fingerprint but may be a section of palm print.

All police departments are requested to check this print against all robbery-rape suspects known to your personnel.

White metal Wittnauer lady's wrist watch, 17 jewel, white face, white gold numerals. Case number unknown. No repair scratch marks. White metal expansion band with white metal crucifix and blue enamel 'Miraculous Medal' attached as illustrated.

White metal Tower boy's waterproof wrist watch, white face, black numerals and hands. No second hand. No movement or case numbers. No repair scratch marks. New clear crystal. White metal expansion band.

Above are illustrations and descriptions of the wrist watches stolen from the robbery victims. All pawn shop and second hand details are requested to check dealers in their jurisdictions for the purchase of the watches. The photograph of suspect is a composite drawing and is believed to be fairly accurate, as described by teen-age victims.

We request you check your MO Files and notify either of the following, telephone collect, immediately.

T. B. DE BERRY, CHIEF OF POLICE, EL SEGUNDO, CALIF., PHONE EASTGATE 22424;
E. W. BISCAILUZ, SHERIFF, LOS ANGELES COUNTY, CALIF., MADISON 69511, EXT. 3615

FIGURE 31.8 Posters describing the victims' missing watches, the composite sketch, and the composite fingerprint were widely circulated in an attempt to identify the killer of the two El Segundo police officers. Investigators recovered the victim's clothing and other property from the stolen vehicle, but these items were determined to be outstanding and believed in the possession of the suspect. They were eventually located not far away where they had been discarded into a backyard as Mason fled the scene.

photographs made. The photographs were then returned to Sears…." The original document was taken by investigators (see Figure 31.12). Decades later, their action would prove a vital link in the forensic document examination that would further prove the killer's guilt.

The investigation determined the Miami address was a gravel pit, yet the victims had reported upon the suspect's distinct Southern drawl. While conducting an investigation throughout the neighborhood surrounding the Sears store, investigators learned that a man had checked into the

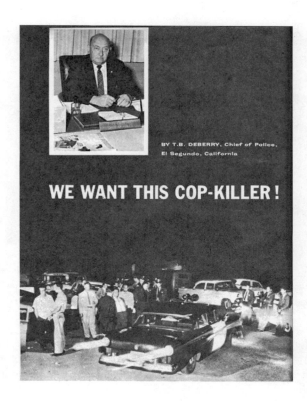

FIGURE 31.9 Road block. Although newspaper accounts describe the use of road blocks to cordon off the surrounding area in an attempt to locate the suspect, *True Detective Magazine* published a photo purportedly of one such roadblock. Review of literature that might have been written about cold case homicides may identify persons, photographs, and other information that is not found in the official file. (Courtesy of El Segundo Police Department)

FIGURE 31.10 One live cartridge and six expended shell casings. Approximately 3 years after the murders, a resident cleaning in his backyard found parts of a pistol that had been taken apart and discarded. The month after the murders, his mother had found a man's broken watch in the same vicinity. She had it repaired and gave it to his son. The resident notified his local police department, and they contacted El Segundo police. A search of the area revealed the missing gun part and the outstanding woman's watch. The discovery of the gun provided the first break in the case. The 9-round cylinder contained six empty cartridge cases and one live round. Each officer had been shot 3 times. In 2002, the resident still resided in the same location.

FIGURE 31.11 The murder weapon. Discovery of the weapon provided investigators with their first lead in the case. The weapon was matched to the fatal bullets. The serial number of the gun allowed it to be traced to a Sears store in Shreveport, Louisiana. (Courtesy of Los Angeles Sheriff's Department)

YMCA in Shreveport on July 17, 1957, signing the guest registry as "George D. Wilson." This location was just two blocks from the Sears store. This individual, believed to be the purchaser of the gun, also gave an address of 2306 NW 34th Street in Miami, Florida. An investigation revealed this address to be bogus. However, the subject's speech, knowledge of the South — specifically the Miami area — now directed investigative interest to this region. Once again, contributing to the chain of evidence that would ultimately culminate in the solution of this crime, the original investigators obtained the original registration card from the YMCA.

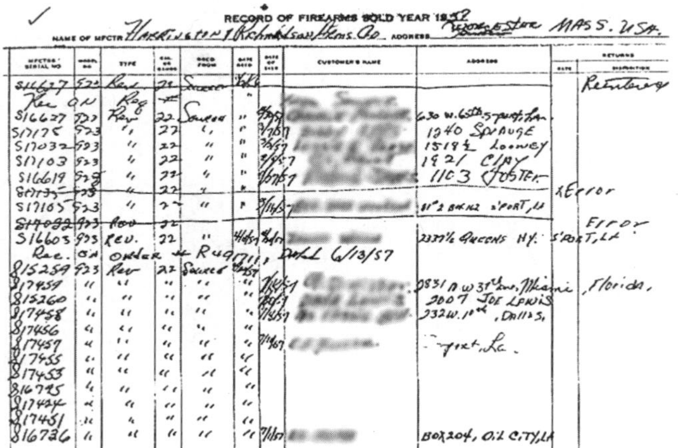

FIGURE 31.12 Investigators located the clerk who sold the gun and obtained the sales records. In 2002, the clerk was relocated and provided additional valuable information regarding the transaction. The sales records were seized, but later lost. Copies of the handwriting were analyzed in 2002 by forensic handwriting expert Paul Edholm. (Courtesy of Los Angeles Sheriff's Department)

As a result of this information, the two agencies requested and received further assistance from the FBI in Miami, Shreveport/New Orleans, and Los Angeles. Every known person identified as or using the name, "George D. Wilson" throughout the United States was located, investigated, and cleared. The Los Angeles County Sheriff's Department amassed several thousand contact cards of individuals looked at as possible suspects during the course of this investigation. These persons were cleared by photo lineups, fingerprint comparisons, and hand-writing comparisons.

The true identity of "G.D. Wilson" could never be ascertained, however. The years passed and original investigators moved on or retired, and the case ultimately languished for lack of follow-up information. To those in law enforcement, however, the case was far from forgotten.

INVESTIGATION REOPENED

On the evening of September 10, 2002, El Segundo Police Lieutenant Craig Cleary was notified by the on-duty watch commander that he had just received a telephone call from a woman who advised that she may have information on the unsolved murder of two police officers in 1957. The woman expressed a belief that a relative may have committed the murders. Lieutenant Cleary immediately contacted the reporting party, and was told of a conversation several years before between the woman and an uncle, who told her that his brother, another uncle, had bragged of killing two police officers when he was a teenager. Her uncle refused to tell his niece any more about it. The informant recently learned that the uncle who told her this was now dying of cancer, and she had gone to visit him. During the visit, the uncle repeated the story, but again refused to provide further details, other than to say he now forgave this other uncle. From another relative she learned that the two officers were from El Segundo, and that the incident occurred during the "summertime in the late 1950s."

Lieutenant Cleary was familiar with this case. It was the only unsolved murder of their police officers. In the mid-1990s, due to the expanding AFIS databases and the suspect's drawl, the composite print had been sent by the LASD to the AFIS systems of numerous Southern states. This search was unsuccessful, however. Not long before this telephone call, one of their crime scene personnel had attended a conference and upon return, updated the lieutenant on the expanded IAFIS system.

Cleary contacted the Homicide Bureau of the Los Angeles County Sheriff's Department and was quickly teamed up by Sheriff's Homicide Bureau Lieutenant Raymond Peavy with veteran LASD homicide detectives Dan McElderry and Kevin Lowe for a joint reinvestigation of these now 45-year-old crimes. These two detectives were experienced homicide investigators, with many years of training and experience behind them as they approached this case. None of the three, however, had faced one of this age and magnitude before.

Although the sheriff's department had changed its case numbering system several decades before, the original case file was located, retrieved from archives, and studied by the three experienced lawmen beginning September 11, 2002. Mindful of the advances in technology since these crimes, the detectives included Identification Deputy Dale Falicon within the investigative group almost immediately.

A check of records in the El Segundo department revealed documents apparently not in the Sheriff's Office file, and all records were compared and combined to ensure that they had all reports. As they reviewed the accumulation of reports, documents, and other records, the three officers looked through a window into law enforcement that had existed before they were born. This was a period when reports were handwritten or typed, of carbon or thermafax copies, and pre-computerization. Index cards memorialized the vast amount of information resulting from individual interviews of thousands of subjects. During this review, they gained an insight into one of the biggest manhunts in history, yet one that had so far been unsuccessful. Over 3000 individuals had been investigated as possible suspects, and cleared. In addition, investigators had reported "…

FIGURE 31.13 Original organized file. Cold case investigation begins with a review of the previous investigation no matter the size. Investigators located the case file and quickly realized the extensive investigation previously accomplished by their predecessors decades before. Learning the old case is necessary to move forward in cold case investigation, and this can be a time consuming effort. (Courtesy of Detectives Dan McElderry and Kevin Lowe, LASD.)

checking more than 14,000 names and handwriting exemplars in the forgery and sex crime file" (see Figure 31.13).

As they reviewed the case, Cleary, McElderry, and Lowe identified past practices that many cold case investigators experience, and that add to the difficulty in reconstructing cold case homicides and locating original witnesses and others. There was a lack of complete identification of the persons in old police reports. This included lack of date of birth, use of nicknames, addresses, and means to locate them. In addition, there was synopsis-oriented report writing.

INVESTIGATION BETTER THAN DOCUMENTATION

The determination and tenacity of the original investigators were apparent as the aging reports were committed to the fresh minds of the three investigators in 2002.

The group brainstormed how to proceed with the case. They separated all reports and arranged them in order, beginning with the Hawthorne crimes, then the homicides. Evidence and property from both agencies were now assimilated into one case file, and all reports were copied to make working three-ring binder files for the investigators. In the end, they had a chronological record, and finally, a picture of events as they unfolded. They ensured that all evidence was reviewed and forwarded to the laboratory for reexamination. Together with Lieutenant Cleary, McElderry and Lowe began reading through the card files, familiarizing themselves with the extent of the investigation and reading the synopsis of those who had been cleared. During their review, they discovered that some earlier investigators had strong disagreement among themselves over focusing on what some perceived as the wrong person. As they continued their review, the investigators came to realize that things that sometimes happen in investigations today also happened back then.

They ultimately rephotographed and relisted all evidence with a new evidence number. Not unlike cold case files elsewhere, articles of the victim's clothing were found in the files and not in evidence. Other items found in the files included the tape used to cover the victims' eyes and mouths. During this review, they considered the potential value of this evidence that might be revealed through DNA analysis or advanced fingerprint detection methods. The tape was taken to the lab with thoughts of retrieving fingerprints, but this avenue eventually proved unfruitful.

During a review of the photo file, they discovered a lack of crime scene photos. Their perspective, however, was that of scene processing in today's law enforcement environment, and perhaps not that of the time and place of the crime. Standards had changed over the years and requirements were now far from those of 45 years earlier. Further searching, however, revealed that someone years before, in an effort to free up storage space, had trashed the evidence. Thus, almost all that remained was what they found in the files. This situation was far from unique.

When reviewing the few photos of the homicide crime scene, the investigators had observed the officer's citation book on the right front fender of the victim's patrol car. Had the suspect touched it? Had he perhaps signed a citation and left it when he fled? As cold case investigators, they were trying to put themselves in the place and time to try to understand events as they unfolded. They wanted to see the cite book. It was still in evidence, but the top copy of the citation was now missing (see Figure 31.14). Also missing was the original YMCA card that had been recovered from the Shreveport YMCA, as well as the original Sears log of the gun sale. All they had was copies of these documents. The new cold case investigators were encountering events, circumstances, and frustrations that have been experienced repeatedly by law enforcement investigators when they return to investigate cold cases.

Pages of laboratory reports revealed that firearms examiners had inspected and eliminated over 400 similar revolvers over the course of the investigation before the murder weapon had been found

FIGURE 31.14 Missing documentary evidence. Analysis of the crime scene photos showed the officer's citation book on the fender as if the victim were in the process of issuing a citation. In 2002, the book remained, but the white or top copy was missing. Investigators would seek to learn whether the suspect signed the citation and then murdered the officers, and this could be revealed by forensic document examination. In this case, the top copy disappeared, and there was no indication the officer had finished completing the form before he and his partner were slain.

FIGURE 31.15 Critical evidence. In 2002, cold case investigators discovered that the original fingerprint evidence had been properly stored and maintained since the original investigation. The fingerprint, when processed through AFIS technology, resulted in a match with the fingerprint of the suspect, Gerald Mason. Original lift cards from pre-1970s may be turning with age and their contents preserved for the future. (Courtesy of Los Angeles Sheriff's Department.)

and positively identified. The weapon would need to be reexamined. Review of the physical evidence revealed the existence of the fingerprints recovered by Deputy Speaks decades before (see Figure 31.15). Fortunately, these prints had been photographed as the original lift cards were now faded beyond usable recognition, victims of time and the materials used then.

They soon discovered that although Deputy Speaks had retired many years before, he was able and willing to rejoin the effort to find the cop killers (see Figure 31.16). As the investigation progressed, they would come to locate other original case participants. Ironically, within days of the initial telephone call from the woman regarding her uncle as a possible suspect, they interviewed the parties, compared prints, and determined that this information was unfounded. Regardless, the case was now reopened and the investigation moved forward.

ROLE OF ADVANCED TECHNOLOGY (AFIS/IAFIS)

Deputy Dale Falicon reexamined the original fingerprint lifts obtained from the stolen 1949 Ford vehicle, and subsequently spoke at length with retired Deputy Speaks. After some digital enhancement, the composite latent image was traced and sent through the new FBI IAFIS fingerprint database Universal Latent Workstation. This database had come on line with a nationwide search capability only months before. Although the FBI IAFIS system had come on line in July 1999, it took several years for different agencies to acquire the hardware and software necessary to interface with the FBI IAFIS system. While the print had previously been checked in the South from Texas to Georgia and Florida, it had not been checked north to South Carolina (see Figure 31.17 and Figure 31.18).

On September 18, 2002, a hit was made on the prints. The number one candidate on the IAFIS list was identified as Gerald F. Mason. His FBI rap sheet revealed that he was an ex-con with a date of birth in 1934, and provided information necessary to begin further investigation. Mason had been arrested and imprisoned in South Carolina for commercial burglary/forgery in 1956, his

FIGURE 31.16 Howard Speaks with evidence. Deputy Speaks retired, but never forgot this case. He was there at the start, conducted exemplary crime scene and evidence processing, and was present for the conclusion of the case 45 years later. (Courtesy of Los Angeles Sheriff's Department.)

only *known* contact with law enforcement. His description at the time reported him as 6'3" tall, weight 195 pounds, with brown hair and brown eyes. The officers soon learned that at the time of this arrest he was living in the YMCA in Columbia, South Carolina.

While technology had prepared a list of possible candidates, the investigation of this case now required old fashioned detective work and "shoe leather." Mason had to be positively linked to the gun and to the crime, and the detectives began an indepth examination of Mason's background.

The name was a start, something previous generations of investigators lacked. To move forward, the detectives needed to confirm Mason's prints, and the best way to do so was with an original

FIGURE 31.17 IAFIS tracing. For entry into IAFIS, the fingerprint is traced and submitted.

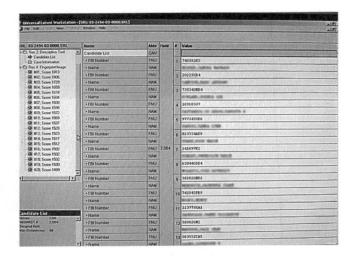

FIGURE 31.18 Universal Latent Workstation. After the print was submitted, a search of fingerprint databases identified Gerald Mason as a candidate for a match. After a "hit" is made, an examiner must match the suspect fingerprint to a known fingerprint of the suspect. Locating an original fingerprint is not always easy, and Detectives Lowe and McElderry traveled across the nation to personally take custody of the only known original fingerprint from Mason's 1956 arrest.

fingerprint ten-print card. Between September 18, 2003 and January 20, 2003, the three investigators would reconstruct not only the crimes, but the persons and a 45-year-old sequence of events, then identify and prove the man responsible for the rape, robbery, kidnappings, and murder of two El Segundo police officers.

A call to Columbia, South Carolina, revealed that Mason's records had been destroyed in a fire years before. Detective Kevin Lowe called the archives unit at the state prison where Mason had been incarcerated, and here their luck began to turn. People skills are as much an attribute of cold case investigators as any other skill, and Lowe's paid off. Rebuffed by others in his attempts to get someone to look for this aged file, he finally found a sympathetic clerk. The woman was offended that a police officer had been murdered, and agreed to search for the official record. After some time, she found Mason's original prison files "Pen Pack," and notified the Los Angeles detectives.

In homicide investigations, time can be of the essence. The same holds true in cold case investigations, and these records were needed to move forward. The detectives flew to South Carolina and took physical custody of Mason's only surviving original fingerprint card and original booking picture (see Figure 31.19 and Figure 31.20). Their personal retrieval of these documents from the custodian of records was important in the continuing chain of custody of the records.

Upon receiving the original ten print card, these original inked fingerprints were compared with the latent prints recovered by Deputy Speaks from the stolen vehicle. The original fingerprints from the hard card matched the prints recovered from the 1949 Ford. The investigators had attempted to determine if the original vehicle might still be in the state motor vehicle system, but its absence was not unexpected. In later contacts with victims, family, and friends of the owner, it would be learned that the young man subsequently sold the vehicle, and it could never be located.

The composite print had been constructed from the two partial prints on the steering wheel. The third print had been recovered from a "chrome strip" but the documentation had not completely described exactly *where* the chrome strip was located in the car. Detective Lowe demonstrated cold case investigator resourcefulness as he "colored outside the box" in his thinking. He went on line, looking for an original, similar 1949 Ford. Cold case investigators may on occasion need to reconstruct aspects of the case, including a physical scene no longer available. Detective Lowe located a Ford car club and through them, a restored, original-condition 1949 Ford. Upon inspection,

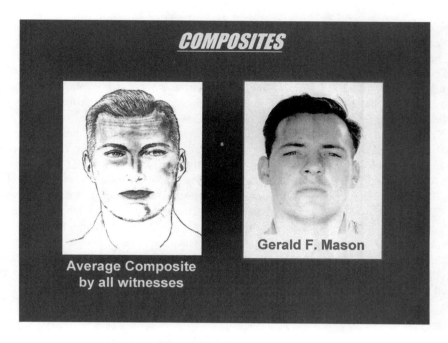

FIGURE 31.19 Comparison of Mason's composite artists sketch and 1956 mug shot. (Courtesy of Los Angeles County District Attorney's Office, Felony Trial Support Division.)

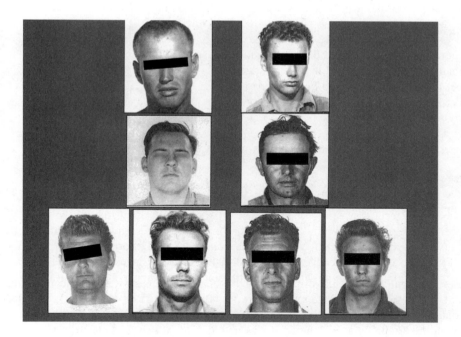

FIGURE 31.20 Print comparison. Latent prints lifted from scene compared to Mason's prison packet prints. Despite the passage of four decades, cold case investigators did not take "no" for an answer when told that Mason's prison prints were gone. People skills proved invaluable as detectives located a sympathetic clerk who put the extra effort into searching for, and finding, Mason's prison pak. (Courtesy of Los Angeles County District Attorney's Office, Felony Trial Support Division.)

they discovered a chrome strip inside the driver's door — a location where it would be reasonable to find the right ring fingerprint left behind by the suspect.

As the case began to come together, they had consulted with the District Attorney's Office. The assigned prosecutor wanted more evidence before the case would be filed and an arrest made, however. While they could now link Mason to the car, it was not proof beyond a reasonable doubt. The detectives and prosecutors realized that he might have offered an "affirmative defense" by saying that his prints were on the vehicle because he was an auto mechanic and had worked on the car. They needed to link Mason to the gun, and to the murders. Mason, now 68 years old, was a retired businessman, a gas station owner with an apparently good reputation. The District Attorney wanted more before he would authorize traveling all the way across the nation to arrest a 68-year-old allegedly respectable member of the community for a 45-year-old crime.

The detectives began to build a profile of the suspect. They wanted to know *who* was Gerald Mason? They returned to South Carolina and began to answer these questions. They learned that Mason was born in Richland County, South Carolina, but was raised in Miami, Florida. That he was Catholic, came as no surprise to the investigators. They recalled reading an early report that said that after being raped, the girl in the front seat had made the sign of the cross, and that Mason did not touch her again. Nor did he take her wallet or money. At the State Archives in South Carolina, they recovered the arrest report and probation/parole information from his 1956 conviction.

RE-INTERVIEW WITNESSES

During the course of the re-investigation, investigators identified critical witnesses involved in the 45-year-old series of crimes and began attempts to locate them. As a result, they learned that while the young boy who owned the 1949 Ford had died, the whereabouts of others involved in the case and investigation became known. In addition to Deputy Speaks, they identified, located, and re-interviewed:

- The gun store clerk who sold the weapon to the suspect
- Original FBI agents involved in the investigation
- Officer Gilbert of El Segundo Police Department
- Officer Porter of El Segundo Police Department
- Surviving Hawthorne victims

Among the resources used to locate these persons were:

- Driver's license checks
- Retired persons or occupation associations
- Past employers
- Friends or family of identified persons
- Law enforcement agency records
- Other databases

Cold case investigation often involves a lot of travel, and this case was no exception. In a Southern state, the investigators located the female Hawthorne victim from the backseat attack. While she could not now identify Mason, she did provide a statement consistent with her original report. Although the young owner of the Ford was now deceased, they learned from friends and family of his fastidious habits of cleaning the car, and began to build a rebuttal to any defense claim that Mason had left his prints on the vehicle when he worked on it.

Reinterviewing witnesses is more than just going over their previous statements. Due to the synopsis-oriented methods of documentation in reports that have been observed in previous generations of law enforcement report writing or other factors, these re-contacts may yield additional information not previously known or documented. When the detectives reinterviewed the gun store

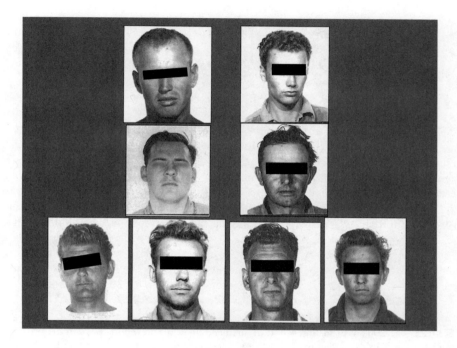

FIGURE 31.21 The 1950s line up in 2002. Detectives assembled a photo line up using mug shots of subjects as they looked at the time of the crime. As time passes, many agencies are purging these older photos, making this process even more difficult. In addition, the detectives enlarged the photos in consideration of the current age of the then-juvenile victims.

clerk, he recalled the events clearly, in part because of his earlier contacts with law enforcement personnel regarding this sale.

Upon reinterview, the clerk provided new information to the investigators. He recalled that the ammunition he sold to the buyer with the gun was a brand known as J.C. Higgins. This was a brand of ammunition sold exclusively through Sears Roebuck and Company, and now found to be consistent with the ammunition and cartridge cases recovered in the weapon. In addition, and without knowing further, he advised the detectives that the subject did not have a "Louisiana accent" but a "Carolina accent."

Investigators also located now-retired Officers Porter and Gilbert, the backup officers to the victim officers moments before they were murdered. As were others, each was shown a photo group of eight period black-and-white photographs that included one of Mason (see Figure 31.21). Although none of the other victims could now identify Mason, the retired officers each recalled that 1 minute or less 45 years before in detail. Both identified Mason's picture as the man they last saw talking to Officer Phillips during the traffic stop.

During these interviews and photo show-up, investigators utilized the 1956 prison photograph of Gerald Mason. This picture depicted his appearance 45 years before, and in doing so, demonstrated a technique that may be beneficial during cold case or other investigations and interviews with now-senior citizens. Instead of the original smaller formatted photographs, they used 8 × 10-inch photos. Agencies may consider the need for retaining back files of mug shots such as these for use when the need arises in cold case investigations.

VISITING THE SCENE

While reading reports may create images of the scene in the minds of cold case investigators, nothing takes the place of visiting the actual location. Locating and inspecting the original 1949

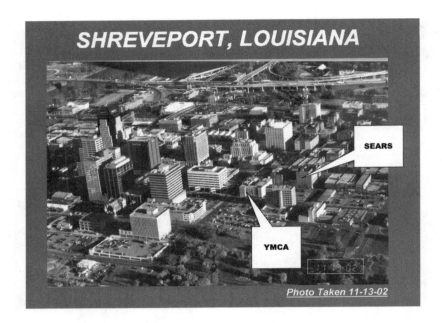

FIGURE 31.22 The 2002 visit to Shreveport. A firsthand visit to Shreveport revealed the proximity of the Sears store and the YMCA, and provided detectives a perspective useful beyond words. This aerial view illustrates this perspective to others. (Courtesy of LADA Felony Trial Support Unit)

Ford assisted the officers in the reconstruction and understanding of events that had taken place over 4 decades before. In November 2002, the investigators flew to Shreveport. On this journey, they realized the discrepancy that can occur as reports are written and then summarized in succeeding years. While an earlier report described the distance between the two locations as being two blocks, later reports described the distance as "two miles." They revisited the location of the Sears store as well as the YMCA. The proximity of these two locations now became truly apparent, a relationship not adequately documented, and that was further revealed by an aerial photograph that depicted their observation of this relationship. (see Figure 31.22).

During their reinvestigation, the investigators had attempted to locate the Hawthorne crime scene, but were unable to do so. The homicide scene, clearly preserved in several of the patrol unit photos, was now a busy city street that bore little resemblance to what it looked like in 1957.

Investigator understanding of the sequence of events is critical in cold case investigation. Revisiting the scenes greatly facilitates this understanding. In addition, the detectives utilized street maps to assist not only their comprehension of distances and relationships, but to demonstrate this at a later date when the case was submitted to others for review and prosecution. Original maps and other sources were utilized to estimate the most logical route from Hawthorne to the homicide scene, and in reconstructing timelines and distances. Sources of potential information were city maps, Public Works maps, and oil company maps.

FORENSIC DOCUMENT EXAMINATION

Document examination offered a strong potential as a solvability factor in this investigation. At the suggestion of the prosecutor, investigators solicited the expertise of forensic document examiner Paul Edholm. A former Beverly Hills Police Department detective, Edholm was a qualified forensic document examiner whose work was recognized by the District Attorney's office and the Superior Courts in Los Angeles. On October 24, 2002, Edholm met with the detectives and Los Angeles County Deputy District Attorney Darren Levine. Levine specialized in crimes against police officers.

DATE IN | RECEIPT NO. | AMOUNT PAID | RATE | REMARKS

ADDRESS 2306 NW 34 st Miami, Fla. MEMBERSHIP

NAME GEORGE D WILSON ROOM NO. 411

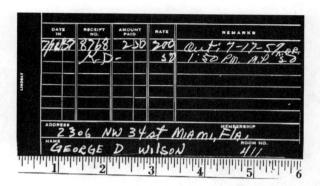

FIGURE 31.23 Photostatic copy of Mason's YMCA registration card. Photocopy machines as we know them did not exist in 1957 and copies produced by this process may be found in some cold case files. (Courtesy of Paul Edholm and Los Angeles County District Attorney's Office, Felony Trial Support Division.)

At this time, the quality of the original investigation and preservation of the case file laid the foundation for the new team to finally close the case.

Although the original had disappeared, Edholm reviewed the remaining photostatic copy of the YMCA registration card signed by the suspect in Shreveport in 1957. He also received from the investigators a copy of Mason's 1999 South Carolina eye examination, required for his driver's license, and an affidavit for a motor vehicle sale. The YMCA document was a photostatic copy, or a paper negative with a black background and white letters (see Figure 31.23 and Figure 31.24). Photocopy machines were not available in 1957. Edholm used Adobe Photoshop® to reverse the image so that the background was now white and the letters black. Now a more conclusive examination could be made (see Figure 31.25 and 31.26).

Edholm compared the 1999 South Carolina Department of Public Safety Report of Eye Examination with the 1957 YMCA document. In addition, he noted other observations in his analysis of the documents. Because only photocopies were available then, Edholm could give only a highly probable opinion (99.9%) that the handwriting in both documents was authored by the same person – Gerald Mason. The match between the two writings indicated to investigators and the prosecutor that Gerald Mason wrote the name "George D. Wilson" on the registry receipt. In conjunction with other information, they also concluded that the case could be made that he was also the individual who purchased the murder weapon at the Sears store in Shreveport, Louisiana, using the name, "G.D. Wilson."

DATE IN | RECEIPT NO. | AMOUNT PAID | RATE | REMARKS

ADDRESS 2306 NW 34 st Miami, Fla. MEMBERSHIP

NAME GEORGE D WILSON ROOM NO. 411

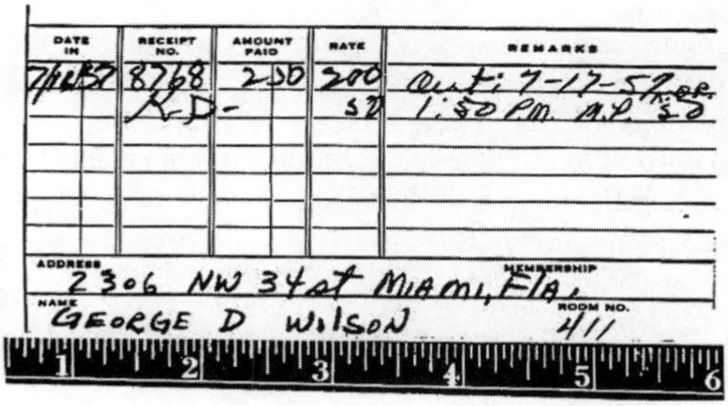

FIGURE 31.24 Reversed photostatic copy of Mason's YMCA registration card. Forensic document examiner Paul Edholm reversed the image shown in Figure 31.23 in his examination process, thus allowing him to conduct a more conclusive examination. (Courtesy of Paul Edholm, Los Angeles County District Attorney's Office, Felony Trial Support Division.)

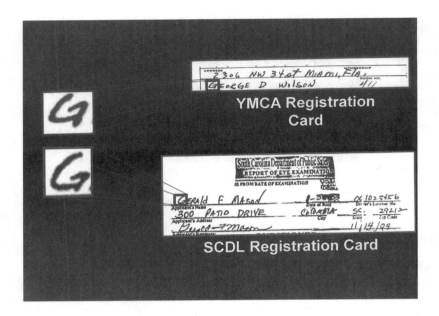

FIGURE 31.25 Similarity between the 1957 YMCA registration card and more recent South Carolina Eye Examination report. (Courtesy of Paul Edholm and Los Angeles County District Attorney's Office, Felony Trial Support Division.)

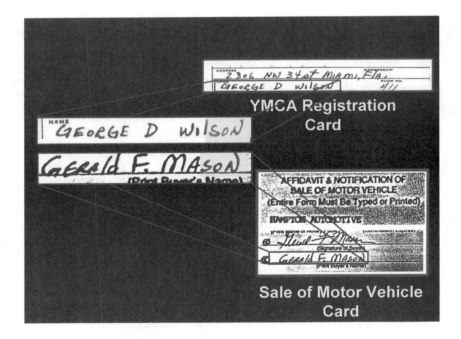

FIGURE 31.26 Similarity between writing on Mason's 1957 YMCA registration card and later Affidavit and Notification of sale of Motor Vehicle. (Courtesy of Paul Edholm, Los Angeles County District Attorney's Office, Felony Trial Support Division.)

Based upon the totality of their investigation, including the identifications made by photo, fingerprints, and handwriting, the investigators now believed Gerald Mason to be the suspect responsible in this murder investigation. Subsequently, they requested a search and arrest warrant for Gerald Mason for the 1957 murders of El Segundo Police Officers Richard Phillips and Milton Curtis.

PREPARING THE CASE FOR REVIEW AND PROSECUTION

Not everyone necessarily understands what may be involved in cold case investigation. This sometimes includes fellow officers and superior officers within one's own agency as well as prosecutors, judges, and juries. These cases often involve a series of events stretched out over a period of years, and styles of investigation and documentation not applicable today. In addition, they usually involve many names and sometimes relationships that need to be explained and understood, as well as evidence and property, forensic examinations, and more. It must be remembered that the prosecutor, who already has a full schedule, must feel confident that the case can be proved beyond a reasonable doubt. The prosecutor must contend with a myriad of issues now compounded by the age of the case, evidence retention, and witness matters. In addition, the prosecutor may also have to deal with potential jury pool perceptions influenced by television and media representations that, in some situations, are less than practically realistic.

Normally, when a homicide investigation is concluded and approved for referral to prosecution, the murder book is submitted for filing. A cold case investigation is the victim's last chance for attention from the criminal justice system and investigators may need to convince their own team as well as the prosecution that *now* is the best time to file and prosecute this case. To do this, investigators should consider other means to best explain and convey the investigation rather than just handing off the "book" and waiting for a response.

PREPARE A ROAD MAP

Investigators of these cases today may consider preparing a computer-generated presentation, such as PowerPoint®. In doing so, they can be expressive and thorough, as well as concise yet complete. Maps, diagrams, photos, and other means that demonstrate people, places, evidence, and relationships all contribute to making such a presentation a success. Use pictures of the victim wherever appropriate, giving the victim a place in the presentation. The prosecutor will want to make the victim come alive for a jury, so make the case come alive for the prosecutor. Everything the investigator can do to help the prosecutor in this regard may come back to pay big dividends for both. In preparing these presentations, consider using the following format, mixing photos *then and now* as appropriate. Highlight information through use of graphics such as lines, arrows, etc.

THE ORIGINAL INVESTIGATION

- Make victim come alive through family pictures and retrace their last days.
  - Victim background.
  - Victim family, including marriage, children, responsibilities.
- Profile suspect.
- Alternate profile between victim's last activities and suspect's activities that brought them together on day of the homicide.
- Identify witnesses or others in the case.
- The crime and investigation as portrayed by:
  - Original crime scene photos.
  - Aerial photos.
  - Maps.

- Calendars.
- Timelines.
- Newspaper clippings.
- Original missing person's report and search efforts.
- Original news video clips.
- Original agency investigation video clips.
- Re-run routes with a video camera and show times and places.
- The killer and the relationship to events and to the victim.
- Suspect's knowledge of the victim.
- Suspect familiarity with crime scene or secondary scenes.
- Introduce the detectives and investigators, the first team.
- Victim's death.
  - Victim's clothing.
  - Victim's remains.
  - Weapon.
  - Crime scene.
  - Victim's living ingress to scene and ultimate egress.
- Forensic review.
  - What was examined and what was done?
  - State of the art of forensics at the time of original analysis.
  - Weapon analysis.
  - Review of reports and criminalistics work.
- Summary of defendants' original statements, if any.
- Summary of original investigation and why case when cold.

REINVESTIGATION

- Cause and reason for start-up
- Discussion of remaining reports, evidence, and any other problems
- Review of role of advanced technology
- Review of role of changes in relationships
- Summary of the current investigation
- Summary to link the suspect to the victim and the evidence

In this case, such a presentation clearly, concisely, and accurately portrayed a 45-year series of events (see Figure 31.27 and Figure 31.28). The presentation presented the case using specific groupings of topics, including:

- Overview of the crimes
  - Hawthorne crimes
  - Murder of two El Segundo police officers
  - Description of crime scenes
- Time sequences
- Physical description of the suspect
- Evidence
- Families of the officer victims
- The initial investigation
  - Composites generated of the suspect
  - Processing and identification of evidence
  - Gun recovery and link to victims and suspect

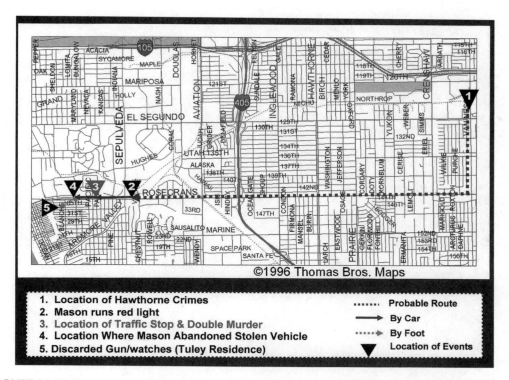

1. **Location of Hawthorne Crimes**
2. **Mason runs red light**
3. **Location of Traffic Stop & Double Murder**
4. **Location Where Mason Abandoned Stolen Vehicle**
5. **Discarded Gun/watches (Tuley Residence)**

....	**Probable Route**
⟶	**By Car**
·····▶	**By Foot**
▼	**Location of Events**

©1996 Thomas Bros. Maps

FIGURE 31.27 Presentations utilizing maps, timelines, and other techniques to illuminate and illustrate the victim, crime, scene, and suspect can be powerful tools to convince others, including defense attorneys and juries. (Courtesy of Los Angeles County District Attorney's Office, Felony Trial Support Division)

07/22/57
Approx. 1:28 A.M.

➢ **Mason runs a red light at Rosecrans & Sepulveda.**

➢ **Mason is pursued by victim Officers Phillips & Curtis of El Segundo Police Department.**

➢ **Mason pulls over and exits the vehicle at Rosecrans & Pacific.**

➢ **During the traffic investigation, a second black & white El Segundo police unit with Officers Porter and Gilbert arrive at the traffic stop and observe Mason. Officer Porter is waived off by officers and leaves the scene at approximately 1:27 a.m.**

➢ **At 1:28 a.m., ESPD dispatch receives a call for ambulance from Officer Curtis ... "OFFICERS SHOT"**

➢ **Officer Curtis is shot 3 times, Officer Phillips is also shot 3 times.**

➢ **Stolen vehicle is found abandoned 4 blocks from location of traffic stop and shooting.**

FIGURE 31.28 Sequence of events timelined and compressed. (Courtesy of Los Angeles County District Attorney's Office, Felony Trial Support Division)

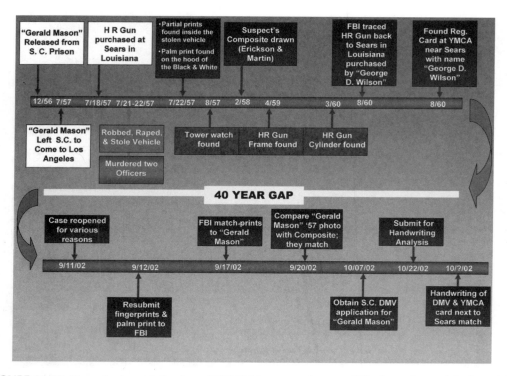

FIGURE 31.29 (See color insert following p. 216.) Cold cases are the most difficult to solve, and the detectives built a compelling case against Mason. In doing so, they utilized many different tools and techniques. Ultimately, advances in technology, supplemented by old-fashioned detective leg work, identified Mason as the killer and built a compelling case to prove it. (Courtesy of Los Angeles County District Attorney's Office, Felony Trial Support Division)

- The re-investigation
  - Show how new information added to the initial case
  - Use of forensic document examination
  - Detailed explanation of how advanced technology used to identify suspect, Gerald Mason
- Further development of Mason as suspect through additional witness interviews, use of original composite drawings, and photo show ups (see Figure 31.29 and Figure 31.30)

Remember, convincing the prosecutor is one more step in the process toward conviction. In this case, the presentation presented by the detectives convinced the prosecutor. Ultimately, the presentation helped convince the defendant to plead guilty to two counts of first degree murder.

SEARCH WARRANTS

Search warrants may be a valuable tool during the investigation and arrest of a suspect in a cold case homicide. We seek these warrants when we conduct a hot homicide investigation, so why not in a cold case investigation? Although the element of time may be a consideration to the prosecution and to the court, and the reasonable expectation to find items sought after the passage of years, this issue may be sufficiently addressed depending upon the circumstances of the case and the investigation.

We seek records and "souvenirs" in a variety of cases. In my opinion and experience, there is not necessarily a reason to believe that a suspect will not, or does not, keep something as a record

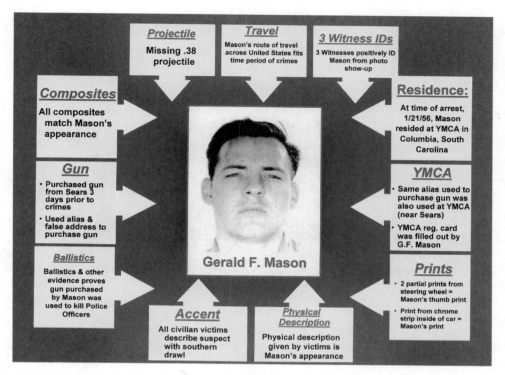

FIGURE 31.30 In 2003, justice caught up with Gerald Mason for his 1957 crime spree. Mason's arrest and conviction was the result of tenacious investigation by a series of investigators for over four decades. Modern investigators built upon the efforts of their predecessors to finally achieve a sense of justice in this case. (Courtesy of Los Angeles County District Attorney's Office, Felony Trial Support Division)

or souvenir of the incident. In white collar and fraud cases, we routinely seek search warrants to find documents that are often many years old. A search warrant may establish other linkages to the crime, as evidenced by the items sought by the investigators in this instance.

In this case, investigators prepared an affidavit for a search warrant and it was transposed to the format acceptable under South Carolina law. In this affidavit, the investigators sought:

- Any papers, photographs, or the like that depicted items sought or believed to be evidence in the case being investigated by this warrant
- Any paperwork, documents, correspondence, receipts, contracts, telephone bills, bank or bank card records that tended to show the purchase of any items believed to be evidence in this case
- Any papers or documents containing suspect Gerald Mason's printing to be collected for examination by handwriting experts and compared with handwriting exemplars already in the possession of the investigators
- Any address books, lists, or single reference to addresses or telephone numbers of persons who may later be determined to be involved with this case
- Any newspaper articles or clippings documenting the murders of Officers Phillips and Curtis and/or robbery/assault victims
- Any documentation of travel to the state of California
- Any photographs of firearms or any paperwork showing the purchase, storage, disposition, or dominion and control of any guns, ammunition, gun cleaning items or kits, holsters, etc.

- Any articles of personal property tending to establish the identity of persons who have dominion and control over the premises, automobiles, or items to be seized, including but not limited to, rent, mortgage receipts, utility bills, miscellaneous addressed personal mail, personal letters, personal identification, keys, purchase/pawn receipts, sales receipts, tax statements, photographs, and vehicle registrations

Los Angeles county investigators also requested by order of this search warrant that suspect Gerald Mason submit a sample of his DNA for comparison to DNA evidence already collected and preserved in this case (i.e., bindings). Investigators also requested that suspect Gerald Mason submit to taking saliva samples from the interior of his mouth. These samples were to be taken utilizing two sterile oral swabs, or Mason could submit to the taking of a blood sample by medical personnel in a medically approved manner. These samples were to be analyzed by Sheriff's Crime Lab personnel for DNA.

On January 24, 2003, Lieutenant Craig Cleary and detectives Kevin Lowe and Dan McElderry presented their case to the Los Angeles County District Attorney's Office, Target Crimes Division. This office subsequently authorized arrest and search warrants for Gerald F. Mason. In the complaint, Mason was charged with 12 felony counts, including two counts of murder in the first degree, four counts of kidnapping, four counts of robbery, and an additional count of kidnapping and one count of rape. The felony counts were filed for extradition and an arrest warrant was signed. Certified copies of the complaint and arrest warrant were provided to investigators.

The detectives then exercised a suggested tactic. The warrant of arrest was *not* entered into warrant systems or NCIC at this time. Rather, the investigators did so only *after* the search warrant was signed in South Carolina and shortly before the service. Cold case investigators may consider the wisdom of this tactic, as it may be troublesome to have the plan in place and ready to proceed only to have the suspect stopped on a routine traffic matter and arrested. In addition, you never know who may know someone after all these years, and for security purposes, this tactic may be advisable.

As an example, I had once obtained a multimillion-dollar bail arrest warrant for a white-collar-crime suspect. The suspect had relocated to a distant jurisdiction and I similarly had withheld the arrest warrant from being entered into NCIC while FBI agents and I were preparing to execute the search and arrest warrants. However it happened, a copy of the arrest warrant was sent to a sheriff's office clerk responsible for the warrant entry. On a quiet Saturday morning, the clerk noticed the warrant and in an attempt to be "helpful," personally notified the uniform division of the police agency to which we were enroute to serve the warrant. Hours before our action, two uniformed officers went to the residence and arrested the suspect on the warrant. He immediately asserted his legal rights and no interview ensued, and no documentation of his immediate reaction or statements were made.

OFFICER SAFETY

The service of any search warrant or arrest warrant poses risk and danger for law enforcement personnel. In my opinion, the service of these warrants in cold cases poses additional risk and uncertainty. Although the suspects may now be older, that does not necessarily mean that they are wiser. Suspects have had many years to think about what they have done, how they may react if confronted, and to estimate the results of their decisions. Flight or fight, prison, or a death penalty. Even *they* do not really know how they will react until it happens. Check available databases for any firearms purchases, updated arrests, or other resources to identify any possible intelligence.

Although these subjects were previously discussed in this textbook, the reality of this situation is most apparent to those who will confront a cold case suspect after the passage of time. The elevated emotions and adrenalin of the moments during and after the crime may be long past, but the consequences of their actions are suddenly a reality. Those who have committed long past crimes may have continued to commit criminal acts and murders, or they may have gone on to become locally "respectable" members of the community. At this stage of the investigation, cold case investigators have been removed from the violence of the crime, and have been immersed in the legal aspects of investigation and liaison with the prosecutor's office. Detectives McElderry and Lowe perhaps summed it up best: "...think like a policeman, not an attorney."

THINK AND PRACTICE OFFICER SAFETY

SEARCH WARRANT SERVICE

On January 27, 2003, the three investigators, accompanied by Los Angeles County Sheriff's Department Homicide Lieutenant Raymond Peavy, traveled to Columbia, South Carolina. Serving out-of-state search warrants involves enlisting the assistance of law enforcement in the jurisdiction where the activity is to occur, and submitting the affidavit for search warrants through local forms and format. The following day, they met with a local magistrate and provided him with copies of the felony complaint and arrest warrant for suspect Gerald Mason. They also provided the court officer with a search warrant affidavit, including statement of probable cause, seeking authorization to search suspect Mason's home for items deemed to be evidence in this case. Agent William Schaekel of the South Carolina Law Enforcement Division (SLED) agreed to act as the affiant on the warrant and prepared the search warrant for Mason's home. The search warrant was approved and authorized by the magistrate. The arrest warrant was now entered into NCIC.

An operations plan for service of the warrants was prepared. In addition to the local agency search warrant and arrest protocol, and, because of the age of the suspect and his wife, the plan included the nearby presence of an ambulance and paramedics.

ARREST AND INTERVIEW

In cold case investigation, as in other investigations, surprise is a valuable asset. South Carolina law enforcement personnel, accompanied by a deputy U.S. marshall assigned to the fugitive task force, contacted Mason at his residence just after 7:00 a.m. on January 29, 2003. Mason was advised of the search warrant. Investigators Cleary, Lowe, and McElderry contacted Mason outside his residence and advised him of the search warrant and arrest warrant from California. A safety sweep of the residence was made, and the suspect's wife was contacted outside the residence by Lt. Peavy, who also informed her of the search and arrest warrants(see Figure 31.31). The home was photographed before and after the search.

FIGURE 31.31 Mason composite then and Mason in 2002. (Courtesy of Los Angeles Sheriff's Department)

After the safety sweep, the investigators sat down with Mason inside his residence — his comfort zone — and again advised him of the search and arrest warrants, and began to conduct a tape-recorded interview. They were well versed in the details of all aspects of the investigation and prepared for an immediate, in-depth interview. Upon being advised of his rights, Mason said he thought he needed an attorney but was willing to hear why investigators had come to his home. Mason was told that the reason for their presence was for the murders of two El Segundo police officers in 1957. As has been noted elsewhere in this text, it is important that investigators note the immediate physical reaction and exact words used by suspects when confronted about a cold case homicide.

Mason "looked stunned" and replied, "My God, you're here for that reason." He sat quietly for about 20 seconds, staring at the investigators. He began breathing heavily, and when asked if he was okay, he responded that he was "stunned" and then said, "I don't understand why you are here." Investigators again explained about the 45-year-old robbery and car stop, and murder of the two officers, and that the suspect had been on the run for all these years. Mason then noted, "And you've come here for me?" When it was reaffirmed, Mason responded that he was certain he needed an attorney. The interview ended.

During this, and subsequent conversations with his wife as he was being transported from the scene, Mason *never denied* being involved in the incident and never offered any explanation as to why he was or was not involved in the incident. In addition, he asked *how* they found him, not *why*. He was advised of the Fugitive From Justice Warrant from the State of South Carolina, and of the extradition process that would follow, as well as of the aka George D. Wilson. Mason said that he did not know a George D. Wilson.

INTERVIEW OF FAMILY AND FRIENDS

When making cold case arrests, it is recommended that investigators interview family members and friends as soon as possible. Information to be sought includes length and depth of their relationships, circumstances and dates or time periods regarding their knowledge of the suspects at or about the times of the crimes, as well as financial, occupational, marital, or other relationship history. This information may be useful in identifying additional crimes, victims, or witnesses, and may also be beneficial to the prosecutors in countering subsequent efforts by the defendants to portray their exemplary characters.

NEWS MEDIA CONSIDERATIONS

In these cases, the news media usually show a high interest. This may be especially elevated in the more sensational cases. As search warrants are served and arrests are made, investigators operate at a steady pace. They usually do not have time to respond to media interest, including questions and interviews. In this instance, the presence of Lieutenant Raymond Peavy (since promoted to captain) provided a number of benefits for the investigation. As a ranking officer, Lieutenant Peavy possessed the authority to made necessary decisions as well as to responsibly respond to media interest and departmental or prosecutorial concerns almost 3000 miles away. In this instance, his command presence operated to the benefit of the investigators, and subsequently, the case investigation.

SEARCH WARRANT FINDINGS

As a result of service of the search warrant, officers seized a number of items covered by the affidavit for the search warrant. Included among these were:

- Passport in name of Gerald Mason
- Marlin .22 rifle
- .38 Special revolver with ammunition

- High Standard .22 revolver and ammunition (9-shot similar to the murder weapon)
- Pistol cleaning kit
- Rifle scope
- 9mm pistol with ammunition
- Numerous rounds of .38 Special ammunition
- Assorted military and union documents in name of Gerald Mason
- Box size 10 1/2 shoes
- Miscellaneous photos and papers
- Two address/phone books and one green notebook
- Photo album with miscellaneous photos of Gerald Mason
- Two wedding photos
- Address book
- Two envelopes with miscellaneous papers
- One Christmas card
- Two oral swabs

Subsequently, the firearms were subject to an ATF firearms trace summary.

SUBSEQUENT COURT PROCEEDINGS

After the arrest of a suspect, it may be advisable for investigators to attend what otherwise might be considered routine hearings to which they might not normally attend. What they see and hear could reveal additional investigation opportunities or provide additional information. At a judicial hearing on March 7, 2003, Mason *admitted* to hitchhiking from the east coast to Shreveport, Louisiana in 1957. He *admitted* to staying at the YMCA in Shreveport and purchasing a revolver from a store in that city. He further *admitted* that he was the same person who wrote the name, "George D. Wilson." on the purchase card. Thereafter, he explained, he hitchhiked to Los Angeles from Shreveport, and remembered being in a field drinking alcohol when he noticed a car stop nearby. "According to the records, Mason admitted that he robbed the occupants in the car and raped one of the young girls … Mason then stole the victim's car and fled the area."

> Suspect Mason admitted that he was stopped a short time later by two police officers. During the traffic stop, Mason exited the stolen car and contacted the officers near the front of the police car. He feared that the officers would discover what he had done and he would be arrested. One of the officers turned his back on Mason and Mason shot the officer three times in the back. Mason then shot the other officer who was seated on the front seat of the police car. After the shooting, Mason reentered the stolen car and drove away. As he fled, one of the officers shot at him and he sustained an injury to his right back. The bullet did not penetrate his body, but did lacerate his skin, which left a scar. He abandoned the stolen vehicle and fled on foot into a nearby neighborhood. He discarded his pistol in a back yard and hid until day break. Mason hitchhiked out of the area and returned to South Carolina.

In short, he admitted to killing the officers because he thought they would learn what he had just done, and he did not want to go back to prison. Lieutenant Cleary had been insistent that Mason's back be examined and photographed, and inspection revealed a scar consistent with a possible wound in the location as may have been caused by one of the fatally wounded officer's bullets.

NEWS CONFERENCE

Announcing the capture of a cold case homicide suspect serves a number of purposes (see Figure 31.32), as has been presented elsewhere in this text. It announces to the public that the

FIGURE 31.32 News conference announcing Mason's arrest. (Courtesy of Los Angeles Sheriff's Department)

crime has not been forgotten and is now solved. In addition, it reaffirms for the public that the agency seeks to continue to safeguard the public, and may stimulate others to come forward with information on this, or other, unsolved homicides.

New Witness

As a result of the revelation of the arrest in this case and media exposure, a heretofore unknown witness contacted the investigators. While he did not wish his name revealed beyond that which was necessary to the detectives, he provided additional information for the case investigation.

The witness was a reporter for a local media outlet. Shortly after the report of the shootings, he responded to the scene. As he neared the scene, a male white individual suddenly appeared at the side of his vehicle and he almost ran over him. In the car headlights, he had a good look at the subject. In the follow-up interview, the detectives showed the eight-picture black-and-white photo spread to the new witness. He identified Mason as looking "… most like the person and has the same physical features."

Postscript

Mason was returned to California. On March 24, 2003, he appeared in the Superior Court in Los Angeles. Represented by a South Carolina attorney and local attorney, Mason pled guilty to two counts of first degree murder for the deaths of El Segundo Police Officers Milton Curtis and Richard Phillips. He was immediately sentenced to two consecutive life terms in the California State Prison.

Immediately after his sentencing, Mason consented to an interview with the three investigators (see Figure 31.33) and provided further information to the detectives about the chain of events which led to his life imprisonment.

FIGURE 31.33 The team. Cold case homicide investigation is teamwork. The teamwork builds on the record of those who originally partnered in the investigation of the crime. This teamwork combines the talents, skills, experience, education, and training of many people engaged in a variety of disciplines. Through the teamwork of detectives, forensic personnel, and prosecutors, cold case homicides may be solved. Left to right, Front row: Howard Speaks (LASD, retired), Detective Dan McElderry (LASD Homicide), Keith Curtis (son of Officer Milton Curtis), Lieutenant Craig Cleary (El Segundo Police Department), Carolyn (Phillips) Stewart (daughter of Officer Richard Phillips), Detective Kevin Lowe (LASD Homicide), Darren Levine (Los Angeles Co. Deputy District Attorney), Reynaldo (Rey) Clara (LASD Lab). Back row: Dale Falicon (LASD Crime Lab) Donald Keir (LASD Crime Lab). (Courtesy of El Segundo Police Department)

ACKNOWLEDGMENTS

This case study is based upon extensive document review and in-depth interviews with the case officers and forensic personnel. I wish to acknowledge and express my gratitude for the extensive assistance, enthusiasm, and cooperation of the LACSD. I especially wish to thank Detectives Kevin Lowe and Dan McElderry, as well as Captain Raymond Peavy of the Los Angeles County Sheriff's Department Homicide Bureau in the preparation of this case study. In addition, I wish to recognize and express my gratitude to Deputy Sheriff Dale Falicon for his assistance and role in this case. All gave freely of their time and experience in homicide investigation and this cold case investigation to share their knowledge for the benefit of others in law enforcement. This assistance is further evidence of the team effort all personnel exhibited during the original and subsequent investigations of this case.

In addition, I also wish to acknowledge and thank Lieutenant Craig Cleary of the El Segundo Police Department for his many hours of assistance and cooperation in the research and preparation of this case study. Lieutenant Cleary's initial familiarity with the case and resolve to solve this crime laid the groundwork for an outstanding investigation by all participants and the generations who had tried before. All of these law enforcement professionals and their respective organizational leadership, represent the tenacity, determination, and dedication that epitomize the best in law enforcement and cold case homicide investigation.

I also wish to acknowledge the outstanding contribution of forensic document examiner Paul Edholm for his role in the solution of this case and contribution to this chapter and this book. Further, I wish to thank Deputy District Attorney Darren Levine for his insights and suggestions that further the team effort so necessary in these investigations. While we sometimes tend to focus on the "identify and arrest" aspects of the cases, we don't always appreciate the remaining hurdles the prosecution must face to finally close these difficult cases. Mr. Levine is a career prosecutor with a long record of successful prosecution of those who offend against those who wear the badge. To each, I offer my respect and gratitude for what you do.

Part IV

Other Resources

32 Other Cold Case Resources

Richard H. Walton

CONTENTS

NATIONAL CENTER FOR MISSING AND EXPLOITED CHILDREN (NCMEC)

BACKGROUND

In 1982, Congress enacted the Missing Children's Act. This legislation authorized the entry of missing child information into the National Crime Information Center (NCIC). Prior to this, guns and vehicles were entered into this national database, but not children.

By an Act of Congress in 1984, the Missing Children's Assistance Act established the National Center for Missing and Exploited Children (NCMEC). This quasi-government agency, an experiment in public–private partnership, was established to serve as a national clearing house and resource center on the issue of missing and exploited children. Today, the agency is funded by public and private sources of revenue, and over 500 corporations donate resources. Expertise comes from many sources, including contributions by the American Coroner's Association, American Academy of Forensic Sciences, Bode Technology Group, Inc., and Vidocq Society. The office works in cooperation with the U.S. Department of Justice's Office of Juvenile Justice and Delinquency Prevention and has offices in six states. The office offers significant services to law enforcement and may be of assistance in cold case homicide investigation.

In the early 1980s, a series of high-profile cases involving missing and abducted children highlighted a defect in the way American law enforcement reacted to reports of missing children. Included in these cases were those of Adam Walsh of Hollywood, Florida, Etan Patz of New York, and 26 missing and murdered children in Atlanta. These cases illuminated the then-common police practice of a mandatory waiting period before agencies would take a missing-children or -persons report. The prevailing wisdom was that children were runaways and if they did not return home within this period, law enforcement would then take a report. When agencies did take a report, however, it was usually handled internally. This may be a significant factor in missing children cases that are still unresolved and have become long-term missing person cases with a high potential to be cold case homicides.

As a result, investigation was delayed and, unfortunately, often nonexistent. There was no national response system among local, state, and federal law enforcement agencies. Communication and coordination among these agencies was lacking, or at most, minimal. For the families of the victims, there was no central resource. The extent of unsolved cases lacking remaining official records in local law enforcement agencies from this period is unknown.

Not unexpectedly, uncleared missing children cases have usually experienced a series of investigators over the intervening years. Similar to cold case homicides, these cases may not have been assigned a high priority for investigation due to the press of current cases and resource utilization. Different investigators brought a different perspective, perhaps a different set of prejudices they set out to prove or disprove, and ultimately interest in the case has diminished and the case has gone cold. These long-term missing-children or missing-person cases are not infrequently assigned for investigation to cold case homicide investigators.

SERVICES OFFERED BY THE NCMEC

The NCMEC provides expert assistance to law enforcement for long-term missing children and unidentified remains cases of persons believed to be under the age of 21. These services are provided at *no cost* to law enforcement agencies. Services offered to cold case homicide investigators by the NCMCE can be classified as forensic or investigative.

Forensic Services

- Computer assisted age progression of the photographs of long-term missing children. Using photo manipulation, NCMEC can age-enhance photographs of children missing 2 years or more so that law enforcement and the public might more easily continue to search for them. Using reference photos from family members of the missing child, they can take a 2-year-old and age progress the individual to age 55.
- Reconstruction of facial images from morgue photographs of unidentified deceased juveniles so that posters can be constructed to aid in the identification of the child.
- Computer assistance in creating artist composites.

- Handwriting comparison and analysis (in conjunction with Forensic Services Division of the U.S. Secret Service).
- Assistance in identifying faces of children from confiscated child pornography.
- Polygraph services.
- AFIS database searches.
- Photographic enhancement.
- DNA. The NCMEC offers free DNA testing of child or juvenile remains for police agencies. Through resources such as Bode Laboratories, they are able to offer mtDNA testing, a procedure currently unavailable at most local and state law enforcement laboratories (excluding California and Texas).

Investigative Assistance

Expert and onsite assistance is offered at no cost to law enforcement through Project ALERT and Team Adam.

Project ALERT (America's Law Enforcement Retiree Team).
This a team of more than 130 retired local, state, and federal law enforcement personnel who volunteer their time and expertise as unpaid consultants to the national law enforcement community. Their purpose is to assist the agency to resolve long-term missing child cases and those cases involving the remains of missing children. This program began in 1992 and is endorsed by 16 leading national law enforcement associations.

In the course of their service with the NCMEC, personnel have received special instruction in cold case investigation. These investigators will provide onsite assistance to the law enforcement agency at no cost to the agency. They offer:

- Immediate assistance
- Long-term case review
- Surveillance
- State-to-state follow-up on leads
- Witness interview assistance
- Public Speakers and roll-call trainers

Team Adam
This program is patterned after the National Transportation Safety Board's method of sending specialists to the scene of transportation incidents. This team is composed of approximately 35 retired law enforcement investigators selected through a formal process. This team is sent to the site of serious child abductions and cases of child sexual exploitation. Services offered include:

- Search
- Analysis
- Technical support
- Investigation
- Equipment/resources

Team Adam also provides assistance and support to family members, including:

- Family advocacy services
- Personal assistance
- Stress management
- Media relations

NCMEC SPECIALIZED CASE UNIT (SCU)

This specialized unit provides expert investigative and technical assistance to law enforcement, medical examiners, and coroners in resolving long-term cases. In partnership with the University of North Texas and the FBI, the SCU is working to obtain DNA samples from relatives of long-term missing and endangered missing children and to enter these profiles into CODIS for comparison with profiles of unidentified remains. They continue to search for missing children as if they were still alive. Other services offered to law enforcement include:

- Cold case review sessions
- Assessing and prioritizing leads and providing law enforcement with the most usable, relevant information possible
- Assistance in the development of investigative strategies
- Working with coroner or medical examiner personnel to provide identification assistance
- Coordination of forensic services
- NCIC off-line search requests and reviews
- Assistance in the development of a regular review protocol for long-term cases
- Surveillance
- Interstate follow-up of leads
- Assistance with witness interviews
- Family liaison

The SCU will also assist in evidence collection, preparation of search warrants and other aspects of investigation and prosecution as a consultant and through the use of Project ALERT resources (see Figure 32.1). The SCU addresses those cases of children missing as a result of a stranger

Endangered missing

Karen Mitchell   Age progressed

DOB: Nov 30, 1980
Missing: Nov 25, 1997
Age Now: 24
Sex: Female
Race: White
Hair: Sandy
Eyes: Blue
Height: 5'5" (165 cm)
Weight: 130 lbs (59 kg)
Missing From: Eureka
CA
United States

Karen's photo is shown aged to 20 years. She was last seen on Broadway across from the Bayshore Mall in Eureka, California. Her eyes are greenish-blue.

Anyone having information should contact
National center for missing & exploited children
1-800-843-5678 (1-800-The-Lost)

Eureka police department (California)-1-707-441-4044

FIGURE 32.1 Karen Mitchell is one of an unknown number of runaway, missing, endangered missing, or murdered children and young adults. The National Center for Missing and Exploited Children offers a number of services to law enforcement to assist in these cold case investigations. (Courtesy of NCMEC)

abduction or ones who are lost, injured, or otherwise missing. There is no specific time limit, just whenever the police or assigned case manager thinks the case is cold. A 5-year limit is applied to the cases of runaways, however. If a child runs away and is still missing after 5 years, the case manager can refer the case to the SCU as the child now fits the description of being lost, injured, or otherwise missing.

Cases are most often referred by the police or medical examiner. The case will be forwarded to the NCMEC SCU. It is prepared as a homicide and not as a missing person. Other assistance to cold case investigators may include:

- *Cold Case Review Panel.* This panel brings in investigators assigned to investigating missing children cases. Similar to the protocol of the Vidocq Society, the panel invites agencies and prosecutors to present unsolved cases to a board comprising forensic and legal experts. In this process they meet with the investigator, who briefs their case before a panel of retired cold case investigators, and they cooperatively build an investigative strategy.
- *Poster Distribution and Media Attention.* The NCMEC partners with major media, corporations, and major television networks to provide broadcast and print material to enhance public awareness and exposure.
- *Serial/Child Homicide Database.* The NCMEC is not a law enforcement agency and does not compile criminal history information. However, if an individual is convicted of a crime against a child, this database contains information about the individual's residential history, employers, vehicles, M.O. and other data.

Other Links

In additional to its in-country resources, the NCMEC has contacts with law enforcement resources around the world. These include:

- The RCMP
- New Scotland Yard in the U.K.
- Office of Children's Issues (U.S. State Department)
- Interpol-USNCB
- The Netherlands Police
- Belgium Police
- Australian National Police
- European Centre (Brussels)
- Interpol-General Secretariat in Lyon, France

The NCMEC accesses communication and databases within the U.S. These include:

- FBI National Crime Information Center (NCIC).
- National Law Enforcement Telecommunications System (NLETS).
- Federal Parent Locator Service (FPLS).
- The Center maintains and operates several databases for the use of law enforcement, including access to nationwide telephone listings, motor vehicle records, employment records, and nationwide school registration.

Other Resources

Win3. This is a free windows-based software program offered by the NCMEC to speed up identification and sorting of remains of missing persons. The agency inputs all unidentified and deceased into this system.

Unidentified Remains Program. The NCMEC has developed software for management of unidentified remains cases for comparing files of those deceased.

CyberTipline. This is a reporting system mandated by Congress. It is an online reporting mechanism for child sexual exploitation. The Web address is www.CyberTipline.com.

Contact Information:

National Center for Missing and Exploited Children
Charles B. Wang International Children's Building
699 Prince Street
Alexandria, Virginia 22314-3175
1-800-843-5678 – National Hotline
http://www.ncmec.org

I wish to express my gratitude to Gerald N. Nance, case manager for The Special Case Unit at the National Center for Missing and Exploited Children for his assistance in the preparation of this section. A former special agent for the U.S. Naval Criminal Investigative Service, Mr. Nance wrote the cold case protocol used by that agency and supervised its cold case squad. Upon retirement, he joined the National Center for Missing and Exploited Children and was instrumental in establishing the Special Case Unit, which addresses long-term missing children and unidentified remains cases of persons believed to be under the age of 21. Mr. Nance gave freely of his time and expertise in the provision of material for this segment as well as review and encouragement.

NATIONAL LAW ENFORCEMENT AND CORRECTIONS TECHNOLOGY CENTER (NLECTC)

The NLECTC is a program of the National Institute of Justice (NIJ), the research and development arm of the U.S. Department of Justice. The NLECTC system engages in research, review, development, and implementation of innovative technologies for regional and national law enforcement, forensics, and public safety. These technologies may be of benefit to cold case homicide investigators.

The NLECTC system offers no-cost assistance in helping agencies both small and large implement current and emerging technologies. The NLECTC system was established in 1994 to deliver information and technology assistance to more than 18,000 police departments, 50 state correctional systems; thousands of prisons, jails, parole and probation departments, and other public safety organizations. The NLECTC system consists of a network of facilities across the nation (see Figure 32.2). These are collocated with an organization or agency that specializes in one or more specific areas of research and development. Each NLECTC facility has a different technology focus. Each center operates independently, yet all support one another and exchange information about their areas of special expertise.

The NLECTC system has been able to deliver expertise in a number of technologies by forming partnerships with such host organizations as the Air Force Research Laboratory, the Space and Naval Warfare Systems Center, and the Aerospace Corporation. Through these partnerships, the NLECTC staff has access to the latest innovations in research and development. The NLECTC system serves as an "honest broker" resource for technology information, assistance, and expertise that includes the following services:

- Technology Identification. The NLECTC system provides information and assistance to help agencies determine the most appropriate and cost-effective technology to solve an administrative or operational problem. It delivers information relating to technology availability, performance, durability, reliability, safety, ease of use, customization capabilities, and interoperability.

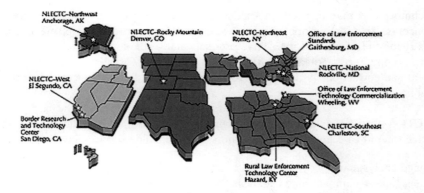

FIGURE 32.2 Regional map for the National Law Enforcement and Corrections Technical Center. (Courtesy of the NLECTC)

- Technology Assistance. The staffs of the NLECTC serve as proxy scientists and engineers. Areas of assistance that may assist cold case homicide investigators include unique evidence analysis (i.e., audio, video, computer, trace, and explosives), systems engineering, and communications and information systems support (i.e., interoperability, propagation studies, and vulnerability assessments). Forensic analysis may include *biological* material (body fluids, tissue, plants, etc.) or *inorganic* (glass, bullets, parts of a knife, etc.) material. The NLECTC may offer assistance in scenario verification, offering resources to suggest whether physical evidence is consistent with a particular sequence of events. *Note*: Evidentiary analysis assistance provided by NLECTC is limited to tasks that cannot be performed by the crime laboratories serving the requesting agency. The NLECTC is *not* a licensed or certified criminalistics laboratory and does *not* conduct DNA testing.
- Technology Implementation. The NLECTC staffs develop technology guides, best practices, and other information resources that are frequently leveraged from hands-on assistance projects and made available to other agencies.
- Property Acquisition. The NLECTC helps departments take advantage of surplus property programs that make Federal excess and surplus property available to law enforcement and corrections agencies at little or no cost.
- Equipment Testing. The NLECTC system oversees standards-based testing programs, including ballistic and stab-resistant body armor, handcuffs, semiautomatic pistols and other law enforcement equipment, and has evaluated emerging products to verify manufacturers' claims.
- Technology Demonstration. The NLECTC system introduces and demonstrates new and emerging technologies. On a limited basis, NLECTC facilitates deployment of new technologies to agencies for operational testing and evaluation.
- Capacity Building. The NLECTC provides hands-on demonstrations of the latest technology to address such operational issues as crime and intelligence analysis, geographic information systems, explosives detection and disablement, inmate disturbances and riots, and computer crime investigation.
- Technology Information. NLECTC disseminates information to the criminal justice community at no cost through educational bulletins, equipment performance reports, guides, consumer product lists, news summaries, meeting and conference reports, videotapes and CD-ROMS. NLECTC also publishes *TechBeat*, a quarterly newsmagazine. Most publications are available in electronic form through JUSTNET at www.justnet.org.
- Technology Commercialization. The system members work with law enforcement and corrections professionals, product and commercialization managers, engineers, and

technical and market research specialists to identify new technologies and product concepts. They then work with innovators and industry to develop, manufacture, and distribute these new and innovative products and technologies.

- Technology Needs Assessment. Members of the NLECTC system work with law enforcement and corrections professionals to ensure that they focus on the real-world needs of public safety agencies.

The NLECTC system offers a variety of resources relative to photographic analysis that may be of assistance to cold case homicide investigators. These include services involving:

- Image analysis
  - Multiple-technique image analysis
  - Temporal relationships
  - Feature analysis
  - Mensuration
- Image Enhancement. Among these capabilities may be:
  - Color enhancement
  - Frame averaging
  - Make image content more apparent
  - Brightness and contrast
  - Sharpen
  - Remove patterns, noise

ASSISTANCE

Assistance occurs when a law enforcement or corrections practitioner requests advice or aid on a technology-related issue. This may also include equipment borrowing, hardware or software evaluation, technology troubleshooting, system setup and updates, information awareness, and much more. Oftentimes the assistance is in the form of directing or putting the practitioner in touch with the appropriate organization or resource to meet their needs.

Because most of the country's law enforcement and correction services are provided at the local level, the NLECTC system is composed of five regional centers and is complemented by several specialty offices and a national center. Most centers are co-located with or supported by federally funded technology partners so that they can leverage unique science and engineering expertise. It is suggested that cold case investigators contact their nearest center to determine the location best suited to provide assistance in their needed arena. These centers are:

NLECTC – National
2277 Research Boulevard
Rockville, MD 20850
800-248-2742
asknlectc@nlectc.org

NLECTC – Northeast
26 Electronic Parkway
Rome, NY 13441-4514
888-338-0584
nlectc_ne@rl.af.mil

NLECTC – Southeast
5300 International Boulevard
North Charleston, SC 29418
800-292-4385
nlectc-se@nlectc-se.org

NLECTC – Rocky Mountain
2050 East Iliff Avenue
Denver, CO 80208
800-416-8086
nlectc@du.edu

NLECTC – West
c/o The Aerospace Corporation
2350 East El Segundo Boulevard
El Segundo, CA 90245-4691
888-548-1618
nlectc@law-west.org

NLECTC – Northwest
3000 C Street, Suite 304
Anchorage, AK 99503-3975
866-569-2969
nlectc_nw@ctsc.net

**Border Research and Technology Center
(BRTC)**
1010 Second Avenue, Suite 1920
San Diego, CA 92101-4912
888-656-2782
info@brtc.nlectc.org

**Rural Law Enforcement Technology Center
(RULETC)**
100 Bulldog Lane
Hazard, KY 41701
866-787-2553
ruletc@aol.com

**Office of Law Enforcement Technology
Commercialization (OLETC)**
2001 Main Street, Suite 500
Wheeling, WV 26003
888-306-5382
oletc@oletc.org

**Office of Law Enforcement Standards
(OLES)**
100 Bureau Drive, Stop 8102
Gaithersburg, MD 20899-8102
301-975-2757
oles@nist.gov

Further information can be obtained at:
800-248-2742
www.justnet.org
asknlectc@nlectc.org

Information courtesy of the National Law Enforcement and Corrections Technology Center System, a program of the National Institute of Justice.

NAVAL CRIMINAL INVESTIGATIVE SERVICE (NCIS)

NCIS is the primary law enforcement and investigative arm of the U.S. Department of the Navy. It has worldwide jurisdiction and works closely with local, state, federal, and foreign law enforcement organizations to counter and investigate serious crimes including terrorism, espionage, computer crime, homicide, rape, robbery, burglary, child abuse, arson, white collar crime, and other criminal violations.

The NCIS traces its roots to 1882, when the Office of Naval Intelligence (ONI) was established. The agency was initially charged with collection of intelligence concerning weaponry and characteristics of enemy weaponry. Their duties expanded during World Wars One and Two, and the agency became responsible for the investigation of sabotage, espionage, and subversive activities considered to pose a threat to the U.S. Navy. The use of civilian special agents began with the Korean War in 1950 and continued through the Cold War.

In 1966, the name Naval Investigative Service was adopted to distinguish the organization from other aspects of the ONI. In 1969, NIS special agents became Excepted Civil Service and were no longer contract employees. After a series of program variations and reorganizations, the NIS was upgraded in 1982 and henceforth reported to the Chief of Naval Operations (CNO). Special Agents began training at the Federal Law Enforcement Training Center (FLETC) in Georgia in 1984, the training center used by most federal investigative agencies except for the FBI.

In January 1995, the NCIS established a Cold Case Homicide Unit. This body was the first federal law enforcement agency to develop a full-time cold case homicide investigation unit. It was formed to:

- Specifically reactivate and reinvestigate unsolved homicides, unresolved and suspicious death investigations and mysterious disappearances pertaining to personnel of the U.S. Navy or Marine Corps.
- Assist other law enforcement agencies with homicide cases.
- Train federal, state, and local law enforcement agencies in cold case homicide investigation methodology.

Since its inception, the unit has played a key role in the resolution of dozens of cases dating to 1968. Many of these have been in concert with local law enforcement agencies. Through seminars, the NCIS Cold Case Homicide Unit provides training in cold case investigation methods to law enforcement personnel from local and state agencies throughout the U.S.

NCIS operates two regional forensic laboratories. These are located in Norfolk, Virginia and San Diego, California. Each of these laboratories contains a consolidated evidence facility that maintains evidence collected by the various field offices and tested at the laboratories. These laboratories provide forensic services to the U.S. Navy, Marine Corps, and other Department of Defense investigative organizations and law enforcement agencies.

Additional technical service offices are located at strategic locations. These are staffed with career personnel who receive extensive training in crime scene examination and processing, electronics, covert video and audio techniques, and photography. The organization provides polygraph examinations through a cadre of trained polygraph examiners.

The NCIS operates field offices in numerous U.S. cities and foreign countries. Each field office has subelements called resident agencies that are further subdivided into resident units. Some of these locations include:

- Atsugi, Japan
- Camp Hansen, Japan
- Iwakuni, Japan
- Misawa, Japan
- Okinawa, Japan
- Sasebo, Japan
- Yokosuka, Japan
- Manama, Bahrain
- Frankfurt, Germany
- Keflavik, Iceland
- Gaeta, Italy
- La Maddelena, Italy
- Rome, Italy
- Sigonella, Italy
- Guantanmo Bay, Cuba
- Chinhae, Korea
- Pusan, Korea
- Seoul, Korea
- Munich, Germany
- Guam
- London, UK
- Manila, RPI
- Marseille, France

- Roosevelt Roads, PR
- Singapore
- Souda Bay, Crete

The Cold Case Homicide Unit is located at:

Washington Field Office
Building 200
Washington, D.C. 20374
(202) 433-3858
www.ncis.navy.mil

VIDOCQ SOCIETY

The Vidocq Society was founded in 1990 in Philadelphia. The three founding members were William Fleisher (retired), then second-in-command special agent for the U.S. Customs Service in that city; well-known forensic sculptor Frank Bender; and Richard Walter (retired), a Michigan state prison psychologist. This trio wanted to establish a venue in which similarly minded persons would gather to discuss and debate crimes and mysteries. Other federal, state, and local law enforcement persons subsequently sought to join the group, and attention grew regarding the criminal investigative expertise of this enlarging body. In time, the society narrowed its mandate to focus on unsolved cold case homicides, and, in some cases, disappearances.

Society membership is limited to 82 regular members, one for each year of the life of the organization's namesake, Eugène François Vidocq, a brilliant 18th-century French crook-turned-cop who rose to become a famous detective and later the first chief of the Sûreté in 1811. Vidocq Society membership is currently in excess of 140 regular and special members from a variety of disciplines, including law enforcement, forensics, psychology, business and other diverse backgrounds. These persons donate their time and efforts for the public good.

Members of the Vidocq Society and invited guests normally meet on the third Thursday of each month. Meetings are normally held over lunch, beginning at noon at the Downtown Club, in the historical Public Ledger Building in Philadelphia. At these meetings, guest presenters share the facts of a case and apply their collective forensic skills and experience to cold case homicides and unsolved deaths. The members evaluate, investigate, refocus, revivify, and attempt to solve the unsolved deaths officially brought to them by representatives of law enforcement organizations or victim's families. The Vidocq Society investigates unsolved deaths and homicides only when law enforcement agencies accept their support, and the investigating agency directs *all* Vidocq Society efforts.

The Vidocq Society has been recognized as a cold case resource by the U.S. Justice Department. An example of its work can be found in Chapter 22, Boulder Jane Doe.

For local and county law enforcement agencies, the Vidocq Society is a forensic resource of great value, a team of experts whose consultative skills and talents are always free. Among the talents and skills Vidocq Society members may offer cold case homicide investigators include:

- Accident Investigation
- Anthropology Reconstruction
- Arson/Bombing Investigation
- Automobile Accident Reconstruction
- Bloodstain Pattern Analysis
- Cardiology
- Critical Mechanical Analysis
- Document Examination

- Financial Investigation
- Firearms
- Forensic Accounting
- Forensic Anthropology and Archeology
- Forensic Odontology
- Periodontics
- Forensic Psychophysiology
- Forensic Pathology
- Homicide Events Reconstruction
- Homicide Investigation
- Handwriting Identification and Analysis
- Interview and Interrogation
- Narcotics Investigation
- Latent Fingerprints
- Organized Crime
- Polygraph
- Post-conviction Investigation
- Crime Assessment and Profiling
- White Collar Crime Investigation

Case Selection

The Society chooses its cases carefully and works closely with local investigators and prosecutors. All work is done at no cost to victim's families or law enforcement and is pro bono as part of the society's commitment to public service.

Case Intake Criteria

The Vidocq Society will undertake a review or investigation only after it is contacted by a family member or a law enforcement agency asking for the Vidocq Society to review an unsolved cold case. A family member making a request must have standing in the case. In all cases, the investigating law enforcement agency must welcome the help of the Vidocq Society.

For the Vidocq Society to consider an unsolved death or homicide case:

- The death must have occurred at least two years prior.
- The victim cannot have been engaged in dangerous or illicit activity of any kind.
- If presented to a meeting by law enforcement or an investigator with standing in the case, no family members may be present.
- The Vidocq Society will not provide progress reports, updates, or other information to the family.

To formally request Vidocq Society review of an unsolved homicide or questionable death, those requesting assistance must read the mission and intake process available at the Vidocq Society World Wide Web page shown below. If the death falls within Vidocq Society guidelines, forward a letter by U.S. Postal service to:

Vidocq Society Case Referrals
1704 Locust Street, Second Floor
Philadelphia, Pennsylvania 19103

The letter should include only photocopies of any police reports, forensic summaries, other relevant documents or newspaper clippings. Prior to submitting required materials by U.S. Mail, questions may be submitted to the Director of Case Management at the Vidocq Society website.

Case Review Process

Upon receipt of the data sent with the request for investigation, along with any other facts gathered independently by the Society personnel, a determination will be made to ascertain whether the case or matter meets Vidocq's basic acceptance criteria. If it is decided that the crime might qualify, the case is assigned to additional experts for further review and analysis. Some cases become Vidocq meeting presentations.

Case Presentation

The presenter of a cold-case homicide or disappearance at a Vidocq Society meeting could be:

- A law enforcement professional who has investigated the murder over the years and continues to carry it on his/her caseload, or his or her successor
- A Vidocq Society member
- A licensed private investigator hired by the murder victim's family

Following the presentation, formal discussions by attending membership include a question-and-answer session. This is a collaborative effort that involves members and invited guests. Case presentations conclude with a call for Vidocq Society members interested in jointly pursuing the matter. In some cases, a "working group" is assembled to more intensively advance that specific investigation.

Confidentiality

Information provided to the Vidocq Society is maintained in a confidential manner. Its policy is to neither confirm nor deny any role in any investigation. The society is a private organization and is not obligated to provide access, information, or explanations to the media or to the public.

Media Concerns

The Vidocq Society recognizes the valuable role the media can afford in the truth-gathering process, and the role that publicity may play in advancing the cause of an investigation of an unsolved death. However, it does not provide real-time media access to investigations. If the society is assisting in any investigation, information would come from the law enforcement agency. At the request of the investigating law enforcement agency, the Vidocq Society will alert local media that a particular death is being presented or investigated. Any case and crime details, however, would be provided by the investigating agency and not the Vidocq Society.

The Vidocq Society publishes *The Vidocq Society Journal* at least four times per year (see Figure 32.3). Articles that appear in this journal do not include confidential Vidocq Society information or matters. Articles may be contributed by members and non-members. Further information can be obtained from the website.

The Vidocq Society is a nonprofit charitable organization under Section 501c (3) of the IRS Code. The society obtains its financial support from membership dues and voluntary contributors willing to help underwrite their pro bono services.

FIGURE 32.3 The Vidocq Society membership contributes pro bono skills in a variety of disciplines to assist law enforcement in solving cold case homicides. This group has been recognized by the U.S. Department of Justice as a cold case resource. While the group does not broadcast its successes, one example of its service can be found in Chapter 22.

Contact Information:

The Vidocq Society
1704 Locust Street, Second Floor
Philadelphia, Pennsylvania 19103
215-545-1450
http://vidocq.org

AMERICAN ACADEMY OF FORENSIC SCIENCES

The American Academy of Forensic Sciences (AAFS), the world's most prestigious forensic science organization, was founded in 1948. The distinguished and diverse membership includes many of the world's leading forensic scientists, and now numbers nearly 6000 members worldwide. The AAFS consists of 10 sections that represent a wide range of forensic disciplines. These include physicians, toxicologists, dentists, physical anthropologists, document examiners, psychiatrists, engineers, criminalists, educators, law enforcement investigators, attorneys, and more, who practice, research, or study in the forensic sciences.

This business is a professional association committed to the application of science to law. In this regard, the AAFS promotes professional development and education in conjunction with the elevation of accuracy, precision, and specificity in the forensic sciences. It accomplishes these goals through annual meetings, seminars, newsletters, and other venues.

The AAFS may assist cold case homicide investigators in a variety of areas through identification of qualified forensic scientists in a wide range of disciplines.

American Academy of Forensic Sciences
410 N. 21st Street
Colorado Springs, CO 80904-2798
(719) 636-1100
http://www.aafs.org

AMERICA'S MOST WANTED

America's Most Wanted (AMW) television broadcast, hosted by John Walsh, premiered on February 7, 1988. On July 27, 1981, Walsh's 6-year-old son Adam Walsh was abducted from a suburban shopping mall and murdered. His remains were found over 100 miles away 16 days later. A prime suspect in the case, Ottis Toole, was never charged with the crime but died in prison while serving life for other crimes. Walsh subsequently became a nationally recognized leader advocating for victim's rights. In 1987, FOX network contacted Walsh about hosting a reality television show designed to track down America's most wanted fugitives by profiling their cases for a national audience. This program profiled active law enforcement cases for public input in attempts to locate fugitives, other wanted felons, and missing persons. The program is broadcast worldwide. Since its inception, AMW has contributed to locating and apprehending over 800 persons.

AMW offers law enforcement and cold case investigators the opportunity for exposure and soliciting information for crimes involving:

- Child and Adult Abduction
- Assault and Battery
- Child Abuse
- Escape
- Homicide
- Narcotics
- Robbery/Burglary
- Sex Crimes
- Serial Homicide/Killers
- Terrorism
- White Collar and Financial Fraud
- Other Crimes

Through its website, AMW offers links for review for advanced search for persons profiled on AMW by geography or last name. Those persons previously profiled may also be searched as:

- Fugitives. This uses a combination of fields to search for fugitive cases on AMW.com. These include:
  - Keyword
  - Name or Nickname
  - Age
  - Gender
  - Region
  - Location
  - Crime Type
  - Victim Name
  - Weapon
  - Vehicle
- Missing Children. This uses a combination of fields to search for missing children profiled on AMW.com. These include:
  - Keyword
  - Name or Nickname
  - Age
  - Race
  - Gender
  - Region
  - Location
  - Missing Since
  - Amber Alert
- Missing Persons. This uses a combination of fields to search for missing persons profiled on AMW.com. These include:
  - Keyword
  - Name or Nickname
  - Age
  - Race
  - Gender
  - Region
  - Location
  - Missing Since
- Captures
- Features
- Victim's Rights

In addition, the *show archive* file lists past episodes to find cases and features. These features may be of interest to cold case homicide investigators when reviewing long-term cases that have experienced a series of investigators. In addition, this may be a source of information when searching for previous persons associated with suspects, victims, or others involved in cold case homicides.

America's Most Wanted Cold Case Unit

AMW formed its own cold case investigation unit in 2000. This unit offers its services to any law enforcement agency in the investigation of unsolved cold case homicides. The program began with the utilization of the service and experience of a retired New York Police Department detective, and now has six investigators. These investigators are retired homicide detectives from such diverse agencies as New York Police Department, Miami Beach Police Department, Washington Metro Police Department, New Orleans Police Department, and the FBI. The program asks these investigators to review cold cases submitted by law enforcement agencies, and each step of their investigation is documented by a camera crew. AMW will broadcast a segment of the investigation, asking the audience to provide leads or other information needed to help solve the case. Further information can be obtained from:

www.amw.com
Confidential Hotline
1-800-CRIME-TV

THE CAROL SUND/CARRINGTON MEMORIAL REWARD FOUNDATION

This foundation was established to memorialize murder victims Carole Sund, her teenage daughter Juli, and their friend, Silvina Pelosso. The trio was murdered while visiting Yosemite National Park in February, 1999. Media attention and a reward offered by the family were credited with providing the first break in their case. This experience led to the fund's establishment by Carole's parents, Francis and Carole Carrington. The foundation is administered by a chairman and board of directors that includes active and retired law enforcement personnel, and is a non-profit 501(c)(3) organization.

The foundation's goal is to help law enforcement officials locate kidnapped or missing persons, return them safely to their homes, and to secure the arrest and conviction of violent criminals in current or cold case homicides. This foundation is unique in this regard and provides resources to families without the economic means to offer rewards for information to help law enforcement officials. In the first 5 years of operation, the Foundation posted rewards in 237 cases totaling $1,941,500 in 36 states. These rewards assisted in the apprehension of 20 murder suspects and one attempted murder suspect, and helped to locate four missing persons.

The foundation publishes a newsletter highlighting missing persons and wanted suspects. In addition, the foundation sponsors public- and media-awareness events to offer support and education for victims of homicide and missing persons.

Criteria for foundation participation include:

- Reward requests must meet established criteria for Foundation participation.
- Victim must be innocent and not involved in illegal activities.
- Rewards are posted for a 6-month period of time.
- Investigating agency must sanction the reward request and qualify the legitimate need.
- Missing persons cases must be at-risk cases, not involving runaways or custody issues.
- Victim's family members, a law enforcement representative, the Foundation and media announce the reward at a designated press conference.
- Following the press conference, awareness will continue with fliers announcing the reward.
- At such time a reward would be given, if appropriate, a press conference will be held to publicize the reward presentation.

Contact information:

The Carole Sund/Carrington Memorial Reward Foundation
301 Downey Avenue
Modesto, California 95354
888-813-8389
www.carolesundfoundation.com

THE DOE NETWORK

The Doe Network is a volunteer organization dedicated to assisting law enforcement in solving cold cases that involve unexplained disappearances and unidentified victims from North America, Europe, and Australia. This organization accomplishes its mission in three ways:

1. Giving cases exposure through its website
2. Use of volunteers to search for clues on cases as well as making possible matches between missing and unidentified persons
3. Attempting to obtain media exposure for cases that need it

The Doe Network website was created in 1999. In 2001, a group of volunteers was put together to try to solve cases found on the website. By December of that year, the group had its first solve. As of 2005, the organization had over 400 volunteers working to solve 840 unidentified victims cases and 2650 missing persons cases on its website.

The group cooperates with missing person organizations, law enforcement agencies, and medical examiner's or coroners offices.

ORGANIZATION

The Doe Network operates in a tiered hierarchy:

- An Administrative Team. Oversees the operation of the organization.
- Area Directors. Serve as the local link to law enforcement agencies and are responsible for maintaining communications with the agencies in their area as well as validation of cases, possible matches with missing and unidentified persons, and information received from the public.
- Local researchers. The organization further utilizes local researchers to check facts and locate additional information about the cases listed on its website.
- Potential Match Panel. This group is responsible for scaling the possibility of each potential match the group makes.

Volunteer members bring specialized skills to the organization and serve in many capacities. In law enforcement, we sometimes tend to think that we are the only persons capable of investigation, ferreting out information, and solving cases. We utilize common sense in a lot of what we do, but common sense is not limited to those who have police training and experience. The Boulder Jane Doe case, found on the Doe Network website, illustrates an example of what a non-police person can accomplish, and what can result when private citizens and law enforcement cooperate.

Projects

The Doe Network currently has a joint effort with NCIC consisting of off-line searches for unidentified victims in cases they have selected to send to this center. In addition, they sponsor Project EDAN (Everyone Deserves a Name), a group of volunteer forensic artists who donate their skills and time to create reconstructions and age progressions of missing and unidentified persons. The artists' work is offered to law enforcement agencies and is also found on the Doe Network's website.

Family Liaison

As a general rule, the Doe Network does not contact victim's families. However, it is receptive to contact by the family of these victims and may be able to offer support or general help, depending upon the circumstances.

Case Criteria

Disappearance cases are those that have been within this category for 9 years or more. Unidentified victims cases are all prior to 2003. The Doe Network does include cases of unidentified victims who have been located after this time period and death was believed to have occurred in 2003 or before.

For further information: http://www.doenetwork.org or DoeNetwork @angelfire.cor

NECROSEARCH

NecroSearch is a nonprofit organization that specializes in the search for clandestine gravesites. The organization utilizes scientists and volunteers with specialized skills to assist law enforcement agencies in the search for and or/recovery of human remains and evidence. NecroSearch does not charge for its services, but requires that involved agencies pay for necessary expenses. This organization can provide specialists in disciplines that include:

- Physical anthropology
- Archaeology
- Botany and plant ecology
- Cadaver dogs
- Criminalistics
- Data processing
- Entomology
- Geology
- Geophysics
- Remote sensing
- Underwater search capabilities

For further information: http://www.NecroSearch.org

33 Conclusion

Richard H. Walton

In his book *Practical Homicide Investigation: Tactics, Procedures, and Forensic Techniques*, Vernon Geberth wrote: "as far as homicide detectives are concerned, there are two types of homicide: one in which the suspect is caught quickly, and the unsolved homicide."

He also noted that murder is the ultimate crime, and that each case deserves a thorough and complete investigation. In most instances, this has probably occurred. In some, it did not, and we would be naïve to assume otherwise. Despite the best efforts of many, however, some homicides have gone unsolved.

Geberth made no reference to *when* we should stop looking, when we should stop investigating. I opine that he did not because we should *never* stop looking. We should *never* cease in our efforts to solve unsolved homicides. We owe it to the victims, to their families, and indeed, to our civilization, that we never cease in our efforts to bring accountability to those who have murdered another human being. In the past 2 decades, many cold cases once thought unsolvable have been solved because dedicated investigators pored through old files and boxes of papers and evidence, followed up on a tip, or reprocessed old evidence and made startling new discoveries.

I further believe that we should never cease in our efforts to learn the truth and to reinvestigate those cases in which, just perhaps, the wrong person was convicted and sentenced. After all, in those instances, someone did get away with murder while someone else paid the penalty.

Unfortunately, many of America's cold case murders may never be solved. Despite this, we can hold out hope that perhaps one day some of these will be solved. As we have seen in this book, time has become our biggest asset in this regard. Through changes in relationships, technological developments, and other factors, cold cases are being solved and will be solved in the future by the dedicated and professional men and women who compose the cold case investigation team: the investigators, the prosecutors, and the laboratories.

In granting Jack Ryan a posthumous pardon on the grounds of innocence in 1996, the governor of California noted:

> We must remember that a just society may not always achieve justice, but it must constantly strive for justice. This means that we must not excuse the guilty nor fail to exonerate the guiltless. As the philosopher Sir Francis Bacon said some 380 years ago, 'If we do not maintain Justice, Justice will not maintain us.'

Acronyms

AAFS	American Academy of Forensic Sciences
AFIS	Automated Fingerprint Identification Systems
AK	Adenylate Kinase
ALS	Alternate Light Source
APB	All Points Bulletin
APIS	Automated Palm Identification System
ASCLD/LAB	American Society of Crime Laboratory Directors/Laboratory Accreditation Board
ATF	Bureau of Alcohol, Tobacco, and Firearms
BATFE	Bureau of Alcohol, Tobacco, Firearms and Explosives
CHRI	Criminal History Record Information
CJIS	Criminal Justice Information System
CJIS APB	Criminal Justice Information System Advisory Policy Board
CJIS WAN	Criminal Justice Information System Wide Area Network
CODIS	Combined DNA Index System
CPM	Critical Path Method
CSI	Crime Scene Investigator
	DAS - Data Acquisition Station
DFO	1,8 Diazafluoren-9-one
DNA	Deoxyribonucleic acid
DQA1	DQ Alpha 1
EAP	Erythrocyte acid phosphatase
ERD	Ending Registration Data
EsD	Esterase D
FBI	Federal Bureau of Investigation
FFT	Fast Fourier Transform
FLS	Forensic Light Source
GRC	General Rifling Characteristics
HITS	Homicide Investigation and Tracking System
IACP	International Association of Chiefs of Police
IAFIS	Integrated Automated Fingerprint Identification System
III	Interstate Identification Index
ITN	Identification Tasking and Networking
LAN	Local Area Network
LDIS	Local DNA Index System
LMG	Leucomalachite green
M.O.	Method of Operation
MOU	Memorandum of Understanding
MtDNA	Mitochondrial DNA
NCAVC	National Center for Analysis of Violent Crime
NCIC	National Crime Information Center
NDIS	National DNA Index System
NFF	National Fingerprint File
NFSTC	National Forensic Science Technology Center

NIBIN	National Integrated Ballistic Information Network
	NIN - Ninhydrin
NIJ	National Institute of Justice
NIST	National Institute of Standards and Technology
NLECTC	National Law Enforcement and Corrections Technology Center
NLETS	National Law Enforcement Telecommunications System
NYSIIS	New York State Identification and Intelligence System
ORI	Originating Agency Identifier
NIBRS	National Incident-Based Reporting Systems
PCR	Polymerase Chain Reaction
PERT	Program Evaluation and Review Techniques
	PGM - Phosphoglucomutase
POF	Protection Order File (in NCIC)
RAIDS	Redundant Array of Independent Drives
RFES	Remote Fingerprint Editing Software
RFLP	Restriction Fragment Length Polymorphism
SCU	Specialized Case Unit
SID	Scientific Investigation Division
SLED	South Carolina Law Enforcement Division
STR	Short Tandem Repeat
SWGDAM	Scientific Working Group on DNA Analysis Methods
	TMB - Tetramethylbenzidine
TraCKRS	Taskforce Aimed at Catching Killers, Rapists, and Sexual Offenders
UCR	Uniform Crime Report
UFAP	Unlawful Flight to Avoid Prosecution
ULW	Universal Latent Workstation
VGTOF	Violent Gang and Terrorist Organization File
VIA	Visual Illustrative Analysis
ViCAP	National Violent Criminal Apprehension Program
VMD	Vacuum Metal Deposition
WAN	Wide Area Network
Y STR	Y chromosome Short Tandem Repeat

Acronyms Part Two (from Ch. 19 onward)

AAFS	American Academy of Forensic Sciences
	AAFS
	AAPP
	AFIC
AMW	America's Most Wanted
APA	American Polygraph Association
ATF	Bureau of Alcohol Tobacco and Firearms
BATFE	Bureau of Alcohol, Tobacco, Firearms, and Explosives
	BPA
	CCTV
	CGT
	CILHI
	CNO
	CSUN
	DAS
	FLETC
	FPLS

FTI	Forensic Technology, Inc.
	GII
IBIS	Integrated Ballistic Identification System
	ICIAF
	IF
	LACSD Los Angeles County Sheriff's Department
LAPD	Los Angeles Police Department
LCV	Leuco Crystal Violet
LMG	Leucomalachite green
MOU	Memorandum of Understanding
	MPS
MUPS	Missing and Unidentified Persons
NCIC	National Crime Information Center
NCMEC	National Center for Missing and Exploited Children
NIJ	National Institute of Justice
NIST	National Institute of Standards and Technology
NLECTC	National Law Enforcement and Corrections Training Center
NLETS	National Law Enforcement Telecommunications System
	ONI
PCR	Polymerase Chain Reaction
	POT
	SCAS
	SCU
	SIC
SID	Scientific Investigation Division
SLED	South Carolina Law Enforcement Division
TMB	Tetramethyl Benzidine

Index